GENERAL PRINCIPLES OF LAW

AS APPLIED BY

INTERNATIONAL COURTS AND TRIBUNALS

Titles published in the Grotius Classic Reprint Series

I. H. Lauterpacht, *The Development of International Law by the International Court*

II. B. Cheng, *General Principles of Law as applied by International Courts and Tribunals*

GENERAL PRINCIPLES OF LAW

as applied by

INTERNATIONAL COURTS AND TRIBUNALS

BY

BIN CHENG, PH.D., LICENCIÉ EN DROIT

Lecturer in International Law
University College, London

WITH A FOREWORD BY

GEORG SCHWARZENBERGER, PH.D., DR.JUR.

Reader in International Law in the University of London;
Vice-Dean of the Faculty of Laws, University College, London

GROTIUS PUBLICATIONS
CAMBRIDGE
UNIVERSITY PRESS

CAMBRIDGE UNIVERSITY PRESS
Cambridge, New York, Melbourne, Madrid, Cape Town, Singapore, São Paulo

Cambridge University Press
The Edinburgh Building, Cambridge CB2 2RU, UK

Published in the United States of America by Cambridge University Press, New York

www.cambridge.org
Information on this title: www.cambridge.org/9780521030007

First published by Stevens & Sons Limited 1953
Reprinted by Grotius Publications Limited 1987
Further reprinted by Cambridge University Press 1994
This digitally printed first paperback version 2006

This work was first published by Stevens & Sons Limited in 1953 as Number 21 in the London Institute of World Affairs' The Library of World Affairs series (Editors: George W. Keeton and Georg Schwarzenberger); was reprinted with kind permission in 1987 by Grotius Publications Limited as Number 2 in their Grotius Classic Reprint series of works of major importance to the international lawyer and political scientist; and again in 1994 by Cambridge University Press following Cambridge's acquisition of Grotius.

A catalogue record for this publication is available from the British Library

ISBN-13 978-0-521-03000-7 paperback
ISBN-10 0-521-03000-5 paperback

TO

MY PARENTS

CONTENTS

PART TWO

THE PRINCIPLE OF GOOD FAITH

PART THREE

GENERAL PRINCIPLES OF LAW IN THE CONCEPT OF RESPONSIBILITY

PART FOUR

GENERAL PRINCIPLES OF LAW IN JUDICIAL PROCEEDINGS

FOREWORD

The draftsmen of the Statute of the Permanent Court of International Justice rendered signal service to international law by incorporating the " general principles of law recognised by civilised nations " as auxiliary rules to be applied by the Court. Whether or not they were fully conscious of all the implications of their action, they achieved at one stroke seven different purposes.

They enabled the Court to replenish, without subterfuge, the rules of international law by principles of law tested within the shelter of more mature and closely integrated legal systems.

They opened a new channel through which concepts of natural law could be received into international law.

They held out to other international judicial institutions a tempting set of rules which these might be encouraged to adopt, as a last resort, in their own practice.

They made it possible for the World Court to strike out a bolder line in its application of international law than, in the absence of such wide reserve powers, the Court might have found it possible to take.

They reduced to silence the prophets of gloom who assumed that, one day, international adjudication would founder on the rock of *non liquet.*

They reintroduced the standard of civilisation into international law and drew a sharp, and necessary, dividing line between civilised and barbarian nations.

Finally, they threw out a challenge to the Doctrine of International Law to sail into new and uncharted seas.

As will become obvious from Dr. Cheng's bibliography, some of this work was undertaken by the inter-war generation of international lawyers. Much, however, still remains to be done.

First of all, it falls to the sociology of international law to establish workable criteria of the meaning of the term *civilised nations*. The issue whether nations organised on the patterns of the police and garrison State have any claim to this epithet has been avoided too long.

Next, the international lawyer must call for succour from his colleagues in the field of comparative law. They alone can provide him with authoritative studies on the scope and limits of the general principles recognised by civilised nations. Only on this basis will he then be able to determine which of these principles of public and private, adjective and substantive, law are applicable in the environment of present-day international society.

Yet even while this preliminary work is in progress, the international lawyer need not sit back in comfort. Dr. Cheng has broken new ground in exploring the practice of international arbitration and has shown that international judicial institutions other than the World Court have found it necessary to have recourse on a much larger scale to this subsidiary source of international law—perhaps for the very reason that, more often than not, they had not been endowed with the additional authority granted to the World Court. Similar work could, and should be, undertaken in the field of State practice, as yet so largely unexplored.

To draw attention to these unperformed tasks is perhaps the only real justification for having acceded to Dr. Cheng's flattering request to write a Foreword to his work; for a teacher and friend must leave it to others, more detached than he can be, to judge this firstling of a highly promising international lawyer.

GEORG SCHWARZENBERGER

University College, London
March, 1953

PREFACE

THE municipal codes of more than a dozen countries expressly provide for the application of the general principles of law in the absence of specific legal provisions or of custom, and Article 38 I (c) of the Statute of the International Court of Justice stipulates that "the general principles of law recognised by civilised nations" constitute one of the sources of international law to be applied by the Court. But, ever since its inclusion in Article 38, sub-paragraph (c) has aroused wide controversy amongst international lawyers as to its exact meaning and scope.

The function of general principles of law has been well stated by the British-United States Claims Arbitral Tribunal of 1910, which was of the opinion that: "International law, as well as domestic law, may not contain, and generally does not contain, express rules decisive of particular cases; but the function of jurisprudence is to resolve the conflict of opposing rights and interests by applying, in default of any specific provisions of law, the corollaries of general principles, and so to find . . . the solution of the problem. This is the method of jurisprudence; it is the method by which the law has been gradually evolved in every country resulting in the definition and settlement of legal relations as well between States as between private individuals."[2]

In the field of international law, where specific rules are relatively few, there is even more occasion for resorting to general principles than in municipal law. There is, however, a danger that these principles, by reason of their general character, may share the fate of natural law, which during the nineteenth century suffered an eclipse from which

[1] See Appendix 2: Municipal Codes which provide for the Application of the General Principles of Law, Equity or Natural Law (*infra*, pp. 400 *et seq.*).
[2] *Eastern Extension, Australasia and China Telegraph Co., Ltd., Case* (1923), Nielsen's *Report*, p. 40, at pp. 75–76.

it is perhaps just beginning to emerge. If, therefore, the general principles of law are not to run the risk of being exploited as an ideological cloak for self-interest, it is essential that their scope and substance be clearly defined and understood. In practice, international tribunals have frequent recourse to these principles, either to guide them in the application of rules of international law, or to decide cases where no specific rule exists. To inquire into the practical application of these principles by international courts and tribunals is the aim of the present study.

In its original form, this work was a thesis submitted to the University of London in 1950 for admission to the degree of Doctor of Philosophy, in the Faculty of Laws. The author wishes to acknowledge his deepest gratitude to Dr. Georg Schwarzenberger, Reader in International Law in the University of London and Vice-Dean of the Faculty of Laws, University College, London, who suggested the subject, supervised the study and kindly wrote the Foreword. It was also through him that the author was made acquainted with the inductive approach to international law.[3]

It is gratifying to find that both the usefulness of studies of this kind and the soundness of the inductive approach have been recognised in official quarters, where the need for a wider and more intensive study of international law as applied by international courts and tribunals has gradually become felt in recent years. Thus, in 1949, the Secretary-General of the United Nations, in a Memorandum submitted to the General Assembly, noted that there was "a growing trend towards an inductive approach" in international law.[4] In another Memorandum, he remarked that "a distinct element of usefulness might attach to any commentary" on Article 38 of the Statute of the International

3 See Schwarzenberger, "The Inductive Approach to International Law," 60 *Harvard L.R.* (1946–47), p. 539; or the same author, *International Law*. Vol. I, *International Law as Applied by International Courts and Tribunals*, 2nd ed., 1949, pp. xliii *et seq.*

4 *Ways and Means of Making the Evidence of Customary International Law More Readily Available*, 1949, U.N. Document A/CN. 4/6, p. 116.

Court of Justice that assembled the accumulated experience of international courts and tribunals "in the application of the various sources of international law."[5]

Since the establishment of the World Court, much has been written on Article 38 of its Statute and many important articles and monographs have been devoted to sub-paragraph (c).[6] Yet, the author ventures to believe that the publication of this work is justified by differences in scope and approach and he hopes that the result of his investigation may, in some small measure, contribute towards a better understanding of the most controversial of the various sources of international law enumerated in Article 38 of the Statute and thus of international law in general. Moreover, since the essence of general principles of law is the fact of their being common to all legal systems, it is further hoped that this work may also be of interest to municipal and comparative lawyers, who themselves have much to contribute to this topic.

In view of the fact that the material relating to international arbitral proceedings is not always readily available, the author owes much to the unfailing assistance of many librarians both in this country and abroad. He is also much indebted to the various Diplomatic and Consular Missions in London for their courtesy and help in his compilation of Appendix 2 relating to municipal codes which provide for the application of the general principles of law, equity or natural law.

Finally, the author wishes to express his very warm thanks to his friends and colleagues, Mr. Leslie C. Green, Lecturer in International Law and Relations, University College, London, Mr. D. H. N. Johnson, formerly Special Lecturer in International Law at the London School of Economics and now Assistant Legal Adviser to the Foreign Office, and Mr. Ivor C. Jackson, Barrister-at-Law, for their

[5] *Survey of International Law*, 1949, U.N. Document, A/CN. 4/1/Rev. 1. p. 22.
[6] See Appendix 3: Bibliography, section B (*infra*, pp. 412–415).

valuable criticisms and suggestions freely given in the course of the preparation of this work for publication.

It goes without saying that responsibility for all shortcomings both in substance and in form lies solely with the author.

Credit for the fine presentation of the book is due to the publishers and printers. For their friendly collaboration, the author wishes to express cordial appreciation. By a happy coincidence, his father's LL.D. thesis was also published by Messrs. Stevens & Sons, Limited, thirty-seven years ago.

B. C.

University College, London
June, 1953

TABLE OF CASES

(Alphabetical)

The letter "C" before the year indicates the year of the compromis, *where it has not been possible to ascertain the date of the decision.*

TABLE OF CASES

(According to Courts and Tribunals)

A. International Courts and Tribunals Established under Multipartite Treaties

PERMANENT COURT OF INTERNATIONAL JUSTICE

HAGUE COMMISSION OF INQUIRY

MIXED ARBITRAL TRIBUNALS

Under the Treaty of Versailles
(June 28, 1919)

Under the Treaty of St. Germain
(September 10, 1919)

Under the Treaty of Neuilly
(November 27, 1919)

Under the Treaty of Trianon
(July 6, 1920)

COLOMBIAN-UNITED STATES CLAIMS COMMISSION (1864)

UNITED STATES-VENEZUELAN CLAIMS COMMISSION (1866)

MEXICAN-UNITED STATES CLAIMS COMMISSION (1868)

BRITISH-UNITED STATES CLAIMS COMMISSION (1871)

SPANISH-UNITED STATES CLAIMS COMMISSION (1871)

MEXICAN-UNITED STATES GENERAL CLAIMS COMMISSION (1923)

C. Ad Hoc International Arbitrations
(In Chronological Order)

D. Municipal Courts and Tribunals

I. International Claims

United States of America

II. Municipal Decisions

British India

Mixed Courts of Egypt

France

Great Britain

United States of America

TABLE OF DIPLOMATIC INCIDENTS

TABLE OF TREATIES

A. Multipartite Treaties

B. Bipartite Treaties

ABBREVIATIONS

A	Series A—Judgments and Orders of the P.C.I.J. (1923–30). 24 fascicles (Nos. 1–24), Leyden, 1923–30.
A/B	Series A/B—Judgments, Orders and Advisory Opinions of the P.C.I.J. (1931–40). 41 fascicles (Nos. 40–80), Leyden, 1931–40.
Ad. & E.	John Leycester Adolphus and Thomas Flower Ellis: *Reports of cases argued and determined in the Courts of King's Bench* (1834–41). 12 vols., London, 1835–42. Reproduced in E.R., vols. 110–3.
Adv.Op.	Advisory Opinion.
A.J.I.L.	*American Journal of International Law.*
Alabama (*Proceedings*)	*Pièces relatives aux délibérations du Tribunal d'arbitrage à Genève.* 2 vols. Vol. I: *Procès-verbaux des Séances.* Vol. II: *La décision du Tribunal et l'Exposé des motifs qui ont empêché Sir Alexander Cockburn d'y adhérer.* London, n.d.
A.S.I.L.	American Society of International Law.
A.S.J.G. (N.T.I.R.)	*Acta Scandinavica Juris Gentium* (*Nordisk Tidsskrift for International Ret*).
Annuaire	*Annuaire de l'Institut de Droit international.*
Annuaire suisse	*Annuaire suisse de droit international—Schweizerisches Jahrbuch für internationales Recht.*
Annual Digest	*Annual Digest* (*and Reports*) *of Public International Law Cases. Being a selection from the decisions of international and national courts and tribunals.*
Arb.int.	A. de La Pradelle et N. Politis: *Recueil des Arbitrages internationaux.* 2 tomes. Paris, 1924, 1932.
B	Series B—Advisory Opinions of the P.C.I.J. (1922–30). 18 fascicles (Nos. 1–18), Leyden, 1922–30.
Bibliotheca Visseriana	*Bibliotheca Visseriana Dissertationum jus Internationale illustrantium.*
B.F.S.P.	*British and Foreign State Papers.*
B.Y.I.L.	*British Year Book of International Law.*
C.	Command Papers, C 1–C 9950 (1870–99).
Cd.	Command Papers, Cd 1–Cd 9239 (1900–18).
Cl.Com.	Claims Commission.
C.I.J.	Cour internationale de Justice.
C.L.P.	*Current Legal Problems.*
Clunet	*Journal de droit international privé* (Clunet).
Cmd.	Command Papers, Cmd. 1– (1919–).
C.O.	Concurring Opinion.
Collection of Decisions	*Amtliche Sammlung von Entscheidungen des Schiedsgerichts für Oberschlesien—Zbior' Urzedowy Orzeczen Trybunalu Rozjemczego dla Górnego Slaska.* 7 vols., 1929–37.
C.P.J.I.	Cour Permanente de Justice Internationale.
Dec. & Op.	German-United States Mixed Claims Commission (1922): *Administrative Decisions and Opinions of a General Nature, and Opinions in Individual Lusitania and Other Cases to October 1, 1926.* Washington, 1928, pp. ii and 885. *Administrative Decisions and Opinions of a General Nature, and Opinions and Decisions in Certain Individual Claims, October 1, 1926–December 31, 1932, with Orders of March 25 and May 7, 1925, and appendices.* Washington, 1933, pp. xciii and 849–1036.

Dec. & Op.	*Opinions and Decisions, January 1, 1933–October 30, 1939 (Excepting Decisions in Sabotage Claims of June 15 and October 30, 1939), and appendix, 1933–39.* Washington, 1940, pp. iv and 1037–1178 and xiv.
Dec. & Op. of Com.	*Decisions and Opinions of the Commissioners, in accordance with the Convention of November 19, 1926, between Great Britain and the United Mexican States, October 5, 1929, to February 15, 1930.* London, 1931.
D.O.	Dissenting Opinion.
Dodson	John Dodson: *Reports of Cases argued and determined in the High Court of Admiralty*, etc. (1811–22). 2 vols., London, 1815, 1828. Reproduced in E.R., vol. 165.
Edw.	Thomas Edwards: *Reports of Cases argued and determined in the High Court of Admiralty*, etc. (1808–12). London, 1912. Reproduced in E.R., vol. 165.
E.R.	*The English Reports* (1220–1865). 176 vols., Edinburgh and London, 1900–30.
Exch.Div.	*Law Reports.* 2nd series, Exchequer Division (1875–80). 5 vols., London, 1876–81.
Further Dec. & Op. of Com.	*Further Decisions and Opinions of the Commissioners, in accordance with the Conventions of November 19, 1926, and December 5, 1930, between Great Britain and the United Mexican States, Subsequent to February 15, 1930.* London, 1933.
G.C.C.	General Claims Commission.
Grotius Transactions	*Transactions* of the Grotius Society, London.
Hague Convention	The Hague Conventions for the Pacific Settlement of International Disputes, 1899, 1907.
Hague Regulations	Regulations respecting the Laws and Customs of War on Land, annex to Hague Convention No. IV concerning the Laws and Customs of War on Land, 1907.
H.C.R.	James Brown Scott: *The Hague Court Reports.* 2 vols. New York, 1916, 1932.
HMSO	Her Majesty's Stationery Office.
Hornby's *Report*	Edmund Hornby: *Report on the Proceedings of the Mixed Commission on Private Claims established under the Convention between Great Britain and the United States of February* 8, 1853; *with the judgments of the Commissioners and Umpire.* London, 1856.
Hunt's *Report*	Bert L. Hunt: *American and Panamanian General Claims Arbitration, Under the Conventions between the United States and Panama of July 28, 1926, and December 17, 1932. Report of Bert L. Hunt.* Washington, 1934.
Hurlstone and Norman	Edwin Tyrrel Hurlstone and John Paxton Norman: *The Exchequer Reports* (1856–62). 7 vols., London 1857–62. Reproduced in E.R., vols. 156–8.
I.C.J.	International Court of Justice.
ICJ Constitution	*Acts and Documents concerning the Organisation of the I.C.J.*
ICJ Jurisdiction	*Collection of Texts Governing the Jurisdiction of the I.C.J.*
ICJ Pleadings	I.C.J.: *Pleadings, Oral Arguments, Documents.*
ICJ Reports	*Reports of Judgments, Advisory Opinions and Orders of the I.C.J.*
ICJ Yearbook	*Yearbook of the I.C.J.*
I.C.L.Q.	*International and Comparative Law Quarterly.*

Id.	*Idem* (as used in this work, denotes the same tribunal as that referred to immediately above).
I.L.A. Rep.	International Law Association: *Report.*
I.L.Q.	*International Law Quarterly.*
I.M.T. (Nuremberg)	International Military Tribunal (Nuremberg).
I.M.T. (*Nuremberg*)	*Trial of the Major War Criminals before the International Military Tribunal, Nuremberg, November 14, 1945–October 1, 1946.* 42 vols. Nuremberg, 1947–49.
I.M.T. (*Proceedings*)	*The Trial of German Major War Criminals. Proceedings of the I.M.T. sitting at Nuremberg, Germany.* 23 vols. London, HMSO, 1946–52.
Int.Adj., A.S.	J. B. Moore: *International Adjudication Ancient and Modern, History and Documents, etc., Ancient Series.* 1 vol. New York, 1936.
Int.Adj., M.S.	J. B. Moore: *International Adjudications, Ancient and Modern, History and Documents, etc., Modern Series.* 6 vols. New York, 1929–33.
Int.Arb.	J. B. Moore: *History and Digest of the International Arbitrations to which the United States has been a party, etc.* 6 vols. Washington, 1898.
Jd.	Jurisdiction.
Jgt.	Judgment.
Jurisprudence	*Jurisprudence de la Commission franco-mexicaine des réclamations (1924–1932).* Paris, 1933.
Jus Gentium (*Revista*)	*Jus Gentium* (*Rivista di diritto internazionale privato*).
L.J.	*Law Journal*, for instance, *Cambridge L.J.*
L.o.N.	League of Nations.
L.N.O.J.	*League of Nations, Official Journal.*
L.o.N.P.	League of Nations Publications.
L.N.T.S.	*League of Nations, Treaty Series.*
L.Q.R.	*Law Quarterly Review.*
L.R.	*Law Review*, for instance, *Harvard L.R.*
Martens, R.	Geo. Fred. de Martens: *Recueil de Traités . . . des Puissances et États de l'Europe . . . depuis 1761, etc.* (1761–1808). 8 vols., Gottingne, 1817–1835.
Martens, N.R.	Geo. Fred. de Martens: *Nouveau Recueil de Traités . . . des Puissances et États de l'Europe . . . depuis 1808, etc.* (1808–39). 16 vols. and 3 supplements, Gottingne, 1817–42.
Martens, N.R.G.	*Nouveau Recueil Général de Traités, Conventions et autres transactions remarquables, servant à la connaissance des rélations étrangères des Puissances et États dans leurs Rapports mutuels . . . depuis 1840. Série I* (1840–73). 20 vols., Gottingne, 1843–75. *Série II* (1873–1906), 35 vols., Leipzig, 1896–1908. *Série III* (1906–), Leipzig, 1908–
M.A.T.	Mixed Arbitral Tribunal.
M.C.C.	Mixed Claims Commission.
Metcalf	T. Metcalf: *Report of Cases argued and determined in the Supreme Judicial Court of Massachusetts* (1840–47), 13 vols. Boston, 1843–51.
Miller, *Treaties*	H. Miller: *Treaties and other International Acts of the U.S.A.* USGPO, 1931–
Moore, *Dig.*	J. B. Moore: *A Digest of International Law, etc.* 8 vols. Washington, 1906.
Nielsen's *Op. & Rep.*	Fred. K. Nielsen: *American–Turkish Claims Settlement, Under the Agreement of December 24, 1923, and Supplemental Agreements between the United States and Turkey. In Accordance with the Act of March 22, 1935 (49 Stat. 67). Opinions and Reports.* Washington, 1937.

Nielsen's *Report*	Fred. K. Nielsen: ***American and British Claims Arbitrations, under the Special Agreement concluded between the United States and Great Britain, August 18, 1910. Report of Fred. K. Nielsen.*** Washington, 1926.
Op. & Dec.	German-United States Mixed Claims Commission (1922): ***Opinions and Decisions in Sabotage Claims Handed Down, June 15, and October 30, 1939, and appendix.*** Washington, 1940.
Op. of Com. 1926–1931	*Opinions of Commissioners, Under the Convention concluded September 10, 1923, between the United States and Mexico, as extended by the Convention concluded August 17, 1929. April 26, 1926, to April 24, 1931.* Washington, 1931.
Op. of Com. 1927	*Opinions of Commissioners, Under the Convention concluded September 8, 1923, between the United States and Mexico. February 4, 1926, to July 23, 1927.* Washington, 1927.
Op. of Com. 1929	*Opinions of Commissioners, Under the Convention concluded September 8, 1923, as extended by the Convention signed August 16, 1927, between the United States and Mexico. September 26, 1928, to May 17, 1929.* Washington, 1929.
Op. of Com. 1931	*Opinions of Commissioners, Under the Convention concluded September 8, 1923, as extended by subsequent conventions, between the United States and Mexico. October, 1930, to July, 1931.* Washington, 1931.
Ö.Z.f.ö.R.	*Österreichische Zeitschrift für öffentliches Recht.*
Pasicrisie int.	H. La Fontaine: *Pasicrisie internationale. Histoire documentaire des arbitrages internationaux.* Berne, 1902.
P.C.A.	Permanent Court of Arbitration.
P.C.I.J.	Permanent Court of International Justice.
PCIJ: 1 *Documents*	PCIJ: Advisory Committee of Jurists: *Documents presented to the Committee relating to existing plans for the establishment of a P.C.I.J.* L.o.N.P.: V.1920.1.
PCIJ: 2 *Documents*	PCIJ: *Documents Concerning the Action taken by the Council of the L.o.N. under Art. 14 of the Covenant and the Adoption by the Assembly of the Statute of the Permanent Court.* L.o.N.P.: V.1920.3.
Procès-verbaux	PCIJ: Advisory Committee of Jurists: *Procès-verbaux of the Proceedings of the Committee, June 16–July 24, 1920, with Annexes.* The Hague, 1920.
Q.B.D.	*Law Reports.* 2nd series, Queen's Bench Division (1875–90). 25 vols. London, 1876–91.
Ralston's *Report*	Jackson H. Ralston and W. T. S. Doyle: *Report of French–Venezuelan Mixed Claims Commission of 1902.* Washington, 1906.
R.D.I.	*Revue de droit international.*
R.D.I. (*égyptienne*)	*Revue égyptienne de droit international.*
R.D.I. (*española*)	*Revista española de derecho internacional.*
R.D.I. (Gve)	*Revue de droit international, de sciences diplomatiques, politiques et sociales.*
R.D.I. (*hellénique*)	*Revue hellénique de droit international.*
R.D.I.L.C.	*Revue de droit international et de législation comparée.*
R.D.P.S.P.	*Revue de droit public et des sciences politiques.*
Recueil Gény	*Recueil d'études sur les sources du droit en l'honneur de François Gény.* 3 tomes, Paris.
Recueil La Haye	*Recueil des cours professés à l'Académie de Droit international de La Haye.* Paris, 1923–

Recueil Sirey	*Recueil générale des lois et des arrêts, Sirey.*
Revista (Buenos Aires)	*Revista de la Facultad de Derecho y Ciencias sociales*, Buenos Aires.
Revista (Habana)	*Revista de Derecho internacional*, Habana.
R.G.D.I.P.	*Revue général de droit international public.*
R.G.P.C.	*Recueil général périodique et critique des décisions, conventions et lois relatives au droit international public et privé.* Paris, 1924–38.
R.I.I.A.	Royal Institute of International Affairs.
Rivista	*Rivista di diritto internazionale*, Roma.
Schwarzenberger, *International Law*	G. Schwarzenberger: *International Law*, Vol. I: *International Law as Applied by International Courts and Tribunals.* London, 1st ed., 1945; 2nd ed., 1949.
S.C.S.	Kingdom of the Serbs, Croats, and Slovenes.
Ser.C	Series C—Acts and Documents relating to Judgments and Advisory Opinions of the P.C.I.J. 92 vols., Leyden, 1923–42.
Ser.D	Series D—Acts and Documents concerning the Organisation of the P.C.I.J. 12 vols., Leyden, 1922–43.
Ser.E	Series E—Annual Reports of the P.C.I.J., Nos. 1-16. 32 vols., Leyden, 1925–45.
Ser.F	Series F—General Indexes. 4 vols., Leyden, 1928–38.
S.O.	Separate Opinion.
T.A.M.	*Recueil des Décisions des Tribunaux arbitraux mixtes institués par les Traités de Paix.* 9 vols. and 1 fasc. Paris, 1922–30.
T.M.E.	*Gazette des Tribunaux mixtes d'Égypte.* Alexandrie.
Traités du XIXe Siècle	Descamps et Renault: *Recueil international des Traités du XIXe Siècle, contenant l'ensemble du Droit conventionnel entre les États et les Sentences arbitrales.* Paris, 1914.
Traités du XXe Siècle	Descamps et Renault: *Recueil international des Traités du XXe Siècle, contenant l'ensemble du Droit conventionnel entre les États et les Sentences arbitrales, 1901–1907.* 7 vols. Paris.
U.N.	United Nations.
UNCIO	U.N. Conference on International Organisation, San Francisco, 1945.
UNCIO: *Documents*	*Documents of the UNCIO.* 16 vols. London, New York.
UNRIAA	*U.N. Reports of International Arbitral Awards.* 4 vols. U.N., 1948–52.
U.N.T.S.	*United Nations, Treaty Series.*
U.S.F.R.	*Papers relating to the Foreign Relations of the United States.* Washington, 1862–
USGPO	United States Government Printing Office.
Ven.Arb. 1903	J. H. Ralston and W. T. S. Doyle: *Venezuelan Arbitrations of 1903, etc.* Washington, 1904.
Y.B.W.A.	*Year Book of World Affairs.*
Z.f.a.ö.R.u.V.	*Zeitschrift für ausländisches öffentliches Recht und Völkerrecht.*
Z.f.P.	*Zeitschrift für ausländisches und internationales Privatrecht.*
Z.f.V.	*Zeitschrift für Völkerrecht.*
Z.I.R.	*Zeitschrift für internationales Recht.*
Z.ö.R.	*Zeitschrift für öffentliches Recht.*

INTRODUCTION

"THE general principles of law recognised by civilised nations" [1] form part of the law to be applied by the permanent forum of the family of nations, the International Court of Justice. The present work is an attempt to apply the inductive method [2] to the study of such principles and to demonstrate their practical application in the field of international law. It is based on an examination of the decisions of international courts and tribunals, which at the present time constitute the most important means for the determination of rules and principles of international law.[3] A consideration of other law-determining agencies of international law, such as State practice or the writings of publicists, is beyond the scope of the present work.

Article 38 of the Statute of the International Court of Justice provides:—

"1. The Court, whose function is to decide in accordance with international law such disputes as are submitted to it, shall apply:

(a) international conventions, whether general or particular, establishing rules expressly recognised by the contesting States;

(b) international custom, as evidence of a general practice accepted as law;

[1] See ICJ Statute, art. 38, para. 1 (*c*).

[2] Mex.-U.S. G.C.C. (1923): *Dujay Case* (1929), *Op. of Com. 1929*, p. 180, at p. 185: "The existence or non-existence of a rule of law is established by a process of inductive reasoning." See Schwarzenberger, "The Inductive Approach to International Law," 60 *Harvard L.R.* (1946–47), p. 539; or the same author, 1 *International Law*, 1949, pp. xliii *et seq.* The Secretary-General of the U.N., in a Memorandum of March 7, 1949, observed that "there is a growing trend towards an inductive approach" (U.N.Doc. A/CN. 4/6, p. 114).

[3] See Schwarzenberger, *op. cit.*, pp. 550 *et seq.*, 9 *et seq.*, respectively on the hierarchy of "law-determining agencies." *Cf.* also the same author, 1 *International Law*, 1st ed., 1945, p. 2: "Compared with the dicta of textbooks and the practice of this or that State, the decisions of international courts have an authority and reality which cannot be surpassed." Sir Arnold D. McNair, now President of the I.C.J., lecturing in 1928 at the *Académie de Droit international* on *La terminaison et la dissolution des traités*, said "We . . . attach more importance in the subject of international law to the practice and decisions of international tribunals than to the opinions of writers. . . . For our part, it is our intention rarely to cite authors" (22 *Recueil La Haye* (1928), p. 459, at p. 463. Transl.).

In view of the fact that some of the international decisions referred to may not be easily, or generally, accessible, actual quotations, instead of mere references, will usually be given. To facilitate reference to writers, a select bibliography is to be found at the end of this volume.

(c) *the general principles of law recognised by civilised nations;*
(d) subject to the provisions of Article 59, judicial decisions and the teachings of the most highly qualified publicists of the various nations, as subsidiary means for the determination of rules of law.

"2. This provision shall not prejudice the power of the Court to decide a case *ex æquo et bono*, if the parties agree thereto."

This Article is the same as Article 38 of the Statute of the Permanent Court of International Justice, except for an alteration in the numbering of the paragraphs and sub-paragraphs [4] and the addition of a few words of no great practical importance in the introductory phrase.[5] The mention of "general principles of law recognised by civilised nations" ("*les principes généraux de droit reconnus par les nations civilisées*") as part of the law to be applied by the Permanent Court of International Justice at once provoked considerable discussion among writers, in which the most divergent views on the character of such principles were expressed.

Some writers consider that the expression refers primarily to general principles of international law and only subsidiarily to principles obtaining in the municipal law of the various States.[6] Others hold that it would have been redundant for the Statute

[4] In the Statute of the P.C.I.J., the paragraphs were not numbered, while the sub-paragraphs were numbered by arabic figures. The present art. 38 I (*c*) was, therefore, referred to, under the old statute, as art. 38 I 3, or often art. 38 3. For the sake of convenience, the new numbering will be used in this work even when referring to the Statute of the P.C.I.J.

[5] The Statute of the P.C.I.J. simply said: "The Court shall apply." The addition is due to the proposal made by the Chilean delegation in Committee I of Commission IV of the San Francisco Conference, 1945 (UNCIO: 13 *Documents*, pp. 284–285, 493). The Report of the Rapporteur of Committee IV/I explained: "The First Committee has adopted an addition to be inserted in the introductory phrase of this article referring to the function of the Court to decide disputes submitted to it in accordance with international law. The *lacuna* in the old Statute with reference to this point did not prevent the P.C.I.J. from regarding itself as an organ of international law; but the addition will accentuate that character of the new Court" (p. 392). As the Chilean delegation itself explained, the proposal was only actuated by a desire to see an express mention of the application of international law by the Court and was in accordance with the reiterated jurisprudence of the P.C.I.J. (p. 493). The amendment was, therefore, not intended, nor is it believed, to restrict the power of the new Court in any way as compared with that of the old. As it stands, however, this article removes any doubt, if any ever existed, that general principles of law recognised by civilised nations form part of international law.

[6] Anzilotti, 1 *Cours de Droit international*, 1929, p. 117. Hudson, *The P.C.I.J., 1920–42*, 1943, p. 611. Castberg, "La méthodologie du droit international public," 43 *Recueil La Haye* (1933), p. 313, at pp. 370 *et seq.* Morelli, "La théorie générale du procès international," 61 *ibid.* (1937), p. 253, at pp. 344 *et seq.*

to require the Court to apply general principles of international law, and that, therefore, this provision can refer only to principles obtaining in municipal law.[7] Some writers even maintain that the expression is intended to refer exclusively to principles of private law.[8]

A difference of opinion also exists as to whether "the general principles of law recognised by civilised nations" are or are not principles of natural law. While certain authors think that they are,[9] others deny categorically that they have any connection with natural law.[10] A leading exponent of the modern doctrine of natural law believes, however, that, while

[7] Strupp, "Le droit du juge international de statuer selon l'équité," 33 *ibid.* (1930), p. 357, at pp. 474–5. Scerni, *I principî generali di diritto riconosciuti dalle nazioni civili*, 1932, pp. 13 *et seq.*

[8] *Cf.* Lauterpacht, *Private Law Sources and Analogies of International Law*, 1927, p. 71: "Those general principles of law are for most practical purposes identical with general principles of private law." See also *ibid.*, p. 85. For a criticism of this exclusive approach, see Le Fur, "Règles générales du droit de la paix." 54 *Recueil La Haye* (1935), p. 5, at pp. 206–7. In his *The Function of Law in the International Community*, 1933, Lauterpacht admitted that they included also general principles of public law, general maxims and principles of jurisprudence.

Grapin, *Valeur internationale des principes généraux du droit*, 1934, pp. 64–6. Ripert, "Règles du droit civil applicables aux rapports internationaux," 44 *Recueil La Haye* (1933), p. 569. Ripert believed that they were principles of municipal law (p. 580) or civil law (pp. 582–3). While he used the term "civil law" first in the sense of municipal law (*jus civile* of the Romans), he seemed to have allowed it subsequently to assume its modern meaning of private law by tracing the evolution of the meaning of the term in France (p. 583). His main object, however, was to ascertain which principles of private law were really principles applicable in all legal systems (p. 569), and he did not appear to maintain that the latter were exclusively to be found in private law.

[9] Spiropoulos, *Die allgemeinen Rechtsgrundsätze im Völkerrecht*, 1928, pp. 20 *et seq.*, 56. *Cf.*, however, his *Théorie générale du droit international*, 1930, pp. 106–7, and *Traité théorique et pratique du droit international public*, 1933, p. 33, where he said that it was only a question of classification whether "general principles of law" were called principles of positive or natural law.

Salvioli, "Observations," 37 *Annuaire* (1932), p. 315. Cavaglieri, "Règles générales du droit de la paix," 26 *Recueil La Haye* (1929), p. 311, at p. 544 (see *infra*, p. 4, note 14).

[10] Strupp, *op. cit.*, p. 452. Maintaining that these principles did not form part of existing international law, although applicable by the Court in virtue of its Statute, Strupp believed that they were principles contained in the positive laws of the various States, and were, therefore, not natural law (pp. 452–74). Strupp did not, however, deny the existence of a natural law with variable content, identifiable with justice or the juridical ideal of a legal community, although he denied it any force of law, either as a source or as a means of interpretation (pp. 457–60).

Wolff in his "Les principes généraux du droit applicables dans les rapports internationaux," 36 *Recueil La Haye* (1931), p. 479, at pp. 485, 496–7. went further. Conceiving law as *quod principi placuit* (p. 492), he denied altogether the possible existence of natural law.

they are not actually principles of natural law, they are derived from it.[11]

Nor do authors agree as to whether " general principles of law " are part of the international legal order, simply because it is a legal order,[12] or because there exists a rule of customary international law according to which such principles are applicable in international relations.[13] Moreover, some writers maintain that " general principles of law " do not form part of existing international law at all, but only form part of the law to be applied by the World Court by virtue of the enabling provision in its Statute.[14]

The greatest conflict of views concerns the part played in international law by these " general principles." While some writers regard them merely as a means for assisting the interpretation and application of international treaty and customary

[11] Le Fur, " La coutume et les principes généraux du droit comme sources du droit international public," 3 *Recueil Gény*, 1936, p. 362, at p. 368. The relevant passage was almost textually reproduced in the same author's " Règles générales, etc.," *loc. cit.*, p. 205.

[12] Scerni, *op. cit.*, pp. 29 *et seq.* F. A. v. der Heydte, " Glossen zu einer Theorie der allgemeinen Rechtsgrundsätze," 33 *Die Friedenswarte* (1933), p. 289, at p. 290. v. der Heydte distinguished two categories of " general principles." He believed that certain " general principles " necessarily formed part of any legal system and, therefore, also of international law (see further, *infra*, p. 5, note 17).

[13] Verdross, *Die Verfassung der Völkerrechtsgemeinschaft*, 1926, p. 59. Lauterpacht, *Private Law Sources, etc.*, 1927, p. 63. Balladore-Pallieri, *I Principii generali di diritto reconosciuti dalle nazioni civili*, 1932, pp. 48 *et seq.*, 60 *et seq.* In his *Diritto internazionale pubblico*, 1937, p. 138, Balladore-Pallieri changed his opinion and derived their validity from the very constitution of the international community. Wolff, *op. cit.*, p. 483.

[14] Cavaglieri, *op. cit.*, p. 323, and particularly at p. 544: "These principles do not, in our opinion, belong to international law. They are rules of justice, of natural law, which, being to a great extent observed in the municipal law of civilised countries, are declared applicable by the Court, in the absence of actual rules of international law, conventional or customary " (Transl.). The above statement seems a rather dangerous one for a positivist like Cavaglieri to make; for he thereby admitted that principles of justice and natural law were to a great extent followed in the municipal law of civilised nations. And if it were shown that these general principles of law were in fact part of existing international law and not merely the law to be applied by the Court in virtue of art. 38 I (*c*), it would mean that, in international law also, principles of justice and natural law were applicable.

Strupp, *op. cit.*, p. 474. In his " Règles générales du droit de la paix," 47 *Recueil La Haye* (1934), p. 263, at pp. 332 *et seq.*, Strupp said that there had been no customary law admitting these general principles of law *in toto*, although a few had been individually adopted.

Gihl, *International Legislation*, 1937, p. 107, and " Lacunes du droit international," 3 (1) A.S.J.G.(N.T.I.R.) (1932), p. 37, at pp. 47 *et seq.*

Morelli, *op. cit.*, pp. 344 *et seq.*, 348 *et seq.* Although Morelli believed that some of these general principles were deducible from rules of international law, he maintained that it was not possible for an international tribunal, in the absence of a special permissive rule, to resort to them.

law,[15] and others consider them as no more than a subsidiary source of international law,[16] some modern authors look upon "general principles" as the embodiment of the highest principles—the "superconstitution"—of international law.[17]

Interesting though this discussion of the character of such "general principles" may be in the theory of international law, it is even more important to know what they in fact represent. For this reason, the purpose of the present study is not to ascertain what they ought to be theoretically, or how they

[15] Salvioli, "La Corte permanente di Giustizia internationale," 15 *Rivista* (1923), p. 11; 16 *ibid.* (1924), p. 272, at pp. 278–84. Makowski, "L'organisation actuelle de l'arbitrage international," 36 *Recueil La Haye* (1931), p. 263, at pp. 360–1.

[16] Lauterpacht, *Private Law Sources*, 1927, p. 69. Scerni, *op. cit.*, 1932, pp. 40–1. Verdross, *op. cit.*, p. 57. The same author as *Rapporteur* of the Institut de Droit International, 37 *Annuaire* (1932), p. 292. *Cf.* next footnote.

[17] Scelle, *Cours* (*Manuel*) *de droit international public*, 1948, p. 580.

Härle adopted a rather curious view in his "Les principes généraux de droit et le droit des gens," 3 (16) R.D.I.L.C. (1935), p. 633. He started from the premise that the general principles of law mentioned in art. 38 I (c) were of a subsidiary character (pp. 679–80). When, however, he discovered that there were some general principles of law "auxquels . . . en droit international comme dans tous les autres systèmes de droit . . . est accordée une importance primordiale," he said: "These principles have in fact acquired such an *absolute* and *indisputable* authority that States *can no longer elaborate rules which are opposed to them.* This particular category of general principles of law . . . (one has only to think . . . of the duty to interpret all obligations deriving from a treaty in good faith, . . . of the nullity of promises obtained through fraud, of the prohibition of the abusive exercise of rights, etc.), . . . does not, however, belong any more to those 'general principles of law' of a subsidiary character mentioned in art. 38, para. 3, but, on account of their inherent legal validity, to *jus cogens*, absolute and valid *vis-à-vis* all States" (p. 680. Transl. Author's italics). It may be pointed out that some of the examples of the special category of general principles of law which, according to Härle, do not belong to the "general principles" mentioned in art. 38 I (c) are precisely those which the framers of the article regarded as typical of this provision, *e.g.*, principle proscribing the abuse of rights (*Procès-verbaux*, p. 315), principle of good faith (*Procès-verbaux*, p. 335). Härle refused, however, to accept v. der Heydte's division of these "general principles" into two categories.

F. A. v. der Heydte distinguished, in art. 38 I (c), between (1) certain legal principles recognised by States as an essential part of any legal order, and (2) certain positive rules of municipal law which, though not forming an essential part of every legal order, were recognised by practically all States *in foro domestico* (*op. cit.*, p. 290, c. 2). He believed that those who maintained the subsidiary character of general principles of law had confused these two distinct kinds of principles (p. 297, c. 1). The first category of "general principles" was considered *jus cogens*, the second category as of a subsidiary character (pp. 297, c. 2; 298, c. 1).

Verdross in his "Les principes généraux dans la jurisprudence internationale" (52 *Recueil La Haye* (1935), p. 191) revised his previous views by accepting the view of Heydte. He now held that "general principles of law take precedence of (*ont la précellence sur le*) positive international law. In effect, they are at the foundation of positive law, from which the rules of the latter cannot derogate" (p. 205. Transl.).

C. de Visscher, "Contribution à l'étude des sources du droit international," 3 *Recueil Gény*, 1936, p. 389, at p. 397.

should be classified, but is primarily intended to determine what they are in substance and the manner in which they have been applied by international tribunals.[18]

As an introduction to this study, the genesis of Article 38 I (c) of the Statute of the World Court may usefully be examined. In February, 1920, at its second meeting, the Council of the League of Nations appointed an Advisory Committee of Jurists for the purpose of preparing plans for the establishment of the Permanent Court of International Justice provided for in Article 14 of the Covenant of the League of Nations. This Advisory Committee[19] held its meetings from June 16 to July 24, 1920,[20] and was able to present its Report together with the Draft Statute of the Court to the Council of the League at its eighth session (July 30—August 5, 1920).

Before the Advisory Committee actually met, a Memorandum was submitted to it by the Secretariat of the League of Nations, together with a number of draft schemes prepared by States and individuals, relating to the establishment of a World Court.[21] In so far as the law to be applied by the Court was concerned, it will be found that none of these drafts took a positivist[22] or voluntarist[23] view. Besides treaties and established rules, the Court was according to these various drafts

[18] *Cf.* Memorandum submitted by the Secretary-General of the U.N., *Survey of International Law*, 1949, A/CN. 4/1/Rev. 1, p. 22. While the Memorandum recognised that in any future codification of international law, no useful purpose would be served by any modification of art. 38 of the Statute of the I.C.J., it added: "A distinct element of usefulness might, however, attach to any commentary accompanying the definition and *assembling the experience of the International Court of Justice and of other international tribunals in the application of the various sources of international law.*"

[19] Members: Mineichiro Adatci, Rafael Altamira, Clovis Bevilaqua (owing to impossibility of attending the meetings, subsequently replaced by Raoul Fernandes), Descamps (Baron), Francis Hagerup, Albert de La Pradelle, Loder, Phillimore (Lord), Arturo Ricci-Busatti, Elihu Root (assisted by James Brown Scott). Secretary-General of the Committee: Dionisio Anzilotti.

[20] The minutes of the meeting were published under the title *P.C.I.J.: Advisory Committee of Jurists, Procès-verbaux of the Proceedings of the Committee, June 16th–July 24th, 1920, with Annexes*, 1920. Herein cited as *Procès-verbaux*.

[21] PCIJ: 1 *Documents*.

[22] As used in this work, "positivism" denotes that school of thought which consider that law "properly so called" consists only of rules derived from a "determinate source" or, in other words, rendered "positive" by means of a formal process (*cf.*, *infra*, p. 23).

[23] As used in this work "voluntarism" denotes that school of thought which emphasises the element of will in the formation of legal norms, either the will of the State, in the form of a command, or the will of the subjects, as manifested by consent.

directed to apply "general principles of law," [24] "general principles of law and equity," [25] "general principles of justice and equity," [26] or even "rules which, in the considered opinion of the Court, should be the rules of international law." [27]

It was, therefore, quite in line with these drafts, which may be considered as a fair indication of the general opinion on the subject, that, when the question of the law to be applied by the Court came up for discussion in the Advisory Committee of Jurists, Baron Descamps, Chairman of the Committee, proposed that, after conventions (clause 1) and commonly recognised custom (clause 2), the Court should apply "the rules of international law as recognised by the legal conscience of civilised nations" (clause 3),[28] or, as they were described in the original French version of the proposal, "*les règles de droit international telles que les reconnaît la conscience juridique des peuples civilisés.*" [29]

Mr. Elihu Root, the American member of the Committee, while not objecting to the application by the Court of conventions and recognised custom (*i.e.*, clauses 1 and 2 of the Descamps proposal), said that he "could not understand the exact meaning of clause 3." He wondered whether it was possible to compel States to submit their disputes to a court, "which would administer not merely law, but also what it deems to be the conscience of civilised peoples." [30]

It may be apposite to point out here that although some words, which are identically spelt in French and English, can be literally transposed from one language into the other, others carry subtle but important differences in meaning in the two

[24] Draft Scheme of Denmark, Norway and Sweden, art. 27 II.

[25] German Draft Scheme, art. 35. Clovis Bevilaqua's Draft Scheme, art. 24 II. Bevilaqua's second category of rules is in fact customary international law. See his Explanatory Notes *ad* art. 24 (PCIJ: 1 *Documents*, p. 371).

[26] Art. 42 of the Swiss Draft Scheme establishes the following three categories: conventions, principles of international law, and the general principles of justice and equity. Art. 12 of the Draft of the Union Juridique Internationale directs the court to apply "law, justice and equity."

[27] Draft Scheme of Denmark, Norway and Sweden, art. 27 II (Alternative). Danish Draft Scheme, art. 15 II. Norwegian Draft Scheme, art. 15 II. Swedish Draft Scheme, art. 17 II. Draft Scheme of the Five Neutral Powers (Denmark, Netherlands, Norway, Sweden, Switzerland), art. 2 II.

[28] Translation of the Secretariat.

[29] The proceedings of the Advisory Committee were conducted in French, except in the case of Elihu Root, who used English. "The English text of the *Procès-verbaux* is to be looked upon as a translation, except in so far as concerns the speeches and remarks of Mr. Root" (*Procès-verbaux*, p. iv).

[30] *Procès-verbaux*, pp. 293–4.

languages so that literal transposition becomes impossible. Thus the word "*conscience*," which exists both in English and in French, while it often conveys the same meaning in both languages, does not invariably do so. "Conscience" has acquired in current English usage a primarily moral and introspective connotation—the sense of what is *morally* right or wrong possessed by an individual or a group *as regards things for which the individual himself*, or the group collectively, *is responsible*.[31]

In French, "*conscience*" denotes also "the sense of what is right or wrong," but not necessarily what is *morally* right or wrong. For instance, the French speak of "*liberté de conscience*" for "freedom of belief," thus distinguishing "*conscience religieuse*" from "*conscience morale*." It follows that "*conscience juridique*" is equally distinguishable from "*conscience morale*." It is a familiar expression with French jurists, meaning "the sense of what is juridically right or wrong."[32]

[31] *Cf. The Oxford English Dictionary, sub voce* "Conscience": "4. The internal acknowledgment or recognition of the moral quality of one's motives and actions; the sense of right or wrong as regards things for which one is responsible; the faculty or principle which pronounces upon the moral quality of one's actions or motives, approving the right and condemning the wrong." *Ibid.*, Note on etymology: "The word is etymologically, as its form shows, a noun of condition or function, like *science*, *prescience*, *intelligence*, *prudence*, etc., and as such originally had no plural: a man or a people had *more* or *less* conscience. But in sense 4 [quoted above] it came gradually to be thought of as an individual entity, a member or organ of the mental system, of which each man possessed *one*, and thus it took *a* and *plural*. So *my* conscience, your *conscience*, was understood to mean no longer our respective shares or amounts of the common quality *conscience*, but to be two distinct individual consciences, mine and yours."

[32] It has to be remembered that the word "*conscience*" in French stands for both "consciousness" and "conscience," and, even when used in the latter sense, it does not *necessarily* bear many of the connotations of the word "conscience" in English. Used in the locution "*conscience juridique*," "*conscience*" in fact conveys an idea covering both its meanings in English.

"*Conscience juridique*" first conveys the meaning of the consciousness, or inward knowledge, of the objective law, or, if preferred, of a standard of judgment of human behaviour which has come to be specified as juridical, as distinct from the moral, religious or similar disciplines of human thought or conduct.

Secondly, it denotes, as a consequence of this knowledge, the sentiment, rising sometimes to conviction, of what is right and wrong according to law (*jus*), *i.e.*, the general principles of the legal system.

The expression "*conscience juridique*" was often used by other members of the Committee coming from Latin countries, as well as by Descamps. Thus Ricci-Busatti, of Italy, used the expression during the discussion of this very article. He said that his "*conscience juridique*" rose against the mention of teachings of writers as a source of law and against the establishment

Furthermore, although " *conscience* " in French also implies the passing of judgment upon human actions and motives, it does not invariably mean an introspective judgment upon one's *own* actions and motives. Thus " *conscience publique* " in French merely means " the people's sense of what is right or wrong " without necessarily implying self-judgment.[33]

For these reasons, the phrase " *la conscience juridique des peuples civilisés* " which figured in the Descamps proposal may be translated into English as " the sense common to all civilised peoples [34] of what is juridically right or wrong," or as " the *opinio juris communis* of civilised mankind." [35]

of a hierarchy among the various sources of law referred to in the draft (see *Procès-verbaux*, p. 332).

Clovis Bevilaqua, of Brazil, also used the expression in his Explanatory Notes to his draft Statute of the P.C.I.J. (see PCIJ: 1 Documents, p. 370). The context in which it was used shows, moreover, that " *conscience juridique* " was identified in nature with the *opinio juris* in a custom. Indeed, *opinio juris communis* is often a suitable translation of the term.

33 *Dictionnaire Larousse du XXe Siècle* defines " *Conscience publique* " as follows, *sub voce* " Conscience ": " Sentiment commun à un groupe, à une classe de personnes: La Conscience *publique*."

Dictionnaire de l'Académie française, sub voce, " Conscience ": " La Conscience publique, Le sentiment qu'un peuple a du bien et du mal. La Conscience du genre humain, Le Sentiment que tous les hommes ont du bien et du mal."

Cf. the following instances where " *conscience publique* " was used. Montesquieu, *Lettres persanes*, 129. Speaking of laws with which one disagrees, Montesquieu said: " Whatever may be these laws, one must always follow them and consider them as ' *la conscience publique*,' to which that [*i.e.*, ' la conscience '] of the individuals must submit." (Transl.) See also the Preamble to the Hague Conventions Concerning the Laws and Customs of War on Land, 1899 and 1907, which speaks of " the rules and principles of the law of nations resulting " from the " *exigences de la conscience publique*."

These quotations demonstrate the intimate connection that is considered to exist between the law and the " *conscience publique*." " *Conscience juridique* " is that part of the " *conscience publique* " which is specifically juridical in nature. It is regarded as the " material source " of the law.

34 It should be noticed that the original proposal of Descamps referred to " peuples civilisés," *i.e.*, " civilised peoples " or " civilised mankind." This is important, because the expressions " civilised nations " and " nations civilisées " which are now to be found in the English and French text of Art. 38 I (c) originate from Root's amendment to the Descamps proposal. This amendment referred to " civilised nations," which was the English translation used by the Committee of Jurists for Descamps' " peuples civilisés." In fact the earlier translation of the Root amendment also used " peuples civilisés " in the French version. Looked at from this angle, the word " nation " in Art. 38 I (c) should be understood not in its politico-legal sense, as it is used in " League of *Nations*," " United *Nations* " or " Inter*nation*al Law," but in its more general sense of a people, as for instance, the Scottish *nation*, the French *nation*, the Maori *nation*, etc. Some further support for this view may be found in the fact that, at certain stages of the drafting of the Article, the word *nation* in clause 3 was written with a small *n*, while the same word in clause 4, in the sense of a country, was written with a capital *N* (see *Texte adopté en Ière Lecture*, Art. 35, *Procès-verbaux*, p. 659, at pp. 665–6).

35 These translations are borne out by Descamps' " Speech on the Rules of Law to be Applied," delivered at the 14th Meeting of the Advisory Committee of

The literal translation of the phrase by "the conscience of civilised nations" would seem to have a different meaning in English, namely, "the moral sense of right and wrong possessed by each civilised nation as regards things for which it is responsible."[36] And, since "conscience" in English denotes an essentially moral quality, the original English translation of the Descamps proposal, which spoke of the "legal conscience of civilised nations," is, if not self-contradictory, at least difficult to understand, as, indeed, Mr. Root found it.[37]

The reason why Mr. Root at first objected to the Descamps proposal was certainly more substantial than one arising from a linguistic misunderstanding,[38] but a proper understanding of the original proposal is nevertheless important.

An examination of the various proposals put forward and opinions expressed during the discussion, concerning the rules of law to be applied by the Court, discloses five distinct views:—

(1) First, a group of proposals refrained from indicating to the Court which rules of law it was to apply.[39]

Jurists (*Procès-verbaux*, pp. 322–5). "*La conscience juridique des nations civilisées*" was considered as the reflex of "objective justice" in man (p. 323), it was "the law of what is just and what is unjust that has been indelibly written and engraved upon the hearts of civilised peoples" (p. 325. Transl.). See also Descamps, *Procès-verbaux*, p. 318, where he identified it with what "*l'opinion universelle*" recognised as "justice."

See *supra*, p. 8, note 32, *in fine*. *Cf. infra*, note 36, *in fine*.

36 *Cf.* the use of the phrase in Oppenheim: *International Law*, Vol. 1, 4th ed., by McNair, London, 1928, p. 14: "The heads of the civilised States, their Governments, their Parliaments, and the public opinion of the whole of civilised humanity, agree and consent that the body of rules for international conduct which is called the Law of Nations shall, if necessary, be enforced by external power, in contradistinction to rules of international morality and courtesy, which are left to the consideration of the *conscience of nations*." "Conscience of nations" is thus clearly recognised as a moral concept and stands in contradistinction to "external power," as morality does to law. "Conscience" is *in pectore* in each nation regulating its own actions. The quotation also shows the contradistinction between the "conscience of nations" and "the public opinion of the whole of civilised humanity." "*La conscience juridique des peuples civilisés*" in fact resembles the latter much more than the former. *Cf. supra*, note 35.

37 See *supra*, p. 7.

38 See *infra*, pp. 12 *et seq.*

39 La Pradelle, following the proposal of the Union-Juridique Internationale, proposed that the Statute should merely provide: "The Court shall judge in accordance with law, justice and equity." He considered that while the judge had to decide according to law, "it was not necessary to define law for him" (*Procès-verbaux*, pp. 295–6). Phillimore was also inclined not to specify the law to be applied by the Court but only to insert in the oath which the judge was to take all that might be considered necessary concerning the law to be applied (*ibid.*, p. 320). Previously he had pointed out that in the English system, the judge took an oath "to do justice according to law" (*ibid.*, p. 315).

(2) Secondly, the various Scandinavian drafts and that of the Five Neutral Powers,[40] inspired by the Swiss Civil Code,[41] directed the Court to apply conventions and recognised rules of international law, and, in default of such rules, to apply what, in its considered opinion, the rule of international law on the subject ought to be. The latter part of this proposal was regarded as conferring on the Court a legislative power,[42] and, since all the members of the Committee were in agreement that a Court should not legislate,[43] this formula did not find any favour.[44]

(3) Thirdly, there was the proposal of Baron Descamps, which was supported by M. Loder and M. Hagerup and received no serious opposition except from Mr. Elihu Root. In order to appreciate how much this view coincides with the fifth view, which was that of Lord Phillimore's,[45] it must be realised that, in his proposal, Baron Descamps defined international custom as "*pratique commune des nations, acceptée par elles comme*

[40] Denmark, Netherlands, Norway, Sweden, Switzerland.

[41] *Cf. Procès-verbaux*, p. 296. For Art. 1 of the Swiss Civil Code, see Appendix 2, *infra*, p. 400, at p. 404.

[42] Phillimore, *Procès-verbaux*, p. 295.

[43] Phillimore, *ibid.*, pp. 295, 316, 584; La Pradelle, *ibid.*, p. 296; Elihu Root, *ibid.*, p. 309; Loder, *ibid.*, p. 311; Ricci-Busatti, *ibid.*, 314; Hagerup, *ibid.*, p. 319; Descamps, *ibid.*, pp. 336, 620.

The view of the Committee on this problem may also be gauged from a study of the evolution of Art. 38 I (d). The text prepared by the drafting committee of the Advisory Committee read: "The Court shall . . . apply . . . 4. rules of law derived from judicial decisions and the teachings of the most highly qualified publicists of the various nations" (*ibid.*, p. 567). At the 27th Meeting of the Advisory Committee (July 19), the following phrase, "as subsidiary means for the determination of rules of law" was added to the end of clause 4 (*ibid.*, p. 584), thus completely altering the meaning of this clause. Judicial decisions and teachings of publicists are no longer regarded as being able to create rules of law applicable to future cases; they serve only as means for the determination of the rules of law. They may properly be called "law-determining agencies" in distinction from "sources of law." See Schwarzenberger, "The Inductive Approach to International Law," 60 *Harvard Law Review* (1946–47), p. 539, at pp. 550 *et seq.*; 1 *International Law*, 1949, pp. 8 *et seq.* This point was further accentuated when at its 30th meeting (July 21), the Advisory Committee deleted the words "rules of law arising from" (*Procès-verbaux*, pp. 620, 655). The subsequent addition of the express reservation of Art. 59 of the Statute was also designed to avoid operative rules of law being drawn from judicial decisions for cases other than the one decided between the parties. From this examination of the origin of clause (d) of Art. 38 I, it emerges clearly that this clause is different in nature from the other three preceding clauses, and it may be concluded that, in the opinion of the framers of the Article, a court does not legislate or create rules of law and that its decisions are not sources, but only evidence or determining agents of the rules of law.

[44] Even the member from Norway, Hagerup, believed, on second thoughts, that it went too far (*Procès-verbaux*, pp. 296, 319).

[45] *Infra*, pp. 13 *et seq.*

loi." As such, his conception of custom was much more restrictive than Lord Phillimore's. According to the Descamps formula, both the *consuetudo* and the *opinio juris*, the two constitutive elements of a custom, have to be *common* to all nations. Adopting so stringent a view of international custom, it is not surprising that Baron Descamps should classify another portion of international law under a third heading, "*les règles de droit international telles que les reconnaît la conscience juridique des peuples civilisés.*" While he conceived these as rules of objective justice, he limited the formula to what the *opinio juris communis* of the civilised world considered as rules of international law. As the formula indicates, they are, in his opinion, already part and parcel of international law.[46] These rules of objective justice, Baron Descamps also called "general principles of law,"[47] and, as an illustration of the principles he had in mind, he cited the case of the application of the principle of *res judicata* in the *Pious Fund Case* by the Permanent Court of Arbitration.[48]

(4) Fourthly, there was the original view of Mr. Root who seemed ready to admit only clauses 1 and 2 of the Descamps proposal, and even entertained some doubt as to clause 2 concerning the application by the Court of commonly recognised custom.[49] The position originally adopted by this distinguished American statesman, who had contributed so much to the establishment of the Permanent Court of International Justice, was, however, actuated more by an earnest wish to see the Statute of the Court accepted by all countries than by strict adherence to juridical principles.[50] In this connection, it should be borne in mind that, at that time, the Advisory

[46] See Descamps' "Speech on the Rules of Law to be Applied" delivered at the 14th Meeting (July 2, 1920), *Procès-verbaux*, pp. 322–5, and his quotation from the Preamble of the Hague Conventions Concerning the Laws and Customs of War on Land, 1899 and 1907. See also Statement of Fernandes (*ibid.*, pp. 345–6).

[47] *Ibid.*, p. 318. Likewise, Fernandes (p. 345).

[48] *Ibid.*, p. 310. *Cf. ibid.*, p. 316, where Phillimore pointed out that the Chairman was referring to the application of the principle of *res judicata*.

[49] *Ibid.*, pp. 293–4. *Cf.* also *ibid.*, pp. 286–7, where, during the discussion relating to the competence of the Court, Root had already maintained the view that "Nations will submit to positive law, but will not to principles as have not been developed into positive rules supported by an accord between all States."

[50] See Root, *ibid.*, pp. 308–9. *Cf.* La Pradelle, *ibid.*, p. 314.

Committee had agreed in principle that the compulsory jurisdiction of the Court should be accepted by all the Members of the League of Nations by the very fact of adhering to the Statute of the Court. Mr. Root rightly linked this aspect of the question with the rules concerning the application of law. However unconnected they may be from a juridical standpoint, their relation is certainly real and substantial from the point of view of States called upon to submit to the jurisdiction of the Court. A restrictive formula with regard to the law to be applied would, in Mr. Root's opinion, have facilitated the acceptance of the step forward in the field of jurisdiction. He was, therefore, disposed to accept the Descamps proposal in respect of all the Court's jurisdiction other than its compulsory jurisdiction.[51] He was even disposed to accept it, where the Court had compulsory jurisdiction, so long as the dispute concerned the interpretation of a treaty, breaches of an obligation, the extent and nature of reparation for breach of an obligation, or the interpretation of judgments; but he was not prepared to accept it where the dispute concerned questions of international law in general.[52]

(5) Finally, there was Lord Phillimore's amended text of the Descamps proposal, elaborated in conjunction with Mr. Root, which was, in fact, the text adopted by the Advisory Committee. On closer examination, Lord Phillimore's views were not so different from those of Baron Descamps.[53] His attitude with regard to the rules concerning the law to be applied by the Court was perhaps even more liberal than that of Baron Descamps; for he was ready to allow that, in the absence of treaty law, the Court should apply the rules of international law in force "from whatever source they may be derived." [54] But, even on the assumption that, by this formula, Lord Phillimore intended the only alternative to treaty law to be customary law,[55] his conception of international custom was much more liberal than that of Baron Descamps; for he declared

[51] *Ibid.*, p. 310.
[52] *Ibid.*, pp. 313–4.
[53] See *supra*, pp. 11 *et seq.*
[54] *Procès-verbaux*, pp. 295, 317.
[55] This does not seem, however, to be the case; for otherwise he would simply have said conventions and custom. *Cf.* also *ibid.*, p. 333, where, on being pressed by Ricci-Busatti, Phillimore said that he admitted doctrine as a source of law.

that, "generally speaking, all the principles of common law are applicable to international relations. They are in fact part of international law." [56] He considered the example cited by Baron Descamps to illustrate "*les règles de droit international telles que les reconnaît la conscience juridique des peuples civilisés,*" namely, the principle of *res judicata*, as one of the principles of common law. "This," he said, "is a principle which has the same character of law as any formulated rule." [57] In other words, there are principles of international law in force which have not yet assumed the form of formulated rules. Indeed, when questioned by Baron Descamps, Lord Phillimore agreed that international law as understood by him resembled natural law.[58] Theoretical niceties apart, there is, therefore, little practical difference between the views of Baron Descamps, who held that international law included certain principles of objective justice, and the views of Lord Phillimore, who held that international law included all the principles of common law, which itself resembled natural law. Furthermore, Lord Phillimore declared himself generally in agreement with M. Ricci-Busatti [59] who had said that the Court should apply "general principles of law." [60] It is, indeed, in this formula that the views of Baron Descamps and Lord Phillimore found their common denominator.[61]

When, therefore, at the 15th Meeting of the Committee (July 3, 1920), the formula "the general principles of law recognised by civilised nations," in lieu of the original clause 3, was actually proposed by Mr. Root, who had, in collaboration with Lord Phillimore, prepared an amended text to the Descamps proposal, it was immediately agreed to by Baron Descamps and the rest of the Committee. This is the origin of the present Article 38 I (c) of the Statute of the International Court of Justice.[62]

Reviewing the discussion in the Advisory Committee, it is

[56] *Ibid.*, p. 316. International custom, thus conceived, would cover a much wider ground than merely "common practice between nations, accepted by them as law."

[57] *Ibid.*, p. 316. See French text.

[58] *Ibid.*, p. 318.

[59] *Ibid.*, p. 333.

[60] *Ibid.*, p. 314.

[61] *Supra*, pp. 11 *et seq.*

[62] *Procès-verbaux*, pp. 331 *et seq.*

quite plain that the Root-Phillimore amendment marked a reversal of Mr. Root's original attitude and his conversion to the views of Lord Phillimore, to whose pen it seems safe to attribute the amended draft.[63]

The views of Phillimore and Descamps being in substance the same, there is no foundation for the assertion that the solution ultimately adopted constituted a rejection of the views of Descamps and the adoption of the original view of Elihu Root.[64] Indeed the exact opposite is the case.[65] Nor is it true to say that the formula finally arrived at was a "compromise of views very far apart."[66] The formula "general principles of law" is in fact the common denominator of two views which were in substance very much alike.[67] With regard to this formula, and also with regard to the article as a whole, it is true to say, in the words of Lord Phillimore, when he moved that the Committee should proceed to the next item of the agenda, that "all the members were in agreement in substance, the criticism was directed only at the form."[68]

[63] The formula was presented by Elihu Root, because at the previous meeting, having expressed his disagreement with the Descamps' proposal, he was asked by Hagerup, who supported Descamps' views, to formulate his thoughts in writing (*ibid.*, pp. 317–31). Having presented the draft, Root does not seem to have said anything more during the discussion, on the subject of the rules governing the application of law. At the 15th Meeting, when the draft was discussed, it was Phillimore who undertook to explain the meaning of the text, who defended its wording, and who consented to its amendment. In one instance, he spoke of the text "which he had formulated in agreement with [*d'accord avec*] Mr. Root" (p. 333. Phillimore spoke in French).

[64] Härle, *op. cit.*, p. 667. He said that because Elihu Root was in the majority, he was asked to draft the article. For the real reason why Elihu Root presented a draft, see preceding footnote.

[65] J. B. Scott, who was present at the meetings of the Advisory Committee as legal adviser to Elihu Root, said in his Presidential address, at the Inaugural Meeting of the Lausanne Session of the Institut de Droit International in 1927 that "the expression general principles of law is only the English version of the phrase, equally precise but more elegant of our Latin friends: '*la conscience juridique des nations civilisées*'" (33 (3) *Annuaire* (1927), p. 34, at p. 54. Transl.).

[66] Kopelmenas, "Quelques Réflexions au sujet de l'Article 38, 3° du Statut de la C.P.J.I.," 43 R.G.D.I.P. (1936), p. 285, at p. 291. The author maintained that even a superficial reading of the proceedings would lead to this conclusion and, therefore, rejected the discussion in the Advisory Committee as of any value for explaining the meaning of Art. 38 I (c). There is, however, a danger of falling into error in a hasty reading. For instance, at p. 291, note 20, by citing *Procès-verbaux*, p. 295, he attributed to Phillimore the view that the application of general principles of law would confer upon the Court a legislative power, while in fact Phillimore was not referring to general principles of law at all but to the last part of Art. 2 of the Draft of the Five Neutral Powers.

[67] *Supra*, p. 14.

[68] *Procès-verbaux*, p. 338.

Indeed, on the general question of the rules governing the application of law by the Court, all members of the Advisory Committee were fundamentally in agreement that the position of the international judge should be the same as that of a national judge.[69] The difference of opinion that existed, as Lord Phillimore pointed out, was one between Continental and Anglo-Saxon lawyers in their different approach to the power of the judge. He said :—

"These divergences arose from the Continental idea of justice; at the outset strict limitations are imposed on the judges, then through fear of restricting them too much they are given complete freedom within these limits. The English system is different: the judge takes an oath 'to do justice according to law'."[70]

This "Continental" attitude towards the power of the judge to which Lord Phillimore referred may be explained in two ways.

First, in codifying rules concerning the application of the law, it is realised in many countries that positive law, even when this includes custom, is insufficient to cover the entire juridical life of the community in all its multifarious and ever-changing aspects. In order to avoid a possible denial of justice, many civil codes expressly provide that the judge, in the absence of express or analogous provisions of positive law, should apply either natural law, as do some earlier codes, or general principles of law, or rules of law which he would lay down if he were himself the legislator.[71]

Secondly, even where the codes did not expressly recognise the existence and applicability of natural law or general principles of law, legal theory on the Continent, especially in Western Europe, witnessed, at the beginning of the twentieth century, a rising reaction against the excessive positivism and attachment to texts so characteristic of the nineteenth century. In place of the theory of the logical plenitude or self-sufficiency of the positive law, the modern theory maintains that the

[69] *Cf.* Loder (*ibid.*, p. 312), La Pradelle (p. 312), Phillimore (pp. 315, 316), Hagerup (p. 317), Ricci-Busatti, as understood by Phillimore, (pp. 316 *in fine*, 333), Fernandes (p. 346).

[70] *Ibid.*, p. 315. *Cf.* also Phillimore, "Scheme for the P.C.I.J.," 6 *Grotius Transactions* (1920), p. 89, at p. 94.

[71] See *infra*, pp. 400 *et seq.*, Appendix 2: Municipal Codes which provide for the Application of General Principles of Law, Equity, or Natural Law.

positive law has always been and always should be guided, supplemented and perhaps even corrected by an unformulated law. The latter is not the product of philosophical speculation as it was in the past, but a real and living force in the life of the legal community. The judge is no longer regarded as an "inanimate being," "which speaks the words of the law,"[72] but as an intelligent collaborator of the legislator in the application of this living law.[73]

[72] Montesquieu, *De l'esprit des lois*, Bk. XI, Chap. VI, where he also spoke of the power of the judge as being "so terrible among men." Montesquieu, with his dogma of separation of powers and J. J. Rousseau, with his theory that the written law represented the "General Will," both contributed to foster the "fetishism of the written law" in the nineteenth century. According to this view, for a judge to supplement or to adapt the law according to circumstances would be to usurp the legislative power or to misapply the general will. At that time, there was also a reaction against the judicial arbitrariness of the *ancien régime*. Portalis, one of the framers of the Code Napoléon, speaking of his own time, said: "One reasons as if the legislators were gods, and as if the judges were not even human beings" (see P. A. Fenet, 6 *Recueil complet des travaux préparatoires du Code Civil*, Paris, 1836, pp. 359–61). Despite Portalis' lamentation, the promulgation of the French Civil Code in 1804 only gave a further impetus to underrate the function of the judge and to exalt the self-sufficiency of the written law (see Bonnecase, *L'Ecole de l'Exégèse en Droit civil*, Paris, 1924). At the end of the nineteenth century, the untenability of this theory in France was evident when the law as applied by the courts clearly went far beyond the original limits set by the written law (see Cruet, *La vie du droit et l'impuissance des lois*, Paris, 1908; G. Morin, *La révolte des faits contre le Code*, Paris, 1920).

[73] An important figure in this new tendency of the twentieth century is no doubt François Gény who in 1899 published his *Méthode d'interprétation et sources en droit privé positif* in which he severely criticised the traditional "fétichisme de la loi," pointing out that Law consisted in more than its mere positive manifestations through the formal sources of law, *i.e.*, written law and custom, and could only be found by a rational interpretation based on scientific methods. Positive law was not complete and sufficient for regulating all the multifarious aspects of the changing life of society. In the absence of positive rules, the judge was himself to find the rule of law applicable, not arbitrarily, but according to the methods which the ideal legislator would have used, by scrutinising the "nature of things" and those social elements which constitute the real sources of law, guided at the same time by legal science and technique. See also his *Science et technique en droit privé positif*, Paris, 1914–1924. His theory which had an immediate influence upon legal thinking in France and beyond, was epigrammatically summed up by himself as "Par le Code civil, mais au-delà du Code civil!" *Cf.* also Hauriou, *Précis de droit constitutionnel*, 1929, p. 236, note 6: "Mettre le juge au-dessous des principes et au-dessus de la loi écrite."

In Belgium, Vander Eycken published his *Méthode positive de l'interprétation juridique* in 1907, advocating the teleological interpretation of the law, that is to say, the interpretation of law in accordance with its social function. *Cf.* also, although these are published after 1920, G. Cornil, *Le Droit privé, essai de sociologie simplifiée*, Paris, 1924, p. 75: "The legislator and the judge are two organs of expression of the law each of which accomplishes an equally important task: that of the legislator satisfies the need of stability in social relations and that of the judge the no less imperative need of flexibility in social relations" (Transl.). H. de Page, *De l'interprétation*

This tendency, which has sometimes been characterised as Juridical or Judicial Modernism, found a clear expression in a speech by M. Fernandes at the 15th Meeting of the Advisory Committee [74] and this speech was regarded by the Chairman of the Committee as coinciding "with the general ideas of the Committee and with the project put forward by Mr. Root." [75] It may be said that, in general, this tendency was reflected in the belief that international judicial decisions would be able to contribute to the development of international law by gradually defining it,[76] and in the constant concern among the various Continental members that if the international judge were permitted to apply only treaties and custom, he might in certain cases be forced to commit a denial of justice by declaring a non-liquet for want of a positive rule.[77] They were anxious to obviate this danger, without, however, attaching too much importance to the formula to be chosen. The two Anglo-Saxon members were apparently the only ones who did not share this general anxiety,[78] largely, no doubt, because the problem had not been so acute a subject of controversy in their

des lois, Bruxelles, Paris, 1925; and *À propos du gouvernement des juges, l'equité en face du droit*, Bruxelles, Paris, 1931.

In Germany, there was the school of Freirecht, of which one of the more outspoken protagonists, H.-U. Kantorowicz, published in 1906 under the name of Gnaeus Flavius, *Der Kampf um die Rechtswissenschaft*, Heidelberg. Kantorowicz cited the example of Bartolus in the Middle Ages who is said to have taught his students in solving a case, first to find the solution in accordance with justice and then to find the juridical justification of the solution (*op. cit.*, p. 21). For a summary survey of this movement in Germany up to 1914, see Gény, 1 *Méthode d'interprétation, etc.*, 2nd ed., 1919, pp. 330–403.

[74] *Procès-verbaux*, pp. 345–346. While agreeing that a judge should not be allowed to create international law, Fernandes declared that, even in municipal law, there were certain incontrovertible principles of law derived from the idea of justice, guiding and giving life to the national law. In many cases, the judge would be unable to find an apposite rule of law, written or customary, governing the case presented to him, and would have to apply directly these general principles. In so doing, he would not be creating the law, but only bringing to light a latent rule of law. The same, he said, was true in the international sphere. To restrict the judge to the mere application of treaties and custom would be to withdraw from him many cases which involved legal relations between States and were, therefore, susceptible of a legal decision. It is clear from this speech that Fernandes considered that, just as in the municipal sphere, there were certain non-positive legal principles forming part of international law and superior to positive rules of law. See also Loder, *ibid.*, p. 294.

[75] *Ibid.*, p. 331.

[76] *Ibid.*, pp. 294, 322, 336. This belief of the Committee is further evidenced by the adoption of Art. 38 I (d). For the significance of this provision, see *supra*, p. 11, note 43.

[77] *Ibid.*, pp. 296, 311, 312, 313, 317, 318, 332.

[78] *Cf.*, however, Ricci-Busatti (*ibid.*, p. 314). But he maintained expressly that the Court had to apply general principles of law.

countries as on the Continent. It was, however, to meet the fear entertained by the members of the Advisory Committee, that they finally agreed to the formula "the general principles of law recognised by civilised nations."[79] As the term "general principles of law" was one of the most usual in codified provisions on the application of law in the municipal sphere—in fact the national law of three of the ten members who drafted the Statute of the Permanent Court of International Justice contained this very formula[80]—it was hardly surprising that when the question of codifying the provisions on the application of law in the international sphere arose, the same term should be adopted.

However, in adopting this provision, the members of the Advisory Committee did not intend to add to the armoury of the international judge a new adjunct to existing international law. Actuated by the belief that existing international law consisted in more than the sum total of positive rules, in adopting the formula "the general principles of law recognised by civilised nations," they were only giving a name to that part of existing international law which is not covered by conventions and custom *sensu stricto*.[81] It was said that the application of these principles had hitherto been a constant practice of international tribunals[82] and although it might be said that the latter, in applying them, brought *latent* rules of law to light, they did not *create* new rules[83]; for the members of the Committee were in agreement that a judge should not legislate.[84] If a State consented to the settlement of its disputes in accordance with international law, no special consent was necessary for the application of these general principles. This point was further confirmed by the discussion of this article in the Committees of the First Assembly of the

[79] *Cf.* Phillimore, "Scheme for the P.C.I.J.," 6 *Grotius Transactions* (1920), p. 89, at p. 94.

[80] *i.e.*, Brazil, Italy, Spain. See Appendix 2, *infra*, p. 400. The member from Brazil, Bevilaqua, proposed the formula in his Draft scheme. The member from Italy, Ricci-Busatti, was actually the first to use the formula during the discussion of the article in the Advisory Committee (*Procès-verbaux*, p. 314).

[81] See the Speeches of Descamps and Fernandes (*ibid.*, pp. 322–5, 345–6). *Cf.* also Loder (*ibid.*, p. 294); Hagerup (pp. 296, 335), Phillimore (*supra*, pp. 13 *et seq.*).

[82] *Ibid.*, p. 310.

[83] *Cf.* Fernandes' speech at the 15th Meeting (*ibid.*, p. 346), Loder (p. 294).

[84] See *supra*, p. 11.

League of Nations, where it was decided that the application of pure equity [85] could not be placed on the same footing as the application of these general principles but must have the express consent of the parties concerned; hence the separate formulation of the provision in Article 38 2 of the Statute which provides that Article 38 1 "shall not prejudice the power of the Court to decide a case *ex aequo et bono*, if the parties agree thereto." [86] *A contrario*, therefore, the application of general principles of law needs no special consent, which means that these principles form part of the existing international law. Furthermore, during the discussion in the Committees of the First Assembly, the words "in the order following" ("*en ordre successif*") in the introductory phrase of the draft article were deleted [87] thus eliminating any notion of hierarchy from the threefold classification of international law.[88]

85 *i.e.*, the application of equity not only *secundum legem* and *praeter legem* but also, if necessary, *contra legem*.

86 At the 7th meeting of the Sub-Committee of the Third Committee of the First Assembly, when the present article came up for discussion, Fromageot raised the question whether under the existing terms, the Court had the power to confirm an arrangement ("*un jugement d'accord*") reached between the parties, and subsequently proposed that clause 3 should read "general principles of law and justice." He explained that the amendment would allow the Court to ground its judgments solely on considerations of equity, although this did not imply that the Court might disregard existing rules (PCIJ: 2 *Documents*, p. 145). This amendment was adopted. At a subsequent meeting of the Sub-Committee, Politis raised the question whether the amended text actually reflected the opinion of the Sub-Committee on the subject. This opinion, according to Politis, was that the right to apply general principles of justice existed only by virtue of an agreement between the parties. He consequently proposed the following formulation: "The general principles of law and, with the consent of the parties, the general principles of justice recognised by civilised nations." After a discussion, the original formulation of the Committee of Jurists was retained, and the insertion of a new sentence was approved which read: "This provision shall not prejudice the power of the Court to decide a case *ex aequo et bono* if the parties agree thereto" (*ibid.*, p. 157).

87 On a proposal of Loder and Fromageot (*ibid.*, p. 145). The following words in the draft of the Advisory Committee were also considered as unnecessary and deleted: "Within the limits of its jurisdiction as defined above" (*ibid.*, p. 145).

88 Already in the Advisory Committee, Ricci-Busatti did not approve of the expression "*ordre successif.*" He thought that the judge should consider the various sources of law simultaneously in relation one to another (*Procès-verbaux*, p. 332). Descamps, however, preferred a classified gradation of sources (pp. 318–9, 336). Phillimore, who proposed the amended version of the article with Root, did not attach much importance to those words which he borrowed from the Descamps proposal. The enumeration was regarded only as following the logical order in which these rules or principles of law would occur to the mind of the judge (p. 333). See also *ibid.*, pp. 337 *et seq.*

During the Meeting of Committee IV/I of the San Francisco Conference of the United Nations, 1945, the question was raised, when Art. 38 of the Statute of the Court came up for discussion, whether this Article, "enumerating the sources of law to be applied by the Court, intends also to stipulate the order

With these modifications,[89] the draft article became Article 38 of the Statute of the Permanent Court of International Justice and was unanimously adopted by the First Assembly of the League of Nations on December 13, 1920. Save for a literal amendment in the French text,[90] the article suffered no modification during the lifetime of the Permanent Court. When the Permanent Court was to be replaced by a new World Court, the general opinion with regard to the provision concerning the application of the law was accurately summarised in the words of the Report of the Informal Inter-Allied Committee on the Future of the Permanent Court:—

> " 140. The law to be applied by the Court is set out in Article 38 of the Statute, and, although the wording of this provision is open to certain criticisms, it has worked well in practice and its retention is recommended (paragraph 62)." [91]

Thus Article 38 of the Statute of the Permanent Court was adopted by the United Nations as Article 38 of the Statute of the International Court of Justice, with the mere addition in the introductory phrase of the words: " whose function is to decide in accordance with international law such disputes as are submitted to it " after " The Court." No new element was thus introduced except perhaps an emphasis on the fact that the various rules and principles enumerated in paragraph I

in which they are to be resorted to. The two observers for the P.C.I.J. [Guerrero and Hudson], invited by the Chairman to comment, agreed that it did not " (UNCIO: 13 *Documents*, p. 164).

As Ricci-Busatti said in the Advisory Committee, " If the expression ' *ordre successif* ' only meant that a convention should be considered before, for instance, customary law, it is unnecessary " (*Procès-verbaux*, p. 337). This is already one of the fundamental principles of law (*ibid.*).

89 Besides the modifications indicated above, there was also an addition to clause 4 of the words " subject to the provision of Art. 57 (bis) " (*i.e.*, Art. 59 of the Statute), by the Council of the League of Nations at its 10th session (Brussels, October, 1920), an addition which did not alter the substance of the article.

90 Before the Revision of the Statute of the P.C.I.J. pursuant to the Protocol of September 14, 1929, there was no equivalent expression in the French text of clause 4 of Art. 38 for the words " of the various nations " which existed in the English text. The two texts were brought into literal conformity during the revision by the insertion of the words " *des diverses nations* " in the French text. L.o.N.P.:C.166.M.66.1929.V. (1929.V.5.), p. 62.

91 *Report of the Informal Inter-Allied Committee on the Future of the P.C.I.J.* (February 10, 1944), Cmd. 6531, 1944, p. 36. This is the conclusion and recommendation of the Committee as contained in Chap. XII of the Report. Paragraph 62 contains the fuller discussion of the subject (pp. 18–19).

Similar views were held by Wang Chung-Hui (a former judge of the P.C.I.J.) and Basdevant (a judge of the I.C.J.) in the United Nations Committee of Jurists (UNCIO: 14 *Documents*, pp. 170–171).

of the Article all form part of existing international law.[92] Further testimony to the declaratory nature of Article 38 of the Statute may be found in a Memorandum of the Secretary-General of the United Nations who, when speaking of the Sources of International Law, said:—

> "The codification of this aspect of international law has been successfully accomplished by the definition of the sources of international law as given in Article 38 of the Statute of the International Court of Justice. That definition has been repeatedly treated as authoritative by international arbitral tribunals." [93]

In some future Code of International Law it may confidently be expected that general principles of law will figure as an integral part of international law in any provision governing the application of law in the international sphere.

Having thus examined the origin of Article 38 I (c) of the Statute of the International Court of Justice, it is now possible to grasp more accurately the meaning of this provision and of the Article as a whole.

Article 38 of the Statute involves a juridical problem which confronts all systems of law, namely, what does law consist of and what are its sources?[94] As the problem is so universal, it is not surprising that the theories and practice developed in municipal systems of law in this connection have exerted their influence upon the minds of those who were called upon to deal with it in the international sphere.

The Article introduced nothing new in substance. It only effected a threefold division of existing international law into conventions, international custom, and general principles of law. The order in which these component parts of international law are enumerated is not, however, intended to represent a juridical hierarchy, but merely to indicate the order in which they would normally present themselves to the mind of an international judge when called upon to decide a dispute in accordance with international law. There is nothing to prevent

[92] See *supra*, p. 2, note 5.
[93] U.N.: *Survey of International Law in Relation to the Work of Codification of the International Law Commission* (Memorandum submitted by the Secretary-General), 1949, A/CN.4/1/Rev.1., p. 22.
[94] *Cf.* La Pradelle, *Procès-vèrbaux*, p. 295.

these three categories of rules or principles of international law from being simultaneously present in the mind of the judge.[95] His task consists precisely in declaring which are the relevant rules applicable to the case, in accordance with international law as a whole.

Since conventions between the parties, international custom, and general principles of law may *all* furnish valid rules operative in the international sphere and capable of solving international legal questions, they constitute "sources" of international law. In distinction to sources of law, judicial decisions and the teachings of publicists, as they do not create rules of law but only serve as means for determining such rules, may properly be called law-determining agencies.[96] The "sources" of law referred to here differ from the so-called "formal sources" of law which imply a special technique of legal formation.[97] The adoption of Article 38 of the Statute of the Court is, in fact, a repudiation of the theory that only rules created by means of a formal process are valid. It upholds the view that, like municipal systems of law, international law contains a number of unformulated principles.[98]

While conventions can be easily distinguished from the two other sources of international law, the line of demarcation between custom and general principles of law recognised by civilised nations is often not very clear, since international custom or customary international law, understood in a broad sense, may include all that is unwritten in international law, *i.e.*, both custom and general principles of law.[99] In Article 38,

95 *Supra*, p. 20.

96 See *supra*, p. 1, note 3, and p. 11, note 43.

97 *Cf.* Kopelmanas, "Essai d'une théorie des sources formelles du droit international," 21 R.D.I. (1938), p. 101. The weakness of this theory consists in its conception of law as a mere bundle of individual and precisely formulated rules each bearing the hall mark of the special process by which it has been produced, thus elevating what is no more than a legal technique to the position of the source of legal validity, the source whence these processes receive their exclusive competence to make law remaining thus unexplained and unexplainable. The theory originates from the municipal sphere where, the technique of law being much more developed, it may have a semblance of truth. It fits very badly, however, into international law where few rules have received a precise formulation. In order to bring his theory more into line with reality, Kopelmanas is forced to give a very wide interpretation to "custom" (*cf.* his "Custom as a Means of the Creation of International Law," 18 B.Y.I.L. (1937), p. 127).

98 *Supra*, pp. 6 *et seq.*, 12, 14, 18–9.

99 Phillimore, for example, understood custom in a very broad sense. He considered all that part of international law which was not convention to be

however, custom is used in a strict sense, being confined to what is a general practice among States accepted by them as law. General practice among nations, as well as the recognition of its legal character, is therefore required. It should be observed that the emphasis in the definition of what constitutes a custom lies not in the rule involved in the general practice, but rather in its being part of objective law as a whole.

In the definition of the third source of international law, there is also the element of recognition on the part of civilised peoples but the requirement of a general practice is absent. The object of recognition is, therefore, no longer the legal character of the rule implied in an international usage, but the existence of certain principles intrinsically legal in nature. This part of international law consists in the general principles of that social phenomenon common to all civilised societies which is called law. Principles are to be distinguished from rules.

> "A rule . . . is essentially practical and, moreover, binding; there are rules of art as there are rules of government, while a principle expresses a general truth, which guides our action, serves as a theoretical basis for the various acts of our life, and the application of which to reality produces a given consequence." [1]

This part of international law does not consist, therefore, in specific rules formulated for practical purposes, but in general propositions underlying the various rules of law which express the essential qualities of juridical truth itself, in short of Law. Thus Lord Phillimore, who proposed the formula, explained that by general principles of law he meant "maxims of law." [2] But how is it possible to ascertain whether a given principle is a principle of law and not of another cognate social discipline, such as religion or morality? The recognition of its legal character by civilised peoples supplies the necessary element of determination. Lord Phillimore also explained that the

customary international law (*Procès-verbaux*, pp. 295–311). But his conception of custom was that of a Common Law (*ibid.*, p. 316; Phillimore, "Scheme for the P.C.I.J.," 6 *Grotius Transactions* (1920), p. 89, at p. 94), which in reality resembled natural law (*Procès-verbaux*, p. 318). *Cf.* also La Pradelle (*ibid.*, p. 335); Raestad, "'Droit coutumier' et principes généraux en droit international," 4 A.S.J.G. (N.T.I.R.) (1933), p. 62, at p. 62.

1 Ital.-Ven. M. C. C. (1903): *Gentini Case*, *Ven.Arb. 1903*, p. 720, at p. 725, the Umpire quoting Bourguignon & Bergerol's *Dictionnaire des Synonymes*. Transl: See *infra*, p. 376.

2 *Procès-verbaux*, p. 335.

principles referred to in Article 38 I (c) were those which were "accepted by all nations *in foro domestico.*" [3] M. de La Pradelle took them to mean that general principles of law were the basis of the municipal law of all or nearly all States.[4] The recognition of these principles in the municipal law of civilised peoples, where the conception of law is already highly developed, gives the necessary confirmation and evidence of the juridical character of the principle concerned. The qualification "recognised by civilised nations" was intended to safeguard against subjectivity and possible arbitrariness on the part of the judge.[5] It should be noticed, however, that the word *nation* was originally used in the sense of "people" rather than "State." [6] The qualifying epithet "civilised" was, therefore, necessary in order to exclude from consideration systems of law of primitive communities which were not yet civilised.[7] At a later stage, however, it would seem that the term was sometimes understood in the sense of States, in which case the word "civilised" must be considered as merely redundant, since any State which is a member of the international society must be considered as civilised.[8] Amongst the examples of these general principles of law recognised by civilised nations, which were cited in the *travaux préparatoires* of the Article, were the principle of *res judicata*, the principle of good faith, certain principles relating to procedure,[9] the principle that what is not forbidden is allowed, the principle proscribing the abuse of

[3] *Ibid.*, p. 335.
[4] *Ibid.*, p. 335.
[5] *Cf.* Descamps (*ibid.*, pp. 311, 323 *et seq.*).
[6] *Cf. supra*, p. 9, note 34.
[7] *Cf.*, however, La Pradelle (*Procès-verbaux*, p. 335) who maintained that law implied civilisation. But see *Abu Dhabi Oil Arbitration* (1951) (1 I.C.L.Q. (1952) p. 247). While recognising that prima facie the concession-contract granted by the Ruler of Abu Dhabi should be governed by the law of Abu Dhabi, the Arbitrator excluded it on the ground that: "The Sheikh administers a purely discretionary justice with the assistance of the Koran; and it would be fanciful to suggest that in this very primitive region there is any settled body of legal principles applicable to the construction of modern commercial instruments" (pp. 250–1). Instead, he applied what were in fact "general principles of law" which he called "a sort of 'modern law of nature'" (p. 251).
[8] *Cf.* Ital.-Ven. M.C.C. (1903): *Sambiaggio Case*, *Ven.-Arb. 1903*, p. 66, at p. 691. ICJ: *Reparation for Injuries suffered in the service of the U.N.* (1949) Adv. Op., D.O. by Krylov, *I.C.J. Reports, 1949*, p. 174, at p. 219. Krylov referred to these principles as "general principles of law (recognised by the nations)" omitting the word "civilised." *Cf.* Krylov, "Les notions principales du Droit des Gens (La doctrine Soviètique du droit international)," 70 *Recueil La Haye* (1947), p. 407, at p. 449.
[9] *Procès-verbaux*, p. 335.

rights, the principle according to which, under special circumstances, the stronger takes rightful precedence over the weaker,[10] and the principle *lex specialis generalibus derogat.*[11]

The ensuing pages are an investigation, based on the decisions of international courts and tribunals, into the substance of such general principles of law, as envisaged by Article 38 I (c) of the Statute of the International Court of Justice, and the limits of their application in international law. Without being exhaustive, the result of this investigation will show four main categories of general principles, which, it is gratifying to note, correspond to or include many of the examples of such principles cited by the framers of the provision. These four categories will be examined in the following order: 1. The principle of Self-Preservation, in which it will be found that what has been called the principle, according to which under special circumstances the stronger takes rightful precedence over the weaker, is but a special aspect; 2. The principle of Good Faith, which includes the principle proscribing the abuse of rights; 3. The juridical concept of Responsibility as an indispensable element in any juridical order and the general principles of law comprised in this concept; 4. Certain general principles of law in Judicial Proceedings.

10 *Ibid.*, pp. 314–5, *per* Ricci-Busatti. La Pradelle was against the last-mentioned principle (p. 315).
11 *Ibid.*, p. 337.

PART ONE

THE PRINCIPLE OF SELF-PRESERVATION

PART ONE

THE PRINCIPLE OF SELF-PRESERVATION

" INTERNATIONAL law governs relations between independent States. The rules of law binding upon States therefore emanate from their own free will as expressed in conventions or by usages generally accepted as expressing principles of law and established in order to regulate the relations between these co-existing independent communities or with a view to the achievement of common aims. Restrictions upon the independence of States cannot therefore be presumed,"[1] even if it be true that " according to ordinary international law, every country is free to renounce its independence and even its existence."[2]

" The right of a State to adopt the course which it considers best suited to the exigencies of its security and to the maintenance of its integrity, is so essential a right that, in case of doubt, treaty stipulations cannot be interpreted as limiting it, even though these stipulations do not conflict with such an interpretation."[3] " This right possessed by all nations, which is based on generally accepted usage, cannot lose its *raison d'être* simply because it may in some cases have been abused."[4]

For the reason given in the preceding paragraph, Judge Anzilotti and Judge Huber in the case of *The Wimbledon* (1923) maintained in their joint dissenting opinion that, since Article 380 of the Treaty of Versailles[5] did not expressly impose a duty on Germany to maintain the Kiel Canal free and open in time of war between third States, she was entitled when her neutrality and internal security were endangered, to adopt extraordinary measures temporarily affecting the application

[1] PCIJ: *The Lotus* (1927), A. 10, p. 18.
[2] PCIJ: *Austro-German Customs Union* (1931), Adv.Op., Ind.Op. by Anzilotti, A/B. 41, p. 59.
[3] PCIJ: *The Wimbledon* (1923), D.O. by Anzilotti and Huber, A. 1, p. 37.
[4] *Ibid.*, p. 36.
[5] " The Kiel Canal and its approaches shall be maintained free and open to the vessels of commerce and of war of all nations at peace with Germany on terms of entire equality."

of the provision in order to protect her neutrality or to ensure her national defence.[6]

Similarly, but even more categorically, in the "*Blockad* " *of Portendic Case* (1843)[7] between Great Britain and France, the British Commissioners declared that they were "prepared to admit, that there are extraordinary cases, no doubt, which ride over ordinary rights, and the necessity of self-preservation, as the French Government in one of its papers properly observes, is one of these."[8]

This overriding interest of self-preservation of the State, the Romans aptly epitomised in the injunction: *Salus Populi Suprema Lex Esto.*[9] This maxim of law has often been invoked before international tribunals and the German-Venezuelan Mixed Claims Commission (1903) conceived it to be the indispensable fundamental law of every civilised country, of which international tribunals should take judicial notice. In fact the Umpire of the Commission in the *Great Venezuelan Railroad Case*[10] held an act performed by a high State official to have been null and void because it "conflicts," in his opinion, "with

[6] *Ibid.*, pp. 36, 37, 40.

[7] This was a dispute which arose out of losses alleged to have been suffered by British merchantmen as a result of the sudden closure by the French of their African port of Portendic in 1835, notwithstanding Art. XI of the Anglo-French Treaty of 1783 (Martens, 3 R., pp. 519 *et seq*) securing to British subjects the right to trade along these coasts, and notwithstanding a verbal assurance of the French Minister of the Navy and the Colonies made in 1834 to the effect that Portendic would not be put under blockade.

The dispute was finally submitted for arbitration to Frederic-William IV, King of Prussia, who made the award in 1843. See 23 B.F.S.P., pp. 543–588; 27 *ibid.*, pp. 1228–1299; 30 *ibid.*, pp. 581–649; 34 *ibid.*, pp. 1036–1108; 42 *ibid.*, p. 1377. See also *infra*, pp. 137 *et seq.*, p. 199, note 25.

Prior to submission to arbitration, a mixed commission was set up in Paris to seek a settlement but failed to reach agreement.

[8] Note of the British Commissioners to the French Commissioners, October 4, 1841 (30 B.F.S.P., p. 619, at p. 643), annexed to the British *Statement* filed with the arbitrator. For the French contention that she had acted under the "right of self-preservation, the most pressing of all, which, in time of war, suspends all those that may come into conflict with it," see 27 *ibid.*, pp. 1237, 1251, 1282–1293.

Although the award did not set out the reasons of the decision, as the British Commissioner of Liquidation, appointed pursuant to the award, reported to the British Foreign Secretary, "the inference is irresistible that, in the opinion of the Royal Arbitrator, the blockade was, under the peculiar circumstances, justifiable," October 9, 1844 (34 *ibid.*, p. 1088, at p. 1102). Damages were, however, awarded on other considerations; see *infra*, pp. 137 *et seq.*

[9] Cicero, *De Legibus*, III, iii, 8. Attributed by some authorities to the XII Tables.

[10] *Ven.Arb. 1903*, p. 632. Claims growing out of transportation of troops or munitions, and suspension of traffic.

the highest law of any nation, the safety of its people." [11] The well-known maxim *Salus populi suprema lex* may thus properly be regarded as one of the general principles of law recognised by civilised nations, within the contemplation of Article 38 I (c) of the Statute of the World Court.

In the present structure of the international society, however, where a State stands on the one hand as a supreme political institution, sovereign within its own boundaries, and on the other hand as a member of a society in which other equally sovereign members co-exist, the application of this principle in international law inevitably assumes a dual significance corresponding to the dual aspect of the State. The present investigation into the principle of self-preservation in international law will, therefore, follow this distinction by dividing the problem into two parts: (1) Territorial application of the principle of self-preservation (acts of self-preservation carried out by the State in territory subject to its authority), (2) External application of the principle of self-preservation.

Generally speaking, it will be seen that, in the former case, the principle *Salus populi suprema lex* permits the welfare and security of the nation as a whole to override the rights and interests of individuals, national or alien, subject to the State's authority; and, in the latter case, it empowers the State to take all necessary measures to protect the nation against external danger and hostility, and, under very exceptional circumstances, even to disregard a minor right of another State or its nationals in order to preserve its own existence. In view, however, of the frequent abuses of the principle of self-preservation, it may be emphasised at the outset that a proper knowledge of the limits and conditions of its application is just as important as knowledge of the existence of the principle itself.

[11] The Umpire held that a contract concluded between the Venezuelan Minister of Public Works and the railroad concerned, " in which the minister attempts to bind the Government for all the injuries which the railroad may suffer because of its performance of a lawful act, if not duty, in transporting troops and material of war to enable the Government to put down a rebellion, is utterly invalid—first, because it is contrary to public policy and conflicts with the highest law of any nation, the safety of its people " (*loc. cit.*, p. 635).

Chapter 1

TERRITORIAL APPLICATION OF THE PRINCIPLE

Inasmuch as the treatment of nationals, at the present stage of development of the international society, does not in principle fall within the purview of international law, except in virtue of treaty provisions,[1] the problem of the municipal application of the principle of self-preservation in international law becomes largely a question connected with aliens. No attempt is made here to undertake even a summary survey of the vast problem of the treatment of aliens. The object is merely to illustrate how, and to what extent, the overriding interest of the State may in certain cases affect their rights and interests.

In the first place, it will be seen that their admission and continued stay in a foreign country is contingent upon the superior interest of the State.

A. Exclusion and Expulsion of Aliens

An examination of cases decided by international courts and tribunals shows that the exclusion or expulsion of aliens by a State finds its juridical basis in the right and duty of the State to safeguard the nation's welfare and security.

Thus in the *Maal Case* (C. 1903),[2] the Umpire stated:—

"There is no question in the mind of the Umpire that the Government of Venezuela in a proper and lawful manner may exclude, or if need be, expel persons dangerous to the welfare of the country, and may exercise large discretionary powers in this regard. Countries differ in their methods and means by which these matters are accomplished, but the right is inherent in all sovereign powers and is one of the attributes of sovereignty, since *it exercises*

[1] *e.g.*, treaty provisions guaranteeing human rights or rights of minorities.

[2] Neth.-Ven. M.C.C. (1903), *Ven.Arb. 1903*, p. 914. The claimant, suspected of conspiracy with the revolutionaries against the government, was expelled. While under arrest, he was subjected to the indignity of being stripped of his clothing and thus made an object of laughter to bystanders.

The letter "C" before the date indicates that the latter refers to the *compromis*, as it has not been possible to ascertain the date of the decision.

it rightfully only in a proper defence of the country from some danger anticipated or actual." [3]

The significance of the right to exclude or expel aliens for reasons of public welfare or security lies in the fact that it cannot be assumed to have been implicitly surrendered by a general convention between two countries which provides that the citizens of each should have the liberty to travel or reside in the territory of the other.

The United States Domestic Commission in the American-Turkish Claims Settlement (1935) held in the *Lazar Rokash Case* (1937) [4] that:—

" The case of the expulsion of a native American, Max Scherpel, from the Free State of Hamburg in 1912 is of interest in connection with the construction of stipulations generally found in so-called commercial treaties relating to residence, conduct of business, and protection of rights of person and property of the nationals of the contracting parties. A question was raised whether Arts. VI and VIII of the Convention of Friendship, Commerce and Navigation concluded December 20, 1827, between the United States and the Hanseatic Republics,[[5]] stood in the way of the expulsion of this

[3] *Loc. cit.*, pp. 914–915. Italics added.
Damages were awarded for indignity suffered, because (and this confirms the thesis that such measures are conditional upon and circumscribed by the need for the protection of the community) " it was not for the protection of Venezuela that he was compelled to suffer this indignity to his person and his feeling " (p. 915).
See also Belg.-Ven. M.C.C. (1903): *Paquet Case, Ven.Arb. 1903*, p. 265 at p. 267 : " That the right to expel foreigners or prohibit their entry into the national territory is generally recognised; that each State reserves to itself the exercise of this right with respect to the person of a foreigner if it considers him dangerous to public order or for considerations of a high political character, but that *its application cannot be invoked except to that end* " (italics added). Damages were awarded for arbitrariness in refusing to state reasons for the measure (p. 267).
See also *Ben Tillet Case* (1898), G. B./Belgium, 92 B.F.S.P., p. 78, Award at pp. 105–9. Expulsion for attempting to ferment a strike at Antwerp and to organise an international federation of dockers. Held: " A State has the undisputed right to forbid its territory to foreigners when their intrigues or presence appear to compromise its security " (at p. 105. Transl.).

[4] Nielsen's *Op. & Rep.*, p. 503. Alleged damage suffered through removal of claimant (American citizen) and members of his family from Jerusalem to Damascus in November, 1917, by the Turkish authorities. Claimant invoked, inter alia, Art. IV of the Treaty of 1830 (*q.v., infra*, p. 34, note 6).

[5] Miller, 3 *Treaties*, 1933, p. 387. Art. VI: " It is, likewise, agreed, that it shall be wholly free for all merchants, commanders of ships, and other citizens of both Parties, to manage, themselves[,] their own business, in all the ports and places subject to the jurisdiction of each other, as well with respect to the consignment and sale of the goods and merchandise, by wholesale or retail, as with respect to the loading, unloading and sending off their ships, submitting themselves to the laws, decrees and usage there established, to which native

citizen. The Department of State observed in an instruction of April 9, 1912, to the American Consul-General at Hamburg: ' that a convention of this nature undoubtedly should not be considered as renouncing such an important attribute of sovereignty as the right of expulsion,' although the Department was of the opinion that the measure had been harshly exercised. It is believed that clearly the much less comprehensive stipulations of the Treaty of 1830 [[6]] between the United States and the Ottoman Empire did not stand in the way of the removal of persons from Jerusalem to Damascus for reasonable purposes, although it is conceivable that arbitrary interference with residence or vocations might result in violations of such stipulations. Furthermore, it is not believed that the so-called capitulary rights stipulated in meagre language in this article prohibited measures taken in time of war to safeguard the public interest, unless of course such measures were shown to be clearly arbitrary and violative of rights of jurisdiction such as are secured by the treaty." [7]

But it also follows from the above that specific treaties must be respected.[8]

As to what constitutes a menace to the welfare and security of the community, the Upper Silesian Arbitral Tribunal in the *Hochbaum Case* (1934) held:—

" Subject to specific treaty, it is the view of the State in question which alone decides whether its internal or external security is at stake. That view may change; it has undoubtedly undergone changes in recent decades in various States and in various circumstances. But in every case it is the consequence of one of the most important rights of the State. . . . The reasonableness of the decision is not subject to review by the Tribunal. If the authority in question is in a position to adduce reasons of a serious nature

citizens are subjected; they being, in all these cases, to be treated as citizens of the Republic in which they reside, or at least, to be placed on a footing with the citizens or subjects of the most favored nation."

Art. VIII : " Both the Contracting Parties promise and engage formally to give their special protection to the persons and property, of the citizens of each other, of all occupations, who may be in the territory subject to the jurisdiction of the one or the other, transient or dwelling therein. . . ."

6 3 *ibid.*, p. 541. Art. IV: " . . . Citizens of the U.S.A., quietly pursuing their commerce, and not being charged or convicted of any crime or offence, shall not be molested; and even when they may have committed some offence they shall not be arrested and put in prison, by the local authorities, but they shall be tried by their Minister or Consul, and punished according to their offence, following in this respect, the usage observed towards other Franks."

7 *Loc. cit.*, p. 509. *Cf.* PCIJ: *The Wimbledon* (1923), Joint D.O. by Anzilotti and Huber, A. 1, p. 37 (quoted *supra*, p. 29).

8 *Cf.* also U.S. Domestic Commission, Mexican Claims (1849): " *Expulsion Cases*," 4 *Int.Arb.* p. 3334.

justifying expulsion, then the Tribunal is not entitled to reject these reasons as unimportant or insufficient.''[9]

In time of war or disturbances, a State may even expel aliens on reasonable suspicion, either from its own territory, for the protection of the safety of the community,[10] or from occupied territory for the protection of its forces of occupation.[11]

[9] 5 *Collection of Decisions* (1935), p. 140, at p. 162; *Annual Digest* (1933–1934), Case 134. Expulsion of a Pole from German Upper Silesia in 1933. It appeared that this Pole formerly belonged to an association called "The Society of the Friends of the Soviet Union." Claim disallowed. The right of residence of Poles in German Upper Silesia was regulated by Art. 43 of the Convention of Geneva, May 15, 1922, but Art. 44 provided that each State retained the right of expulsion for reasons of internal or external security or on account of police regulations. The Tribunal held that: "This amounts to a recognition without any qualification, of the fundamental right of every sovereign State to decide in its free discretion as to continued residence of aliens in its territory." See also Kaeckenbeeck, *The International Experiment of Upper Silesia*, 1942, pp. 207–212, also Appendix III, pp. 567–822, where the Geneva Convention is reproduced.

Ben Tillet Case (1898) 92 B.F.S.P., p. 78, at p. 105. "The State determines in the plenitude of its sovereignty, whether the facts warrant such a prohibition" (Transl.).

Cf. Span.-U.S. Cl.Com. (1871): *Casanova Case* (1882), 4 *Int.Arb.*, p. 3353.

In Belg.-Ven. M.C.C. (1903): *Paquet Case* (*Ven.Arb. 1903*, p. 265, at p. 267), the umpire merely said: "The general practice among governments is to give explanations to the government of the person expelled if it asks them." A refusal gives rise to a presumption of arbitrary conduct.

It does not seem that in substance, the *Boffolo Case*, decided by the Ital.-Ven. M.C.C. (1903) (*Ven.Arb. 1903*, p. 696) is materially in contradiction with the above cases. All that the umpire required was that "the country exercising the power must, when occasion demands, state the reason of such expulsion before an international tribunal, and an inefficient reason or none being advanced, accepts the consequences" (p. 705). An Italian was expelled. The umpire tried to conjecture the reasons of the measure but found all the possible excuses would be invalid by Venezuelan law. Damages were awarded apparently because: "The umpire is more disposed to believe that for public reasons satisfactory to itself the [Venezuelan] Government has chosen not to offer the basis of its action, rather preferring to submit to such judgment as to this Commission might seem meet in the case" (p. 705). The *ratio decidendi* is therefore the absence of any reasons being adduced.

Cf. contra Mex.-U.S. Cl.Com. (1868): *Zerman Case*, 4 *Int.Arb.*, p. 3348: "In the present instance there was no war, and reasons of safety could not be put forward as a ground for the expulsion of the claimant without charges preferred against him or trial; but if the Mexican Government had grounds for such expulsion it was at least under the obligation of proving charges before this commission."

[10] *Zerman Case, loc. cit.*: "The President of the Republic of Mexico had the right to expel a foreigner from its territory who might be considered dangerous, and that during war or disturbances it may be necessary to exercise this right even upon bare suspicion."

Mex.-U.S. Cl.Com. (1868): *De Rijon Case* (1876), 4 *Int.Arb.* pp. 3348–9. Expulsion of a Mexican from the zone of military operations during the American Civil War. "The right which General Herron claimed of turning anyone out of his lines when he thought proper to do so was the undoubted right of any officer in the position held by General Herron. . . . An officer in command in such a position is not always bound in time of war to give his precise reasons for such steps" (pp. 3348–49).

[11] P.C.A.: *Chevreau Case* (1931), France/Great Britain, 2 UNRIAA, p. 1113. During the first world war, British forces occupying Persia deported a French

To enemy nationals found within the national territory at the outbreak of war, a State may apply a great number of measures of self-protection and, in principle, it has the right to expel them all.[12]

In all the above cases, however, this right, discretionary though it is, must be exercised in good faith.[13] It must not be arbitrary,[14] nor accompanied by unnecessary indignity or hardship.[15]

B. Measures to Promote Public Welfare

" In application of a generally accepted principle, any person taking up residence or investing capital in a foreign country must assume the concomitant risks and must submit, under

citizen. There was considerable armed resistance in this district. " Under these circumstances the arbitrator deems that he cannot deny to the British forces operating in Persia the right to take the measures necessary to protect themselves against the activities of the civilian population which were of a kind harmful to their operations or favourable to the enemy, a right which in general, according to international law, belongs to belligerent forces occupying enemy territory. . . . The arbitrary arrest, detention or deportation of a foreigner may give rise to a claim in international law. But the claim is not justified if these measures have been taken in good faith and upon reasonable suspicion, especially if a zone of military operations is involved " (at p. 1123. Transl.).

12 Fran.-Mex. Arbitration (C. 1839), decided by Queen Victoria (1844), 5 *Int. Arb.* p. 4865. On the wholesale expulsion of Frenchmen from Mexico on the outbreak of hostilities in 1838, the arbitrator was of opinion that no indemnity was due to France, the act " being justified by the state of hostilities between them " (p. 4866).

See 4 *Int.Arb.*, pp. 3334 *et seq.* for limitation of this right by treaties and customs.

Cf. also Mex.-U.S. G.C.C. (1923): *E. R. Kelly Case* (1930), *infra*, pp. 53 *et seq.*, for measures of self-protection applicable to enemy nationals.

13 See *Chevreau Case* (1931), *supra*, p. 35, note 11 *in fine.*

14 *Chevreau Case* (1931), *loc. cit.*, at p. 1123: " The arbitrary arrest, detention or deportation of a foreigner may give rise to a claim in international law " (Transl.).

Belg.-Ven. M.C.C. (1903): *Paquet Case*, *Ven.Arb. 1903*, p. 265. The umpire held that, the reasons for the expulsion having been asked for and refused, " the expulsion can be considered as an arbitrary act of such a nature as to entail reparation " (p. 267).

15 It is true that the arbitrator in the *Ben Tillet Case* (1898) pointed out that " in recognising the right of the State to expel, one cannot at the same time deny it the means of making its injunctions effective " (*loc. cit.*, p. 105. Transl.). But, as the Neth.-Ven. M.C.C. (1903) said in the *Maal Case*, where damages were awarded because the claimant was stripped in public, " There was no possible occasion for the public stripping, or private stripping, in fact, of the claimant. It was not for the protection of Venezuela that he was compelled to suffer this indignity to his person and to his feelings " (*loc. cit.*, p. 915).

In case of detention, " the detained person must be treated in a manner appropriate to his station, and conforming in the standards habitually practised among civilised nations. If this rule is not observed, there is ground for a claim " (*Chevreau Case* (1931), *loc. cit.*, at p. 1123. Transl.).

reservation of any measures of discrimination against him as a foreigner, to all the laws of that country." [16]

One of the risks is that, at any moment, a public need may arise either for the ownership or user of the alien's property and his right will then have to give way to the needs of the community, in the same way as other members of the community may be deprived of their property in similar circumstances. " The law of nations demands respect for private property, but it recognises the right of the State to derogate from this principle, when its superior interest so requires. Thus it allows expropriation for reasons of public utility in time of peace and requisition in time of war." [17]

I. EXPROPRIATION

Expropriation of private property, whether national or foreign, for reasons of public utility was recognised by the Permanent Court of International Justice [18] and the subject received detailed examination from the Permanent Court of Arbitration in the *Norwegian Claims Case* (1922).[19] The right was described by the latter as:—

[16] *Standard Oil Co. Case* (1926), Reparation Commission/U.S.A., 2 UNRIAA, p. 777 (*vide* " *The Deutsche Amerikanische Petroleum Gesellschaft Oil Tankers* " *Case*), at p. 794. Requisition by Germany of vessels belonging to a German company, for delivery to the Reparation Commission under the Treaty of Versailles. Standard Oil Co. claimed beneficial ownership over the vessels and contended that they should not be delivered. Claim disallowed.

[17] Portugo-German Arbitration (1919): *Award II* (1930), 2 UNRIAA, p. 1035, at p. 1039 (Transl.). Some of the cases decided concerned requisition by Germany of property belonging to Portuguese nationals in Belgium while Portugal was still neutral.

A passage extremely similar to that quoted in the text appears in Rumano-German Arbitration (1919): *David Goldenberg & Sons Case* (1928), 2 UNRIAA, p. 901, at p. 909. Requisition by Germany, in 1915, of 30 tons of tin, in occupied Belgium, belonging to the claimants (neutral). Payment of compensation in 1921 in paper marks represented only one sixth of the real value. Claim for balance allowed.

[18] *German Interests Case* (Merits) (1926), Germany *v.* Poland, A. 7, p. 22. On the subject of expropriation of foreign property, see further Schwarzenberger, " The Protection of British Property Abroad," 5 C.L.P. (1952) p. 295, and the present writer's " The Anglo-Iranian Dispute," 5 *World Affairs* (N.S.) (1951) p. 387.

[19] Norway/U.S.A., 2 H.C.R., p. 40. The court held: " This is a case of expropriation " (p. 77). " This is not a case of ' requisition of neutral property ' in the special meaning of that term in the laws and customs of war " (p. 72). Having been exercised by a belligerent for the need of national defence, this taking of property falls no doubt within the " general " notion of requisition (*cf. infra*, pp. 40 *et seq.*). The measure may also be considered as an exercise of the right of angary, at least as regards those contracts which conferred upon the purchaser real rights in the vessels under construction (*cf. infra*, pp. 42 *et seq.*). This is only a further instance showing the intimate relation between, and the basic identity of, the rights of expropriation, requisition and angary.

" the power of a sovereign State to expropriate, take or authorise the taking of any property within its jurisdiction which may be required for the ' public good ' or for the ' general welfare '." [20]

The right to expropriate, therefore, finds its juridical basis in the requirements of the " public good " or the " general welfare " of the community.

In case of a dispute, according to the Permanent Court of Arbitration, an international tribunal is competent to, and should, decide whether the " ' taking ' is justified by public needs." [21] The logical consequence of this is that any taking not so justified must be regarded as an unlawful act. It also follows logically that, if an expropriation has not been intended to be a definite assumption of ownership but merely a temporary measure to meet some passing requirement, the continued retention of the property, when the need has ceased, constitutes an unlawful act. The decisions of international tribunals in the *Walter F. Smith Case* (1929),[22] and in the *Norwegian Claims Case* (1922),[23] which respectively upheld these conclusions are clear examples showing that the right of the State to expropriate is not only founded on, but also strictly circumscribed by, the public interest.

20 *Loc. cit.*, p. 66.

21 *Loc. cit.*, p. 66.

22 See *infra*, p. 39.

23 *Loc. cit.*, at p. 63: " The Tribunal is of opinion that, whatever may be said in favour of the taking for title of the claimants' property during the war, there was no sufficient reason for keeping these ships after the signature of the Versailles Treaty in June, 1919. The reasons which have been given afford no legal interest which this International Tribunal could recognise as being superior to the rights of private foreign citizens in their own property," and it spoke of the " unlawful retaining of the title and use of the ships after all emergency ceased " (p. 75). This apparently applies only to those cases where expropriation for use " was possible without destroying the property, according to the contract, state of completion of ships, etc." (*ibid.*). Some of the contracts were taken for good and Norwegian property destroyed when they were first requisitioned on October 6, 1917. The duality of the position is shown by the two systems of computation of compensation envisaged by the Tribunal (*ibid.*).

Cf. Germ.-U.S. M.C.C. (1922): *Opinion Construing the Phrase " Naval and Military Works or Materials " as Applied to Hull Losses and also dealing with Requisitioned Dutch ships* (1924), *Dec. and Op.*, p. 75, at pp. 93–4: " They [the requisitioned ships] were lawfully in its possession . . . during an emergency the duration of which the United States alone could determine "; " Return them, at a time to be determined by it [the requisitioning State]." See *infra*, p. 45.

Cf. also the American reservation to the award in the *Norwegian Claims Case* (1922), letter of the Secretary of State to the Norwegian Minister at Washington, February 26, 1923: " The requisitioning State is free to determine the extent and duration of its own emergency " (*loc. cit.*, p. 81).

See *infra*, pp. 43 *et seq.*

What constitutes a public need [24] is obviously not a static notion, but one which evolves according to the practice of nations. The building of highways [25] and railroads,[26] of military barracks and public cemeteries,[27] the fulfilment of an international obligation,[28] the secularisation of religious property,[29] the mobilisation of commercial and industrial resources for the prosecution of a war [30] are only some of the instances which international tribunals have accepted as clear cases of genuine public need.[31] In such cases, they do not inquire into the intrinsic merits of the needs, as international law is not concerned with the internal administration of the State.

But international law, like law in general, must look at the facts [32]: *non ex nomine sed ex re.*

Thus, in the *Walter F. Smith Case* (1929), the Arbitrator did not hesitate to point out that:—

" The expropriation proceedings were not, in good faith, for the purpose of public utility. . . . While the proceedings were municipal in form, the properties seized were turned over immediately to the defendant company, ostensibly for public purposes, but, in fact, to be used by the defendant for purposes of amusement and private profit, without any reference to public utility." [33]

It may, therefore, be said that the public welfare of the community is considered by international law to be of such overriding importance that it is allowed to derogate from the

24 Although admittedly of a different character and related to the interpretation of a specific treaty, the judgment of the P.C.I.J. in the *German Interests Case* (Merits) (1926) A. 7, relating to what constitutes the " needs " of an industrial enterprise (pp. 49 *et seq.*) is highly instructive, *e.g.*, the needs must be genuine and not fictitious or imaginary; they may be temporary or future, etc.

25 Spanish Zone of Morocco Claims (1923): Claim No. 21, *Holliday (Ouad Hélu)* (1924) 2 UNRIAA, p. 615, at pp. 679–80.

26 *Id.*: Claim No. 15, *Forde (Chemin de Fer Larache-Alcazar)* (1924) 2 *ibid.*, p. 615, at pp. 679–80.

27 *Id.*: Claim No. 6, *Rzini (Ras-El-Karaber)* (1924) 2 *ibid.*, p. 615, at pp. 664 *et seq.*

28 *Standard Oil Co. Case* (1926), *loc. cit.* See *supra*, p. 37, note 16.

29 P.C.A.: *Expropriated Religious Properties Case* (1920) France, G.B., Spain, Portugal, 2 H.C.R., p. 1.

30 *Norwegian Claims Case* (1922) *loc. cit.*, at pp. 46, 72.

31 On nationalisation or socialisation as an object of expropriation, see the present writer's " The Anglo-Iranian Dispute," 5 *World Affairs* (N.S.) (1951), p. 387, at p. 391.

32 PCIJ : *German Interests Case* (Merits) (1926), A. 7, p. 22: " The legal designation applied by one or other of the interested parties to the act in dispute is irrelevant if the measure in fact affects German nationals in a manner contrary to the principles enunciated above."

33 U.S.A./Cuba, 2 UNRIAA, p. 913, at pp. 917–8. Seizure held unlawful.

principle of respect of private rights. Such derogation is, however, conditional upon the presence of a genuine public need, and is governed by the principle of good faith.[34]

II. REQUISITION

"Military requisition is a form *sui generis* of expropriation for reasons of public utility. The latter is a permitted derogation from the principle of the respect for private property. The same applies to requisition." [35] What has been said of expropriation applies, therefore, *mutatis mutandis*, to requisition and vice versa.

Requisition has been defined as follows:—

> "Requisition is the manifestation of the unilateral will of the authorities exercising their powers of employing the resources found within the country for purposes of national defence. It finds sufficient justification in the necessity created by the war." [36]

Requisition is, therefore, distinguishable from other forms of expropriation by the kind of national need which it is called upon to serve—the requirements of national defence created by a state of war. War is, however, not to be interpreted in a formal sense. As was stated by the Umpire in the *Georges Pinson Case* (1928),

> "I believe that the right of requisition ought to be conceded to every government, even where the insurgents have not previously been recognised as belligerents, on condition that adequate compensation is paid.",[37]

Owing to the pressing and vital character of the military needs of a nation at war, it is only true to say that States have in practice been allowed to appropriate almost any form of

[34] On the question of compensation and the practical consequence of the distinction whether the taking is lawful or not, see *infra*, pp. 47 *et seq*.

[35] Rum.-Germ. Arb. (1919): *David Goldenberg & Sons Case* (1928) 2 UNRIAA, p. 901, at p. 909. (Transl.)

[36] Greco-Turk. M.A.T.: *Polyxène Plessa Case* (1928), 8 T.A.M. p. 224, at p. 230. (Transl.) *Cf. Finnish Vessels Case* (1934) 3 UNRIAA, p. 1479, at pp. 1530, 1542.

[37] Fran.-Mex. Cl.Com. (1924), *Jurisprudence*, p. 1, at p. 137, note 2. (Transl.). Requisition and destruction of property in time of revolution. Test case for a number of others. The view of A. Rougier in his *Les Guerres civiles et le Droit des Gens*, 1903, p. 476, to the contrary was expressly rejected by the Umpire.

private property situated in territory subject to their authority that might be useful for the conduct of military operations or for the maintenance of their armed forces. Sometimes, therefore, requisition is hardly distinguishable from the unlawful taking of property, except by reference to the use to which the appropriated articles have been put.[38]

By specific treaties, however, States may voluntarily curtail their wide discretionary power of requisition.[39] The Hague Regulations concerning the Laws and Customs of War on Land constitute a notable example in that inter alia they limit the power of requisition in hostile territory to the necessities (*besoins*) of the army of occupation.[40] Although such treaties are restrictively interpreted, there can be no doubt that violations of specific provisions constitute unlawful acts.[41] The very

[38] *Cf. e.g.*, Portugo-German Arbitration (1919): *Award II* (1930), Group A, Claim 22, 2 UNRIAA, p. 1035, at pp. 1046–7. Furniture belonging to a Portuguese (neutral) taken by German troops in occupied Belgium. "There could have been either requisition effected without the usual delivery of receipts, or acts of pillage. . . . In case of doubt, the arbitrators consider that they should calculate the damages as if there had been a requisition" (at p. 1046. Transl.).

Cf. also Mex.-U.S. Cl.Com. (1868): *Thomas C. Baker Case*, 4 *Int.Arb.*, p. 3668.

[39] *e.g.*, Treaty between Spain and the U.S.A., 1795, Art. VIII (Miller, 2 *Treaties*, 1931, p. 323); Franco-Mexican Treaty of Friendship, Commerce and Navigation, Nov. 27, 1886, Art. 7 (1) (2(15) Martens, N.R.G. (1879–90), pp. 840 *et seq.*); Treaty between Great Britain and Nicaragua, 1905. (*Handbook of Commercial Treaties*, 1931, p. 475.)

[40] Art. 52. See also Art. 53 and also Arts. 46, 47, 54, 56. *Cf.* Draft of International Declaration concerning the Laws and Customs of War adopted by the Conference of Brussels, Aug. 22, 1874, Arts. 6–8.

[41] Fran.-Mex. Cl.Com. (1924): *Pinson Case* (1928). The umpire conceded to States the right of requisition not only in international wars but also in unrecognised civil wars. But prima facie he did not consider a treaty exempting the citizens of the other contracting party from requisitions of war as applicable in case of a civil war, although he recognised that such an interpretation was perfectly reasonable. If it were to apply the requisition will be an unlawful act (*loc. cit.*, p. 137 *in fine* and note 2).

For the practical consequences in the distinction between a lawful and an unlawful taking of private property, see *infra*, pp. 50 *et seq.*

In regard to the legal effect of a violation of Art. 52 of the Hague Regulations, contradictory decisions seem to have been rendered by different M.A.T. In chronological order:—Brit.-Germ. M.A.T.: *Tesdorpf & Co. Case* (1923), 3 T.A.M., p. 22. Requisition of coffee belonging to British subject in warehouse, Antwerp, 1916. Coffee sent to Germany for distribution to army. Though recognising that the limits of Art. 52 of the Hague Regulations had been exceeded (p. 27), stressing inter alia the military character of the requisition (p. 26) and the nature of the goods, which, being goods that could not be used without being consumed, implied an immediate appropriation (p. 26), the M.A.T. refused to consider that the requisition was void and of no effect or that ownership of the property had not been transferred to Germany (p. 28).

Id.: *Ralli Brothers' Case* (1923, 1924) 4 T.A.M., p. 41. Cotton, hide, and linseed seized at Antwerp and sent to War Raw Material Dept., Germany. Held act contrary to Art. 52, but there was immediate appropriation. Act not devoid of legal effect.

Belgo-Germ. M.A.T.: *Zurstrassen & Cie. Case* (1924) 4 T.A.M., p. 326. Wool

existence of all these restrictions, however, confirms rather than disproves the original right of the State to requisition private property for military purposes.

Mention may be conveniently made here of a special form of requisition, the *jus angariae*, which the Greco-Bulgarian Mixed Arbitral Tribunal in the *Arakas* (*The Georgios*) *Case* (1927) [42] held to be a universally recognised doctrine sanctioned

seized in Poland and sent to Germany. Held act contrary to Art. 52 and, as an exceptional war measure, null on account of Treaty of Versailles, annex to Art. 297, § I (2) (pp. 328–9). Ownership not transferred to Germany (p. 329).

Fran.-Germ. M.A.T.: *Gros Roman & Cie.* (1924) 4 T.A.M., p. 753. Muslin-de-laine seized at Antwerp and sent to Germany. Act null. Ownership not transferred. Grounds same as above. This decision expressly mentioned the *Ralli Brothers' Case* (p. 756) and, therefore, must be considered to have knowingly differed from it.

On the whole, it would seem more consonant with general principles to deny to an unlawful act the effect of transferring ownership (*l'effet translatif de propriété*). A careful reading of the decision in the *Tesdorpf & Co. Case* (1923) suggests that the Brit.-Germ. M.A.T. did not in principle disagree with such a solution. " The Tribunal are not of opinion that in the absence of an express provision avoiding unlawful acts, such a sanction [*i.e.*, *nullity*] is to be excluded altogether. This is a point which must be decided according to the general rules and the spirit of international law and having regard to the actual circumstances of each case " (*loc. cit.*, p. 27). The Tribunal seemed to have given a rather subtle interpretation to Arts. 52, 53 of the Hague Regulations, distinguishing from the rest certain requisitions which had for their object consumption goods susceptible of being used by the army. In these cases, there was held to be an " immediate appropriation." If by this the Tribunal meant that there was an immediate transfer of ownership, then it would be quite logical to hold that the subsequent abuse, consisting in removing the validly requisitioned goods from the occupied territory to be used by units stationed outside the occupied territory, constituted an independent contravention of the Hague Regulations, no longer affecting the question of ownership over these goods, but falling only under Art. 3 of the Convention proper. The following passage of the decision seems to lend some additional colour to this interpretation of the award: " Considering that the requisition took place in fact for needs of the army and with regard to stores of food which were warehoused in an important commercial seaport, the Tribunal cannot come to the conclusion that the mere fact of the allocation of the coffee for the use of other parts of the German army than that part which occupied Belgium, is sufficient to deprive the requisition of the character and effects which as such it has according to international law and the very nature of the things seized " (*loc. cit.*, pp. 27–8). *A contrario* it seems that where, by their nature, the goods are not susceptible of direct use by the army and where the requisition is not of a military character, the seizure would be manifestly and *ab initio* contrary to the Hague Regulations, and thus devoid of all legal effect.

[42] 7 T.A.M., p. 39. This case, decided on January 31, 1927, is wrongly placed under the heading *Vlassios D. Katrantsios* c. *État bulgare* (July 23, 1926) in the T.A.M. The *Georgios*, a neutral vessel flying the Samiote flag was seized by the Bulgarian army occupying the port of Eregli (*Heraclée*) in December, 1912, during the first Balkan War. A cargo of wood was requisitioned and the vessel was subsequently sunk by order of the Bulgarian military authorities. Held: " The Case of *The Georgios* constitutes an application of the right of angary " (p. 46, Transl.).

Cf. the Greco-Germ. M.A.T.: *S.A. hellénique maritime* (*The Kerveros*) *Case* (1926) 7 T.A.M., p. 33. Held: embargo on a Greek ship in a German port while Greece was still neutral was an unlawful act. But it must be by positive law.[43] The Tribunal seemed to conceive angary as the right of a belligerent State, for military purposes, to requisition neutral vessels and their cargo, or rolling stock belonging to neutral countries,[44] found within the limits of its authority, either for use or, if need be, for destruction.[45] It added that the right should be restricted solely to "cases of serious necessity," [46] and that its exercise involved the inescapable duty of paying adequate compensation to the owners.[47]

By conceding to States the right of requisition and angary, international law allows a nation's military needs to take precedence over private property rights situated in territory subject to its authority. Apart from specific treaty restrictions upon its exercise, the existence of this right of requisition and angary is strictly conditional upon, and circumscribed by, the presence of such military needs. How they may best be met is, of necessity, a matter to be decided by the State alone.

A special problem arises in connection with property which a State, in requisitioning, does not intend to appropriate definitively. In such a case international tribunals are in agreement that, since requisition is justified only by the superior need of the community, the property requisitioned should be restored immediately after such need has ceased to exist. There is, however, no unanimity of opinion as to whether an international tribunal is competent to determine the duration of these public needs of a State. The German-U.S. Mixed Claims Commission (1922) was definitely of the opinion that the State was alone competent to decide.[48] It is believed, however, that, while this

pointed out that in this case the ship which was under a German crew was ordered out of a Dutch port by a German coastguard vessel to return to Germany where it was seized.

43 *Loc. cit.*, pp. 45, 46.

44 Hague Convention II, 1899, Regulations, Art. 54; Hague Convention IV, 1907, Regulations, Art 19.

45 *Loc. cit.*, pp. 45–6.

46 *Loc. cit.*, p. 46. The Tribunal did not indicate, however, in this case any special necessity beyond military needs, and the exercise was considered rightful. *Cf. The Kronprins Gustav Adolf Case* (1932) 2 UNRIAA, p. 1239, at p. 1257: "The word 'angary' refers to the requisition and use of goods and to the justification of such a measure by the emergency which makes it necessary."

47 *Loc. cit.*, p. 46. *Cf.* Bullock, "Angary," 3 B.Y.I.L. (1922–23), p. 99. See also Le Clère, *Les mesures coercitives sur les navires de commerce étrangers: Angarie, Embargo, Arrêt de Prince*, Paris, 1949.

48 *Opinion Construing the Phrase "Naval and Military Works or Materials" as applied to Hull Losses and also Dealing with Requisitioned Dutch Ships* (1924), *Dec. & Op.*, p. 75, at pp. 93–4. See *supra*, p. 38, note 23.

is correct in principle, international tribunals are competent to intervene in case of evident arbitrariness—discrimination [49] or abuse.

The United States-Venezuelan Claims Commission (1885) held in the *Willet Case*:—

"Admitting fully the doctrine that the safety of the State is the supreme law, and that the property and person of the citizen [50] are subject to be taken for the public service whenever the exigency is sufficient to justify it, of which the State itself, by the necessity of the case, must be the only judge, yet we cannot perceive that there was any necessary connection between the seizure of the warehouse for purposes of defence and the consequent pillage and destruction of the property which ensued.

"Besides, while the seizure of the building was lawful in the first instance for the purpose of repelling an attack or guarding the arsenal, which was in the near neighbourhood, no reason has been assigned for its continued use and occupation as barracks long after the emergency had ceased to operate." [51]

The decision of the Permanent Court of Arbitration in the *Norwegian Claims Case* (1922) contained a very similar passage.[52]

Again the question whether property should be requisitioned definitively or only temporarily seems to be left to the exclusive judgment of the State. This, as well as the nature of the right over requisitioned property, may be gathered from the following passage in a decision of the German-U.S. Mixed Claims Commission (1922) in the cases of the *S.S. Merak* and *Texel* (1924), Dutch vessels requisitioned by the United States:—

[49] The *ratio decidendi* of the *Norwegian Claims Case* (1922) lies indeed in discrimination against friendly aliens, for it was held by the P.C.A.: "The United States are responsible for having thus made a discriminating use of the power of eminent domain towards citizens of a friendly nation, and they are liable for the damaging action of their officials and agents towards these citizens of the Kingdom of Norway" (2 H.C.R., p. 40, at p. 74).

[50] The case in fact concerned an alien.

[51] 4 *Int.Arb.*, p. 3743. at p. 3743. U.S. citizen, domiciled in Venezuela, had his warehouse occupied for many years after it had first been used as a kind of fort by the Government troops against the revolutionaries, everything of value in the building being in the meantime either destroyed or consumed.

[52] 2 H.C.R., p. 40, at p. 63. See *supra*, p. 38, note 23. It may be pointed out that in this case the P.C.A. considered that the U.S. had by its own acts shown that the emergency had at a certain moment ceased. "As early as February, 1919, the Emergency Fleet Corporation was giving back to their former owners some of the ships which had been needed during the war. but for which there was no further use" (p. 63). See also *The Edna* (1934) 3 UNRIAA, p. 1592, at pp. 1601 *et seq.*

" The right of the United States to possess and use them against all the world was absolute and superior to any possible contingent rights or interests of those Dutch nationals who owned them at the time they were requisitioned . . . As the United States had the absolute right against the whole world to possess these ships and use them as it saw fit, conditioned only upon the duty to make adequate compensation for their use and to return them, at a time to be determined by it or in the alternative to make adequate compensation, to the Dutch nationals who owned them at the time they were requisitioned, certain it is that this amounted to a special or qualified property in the ships tantamount to absolute ownership thereof for the time being. The possession of the United States was analogous to that of a grantee having an estate defeasible upon the happening of some event completely within his control." [53]

It also follows from the above that the risks, to which the property, even when temporarily requisitioned, may be exposed, lie with the requisitioning State.[54] Should the property perish while under requisition, the obligation of the State towards the owners, if it has not already been performed, is not thereby dissolved. In fact, frequent cases occur in which property is "requisitioned to be destroyed," a case which is to be distinguished from destruction incidental to military operations.

[53] *Opinion construing the Phrase " Naval and Military Works or Materials " as applied to Hull Losses and also Dealing with Requisitioned Dutch ships* (1924), *Dec. & Op.*, p. 75, at pp. 93–4.

The freedom of choice may be restricted in certain cases by conventional or customary international law. *Cf.* Hague Regulations, Art. 53, II. It may also be impaired by other considerations. For instance, it seems reasonable to consider that the P.C.A., in the *Norwegian Claims Case* (1922), regarded the freedom of choice of the U.S. as having been prejudiced by the fact that the progress payments made by the purchasers were not refunded by the U.S. when it requisitioned the contracts. "The necessary consequence," said the court, " is that the Corporation took over the rights and duties of the shipbuilders towards the shipowners " (2 H.C.R., p. 40, at p. 56). The duties of the shipbuilders can be no other than those of building and delivering the ships to their owners.

[54] The purpose of the decision was in fact to show that the U.S. had a claim against Germany for the unlawful destruction of these vessels.

See also *Cession of Vessels and Tugs for Navigation on the Danube* (1921) 1 UNRIAA, p. 97, at pp. 107–8: " In cases where a belligerent State has employed private property for military purposes under arrangements whereby the State undertakes to return the property to its owner, the appropriation of the property by the Enemy State would not place the burden of the loss upon the private owner, but would place it upon the owner's State which would be under an obligation to make compensation to the owner."

Mex.-U.S. Cl.Com. (1868): *Putegnat's Heirs Case* (1871) 4 *Int.Arb.*, p. 3718, pp. 3719–20: " The enemy destroyed the property indeed, but only after the government had taken it for public use, by being used by the government, and because it was so used."

The theoretical distinction was clearly drawn by the Mexican-U.S. Claims Commission (1868) in the *Putegnat's Heirs Case* (1871):—

"I conceive that the Government of Mexico is not liable for property destroyed by the enemy during the siege of a town without any complicity on its part; nor for property necessarily and incidentally destroyed by the government in its fire upon an enemy. To make the government responsible, the property must be taken by its authority to be used against the enemy (to assist an attack or make good a defence, for instance) or destroyed or carried away to prevent the enemy from using it. This is what Vattel calls taking deliberately or by way of precaution . . . Property taken or destroyed for the public use lawfully by the civil or military authorities must be paid for by the government . . . It is the seizure of private property for the public use and its loss or destruction while so employed, whether by the enemy or the government, that entitles the owner to payment. Even if it be morally certain that the enemy would himself take the property and use it, depriving the owner of it for ever, still its destruction by the government entitles the party to compensation . . . We must hold, even in such a case, that the public has received the value of the property, by embarrassing its enemy by its destruction, and is bound to make just compensation. It can never be just that the loss should fall exclusively on one man where the property has been lawfully used or destroyed for the benefit of all." [55]

This leads us conveniently to the problem of compensation.

[55] *Loc. cit.*, at pp. 3719–20. Mexican general turned claimant's store-house into fortification and forbade the removal of property to safety.

See also Brit.-U.S. Cl.Com. (1871): *John Turner Case*, 4 *Int.Arb.*, p. 3684. Destruction of house to prevent accumulated medical supplies from falling into hands of advancing enemy. Fran.-U.S. Cl.Com. (1880): *Bertrand Case*, 4 *ibid.*, p. 3705. Destruction of cotton to prevent it falling into the hands of the enemy. *Id.*: *Labrot Case*, 4 *ibid.*, p. 3706. Trees cut to give free range to guns defending position during American Civil War. Brit.-U.S. Cl.Com. (1871): *The Labuan Case*, 4 *ibid.*, p. 3791. Detention of ships in port for reasons of military security also considered as a taking of private property for public use. In all the above cases, damages were awarded.

Cf. also Brit.-U.S. Cl.Com. (1871), *McDonald Case* (4 *ibid.*, p. 3683), with the other claims for cotton destroyed during the American Civil War presented to the same Commission (4 *ibid.*, pp. 3679–83). It would seem therefrom that within one's own lines the notion of taking private property for public use covers some of the cases that would be considered as military necessity, *e.g.*, destruction to prevent enemy capture, in enemy territory.

Cf. Belgo-Hung. M.A.T.: *Sucrerie de Roustchouk Case* (1925) 5 T.A.M., p. 772. The destruction of vessels on the Danube to anticipate crossing by Serb troops was not considered as destruction following requisition, but purely as a military measure, having a strategic or tactical aim and nature. The use of one of the vessels after it had been refloated was considered as a measure of requisition requiring compensation. The case also illustrates the intimate connection between the benefit received and the compensation to be paid.

III. COMPENSATION

Both as regards expropriation and requisition, the payment of compensation to the individuals who have been deprived of their property is now considered indispensable.[56] The duty to pay compensation has either been based upon respect for private property,[57] or upon the enrichment of the community at the expense of isolated individuals, or classes of individuals, by a definite act of appropriation without any fault on the part of the individual.[58] There is much to be said in favour of the

[56] *e.g.*, U.S.-Ven. M.C.C. (1903): *Upton Case, Ven.Arb. 1903*, p. 172, at p. 174: " The right of the State, under the stress of necessity, to appropriate private property for public use is unquestioned, but always with the corresponding obligation to make just compensation to the owner thereof." See also p. 173. Panamanian-U.S. G.C.C. (1926): *De Sabla Case* (1933), Hunt's *Report*, 379, at p. 447: " It is axiomatic that acts of a government in depriving an alien of his property without compensation impose international responsibility."

The Brit.-U.S. Cl.Arb. (1910): *Eastern Extension Australasia and China Telegraph Co., Ltd. Case* (1923) (Nielsen's *Report*, p. 40, at p. 76) considered that the right of expropriation, requisition or angary " is in reality only itself acquired in consideration of the payment of compensation, and has no existence as a right apart from the obligation to make compensation."

The following cases considered a requisition not followed by complete compensation as an unlawful act:—

Greco-Germ. M.A.T.: *Karmatzucas Case* (1926), 7 T.A.M., p. 17. Requisition in Rumania by Germany of wheat belonging to claimant (neutral). Receipt given, but only part payment made. Held illegal on the basis of Hague Regulations, Art. 52. *Id*: *Kotzias Case* (1929), 9 *ibid.*, p. 701. *Id. Evghenides Case* (1929), 9 *ibid.*, p. 692. In this case, Hague Regulations, Art. 52 was in fact inapplicable, because the so-called " requisition " took place in the belligerent's own territory. But the M.A.T. simply followed the decision in the *Karmatzucas Case* (1926). Rum.-Germ. Arbitration (1919): *David Goldenberg & Sons Case* (1928), 2 UNRIAA, p. 901, at p. 909. Portugo-Germ. Arbitration (1919): *Award II* (1930), 2 *ibid.*, p. 1035, at p. 1039.

[57] *e.g.*, P.C.A.: *Norwegian Claims Case* (1922), 2 H.C.R., p. 40, at p. 69: " Whether the action of the United States was lawful or not, just compensation is due to the claimants under the municipal law of the United States, as well as under international law, based upon the respect for private property." Rum.-Germ. Arbitration (1919): *David Goldenberg & Sons Case* (1928), *loc. cit.*, at p. 909. Portugo-Germ. Arbitration (1919): *Award* II (1930), *loc. cit.*, at p. 1039.

It is true that the P.C.I.J. staunchly defended the principle of " respect for vested rights " (*e.g.*, A. 7, pp. 21, 22; A. 9, p. 27), but it also admitted that expropriation for reasons of public utility was a permitted derogation from the principle (A. 7, p. 22). It is doubtful whether the P.C.I.J. can be regarded as having subscribed to this opinion.

[58] Mex.-U.S. Cl.Com. (1868): *Putegnat's Heirs Case* (1871), already quoted *in extenso*, above (p. 46) is a good example of this theory, the salient points of which may be recalled: " Property taken or destroyed for the public use lawfully by the civil or military authorities must be paid for by the government. . . . The public has received the value of the property . . . and is bound to make just compensation. It can never be just that the loss should fall exclusively on one man where the property has been lawfully used or destroyed for the benefit of all." (4 *Int.Arb.*, p. 3718, at pp. 3719–3720.) Cited by U.S.-Ven. M.C.C. (1903): *American Electric and Manufacturing Co Case, Ven.Arb. 1903*, p. 35, at p. 36. U.S.A.: Spanish Treaty Claims Commission, established under Act of March 2, 1901, 24 *Spanish Treaty*

second solution. In the difficult problem of fixing the amount of compensation, this view may yet be of help in discovering a satisfactory solution. Indeed the second view seems to be more in conformity with the basic conception of expropriation and of requisition as the taking of private property for public use, and also with the principles of political economy. For it should be remembered that, whilst an individual should be compensated for his property which has been used for the general welfare, as a member of the community, he may at the same time have to pay for property that other members have similarly been deprived of. In such cases, there may well be a set-off of the mutual debts. If this is true, it becomes easy to explain why the rate of compensation may decrease as the circle of persons affected widens. The justice of this decrease has often been felt, but has rarely been articulately expressed. Thus when the *Rapporteur* on the Spanish Zone of Morocco Claims (1923) said that " an alien may not be deprived of his property without just compensation," he added: " This is true particularly when the restriction imposed upon the free exercise of the right of property is the result of a measure directed only at specific persons, and not at all owners of property similarly situated." [59] If compensation is based on respect for private property, it does not seem logical to introduce such refinements. Indeed, the theory of compensation based on enrichment is much more flexible. It permits the taking into consideration of equities in favour not only of the individual, but also of the community. The Permanent Court of International Justice has said that in case of expropriation a " fair compensation " (" *une indemnité équitable* ") should be paid.[60] True equity, said the Umpire of the Franco-Mexican Mixed Claims Commission (1924), consists

Claims Commission (1910), p. 150: " The Commission made an allowance in every case where property was used or consumed by the Spanish forces for their benefit, the theory being that whenever it appeared that the Spanish forces had been advantaged by the use or consumption of private property it should be paid for." ICJ: *Anglo-Iranian Oil Co. Case* (Jd.) (1952), D.O. of Levi Carneiro, *ICJ Reports, 1952*, p. 93, at p. 162: " Where damage has been suffered by a member of the community in the interests of the latter, it would be unjust that that member alone should bear the full burden of the sacrifice."

See also Mex.-U.S. Cl.Com. (1868): *Thomas C. Baker Case*, 4 *Int.Arb.*, p. 3668. Belgo.-Hung. M.A.T.: *Sucrerie de Roustchouk Case*. (1925), *loc. cit., supra*, p. 46, note 55 *in fine*.

59 *Rapport III* (1924), 2 UNRIAA, p. 615, at p. 647. Transl.

60 *Chorzów Factory Case* (Indemnity: Merits) (1928) A. 17, p. 46.

in holding in the best equilibrium the considerations of equity invoked by both parties.[61]

IV. CONCLUSIONS

In the preceding pages, one aspect of the application in international law of the general principle *Salus Populi Suprema Lex* has been briefly examined. In application of this general principle, international law, in common with the public law of all nations, allows the interest of the State, for the promotion of the communal welfare, to take precedence over the proprietary rights of private individuals situated in territory subject to its authority. International law recognises the superiority of the collective interest, when it gives expropriation the status of a legal right, albeit a right conditional upon the payment of compensation and strictly circumscribed by the collective needs which alone justify it. This right, like every other right of the State must be exercised by its competent organs in accordance with the requirements of good faith and, in particular, there must be no undue discrimination against aliens.[62] Moreover, when exercising such a right, it is incumbent upon the State, as much as possible, to safeguard the rights and interests of the individual,[63] to respect educational institutions,[64] places and objects of worship,[65] and to conform to the dictates

[61] *Pinson Case* (1928), *Jurisprudence*, p. 1, at p. 133.

[62] *Supra*, pp. 39 *et seq.*, 44 *et seq.* See *Standard Oil Co. Case* (1926) quoted *supra*, pp. 36–7.

[63] In the Spanish Zone of Morocco Claims (1923): Claim 21: *Holliday* (*Ouad Hélu*) *Case* (1924), the land was expropriated for the construction of a highway and the claimant's survey was erroneous in that its figures were less than the actual area involved. The *Rapporteur* declared: "*In a case of expropriation, where the authorities should have prepared the surveys*, an error committed by the owner during the establishment of a private survey should not cause him any disadvantage" (2 UNRIAA, p. 615, at p. 692. Italics added. Transl.). The objection of *ultra petita* was set aside.

PCA: *Norwegian Claims Case* (1922), 2 H. C. R., p. 39, at p. 72: "The just compensation to which they are entitled includes not only the items which have been duly proved, but also those which could have been proved and estimated if the officials of the belligerent State had, in the interest of both parties, paid or offered payment, or at least required contradictory expert evaluation and inventory, of the neutral property taken."

[64] PCA: *Expropriated Religious Property Case* (1920), 2 H.C.R., p. 1. Among the French claims, in one case where the land of a girls' school was involved, the PCA decided that the land should not pass to Portugal till the school had finished its use of the land (p. 5).

Cf. Hague Regulations, Art. 56.

[65] *Expropriated Religious Property Case* (1920). The court ordered the Chapel of Picoas, together with all the objects and ornaments for the practice of worship, to be restored to the claimant (*loc. cit.*, p. 5).

Cf. Hague Regulations, Art. 56; Hague Convention XI of 1907, Art. 4.

of humanity.[66] This right may also be restricted by specific rules of international treaty or customary law, which must of course be respected.[67]

The recognition that public needs constitute a legal right is of no mere academic interest; for it entails legal consequences of practical importance. As the Permanent Court of International Justice pointed out in the *Chorzów Factory Case* (Merits) (1928), a clear distinction should be drawn between expropriation and the unlawful taking of private property.[68] While the taking of private property for public use requires only the payment of "fair compensation" ("*indemnité équitable*") to make it lawful,[69] an unjustified taking of the private property of an alien is an internationally illegal act.

If the taking is unlawful, the State may, in the first place, be called upon to restore the property and at the same time to repair any damage not covered by the restitution.[70] If this is

[66] Mex.-U.S. G.C.C. (1923): *Bond Coleman Case* (1928). A boat chartered to take a wounded man to a town where he could receive proper medical treatment was seized by a Mexican general for troop transportation. "At a time when the dictates of humanity should have prompted assistance to the claimant, measures taken for his relief were frustrated. No imperative necessity for taking the boat has been shown." (*Op. of Com. 1929*, p. 56, at pp. 60–61). Seizure held a wrongful act and compensation awarded. Had public needs imperatively required it, the boat, it seems, might yet have been lawfully taken. But a State must not act in disregard of humanitarian considerations.

Cf. Preamble to Hague Conventions II and IV of 1899 and 1907 respectively.

[67] *Supra*, pp. 41 *et seq.* See also Spanish Zone of Morocco Claims (1923): Claim 51: *British Government* (*Aduana Vieja*) *Case* (1924). Spanish troops wanted to quarter in a British consular residence in Morocco and, finding it too dilapidated, destroyed it. Recalling the inviolability of consular residence in a country submitted to capitulations, the *Rapporteur* declared that the quartering of troops in the building was in the first instance illegal (2 UNRIAA, p. 615, at pp. 725–726).

[68] A. 17, pp. 46 *et seq.*

[69] It seems that, unless the national standard of compensation be higher (*Cf. Norwegian Claims Case* (1922), at p. 74: "Just compensation, as it is understood in the United States, should be liberally awarded"), the amount of compensation does not exceed the value of the property at the moment of dispossession plus interest to the day of payment (*Cf.* PCIJ: *Chorzów Factory Case* (Merits) (1928), A. 17, p. 47). *Lucrum cessans* is not compensated (*Cf. infra*, p. 51, note 71). The umpire of the Fran.-Mex. Cl.Com. (1924) even refused to allow interest "on the value of the requisitioned articles either from the date of requisition, or from that of the official notification of the claim to the government of the debtor State" (*Pinson Case* (1928), *Jurisprudence*, p. 1, at pp. 137–138). International Tribunals may, however, also take into account other equities, *e.g.*, Rum.-Germ. Arbitration (1919): *David Goldenberg & Sons Case* (1928), 2 UNRIAA, p. 901, at p. 910.

On the theoretical basis of compensation, see *supra*, pp. 47 *et seq.*

[70] *Chorzów Factory Case* (Merits) (1928), A. 17, p. 47. *Cf. Walter Fletcher Smith Case* (1929), 2 UNRIAA, p. 913, at p. 918: "The Arbitrator believes that it would be not inappropriate to find that, according to law, the property should be restored to the claimant." *Cf. supra*, p. 41, note 41, with regard to requisition in violation of Art. 52 of the Hague Regulations.

not possible, reparation would then have to be made in money, which, in this eventuality, would include any ascertainable *lucrum cessans* of the individual so injured by the unlawful act.[71]

C. Measures to Ensure Public Safety

The *Rapporteur* on the Spanish Zone of Morocco Claims (1923) conceived "the maintenance of internal peace and social order" to be the prime object and duty of every State.[72] The State cannot, therefore, be reasonably denied the means of realising this object and fulfilling its duty.

The undisputed principle of the absolute and exclusive jurisdiction of a sovereign State within its national territory requires no recapitulation here.[73] The substantive question is to what extent a State may take exceptional measures affecting the rights and interests of aliens when the safety of the community is endangered.

A general answer may be found in the decision of the Mexican-U.S. General Claims Commission (1923) in the *Dickson Car Wheel Co. Case* (1931):—

"States have always resorted to extraordinary measures to save themselves from imminent dangers, and the injuries to foreigners resulting from these measures do not generally afford a basis for claims . . . The foreigner, residing in a country which, by reason of natural, social or international calamities is obliged to adopt those measures, must suffer the natural detriment to his affairs without any remedy." [74]

[71] *Chorzów Factory Case* (Merits) (1928), A. 17, p. 47. See *infra*, pp. 233 *et seq.*: The Principle of Integral Reparation. See, however, on the other hand, Spanish Zone of Morocco Claims (1923): Claim No. 6: *Rzini* (*Ras-El-Karaber*) *Case* (1924), 2 UNRIAA, p. 615, at pp. 664 *et seq.* The *Rapporteur* held that, the land having been taken for public utility, only the price of the land at the time of dispossession plus normal interest should be paid. He would not take into account any particularly high price which the land might have fetched since the day of expropriation to the day of the decision (pp. 665–6).

[72] *Rapport III* (1924) 2 UNRIAA, p. 615, at p. 642. See also PCA: *Palmas Case* (1928), U.S./Neth., 2 H.C.R., p. 84, at p. 93.

[73] See, *e.g.*, *Palmas Case* (1928), *loc. cit.*, p. 92; PCIJ: *The Lotus Case* (1927), A. 10, pp. 44, 69, 94.

[74] *Op. of Com. 1931*, p. 175, at pp. 192–193. Claims for railway wheels sold to Mexican railroads before latter taken over by Mexican Government as an emergency measure. As an example, the Commission said, "Moratoriums imposed upon National Banks are measures of this character, and there is no precedent showing that international indemnities have been awarded on this ground." (p. 192.)

Irrespective of the source of danger, therefore, a State may take all necessary steps to ensure the safety and welfare of the community.

I. ADMINISTRATIVE MEASURES

If necessary, a State may "prevent the passage of persons either for travel or business" in territory under its control, "suspend traffic upon any line of transportation,"[75] prohibit navigation on its own rivers, even though permission to navigate them has previously been given.[76] It may close its harbours and ports, even though there exists a treaty granting aliens the right of call,[77] or a concession conferring special rights of user.[78] It may impose a moratorium on its banks,[79]

[75] Germ.-Ven. M.C.C. (1903): *Great Venezuelan Railroad Case, Ven.Arb. 1903*, p. 632, at p. 636.

[76] Germ.-Ven. M.C.C. (1903): *Faber Case, Ven.Arb. 1903*, p. 600, at pp. 626 and 630. Claims on behalf of German nationals in Colombia, who had a commercial interest in navigating the Catatumbo and the Zulia rivers.

U.S.-Ven. M.C.C. (1903): *Orinoco Steamship Co. Case* (1904), *Ven.Arb. 1903*, p. 72 *et seq.*; 1 H.C.R., p. 240, at pp. 272–3: "The right to open and close, as a sovereign on its own territory, certain harbours, ports and rivers in order to prevent the trespassing of fiscal laws is not and could not be denied to the Venezuelan Government, much less this right can be denied when used in defence not only of some fiscal rights, but in defence of the very existence of the Government; . . . The temporary closing of the Orinoco River (the so-called 'blockade') in reality was only a prohibition to navigate that river in order to prevent communication with the revolutionists in Ciudad Bolivar and on the shores of the river, this lawful act by itself could never give a right to claims for damages to the ships that used to navigate the river." In this case there had previously been an express written permission to navigate the river, which the claimants alleged to be a granted "monopoly." Case was first decided by the above mentioned Claims Commission; was subsequently submitted again to the P.C.A. at the instance of the U.S. and by means of a special agreement of 1909 (1 H.C.R. at pp. 226 *et seq.*). While some counts of the original award were reversed for disregard of the *compromis*, others were allowed to stand. The part of the award from which the above passage was extracted was in no way affected.

[77] "*Blockade*" *of Portendic Case* (1843), *supra*, p. 30. Note particularly that the *Meta* and the *Marmion* were not awarded damages. See Report of the British Commissioner of Liquidation, 34 B.F.S.P. 1088, at pp. 1101–2: "According to the terms of the royal award, the fact of the blockade does not constitute a ground for compensation. . . . The inference is irresistible, that in the opinion of the Royal Arbitrator, the blockade was under the circumstances, justifiable." See also Ital.-Ven. M.C.C. (1903): *Poggioli Case, Ven.Arb. 1903*, p. 847, at p. 870.

[78] Fran.-Ven. M.C.C. (1902): *Compagnie générale de l'Orénoque Case* (1905), Ralston's *Report*, p. 244, at p. 360, quoted *infra*, p. 55.

Ital.-Ven. M.C.C. (1903): *Martini Case, Ven.Arb. 1903*, p. 819, at p. 843: "This closure, while entirely legal and within the power of the Government as against the world at large . . ."

[79] Mex.-U.S. G.C.C. (1923): *Dickson Car Wheel Co. Case* (1931), *loc. cit.*, p. 192. *Supra*, p. 51, note 74.

or prohibit the exportation of certain articles, notwithstanding a treaty provision securing liberty to trade.[80]

On the principle of *Salus populi suprema lex esto*, the Mixed Courts of Egypt, in 1921, recognised the right of the Commander-in-Chief of the British Forces in Egypt, as representing the protecting power, to proclaim a "political state of siege ('*état de siège politique*')," concentrating in the hands of the military authorities the powers of State, and allowing them to take measures not only of police and order, but also measures extending to economic, legal and social fields, thereby affecting the interests and rights of aliens normally enjoying extraterritoriality.[81] A political state of siege was considered to be "a measure of an internal character concerning public order and social peace, adopted on account of necessity and not in view of a foreign war." [82]

In case of war, however, there is a natural presumption of national emergency. In particular, a state of war brings about a special relationship between the belligerent State and enemy nationals, and permits the former to take all necessary measures in relation to the latter so as to prevent them from engaging in any activity harmful to its welfare or security. The position was discussed at length by the Mexican-United States General Claims Commission (1923), in the *Kelly Case* (1930) [83]:—

"During the last century there has been a world wide effort to mitigate the horrors of war. The principle has been acknowledged more and more that the unarmed citizens should be spared in person, property and honour, as much as the exigencies of war will permit." [84]

"There are well defined rules of international law for the safeguarding of rights of non-combatants. But there are, of course, many ways in which non-combatants may, without being entitled to

[80] Brit.-U.S. Cl.Com. (1871): *The Daring, The Templar, The Patmos* ("*Calcutta Saltpetre Cases*"). Prohibition of export of saltpetre described by counsel for Great Britain as a measure of self-defence, especially when war threatened between the two countries. Claims dismissed (4 *Int.Arb.*, p. 4379, at p. 4383).

[81] *Ismail Pasha Sedky* v. *Sidarous Bichara* (1921) 11 T.M.E. (1920–1), pp. 162–3.

[82] *Loc. cit.*, p. 163, c. 2. Transl.

[83] *Op. of Com. 1931*, p. 82. Removal of a U.S. citizen from a responsible position in the Mexican railroads when the U.S., without actual declaration of war, landed forces at Vera Cruz in 1914 and extensive hostilities took place. The Commission, without actually deciding whether these hostilities constituted a state of war, assimilated U.S. nationals to enemy aliens.

[84] *Loc. cit.*, p. 90.

compensation, suffer losses incident to the proper conduct of hostile operations. And a government has recourse to a great many measures of self-protection distinct from actual military operations such as the segregation or internment of enemy nationals, the elimination of such persons from any position in which they might be a source of danger, and their exclusion from prescribed locations." [85]

"As is shown by precedents that have been cited and others that might be mentioned, there is a wide range of defensive measures in time of hostilities. Undoubtedly, the justification of such measures must be found in the nature of the emergency in each given case and of the methods employed to meet the situation." [86]

"Payment must be made for property appropriated for use by belligerent forces. Unnecessary destruction is forbidden. Compensation is due for the benefits resulting from ownership or user. In dealing with the precise question under consideration by such analogous reasoning as we consider it to be proper to employ, we must take account of things which in the light of international practice have been regarded as proper, strictly defensive measures employed in the interest of public safety. Generally speaking, international law does not require that even nationals of neutral countries be compensated for losses resulting from such measures." [87]

It may, therefore, be said that whenever the safety of the State is threatened, whatever may be the cause, it has a right to take the requisite measures, in territory subject to its authority, in order to ensure the safety of the community.

The opportuneness of these measures is not subject to review by an international tribunal. In the words of the Umpire in the *Faber Case* (C. 1903):—

"What is necessary to peace, safety, and convenience of her own citizens she must judge, and it seems to the Umpire quite clear that in any case calling for an exercise of that judgment her decision is final." [88]

[85] *Loc. cit.*, p. 85.
[86] *Loc. cit.*, p. 91.
[87] *Loc. cit.*, pp. 92–3; claim disallowed.
See Rum.-Germ. M.A.T.: *Rosenstein Case* (Merits) (1930), 10 T.A.M., p. 122, at p. 127: "Undoubtedly, we have, in principle, to admit the right of a Sovereign State, for reasons of public interest, to withdraw public works from a contractor who, as the result of a declaration of war, has become the subject of an enemy State and, as such, not only suspect, but also liable to be interned at any time" (Transl.). No indemnity was held to be due.
[88] *Ven.Arb. 1903*, p. 600, at p. 626, reiterated at p. 630. See also Ital. Ven. M.C.C. (1903): *Poggioli Case*, *Ven.Arb. 1903*, p. 847, at p. 870: "The Umpire has nothing whatever to do with the reasons inducing the government to close

It seems sufficient for the State to show that there existed in fact "a case for the exercise of this discretion," [89] in other words, that the safety of the community was threatened.

With regard to the question how far these exceptional measures may be compatible with a State's legal undertakings, a distinction has to be drawn between contracts under municipal law and treaties under international law. The former cannot limit the State's right to resort to exceptional measures for its safety. The State may elect to pay compensation instead of performing its obligations under a contract, whenever its interest of self-preservation so requires. Thus the Franco-Venezuelan Mixed Claims Commission (1902) declared in the case of the *Compagnie générale de l'Orénoque* (1905):—

"As the Government of Venezuela, whose duty of self-preservation rose superior to any question of contract, it had the power to abrogate the contract in whole or in part. It exercised that power and cancelled the provision of unrestricted assignment. It considered the peril superior to the obligation and substituted therefor the duty of compensation." [90]

With regard to treaties, it is necessary to bear in mind the following reservation contained in the joint dissenting opinion by Judges Anzilotti and Huber in *The Wimbledon Case* (1923), which appears to be corroborated by decisions of other international tribunals:—

"In this respect, it must be remembered that international conventions and more particularly those relating to commerce and communications are generally concluded having regard to normal peace conditions. If, as the result of a war, a neutral or belligerent State is faced with the necessity of taking extraordinary measures

the port." PCIJ: *Oscar Chinn Case* (1934), U.K./Belgium, A/B. 63. Speaking of the economic crisis in Belgian Congo, the P.C.I.J. said: "The Belgian Government was the sole judge of this critical situation and of the remedies that it called for—subject of course to its duty of respecting its international obligations" (p. 79).

[89] *Faber Case*, *loc. cit.*, pp. 626, 630.

[90] Ralston's *Report*, p. 244, at p. 360. The contract-concession originally permitted unrestricted assignment. When in 1890, the claimant company succeeded in interesting an English company in taking over the concession, the Venezuelan Government absolutely refused to permit the transfer, on account of a very serious and threatening dispute between Great Britain and Venezuela over part of the territory covered by the concession.

Cf. also Ital.-Ven. M.C.C. (1903): *Martini Case*, *Ven.Arb. 1903*, p. 819, at p. 843. Fran.-Ven. M.C.C. (1902): *Pieri Dominique & Co. Case* (1905), Ralston's *Report*, p. 185, at p. 205 (*f*).

temporarily affecting the application of such conventions in order to protect its neutrality or for the purposes of national defence, it is entitled to do so even if no express reservations are made in the convention. This right possessed by all nations, which is based on generally accepted usage, cannot lose its *raison d'être* simply because it may in some cases have been abused. . . .

" The right of a State to adopt the course which it considers best suited to the exigencies of its security and to the maintenance of its integrity, is so essential a right that, in case of doubt, treaty stipulations cannot be interpreted as limiting it, even though these stipulations do not conflict with such an interpretation." [91]

But as Judges Anzilotti and Huber themselves acknowledged:—

" The foregoing considerations could not be effective against a definite provision expressly referring to the circumstances arising out of a war." [92]

Any violation of such a provision would undoubtedly be an unlawful act.

Express treaty provisions apart, the only legal limitation on the discretion of the State appears to be the principle of good faith. The measures taken should be reasonable and must not be arbitrary,[93] oppressive, or maintained for longer than necessary.[94] Indeed, as the Mexican-United States General Claims Commission (1923) observed in the *E. R. Kelly Case* (1930):—

" Undoubtedly the justification of such measures must be found in the nature of the emergency in each given case and of the methods to meet the situation." [95]

In determining what is meet and proper in a given case, it is necessary to

[91] PCIJ: A. 1, pp. 36–7. See "*Blockade*" *of Portendic Case* (1843), *supra*, pp. 30, 52.

[92] *Loc. cit.*, p. 37. See also PCIJ: *Oscar Chinn Case* (1934), A/B. 63, p. 79.

[93] PCIJ: *The Wimbledon* (1923), D.O. by Anzilotti and Huber, A. 1, pp. 40–1: "For these reasons, we are of opinion that the only question to be decided is whether the application to the Kiel Canal of the neutrality regulations adopted by Germany was an arbitrary act calculated unnecessarily to impede traffic."

[94] *Carlos Butterfield Case* (1890) U.S./Den., 2 *Int.Arb.*, p. 1185. In dismissing the claim, the Arbitrator, speaking of the Danish measures for protecting her neutrality, said: "The Arbitrator is of opinion that these measures were reasonable, and in no sense oppressive" and "the precautionary measures were not maintained longer than was necessary" (p. 1206).

[95] *Op. of Com. 1931*, p. 82, at p. 91.

"take account of things which in the light of international practice have been regarded as proper, strictly defensive measures employed in the interest of public safety." [96]

This practice may, and indeed does, vary with time and circumstances.[97]

Generally speaking, measures taken in time of peace or in time of war to ensure the safety of the community give rise to no compensation, even if the interests of friendly aliens are thereby directly affected,[98] and this is so, *a fortiori*, when the damage has resulted from measures primarily affecting the State's own nationals.[99, 1] Exceptions to this general rule, it seems, are confined to three instances:—

1. Where a contract with individuals has to be disregarded.[2]
2. Where private property has been taken for public use.[3]

[96] *Ibid.*, at p. 92–3.

[97] *Cf.* Mixed Courts of Egypt: *Ismail Pasha Sedky* v. *Sidarous Bichara* (1921) 11 T.M.E. (1920–21), p. 162, at p. 163, c. 2: "It is sufficient to recall in this connection that the Great War has profoundly upset a great number of principles of public and private law, however intangible [*sic! infrangible?*] they may have been considered up to the present. Similarly, and as an inevitable consequence, it has affected the traditional principles which, during a state of siege, limited the powers of the military authorities to mere measures of police and order. It has extended them to the economic, juridical and social fields, as is shown by the numerous measures dictated by the exceptional circumstances of the moment and enacted more or less everywhere to avert all kinds of difficulties" (Transl.).

[98] Mex.-U.S. G.C.C. (1923): *Dickson Car Wheel Co. Case* (1931), *Op. of Com. 1931*, p. 175, at pp. 192–3; *Id.*: *Kelly Case* (1930) *ibid.*, p. 82, at pp. 92 *et seq.*; and other cases mentioned in the present section.

[99] *Dickson Car Wheel Co. Case* (1931), *loc. cit.*; at pp. 188 *et seq.* See also Mex.-U.S. Cl.Com. (1868): *Siempre Viva Silver Mining Co. Case* (1874) 4 *Int.Arb.* p. 3784; *Id.*: *John Cole Case* (1876) 4 *ibid.*, at p. 3785. An alien cannot complain if his interests are affected because nationals have been called up for national service. *Cf. contra* Greco-Germ. M.A.T.: *Evghenides Case* (1929) 9 T.A.M., p. 692.

[1] In the light of the above, the decision of the Mex.-U.S. Special Cl.Com. (1923) in the *Santa Isabel Cases* (1926) (*Op. of Com. 1926–31*, p. 1, at pp. 11–12) becomes easily understandable and also serves to illustrate the above proposition. While an amnesty to malefactors guilty of crimes against aliens is usually regarded as a failure of justice involving the responsibility of the State, the Commission in this case considered the action of the Mexican Government "a supreme effort for achieving, by any means whatsoever, the pacification of the country," and refused to hold it to be an act of leniency entailing the responsibility of Mexico.

[2] *Supra*, p. 55.

[3] *Supra*, pp. 36–51.

3. Generally where there has been a tangible enrichment of the State to the detriment of individuals without any fault on their part.[4]

II. FORCIBLE MEASURES

So far only administrative measures have been mentioned. There can be no doubt, however, that a State may also use force of arms to ensure the safety and welfare of the community, when circumstances so require. In the words of the Arbitrator in *The Montijo Case* (1875):—

> "The first duty of every government is to make itself respected both at home and abroad."[5]

Force may thus be used to compel obedience to the law. As the sole Arbitrator said in the *James Pugh Case* (1933):—

> "The right of the individual must ever be maintained, but the right of society is superior. A fundamental right of society is the right to law and order and the further right to compel obedience thereto by the individual. . . . Obedience to law is not a matter of individual choice, but is a matter of compulsion. Such being the necessary situation in organised society, the obedience must be compelled by the use of force when that becomes necessary."[6]

If an individual should resist the arm of the law, the State is not responsible for the consequences of the use of necessary

[4] *Kelly Case* (1930), *loc. cit.*, at p. 92: "Compensation is due for the benefits resulting from ownership or user."
However, in such cases, it is essential to determine the person to whose detriment in fact and in law the benefit has been obtained. If a person has supplied materials to a railroad company and the line is taken over and operated by the State in an emergency, the user of these materials is not to his detriment but to that of the Company, since he no longer has a right over them, but has only a contractual right against the railroad company. See *Dickson Car Wheel Co. Case* (1931), *loc. cit.*, pp. 185–6; *cf.* pp. 191–2.

[5] U.S.A./Colombia, 2 *Int.Arb.*, p. 1421, at p. 1444. Seizure of ships by revolutionaries. It may be mentioned, however, that the Umpire in this case established an absolute responsibility for the protection of aliens, while modern international jurisprudence is content with *diligentia quam in suis*. See Spanish Zone of Morocco Claims (1923): *Rapport III* (1924), 2 UNRIAA, p. 615, at pp. 643 *et seq.*; *infra*, pp. 220 *et seq.*

[6] *U.K.* (*for Irish Free State*) v. *Panama*, 3 UNRIAA, p. 1439, at pp. 1447–8. Pugh, a citizen of the Irish Free State, met his death as a result of clubbing by the Panamanian police. "What the record discloses to us is the unfortunate and accidental death of Pugh brought on by himself by reason of his resistance to arrest, his striking the police and the consequent lawful use of their clubs on him, without any intent, actual or constructive, of killing him but for the sole purpose of lawfully compelling his submission and of defending themselves" (p. 1451). Claim disallowed.

and reasonable force to vindicate its lawful authority.[7] Moreover, even where there is no fault on the part of the victim, a State is not responsible for injuries, even when fatal, caused to aliens incidentally in the enforcement of its laws by the use of arms, provided that such use is in accordance with the local law.[8] In every case, however, the use of force must be justified by necessity and the amount of force and the manner in which it is employed must be reasonable.[9] Furthermore, what is necessary and reasonable, although largely dependent

[7] See *Pugh Case* (1933), *supra*, p. 58.

See also Peruv.-U.S. Cl.Com. (1863): *Brand Case*, 2 *Int.Arb.*, p. 1625, at p. 1625: " Mr. Brand received his injuries in consequence of the violent armed opposition to legal authority by the resistance offered on the deck of the *Ganges*. . . . If he had been shot dead by one of the soldiers under the circumstances the Government of Peru would not have been accountable."

Cf. also *The I'm Alone* (1933, 1935), Canada/U.S., Joint Interim Report of the Commissioners (1933) 3 UNRIAA, p. 1609, at p. 1615: "On the assumptions stated in the question [*i.e.*, the right of hot pursuit existed in the circumstances], the United States might, consistently with the Convention, use necessary and reasonable force for the purpose of effecting the objects of boarding, searching, seizing and bringing into port the suspected vessel; and if sinking should occur incidentally, as a result of the exercise of necessary and reasonable force for such purpose, the pursuing vessel might be entirely blameless." *In casu*, the admittedly intentional sinking of the Canadian schooner by the U.S. was considered unjustified.

[8] Brit.-U.S. Cl.Arb. (1910): *Cadenhead Case* (1914) Nielsen's *Report*, p. 505. Tribunal disallowed a claim for accidental killing of a British subject by a United States soldier firing at a military prisoner escaping from a Michigan prison. The soldier was found to have acted in conformity with military orders and regulations. The Tribunal, however, recommended an *ex gratia* payment of compensation. *Cf. infra*, p. 64.

[9] *Cf. La Masica Case* (1916) *G.B.* v. *Honduras*, 121 B.F.S.P. (1925), p. 784, at pp. 792–793: " If the attitude of the negroes [British subjects] and their refusal to come down from the engine to be arrested cannot justify the public force [of Honduras] having discharged their rifles at them, the same cannot be said with respect to the action taken in the case of Joseph Holland because, as it is admitted by the two high parties that there was an affray and that the negroes refused to come down from the engine, the employment of force to compel them to do so was justified within certain limits, and there is no reason to think that these limits were exceeded in the case of Holland." Honduras held liable for the death of the negroes, but not for the injuries inflicted upon Holland.

In the *Pugh Case* (1933), the Arbitrator examined at length whether the circumstances justified the Panamanian police in using their clubs on Pugh and whether in so doing they committed any excess (*loc. cit.*, pp. 1447 *et seq.*).

Mex.-U.S. G.C.C. (1923): *Mallén Case* (1927), *Op. of Com. 1927*, p. 254. The U.S. was held liable for injuries inflicted by a deputy constable who, partly to satisfy a private vengeance, in effecting an arrest of doubtful legality, acted in a savage, brutal and humiliating manner (*cf. ibid.*, pp. 259, 260). As the U.S. Commissioner said in his concurring opinion: " The award of the Commission must be based on the character of the injuries inflicted upon the consul as a result of *force and violence not necessary to effect his arrest* " (p. 266).

Cf. also *Id.*: *Koch Case* (1928) *Op. of Com. 1929*, p. 118, at p. 119.

upon the circumstances of each case, is to be determined in accordance with international standards.[10]

The same principle also applies when a State is obliged to have recourse to arms for the suppression of organised resistance to its authority inside its territory or for the defence of the community against foreign invasion. Thus the *Rapporteur* on the Spanish Zone of Morocco Claims (1923) stated:—

"It has been said [11] that the State may not be held responsible for the fact that a revolution breaks out in its territory, or that the

[10] "Indemnities have been awarded in cases in which it has been considered that soldiers or police officials acted improperly in attempting to make arrests, when persons have failed to respond to a summons to halt. Domestic laws throughout the world seem none too certain with respect to the action of officers relative to such matters. It seems reasonable to suppose that such is the fact because it is considered inadvisable or impracticable to frame legislation tending on the one hand to tie too rigidly the hands of officials, or on the other hand, to give them too great latitude, and that therefore considerable discretion is left to them" (Mex.-U.S. G.C.C. (1923): *Kling Case* (1930), *Op. of Com. 1931*, p. 36, at p. 41). This shows the difficulty in formulating any hard and fast rules. The Arbitrator in the *Pugh Case* (1933) stated: "We reiterate that it is impossible to set forth the situations which demand and justify the use of a club by a policeman. Rather can we arrive at a conclusion by a study of a particular case" (*loc. cit.*, p. 1448). In the *Kling Case* (1930), the Mex.-U.S. G.C.C. (1923), *per* the American Commissioner, held Mexico liable for "indiscreet, unnecessary and unwarranted" use of firearms by Mexican soldiers when a party of Americans of the Texas Co. of Mexico, S.A., returning from a nearby town to the camp of their company, fired their revolvers into the air for fun. In the *Garcia and Garza Case* (1926), the Commission recognised that there existed an "international standard concerning the taking of human life." And it declared: "If this international standard of appraising human life exists, it is the duty not only of municipal authorities but of international tribunals as well to obviate any reckless use of firearms" (*Op. of Com. 1927*, p. 163, at p. 166). With particular reference to the use of firearms in the enforcement of law along an international border, the Commission formulated the following rule: "In order to consider shooting on the border by armed officials of either government (soldiers, river guards, custom guards) justified, a combination of four requirements would seem to be necessary: (a) the act of firing, always dangerous in itself, should not be indulged in unless the delinquency is sufficiently well stated; (b) it should not be indulged in unless the importance of preventing or repressing the delinquency by firing is in reasonable proportion to the danger arising from it to the lives of the culprits and other persons in their neighbourhood; (c) it should not be indulged in whenever other practicable ways of preventing or repressing the delinquency might be available; (d) it should be done with sufficient precaution not to create unnecessary danger, unless it be the official's intention to hit, wound, or kill" (p. 167; see also *Id.*: *Falcón Case* (1926), *Op. of Com. 1927* p. 140). *Cf.* these four requirements with the conditions governing Self-Defence and Reprisals, *infra*, pp. 94 *et seq.*, 98 *et seq.*

[11] *Rapport III* (1924), 2 UNRIAA, p. 615, at p. 642: "It seems beyond dispute that the State is not responsible for the occurrence of a riot, revolt, civil war or international war, nor for the fact that these happenings cause damage in its territory. It might be more or less possible to prove mistakes on the part of the government, but, in the absence of specific agreements or treaty provisions, the necessary investigation to this end is not permissible. These events must be considered as cases of *vis major*. The principle of the independence of States excludes the possibility of their domestic or foreign policy being made, in case of doubt, the subject of international judicial enquiry" (Transl.).

State is involved in a war. From this premise, it follows logically that a State can also not be held responsible for the consequences of its effort to re-establish order or to combat the enemy by the force of arms. In acting thus, the State is only fulfilling a primordial duty. In this matter, it seems that there exists a quite generally recognised rule: The State is not even responsible for damage caused by the military operations of its own forces." [12]

And in the *Luzon Sugar Refining Co. Case* (1925), which involved a claim for damages suffered in 1899 during the American campaign against the Philippine insurrectionists, it was held that:

"The foreign residents, whose property unhappily chanced to stand in the fields of those operations, have no ground of complaint against the United States which had no choice but to conduct them where the enemy was to be found." [13]

"The rule that neutral property in belligerent territory is liable to the fortunes of war equally with that of subjects of the State applies in the case of civil as well as international war." [14]

Under traditional international law, all damages incidental to military operations is considered as mere *casus fortuitus* for which neither of the belligerents is responsible.[15] Military necessity, whatever its cause or origin, absolves the State from liability for damage resulting therefrom. As, however, the *Rapporteur* on the Spanish Zone of Morocco Claims (1923) pointed out, the absence of liability for the State for damage caused through military operations proceeds juridically from the premise that, as a rule, international tribunals lack jurisdiction to determine responsibility for the existence of a state of war, whether civil or international.[16] But when an international tribunal is expressly empowered to establish this responsibility, there is juridically no obstacle to holding the State liable for the damage caused by its unlawful military

[12] *Rapport III* (1924), *ibid.*, at p. 645. (Transl.)

[13] Brit.-U.S. Cl.Arb. (1910), Nielsen's *Report*, p. 586, at p. 586. See also U.S.-Ven. M.C.C. (1903): *American Electric and Manufacturing Co. Case*, *Ven.Arb. 1903*, p. 35, at p. 36.

[14] U.S.-Ven. M.C.C. (1903): *Volkmar Case*, *Ven.Arb. 1903*, p. 258, at p. 259. See also *Rosa Gelbtrunk Case* (1902), U.S.F.R. (1902), p. 876, at p. 879.

[15] See also Mex.-U.S. Cl.Com. (1868): *Shuttuck Case*, 4 *Int.Arb.*, p. 3668. Brit.-U.S. Cl.Arb. (1910): *Hardman Case* (1913), Nielsen's *Report*, p. 465 (see *infra*, p. 64).

[16] *Supra*, p. 60, particularly note 11.

operations.[17] Indeed, in the Portugo-German Arbitration of 1919, certain German military incursions in 1914 into Portuguese possessions in Africa were found to be unlawful and Germany was held liable for all the proximate consequences of these acts,[18] according to principles governing unlawful acts in general.[19] However this may be, it seems certain that there is, at all events, exemption from responsibility in the case of military operations undertaken by the State to quell internal disorder[20] or to resist external aggression.[21]

[17] *Cf.* Fran.-Germ. M.A.T.: *Franz Case* (1922), 1 T.A.M., p. 781, at p. 785; *Id.*: *Hourcade Case* (1922), *ibid.*, p. 786, at p. 788: "By the terms of Art. 231 of the Treaty (of Versailles), Germany has admitted responsibility for the war and its consequences; . . . it follows that if, according to German municipal law, the war may be invoked as a case of *vis major*, not only by private individuals but also by those States which have taken part in it—a question which it is unnecessary to decide in the present case—the German Government can, in no way, benefit from such a defence in its disputes with allied nationals; . . . it is indeed an undisputed and indisputable principle that no one can invoke, in his own defence, the existence of a fact for which he is himself alone responsible" (Transl.).

Cf. also the I.M.T. at Nuremberg (1945) which, empowered to try individuals accused inter alia of crimes against peace, had to investigate the legality of the wars in which the European Axis Countries were engaged. It found that the German military operations against Poland, Denmark, Norway, Belgium, The Netherlands, Luxembourg, Yugoslavia, Greece, the U.S.S.R., and the U.S. to be aggressive wars (1 *I.M.T.* (*Nuremburg*), pp. 198–216).

[18] Portugo-Germ.Arb. (1919): *Maziua Case* (1928), (1930), 2 UNRIAA, p. 1011. On August 24, 1914, the German garrison at the small frontier post of Sasabara, German East Africa, erroneously believing that Portugal was at war with Germany, attacked the Portuguese garrison across the border at Maziua. On learning of the mistake, the Governor of German East Africa apologized to the Portuguese authorities and offered to restore the arms and munitions captured. Germany admitted responsibility for this unjustified attack (p. 1015). Damages allowed included compensation for injuries to persons and damage to property, both private and public (p. 1018).

Portugo-Germ.Arb. (1919): *Angola Case* (1928), (1930), 2 *ibid.*, p. 1011. A German official and two German officers having been killed in the Portuguese garrison post of Naulilaa, Germany, allegedly in reprisal therefor, sent military expeditions into Angola at several points in November-December, 1914, (p. 1014. The UNRIAA erroneously reports 1915, *cf.* 8 T.A.M., p. 409, at p. 410). Portugal was not held legally responsible for the unfortunate incident at Naulilaa (pp. 1019 *et seq.*), and the German attacks were held unlawful (pp. 1025 *et seq.*). For the computation of the damages which amounted to 47 million gold marks covering both the *Maziua* and the *Angola Cases*, see pp. 1029 *et seq.*; pp. 1068 *et seq.*

[19] See *infra*, pp. 241 *et seq.*

[20] *e.g.*, Neth.-Ven. M.C.C. (1903): *Bembelista Case*, *Ven.Arb. 1903*, p. 900, at pp. 900–1: "His injuries were received in the course of battle and in the rightful and successful endeavour of the Government to repossess itself of one of its important towns and ports. The Government owed a duty to the claimant and to all the inhabitants of Puerto Cabello to become the government in fact of the town in question. And as their repossession of it was resisted by the troops then in charge it became the due course of war to take and carry the intrenchments of the town. It was the misfortune of the claimant that his building was so near to one of the principal intrenchments, where there was the most serious resistance, and the injuries occasioned his property were one of the ordinary incidents of battle."

[21] Mex. U.S. Cl.Com. (1868): *Blumenkron Case*, 4 *Int.Arb.*, p. 3669, at p. 3669: "Neither can the Mexican Government be expected to compensate foreigners

The uncompensated sacrifices demanded of individuals in such circumstances find their juridical justification in the superior interest of the State in ensuring the security and peace of the community.

" The interest of a government, like that of an individual, lies in its preservation . . . To say that a government is . . . responsible for the acts it commits in an attempt . . . to maintain its own existence . . . is a proposition difficult to maintain." [22]

However, as the *Rapporteur* on the Spanish Zone of Morocco Claims (1923) observed, when speaking of the rule that a State is not responsible for damages caused by military operations of its own troops:—

" It is not possible to include within this rule all measures having some connection with military operations, nor is it possible to include therein all acts committed by the troops." [23]

In fact, military operations should be conducted in accordance with the rules and customs of warfare. Acts which are contrary to these rules, although they may be justifiable and advantageous from the military point of view, are considered as unlawful [24] or even criminal.[25] In referring to the Hague Convention IV of 1907 concerning the Laws and Customs of War on Land, the *Rapporteur* said:—

" The principle which it establishes deserves to be retained even in military operations falling outside the scope of a war properly

for damages done to their real property by reason of actual hostilities for the purpose of delivering the country from a foreign enemy."

22 Ital.-Ven. M.C.C. (1903): *Sambiaggio Case*, *Ven.Arb. 1903*, p. 666, at p. 680. Claims arising out of damage caused by revolution.

23 *Rapport III* (1924), 2 UNRIAA, p. 615, at p. 645. (Transl.)

24 See Greco-Germ. M.A.T.: *Coenca Brothers Case* (1927) 7 T.A.M., p. 683, at p. 687. Aerial bombardment without warning held unlawful, being contrary to generally accepted principles of warfare, even though from the military point of view such bombardment should be carried out by surprise.

Cf. also U.S.-Ven. M.C.C. (1903): *American Electric and Manufacturing Co. Case*, *Ven.Arb. 1903*, p. 35, at p. 36: " The general principles of international law which established the non-responsibility of the Government for damages suffered by neutral property owing to imperious necessities of military operations within the radius of said operations, or as a consequence of the damages of a battle, incidentally caused by the *means of destruction* employed in the war *which are not disapproved by the law of nations*, are well known " (Italics added).

25 The Charter of the International Military Tribunal (Nuremberg), Art. 6 II (b), defines " War Crimes " *stricto sensu* as " violations of the laws or customs of war." The Charter of the International Military Tribunal for the Far East calls them " Conventional War Crimes " (Art. 5 II (b)).

so-called. This being admitted, it must also be remembered that the said Convention . . . makes considerable allowance for military necessity." [26]

A belligerent is liable for damages caused in violation of the rules and customs of warfare [27] and individuals committing the offence may be prosecuted as war criminals.[28] The absence of responsibility of the State is confined to " damages suffered . . . owing to imperious necessities of military operations within the radius of said operations, or as a consequence of the damages of a battle, incidentally caused by the means of destruction employed in the war which are not disapproved by the law of nations." [29] Even in such an event, meritorious cases may create a moral duty on the part of the State to grant an *ex gratia* indemnity.[30]

26 *Rapport III* (1924) 2 UNRIAA, p. 615, at p. 645. (Transl.)

27 Hague Convention IV, 1907, Art. 3. The Fran.-Mex. Cl.Com. (1924) (*Caire Case* (1929) *Jurisprudence*, p. 207, at p. 219) was of the opinion that, *de lege lata*, Art. 3 of the Hague Convention IV, 1907, was not applicable *in a general manner* to *all* the acts of the troops of a State (the English summary of the case in *Annual Digest* (1929–30), Case No. 91, at p. 148, goes further than the original French version of the decision would seem to warrant). However, the decision appears, erroneously it is believed, to consider that Art. 3 establishes an objective responsibility (p. 219, particularly note 1). This is due, in turn, to what is regarded as the Commission's erroneous conception of the notion of imputability in international law, hence its exaggerated notion of objective responsibility. See *infra*, pp. 204 *et seq*. Art. 3, it is submitted, is merely declaratory of the ordinary principles of State responsibility for the acts of its agents.

28 International penal law is still in the embryonic stage. The Charters of the International Military Tribunals (Nuremberg, Art. 6 II (b); Far East, Art. 5 II (b)) define as war crimes all " violations of the laws and customs of war." The Judgment of Nuremberg (1946), while accepting as law the general definition of the Charter, referred more specifically to Arts. 46, 50, 52 and 56 of the Hague Regulations of 1907, and Arts. 2, 3, 4, 46 and 51 of the Geneva Convention of 1929 regarding the treatment of prisoners of war. It held: " That violations of these provisions constituted crimes for which the guilty individuals were punishable is too well settled to admit of argument " (1 *I.M.T.* (*Nuremberg*), p. 171, at p. 253). The Tribunal also convicted Dönitz on the count of " war crimes " for violations of the Naval Protocol of 1936 (p. 311 *et seq*.). In this matter, it seems preferable to establish, if possible, an international military criminal code distinct from, and more restrictive than, the rules intended to govern what is in fact the " civil " responsibility of States. *Cf*. Schwarzenberger: " The Problem of an International Criminal Law," 3 C.L.P. (1950) p. 263.

29 U.S.-Ven. M.C.C. (1903): *American Electric and Manufacturing Co. Case*, *Ven.Arb. 1903*, p. 35, at p. 36.

30 Brit.-U.S. Cl.Arb. (1910): *Hardman Case* (1913), Nielsen's *Report*, pp. 495, 497: " Notwithstanding the principle generally recognised in international law that necessary acts of war do not imply the belligerent's legal obligation to compensate, there is, nevertheless, a certain humanitary conduct generally followed by nations to compensate the private war losses as a matter purely of grace and favour, when in their own judgment they feel able to do so, and when the sufferer appears to be specially worthy of interest. Although there is no

" 'Military necessity, as understood by modern civilised nations, consists in the necessity of those measures which are indispensable for securing the ends of the war, and which are lawful according to the modern law and usages of war.

" 'Military necessity admits of all direct destruction of life or limb of *armed* enemies, and of other persons whose destruction is incidentally *unavoidable* in the armed contests of the war.' "[31]

The British-United States Claims Arbitral Tribunal (1910) also gave the following definition of military necessity:—

"In law, an act of war is an act of defence or attack against the enemy and a necessity of war is an act which is made necessary by the defence or attack and assumes the character of *vis major*."[32]

"The determination of these necessities ought to be left in a large measure to the very persons who are called upon to act in difficult situations, as well as to their military commanders. A non-military tribunal, and above all an international tribunal, could not intervene in this field save in case of manifest abuse of this freedom of judgment."[33]

While a large discretion is thus left to the State, this must not be abused. Indeed, destruction not justified by military

legal obligation to act in that way, there may be a moral duty which cannot be covered by law, because it is grounded only on an inmost sense of human assistance, and because its fulfilment depends on the economical and political condition of a nation, each nation being its own judge in that respect."

This moral obligation can naturally be transformed into a legal obligation by an agreement between the countries concerned in regard to damages suffered by their nationals as a result of military operations conducted by the other. P.C.A.: *Russian Indemnity Case* (1912) Russia/Turkey, 1 H.C.R. p. 297, at p. 319. See further, *infra*, p. 164, note 4.

[31] Fran.-Ven. M.C.C. (1902): *Brun Case* (1905) Ralston's *Report*, p. 5, at p. 27, quoting *Instructions for the Government of Armies of the U.S. in the Field*, April 24, 1863, paras. 14–15.

[32] *Hardman Case* (1913), *loc. cit.*, at p. 497. Destruction of claimant's personal property through houses being set on fire by American military authorities to prevent the spread of yellow fever threatening the health of American forces who were fighting the Spaniards in Cuba. The British contention was that the act was not a necessity of war, but a measure for better securing the comfort and health of the U.S. troops and therefore the claimant (British) was entitled to compensation. Held: "In the present case, the necessity of war was the occupation of Siboney, and that occupation . . . involved the necessity . . . of taking the said sanitary measures. . . . The presence of the U.S. troops at Siboney was a necessity of war and the destruction required for their safety was consequently a necessity of war" (p. 497).

The *Rapporteur* on the Spanish Zone of Morocco Claims (1923) conceived the notion of military operations, for the consequence of which a State is not responsible, to mean only acts having a tactical object. See Claim No. 44: *Rzini* (*Dar Ben Karrish, Harvest*) *Case* (1924), 2 UNRIAA, p. 615, at pp. 716–7. *Cf. supra*, p. 46, note 55.

[33] Spanish Zone of Morocco Claims (1923): *Rapport III* (1924), 2 UNRIAA, p. 615, at p. 645. (Transl.).

necessity or wanton devastation has long been condemned by international tribunals[34] and is now even regarded as a war crime.[35] In all events, a duty always falls upon States, when conducting military operations to take every care to safeguard the interests of private individuals[36] and of cultural or humanitarian institutions.[37]

[34] Mex.-U.S. Cl.Com. (1868): *Johnston Case* (1874), 4 *Int.Arb.*, p. 3673, at p. 3673: "As the defendants have not proved that the requirements of war rendered that damage necessary, it must therefore be considered to have been unnecessary; and that therefore the claimants are, on account of that damage, entitled to compensation." *Id.*: *Brooks Case*, 4 *Int.Arb.*, p. 3672. Opinion of U.S. Commissioner: "I do not know anything more criminal or more stupid than the wanton destruction of the labours of the farmer by the military who possess the district where he resides" (pp. 3672–73). $4,000 awarded as damages. Fran.-Ven. M.C.C. (1903): *Brun Case* (1905), Ralston's *Report*, p. 5, and precedents cited therein at p. 26.

[35] See Charter of the International Military Tribunal (Nuremberg), Art. 6 II (*b*). By Resolution 95 (I) of December 11, 1946, the General Assembly of the United Nations unanimously "affirms the principles of international law recognised by Charter of the Nürnberg Tribunal and the judgment of the Tribunal."

[36] Spanish Zone of Morocco Claims (1923): Claim 25: *Rzini* (*Beni-Madan, Cattle*) *Case* (1924), 2 UNRIAA, p. 615, at pp. 696–97. In a drive against hostile tribes, Spanish authorities seized and slaughtered 190 head of cattle and sheep belonging to the claimant. *Rapporteur* said: "The responsibility of the Spanish authorities must in this case be admitted . . . because without prejudicing the military operation, it would have been possible, once the animals had been seized, to separate those belonging to peaceful natives from those belonging to the hostile tribe against which the raid was directed. But all the cattle were indiscriminately killed. Whilst the raid, as such, has been recognised as falling within the notion of military operations, . . . it is nonetheless true that the failure to take all measures for safeguarding the interests of peaceful owners and the immediate slaughter of all the captured cattle could not be justified by any military necessity" (p. 696. Transl.).

Greco-Germ. M.A.T.: *Coenca Brothers Case* (1927), 7 T.A.M., p. 683, at p. 687: "It is one of the generally recognised principles of the law of nations that belligerents should respect, as much as possible, the civil population and property belonging to civilians" (Transl.). *Id.*: *Kiriadolou Case* (1930), 10 *ibid.*, p. 100, at p. 103.

Fran.-Ven. M.C.C. (1903): *Brun Case* (1905), Ralston's *Report*, p. 5. See authorities cited at pp. 26 *et seq.* Also Headnote to the decision subsequently prepared by the Umpire: "A city not in revolt, but temporarily occupied by insurgent forces, is entitled to receive from the Government the *utmost care and protection* not inconsistent with the retaking of the town from the insurgent forces, and is subject only to the *inevitable* contingencies attending such an undertaking" (p. 5. Original italics.).

[37] Fran.-Ven. M.C.C. (1903): *Brun Case* (1905), Ralston's *Report*, p. 5, at p. 27: "Even in bombardments it is now deemed necessary to avoid as far as possible injuries to churches, museums, and hospitals, and not to direct the artillery upon the quarter inhabited by civilians, unless it is impossible to avoid them while firing at the fortifications and military buildings."

See Hague Regulations, Art. 27. Hague Convention IX of 1907, Art. 5. See also Hague Convention Concerning the Laws and Customs of War on Land, Preamble: "Until a more complete code of the laws of war can be issued, the High Contracting Parties think it expedient to declare that in cases not included in the Regulations adopted by them, populations and belligerents *remain* under the protection and the rules of the principles of the law of nations, as they result from the usages established between civilised nations, from the *laws of humanity, and the requirements of the public conscience.*" (Italics added.)

D. Conclusions

In the above survey, a single theme seems to emerge from the decisions of various international courts and tribunals. Within the territorial limits of the State's authority, the interest of the community is superior to that of individuals whether national or alien. For the welfare and safety of the community, a State may adopt a variety of measures appropriate to the needs and circumstances of the case, even though such measures may amount to an encroachment upon private rights which ordinarily must be respected. If the State, by any of these measures, should procure a material enrichment of the community at the expense of isolated individuals, or groups of individuals, there is a duty to compensate.[38] Incidental damage to the rights and interests of individuals, however, gives rise to no compensation, although, morally, compensation may be justifiable in certain cases.[39]

By reason of the fundamental importance of national self-preservation, it seems that a State is presumed not to have undertaken obligations towards private individuals in derogation of this vital interest. An organ of the State which acts otherwise is considered to have violated the fundamental law of the State and its act is consequently void.[40] Other obligations towards individuals may also be abrogated by the State whenever the national interest of self-preservation so demands.[41]

With regard to international obligations, the right of the State to adopt measures necessary to ensure the welfare and security of the community in exceptional circumstances cannot be considered as being impaired by general provisions contained in treaties entered into with reference to normal circumstances.[42] But, as States may even renounce their political existence,[43] international tribunals are agreed that a specific treaty provision, intended by the parties to apply even in exceptional circumstances, must always be respected.[44]

Since the State's power to resort to such extraordinary

[38] *Supra*, pp. 47–9, 57–8.
[39] *Supra*, pp. 59, note 8; 64.
[40] *Supra*, pp. 30–1.
[41] *Supra*, p. 55.
[42] *Supra*, pp. 29–30, 33–4, 52–3, 55–6.
[43] *Supra*, p. 29, note 2.
[44] *Supra*, pp. 34, 41, 50, 56, 63–4.

measures is justified only by the necessity of self-preservation, the legality of the measures taken, as regards their nature, extent and duration, is strictly circumscribed by the needs of each particular case.[45] The determination of the existence of the need and the methods best calculated to meet the contingency are, however, left to the discretion of the State.[46] International tribunals only require the State to prove the existence of a contingency warranting the exercise of this discretion. They will, however, intervene in cases of abuse.[47]

In reviewing such measures international tribunals will be guided by current international practice. This practice naturally varies according to time, place, and circumstance; and, with the prevailing trend of greater social integration, the sphere of State activity is constantly being enlarged.[48]

In every case, the State must, however, so far as circumstances permit, take every care to safeguard the interests of private individuals, to respect the human personality and to protect the spiritual values of humanity.[49]

[45] *Supra*, pp. 33, note 3; 38–40, 43–6, 49, 54, 56–7, 59–60, 65–6.
[46] *Supra*, pp. 34–5, 39, 43, 45, 54–5, 65.
[47] *Supra*, pp. 32, note 2; 33, note 3; 36, 38, 39, 44, 46, 59–60, 66.
[48] *Supra*, pp. 39, 57, particularly note 97.
[49] *Supra*, pp. 36, 49–50, 66.

Chapter 2

EXTERNAL APPLICATION OF THE PRINCIPLE

A. Necessity

In the *Faber Case* (C. 1903),[1] the German Commissioner maintained:—

"When a river constitutes the only way of communication, indispensable for the subsistence of another nation, or part of it, its use cannot be entirely prohibited."[2]

But the Umpire held:—

"It certainly is a novel proposition that because one may be so situated that the use of the property of another will be of special advantage to him he may on that ground demand such use *as a right*. The rights of an individual are not created or determined by his wants or even his necessities. The starving man who takes the bread of another without right is none the less a thief, legally, although the immorality of the act is so slight as to justify it. Wants or necessities of individuals cannot create legal rights for them, or infringe the existing rights of others . . ."[3]

Even in this case, however, the Umpire, before arriving at his final conclusion, wanted to be assured that:—

"It is not accurate . . . to say that the Zulia River is indispensable to the existence of Santander, or that it is the only route of communication of Santander through the Republic of Colombia to the sea."[4]

[1] Germ.-Ven. M.C.C. (1903), *Ven.Arb. 1903*, p. 600.

[2] *Loc. cit.*, p. 605.

[3] *Loc. cit.*, pp. 629–30.

An example of the starving man is the *Louise Ménard Case* (1898), in France. The woman, out of hunger, stole from a bakery. She was absolved by the "*bon juge Magnaud*" at the Correctional Court of Château-Thierry (H. Leyret, 1 *Les Jugements du Président Magnaud*, Paris, 1900, pp. 14–15). The decision was upheld in the Court of Appeal of Amiens (*Recueil Sirey* (1899), 2*e partie*, p. 1).

The *jus necessitatis* is, in France, a creation of the courts ("*l'état de nécessité*"), while in Germany ("*Notstand*"), Switzerland and Italy ("*lo stato di necessità*"), it has been sanctioned by the written law. As to English law, see Glanville Williams, "The Defence of Necessity," 6 C.L.P. (1953), p. 216.

[4] *Loc. cit.*, p. 624.

The example of the starving man mentioned in the award of the Umpire finds its international counterpart in the case of *The Neptune* (1797) which was decided by the Arbitral Commission established under Art. VII of the Jay Treaty (1794) between Great Britain and the United States.[5]

The *Neptune* was an American vessel laden with provisions bound for Bordeaux from the United States. She was captured by a British frigate in 1795 in pursuance of a general order of April of that year directing the bringing into British ports of all neutral vessels bound with provisions for ports of the enemy.

On being libelled in the High Court of Admiralty the vessel was released, but the cargo was taken over for the British Government, the owners being allowed the invoice price plus a mercantile profit of 10 per cent. This was less than the goods were then worth in London, and much less than they were worth in Bordeaux. The owners claimed the difference between what was paid to them and the price the goods would have fetched at Bordeaux, had they not been seized.

One of the arguments advanced to justify the order of April, 1795, was that it imposed a blockade in order to reduce the enemy by famine. The other argument was that of necessity, since Great Britain was threatened with a scarcity of provisions at the time when the order was made. The first argument was rejected by the majority of the commissioners. As regards the second argument, the Fifth Commissioner, Mr. Trumbull, stated in his opinion that:—

"It only remains to inquire whether there existed at the time any necessity on the part of the captor so pressing as to justify the act.

"The necessity which can be admitted to supersede all laws and to dissolve the distinctions of property and right must be absolute and irresistible, and we cannot, until all other means of self-preservation shall have been exhausted, justify by the plea of necessity the seizure and application to our own use of that which belongs to others. Did any such state of things exist in Great Britain in April, 1795? Were any means employed to guard against an apprehended, rather than an existing, scarcity before the measure in question was adopted? And when a degree of scarcity was felt a few months later in the year was not the obvious and inoffensive

[5] 4 *Int.Adj.*, M.S., p. 372.

measure of offering a bounty on corn imported effectual, and that speedily? It cannot, then, be presumed that the capture in question is any more to be justified by the plea of necessity than it is by that of right, and I must, therefore, conclude that the neutral claimant has in this case suffered loss and damage by reason of an irregular and illegal capture." [6]

Several rules may be deduced from the above case regarding the plea of necessity: —

1. When the existence of a State is in peril, the necessity of self-preservation may be a good defence for certain acts which would otherwise be unlawful.

2. This necessity "supersedes all laws," "dissolves the distinctions of property and rights" and justifies the "seizure and application to our own use of that which belongs to others." Although the language used in the decision is very general, it may perhaps be inferred from the emphasis on property that it is essentially the proprietary rights of others which may be disregarded in case of an irresistible and absolute necessity.

3. This necessity must be "absolute" in that the very existence of the State is in peril.

4. This necessity must be "irresistible" in that all legitimate means of self-preservation have been exhausted and proved to be of no avail.

5. This necessity must be actual and not merely apprehended.

6. Whether or not the above conditions are fulfilled in a given case, is a proper subject of judicial inquiry. If they are not, the act will be regarded as unlawful and damages will be assessed in accordance with principles governing reparation for unlawful acts.

The above rules correspond to those that have been elaborated by various other international tribunals as regards the plea of necessity in relation to treaty obligations.

In his Individual Opinion in the *Oscar Chinn Case* (1934), Judge Anzilotti said: —

> "Necessity may excuse the non-observance of international obligations." [7]

[6] *Loc. cit.*, p. 433.
[7] PCIJ: A/B.63, p. 113.

The German agent in the case of *The Wimbledon* (1923), in denying that Germany was invoking the *jus necessitatis*, made the following observation, which helps to elucidate the notion of necessity:—

"There was neither an impossibility for her to comply with the provisions of the Treaty of Versailles, nor a situation absolutely preventing her from fulfilling her obligations." [8]

As regards treaty obligations, therefore, the plea of necessity is equivalent to a plea of impossibility of performance, whether objective or subjective. In the *Serbian and Brazilian Loans Cases* (1929), the Permanent Court of International Justice grouped these two forms of impossibility of performance under the single heading of *force majeure*.[9]

Objective impossibility would no doubt extinguish an obligation, but the Court emphasised that the impossibility must relate to the very substance of the obligation. Consequently, when the obligation specifies that payment should be made in gold francs taken as a standard of value, the impossibility of procuring gold francs *in specie* does not dissolve the obligation.[10]

The extinction of obligations by subjective impossibility was admitted in principle by the Permanent Court of Arbitration in the *Russian Indemnity Case* (1912), in which it held that:—

"The exception of *vis major*, invoked as the first line of defence, may be pleaded in public international law as well as in private law; international law has to adapt itself to political necessities. The Imperial Russian Government expressly admits (Russian Reply, p. 33 and note 2) that the obligation of a State to carry out treaties may give way 'if the very existence of the State is endangered, if the observance of the international duty is . . . self-destructive.'" [11]

[8] PCIJ: Ser.C. 3–I, p. 306. Quotation translated from the French version which is more complete than the English summary.

[9] PCIJ: A.20/21, pp. 39–40, 120. See further, *infra*, pp. 223 *et seq.*

[10] *Ibid.*, at pp. 40, 120.

[11] 1 H.C.R., p. 532, at p. 546. (Transl.)

Cf. Fran.-Turk. M.A.T.: *Cillière Case* and *Lejosne Case* (1927), 7 T.A.M., p. 930, at p. 933 and at pp. 935–6: "According to the present conception of the notion of *vis major*, it is sufficient that the circumstances in which a contract has to be performed are such that in good justice and in all equity, this performance could not be exacted" (Transl.).

But the concept of necessity, or *vis major*, differs considerably from that of national interest[12] and does not signify the mere existence of grave difficulties in the performance of an obligation.[13]

As Judge Anzilotti said in his Individual Opinion, already referred to:—

"The plea of necessity, . . . by definition, implies the impossibility of proceeding by any other method than the one contrary to law."[14]

Finally, Judge Anzilotti also held that the plea of necessity involved an issue of fact. In case of a dispute, the burden of proof is upon the party raising it.[15]

From the above survey it is therefore apparent that the international judicial decisions of the twentieth century are in complete accord with the principles laid down in *The Neptune Case* decided at the end of the eighteenth.[16]

If there is absolutely no conceivable manner in which a State can fulfil an international obligation without endangering

12 PCIJ: *Oscar Chinn Case* (1934), Ind.Op. by Anzilotti, A/B 63, p. 112: "International law would be merely an empty phrase if it sufficed for a State to invoke the public interest in order to evade the fulfilment of its engagements."

13 *Russian Indemnity Case* (1912), 1 H.C.R., p. 532, at pp. 546–47: "In support of its plea of *force majeure*, the Sublime Porte has undoubtedly proved that Turkey from 1881 to 1902 was contending with financial difficulties of the utmost seriousness, aggravated by domestic and foreign troubles (insurrections, wars) which forced her to apply a considerable amount of her revenues for special purposes, to submit to the foreign control of part of her finances, and even to grant a moratorium to the Ottoman Bank, and generally to fulfil her obligations only imperfectly or with delay and, even then, at great sacrifice. But, it has been proved, on the other hand, that, during this same period, and especially following the creation of the Ottoman Bank, Turkey was able to obtain loans at favourable rates, to redeem others, and, finally, to pay off an important part of her public debt, estimated at 350 million francs. It would be clearly an exaggeration to admit that the payment (or the raising of a loan for the payment) of the comparatively small amount of about 6 million francs to the Russian claimants, would have imperilled the existence of the Ottoman Empire or seriously compromised its internal or international position. The plea of *force majeure* is, therefore, inadmissible" (Transl.).

Cf. also the rejection of the plea of *force majeure* by the PCIJ in the cases of the *Serbian and Brazilian Loans* (1929), A. 20/21, pp. 39–40, and p. 120. It is only fair to mention, however, that it seems that the parties did not invoke the plea. Mention of economic difficulties after the war was made by the Serb-Croat-Slovene Kingdom under the heading of "Equity" (Ser. C. 16–III, pp. 457 *et seq.*, at p. 470). By Art. II of the special agreement, the P.C.I.J. was informed that considerations of equity would be separately considered after the Court should have rendered its decision. The mention of economic difficulties was even more vague in the Brazilian case (*Cf.* Ser. C. 16–III, pp. 168 and 130–1).

14 A/B 63, p. 114.

15 *Ibid.*, p. 113.

16 *Supra*, pp. 70 *et seq.*

its very existence, that State is justified in disregarding its obligation, in order to preserve its existence.

If, after every conceivable legal means of self-preservation has first been exhausted, the very existence of the State is still in danger, and if there exists only one single means of escaping from such danger, the State is justified in having recourse to that means in self-preservation, even though it may otherwise be unlawful.

In every case, the questions whether such a danger to the very existence of the State really existed, whether there was such a lack of choice of means, and whether there was such a necessity for resorting to the otherwise unlawful means of self-preservation, are all issues of fact. The burden of proof lies with the party invoking the plea of necessity. If the matter is submitted to an international tribunal, the latter is competent to review the facts and circumstances in order to determine whether such a state of absolute and irresistible necessity did in fact exist.

In reaching this conclusion, however, the words of the Umpire in the *Faber Case* (C. 1903) must be borne in mind:—

> "The rights of an individual are not created or determined by his wants or even his necessities. The starving man who takes the bread of another without right is none the less a thief, legally, although the immorality of the act is so slight as to justify it."[17]

The necessity of self-preservation justifies and excuses an otherwise unlawful act, exempting it from the legal consequences normally resulting from acts of this kind. But it does not render the commission of the act a matter of right.[18] The law of necessity is a means of preserving social values. It is the great disparity in the importance of the interests actually in conflict that alone justifies a reversal of the legal protection normally accorded to these interests, so that a socially important interest shall not perish for the sake of respect for an objectively minor right. In every case, a comparison of the conflicting interests appears to be indispensable. At all events, it would appear that it can never be justifiable to endanger the existence

[17] *Ven.Arb. 1903*, p. 600, at p. 630.
[18] *Cf.* The *Neptune* (1797), last sentence in the above quoted passage, *supra*, p. 71. *Cf.* Anzilotti, *supra*, p. 71.

of one State in order to preserve the existence of another. As States are equal, the conflicting interests are thus also of equal importance.[19]

Lastly, it appears from the voluntary action of Great Britain in the case of *The Neptune* (1797) that any material enrichment obtained as a result of the self-preservative act must be compensated.[20]

VESSELS IN DISTRESS

A special application of the plea of necessity in international law relates to vessels in distress, where the principles involved are substantially the same, although perhaps less stringent. The Mexican-United States General Claims Commission (1923) in the *Hoff (The Rebecca) Case* (1929) stated that:—

'The enlightened principle of comity which exempts a merchant vessel, at least to a certain extent, from the operation of local laws has been generally stated to apply to vessels forced into ports by storm, or compelled to seek refuge by vital repairs or for provisioning, or carried into port by mutineers." [21]

As to what constitutes necessity justifying such a disregard of local laws, the same Commission added:—

"It has been said that the necessity must be urgent. It seems possible to formulate certain reasonably concrete criteria applicable and controlling in the instant case. Assuredly a ship floundering in

[19] *Cf.* England, Queen's Bench Division: *The Queen* v. *Dudley and Stephens* (1884) 14 Q.B.D., p. 273. Self-preservation is no defence to the killing of another shipwrecked person and eating his flesh in order to escape starvation.

[20] *Supra*, p. 70.

[21] *Op. of Com. 1929*, p. 174, at p. 177.

The Commission called it a rule of comity. *Cf.*, however, Brit.-U.S. Cl. Com. (1853): *The Enterprize Case* (1854) (Hornby's *Report*, p. 332); probably the case of reprovisioning which the Mex.-U.S. G.C.C. (1923) had in mind. In that case, the U.S. Commissioner held that: "The entrance of a vessel into a foreign harbour, when compelled by stress of weather, is a matter of right" (p. 368), although the Umpire did not specifically deal with this point. The Umpire, however, in another case which was brought before the same Commission, the case of the *Creole* (1855), which was taken into port by mutineers, stated expressly: "These rights, sanctioned by the law of nations, *viz.*, the right to navigate the ocean and to seek shelter in case of distress or other unavoidable circumstances, and to retain over the ships, her cargo, and passengers, the laws of her own country, must be respected by all nations, for no independent nation would submit to their violation" (Hornby's *Report*, p. 376, at p. 392).

Cf. the Mex.-U.S. G.C.C. (1923), when speaking of the "immunity" of the ship, said: "Perhaps it may be said in a more concrete and emphatic manner" (*loc. cit.*, p. 177). Such an involuntary entry is certainly "*straflos*," if indeed not of right. *Cf. infra*, p. 76, note 23.

distress, resulting either from the weather or from other causes affecting management of the vessel, need not be in such a condition that it is dashed helplessly on the shore or against rocks before a claim of distress can properly be invoked in its behalf. The fact that it may be able to come into port under its own power can obviously not be cited as conclusive evidence that the plea is unjustifiable. If a captain delayed seeking refuge until his ship was wrecked, obviously he would not be using his best judgment with a view to the preservation of the ship, the cargo and the lives of people on board." [22]

The above passage also corroborates the view that the object of the principle of self-preservation is essentially to permit a person to have recourse to extraordinary measures to avert an imminent and irresistible danger. Its purpose is preventive. It is, therefore, not necessary to wait until the danger has materialised and the harm has been done.

Moreover, the concluding sentence of the above quotation shows that necessity is not an independent notion. It rests upon the principle of self-preservation. When applied to a vessel, it aims at the preservation of the ship, the cargo, and the lives of the people on board.

This point is further illustrated by the following passage which makes it clear that the principle of necessity cannot be invoked to justify actions taken for reasons of pure convenience:—

" A mere matter of convenience in making repairs or in avoiding a measure of difficulty in navigation cannot justify a disregard of local laws." [23]

[22] *Loc. cit.*, p. 178.

[23] *Hoff* (*The Rebecca*) *Case* (1929), *loc. cit.*, at p. 178. *Cf.* England, High Court of Admiralty: *The Eleanor* (1809), Edw., p. 135, at p. 161.

When the Mex.-U.S. G.C.C. (1923) spoke of "disregard of local laws," it must not be taken to mean a total disregard of the local laws, but only that the vessel should not be made to suffer for having made an involuntary entry. The Commission itself had earlier spoken only of " the enlightened principle of comity which exempts a merchant vessel, *at least to a certain extent*, from the operation of local laws. . . ." (*loc. cit.*, p. 177. Italics added.)

The cases of the *Enterprize*, the *Hermosa* and the *Creole* before the Brit-U.S. Cl.Com. (1853) (Hornby's *Report*, pp. 332–395) show, on the other hand, that the exemption is not solely from customs regulations. Slavery was then abolished in G.B. and colonies, but still permitted in the U.S. and under international law. The freeing of slaves on board these American ships which, sailing between American ports, entered British harbours in distress was held unlawful. *Cf. Id.*: *The Lawrence* (1855), *ibid.*, p. 397, where ship engaged in African slave trade, then prohibited by American, British and international law, claim was dismissed.

With regard to the determination of the existence of the necessity and the choice of means, the Commission, having pointed out that the ship, in a crippled condition, had been contending with a storm for three days, stated:—

"In such a case a captain's judgment would scarcely seem subject to question. It may also be concluded from the evidence in the case that a well grounded apprehension of the loss of the vessel and cargo and persons on board prompted the captain to turn south to Tampico." [24]

Thus, where a prima facie case existed, the decision of the person who had to act in such circumstances may be presumed to have been well founded. But an international tribunal is also competent to draw its own conclusions from the facts of the case. In so doing, it only seeks to ascertain whether at the crucial moment, there was a good reason to believe that a state of vital danger existed.

Another important condition governing the law of necessity, as the Commission has pointed out, is that the person who invokes it must be in good faith. *Fraus omnia corrumpit.*[25] It can hardly be doubted that this last condition also governs the entire application of the principle of self-preservation in inter-State relations.

B. Self-Defence

I. ON THE HIGH SEAS

For the purpose of self-defence, a State may be authorised to overstep its territorial limits and interfere with navigation of other States on the high seas. As Judge Moore observed in his Dissenting Opinion in the case of *The Lotus* (1927):—

"No State is authorised to interfere with the navigation of other States on the high seas in time of peace *except . . . in extraordinary cases of self-defence* (*Le Louis* (1817) 2 Dodson, 210, 243–244)." [26]

[24] *Hoff* (*The Rebecca*) *Case* (1929), *loc. cit.*, at p. 178.

[25] *Ibid.*, at p. 178: "Clearly an important consideration may be the determination of the question whether there is any evidence in a given case of a fraudulent attempt to circumvent local laws."

Cf. The Eleanor (1809), Edw., p. 135, at p. 161: "Then, again, where the party justifies the act upon the plea of distress, it must not be a distress, which he has created himself, by putting on board an insufficient quantity of water or of provisions for such a voyage, for there the distress is only a part of the mechanism of the fraud, and cannot be set up in excuse for it."

[26] PCIJ: A. 10, p. 69. Italics added.

In the case of the *Le Louis* (1817), to which Judge Moore referred in support of his statement, Lord Stowell said:—

"I can find no authority that gives the right of interruption to the navigation of States in amity upon the high seas, excepting that which the rights of war give to both belligerents against neutrals. This right, incommodious as its exercise may occasionally be to those who are subjected to it, has been fully established in the legal practice of nations, having for its foundation the necessities of self-defence, in preventing the enemy from being supplied with the instruments of war, and from having his means of annoyance augmented by the advantages of maritime commerce. Against the property of his enemy each belligerent has the extreme right of war. Against that of neutrals, the friends of both, each has the right of visitation and search, and of pursuing an inquiry whether they are employed in the service of his enemy, the right being subject, in almost all cases of an inquiry wrongfully pursued, to a compensation in costs and damages . . .

"If it be asked why the right of search does not exist in time of peace as well as in war, the answer is prompt; that it has not the same foundation on which alone it is tolerated in war—the necessities of self-defence." [27]

Although formally the distinction is between time of peace and time of war, in substance the question whether a State has a right to interrupt navigation of friendly States on the high seas depends upon whether the conditions justifying the valid exercise of the right of self-defence do or do not exist.[28]

It seems, therefore, that Judge Moore has drawn the logical conclusion from the judgment of Lord Stowell in holding that,

[27] England, High Court of Admiralty: *The Le Louis Case* (1817), 2 Dodson, p. 210, at p. 243–5. Capture of a French vessel engaged in slave trade by British cruiser on the high seas.

[28] *Fur Seal Arbitration* (1893), G.B./U.S. 1 *Int.Arb.*, p. 755. Oral argument of U.S. counsel: "What is said upon the other side? They agree that all these things may be done. What do they say? Well, they say that they cannot be done in time of *peace*; that you cannot defend yourself by the exercise of force on the high seas in time of peace. . . . There is no substance in that. The right exists in time of peace just as well. Whenever the necessity arises, the right arises, whether it be in time of war or time of peace. . . . In point of fact, the principal occasions, and the most frequent occasions, for the exercise of this right *happen to occur* in time of war, and, therefore, the instances in which it is exercised, and the rules which govern its exercise, are found in belligerent conditions far more than in conditions of peace. The absence of the *occasion* is the reason why we find less discussion of these rights in time of peace, and a want of rules for regulating them; but, nevertheless, the occasion may arise, and when it does arise, then the power must be put in force" (p. 868. Original italics).

in special circumstances, self-defence would justify interference with shipping of other States on the high seas even in time of peace. Indeed, Lord Stowell also recognised that:—

> "This right . . . has been distinctly admitted not to exist generally in time of peace . . . Wherever it has existed, it has existed upon the ground of repelling injury, and as a measure of self-defence." [29]

The words "repelling injury" should be noted; for the exercise of the right of self-defence, which requires no compensation for the damage it may cause, is only justified in repelling or forestalling an unjustified attack.

1. *In Time of Peace*

A case where a State, if not actually at peace, was likewise not at war in the technical sense, but nevertheless exercised the right of capture on the high seas on the plea of self-defence, came before the Spanish-United States Claims Commission (1871).[30]

The American brig *Mary Lowell* left New York early in 1869 with a cargo of arms and ammunition, the destination given being Vera Cruz in Mexico. En route, she put into Ragged Island, reporting herself to be in distress. While there she was watched by the Spanish man-of-war *Andaluza*, in consequence of information that her cargo was destined for the insurgents in Cuba. On March 15, 1869, when the *Mary Lowell* left Ragged Island "for a neighbouring harbour of greater security," she was seized by the *Andaluza* on the high seas and conducted to Havana where she was condemned together with her cargo.

The Umpire held in two successive awards that:—

> "As the cargo, consisting of arms, ammunition, and other military supplies, was admittedly intended by its owner, A. A. Arango, for the benefit of the insurgents against the Spanish Government, and as the brig was allowed by C. H. Campbell, either wilfully or negligently, to fall into the hands of parties actively interested in promoting the insurrection, the claimants forfeited their right to the protection of the American flag, and are estopped

[29] *The Le Louis* (1817), *loc. cit.*, at p. 246.
[30] *The Mary Lowell* (1879), 3 *Int.Arb.*, p. 2772.

from asserting any of the privileges of lawful intercourse in time of peace and any title to individual benefit of indemnity as against the acts of the Spanish authorities done in self-defence." [31]

While this case only concerns hostile acts of alien individuals, it cannot be doubted that the principle applies equally to hostile acts of a foreign State, with the additional consequence that the assailant State will be completely estopped from complaining about the consequences of acts done in self-defence by the other State.

2. *In Time of War*

It has already been seen that in time of war the necessities of self-defence create for the belligerents a number of rights over neutrals on the high seas.[32] In fact, the decision in the *Eastern Extension, Australasia and China Telegraph Co., Ltd., Case* (1923) seems to indicate that all belligerent rights are based upon the principle of self-defence. It spoke of:—

"[The] right of legitimate defence which forms the basis of the rights of any belligerent nation." [33]

[31] *Ibid.*, at pp. 2774–5. It is true that in the second award reaffirming the first, the Umpire pointed out that: "The Umpire must be understood as applying the rule of estoppel only against the private claims of C. H. Campbell and A. A. Arango, as claimants of an indemnity for their own individual account, . . . The Umpire cannot be legitimately called upon to treat this as a case of the United States against Spain having for its direct object a suitable reparation for the offended dignity of their flag. In such a case the regularity of the capture would constitute the principal question to be considered, the personal situation of the owners of the property becoming subordinate" (pp. 2776–7). But the attitude of the U.S. in acquiescing in this decision and considering it as finally disposing of the dispute would seem to indicate that they accepted the Spanish action as legal.

Cf. The Virginius Incident (1873) (Moore, 2 *Dig.*, pp. 895 *et seq.*, 967, 980; also 65 B.F.S.P. (1873–4), pp. 98–229), where the case differs only in that the crew and other persons on board were summarily court-martialled and some executed, including Americans, British and Cubans. In this case the American request for a salute of the American flag was dropped when it was proved that the ship carried the American flag illegally. In *The Mary Lowell Case*, it must be remembered that the Umpire decided that she "forfeited the right to the protection of the American flag."

The British attitude towards *The Virginius Incident* confirms that the Spanish action in *The Mary Lowell Case* was lawful or, at least, not unlawful. In his instruction to the British Minister in Madrid directing him to make a claim for the British crew that were executed, the British Foreign Secretary stated: "Much may be excused in acts done under the expectation of instant danger in self-defence by a nation as well as by an individual. But, after the capture of the *Virginius* and the detention of the crew was effected, no pretence of imminent necessity of self-defence could be alleged" (65 B.F.S.P. (1873–4), p. 217). The second sentence also confirms that acts in legitimate self-defence should be of a purely preventive character.

[32] *The Le Louis* (1817), *supra*, p. 78.

[33] Brit.-U.S. Cl.Arb. (1910), Nielsen's *Report*, p. 40, at p. 76.

Such belligerent rights being absolute rights, the Tribunal decided that no compensation was legally due in respect of their exercise.[34]

The case was concerned with the cutting of submarine cables belonging to a neutral company linking a belligerent territory with a neutral possession. At first sight, it might be wondered whether, in such a case, there had been any improper attack or injury upon the belligerents for which the neutral was responsible. If there were not, it would appear that either this is, properly speaking, not a case of self-defence, or that the proposition made above that self-defence is permissible only against an unjustified attack, or threat of attack, requires qualification.[35] This, however, is not the view taken by international law. Apart from the fact that in the case in question the Tribunal found that the claimant company possessed the character of an enemy public service,[36] it also held that all acts of neutrals using the high seas "to afford assistance to the enemy either by carrying contraband, by communicating with blockaded coasts, or by transporting hostile despatches, troops, enemy agents, and so on" are "*impressed with a hostile character*," although it added that in such cases "the neutrals do not, properly speaking, lose their neutral character." [37]

This construction is confirmed and further illustrated by the decision of the United States Court of Claims in the case of the sloop *Ralph* (1904), which concerned the seizure of a contraband vessel on her return voyage:—

"The transportation of contraband articles to one of the belligerents is in itself an assault for the time being upon the other belligerents, in the fact that it may furnish them with the weapons of war and thereby increase the resources of their power as against their adversary; and for that reason, upon the broad ground of self-preservation incident to nations as well as to individuals, the parties against whom the quasi-assault is made have the right to defend themselves against the threatened blow by seizing the weapon before it reaches the possession and control of their enemy." [38]

[34] *Ibid.*, at p. 76.
[35] *Supra*, p. 79.
[36] *Loc. cit.*, p. 79.
[37] *Loc. cit.*, p. 76. Italics added.
[38] USA, 39 *U.S. Court of Claims*, p. 204, at p. 207. In this case the seizure of the vessel on its return voyage after carrying contraband was held illegal, since

In the light of the above interpretation, it is easy to understand why the rights of belligerents over neutrals on the high seas can be said to be based upon the principle of self-defence. Any act or installation on the high seas which is calculated to assist the enemy is stamped with a hostile character and considered to be an assault, or instrument of assault, against the belligerent State, thus justifying the taking of appropriate measures of self-defence in respect of such act or installation. The proposition that self-defence presupposes an improper attack is thus confirmed rather than disproved.

In considering the wide extent of these belligerent rights, it is necessary not to lose sight of the fact, which the British-United States Claims Arbitral Tribunal (1910) recalled in the case of the *Eastern Extension, Australasia and China Telegraph Co., Ltd.* (1923), that the high seas are considered as *res nullius* or *res communis*.[39] Another tribunal has said: " The rights of war may be exercised on the high seas, because war is carried on upon the high seas." [40] Indeed it follows from the " characteristic feature of the legal situation pertaining to those parts of the globe, which, like the high seas or lands without a master, cannot or do not yet form the territory of a State " [40a] that in this space there is no one to whom the State can appeal for the protection of its rights and safety. Of necessity, the duty falls upon the State itself. Referring to neutral shipping

the paramount purpose of seizing a contraband vessel and its cargo is preventive, as in self-defence generally. When the danger has passed, self-defence loses its *raison d'être*.

PCIJ: *The Wimbledon* (1923), D.O. by Anzilotti and Huber, A. 1, p. 42: " Commerce in and transport of contraband, although not necessarily affecting the neutrality of States, is regarded under the law of nations as unlawful because it assumes the guise of peaceful commerce for warlike purposes."

Cf. also *The Le Louis* (1817), *supra*, p. 78.

See also the unratified Declaration of London, 1909, Art. 46: "A neutral vessel will be condemned, and in a general way receive the same treatment as would be applicable to her if she were an enemy merchant vessel: (1) If she takes a direct part in the hostilities. (2) If she is under the orders or control of an agent placed on board by the enemy government. (3) If she is in the exclusive employment of the enemy government. (4) If she is exclusively engaged at the time either in the transport of enemy troops or in the transmission of intelligence in the interest of the enemy." Rule applied by Greco-Germ. M.A.T.: *Marouli (The Kyma) Case* (1928), 8 T.A.M., p. 345; *Id.*: *Costomenis (The India) Case* (1929), *ibid.*, p. 848; *Id.*: *Embiricos (The Eirini) Case* (1930), 10 *ibid.*, p. 104.

39 *Loc. cit.*, p. 76.

40 Chil.-U.S. Cl.Com. (1892): *The Itata*, 3 *Int.Arb.*, p. 3067, at p. 3071. Seizure of vessel in foreign territorial waters. Sentence appears in a quotation from a decision of the U.S. Supreme Court.

40a PCA: *Palmas Case* (1928), 2 H.C.R. p. 84, at p. 92.

in the First World War, the Greco-German Mixed Arbitral Tribunal held, in the *Kyriakides Case* (1928):—

"In those cases where the ships of neutral commerce wish to protect themselves against German submarines, they should appeal to their own government in order to obtain a convoy for their flag." [41]

Thus, by implication, force may be used to repel any unlawful attack on the high seas.

II. IN FOREIGN TERRITORY

The situation is different with regard to acts of self-defence carried out in the territory of another State. Juridically all the rights of a State within the territory of another State are protected by the latter. As a corollary to its right to display the activities of a State within its territorial limits, each State is subject to "the obligation to protect within the territory the rights of other States, in particular their right to integrity and inviolability in peace and in war, together with the rights which each State may claim for its nationals in foreign territory." [42]

"'A State owes at all times a duty to protect other States against injurious acts by individuals from within its jurisdiction.'" [43]

For example, no State may tolerate the organisation of marauders along its borders for the purpose of invading a friendly nation.[44] A State may not even use or permit the use of its territory in such a manner as to cause serious injury by fumes in or to the territory of another or to persons or property situated therein.[45] Moreover, an elaborate set of rules has grown up regarding the duties of a neutral State in

[41] 8 T.A.M., p. 349, at p. 351. Transl. Torpedoing of neutral vessels under belligerent convoy.

[42] PCA: *Palmas Case* (1928), 2 H.C.R., p. 84, at p. 93.

[43] Trail Smelter Arbitration (1935): *Award II* (1941), 3 UNRIAA, p. 1905, at p. 1963, quoting with approval Eagleton's *Responsibility of States*, 1928, p. 80. PCIJ: *The Lotus* (1927) S.O. by Moore, A. 10, p. 88: "It is well settled that a State is bound to use due diligence to prevent the commission within its dominions of criminal acts against another nation or its people."

[44] See Spanish Zone of Morocco Claims (1923): Claim 28: *Haj Mohamed Harrej (Tangier, horses) Case* (1924), 2 UNRIAA, p. 615, at pp. 699–700.

[45] Trail Smelter Arbitration (1935): *Award II* (1941), *loc. cit.*, p. 1965.

time of war.[46] Normally, therefore, a State need not and, indeed, should not defend its rights in the territory of another State by its own action, but should only call upon the latter to afford the necessary protection.

Even in foreign territory, however, a State may sometimes be permitted to take "warlike measures, strictly and purely defensive, in case of an exigency, which admit of no delay," in the words of the Supreme Judicial Court of Massachusetts in the case of *Commonwealth* v. *William P. Blodgett* (1846).[47] In that case, some soldiers in the service of the state of Rhode Island, penetrated into the state of Massachusetts, without prior permission from the latter, and arrested several rebels who had been taking refuge there. The soldiers were tried in Massachusetts and the Court, in directing the jury that the arrest of the rebels would be a criminal offence if the facts were proved, qualified its directions thus:—

> "If there existed a necessity, for the defence or protection of the lives and property of the citizens of Rhode Island, or for the defence of the State of Rhode Island, that the defendants should do the acts complained of in the indictment, or if there was probable cause to suppose, at the time, the existence of such a necessity, and the jury found such necessity, or probable cause, they were to acquit them."[48]

Indeed, as the International Military Tribunal at Nuremberg stated in its Judgment (1946):—

> "It must be remembered that preventive action in foreign territory is justified only in case of 'an instant and overwhelming necessity for self-defence, leaving no choice of means, and no moment of deliberation' (*The Caroline Case*, Moore's *Digest of International Law*, II, 412)."[49]

The *Caroline Incident* (1837),[50] to which the Tribunal referred, occurred on the night of December 29–30, 1837, the

[46] See, *e.g.*, *Jay Treaty* (Art. VII) Arbitration (1794), 4 *Int.Adj.*, M.S. (*Compensation for Losses and Damages caused by the Violation of neutral Rights, and by the Failure to perform neutral Duties, Mixed Commission under Art. VII of the Treaty between Great Britain and the U.S. of November 19, 1794*), 1931, and *The Alabama* (1872), 1 *Int.Arb.*, p. 495.

[47] 12 Metcalf, p. 56, at p. 82.

[48] *Ibid.*, at p. 84.

[49] 1 *I.M.T.* (*Nuremberg*), p. 171, at p. 207. See *infra*, pp. 88 *et seq.*

[50] Moore, 2 *Dig.*, pp. 412–4; 3 *Int.Arb.*, pp. 2419–28; 26 B.F.S.P. (1837–8), pp. 1372–7; 29 *ibid.* (1840–1), pp. 1126–1142; 30 *ibid.* (1841–2), pp. 193–203; R. Y. Jennings, *The Caroline and McLeod Cases*, 32 A.J.I.L. (1938), p. 82.

United States and Great Britain being then at peace. Certain British soldiers in Canada crossed the Niagara River, which formed the international boundary, boarded by force the American ship *Caroline* lying by Schlosser in United States territory, set the steamer on fire, cut her loose, and sent her adrift over the Niagara Falls.[51]

This was during the Canadian Rebellion of 1837. It appears from the documents that, for some time and in many parts of the United States, Canadian rebels and United States citizens were actively advocating and organising aid to the insurgents. The movement was particularly strong along the Canadian border and the local American authorities were unable effectively to enforce the laws of neutrality.[52] The climax was reached when some 1,000 men, well armed, coming mostly in small groups from the American side of the Niagara River, entrenched themselves on Navy Island, on the Canadian side of the border. On the eve of the incident, the *Caroline*, flying American colours, made several voyages to Navy Island " landing passengers and freight " and returned finally to berth at Schlosser where during the evening some more " passengers " came on board for the night. It was towards midnight that the above incident took place.

The dispute arising out of the incident was not finally settled until 1842, after a special plenipotentiary, Lord Ashburton, had been sent from Great Britain.[53] In a Note to the British Plenipotentiary, the American Secretary of State, Mr. Webster, set out the legal principles governing the case, which appear to have been admitted by the British, and in which the passage quoted by the International Military

[51] Some injuries were caused, two cases being fatal, by shots fired while the occupants were escaping from the vessel during the mêlée.

[52] See letter from the Mayor of Buffalo to the President, Dec. 14, 1837: " The civil authorities have no adequate force to control these men " (H.Ex.Doc. 74, 25 Cong. 2 sess., quoted in 3 *Int.Arb.*, p. 2426); Report of the Marshal of the U.S. for the Northern District of New York, Dec. 27, 1827 to the effect that warrants had been issued for the arrest of the men, but could not be served (H.Ex.Doc. 64, 25 Cong. 2 sess., quoted *op. cit.*, p. 2426); President Van Buren's message to Congress of Jan. 5, 1838, after the incident, admitting that the existing laws were insufficient to cope with hostile invasions from the U.S. of the territory of neighbouring and friendly nations, and requesting full powers for the executive in the matter (H.Ex.Doc. 64, 25 Cong. 2 sess., quoted *op.cit.*, p. 2427).

[53] Ramifications of the incident were not finally disposed of, however, until the Brit.-U.S. Cl.Com. (1853) rendered its decision on the *McLeod Case* (1855) (Hornby's *Report*, p. 428. See also 3 *Int.Arb.*, p. 2419).

Tribunal first appeared.[54] In this Note, Secretary of State Webster challenged Her Majesty's Government to show

"a necessity of self-defence, instant, overwhelming, leaving no choice of means, and no moment for deliberation. It will be for it to show, also, that the local authorities of Canada, even supposing the necessity of the moment authorised them to enter the territories of the United States at all, did nothing unreasonable or excessive; since the act, justified by the necessity of self-defence, must be limited by that necessity, and kept clearly within it. It must be shown that admonition or remonstrance to the persons on board the *Caroline* was impracticable, or would have been unavailing; it must be shown that daylight could not be waited for; that there could be no attempt at discrimination between the innocent and the guilty; that it would not have been enough to seize and detain the vessel; but that there was a necessity, present and inevitable, for attacking her in the darkness of the night, while moored to the shore, and while unarmed men were asleep on board, killing some and wounding others, and then drawing her into the current, above the cataract, setting her on fire, and, careless to know whether there might not be in her the innocent with the guilty, or the living with the dead, committing her to a fate which fills the imagination with horror. A necessity for all this, the Government of the United States cannot believe to have existed." [55]

In his reply, the British Plenipotentiary sought to show point by point that such a necessity did in fact exist, after recalling the inability of the American authorities to prevent the organisation of forces hostile to Britain in American territory.[56] Having also received an expression of regret from the British Plenipotentiary on behalf of the British Government, the United States Secretary of State declared the incident closed. He, furthermore, expressed the satisfaction of the President that there was agreement between the two countries on the principle of the inviolability of the territory of independent States, except in cases of self-defence, where the "necessity of that self-defence is instant, overwhelming

[54] The Note had first been sent to the British Minister Fox, on April 24, 1841 (29 B.F.S.P., p. 1129, at p. 1138). But it was sent again to the British Special Plenipotentiary Ashburton by Webster in his Note of July 27, 1842, as enclosure I (30 B.F.S.P., pp. 193 *et seq.*). It was Ashburton who answered it on July 28, 1842 (30 B.F.S.P., pp. 195 *et seq.*).

[55] 29 B.F.S.P., p. 1129, at p. 1138.

[56] Ashburton to Webster, July 28, 1842 (30 B.F.S.P., pp. 195–200).

and leaving no choice of means, and no moment for deliberation."[57] It was from this diplomatic note that the International Military Tribunal (Nuremberg) took its quotation.

The rule of law evolved from the *Caroline Incident* (1837), which has long been regarded as the *locus classicus* of the principle of self-defence in international law,[58] thus received a further confirmation from the Judgment of Nuremberg (1946).

In case of an "instant and overwhelming necessity," a State is thus allowed to take defensive measures against hostile acts of private individuals in the territory of a friendly foreign State, when the latter is unable to afford the necessary protection to its rights. *A fortiori* a State may also take the appropriate and necessary defensive measures against hostile acts emanating from the foreign State itself, provided that such acts are unlawful and that no pacific or other lawful means exist for preventing or suppressing them. It may use force to repel an overt and unlawful attack by another State.[59] The State acting in self-defence is not responsible for injuries thus caused to the wrongful attacker, or for incidental damage to individuals of third States, either in its own territory or in the territory of the offending State, or on the high seas.[60]

As regards hostile acts of one State against another State within the territory of a third State, the situation of a neutral in time of war may be considered. It has already been said that the rights of a State within the territory of another State, including the right to integrity and inviolability, are in principle under the protection of the territorial sovereign. Either belligerent has a right to expect that no hostile act will

[57] Webster to Ashburton, August 6, 1842 (Moore, 2 *Dig.*, p. 412. For full text, see 30 B.F.S.P., pp. 201–2).

[58] It was referred to in many international judicial proceedings, *e.g.*, in *The Mary Lowell Case* (1879) by the Spanish Government (3 *Int.Arb.*, p. 2774), by both sides in the *Fur Seal Arbitration* (1893) (1 *Int.Arb.*, p. 755, at pp. 841, 895 *et seq.*). See also in the latter case, p. 894, where counsel for G.B. adopted the Webster-Ashburton formula to measure the case of the U.S. Counsel for the U.S. referred to it in the *Kelly Case* (1930), before the Mex.-U.S. G.C.C. (1923) and it was examined by the Commission at some length (*Op. of Com.*, *1931*, p. 82, at p. 92).

[59] See for instance Portugo-German Arbitration (1919): *Angola Case* (1928, 1930), 2 UNRIAA, p. 1011. Germany unlawfully invaded Portuguese Angola. No question was raised as to the legality of the military defence by Portugal. On the contrary, Germany was held responsible inter alia for the additional expenses incurred by Portugal in expediting the arrival of a military convoy at the colony (pp. 1070–1), death of officers and men killed in action (pp. 1072–3), etc.

[60] See *supra*, pp. 53 *et seq.*, 60 *et seq.*, 79 *et seq.*

emanate from neutral territory. Should the neutral be unable or unwilling to protect this right of the belligerents, the latter may take the necessary measures in self-defence.

Examining the legality of the German air raid on Salonika in January, 1916, the Greco-German Mixed Arbitral Tribunal considered that:—

> "... the occupation of Salonika by the armed forces of the Entente in the Autumn of 1915, at a time when Greece was not yet a party to the war, constitutes a violation of that country's neutrality; ... It is unnecessary to consider whether the Hellenic Government protested against the said occupation or whether it consented to it, either expressly or impliedly; ... In either case, the occupation of Salonika was, as regards Germany, an unlawful act, which authorised her to resort to all measures of war necessary for her own defence, even upon Greek soil." [61]

The Tribunal added:—

> "The right of Germany to defend herself against the occupation of Greek territory by forces of the Entente did not relieve her of the duty of observing the rules laid down by international law." [62]

Attention may be drawn to two points in this decision. First the act of self-defence is justified only by the existence of an unlawful act in regard to the belligerent State concerned. Secondly, the measures of war permitted under such circumstances are measures necessary for the defence of that State.

One of the legal problems which arose at the trial of the "German Major War Criminals" (1945–1946) was whether or not the taking of preventive measures in a neutral country is permissible when it is certain that the neutral is on the point of being, but is not yet, invaded by the enemy. The question arose in connection with the German invasion of Norway launched on April 9, 1940, for which the defendant Erich Raeder was charged with criminal responsibility.

Counsel for the defendant invoked "the right of self-defence," [63] and argued that the object of the German invasion

61 *Coenca Brothers Case* (1927), 7 T.A.M., p. 683. at pp. 686–7. (Transl.).

62 *Ibid.*, at p. 687. (Transl.) The Tribunal had in mind principally the rules of warfare.

63 "*Das Recht der Selbsterhaltung,*" "*le droit de défence personnelle*" (18 *I.M.T.* (*Nuremberg*), p. 417 (July 17, 1946)).

was to forestall an imminent British invasion of Norway. "Documents which were subsequently captured by the Germans are relied on to show that the Allied plan to occupy harbours and airports in Western Norway was a definite plan, although in all points considerably behind the German plans under which the invasion was actually carried out. These documents indicate that an altered plan had been finally agreed upon on March 20, 1940, that a convoy should leave England on April 5, and that mining in Norwegian waters would begin the same day; and that on April 5 the sailing time had been postponed until April 8." [64]

"Thus," defence counsel contended, "factual evidence of imminent neutrality violations existed from the point of view of international law; and neutrality violation had indeed been already committed to a certain extent as by mine-laying. This was the point where Germany, in accordance with the international concept of the right of self-defence, was entitled to resort to equivalent counter measures, that is, to occupy Norway in order to prevent the impending occupation by other belligerent States." [65]

"Preventive counter measures are permissible, and an impending violation of neutrality, which can be expected with certainty, is considered equal to a completed violation of neutrality."[66]

In its Judgment, the International Military Tribunal (Nuremberg) chose not to express a definite opinion on this issue, basing its decision on a lack of causal connection between the Allied plan and the German invasion. It held that:—

"When the [German] plans for an attack on Norway were being made, they were not made for the purpose of forestalling an imminent Allied landing, but, at the most, that they might prevent an Allied occupation at some future date." [67]

Referring to the Allied plans for the occupation of bases in Western Norway, the Tribunal said:—

[64] I.M.T. (Nuremberg) (1945): *France, U.S.S.R., U.K., U.S.A.* v. *Hermann W. Göring and others* ("*German Major War Criminals Case*") (1946), 1 *I.M.T.* (*Nuremberg*), p. 171, at p. 208. British ("Plan R.4") and German ("Weser Exercise") military plans regarding Norway during the Second World War are described in T K. Derry's *The Campaign in Norway*, London, H.M.S.O., 1952, Chapter 2. Defence counsel at Nuremberg referred to the Allied plan as the "Stratford Plan."

[65] 18 *ibid.*, p. 419 (July 17, 1946).

[66] Defence counsel's contention (*ibid.*, at p. 413).

[67] "*German Major War Criminals Case*" (1946), 1 *I.M.T.* (*Nuremberg*), p. 171, at p. 207.

" But these plans were not the cause of the German invasion of Norway. Norway was occupied by Germany to afford her bases from which a more effective attack on England and France might be made, pursuant to plans prepared long in advance of the Allied plans which are now relied on to support the argument of self-defence." [68]

As the Germans, at the time of their invasion of Norway, had no definite information regarding the so-called " Stratford Plan," of which they learned only subsequently through captured documents, and did not even consider an Allied invasion of Norway imminent,[69] the Tribunal was no doubt right in applying a principle of logic as well as of law that something which is not known at the time of an action or decision, but only learned of subsequently, cannot be invoked as a motive for such action or decision.[70] But by its failure to refute categorically the German contention that an impending violation of neutrality by one of the belligerents, which could be expected with certainty, was equivalent to an actual violation entitling the other belligerent to take preventive military measures in the neutral's territory, and furthermore by the very fact of basing this point of its decision on the lack of causal connection between the impending violation by one of the belligerents and the actual violation by the other, the Tribunal laid itself open to the serious charge that in principle it admitted the German contention.

This German contention was anticipated and contested by the prosecution. Sir Hartley Shawcross, the British Chief Prosecutor, speaking of the German allegations concerning the impending Allied invasion of Norway said:—

" I do not propose to argue the question whether or not these allegations were true or false. That question is irrelevant to the issues before this Court. Even if the allegations were true—and they were patently false—they would afford no conceivable justification for the action of invading without warning, without

[68] *Ibid.*, at p. 208.

[69] This was the finding of the I.M.T. (Nuremberg) (*ibid.*, at p. 208).

[70] The same principle was applied by the P.C.A. in the case of *The Carthage* (1913), France/Italy, 1 H.C.R., p. 556, at p. 559: " The despatch from Marseilles, relating certain remarks by the mechanician of the said Duval, did not reach the Italian authorities until after the *Carthage* had been stopped and taken to Cagliari and could not, therefore, have been the reason for [' *motiver* '] these measures " (Transl.).

declaration of war, without any attempt at mediation or conciliation. Aggressive war is none the less aggressive war because the State which wages it believes—rightly or wrongly—that other States might, in the future, take similar action. The rape of a nation is not justified because it is thought she may be raped by another. Nor even in self-defence are warlike measures justified except after all means of mediation have been tried and failed, and force is actually being exercised against the State concerned." [71]

It is submitted that the view of the prosecution is substantially correct. Indeed, if the German contention were correct, it would lead to the untenable conclusion that whilst the violation of the neutrality of a State is unlawful, it becomes lawful if both belligerents are bent on violating it, merely on the ground that the object of each side is to forestall the action of the other.

Moreover, the German contention appears to be incompatible with the Webster-Ashburton Rule on self-defence, accepted in principle by the Nuremberg Tribunal. In this connection, it must be remembered that the impending violation of a State's neutrality, even if its ultimate object is to injure the opposing belligerent, constitutes primarily a direct threat to the neutral State, and only a secondary and indirect threat to the rights of the opposing belligerent. Such a secondary and indirect danger cannot be said to create that " instant and overwhelming necessity " of self-defence required by the Rule. Furthermore, as has already been pointed out, the right of the belligerent to expect the neutral State to maintain its neutrality and to prevent its territory from being used for warlike purposes by the other belligerent, is a right primarily under the protection of the neutral State. If this right should thus become indirectly threatened, it is always possible to remind the neutral of its duty. The latter must be presumed willing and able to fulfil its international obligations. Until the neutral has definitely proved itself unwilling or unable to do so by the tangible fact that its territory is actually being used for belligerent purposes by one of the belligerent parties, and there remains no alternative but for the opposing party to undertake its own defence against hostile acts emanating from that

[71] 2 *I.M.T. (Proceedings)*, p. 74 (Dec. 4, 1945); or 3 *I.M.T. (Nuremberg)*, p. 129.

territory, it cannot be said that there is "no choice of means." Moreover, besides the protection afforded by the legal sanctity of neutrality and the neutral State's own forces, it is always open to the belligerent, whose enemy is about to invade a neutral State, to protect the latter's neutrality from violation by all lawful measures of warfare directed against its enemy, for instance, by destroying the concentration of troops massed for the invasion. It appears, therefore, that the impending violation of the neutrality of a State by one of the belligerents can in no wise be considered as creating an "instant and overwhelming necessity for self-defence, leaving no choice of means, and no moment of deliberation," thus authorising the prior invasion of the neutral State by the other belligerent.[72]

The attempt to justify the German invasion of Norway on the ground of self-defence is perhaps a typical example of the abuses to which the principle of self-preservation may sometimes give rise. A clear refutation of the German contention by the International Military Tribunal (Nuremberg) would, therefore, have rendered a great service to international law by clarifying the notion of self-defence.

III. SELF-DEFENCE AS A JURIDICAL CONCEPT

1. *Meaning*

Self-defence, in law, possesses a technical meaning and denotes the recourse by a person to means not normally permitted by law for his own protection against an imminent danger under conditions which the law prescribes. In some international decisions, therefore, the expression "legitimate

[72] For the same reasons, the present writer is unable to endorse the view of Charles de Visscher ("Des lois de la guerre et la théorie de la nécessité," 24 R.G.D.I.P. (1917), p. 74), who gave the example of a belligerent which was able to prove that its enemy was about to invade a neutral country that was evidently incapable of defending its neutrality. He said: "No one would challenge its right, in the absence of any other means of defence, to forestall the aggression threatening it by occupying the neutral territory which its enemy was about to turn into a base of military operations" (pp. 76–77. Transl.). He added, however, that: "The justification of this act is not to be found, as the German doctrine wrongly maintains, in an alleged right of self-preservation (*Selbsterhaltungsrecht*) or of necessity (*Notrecht*); it resides solely in the *unlawful* character of the aggression which has to be averted" (p. 77. Transl.). The discussion in the text already presupposes that the occupation or use of the neutral territory by either of the belligerents would be unlawful.

defence" instead of merely "self-defence" is to be found.[73] When exercised under conditions prescribed by law, self-defence is a matter of right. The Charter of the United Nations recognises it as an "inherent right."[74]

2. *Object*

International tribunals sometimes have occasion to recognise the right of individuals to resort to self-defence for the preservation of their lives.[75] In so far as States are concerned, as set out in the court's directions to the jury in the *Blodgett Case* (1846), self-defence has for its object the protection of the State itself and the lives and property of its nationals.[76] In any event, self-defence must be confined to the defence of acknowledged rights of the State.

The malady of international relations is due in no small measure to the claim that States may defend by force such of their "interests" as are "important enough to be defended."[77] But as was pointed out by Lord Russell of Killowen, who was counsel for Great Britain in the *Fur Seal Arbitration* (1893), the inevitable upshot of such a claim is war,[78] and he rightly said: "That is not international law, or international right."[79]

73 *e.g.*, Brit.-U.S. Cl.Arb. (1910): *Eastern Extension, Australasia and China Telegraph Co., Ltd. Case* (1923), Nielsen's *Report*, p. 40, at p. 76, *supra*, p. 80. The use of the expression is probably due to the fact that the President of the Tribunal was a French jurist. In France and many other Latin countries, the expression is legitimate defence, just as the Canonists spoke of *defensio legitima*.

74 Art. 51. The Spanish text uses an identical expression and speaks of "*el derecho inmanente*." The Chinese and the French texts speak of "natural right," while the Russian text uses the expression "imprescriptible right."
See also U.S. Court of Claims: *The Sloop Ralph* (1904), *supra*, p. 81. *Cf.* Span.-U.S. Cl.Com. (1871): *The Mary Lowell* (1872), *supra*, p. 80, note 31.

75 Portugo-German Arbitration (1919): *Naulilaa Case* (1928), 2 UNRIAA, p. 1011, at p. 1025.

76 12 Metcalf, p. 56, at p. 84; *supra*, p. 84.

77 *Cf.*, *e.g.*, U.S. contention in the *Fur Seal Arbitration* (1893), 1 *Int.Arb.*, p. 755, at pp. 839–40: "It [the U.S. Government] asserts that the right of self-defence on the part of a nation is a perfect and paramount right to which all others are subordinate, and which upon no admitted theory of international law has ever been surrendered; that it extends to all the material interests of a nation important to be defended; that in the time, the place, the manner, and the extent of its execution it is limited only by the actual necessity of the particular case; that it may, therefore, be exercised upon the high sea as well as upon the land, and even upon the territory of other and friendly nations, provided only that the necessity for it plainly appears." Counsel for the U.S. pursued his theory to its logical conclusion (pp. 835–54), which, by its very extravagance, only serves as condemnation of the theory itself.

78 *Ibid.*, at p. 894–5.

79 Oral Argument delivered by Sir Charles Russell (as he then was): "I may be asked, finally: May there not be cases in which, although it may not be

It is lawlessness. The award of the Tribunal in the *Fur Seal Arbitration* (1893), which rejected such an extravagant contention [80] and which resulted in the payment of damages for unjustified measures taken allegedly in self-defence [81] may be said to have pronounced the doom of this dangerous doctrine.

3. *Conditions Governing its Existence and Exercise*

(a) *Instant Danger*:—The existence of an "instant and overwhelming" danger to the safety of the State or the lives or property of its nationals is the condition *sine qua non* of legitimate defence.[82] In the words of the decision in the case of the sloop *Ralph* (1904):—

"When the act is accomplished, damage suffered, and the danger passed, then the incidents of self-defence cease." [83]

This condition explains the essentially preventive and non-retributive character of self-defence. Its purpose is limited to

possible to formulate the interests of a nation under any recognised head of law, municipally or internationally regarded; yet may there not be cases in which there may be great interests of a nation which yet call for and morally justify that nation in acting, and acting in assertion of those interests and in defence of them? Yes; there are such cases; but what are they? These are cases which rest upon the very same principle upon which nations have been driven, sometimes justly, sometimes unjustly, to defend territory which they have acquired, or to acquire territory in which they have by international law no right, but which, either in pursuit of a great ambition, or in the gratification of racial antipathy, or under the influence of a great potentate, they choose to think is necessary for the well-being and safety of the nation. But that is not international law, or international right. That is war, and is defended as war, and justified as war alone" (*ibid.*, at p. 894, see also pp. 894–5). *Cf.* Brierly, *The Outlook for International Law*, 1944, pp. 32 *et seq.*, for a discussion of the relation between the "vital interests" of the subjects of the law, particularly powerful subjects, and the law itself. The free pursuit of what each State considers to be its "vital interest" would indeed throw us back, as Brierly says, to the "law of the jungle" (p. 38).

80 See the award of the Tribunal on the last of the five points submitted to it, denying the U.S. any right of protection to the fur seals in the Behring Sea beyond the ordinary 3-mile limit (*loc. cit.*, p. 949). See more particularly the rejection of the alternative draft to this part of the award submitted by the American members of this Tribunal, whereby they wished to alter the award into saying that the U.S. had no *special* right "beyond the rights that all nations have, under the international law, in respect of self-protection and self-defence" (pp. 919 and 920).

81 By a convention of 1896, a Mixed Commission was set up to deal with damages arising out of the seizure of British vessels in the Behring Sea before the submission of the dispute to arbitration, in the light of the award rendered by the Fur Seal Tribunal. By an award of Dec. 17, 1897, a total sum of $473,151.26 was allowed for the various claims (2 *Int.Arb.*, pp. 2123–31).

82 *Cf.* Counsel for G.B. in the *Fur Seal Arbitration* (1893) where he pointed out that the true basis of all exceptional acts of self-defence or self-preservation rests upon "the genuine emergency of danger" (1 *Int.Arb.*, p. 755, at p. 892).

83 39 *U.S. Court of Claims*, p. 204, at p. 207.

averting the instant danger threatening the safety of the State or its nationals. Acts committed in excess of what is necessary for that purpose are unlawful.[84]

(b) *Unjustifiable Character of the Danger*:—The danger must be unlawful or unjustified. It is this character of the danger which purges the unlawful means employed to avert it of its illegality.[85]

(c) *Absence of Lawful Means of Protection*:—Another condition governing the existence of the right to resort to extraordinary means for self-defence is that the desired object of averting the imminent danger cannot, in the circumstances, be achieved by lawful and pacific means. In other words, there should be "no choice of means." It is not a case of necessary or legitimate self-defence if the danger can be averted by such lawful means as admonition, protest or diplomatic representation.[86] It is only when such means are impracticable or have proved unavailing that the State is justified in resorting to means which would otherwise be unlawful.

This requirement explains the greater stringency governing the case of self-defence in the territory of a friendly State than on the high seas. For while on the high seas the duty of protecting one's rights falls primarily on the State itself,[87] in the territory of another the duty falls primarily on the territorial sovereign.[88] From this point of view, acts of self-defence in the territory of a friendly nation are permissible only when the prevention of the danger emanating from that territory admits of no delay,[89] or when the local sovereign has proved either

[84] See *The Sloop Ralph* (1904), *supra*, 81, note 38. In *The Caroline Incident* (1837–42), the British Law Officers of the Crown thus advised the Foreign Secretary in their opinion dated March 25, 1839: "We feel bound to suggest to your Lordship that the grounds on which we consider the conduct of the British authorities to be justified is that it was absolutely necessary as a measure of precaution *for the future* and not as a measure of retaliation *for the past*. What had been done previously is only important as affording irresistible evidence of what would occur afterwards. We call your Lordship's attention to this distinction as it is very important to be alluded to in any communication which your Lordship may make to the American Minister" (Record Office, F.O. 83/2207).

[85] *Cf. supra*, pp. 79, 80, 81–82, 88, 89, 92, note 72.

[86] *Supra*, pp. 86, 91. *Cf.* also 1 *Int.Arb.*, p. 894.

These lawful means for averting an impending danger also include the offer of arbitration and, for members of any collective organisation providing means for the pacific settlement of disputes, the recourse to such means.

[87] *Supra*, pp. 82 *et seq.*

[88] *Supra*, pp. 83 *et seq.*

[89] *Supra*, pp. 84 *et seq.*

unable or unwilling to afford the necessary protection,[90] and still on the basis that no other lawful means exist for compelling that State to fulfil its obligations.

(d) *Reasonableness in its Exercise*:—In the *Blodgett Case* (1846), the Court recognised that it would be impracticable to "attempt drawing any exact line of distinction as to the measures which such necessary defence would warrant . . . ; because it must depend much on the circumstances of each case."[91] But "the act, justified by the necessity of self-defence, must be limited by that necessity, and kept clearly within it."[92] Consequently, there should be "nothing unreasonable or excessive."[93] In short the exercise must be in good faith.[94]

4. *Self-Defence as a Justiciable Issue*

The International Military Tribunal (Nuremberg), in the trial of the "*German Major War Criminals*," held in its Judgment (1946) that:—

"Whether action taken under the claim of self-defence was in fact aggressive or defensive must ultimately be subject to investigation and adjudication if international law is ever to be enforced."[95]

90 See *supra*, pp. 87, 88 *et seq.*, 91. It seems clear that in *The Caroline Incident* (1837–42), the U.S. Government implicitly admitted its failure to protect the rights of Great Britain. In the Note of July 27, 1842, of Webster to Ashburton, in which he enclosed the Note already mentioned above (*supra*, p. 86) he also enclosed the following extract from a message of the U.S. President to Congress, of Dec. 7, 1841: "This Government can never concede to any foreign Government the power, except in a case of the most urgent and extreme necessity, of invading its territory, either to arrest the persons or destroy the property of those who may have violated the municipal laws of such foreign Government, or have disregarded their obligations arising under the law of nations. The territory of the United States must be regarded as sacredly secure against all such invasions, until they shall voluntarily acknowledge inability to acquit themselves of their duties to others" (30 B.F.S.P., p. 194). It is perhaps too much to expect any Government to make a voluntary acknowledgment of its inability to acquit itself of its duties, but the fact of enclosing this extract was a hint which Ashburton did not fail to take; for in his reply he first of all mentioned the failure of the U.S. Government to suppress the activities complained of. *Cf. supra*, p. 85, note 52.

91 12 Metcalf, p. 56, at p. 84.

92 Webster's Note (29 B.F.S.P., p. 1136, at p. 1138).

93 *Ibid. Cf.* also *The Virginius Incident* (*supra*, p. 80, note 31 *in fine*).

94 See *infra*, pp. 132 *et seq.*

95 1 *I.M.T.* (*Nuremberg*), p. 171, at p. 208. Used in the legal, and not the military or tactical, sense of these words, aggressive self-defence is indeed a contradiction. What the I.M.T. meant, therefore, was that whether or not an act carried out allegedly in self-defence fulfilled the legal conditions governing legitimate self-defence could and must ultimately be subject to judicial investigation in case of dispute.

In this case, it examined and rejected the plea that Germany in invading Norway on April 9, 1940, acted in self-defence.[95a]

C. Self-Help

In the preceding section, it was seen that legitimate self-defence is of a strictly preventive character.[96] There can be no self-defence against an unlawful *fait accompli*, unless it continues to present a grave threat to the safety of the State. In the absence of an effective system of collective protection against wrongful acts, these measures of self-defence cannot always be said to ensure full protection of a State's rights.

The Permanent Court of Arbitration in the *North Atlantic Coast Fisheries Case* (1910) enumerated the sanctions of traditional international law:—

"Such sanctions are, for instance, appeal to public opinion, publication of correspondence, censure by parliamentary vote, demand for arbitration and the odium attendant on a refusal to arbitrate, rupture of relations, reprisals, etc." [97]

The only sanction that needs mention here is reprisal, by reason of the exceptional power that it confers upon a State.

In the *Angola Case* (1928, 1930), the Portugo-German Arbitral Tribunal examined the question of reprisals and found that:—

"The most recent doctrine, especially the German doctrine, defines reprisals in the following terms:—

"*Reprisal* is a measure of self-help (*Selbsthilfehandlung*) taken by the injured State in reply to an act contrary to the law of nations on the part of the offending State—*after summons which proves unavailing*. Its effect is to suspend temporarily the observance of a particular rule of the law of nations in the relations between two States. It is *limited* by the experiences of humanity and by the rules of good faith, applicable in international relations. *It would be illegal if a previous act, contrary to international law*, had not provided its justification. Its object is to compel the offending State to make reparation for the injury or to return to legality, by avoiding further offences.

[95a] See *supra*, p. 90.
[96] *Supra*, p. 80, note 31 *in fine*; p. 81, note 38, p. 95, especially note 84.
[97] 1 H.C.R., p. 146, at p. 167.

"This definition does not require that the act of reprisal should be strictly *proportionate* to the first unlawful act. On this point, authors, unanimous until a few years ago, begin to be divided in opinion. The majority regard a certain proportion between the offence and the act of reprisal as a necessary condition to the legality of the latter. Others, amongst more recent writers, no longer require this condition. As regards the new trend in international law which is undergoing transformation pursuant to the experiences of the last war, it certainly tends to restrict the notion of legitimate reprisal and to forbid any excess." [98]

The rules governing this form of self-help among States are, therefore, as follows:—

(a) "The first condition—*sine qua non*—of the right to take reprisals is a justification provided by a previous act contrary to the law of nations." [99]

(b) "Reprisals are not permissible except against the offending State. It is, indeed, possible that legitimate reprisals taken against an offending State may affect the nationals of an innocent State (*e.g.*, the bombardment of a town, carried out in reprisal for a similar act, may cause casualties among nationals of neutral States, against whom the reprisal was not directed. J. Hatschek, *Völkerrecht*, p. 408, III). But this is an indirect and involuntary consequence which the injured State would always endeavour to avoid in practice or to limit as much as possible." [1]

(c) "The reprisal is only lawful if it is preceded by a summons which proves to be of no avail." [2]

(d) "The use of force is only justifiable by its being necessary." [3]

(e) "Even if one were to concede that the law of nations does not require the reprisal to be approximately proportionate to the offence, reprisals out of all proportion to the act which had prompted them ought certainly to be considered as excessive and hence unlawful." [4]

If the above conditions were fulfilled, it would seem from the Portugo-German Arbitration (1919) that a State might even

[98] 2 UNRIAA, p. 1011, at pp. 1025–26. (Transl.) Italics of the Tribunal. German military expedition in 1914 into Portuguese (neutral) territory in Africa allegedly in reprisal for the Naulilaa incident. Legal conditions for reprisal held not fulfilled. Germany held liable for damage caused by her unlawful act.

[99] *Ibid.*, at p. 1027. (Transl.)

[1] *Id.*: *The Cysne* (1930), 2 UNRIAA, p. 1035, at p. 1057. (Transl.)

[2] *Angola Case* (1928), *loc. cit.*, p. 1027. (Transl.)

[3] *Ibid.* (Transl.)

[4] *Ibid.*, at p. 1028. (Transl.)

be permitted to adopt military measures against a country with which it is formally at peace. Such a state of things would in fact differ little from a state of war.[5] Indeed, war itself may be regarded as the extreme form of self-help. The Permanent Court of Arbitration, in the *Norwegian Claims Case* (1922), speaking of the First World War, observed:—

> "Belligerents and neutrals alike were fearful for their existence. The hardships of neutrality were felt so deeply by the United States themselves that they declared war on Germany as the only means of defence against its 'repeated acts of war against the government and people of the United States of America.'"[6]

War, the *ultima ratio regum,* is the last means of national self-preservation.

D. Conclusions

While the case of necessity (*l'état de nécessité, Notstand*), by its very exceptional character stands in a class by itself, the above survey has shown that it is possible to deduce certain basic principles governing the use of extraordinary measures by a State for its self-preservation, either in self-defence or in self-help. These basic principles will now be briefly summarised.

The cardinal point to be noted is that, for these measures to be legitimate, they must be taken for an essentially defensive and preventive purpose, although, in their actual application, they may assume an offensive and even punitive character. Their purpose must be either to avert an imminent injury or, by exacting reparation for an unredressed wrong, to prevent the occurrence of further unlawful acts. It is not possible to determine in advance the appropriate measures in each contingency, but no otherwise unlawful measures should be resorted to, unless and until all pacific and lawful means of protection are proved to be of no avail. "The use of force is justifiable only by its being necessary." In its attempt at self-preservation, the State should be guided by the principles of good faith and the dictates of humanity. In particular, there should be "nothing unreasonable or excessive," going beyond

[5] *Cf.* Mex.U.S. G.C.C. (1923): *Kelly Case* (1930), *Op. of Com. 1931*, p. 82.
[6] 2 H.C.R., p. 40, at p. 75.

the needs of the case and out of all proportion to the injury which the State has first set out to avert or to redress. As is demonstrated by the precedents, such cases are capable of review by an international tribunal which can determine from the facts of the case whether the legal conditions justifying the measures taken have been fulfilled. Should the finding of the tribunal concerned be in the negative, the act will be considered unlawful and the State held liable for all its proximate consequences.

Under these conditions, traditional international law, adapting itself to the political necessities of international life, and basing itself on the principle of self-preservation, permits States a wide range of action to ensure the protection of their own rights, safety and existence.

The recognition of the principle of self-preservation in international law is of course no implied authority for its abuse. In particular, the principle of self-preservation does not permit recourse to unlawful acts and means, especially to violence, for the protection or enforcement of what are not a State's rights, but merely its interests and aspirations.

On the other hand, the principle of self-preservation, in its various manifestations, is so fundamental that no system of law can possibly ignore it. The present generation, which has twice suffered from the terrible scourge of war and is living in an age in which the instruments of death and destruction have been perfected at a pace and to a degree almost defying imagination, is perhaps more bent than any previous generation on proscribing the use of force in international relations. By the Pact of Paris, the signatory nations solemnly renounced war as an instrument of national policy, thereby declaring such a war to be illegal under international law.[7] This was, perhaps, merely the solemn affirmation of existing principles of law,[8] which hitherto had never been enforced, owing to the fact that the external policies of States were traditionally regarded as not being subject to review by international tribunals.[9] The Charter of the United Nations has apparently gone further.[10]

[7] I.M.T. (Nuremberg): "*German Major War Criminals Case*" (1946), 1 *I.M.T. (Nuremberg)*, p. 171, at p. 220.
[8] *Cf. ibid.*, at p. 221.
[9] See *supra*, p. 60, note 11.
[10] U.N. Charter, Art. 2, para. 4.

It has been considered that, under the Charter, self-help is no longer permissible.[11] Self-defence is, however, expressly recognised by the Charter as a natural, inherent or imprescriptible right of nations.[12] It is believed that, unless and until the system of pacific settlement of international disputes and collective security established by the Charter can be rendered effective, the traditional methods of self-preservation would still have to be admitted in the last resort, subject to the conditions described above.[13]

In this connection, it may be instructive to look at an example of international organisation on a smaller scale. It will be seen that, in the absence of an effective protection afforded by the Federal Government, the principle of self-preservation will override even so venerable an instrument as the American Constitution allowing states subject to it ultimately to resort to force for their own preservation. The Supreme Judicial Court of Massachusetts, speaking of the states within the American Union, thus observed:—

"They are, therefore, in the condition of States sovereign to some purposes, but who have by compact renounced and relinquished their sovereign powers, in regard to war and peace, and, of course, to the regulation and control of the incidents to war and peace, except the power of taking warlike measures, strictly and purely defensive, in case of an exigency, which admit of no delay. In all other respects, the power of making war and peace, of treaties and alliances, is vested absolutely and exclusively in the general government, with their incidents. But as a compensation for this surrender, the general government of the United States is bound to protect each State against invasion and against domestic violence. The Constitution of the United States is to be taken as a whole; whilst it restrains the States from making war and peace, and exercising powers incidental thereto, it assumes that the general

[11] ICJ: *Corfu Channel Case* (Merits) (1949), U.K./Albania, D.O. by Krylov, *ICJ Reports, 1949*, p. 4, at p. 77: "Since 1945, *i.e.*, after the coming into force of the Charter, the so-called right of self-help, also known as the law of necessity (*Notrecht*), which used to be upheld by a number of German authors, can no longer be invoked. It must be regarded as obsolete. The employment of force in this way, or of the threat of force, is forbidden by the Charter (para. 4 of Art. 2)." *Cf.* majority decision (*ibid.*, at p. 35).

[12] Art. 51 (see *supra*, p. 93, note 74).

[13] *Cf. Statement Relating to Defence*, 1948, presented by His Britannic Majesty's Minister to Parliament, February, 1948, paragraph 52: ". . . In the present situation, where the United Nations Organisation is not yet able to enforce peace, the best deterrent to war is tangible evidence of our intention and ability to withstand attack" (Cmd. 7327).

government will do its duty, and effectually secure to each State that immunity from all violence, foreign and domestic, which was the obvious consideration for the surrender of these great powers. It is useless to speculate upon the contingency, as to what would be the rights of the States in case the general government should fail to afford that protection to States which the Constitution guarantees to them. Such a state of things is not to be supposed. It would be one of revolution and anarchy, in which a regard to self-defence and public safety would constitute an exigency that would warrant such measures as the necessity of the case might require, under the maxim *Salus populi suprema est lex*. The necessity, which would create such an exigency, must limit and direct the means of meeting it.'' [14]

[14] *Commonwealth* v. *William P. Blodgett and Another* (1846) 12 Metcalf, p. 56, at pp. 82–3.

PART TWO

THE PRINCIPLE OF GOOD FAITH

PART TWO

THE PRINCIPLE OF GOOD FAITH

THE sole Arbitrator in the *Metzger & Co. Case* (1900) held that: "It cannot be that good faith is less obligatory upon nations than upon individuals in carrying out agreements."[1] There was little doubt in the mind of the Arbitrator as to the binding character of the principle of good faith upon individuals living under the rule of law and he held that it was equally binding upon nations. The Permanent Court of Arbitration, in the *Venezuelan Preferential Claims Case* (1904), also expressly affirmed that the principle of good faith "ought to govern international relations."[2] The sole Arbitrator in the Germano-Lithuanian Arbitration (1936) held that: "A State must fulfil its international obligations bona fide."[3] The principle of good faith is thus equally applicable to relations between individuals and to relations between nations. Indeed, the Greco-Turkish Arbitral Tribunal considered the principle of good faith to be "the foundation of all law and all conventions."[4] It should, therefore, be the fundamental principle of every legal system.

What exactly this principle implies is perhaps difficult to define. As an English judge once said, such rudimentary terms applicable to human conduct as "Good Faith," "Honesty," or "Malice" elude *a priori* definition. "They can be illustrated but not defined."[5] Part Two will be an attempt to illustrate, by means of international judicial decisions, the application of this essential principle of law in the international legal order.

[1] U.S./Haiti, U.S.F.R. (1901), p. 262, at p. 271.
[2] Germany, Great Britain, Italy/Venezuela *et al.*, 1 H.C.R., p. 55, at p. 60.
[3] *Award* (1937) 3 UNRIAA, p. 1719, at p. 1751. (Transl.)
[4] *Megalidis Case* (1928) 8 T.A.M., p. 386, at p. 395.
[5] Lord Hobhouse (England, House of Lords: *Russell* v. *Russell* [1897] A.C. p. 395, at p. 436).

CHAPTER 3

GOOD FAITH IN TREATY RELATIONS

THE law of treaties is closely bound with the principle of good faith, if indeed not based on it; for this principle governs treaties from the time of their formation to the time of their extinction.

A. Formation of Treaties

"Contracting parties are always assumed to be acting honestly and in good faith. That is a legal principle, which is recognised in private law and cannot be ignored in international law." [1]

States in negotiating and concluding treaties are, therefore, presumed to have proposed nothing which is illusory [2] or merely nominal.[3] Indeed,

> " No construction shall be admitted which renders a treaty null and illusive, nor which leaves it in the discretion of the party promising to fulfil or not his promise." [4]

Nor can the contracting parties be presumed to have intended anything which would, under the circumstances, have been unreasonable,[5] absurd or contradictory,[6] or which leads to impossible consequences.[7]

1 PCIJ: *Lighthouses Case* (1934), France/Greece, S.O. by Séfériadès, A/B 62, p. 47.

2 Jay Treaty (Art. VII) Arbitration (1794): *The Betsey* (1797) 4 *Int.Adj.*, M.S., p. 179, at p. 239. In rejecting the British contentions, Commissioner Gore held inter alia that they " raise objections which render the provisions of the article [constituting the Commission] illusory—a consequence not to be admitted in the most trifling contract, if by any way it can be avoided; still more admissible in a solemn bargain between two wise and respectable nations."

3 Brit.-U.S. Cl.Arb. (1910): *Cayuga Indians Case* (1926) Nielsen's *Report*, p. 203, at p. 322. The U.S. argued, on the basis of the history of the negotiations leading to Art. IX of the Treaty of Ghent that the " article was only a ' nominal ' provision, not intended to have any application," " that the promise has no meaning but was . . . a provision inserted to save the face of the negotiators." The Tribunal refused to subscribe to such an interpretation, and relied on the provision for the decision of the case.

4 Jay Treaty (Art. VII) Arb. (1794): *The Sally*, Hayes, Master (1803) 4 *Int. Adj.*, M.S., p. 459, at p. 478.

5 PCIJ: *Meuse Case* (1937), Neth./Belg., D.O. by Anzilotti. He would not enforce what " would be going beyond the reasonable intentions of the Parties " (A/B. 70, p. 47).

6 PCIJ: *Polish Postal Service in Danzig* (1925) Adv.Op., B. 11, p. 39.

7 PCIJ: *The Wimbledon* (1923) D.O. by Anzilotti and Huber, A. 1, p. 36: " It must not be presumed that the intention was to express an idea which

" 'In case of doubt, treaties ought to be interpreted conformably with the real mutual intention, and conformably to what can be presumed, between parties acting loyally and with reason, was promised by one to the other according to the words used.' "[8]

As to the terms that a party employs, these are presumed to have been used in the contemporary[9] and general sense in which the other party would have understood them at the time the treaty was concluded.[10] If, therefore, a party wishes to use words in a special or a restricted sense, it must expressly say so. And "when one has made a promise and then excepted from its extent what the words might naturally have conveyed it is evident that he was aware of the effect of his language, and took from its comprehension all that was within his intention to except."[11]

In short, good faith requires that one party should be able to place confidence in the words of the other, as a reasonable man might be taken to have understood them in the circumstances.

Thus, in 1903, after three of Venezuela's many creditors had staged a blockade of her ports, Venezuela sent a representative to Washington with full powers to negotiate with the creditor Powers. In the course of the negotiations, the Venezuelan representative proposed to the representatives of the blockading Powers that "all claims against Venezuela" should be offered special guarantees.[12] A controversy arose as to whether the

leads to contradictory or impossible consequences or which, in the circumstances, must be regarded as going beyond the intention of the parties. The purely grammatical interpretation of every contract, and more especially of international treaties, must stop at this point."

[8] P.C.A.: *Timor Case* (1914) Neth./Port. 1 H.C.R., p. 354, at p. 365, quoting Heffter: *Völkerrecht*, § 90. Quoted also in Greco.-Bulg. M.A.T.: *Sarropoulos Case* (1927) 7 T.A.M., p. 47, at p. 52.

[9] *Cravairola Boundary Case* (1874) Swit./Italy, 2 *Int.Arb.*, p. 2027, at p. 2046. *Abu Dhabi Oil Arbitration* (1951) 1 I.C.L.Q. (1952), p. 247, at pp. 252–3.

[10] P.C.A.: *North Atlantic Coast Fisheries Case* (1910) 1 H.C.R., p. 141, at p. 181. "Now, considering that the Treaty used the general term 'bays' without qualification, the tribunal is of opinion that these words of the treaty must be interpreted in a general sense as applying to every bay on the coast in question that *might be reasonably supposed to have been considered as a bay by the negotiators of the treaty under the general conditions prevailing*, unless the U.S. can adduce satisfactory proof that any restrictions or qualifications of the general use of the term were or should have been present to their minds" (italics added). See also *ibid.*, pp. 184, 187.

[11] Jay Treaty (Art. VII) Arb. (1794): *The Betsey* (1797) 4 *Int.Adj.*, M.S., p. 179, at pp. 217–8.

[12] *Venezuelan Preferential Claims Case* (1904) 1 H.C.R., p. 55, at p. 61, note 1.

words "all claims" referred to all the claims of the allied and blockading Powers, or to all the claims of every country, creditor of Venezuela. The Permanent Court of Arbitration decided:—

"The good faith which ought to govern international relations imposes the duty of stating that the words 'all claims' used by the representative of the Government of Venezuela in his conferences with the representatives of the allied Powers . . . could only mean the claims of these latter and could only refer to them." [13]

In case of doubt, words are to be interpreted against the party which has proposed them, and according to the meaning that the other party would reasonably and naturally have understood.[14] In contracting with a party labouring under a special handicap, *e.g.*, Red Indians, terms should no longer be used in their technical meaning, but only in the meaning which can be understood by that party; for in case of dispute it is not the technical meaning of the terms of the covenant that an international tribunal would enforce, but only the "sense in which they would naturally be understood by the Indians." [15]

How far are States bound in good faith, pending the negotiation for a Special Agreement, to abstain from any surprise action capable of modifying the existing situation at law, or from resort to any tactical measures? The question arose to a limited extent in the *Eastern Greenland Case* (1933), but

[13] *Ibid.*, at pp. 60–1.

[14] Rum.-Germ. Arb. (1919): *David Goldenberg & Sons Case* (1928) 2 UNRIAA, p. 901, at p. 907. The question was raised whether § 4 of the annex to Arts. 297 and 298 of the Treaty of Versailles in obliging Germany to make reparation for "acts committed" meant only unlawful acts or any act done by Germany. Held: "The provision in question imposes an obligation on Germany. According to the rule constantly followed by the Rumano-German M.A.T., provisions of this kind should not be extended, by way of interpretation, beyond *the meaning which Germany could reasonably have attributed to the text submitted for her acceptance.* An ambiguous provision is, in principle, interpreted against the party which has drafted it" (Transl. Italics added).

PCIJ: *Brazilian Loans Case* (1929) A.20/21, p. 114: "There is a familiar rule for the construction of instruments that, where they are found to be ambiguous, they should be taken *contra proferentem.* In this case, as the Brazilian Government by its representative assumed responsibility for the prospectus, which this representative, who had signed the bonds, had 'seen and approved,' it would seem to be proper to construe them in case of doubt *contra proferentem* and to ascribe to them the meaning which they would naturally carry to those taking the bonds under the prospectus."

Cf. Abu Dhabi Oil Arbitration (1951) 1 I.C.L.Q. (1952) p. 247, at p. 251.

[15] Brit.-U.S. Cl.Arb. (1910): *Cayuga Indians Case* (1926) Nielsen's *Report*, p. 203, at p. 326, quoting an American decision.

unfortunately the Permanent Court of International Justice had no occasion to consider it.[16] In the present state of international law, however, it does not seem that such an obligation exists, except perhaps in very special circumstances.

B. Treaties sub spe rati

The question whether treaties come into force on signature or on ratification depends, in each individual case, upon the intention of the parties. According to present practice, the greater number of treaties are "binding only by virtue of their ratification." [17] The International Court of Justice held in the *Ambatielos Case* (1952) that:—

> "The ratification of a treaty which provides for ratification . . . is an indispensable condition for bringing it into operation." [18]

Yet, it may well be asked whether, before ratification, such a treaty, solemnly signed by plenipotentiaries of States, is of absolutely no legal effect. In the first place, it cannot be denied that that part of the treaty relating to ratification and its coming into force must necessarily be considered as validly concluded and binding upon the parties upon signature.[19] Secondly, the signing of a treaty at least "establishes," in the words of the International Court of Justice, "a provisional status" between the signatories, which would terminate either if the signature is not followed by ratification, or when the treaty becomes effective on ratification.[20]

It is perfectly true, as counsel for the United States in the *Iloilo Claims* (1925) maintained before the British-United States Claims Arbitral Tribunal (1910), that "when there still remains ratification and exchange of ratification or deposit of ratification as the case may be, it is utterly meaningless to say that a

[16] Denmark/Norway, A/B.53, pp. 43, 74.

[17] *Cf.* PCIJ: *International Commission of the River Oder Case* (1929) U.K., Czech., Denmark, France, Germany, Sweden/Poland, A.23, p. 20.

[18] Greece/U.K., *ICJ Reports, 1952*, p. 28, at p. 43. The I.C.J. recognised at the same time, however, that "such a conclusion might have been rebutted if there had been any special clause or any *special object* [" *une raison particulière* "] necessitating retroactive interpretation" (p. 40. Italics added). *Cf.* PCA: *Muscat Dhows Case* (1905), France/G.B., 1 H.C.R., p. 93, at p. 99.

[19] See Nisot, "La force obligatoire des traités signés, non encore ratifiés," 57 *Clunet* (1930) p. 878.

[20] See *Reservations to the Convention on Genocide* (1951) Adv.Op., *ICJ Reports, 1951*, p. 15, at p. 28.

treaty is binding from the time of signature."[21] As he admitted, however, there may be "some questions that may seem a little vexatious as to the effect of the signing of a treaty. . . . What is the vexatious question which has sometimes troubled courts a little and perhaps administrative officials? It deals with the maintenance, I should say, of the status quo between the time of the signing and the time of the exchange of ratification. If Germany by treaty cedes territory to Poland or to France, obviously Germany cannot prior to ratification proceed to cede that territory to some other nation, even though the treaty obviously is not, in accordance with its terms, in effect. If Germany is obliged to deliver commodities in kind, as we used to say in Paris, whether it be cattle or machinery, or pictures, she cannot dispose of those things to some other nations pending a certain period of time for ratification. If she does, that is a fraud on the other party to a treaty."[22]

Events similar to the above hypothesis arose in the case concerning certain *German Interests in Polish Upper Silesia* which was decided by the Permanent Court of International Justice in the following year (1926). In this case, Poland complained of certain transactions of the German Government regarding the latter's property in Upper Silesia as being in violation of the signed, but yet unratified, Treaty of Versailles (Art. 256, I, II).

"As, after its ratification, the Treaty did not, in the Court's opinion, impose on Germany such obligation to refrain from alienation, it is *a fortiori*, impossible to regard as an infraction of the principle of good faith Germany's action in alienating the property before the coming into force of the Treaty which had already been signed. In these circumstances, the Court need not consider the question whether, and if so how far, the signatories of a treaty are under an obligation to refrain from any action likely to interfere with its execution when ratification has taken place."[23]

It seems, however, even from the above passage, and from the rest of the Judgment that, in the opinion of the Court,

21 Nielsen's *Report*, p. 382, at p. 398.
22 *Ibid.*, at pp. 398–399.
23 (Merits), A.7, pp. 39–40. For the facts of the case, see *infra*, pp. 126 *et seq.*

during the period in question, the parties must not act against the principle of good faith.[24]

The Greco-Turkish Arbitral Tribunal in an award delivered a few months later was even more explicit:—

"It is a principle of law that already with the signature of a treaty and before its entry into force, there exists for the contracting parties an obligation to do nothing which may injure the Treaty by reducing the importance of its provisions. . . . It is of interest to state that this principle—which really is only an expression of the principle of good faith which is the foundation of all law and all conventions—has received application in a number of treaties." [25]

Umpire Lieber of the Mexican-United States Claims Commission (1868) was of the opinion that:—

"If a peace were signed with a moral certainty of its ratification and one of the belligerents were, after this, making grants of land in a province which is to be ceded, before the final ratification, it would certainly be considered by every honest jurist a fraudulent and invalid transaction." [26]

Pending the ratification of a treaty,[27] therefore, the principle of good faith requires that each party should abstain from acts which would prejudice the rights—imperfect perhaps, but none the less rights—of the other party, as established by the signed treaty. Acts which violate the principle are fraudulent and invalid in the eyes of the law.[28]

[24] *Cf. ibid.*, at pp. 30, 37–9. See also Anzilotti, *Cours de droit international public*, Paris, 1929, p. 373. Anzilotti was one of the judges who decided the *German Interests Case* (Merits) (1926). *Cf.* also *Interpretation of Art. 260 of the Peace Treaty of Versailles Case* (1924), Germany/Reparation Commission, 1 UNRIAA, p. 429, at pp. 521–3.

[25] *Megalidis Case* (1926), 8 T.A.M., p. 390, at p. 395. (Transl.)
For examples of treaties, other than that given by the Tribunal, see Art. 38 of the General Act of Berlin, 1885 (Martens, II (10) N.R.G., p. 414); Protocol to the Convention for the Control of Trade in Arms and Ammunition, St. German-en-Laye, 1919 (Hudson: 1 *Int.Leg.*, p. 343).

[26] *Ignacio Torres Case*, 4 *Int.Arb.*, p. 3798, at p. 3801. On the effect of the signature of a treaty of peace on the permissibility of further hostilities pending ratification of the treaty, see *ibid.*, pp. 3800–1. See also *Id.*: *Anaya Case*, *per* Umpire Thornton, *ibid.*, pp. 3804–5.

[27] This excludes the case when it is certain that a treaty is not to be ratified. The principle of good faith does not necessarily condemn a refusal to ratify a signed treaty, when the ratifying authority deems it unsatisfactory, even if the treaty had been concluded pursuant to a *pactum de contrahendo*. See *Tacna-Arica Arbitration* (1925), Chile/Peru, 2 UNRIAA, p. 921, at p. 929.

[28] See *Harvard Research* (1935, Part III): *Draft Convention on the Law of Treaties*, Art. 9 and *Comment* thereon. Supplement to 29 A.J.I.L. (1935), pp. 778–87. The *Comment* is no doubt right in saying that whether an action indicates bad faith or not "depends entirely upon the circumstances of the

C. Pacta sunt servanda

"A treaty is a solemn compact between nations. It possesses in ordinary the same essential qualities as a contract between individuals, enhanced by the weightier quality of the parties and by the greater magnitude of the subject-matter. To be valid, it imports a mutual assent." [29]

"It need hardly be stated that the obligations of a treaty are as binding upon nations as are private contracts upon individuals. This principle has been too often cited by publicists and enforced by international decisions to need amplification here." [30]

"It cannot be that good faith is less obligatory upon nations than upon individuals in carrying out agreements." [31]

"From the standpoint of the obligatory character of international engagements, it is well known that such engagements may be taken in the form of treaties, conventions, declarations, agreements, protocols, or exchange of notes." [32]

"'Treaties of every kind, when made by the competent authority, are as obligatory upon nations as private contracts are binding upon individuals . . . and to be kept with the most scrupulous good faith.'" [33]

case" (p. 782). We cannot agree, however, that the obligation to abstain from acts of bad faith is purely moral and non-legal (pp. 781 *et seq.*). The draft to a certain extent betrays the usual confusion between the coming into force of the substantive provisions of the treaty and the abstention from acts of bad faith pending ratification. This can be seen from the examples which the *Comment* gives of "hypothetical cases wherein the obligation of good faith referred to in Art. 9 might be regarded as being ignored." The first example is as follows: "A treaty contains an undertaking on the part of the signatory that it will not fortify a particular place on its frontier or that it will demilitarise a designated zone in that region. Shortly thereafter, while ratification is still pending, it proceeds to erect the forbidden fortifications or to increase its armament within the zone referred to" (p. 781). The act is plainly in violation of the terms of the treaty if the substantive provisions have come in force. But before that date, however, it cannot be said that the act was designed to prejudice the eventual execution of the treaty, nor to injure the inchoate rights of the other party, in case the treaty becomes ratified. In fact, the only party which would suffer, if the treaty is ratified, would be the State erecting these fortifications, because it would have to demolish them. The situation would be totally different if the treaty had provided not for demilitarisation, but for the maintenance of the military *status quo* in a given area. In such a case, the act of increasing the fortification in the area concerned during the interval between signature and ratification would indeed be an act of bad faith, and such an act, it is submitted, cannot be sanctioned, either by morality or by law.

29 Fran.-Ven. M.C.C. (1902): *Maninat Case* (1905), Ralston's *Report*, p. 44, at p. 73.

30 *Metzger & Co. Case* (1900), U.S.F.R. (1901), p. 262, at p. 276.

31 *Metzger & Co. Case* (1900), *ibid.*, at p. 271.

32 PCIJ: *Austria-German Customs Union* (1931), Adv.Op., A/B. 41, p. 47.

33 *Van Bokkelen Case* (1888), 2 *Int.Arb.*, p. 1807, at pp. 1849–50, quoting Kent's *Commentaries*.

Pacta sunt servanda, now an indisputable rule of international law,[34] is but an expression of the principle of good faith which above all signifies the keeping of faith,[35] the pledged faith of nations as well as that of individuals. Without this rule, "International law as well as civil law would be a mere mockery." [36]

A party may not unilaterally "free itself from the engagements of a treaty, or modify the stipulations thereof, except by the consent of the contracting parties, through a friendly understanding." [37] "As long as the Treaty remains in force, it must be observed as it stands. It is not for the Treaty to adapt itself to conditions. But if the latter are of a compelling nature, compliance with them would necessitate another legal instrument." [38] The doctrine of *clausula rebus sic stantibus* has, therefore, no application in international law in the sense that what has been mutually agreed to by the parties can cease to be binding merely on account of changed circumstances. On the other hand, the doctrine is applicable in the sense that a treaty or contract cannot be invoked to cover cases which could not have been reasonably contemplated at the time of its conclusion.[39]

"Reparation is the indispensable complement of a failure to apply a convention, and there is no necessity for this to be stated in the convention itself." [40] It is, indeed, "a general conception of law, that any breach of an engagement involves an obligation to make reparation," [41] however short the breach

[34] See *Harvard Research* (1935 Part III), Supplement to 29 A.J.I.L. (1935), pp. 671–85; Kunz, "The Meaning and the Range of the Norm Pacta sunt Servanda" 39 A.J.I.L. (1945), pp. 180–97; and literature cited in both.

[35] See *e.g.*, Grotius, *De Jure Pacis et Belli*, III, xix–xxv; Bynkershoek, *Quaestionum Juris Publici*, II, x: "Pacta privatorum tuetur jus civile, pacta principum bona fides"; Vattel, *Le droit des gens*, II, xv, § 220.

[36] Ven.-U.S. M.C.C. (1903): *Rudloff Case* (Interlocutory Decision), *Ven.Arb. 1903*, p. 182, at p. 194. *Cf. Id.*: *Turnbull/Manoa Co., Ltd./Orinoco Co., Ltd. Cases*, *ibid.*, p. 200, at p. 244.

[37] The Protocol of London of 1871. See PCIJ: *Oscar Chinn Case* (1934), S.O. by van Eysinga, A/B. 63, p. 134. The Protocol of London of 1871 is found in Martens, 18 N.R.G., p. 278. See also *Chilean-Peruvian Accounts Case* (1875) 2 *Int.Arb.*, p. 2085, at pp. 2095, 2102.

[38] PCIJ: *Meuse Case* (1937), S.O. by Altimira, A/B. 70, p. 43. *Cf. contra*, ICJ: *Anglo-Iranian Oil Co. Case* (Jd.) (1952), U.K./Iran, D.O. by Alvarez, *ICJ Reports, 1952*, p. 93, at p. 126. Judge Alvarez' "New International law" is, however, still largely *de lege ferenda*.

[39] See *infra*, pp. 118–119.

[40] PCIJ: *Chorzów Factory Case* (Merits) (1928) A. 17, p. 29.

[41] *Ibid.*

may be in duration [42] and however relative it may be in importance, so that each party may "place entire confidence in the good faith of the other." [43]

D. Performance of Treaty Obligations

The principle that treaty obligations should be fulfilled in good faith and not merely in accordance with the letter of the treaty has long been recognised by international tribunals and is reaffirmed by the United Nations [44] "as an act of faith." [45]

In the *North Atlantic Coast Fisheries Case* (1910) the Permanent Court of Arbitration expressly affirmed that:—

> "Every State has to execute the obligations incurred by treaty bona fide, and is urged thereto by the ordinary sanctions of international law in regard to observance of treaty obligations." [46]

This means, essentially, that treaty obligations should be carried out according to the common and real intention of the parties at the time the treaty was concluded, that is to say, the spirit of the treaty and not its mere literal meaning.[47]

[42] PCIJ: *Oscar Chinn Case* (1934), D. O. by Sir Cecil Hurst, A/B. 63, p. 119: "If a State is subject to engagement to do or not to do a certain thing, there cannot be read into it a provision that for short periods there shall be liberty to violate the engagement."

[43] Peruv.-U.S. Cl.Com. (1863): *Sartori Case*, 3 *Int.Arb.*, p. 3120, at p. 3123: "On the principle that reparation ought to be made in cases where responsibility is incurred, however small it may be, for non-compliance with the treaty, in order that each Government may place entire confidence in the good faith of the other, it seems to me that an equitable and reasonable indemnity ought to be granted to Mr. Sartori."

[44] U.N. Charter, Art. 2 (2).

[45] *Cf* UNCIO: 6 *Documents*, p. 79.

[46] 1 H.C.R., p. 143, at p. 167.

[47] PCA: *Timor Case* (1914) 1 H.C.R., p. 354, at p. 365.

Cf. UNCIO: 6 *Documents*, pp. 74–75. With regard to the term good faith, Dean Gildersleeve explained in Commission I of the UNCIO: "This is a customary phrase, which to our friends of the Latin countries, especially, conveys the meaning that we are all to observe these obligations, not merely the letter of them, but the spirit of them, and that these words do convey an assurance without which the principle would seem unsatisfactory to these friends of ours."

See also Planiol et Ripert, 6 *Traité pratique de droit civil français*, 1930, § 379: "... all our contracts are contracts *bonæ fidei*, which imply the obligation to behave like an honest and conscientious man not only in the formation, but also in the performance of the contract, and not to cling to its literal meaning. ... To determine what is due [under the contract], we must ascertain what honesty allows us to demand as well as what it obliges us to do" (Transl.).

Harvard Research (1935, Part III): Draft Convention on the Law of Treaties, Comment *ad* Art. 20: "The obligation to fulfil in good faith a treaty engagement requires that its stipulations be observed in their spirit as

This is one of the most important aspects of the principle of good faith and is in accordance with the notion that a treaty is an accord of will between contracting parties. As was held by the Franco-Venezuelan Mixed Claims Commission (1902):—

"A treaty is a solemn compact between nations. . . . To be valid, it imports a mutual assent, and in order that there may be such mutual assent there must be a similar understanding of the several matters involved. It can never be what one party understands, but it always must be what both parties understood to be the matters agreed upon and what in fact was the agreement of the parties concerning the matters now in dispute." [48]

Performance of a treaty obligation in good faith means carrying out the substance of this mutual understanding honestly and loyally.

As the ascertainment of this mutual understanding, *i.e.*, the real and common intention of the parties, is a matter of interpretation, it is also said that treaty interpretation is governed by the principle of good faith. Thus the Arbitrator observed in the *Timor Case* (1914), quoting the words of Rivier:—

"Above all, the common intention of the parties must be established: *id quod actum est*. . . . Good faith prevailing throughout this subject, treaties ought not to be interpreted exclusively according to their letter, but according to their spirit . . . . Principles of treaty interpretation are, by and large, and *mutatis mutandis*, those of the interpretation of agreements *between individuals*, principles of common sense and experience, already formulated by the Prudents of Rome." [49]

well as according to their letters and that what has been promised be performed without evasion or subterfuge honestly and to the best of the ability of the party which made the promise" (Supplement to 29 A.J.I.L. (1935), p. 987).

[48] *Maninat Case* (1905), Ralston's *Report*, p. 44, at p. 73.

Agreement must exist with regard to the *negotia essentialia* of the treaty. A treaty is not, however, vitiated because on a minor point the parties may have understood the words which they used in different meanings. See, *e.g.*, PCIJ: *Lighthouses Case* (1934), France/Greece, A/B. 62. In that case, the Court had to decide the exact meaning of "Contract duly entered into" in the Special Agreement between the parties. The parties agreed that the words were taken from Art. 1 of Protocol XII of Lausanne (pp. 16–17). But they understood the meaning of these words in the Protocol differently. France understood them as meaning only formalities under Ottoman law, while Greece took them to include objections of an international character (p. 17). This misunderstanding did not affect the validity of the treaty or of the provision.

[49] *Loc. cit.*, p. 365. *Cf.* Yü, *The Interpretation of Treaties*, 1927, Chap. V: "The so-called Rules of Construction and the doctrine of Uberrima Fides," pp. 203 *et seq.*

Cf. PCIJ: *The Wimbledon Case* (1923), D.O. by Anzilotti and Huber,

Indeed, he considered that there was "entire coincidence of private and international law on this point."[50] It should be pointed out, however, that where this common intention has been reduced to writing, it is primarily the common intention as set out in the text which is to be enforced.[51] The text of a treaty cannot be "enlarged by reading into it stipulations which are said to result from the proclaimed intentions of the authors of the treaty, but for which no provision is made in the text itself."[52] But "the intention of the parties must be sought out and enforced even though this should lead to an interpretation running counter to the literal terms of an isolated phrase, which read in connection with its context is susceptible of a different construction."[53] Moreover, the Permanent Court of International Justice has developed the teleological approach of interpreting the intention of the parties so that it is the real and practical aim pursued by the contracting parties that is enforced.[54]

A. 1, p. 36: "Though it is true that when the wording of a treaty is clear its literal meaning must be accepted as it stands, without limitation or extension, it is equally true that the *words have no value except in so far as they express an idea. . . .*" Italics added. See also PCIJ: *Meuse Case* (1937), D.O. by Anzilotti, A/B. 70, p. 46.

50 *Timor Case* (1914), *loc. cit.*, p. 366.

51 Thus in the *Lighthouses Case* (1934), although it was the common intention of the parties that the meaning of the words "contracts duly entered into" was the same in Art. 1 of Protocol XII of Lausanne as in the Special Agreement (A/B. 62, pp. 16–17), the P.C.I.J. by the method of systematic or organic interpretation arrived at the conclusion that, in the Protocol, these words referred to formalities in Ottoman law (p. 15), while, in the Special Agreement, because the question whether the contract was "duly entered into" or not was linked with the question of enforceability against Greece, these words, in the intention of the parties, also referred to objections of an international character (pp. 13–16). Thus though the common intention was that the same words were to have the same meaning in both instruments, because they were expressed in different contexts, different meanings were attributed to them.

52 PCIJ: *Polish War Vessels in Danzig* (1931) Adv.Op., A/B. 43, p. 144. *Cf.* the importance to be attached to matters of form in treaty interpretation, ICJ: *Ambatielos Case* (1952), D.O. by Basdevant, *ICJ Reports, 1952*, p. 28, at pp. 69–70.

53 Germ.-U.S. M.C.C. (1922): *Mendel Case* (1926) *Dec. & Op.*, p. 772, at p. 791. For facts of the case, see *infra*, pp. 212 *et seq.* See also *Chevreau Case* (1931) 2 UNRIAA, p. 1113, at pp. 1137–8.

54 See *e.g.*, PCIJ: *Chorzów Factory Case* (Jd.) (1927) A. 9, pp. 24, 25; *Minority Schools in Albania* (1935) Adv.Op., A/B. 64, p. 17; *Electricity Co. of Sofia and Bulgaria Case* (Prel.Obj.) (1939) A/B. 77, p. 76; *Competence of the International Labor Organization (Personal Work of the Employer)* (1926) Adv.Op., B. 13, p. 18; *Greco-Bulgarian "Communities"* (1930) Adv.Op. B. 17, pp. 19 *et seq.* In many cases, Anzilotti would have preferred to go much further than the Court, a fact which explains many of his dissenting opinions, see *e.g.*, *The Wimbledon Case* (1923), Joint D.O. by Anzilotti and Huber, A. 1, pp. 36, 38; *Interpretation of the 1919 Convention concerning*

From the fact that it is the common intention of the parties or the spirit of the treaty that has to be respected, it follows that it is not permissible, whilst observing the letter of the agreement, to evade treaty obligations by—what the Permanent Court has called—"indirect means." If, for instance, it is the intention of the parties that freedom of navigation and commerce should be established in certain parts of their territory, it is not permissible for one party, while respecting the letter of the agreement, to evade its obligations in effect by an exaggerated exercise of its right to manage its national shipping.[55] Similarly, if State A has, by treaty with State B, granted to the inhabitants of State B the right to fish in certain parts of its coastal waters in common with its own nationals, and to enter its bays and harbours for the purpose of repairs, etc., State A may not, by an unreasonable exercise of its sovereign right to legislate for the preservation and protection of its fisheries, deprive the grant of its practical effect.[56] The unreasonable exercise of a right in such cases constitutes an abuse of right,[57] which being an act that is inconsistent with the duty to carry out the treaty in good faith, is considered as unlawful.

Again, if parties agree that disputes shall be submitted to judicial settlement only if they "cannot be settled by negotiation," "the condition in question does not mean . . . that resort to the Court is precluded so long as the alleged wrongdoer may profess a willingness to negotiate." [58] A party which is bound by a *pactum de contrahendo* to negotiate a certain treaty is responsible for the consequences of its acts of bad

Employment of Women During the Night (1932) Adv. Op., A/B. 50; *Oscar Chinn Case* (1934) A/B. 63; *Meuse Case* (1937) A/B. 70.

See also ICJ: *Reparation for Injuries Suffered in the Service of the UN* (1949) Adv.Op., *ICJ Reports, 1949*, p. 174, at pp. 177 *et seq.*, 182 *et seq.*; *United States Nationals in Morocco Case* (1952) *ICJ Reports, 1952*, p. 176, at p. 197.

[55] PCIJ: *Oscar Chinn Case* (1934) A/B. 63, p. 86. The claim was dismissed because "The circumstances in which the impugned measures were taken are such as to preclude any idea that the Belgian Government intended by indirect means to escape the obligations incumbent on it." See also PCIJ: *Free Zones Case* (Jgt.) (1932) A/B. 46, pp. 167 *et seq.*

[56] P.C.A.: *North Atlantic Coast Fisheries Case* (1910) 1 H.C.R., p. 141, see pp. 168, 169, 170, 171.

[57] See *infra*, pp. 123 *et seq.*

[58] PCIJ.: *Mavrommatis Palestine Concessions Case* (1924), D.O. by Moore, A. 2, p. 62.

faith.[59] It may be said that in such cases good faith consists in a sincere and honest desire, as evidenced by a genuine effort, to fulfil the substance of the mutual agreement. It is essentially a moral quality or perhaps what Judge Moore has described as the "ordinary conceptions of fair dealing as between man and man." [60] The enforcement of the principle of good faith may be considered as the enforcement of that degree of morality which is necessary for the functioning of the legal system.

Also, since it is the common intention of the parties and the spirit, rather than the letter, of the treaty which have to be observed, a party may not be allowed to make capital out of inexact expressions or mistaken descriptions in a treaty, when the real and common intention can be ascertained and the error established. *Falsa demonstratio non nocet.*[61]

While the principle of good faith prohibits the evasion of an obligation as established by the common intention of the parties, it also prohibits a party from exacting from the other party advantages which go beyond their common and reasonable intention at the time of the conclusion of the treaty, as, for example, by invoking the treaty to cover cases which could not reasonably have been in the contemplation of the parties at the time of its conclusion.[62] In this limited sense, the doctrine of

[59] *Cf. Tacna-Arica Arbitration* (1925) 2 UNRIAA, p. 921, at p. 930. See also *passim*, for the repeated emphasis on the requirement of good faith in executing the obligations resulting from a *pactum de contrahendo.*

[60] *Cf. Mavrommatis Palestine Concessions* (1924), D.O. by Moore, A. 2, p. 61.

[61] See P.C.A.: *Timor Case* (1914) 1 H.C.R. p. 354, Pt. VI, No. 4; Pt. VII, No. 7 of Award. PCIJ: *European Danube Commission* (1927) Adv.Op., B. 14, pp. 31–32. *Cf.* also P.C.A. *Chevreau Case* (1931) 2 UNRIAA, p. 1113, at pp. 1137–1138.

[62] An instance where a State considered it contrary to the principle of good faith for it to insist upon the letter of the treaty in order to gain advantages not in the mind of the parties at the time of the conclusion of the treaty may be seen from the Report of the Law Officers of the Crown to Earl Granville, February 24, 1872, quoted in McNair, *The Law of Treaties, British Practice and Opinions*, 1938, pp. 190–1, at p. 191.

Cf. PCIJ: *Meuse Case* (1937) Neth./Belg. The Belgian Government, in its written rejoinder (Ser. C. 81, pp. 180 *et seq.*), prayed the Court alternatively: "In case the Court should be unable on certain points to find in accordance with the submissions of the Respondent, to declare in any case that the Applicant is committing an abuse of right (*abus de droit*) in invoking the Treaty of May 12, 1863, in order to protect new interests (the Juliana canal and the canalised Meuse) which were not contemplated at the time of the conclusion of that Treaty, while the interests which that Treaty was intended to protect are not in any way threatened" (A/B. 70, p. 8). See also Ser. C. 81, pp. 208–9.

Cf. also PCIJ: *Free Zones Case* (Jgt.) (1932) A/B, 46 pp. 156–8. *Pensions of Officials of the Saar Territory Case* (1934) 3 UNRIAA, p. 1553, at p. 1566. *Abu Dhabi Oil Arbitration* (1951) 1 I.C.L.Q. (1952), p. 247, at p. 253.

clausula rebus sic stantibus is founded on the principle of good faith and is recognised by international law.[63]

Finally, the principle of good faith requires a party to refrain from abusing such rights as are conferred upon it by the treaty.[64]

E. Denunciation of Treaties

Where a party is free to denounce a treaty at any time, it should not do so immediately on learning that the other party wishes to invoke the treaty; for otherwise the treaty would, contrary to the true intention of the parties, be deprived of all practical effect. If, however, this right does not exist except at periodic intervals, a party may denounce the treaty at the end of a period even if it is at the same time notified that the other party wishes to invoke the treaty.[65]

Good faith in contractual relations thus implies the observance by the parties of a certain standard of fair dealing, sincerity, honesty, loyalty, in short, of morality, throughout their dealings. All these qualities may escape precise definition, but they may be considered as inherent in, or at least perceptible to, every common man. International law applies this standard in treaty relations between States to the extent described above, much as municipal law in contractual relations between individuals. In particular, all systems of law in accordance with the principle of good faith prescribe that promises should be scrupulously kept so that the confidence that may reasonably be placed upon them should not be abused. The importance

63 *Cf.* D.O. by Alvarez in I.C.J.: *Competence of Assembly regarding Admission to the U.N.* (1950) Adv.Op., *ICJ Reports, 1950*, p. 4, at p. 17; also in *Anglo-Iranian Oil Co. Case* (Jd.) (1952) *ICJ Reports, 1952*, p. 93, at p. 126; D.O. by Winiarski in I.C.J.: *Interpretation of Peace Treaties* (1st Phase) (1950) Adv. Op., *ICJ Reports, 1950*, p. 65, at p. 94. Both learned judges, it is submitted, however, failed to distinguish the two different meanings of the *clausula*, wherein lies the main flaw in their argument. See further *supra*, pp. 113 *et seq.* and note 38.

64 Peruv.-U.S. Cl.Com. (1863): *Sartori Case*, 3 *Int.Arb.* 3120, at p. 3122: "The honour and interests of the two republics represented in the joint commission require them to give proofs of the good faith with which each of the two countries fulfils the stipulations of the public treaty that binds them and requires that neither government shall allow the citizens so to abuse the protection and guarantees conceded to them by the treaty as to consider them a species of immunity under which they may infringe the laws."

65 PCIJ: *Electricity Co. of Sofia and Bulgaria Case* (Prel.Obj.) (1939), D.O. by Anzilotti, A/B. 77, pp. 97–8; *Cf.* Ser. C. 88, pp. 430–1.

of this principle in any system of law and society cannot be over-emphasised. Indeed, as Aristotle said, most of our daily relations—namely, those that are voluntary—are regulated by contracts, and if these lose their binding force, human intercourse would cease to exist.[66] And the smoothness of this intercourse depends in large measure upon the degree of good faith with which our contractual or treaty relations are observed.

[66] *Rhetorica*, I, xv, 22.

Chapter 4

GOOD FAITH IN THE EXERCISE OF RIGHTS (THE THEORY OF ABUSE OF RIGHTS)

The principle of good faith which governs international relations controls also the exercise of rights by States. The theory of abuse of rights (*abus de droit*), recognised in principle both by the Permanent Court of International Justice [1] and the International Court of Justice,[2] is merely an application of this principle to the exercise of rights.

A. The Malicious Exercise of a Right

The prohibition of malicious injury is an important aspect of the theory of abuse of right as it has been applied in most Continental legal systems.[3] In the international sphere, attention may be drawn to the following extract from the proceedings of the Fur Seal Arbitral Tribunal (1892), which clearly shows that the President of the Tribunal entertained no doubt as to its applicability in international law and that counsel for Great Britain was not indisposed to admit it. The question raised was whether the United States had a right to complain of the hunting of fur seals by British fishermen in that part of the Behring Sea adjacent to the American Pribilof Islands.

" Sir Charles Russell: Where is the right that is invaded by that pelagic sealing? . . . It is not enough to prove that their industry (if I must use that phrase) may be less profitable to them because other persons, in the exercise of the right of sealing on the high seas, may intercept seals that come to them—that may be what lawyers

[1] *Cf. infra*, pp. 123, 127.

[2] *Anglo-Norwegian Fisheries Case* (1951), U.K./Norway, *ICJ Reports, 1951*, p. 116, at p. 142. See *infra*, p. 134, note 42. The theory of abuse of rights has been frequently referred to by judges of the I.C.J. in their separate and dissenting opinions. See *ICJ Reports, 1947–1948*, pp. 69, 71, 79 *et seq.*, 91, 92, 93, 103, 115; *ICJ Reports, 1949*, pp. 46, 47 *et seq.*, 75, 129 *et seq.*; *ICJ Reports, 1950*, pp. 14 *et seq.*, 19, 20, 29, 148, 348, 349; *ICJ Reports, 1951*, pp. 149 *et seq.*; *ICJ Reports, 1952*, pp. 56, 128, 133, 135.

[3] *Cf.* H. C. Gutteridge, " Abuse of Rights," 5 *Cambridge L.J.* (1933), p. 22.

call a damnum, but it is not an injuria . . . ; but a damnum does not give a legal right of action. . . .

"The PRESIDENT: Unless done maliciously.

"Sir CHARLES RUSSELL: You are good enough, Mr. President, to anticipate the very next topic. . . . They would have a right to complain . . . if it could be truly asserted that any class or set of men had, for the malicious purpose of injuring the lessees of the Pribilof Islands and not in regard to their own profit and interest and in exercise of their own supposed rights, committed a series of acts injurious to the tenants of the Pribilof Islands, I agree that that would probably give a cause of action; and, therefore, they have the further right (what I might call the negative right) of being protected against malicious injury. . . ."[4]

The exercise of a right—or supposed right, since the right no longer exists—for the sole purpose of causing injury to another is thus prohibited. Every right is the legal protection of a legitimate interest. An alleged exercise of a right not in furtherance of such interest, but with the malicious purpose of injuring others can no longer claim the protection of the law.[5] *Malitiis non est indulgendum.*[6]

B. The Fictitious Exercise of a Right

I. EVASION OF THE LAW

Ex re sed non ex nomine is a principle of good faith.[7] By looking to the real state of things and not attaching decisive importance to the legal denominations which the parties may give to their actions, this principle inter alia precludes the form of the law from being used to cover the commission of what in fact is an unlawful act. If international law prescribes respect for private property, but allows expropriation for

[4] *Fur Seal Arbitration* (1893) G.B./U.S., 1 *Int.Arb.*, p. 755, at pp. 889–890. *Cf.* American contention that the high seas were "free only for innocent and inoffensive use, not injurious to the just interests of any nation which borders upon it" (p. 839). See also *ibid.*, p. 892.

[5] *Cf.* PCIJ: *German Interests Case* (Merits) (1926), Speech of German Agent (Ser. C. 11–I, pp. 136 *et seq.*) and German Memorial (pp. 375 *et seq.*), where the German Government admitted that the exercise of no right can be unlimited, and that the exercise of a right for no serious motive except the purpose of injuring others constituted an abuse of right.

[6] *Digest*: VI.i. *De rei vindic*, 38.

[7] *Cf.* PCIJ: *Chorzów Factory Case* (Merits) (1928), D.O. by Ehrlich, A. 17, p. 87. See *supra*, p. 39.

reasons of public utility[8] it is not permissible for a State to go through the forms of an expropriation procedure in order to seize private property not for public purposes, but for the use of some individuals for private profit. This occurred in the *Walter F. Smith Case* (1929) and the act was considered contrary to the principle of good faith and held to be unlawful.[9]

II. EVASION OF TREATY OBLIGATIONS

By application of the same principle, international law prohibits the evasion of a treaty obligation under the guise of an alleged exercise of a right. In the *Free Zones Case* (Jgt.) (1932), France was under treaty obligations to maintain certain frontier zones with Switzerland free from customs barriers. The Permanent Court of International Justice while recognising that France had the sovereign and undoubted right to establish a police cordon at the political frontier, for the control of traffic and even for the imposition of fiscal taxes other than customs duties, held that:—

> "A reservation must be made as regards the case of abuses of a right ["*les cas d'abus de droit*"], since it is certain that France must not evade the obligation to maintain the zones by erecting a customs barrier under the guise of a control cordon." [10]

The principle of good faith thus requires every right to be exercised honestly and loyally. Any fictitious exercise of a right for the purpose of evading either a rule of law or a contractual obligation will not be tolerated. Such an exercise constitutes an abuse of the right, prohibited by law.

C. Interdependence of Rights and Obligations

I. RIGHTS AND TREATY OBLIGATIONS

When a State assumes a treaty obligation, those of its rights which are directly in conflict with this obligation are, to that extent, restricted or renounced. Thus, if Great Britain agrees

[8] *Supra*, p. 37.
[9] *Supra*, p. 39.
[10] A/B. 46, p. 167. See also the Court's Order of December 6, 1930, in the same case, A. 24, p. 12; and *Oscar Chinn Case* (1934), A/B. 63, p. 86 (see *supra*, p. 117).

that inhabitants of the United States shall have the right to fish in certain of her territorial waters, she has to that extent deprived herself of the right to prohibit foreigners from fishing in those waters. But the other rights of Great Britain, for example, her right as local sovereign to legislate for the protection and preservation of fisheries, are apparently not considered as having been affected by this obligation. Thus in the *North Atlantic Coast Fisheries Case* (1910) where the facts were as related above, the Permanent Court of Arbitration said:—

> ". . . the line by which the respective rights of both parties accruing out of the treaty are to be circumscribed, can refer only to the right granted by the treaty; that is to say the liberty of taking, drying, and curing fish by the American inhabitants in certain British waters in common with British subjects, and not to the exercise of rights of legislation by Great Britain not referred to in the treaty.
>
> ". . . a line which would limit the exercise of sovereignty of a State within the limits of its own territory, can be drawn only on the ground of express stipulation, and not by implication from stipulations concerning a different subject-matter." [11]

The non-limitation of the right is, however, only apparent. It is submitted that, in reality, with the assumption of every obligation, all the rights of the State suffer a limitation to a greater or lesser extent. When a State assumes a treaty obligation, the principle of good faith—which governs the performance of treaty obligations—imposes a general limitation on every right of the State so that none may be exercised in a manner incompatible with the bona fide execution of the obligation assumed. Thus in the same decision, the Permanent Court of Arbitration added:—

> "The line in question is drawn according to the principle of international law that treaty obligations are to be executed in perfect good faith, therefore excluding the right to legislate *at will* concerning the subject-matter of the treaty, and *limiting the exercise of sovereignty of the State bound by a treaty with respect to that subject-matter to such acts as are consistent with the treaty.*" [12]

[11] 1 H.C.R., p. 141, at p. 169.
[12] *Ibid.*, at p. 169. Italics added.

In other words,

"The exercise of that right [*i.e.*, to legislate] by Great Britain is, however, limited by the said treaty in respect of the said liberties therein granted to the inhabitants of the United States in that such regulations must be made bona fide and must not be in violation of the said treaty.

"Regulations which are (1) appropriate or necessary for the protection and preservation of such fisheries, or (2) desirable or necessary on grounds of public order and morals without unnecessarily interfering with the fishery itself, and in both cases equitable and fair as between local and American fishermen, and not so framed as to give unfairly an advantage to the former over the latter class, are not inconsistent with the obligation to execute the treaty in good faith and are therefore reasonable and not in violation of the treaty." [13]

Whatever the limits of the right might have been before the assumption of the obligation, from then onwards, the right is subject to a restriction. Henceforth, whenever its exercise impinges on the field covered by the treaty obligation, it must be exercised bona fide, that is to say reasonably. A reasonable and bona fide exercise of a right in such a case is one which is appropriate and necessary for the purpose of the right (*i.e.*, in furtherance of the interests which the right is intended to protect). It should at the same time be fair and equitable as between the parties and not one which is calculated to procure for one of them an unfair advantage in the light of the obligation assumed. A reasonable exercise of the right is regarded as compatible with the obligation. But the exercise of the right in such a manner as to prejudice the interests of the other contracting party arising out of the treaty is unreasonable and is considered as inconsistent with the bona fide execution of the treaty obligation, and a breach of the treaty. In this way, the principle of good faith establishes an interdependence between the rights of a State and its obligations. By weighing the conflicting interests covered by the right and the obligation, it delimits them in such a way as to render the exercise of the right compatible with the spirit of the obligation.

Another, though more complicated, example, illustrating the interdependence of rights and treaty obligations, is to be found

[13] *Ibid.*, at p. 171.

in the *German Interests Case* (Merits) (1926). The relevant facts may be briefly recalled. The case was concerned inter alia with the nitrate factory at Chorzów, Polish Upper Silesia. Both the factory and the territory formerly belonged to the German Empire. By the Treaty of Versailles, Germany agreed that a plebiscite should be held in Upper Silesia and in advance renounced in favour of Poland all rights and titles over that portion of Upper Silesia lying beyond the frontier line to be fixed by the Principal Allied and Associated Powers as the result of the plebiscite (Art. 88). Article 256 of the Treaty provided that Powers to which German territory was to be ceded were to acquire the property and possessions situated therein belonging to the German Empire. The value of such acquisitions was to be fixed by the Reparation Commission, and paid to the latter by the State acquiring the territory, to be credited to the German Government on account of the sums due in respect of reparations. Poland, however, was not entitled to reparations. The Treaty was signed on June 28, 1919, but did not come into force between Germany and Poland until January 10, 1920. On December 24, 1919, *i.e.*, between the date of signature of the Treaty and its coming into force, a series of legal instruments were signed and legalised in Berlin. By these instruments a private company was formed and to it the Reich sold the factory at Chorzów. Ownership was transferred only on January 28–29, 1920, at a time when the Treaty had already come into force. After that part of Upper Silesia in which the factory was situated had been allotted to Poland (October 20, 1921), Poland, considering the sale to be null and void, declared that the factory had become Polish State property in accordance with Article 256 of the Treaty of Versailles. Germany contested the legality of this measure.

In the opinion of the Permanent Court of International Justice, Article 88 of the Treaty of Versailles merely contemplated the possible renunciation of sovereignty over the territories in question and Article 256 did not operate in this case until the effective transfer of sovereignty. It held that:—

> "Germany undoubtedly retained until the actual transfer of sovereignty the right to dispose of her property." [14]

[14] A. 7, p. 30.

The treaty obligations assumed by Germany did not, therefore, directly affect her proprietary rights, including the right of alienating property in the plebiscite area. The Court added, however:—

"And only a misuse of this right could [' *ce n'est qu'un abus de ce droit ou un manquement au principe de la bonne foi qui pourraient* '] endow an act of alienation with the character of a breach of the Treaty." [15]

It follows, therefore, that a legitimate exercise of the right of alienation was compatible with the treaty obligations, while an abuse of this right, *i.e.*, an exercise of the right contrary to the principle of good faith, would be incompatible therewith.

In considering "whether Poland can rely as against Germany on the contention that there has been a misuse of the right [' *un abus du droit* '] possessed by the latter to alienate property situated in the plebiscite area, before the transfer of sovereignty," [16] the Court arrived at the conclusion that:—

"Such misuse [' *un tel abus* '] has not taken place in the present case. The act in question does not overstep the limits of the normal administration of public property and was not designed to procure for one of the interested Parties an illicit advantage and to deprive the other of an advantage to which he was entitled." [17]

In the opinion of the Court, "the abandonment by the Reich of an enterprise showing a serious deficit, by means of a sale under conditions offering a reasonable guarantee that the capital invested would eventually be recovered" "appears in fact to have fulfilled a legitimate object of the administration," and no sufficient reasons had been shown why the transaction should not be regarded as genuine.[18]

"Again, the Court cannot regard the alienation as an act calculated to prejudice Poland's rights. At the time when the alienation took place (*Auflassung* and entry in the land register, January 28–29, 1920), the Treaty of Versailles was already in force. *An opinion must therefore be formed regarding the good faith of the Government of the Reich in the light of the obligations arising out of this*

[15] *Ibid.*, at p. 30. The French text is authoritative.
[16] *Ibid.*, at p. 37.
[17] *Ibid.*, at pp. 37–38.
[18] *Ibid.*, at p. 38.

Treaty, and not on the basis of other international agreements—such as for instance the Geneva Convention—which did not exist at that date and the conclusion of which could not even be foreseen. Now, under the Treaty of Versailles, Germany could only foresee two possibilities, either that Poland would claim the factory as Reich property, or that she would claim the right to liquidate it as belonging to a company controlled by German nationals, such as the Oberschlesische. The advantage for Poland of the former alternative over the latter would have consisted in the possibility of directly acquiring the ownership under Article 256, at a price to be fixed by the Reparation Commission instead of obtaining it by application of the liquidation procedure referred to in Article 297. This difference, however, cannot suffice to justify the view that the alienation was contrary to the obligations arising under the Treaty of Versailles and that it was even null and void or contrary to the principles of good faith." [19]

This case, and especially the last quotation from the judgment, shows the intimate, one might almost say the intricate, interdependence of a State's rights and obligations, established by the principle of good faith. On the one hand, there was the undoubted right of Germany to dispose of her property in the plebiscite area until the actual transfer of sovereignty. On the other, there were the obligations assumed by Germany under the Treaty of Versailles. These obligations did not prohibit Germany from alienating her property. With the assumption of these obligations, however, the right of disposition implicitly suffered certain restrictions. It could no longer be exercised at will. While the bona fide exercise of the right would be compatible with Germany's treaty obligations, its exercise contrary to the principle of good faith would constitute an abuse of right and a breach of these obligations, *i.e.*, an unlawful act. In such cases, in deciding whether or not the right was exercised in good faith, an international tribunal must examine whether the exercise of the right was in pursuit of the legitimate interests protected by it [20] and whether, in the light of the obligations assumed by the State, the exercise of

[19] *Ibid.*, at pp. 38–39. Italics added.

[20] It must be remembered that, in this case, the right of disposition is merely an attribute of the right of ownership, which determines the object of the right.

the right was calculated to prejudice the rights and legitimate interests of the other party under the Treaty.

In this way, the principle of good faith governing the exercise of rights, sometimes called the theory of abuse of rights, while protecting the legitimate interests of the owner of the right, imposes such limitations upon the right as will render its exercise compatible with that party's treaty obligations, or, in other words, with the legitimate interests of the other contracting party. Thus a fair balance is kept between the respective interests of the parties and a line is drawn delimiting their respective rights. Any overstepping of this line by a party in the exercise of his right would constitute a breach of good faith, an abuse of right, and a violation of his obligation.

II. RIGHTS AND OBLIGATIONS UNDER GENERAL INTERNATIONAL LAW

The Mexican-United States General Claims Commission (1923) in the *North American Dredging Co. of Texas Case* (1926) said:—

"If it were necessary to demonstrate how legitimate are the fears of certain nations with respect to abuses of the right of protection and how seriously the sovereignty of those nations within their own boundaries would be impaired if some extreme conceptions of this right were recognised and enforced, the present case would furnish an illuminating example." [21]

Speaking of the "world-wide abuses either of the right of national protection or of the right of national jurisdiction," the Commission declared:—

"The present stage of international law imposes upon every international tribunal the solemn duty of seeking for a proper and adequate balance between the sovereign right of national jurisdiction, on the one hand, and the sovereign right of national protection of citizens on the other. No international tribunal should or may evade the task of *finding such limitations of both rights as will render them compatible with the general rules and principles of international law.*" [22]

[21] *Op. of Com. 1927*, p. 21, at p. 29.
[22] *Ibid.*, at p. 23. Italics added.

This approach to the problem of the limitation of rights clearly shows that what has so far been said regarding the interdependence of rights and obligations applies not only to treaty obligations but also to obligations derived from the general law. Every right is subject to such limitations as are necessary to render it compatible both with a party's contractual obligations and with his obligations under the general law.

This process of adjusting the rights and obligations of a State may also be illustrated by the Trail Smelter Arbitration (1935). In this case, there was, on the one hand, the right of a State to make use of its own territory, and, on the other hand, the duty of a State at all times "to protect other States against injurious acts by individuals from within its jurisdiction." [23] Taking into account the conflicting interests at stake [24] and analogous cases in municipal law,[25] the Arbitral Tribunal arrived at the conclusion that:—

> "No State has the right to use or permit the use of its territory in such a manner as to cause injury by fumes in or to the territory of another or the properties or persons therein, when the case is of serious consequence and the injury is established by clear and convincing evidence." [26]

Thus, instead of recognising and enforcing some extreme views concerning the use of territory, the Tribunal struck a proper balance between a State's rights and obligations. Any overstepping of this limit would constitute an abuse of right, a violation of the obligation to protect other States from injuries emanating from its territory and an unlawful act.

The recognition of the interdependence of a person's rights and obligations is one of the most important features of the principle of good faith governing the exercise of rights. The rights enjoyed by a person become correlated with his obligations. Generally, each right suffers such limitations as would render its exercise compatible with the obligations arising from the general rules and principles of the legal order. Its limits vary, therefore, with the changing contents of these rules and

[23] *Award II* (1941), 3 UNRIAA, p. 1905, at p. 1963.
[24] *Cf. ibid.*, at pp. 1938, 1939.
[25] *Ibid.*, at pp. 1963 *et seq.*
[26] *Ibid.*, at p. 1965.

principles. As a society becomes more integrated more obligations are laid upon its members and the rights of each subject of law become also more restricted. Whenever the owner of the right contracts additional obligations, these place further limitations upon its exercise, even though this may not be expressly laid down. The right may no longer be exercised in a manner incompatible with the bona fide performance of these obligations. Hence the exact limits of a right may differ from person to person, according to the amount and contents of each person's obligations. In this sense, rights can no longer be regarded as absolute,[27] but are essentially relative.[28]

Good faith in the exercise of rights, in this connection, means that a State's rights must be exercised in a manner compatible with its various obligations arising either from treaties or from the general law. It follows from this interdependence of rights and obligations that rights must be reasonably exercised. The reasonable and bona fide exercise of a right implies an exercise which is genuinely in pursuit of those interests which the right is destined to protect and which

[27] *Cf. North American Dredging Co. of Texas Case* (1926), *Op. of Com. 1927*, p. 21 at p. 26. What the Commission here wished to refute appears to be not so much the law of nature, but the view that certain rights are "inalienable," or "uncurtailable."

[28] *Cf.* ICJ: *Admission of a State to the U.N.* (1948) Adv.Op., Ind.Op. by Azevedo, *ICJ Reports, 1947–1948*, p. 57, at p. 79. See also p. 80. It is believed, however, that the learned judge used the term "relativity of rights" in the sense generally employed by writers, *i.e.*, rights must be exercised in conformity with the social purpose of the rule of law which creates them. (See, *e.g.*, L. Josserand, *De l'esprit des lois et de leur relativité; Théorie de l'abus de droit*, 1927).

Among international publicists, the view is quite widely held that an abuse of right is an anti-social exercise of the right. See *e.g.*, Politis, "Le problème des limitations de la souveraineté et la théorie de l'abus des droits dans les rapports internationaux," 6 *Recueil La Haye* (1925), p. 1, at p. 81 *et passim*, and following him, Lauterpacht, *The Function of Law in the International Community*, 1933, pp. 286 *et seq.* T. Selea, in his *La notion de l'abus du droit dans le droit international*, 1940, though in substance following closely the above-cited work of Politis, went further and considered as an abuse of right any exercise of a right which deviates from the social function or social purpose of the right (pp. 57 *et seq.*, 101 *et seq.*, 177). This, however, is going too far. Money thrown into the sea would presumably not be fulfilling its destined social function, but it is doubtful whether a State acting in this way would be legally chargeable with an abuse of right. The functional criterion is above all inadequate. It affords no juridical explanation why an unsocial or anti-social exercise of a right is unlawful. It fails completely to explain such cases of abuse of right as those envisaged by the *German Interests Case* (Merits) (1926) and the *Free Zones Case* (Jgt.) (1932). The correlation is, therefore, in the writer's opinion, between a person's rights and his obligations, and not between rights and the public interest. The existence of the obligation explains the illegality of the abusive exercise of the right.

is not calculated to cause any unfair prejudice to the legitimate interests of another State, whether these interests be secured by treaty or by general international law. The exact line dividing the right from the obligation, or, in other words, the line delimiting the rights of both parties is traced at a point where there is a reasonable balance between the conflicting interests involved. This becomes the limit between the right and the obligation, and constitutes, in effect, the limit between the respective rights of the parties. The protection of the law extends as far as this limit, which is the more often undefined save by the principle of good faith. Any violation of this limit constitutes an abuse of right and a breach of the obligation—an unlawful act. In this way, the principle of good faith, by recognising their interdependence, harmonises the rights and obligations of every person, as well as all the rights and obligations within the legal order as a whole.

D. Abuse of Discretion

In the complexities of human society, either of individuals or of nations, law cannot precisely delimit every right in advance. Certain rights may indeed be rigidly circumscribed, as, for instance, the right of self-defence in the territory of a friendly State. This right is limited to the taking of the only available means of self-defence imperatively demanded by the circumstances.[29] But, in a great number of cases, the law allows the individual or the State a wide discretion in the exercise of a right. Thus we have seen, when examining the principle of self-preservation, that the State enjoys a wide discretion in the exercise of its right of expropriation and requisition, its right to admit and expel aliens, and, generally speaking, all its rights of self-preservation in territory subject to its authority. This discretion extends to the determination of the nature, extent and duration of the State's requirements and the methods best calculated to meet the various contingencies.[30]

But wherever the law leaves a matter to the judgment of the person exercising the right, this discretion must be exercised in good faith, and the law will intervene in all cases where this

[29] *Supra*, pp. 83 *et seq.*
[30] See *supra*, pp. 67–68, and references therein.

discretion is abused.[31] As Judge Azevedo said in one of his individual opinions:—

"Any legal system involves limitations and is founded on definite rules which are always ready to reappear as the constant element of the construction, whenever the field of action of discretionary principles, adopted in exceptional circumstances, is overstepped. This is a long-established principle, and has served, during centuries, to limit the scope of the principle of *qui suo jure utitur neminem laedit.*" [32]

Thus in cases concerning the expulsion of aliens, an international tribunal would normally accept as conclusive the reasons of a serious nature adduced by the State as justifying such action.[33] It would, however, regard as unlawful measures of expulsion those which are arbitrary,[34] or accompanied by unnecessary hardship.[35] Where private property is taken for public use, although it is primarily for the State to decide what are its needs, as well as their extent and duration,[36] international tribunals would intervene when the need is plainly not one of a public character,[37] or when the property is retained clearly beyond the time required by the public need.[38] Furthermore, while it is left to the State conducting military operations to determine what are military necessities, international tribunals are entitled to intervene in cases of manifest abuse of this discretion, causing wanton destruction or injury.[39] Again, while a State taking reprisals against another is not bound to relate its measures closely to the offence,[40] it has been held that "reprisals out of all proportion to the act which had prompted them ought certainly to be considered as excessive and hence unlawful." [41]

Whenever, therefore, the owner of a right enjoys a certain discretionary power, this must be exercised in good faith, which

[31] See *supra*, p. 68, and references therein.
[32] ICJ: *Admission of a State to the U.N.* (1948), Adv.Op., *ICJ Reports, 1947–1948*, p. 57, at p. 80.
[33] *Supra*, pp. 34–35.
[34] *Supra*, p. 35, note 9, and p. 36.
[35] *Supra*, p. 36.
[36] *Supra*, pp. 39, 40–41, 43–45.
[37] *Supra*, p. 39.
[38] *Supra*, p. 44.
[39] *Supra*, pp. 65 *et seq.*
[40] *Supra*, p. 98.
[41] *Supra*, p. 98.

means that it must be exercised reasonably, honestly, in conformity with the spirit of the law and with due regard to the interests of others. But since discretion implies subjective judgment, it is often difficult to determine categorically that the discretion has been abused. Each case must be judged according to its particular circumstances by looking either at the intention or motive of the doer or the objective result of the act, in the light of international practice and human experience. When either an unlawful intention or design can be established, or the act is clearly unreasonable,[42] there is an abuse prohibited by law.

In some cases, however, the existence of an abuse is particularly difficult to determine. This is well illustrated by the case contemplated in the first Advisory Opinion delivered by the International Court of Justice. The question put to the Court was whether a member of the United Nations which was called upon, in virtue of Article 4 of the Charter, to vote, either in the Security Council or in the General Assembly, on the admission of a State to membership in the United Nations, was juridically entitled to make its consent to the admission dependent on conditions not expressly provided by paragraph I of the said Article. A majority of nine judges considered that the conditions laid down in Article 4 I of the Charter were the only conditions to be taken into account,[43] while a minority of six considered that these were merely the indispensable conditions of admission.[44] In determining whether or not a particular condition is fulfilled by an applicant, the State which is called upon to vote naturally enjoys freedom of judgment. But it follows from the above Advisory Opinion that, in the view of the Court, this freedom is to be exercised within the scope of the prescribed conditions of Article 4 I, while in the opinion of the dissenting Judges this freedom is not so circumscribed,

[42] See also the application of the test of " reasonableness " and " moderation " by the I.C.J. in the *Anglo-Norwegian Fisheries Case* (1951) in determining whether Norway committed a " manifest abuse " in delimiting the base line of the Lopphavet Basin (*ICJ Reports, 1951*, p. 116, at pp. 141–142; *cf.* pp. 150. 153, 156, 167 *et seq.*) See also ICJ: *United States Nationals in Morocco Case* (1952), *ICJ Reports, 1952*, p. 176, at p. 212.

[43] *Admission of a State to the U.N.* (1948), Adv.Op., *ICJ Reports 1947–1948*, p. 57, at p. 65.

[44] *Ibid.*, at pp. 90, 104, 109 *et seq.*

but may be exercised within the general purposes and principles of the Charter of the United Nations.[45]

But, as was pointed out by some of the dissenting Judges, however circumscribed, the exercise of this discretion is extremely difficult, if not impossible, to control.[46] For the only result of its exercise is a vote of "yes" or "no," and there is no rule of law which obliges a member, in casting his vote, to give his reasons. Even if the reasons may be gathered from the discussions preceding the vote, a member might change his views between the time of the discussions and the time of the vote. Furthermore, whatever juridical limits may have been set to the type of consideration that may be taken into account, there is no means of verifying whether the reasons advanced during the discussion are genuine and decisive, and, even if they are, whether they are the exclusive ones. As one of the Judges said in an individual opinion "all kinds of prejudices, and even physical repugnance will find a way of influencing the decision, either by an act of the will or even through the action of the subconscious." [47]

It is especially on account of this difficulty of controlling the exercise of discretionary powers that the Judges, whether they were of the opinion that the discretion should be exercised within the limits of Article 4 I or within the wider limits of the general purposes and principles of the United Nations Charter, all agreed in stressing that the discretion inherent in the right to vote must be exercised in good faith.[48] Good faith in the exercise of the discretionary power inherent in a right seems thus to imply a genuine disposition on the part of the owner of the right to use the discretion in a reasonable, honest and sincere manner in conformity with the spirit and purpose, as well as the letter, of the law. It may also be called a spontaneous sense of duty scrupulously to observe the law. In this present case, there is practically no means of controlling the exercise of the discretion. It is, therefore, essential that it should be possible to place reliance on the State's own sense of respect for the law.

[45] *Ibid.*, at pp. 91–2, 93, 103, 115.
[46] *Ibid.*, at pp. 102 *et seq.*, 111 *et seq.*
[47] Judge Azevedo, *ibid.*, at p. 78.
[48] *Ibid.*, at pp. 63, 71, 79 *et seq.*, 91, 92, 93, 103, 115.

The present instance clearly shows how important, and indeed how indispensable, it is to any legal system for the discretionary power inherent in every right to be exercised in good faith.[49] For, unless this discretion is normally exercised by every subject of law spontaneously in a bona fide manner well within the limit beyond which the exercise may be regarded as an abuse, even if the law is able ultimately to prevent certain manifest abuses, the legal system will be strained to breaking point.

In the preceding pages we have seen the various ways in which the principle of good faith governs the exercise of rights. Where the right confers upon its owner a discretionary power, this must be exercised honestly, sincerely, reasonably, in conformity with the spirit of the law and with due regard to the interests of others. All rights have to be exercised reasonably and in a manner compatible with both the contractual obligations of the party exercising them and the general rules and principles of the legal order. They must not be exercised fictitiously so as to evade such obligations or rules of law, or maliciously so as to injure others. Violations of these requirements of the principle of good faith constitute abuses of right, prohibited by law. It follows, however, from the general presumption of good faith that abuses of right cannot be presumed.[50]

The importance of the principle of good faith governing the exercise of rights naturally goes beyond the prohibition of abuses. In recognising the interdependence of rights and obligations, it reconciles conflicting interests, establishes the proper limits of rights, and secures harmony in the legal order. By infusing such qualities as honesty, sincerity, reasonableness and moderation into the exercise of rights, it promotes the smooth and proper functioning of the legal system.

[49] See also ICJ: *United States Nationals in Morocco Case* (1952), *ICJ Reports, 1952*, p. 176, at pp. 207–212, especially p. 212.

[50] PCIJ: *German Interests Case* (Merits) (1926), A. 7, p. 30; *Id.*: *Free Zones Case* (Second Phase: Order) (1930), A. 24, p. 12; Same Case (Jgt.) (1932), A/B 46, p. 167.

CHAPTER 5

OTHER APPLICATIONS OF THE PRINCIPLE

A. Duty to Notify a Change in Policy

ORDINARILY, a State is free to pursue its own policy, domestic and foreign, and to alter it as it deems fit. In certain circumstances, however, a State may be obliged by the principle of good faith to notify another of a proposed change in policy.

With regard to good faith in treaty relations,[1] it has already been seen how very far the principle of good faith protects the confidence that one nation may reasonably place in the promise of another. The protection of good faith extends equally to the confidence and reliance that can reasonably be placed not only in agreements but also in communications or other conclusive acts from another State. If State A has knowingly led State B to believe that it will pursue a certain policy, and State B acts upon this belief, as soon as State A decides to change its policy—although it is at perfect liberty to do so—it is under a duty to inform State B of this proposed change. Failure to do so, when it knows or should have known that State B would continue to act upon this belief, gives rise to a duty to indemnify State B for any damage it may incur. What the principle of good faith protects is the confidence that State B may reasonably place in State A. Therefore, once State B has learned of the altered circumstances—it matters not from what source—it can no longer claim indemnification for any further losses it may incur; for, being in possession of the facts, it is no longer acting under an erroneous belief and its continued reliance upon the previous communication from State A is no longer justified.

In the "*Blockade*" *of Portendic Case* (1843) between Great Britain and France,[2] the French Minister of Marine and Colonies had informed the British Ambassador, some ten months

[1] *Supra*, pp. 106 *et seq.*
[2] See 42 B.F.S.P., pp. 1377–1378; 23 *ibid.*, pp. 543–588; 27 *ibid.*, pp. 1228–1299; 30 *ibid.*, pp. 581–649; 34 *ibid.*, pp. 1036–1108. See also *supra*, p. 30.

prior to the closure (called a blockade) of Portendic, that no intention existed to close that port. The operative part of the Award reads as follows:—

"We are of the opinion that France should indemnify the claimants for damages and losses to which they would not have been exposed if the said Government, in sending the Governor of Senegal the order to establish the blockade, had simultaneously notified the British Government of this measure; that France, on the other hand, notwithstanding the failure to send this official notification of the blockade, owes no indemnity to those claimants who had incurred losses in their commercial pursuits after they had positively learned, from other sources, of the establishment of the blockade of Portendic, or at least, after they could have been informed of it as a result of authentic news received by the British Government from any of its agents in Africa." [3]

This decision corresponds with the main British argument in the case:—

"The Minister of Marine may not be able to engage his Government as to what it will do, but he may be perfectly able to say what that Government, in the department over which he presides, is not going to do. There is not (precisely speaking) an engagement in this case, but there is a confidential communication, which communication, in all good faith, is to be believed, until otherwise explained or contradicted.

"The undersigned, therefore, still affirm, that where a Minister of the French Government has made an official communication, relative to his own department, the Government of Great Britain is justified by all the rules and constant usage subsisting in the intercourse between civilised nations, to give trust and confidence to such declaration; and that if the French Government should think fit, afterwards, to act contrary to the assurances of its own official organ, that then, in common justice, the British Government have a fair right to expect the earliest communication of such intention.

"It is quite obvious, that unless these principles be rigidly adhered to, the ordinary intercourse between two nations must be exposed to difficulties and impediments, equally destructive to the interests of both." [4]

[3] 42 *ibid.*, p. 1378. (Transl.)

[4] 30 B.F.S.P., p. 619, at p. 641. Appendix to the British *Statement* (34 *ibid.*, pp. 1071 *et seq.*, see p. 1076). *Cf.* Ven.-U.S. Cl.Com (1885): *Gowen and Copeland Case*, 4 *Int.Arb.*, p. 3354, at pp. 3358–9.

Attention may be drawn to the following points:—

1. The communication or assurance in the first instance must have emanated from an official of the State acting in his official capacity. In other words, it must be imputable to the State.[5]

2. The assurance in no way affects the validity or legality of the decision to act otherwise. In the above case, the British member of the Mixed Commission of Liquidation, established after the arbitration, reported to the Earl of Aberdeen that: "The inference is irresistible, that, in the opinion of the Royal Arbitrator, the blockade was, under the peculiar circumstances, justifiable." [6]

3. The assurance gives rise to a duty to notify the other State of any impending change in policy. The duty, however, only requires the information to be given at the earliest possible moment. Thus the claims in respect of the first two ships to be affected by the closure (the *Meta* and the *Marmion*) were not allowed, because these ships had actually set sail for Africa before the French Government decided to close the port and sent out instructions accordingly, and could not therefore have been warned in time in any event.[7]

4. As has already been indicated, the object of the protection in such a case is the trust and confidence that a State may reasonably place in the word of another. Indeed, it is one of the most important aspects of the principle of good faith that promises and assurances should be faithfully adhered to so

[5] See *infra*, p. 199, note 25. *Cf.* Mex.-U.S. Special Cl.Com. (1923): *Santa Isabel Cases* (1926) *Op. of Com. 1926–1931*, p. 1, see pp. 12 *et seq.*; *cf.* p. 26. The declaration by the Commander-in-Chief of a country at an unofficial banquet to the effect that conditions of the country were safe for foreigners to return and bidding them to do so can not be a ground of State responsibility, if, after their return, these foreigners are attacked by bandits or revolutionaries.

[6] 34 B.F.S.P., p. 1088, at p. 1102 (Oct. 9, 1844).

[7] *Ibid.*, p. 1095, at p. 1103. The exclusion of these two ships from indemnity lends further support to what is submitted to be the *ratio decidendi* of the decision, and tends to discredit the view that it was based simply upon France's failure to notify the closure (see 1 *Arb.Int.*, p. 512, at pp. 539, *et seq.*; 2 *ibid.*, p. 665). Furthermore, Great Britain herself admitted that an emergency might justify a blockade on the spot (30 B.F.S.P., p. 612), the establishment of which could not possibly be previously notified. It is submitted, therefore, that the "*Blockade*" *of Portendic Case* (1843) is perfectly reconcilable with the *Closure of Buenos-Aires Case* (1870), G.B./Argentina (2 *Arb.Int.*, p. 637), where notification was held to be unnecessary. Since Great Britain did not invoke the case of 1843 before the arbitrator in the arbitration of 1870, it would seem that she was also of the same opinion.

that the trust that others may reasonably place in them shall not be betrayed. This is probably the most prominent feature of the Germanic conception of good faith: *Treu und Glauben.*

B. Duty to Maintain the Status Quo

In a previous Chapter mention was made of the duty of the parties to a treaty which is *sub spe rati* to refrain from any act which may prejudice the eventual execution of the treaty.[8] A similar duty is that of the parties to a judicial process.

> "Parties to a case must abstain from any measure capable of exercising a prejudicial effect in regard to the execution of the decision to be given and, in general, not to allow any step of any kind to be taken which might aggravate or extend the dispute."[9]

The provisions in the Statute and in the Rules of the World Court which permit it to "indicate" interim measures of protection[10] are, in the opinion of the Permanent Court, but an application of this principle "universally accepted by international tribunals."[11]

There are other circumstances in which States are required by the principle of good faith to maintain the *status quo* during a period between two events. The Arbitrator in the *Samoa Claims Case* (Preliminary Decision) (1902) had occasion to consider a situation of this nature. At the time in question, there were two contending parties in Samoa, the Mataafans and the Malietoans. On December 31, 1898, the Chief Justice of Samoa, in a decision, declared Malietoa Tanumafili King of Samoa. The parties to the dispute submitted to arbitration were Germany on the one hand and the United Kingdom and the United States on the other, *i.e.*, the three treaty Powers in Samoa. The question at issue was the legality of certain military measures taken unilaterally by the United Kingdom

[8] *Supra*, pp. 109 *et seq.*

[9] PCIJ: *Electricity Company of Sofia and Bulgaria Case* (Interim Protection) (1939), A/B. 79, p. 199. See also *Id.*: *South Eastern Greenland Case* (Order of August 3, 1932), A/B. 48, pp. 287 *et seq.*; ICJ: *Anglo-Iranian Oil Co. Case* (Interim Protection) (1951), *ICJ Reports 1951*, p. 89.

[10] ICJ (also PCIJ): Statute, Art. 41; Rules, Art. 61. See *infra*, p. 268.

[11] *Electricity Company of Sofia and Bulgaria Case* (Interim Protection), (1939), *loc. cit.*, p. 199. See *infra*, pp. 267 *et seq.*

and the United States in support of the Malietoans against the Mataafans in March, 1899. Beside finding that the three treaty Powers should always act in common accord, the Arbitrator held:—

"Furthermore, by proclamation issued on the 4th of January, 1899, the Consular representatives of the treaty powers in Samoa, owing to the then disturbed state of affairs and to the urgent necessity to establish a strong provisional government, recognised the Mataafa party, represented by the High Chief Mataafa and 13 of his chiefs, to be the provisional government of Samoa pending instruction from the three treaty powers, and thus *those powers were bound upon principles of international good faith to maintain the situation* thereby created until by common accord they had otherwise decided . . .

". . . That being so, the military action in question undertaken by the British and American military authorities before the arrival of the instructions mentioned in the proclamation, and tending to overthrow the provisional government thereby established, was contrary to the aforesaid obligation." [12]

The military measures were, therefore, considered unlawful, and the United Kingdom and the United States were held liable for their consequences.

It would appear from the cases just considered that whenever the parties have agreed to await a final decision concerning a certain matter, or are under an obligation to do so—a decision depending either upon the parties themselves or upon an independent third party—the principle of good faith obliges them to maintain the existing situation as far as possible so that the final decision, if taken on the basis of the *status quo*, would not be prejudiced in its effects by a unilateral act of one of the parties during the inevitable lapse of time.

C. Allegans Contraria Non Est Audiendus

It is a principle of good faith that "a man shall not be allowed to blow hot and cold—to affirm at one time and deny at another. . . . Such a principle has its basis in common sense and common justice, and whether it is called 'estoppel,' or by

[12] U.S.F.R. (1902), p. 444, at p. 446. Italics added.

any other name, it is one which courts of law have in modern times most usefully adopted." [13]

In the international sphere, this principle has been applied in a variety of cases. In the case of *The Lisman* (1937), concerning an American vessel which was seized in London in June, 1915, the claimant's original contention before the British prize court "was not that there was not reasonable cause for seizure, or for requiring the goods to be discharged, but that there was undue delay on the part of the Crown in taking the steps they were entitled to take as belligerents." [14] In a subsequent arbitration in 1937, which took the place of diplomatic claims by the United States against Great Britain, the sole Arbitrator held that:—

"By the position he deliberately took in the British Prize Court, that the seizure of the goods and the detention of the ship were lawful, and that he did not complain of them, but only of undue delay from the failure of the Government to act promptly, *claimant affirmed what he now denies, and thereby prevented himself from recovering there or here upon the claim he now stands on*, that these acts were unlawful, and constitute the basis of his claim." [15]

This principle has also been applied to admissions relating to the existence of rules of international law. Thus in the case of *The Mechanic* (C. 1862), it was held that:—

"Ecuador . . . having fully recognised and claimed the principle on which the case now before us turns, whenever from such a recognition rights or advantages were to be derived, could not in honour and good faith deny the principle when it imposed an obligation." [16]

In the *Meuse Case* (1937), it was held that, where two States were bound by the same treaty obligations, State A could not complain of an act by State B of which it itself had set an example in the past.[17] Nor indeed may a State, while denying

[13] England, Court of Exchequer: *Cave* v. *Mills* (1862) 7 Hurlstone & Norman, p. 913, at p. 927.

[14] 3 UNRIAA, p. 1767, at p. 1779.

[15] *Ibid.*, at p. 1790.

[16] Ecua.-U.S. Cl.Com. (1862): *Atlantic and Hope Insurance Companies (The Mechanic) Case*, 3 *Int.Arb.*, p. 3221, at p. 3226.

[17] PCIJ: A/B. 70, p. 25. *Cf.* also the apparently contradictory attitude of the Netherlands in the same case as to whether the *possibility* of an infraction constitutes an infraction (pp. 5 and 8) and the Dutch explanation (Ser. C. 81, pp. 137 *et seq.*).

that a certain treaty is applicable to the case, contend at the same time that the other party in regard to the matter in dispute has not complied with certain provisions of that treaty.[18]

This principle was also applied by the German-United States Mixed Claims Commission (1922) in the *Life-Insurance Claims Case* (1924) to preclude a State from asserting claims which, on general principles of law, its own courts would not admit, for instance, claims involving damages which its own municipal courts, in similar cases, would consider too remote.[19] Incidentally, this case also shows one of the means whereby general principles of law find their application in the international sphere. A State may not disregard such principles as it recognises in its own municipal system, except of course where there is a rule of international law to the contrary.

In the *Shufeldt Case* (1930), the United States contended that Guatemala, having for six years recognised the validity of the claimant's contract, and received all the benefits to which she was entitled thereunder, and having allowed Shufeldt to continue to spend money on the concession, was precluded from denying its validity, even if the contract had not received the necessary approval of the Guatemalan legislature.[20] The Arbitrator held the contention to be "sound and in keeping with the principles of international law." [21]

This case is a clear application in the international sphere of the principle known in Anglo-Saxon jurisprudence as estoppel in pais or equitable estoppel, the application of which was also considered in the *Serbian Loans Case* (1929) and in the *Aguilar-Amory and Royal Bank of Canada (Tinoco) Case* (1923). It appears, from the discussion of this principle in the last two mentioned cases, that it precludes person A from averring a particular state of things against person B if A had previously, by words or conduct, unambiguously represented to B the existence of a different state of things, and if, on the faith of that representation, B had so altered his position that the

[18] PCIJ: *Mavrommatis Palestine Concessions Case* (1924), A. 2, p. 33. *Id.*: *Chorzów Factory Case* (Jd.) (1927), A. 9, p. 31.

[19] *Dec. & Op.*, p. 103, at p. 139. *Id.*: *Hickson Case* (1924), *ibid.*, p. 439, at p. 443.

[20] See *Case of the U.S.*, Part II, Point II (*Shufeldt Claim*, USGPO, 1932, pp. 57 *et seq.*).

[21] *Ibid.*, at pp. 869–70; or 2 UNRIAA, p. 1079, at p. 1094.

establishment of the truth would injure him.[22] An intent to deceive or defraud is, however, not necessary. The principle is yet another instance of the protection which law accords to the faith and confidence that a party may reasonably place in another, which, as mentioned before, constitutes one of the most important aspects of the principle of good faith.

In its Advisory Opinion No. 14, the Permanent Court of International Justice was of the opinion that where States, acting under a multipartite convention, to which they are all parties, have concluded certain arrangements, they cannot, as between themselves, contend that some of the provisions in the latter are void as being outside the mandate conferred by the previous convention.[23]

The principle applies equally, though perhaps not with the same force, to other admissions of a State which do not give rise to an equitable estoppel. Thus it has been held that a State cannot be heard to repudiate liability for a collision after its authorities on the spot had at the time admitted liability and sought throughout to make the most advantageous arrangements for the Government under the circumstances.[24] Again, if a State, having been fully informed of the circumstances, has accepted a person's claim to the ownership of certain property and entered into negotiation with him for its purchase, it becomes "very difficult, if not impossible" for that State subsequently to allege that he had no title at the time.[25] If a State, which is

[22] PCIJ: *Serbian Loans Case* (1929), A. 20/21, pp. 38–39. *Aguilar-Amory and Royal Bank of Canada (Tinoco) Case* (1923), 1 UNRIAA, p. 369, at pp. 383–4. See also *Shufeldt Case* (1930), *Case of the U.S.*, Part II, Point II (*loc. cit.*) and the definition of estoppel by conduct of Lord Denman C.J. in *Pickard* v. *Sears* (1837) (6 Ad. & E., p. 469, at p. 474) therein cited.

See further Halsbury, *Laws of England*, *sub voce* Estoppel, §§ 538, 541, 547; Phipson, *The Law of Evidence*, 1952, pp. 704–710; Broom's *Legal Maxims*, 1939; M. Cababe, *Principles of Estoppel*, 1888; L. F. Everest and E. Strode, *Law of Estoppel*, 1923.

[23] *European Danube Commission* (1927), B. 14, p. 23.

See also *Costa Rica–Nicaragua Boundary Case* (1888), 2 *Int.Arb.*, p. 1945, at p. 1961.

[24] Brit.-U.S. Cl.Arb. (1910): *The Eastry* (1914), Nielson's *Report*, p. 499. See also *Id.*: *The Kate* (1921), *ibid.*, p. 472, *The Lindisfarne* (1913), *ibid.*, 483. *Cf.* Art. 2 of the Terms of Submission, *ibid.*, p. 9. Mex.-U.S. Cl.Com. (1868): *Hammaken Case*, 4 *Int.Arb.*, p. 3470, at p. 3471.

Cf. decisions of the Granadine-U.S. Cl.Com. (1857): "*Panama Riots Cases*" (2 *Int.Arb.*, p. 1361) with *U.S. and Paraguay Navigation Co. Case* (1860) (*ibid.*, 1485) as to whether the agreement to submit claims to arbitration is an admission of liability.

[25] Brit.-U.S. Cl.Arb. (1910): *Union Bridge Co. Case* (1924), Nielsen's *Report*, p. 371, at p. 378.

the lessee of a property owned by two joint owners, has, after the death of one of them, paid the entire rent to the other, who claims to have become the sole owner, " this act can not be interpreted otherwise than as a recognition by the authorities of the fact that the right of ownership of Hassar [the deceased] has passed to Rzini [the claimant]." [26] Where a party negotiates for the sublease of a concession granted by a State, it thereby recognises the validity of the concession and the right of the State to grant it.[27] Again, if a State in the past had dealings with the inhabitants of a certain territory only through, and in the presence of, the representative of another State [28] or if it has applied to that other State for protection against the molestations of its interests or those of its nationals in that territory by the acts of a third State,[29] it should not dispute a claim to jurisdiction over the territory in question advanced by the other State. In the *Eastern Greenland Case* (1933), the Permanent Court of International Justice held that:—

> " Norway reaffirmed that she recognised the whole of Greenland as Danish; and thereby she has debarred herself from contesting Danish sovereignty over the whole of Greenland." [30]

[26] Spanish Zone of Morocco Claims (1923): *Claims Nos. 18–20* (1924), 2 UNRIAA, p. 685, at p. 686. (Transl.) The recognition was considered as sufficient evidence to establish ownership over the whole property, for the purpose of the particular case, but it was not regarded as irrebuttable. The question of ownership being merely incidental, the *Rapporteur* made a reservation with regard to the case where the claimant should be evicted from the property by a competent tribunal (see *infra*, p. 354, note 63).

[27] U.S.-Ven. Cl.Com. (1885): *Gowen and Copeland Case*, 4 *Int.Arb.*, p. 3354, at p. 3357.

[28] *Dutch and French Boundary Dispute concerning Guiana* (1891), 5 *Int.Arb.*, p. 4869, at p. 4870.

[29] P.C.A.: *North Atlantic Coast Fisheries Case* (1910), 1 H.C.R., p. 141, at p. 186.

[30] A/B. 53, pp. 68–9. The various acts constituting admissions and their reaffirmations were, in this case:—

1. The formal withdrawal of a claim over the contested territory and the statement that it was lost to Norway (Holst Declaration) (pp. 64–6).

2. During a previous mediation in the matter between the Kingdom of Sweden and Norway on the one hand, and Denmark on the other, the Foreign Minister of the former mentioned in two different communications to the mediator that his sovereign on behalf of Norway renounced all claims to Greenland in favour of the Crown of Denmark (p. 66).

3. The Convention of Sept. 1, 1819, signed by the King of Sweden and Norway in his capacity as King of Norway, and the King of Denmark expressly stated that " everything in connection with the Treaty of Kiel " of 1814, which inter alia reserved Greenland to Denmark, was to be regarded as completely settled (pp. 66–8).

4. Norway reaffirmed her previous admissions by affixing her signature to, and accepting as binding upon herself, bipartite agreements between Norway and Denmark, and various other multipartite agreements to which both Denmark and Norway were parties, in which Greenland was described as a Danish colony or as forming part of Denmark, or Denmark was allowed to exclude Greenland from the operation of the agreements (pp. 68–9).

In the *Anglo-Norwegian Fisheries Case* (1951), the International Court of Justice went further and considered that the " prolonged abstention " of the United Kingdom from protesting against the Norwegian system of straight base lines in delimiting territorial waters was one of the factors which, together with " the notoriety of the facts, the general toleration of the international community, Great Britain's position in the North Sea, her own interest in the question, and her prolonged abstention would in any case warrant Norway's enforcement of her system against the United Kingdom." [31]

In the same case, however, the International Court of Justice considered that:—

> " Too much importance need not be attached to the few uncertainties or contradictions, real or apparent, which the United Kingdom Government claims to have discovered in Norwegian practice. They may be easily understood in the light of the variety of the facts and conditions prevailing in the long period which has elapsed since 1812, and are not such as to modify the conclusions reached by the Court." [32]

Similarly, in the *Eastern Greenland Case* (1933), the Permanent Court found that, although Denmark, in some of her Notes to foreign powers, seeking their recognition of Danish sovereignty over the whole of Greenland, used the expression " *extension* of Danish sovereignty," she was in reality seeking their recognition of an existing state of things, and held that:—

> " In these circumstances, there can be no ground for holding that, by the attitude which the Danish Government adopted, it admitted that it possessed no sovereignty over the uncolonised part of Greenland, nor for holding that it is estopped [*empêché*] from claiming, as it claims in the present case, that Denmark possesses an old established sovereignty over all Greenland." [33]

31 *ICJ Reports 1951*, p. 116, at p. 139.

32 *Ibid.*, at p. 138. See also ICJ: *United States Nationals in Morocco Case* (1952), *ICJ Reports, 1952*, p. 176, at p. 200: " There are isolated expressions to be found in the diplomatic correspondence which, if considered without regard to their context, might be regarded as acknowledgments of United States claims to exercise consular jurisdiction and other capitulary rights. On the other hand, the Court cannot ignore the general tenor of the correspondence, which indicates that at all times France and the United States were looking for a solution based upon mutual agreement and that neither party intended to concede its legal position."

33 A/B. 53, p. 62 (English text authoritative). See also pp. 54 *et seq.* *Cf.* D.O. by Anzilotti (pp. 82, 94). *Cf.* ICJ: *Asylum Case* (1950), *infra*, p. 300, note 5.

The application of this principle to such cases of admission, sometimes also called " estoppel," or described under the maxim "*non concedit venire contra factum proprium,*" does not, however, have the same effect as an equitable estoppel mentioned earlier in this section. Unlike the latter, an admission does not peremptorily preclude a party from averring the truth. It has rather the effect of an *argumentum ad hominem*, which is directed at a person's sense of consistency, or what in logic is paradoxically called the " principle of contradiction." An admission is not necessarily conclusive as regards the facts admitted. Its force may vary according to the circumstances.

Thus, in the *Salvador Commercial Co. Case* (1902), the Arbitral Tribunal, in dealing with the Salvadorian contention that the Company did not comply with the terms of the concession, held that:—

> " It is of course obvious that the Salvador Government should be estopped from going behind those reports of its own officers on the subject and from attacking their correctness without supplementary evidence tending to show that such reports were induced by mistake or were procured by fraud or undue influence. No evidence of this kind is introduced." [34]

In the *Kling Case* (1930), however, where the United States Government was asserting that a certain occurrence involved the direct responsibility of Mexico, although one of its consuls had previously reported to the State Department that it was an accident, the Mexican-United States General Claims Commission (1923) held the report to be only ordinary evidence and, in this case, being based on scanty information, to be of little value.[35]

In this connection, it may be noted that there is a growing tendency among international tribunals not always to regard the recognition of Governments as an admission of the effective status of a régime, but often as a political act grounded on political considerations. In such a case, the recognition or non-recognition carries little evidential weight in regard to the actual status of the régime.[36] This appears to be the reason

[34] U.S.F.R. (1902), p. 838, at p. 866.

[35] *Op. of Com. 1931*, p. 36, at p. 47.

[36] *Cf. Aguilar-Amory and Royal Bank of Canada (Tinoco) Case*, 2 UNRIAA, p. 369, at p. 381; Mex.-U.S. G.C.C. (1923): *Hopkins Case* (1926, 1927), *Op. of Com. 1927*, pp. 42 and 329, at p. 50. Fran.-Mex. M.C.C. (1924): *Pinson Case* (1928), *Jurisprudence*, p. 1, at p. 106.

why the non-recognition of a Government has been held not to estop a foreign State from subsequently asserting that a régime not recognised by it was the effective Government of a country.[37]

As regards admissions in general, it may be said that they must have been made by responsible agents of the State acting in their official capacity,[38] on behalf of the State.[39] Admissions may be vitiated by duress,[40] excusable error,[41] fraud or undue influence.[42] In the *Serbian Loans Case* (1929), the Permanent Court of International Justice was faced with the plea of admission on the ground that for many years the creditors had accepted payment in paper francs. The Court rejected the

[37] *Aguilar-Amory and Royal Bank of Canada (Tinoco) Case* (1923), *loc. cit.*, p. 384; *Hopkins Case* (1926, 1927), *loc. cit.*, p. 50. *Cf.* also *Pinson Case* (1928), *loc. cit.*, pp. 106–7. In the last mentioned case, the Umpire did not in reality commit himself. See also *infra*, p. 189, note 91.

[38] *Cf.* Brit.-U.S. Cl.Arb. (1910): *The Newchwang* (1921), Nielsen's *Report*, p. 411. A private recommendation by the U.S. Secretary of the Navy to the Chairman of the House of Representatives Committee on Claims expressing views favourable to the claim held not to constitute an admission of liability on the part of the U.S. See *infra*, pp. 200 *et seq.*, 208 *et seq.*

[39] One of the reasons why the Senate of Hamburg, in the *Croft Case* (1856) (2 *Arb.Int.*, pp. 1–37), refused, after much deliberation and hesitation (pp. 21–2), to regard as admissions statements in a Portuguese Government memorial, filed with the Portuguese Council of State, was that the Portuguese Government was only adopting the arguments of the claimants and acting as if it were their counsel (pp. 24–25).

[40] Mex.-U.S. Cl.Com (1868): *Cuculla Case*, 3 *Int.Arb.*, p. 2873. Counsel for the U.S. contended that Mexico should be held responsible to the U.S. for acts of the Zuloaga Government, since she had previously admitted liability to France and England. The U.S. Commissioner held: "These concessions, extorted by a duress as actual and relentless as ever pressed upon an embarrassed and exhausted Government, were made to buy its peace and, rejected by its powerful adversaries, cannot now furnish any assistance to this commission in determining the interesting question presented in this case" (p. 2879).

In the *Croft Case* (1856), the Portuguese pleaded compulsion with regard to certain statements that they had made and the tribunal admitted that these statements were made at the "pressing instances" of the British Government in an attempt to "appease" the latter (*loc cit.*, p. 24).

[41] PCIJ: *Mavrommatis Jerusalem Concessions Case* (1925), A. 5, p. 31. The PCIJ inquired into the question "Whether the fact that M. Mavrommatis is described in the concession as an Ottoman subject, though not invalidating the concession itself, might deprive him of the right to benefit by the terms of Art. 9 of the Protocol"; for Mavrommatis now claimed to be a Greek subject, entitled to the intervention of the Greek Government. But it answered the question in the negative; for it held that the description Ottoman national "was in error set down in the concessionary contracts."

Closure of Buenos-Aires Case (1870), Argentina/G.B., 2 *Arb.Int.*, p. 637. It was considered an excusable error not constituting an admission, the fact that the Argentine Government confirmed the decisions of a mixed commission which wrongly interpreted certain conventions, apparently because the State archives, in which the texts of these conventions were kept, were at that time in the hands of revolutionaries "and it is not surprising that the Commission and the Government did not know the terms of the conventions" (p. 654).

[42] *Salvador Commercial Co. Case* (1902), *loc. cit.* at p. 866. See *supra*, p. 147.

plea on the ground that: "It does not even appear that the bondholders could have effectively asserted their rights earlier than they did, much less that there is any ground for concluding that they deliberately surrendered them."[43] Conduct, in order to constitute an admission, must not, therefore, be due to an impossibility of acting otherwise.

Finally, it should be added that declarations, admissions, or proposals made in the course of negotiations which have not led to an agreement do not constitute admissions which could eventually prejudice the rights of the party making them.[44]

D. Nullus Commodum Capere De Sua Injuria Propria

"No one can be allowed to take advantage of his own wrong," declared the Umpire in *The Montijo Case* (1875).[45]

A State may not invoke its own illegal act to diminish its own liability. Commissioner Pinkney, in *The Betsy Case* (1797), called it "the most exceptionable of all principles, that he who does wrong shall be at liberty to plead his own illegal conduct on other occasions as a partial excuse."[46]

The Permanent Court of International Justice, in its Advisory Opinion No. 15 (1928), said that "Poland could not avail herself of an objection which . . . would amount to relying upon the non-fulfilment of an obligation imposed upon her by an international agreement,"[47] and in the *Chorzów Factory Case* (Jd.) (1927), the Court held:—

"It is, moreover, a principle generally accepted in the jurisprudence of international arbitration, as well as by municipal courts, that one party cannot avail himself of the fact that the other has not fulfilled some obligation or has not had recourse to some means of redress, if the former party has, by some illegal act, prevented the latter from fulfilling the obligation in question, or from having recourse to the tribunal which would have been open, to him."[48]

[43] A. 20/21, p. 39.

[44] PCIJ: *Chorzow Factory Case* (Jd.) (1927), A. 9, p. 19; (Merits) (1928), A. 17, pp. 51, 62. Rum.-Hung. M.A.T.: *Emeric Kulin Case* (Jd.) (1927), 7 T.A.M., p. 138, at p. 149.

[45] 2 *Int.Arb.*, p. 1421, at p. 1437.

[46] Jay Treaty (Art. VII) Arb. (1794): 4 *Int.Adj.*, M.S., p. 179, at p. 277.

[47] PCIJ: *Jurisdiction of the Danzig Courts* (1928), Adv.Op., B. 15, pp. 26–27. Poland could not "contend that the Danzig courts could not apply the provisions of the *Beamtenabkommen* because they were not duly inserted in the Polish national law."

[48] A. 9, p. 31.

The application of this principle is well illustrated by the *Chorzów Factory Case* (Jd.) (1927). The Polish Government had appropriated the Chorzów Factory in virtue of her laws of July 14, 1920, and June 16, 1922, without following the procedure laid down in the Geneva Convention of 1922.[49] As regards procedure, the Convention had provided that no dispossession should take place without prior notice to the real or apparent owner, thus affording him an opportunity of appealing to the Germano-Polish Mixed Arbitral Tribunal (Art. 19). Poland, by failing to follow the procedure laid down in the Geneva Convention, had illegally deprived the other party of the opportunity of appealing to the Mixed Arbitral Tribunal. The Permanent Court held that Poland could not now prevent him, or rather his home State, from applying to the Court, on the ground that the Mixed Arbitral Tribunal was competent and that, since no appeal had been made to that Tribunal, the Convention had not been complied with.[50]

Another instance where the same principle was applied is *The Tattler Case* (1920), where the Tribunal held that:—

"It is difficult to admit that a foreign ship may be seized for not having a certain document when the document has been refused to it by the very authorities who required that it should be obtained."[51]

The refusal was wrongful.

In the *Frances Irene Roberts Case*, the United States-Venezuelan Mixed Claims Commission (1903), in rejecting a plea of prescription in a case which, though diligently prosecuted by the claimants for over 30 years, had not yet been settled, held:—

"The contention that this claim is barred by the lapse of time would, if admitted, allow the Venezuelan Government to reap advantage from its own wrong in failing to make just reparation to Mr. Quirk at the time the claim arose."[52]

No one should be allowed to reap advantages from his own wrong.

The situation is slightly different where a State's acquiescence in a breach of its own law amounts to connivance. In such a

[49] Martens, III (16) N.R.G., p. 645.
[50] *Loc. cit.*, p. 31.
[51] Brit.-U.S. Cl.Arb. (1910): Nielsen's *Report*, p. 489, at p. 493.
[52] *Ven.Arb. 1903*, p. 142, at p. 144. See also Mex.-U.S. G.C.C. (1923): *G. W. Cook Case* (Dock. 663) (1927), *Op. of Com. 1927*, p. 318, at p. 319.

case the State is prevented from invoking the breach to the disadvantage of the other party either to found a right or as a defence.[53]

A fortiori, where a State has directly requested another to do a certain thing it may not subsequently put forward a claim against the latter founded on this very act. Thus, if the President of a State has requested the naval authorities of another State to help capture a rebel, declared to be a pirate, his State may not afterwards present a claim in respect of his capture. As Commissioner Wadsworth of the Mexican-United States Claims Commission (1868) held, the State would be "estopped." [54] This kind of estoppel is but an application of the principle *nullus commodum capere de sua injuria propria.*[55]

In the Advisory Opinion on the *Interpretation of Peace Treaties* (2nd Phase) (1950), Judge Read, in a dissenting opinion used the term "estoppel" in the same sense and was of the view that "in any proceedings which recognised the principles of justice," no government would be allowed to raise an objection which would "let such a government profit from its own wrong." [56]

The International Court of Justice, in that case, was concerned with the interpretation of the following provision of the Peace Treaties of 1947 [57]:—

". . . any dispute concerning the interpretation or execution of the Treaty, which is not settled by direct diplomatic negotiations, shall be referred to the Three Heads of Mission acting under Article

[53] *Shufeldt Case* (1930) 2 UNRIAA, p. 1079. Guatemala cancelled a concession to extract chicle. One of the contentions put forward when the case was submitted to arbitration was that the claimants used machetes instead of a scratcher to bleed the chicle, in violation of Guatemalan law and fiscal regulations. Held: "The Government never having taken any steps to put a stop to this practice which they must have known existed either under the law or by arbitration under the contract, and never having declared the contract cancelled therefor, and having recognised the contract all through, and thus making themselves *particeps criminis* in such breach (if any) of the law, cannot now in my opinion avail themselves of this contention" (p. 1097).
See also Brit.-U.S. Cl.Arb. (1910): *Yukon Lumber Co. Case* (1913) Nielsen's *Report*, p. 438, at p. 442. *Cf.* also *The Montijo* (1875) 2 *Int.Arb.* p. 1421.

[54] *Marin Case*, 3 *Int.Arb.*, p. 2885, at p. 2886.

[55] See Broom's *Legal Maxims*, 1939, under *nullus commodum capere potest de sua injuria propria.*

[56] *ICJ Reports 1950*, p. 221, at p. 244.

[57] Art. 36 of the Treaty with Bulgaria, to which correspond *mutatis mutandis* Art. 40 of the Treaty with Hungary and Art. 38 of the Treaty with Rumania. Italics added.

35\. . . . Any such dispute not resolved by them within a period of two months shall, unless the parties to the dispute mutually agree upon another means of settlement, be referred at the request of either party to the dispute to a Commission composed of one *representative* of each party and a third member [*un tiers membre*] selected by mutual agreement of the two *parties* from nationals of a third country [*un pays tiers*]. Should the two *parties* fail to agree within a period of one month upon the appointment of the third member [*ce tiers membre*], the Secretary-General of the United Nations may be requested by either party to make the appointment."

The majority of the Court, from whom Judge Read and Judge Azevedo differed, was of the opinion that:—

> "If one party fails to appoint a representative to a Treaty Commission under the Peace Treaties . . . where that party is obligated to appoint a representative . . . , the Secretary-General . . . is not authorised to appoint the third member of the Commission upon the request of the other party to a dispute." [58]

It is submitted that a different interpretation of the Peace Treaties is possible, without recourse to the principle that no one can benefit from his own wrong, invoked by Judge Read.

The Court considered that "the text of the Treaties [did] *not* admit" of the interpretation,

> "that the term 'third member' is used here simply to distinguish the neutral member from the two Commissioners appointed by the parties without implying that the third member can be appointed only when the two national Commissioners have already been appointed, and that therefore the mere fact of the failure of the parties, within the stipulated period, to select the third member by mutual agreement satisfies the condition required for the appointment of the latter by the Secretary-General." [59]

But the Court also conceded that "the text in its literal sense does not completely exclude the possibility of the appointment of the third member before the appointment of both national Commissioners." [60] This interpretation could indeed

[58] *ICJ Reports 1950*, p. 221, at p. 230.
[59] *Loc. cit.*, p. 227.
[60] *Loc. cit.*, p. 227.

have been upheld as being more in accordance with both the letter and the spirit of the provision. Contrary to the opinion of the Court,[61] the literal interpretation of the text does not disclose any contemplated " sequence " in the appointment of the three members. Nor, it is submitted, can such a " sequence " be regarded as " natural and ordinary " in view of the " normal practice of arbitration "; for it has possibly been overlooked that the Treaty Commission is by no means a " normal " arbitral commission, where the national Commissioners are appointed as independent arbitrators and not as national representatives.[62] In the case of the Treaty Commission, they are expressly stated to be " representatives " of their respective Governments. Consequently, their position, even though they have the right to vote, is more akin to that of agents than judges, while the neutral member fulfils the function of a sole arbitrator rather than an umpire. Although it may be the normal practice to appoint first the arbitrators and then the umpire, it is equally normal first to select the sole arbitrator before appointing the agents. Moreover, as contemplated by the Peace Treaties, the Treaty Commission is the last resort to break any deadlock which might arise between the parties in case of a dispute and it represents a machinery to be set in motion essentially by unilateral action " at the request of either party." This is so with regard to the reference of the dispute to the Commission, and also to the eventual appointment of the third member by the Secretary-General. The intention is that this ultimate means of settlement should not fail on account of either the indifference or the recalcitrance of one of the parties.

It is submitted, therefore, that the interpretation: " the mere fact of the failure of the parties, within the stipulated period, to select the third member by mutual agreement satisfies the condition required for the appointment of the latter by the Secretary-General," besides being in strict conformity with the terms of the provision, would be more in accordance with the intention of the parties, and with the principles of good faith,[63] and more in the interest of the rule of law in international

61 *Loc. cit.*, p. 227. See also the French (authoritative) text of the Adv.Op.
62 See *infra*, pp. 279 *et seq.*, esp. pp. 280 *et seq.*
63 See *supra*, pp. 105 *et seq.*

relations.[64] If this interpretation were accepted, the failure of one of the parties to appoint its representative to the Commission would not affect the power of the Secretary-General to make the appointment. That the defaulting party may or may not have thereby violated a treaty obligation thus becomes immaterial and there is, therefore, no occasion for applying the principle *nullus commodum capere de sua injuria propria.*

The problem of the application of this principle might have arisen, however, if the condition required by the Peace Treaties for the appointment of the neutral member by the Secretary-General is not the failure of the *parties* to agree upon the appointment, but the failure of the two *national Commissioners.* In such a case, if one of the parties refuses to appoint its national Commissioner, albeit unlawfully, *i.e.*, in violation of its treaty obligations, it would be necessary to agree with the Court, though perhaps for different reasons, that "nevertheless, such a refusal cannot alter the conditions contemplated in the Treaties for the exercise by the Secretary-General of his power of appointment."[65]

The Court was not altogether explicit as to the reasons for this statement. It is submitted that the reason is not that the principle that no one can benefit from his own wrong cannot be applied, but that the Secretary-General cannot, on the basis of his power of appointment, assume the right to pass judgment upon the violation *vel non* by States of their international obligations. It was pointed out by the United States before the Court that in the municipal law of the great majority of nations, "provision is made for the appointment of an arbitrator (*often by the court*) if one of the parties to a dispute refuses or fails to appoint its arbitrator under an arbitration agreement."[66] It is submitted that this is possible principally because, generally speaking, a municipal court has jurisdiction over the parties. It can determine their responsibility for any violation of their contractual obligations and has also the power to order relief *in natura.*[67] Similarly, an international tribunal would also have the power, if it has jurisdiction over the issue,

64 *Cf.* Schwarzenberger, "Trends in the Practice of the World Court," 4 C.L.P. (1951), p. 1, at pp. 11 *et seq.*
65 *Loc. cit.*, p. 228.
66 *Interpretation of Peace Treaties* (1950), *ICJ Pleadings*, pp. 235, 294, 360.
67 See *ibid.*, p. 294.

both *ratione personae* and *ratione materiae*. In such a case, should the defaulting party object that one of the conditions required by the treaty had not been fulfilled, the tribunal would and should hold, as Judge Read said, "that it was estopped from alleging its own treaty violation in support of its own contention." [68]

EX DELICTO NON ORITUR ACTIO

Another manifestation of the principle *nullus commodum capere de sua injuria propria* is that

"an unlawful act cannot serve as the basis of an action in law." [69]

The principle *ex delicto non oritur actio* is generally upheld by international tribunals [70] and it may be of interest to illustrate it with a case which lasted nearly 70 years from the date the events occurred, going through four different international tribunals, *viz.*, the case of Capt. Clark, known also as *The Medea* and *The Good Return Cases*.

Capt. Clark was a citizen of the United States, who in 1817, obtained a letter of marque from Oriental Banda (as Uruguay was then called) in the war then being fought between Portugal and Spain on the one side and Oriental Banda and Venezuela on the other. Some of the Spanish vessels captured by Clark were seized by Venezuela. Venezuela later combined with New Granada to form the Republic of Colombia, which, in turn, split into three separate States, New Granada, Venezuela and Ecuador.

When claims commissions were constituted between the United States on the one hand and New Granada, Ecuador and

[68] *ICJ Reports 1950*, p. 221, at p. 244. N.B. in advisory procedure, the Court does not and should not pass judgment on an actual dispute without the consent of the parties, PCIJ: *Eastern Carelia Case* (1923), B. 5, pp. 27–9; ICJ: *Interpretation of Peace Treaties* (1st Phase) (1950), *ICJ Reports 1950*, p. 65, at p. 72: "The legal position of the parties to these disputes cannot be in any way compromised by the answers that the Court may give to the questions put to it." See also p. 71.

[69] PCIJ: *Eastern Greenland Case* (1933), D.O. by Anzilotti, A/B. 53, p. 95.

[70] *e.g.*, Brit.-U.S. Cl.Com. (1853): *The Lawrence* (1855), Hornby's *Report*, p. 397. Seizure of ship engaged in slave trade, act prohibited by the law of the claimant's own State and by the law of nations. "The owners of the 'Lawrence' could not claim the protection of their own Government, and, therefore, in my judgment, can have no claim before this commission" (p. 398). Mex.-U.S. Cl.Com. (1868): *Brannan Case*, 3 *Int.Arb.*, p. 2757, at p. 2758: "The Umpire cannot believe that this international commission is justified in countenancing a claim founded upon the contempt and infraction of the laws of one of the nations concerned." Claim arising out of unneutral services rendered in violation of the laws of the claimant's own State.

Venezuela on the other hand, the claims of Capt. Clark were successively and separately put forward before these commissions.

These claims were allowed by Umpire Upham before the Granadine-United States Claims Commission (1857).[71]

The Ecuadorian-United States Claims Commission (1862), however, rejected them. The American Commissioner Hassaurek, after pointing out that the conduct of Clark was in violation of both United States municipal law and treaty provisions between the United States and Spain, the latter considering such conduct as piracy, asked:—

"What right, under these circumstances, has Captain Clark, or his representatives, to call upon the United States to enforce his claim on the Colombian Republics? Can he be allowed, as far as the United States are concerned, to profit by his own wrong? *Nemo ex suo delicto meliorem suam conditionem facit.* He has violated the laws of our land. He has disregarded solemn treaty stipulations. He has compromised our neutrality. . . . What would be the object of enacting penal laws, if their transgression were to entitle the offender to a premium instead of a punishment? . . . I hold it to be the duty of the American Government and my own duty as commissioner to state that in this case Mr. Clark has no standing as an American citizen. A party who asks for redress must present himself with clean hands." [72]

Subsequently a new Claims Commission (1864) was set up between the United States and New Granada (which had by then changed its name to Columbia). Sir Frederick Bruce, the Umpire of this Commission, adopted the views of Commissioner Hassaurek and reversed the decision of Umpire Upham.[73]

Finally, on the same principle, the case was dismissed by Umpire Findlay before the United States-Venezuelan Claims Commission (1885).[74]

[71] 3 *Int.Arb.*, p. 2730.

[72] *Ibid.*, p. 2731, at pp. 2738–9.

[73] *Ibid.*, p. 2743.

[74] *Ibid.*, p. 2743, at p. 2749. Hassaurek's opinion was cited and the same principle was applied in U.S.-Ven.M.C.C. (1903): *Jarvis Case*, *Ven.Arb.1903*, p. 145. See also Span.-U.S. Cl.Com. (1871): *The Mary Lowell* (1879) 3 *Int.Arb.*, p. 2772. Claimants who aided insurgents by supplying arms were estopped from claiming damages for capture of these arms on the high seas by the Spanish Government (pp. 2774, 2775, 2776). "On those principles of equity which the Umpire does not feel at liberty to disregard he is bound to decide that the owners of the ship and cargo are, as such, estopped in their present claim to indemnity for the consequences of their unlawful venture" (p. 2776). *Cf.* also Mex.-U.S. Cl.Com. (1868): *Cucullu* [*i.e.*, *Cuculla*] *Case*, 4 *Int.Arb.*, p. 3477, at p. 3479.

The principle does not, however, appear to be *jus cogens*. For although a Government

" could not be justified, under the law of nations, in interposing its authority to enforce a claim of one of its citizens growing out of services rendered in violation of its own laws, and its duties as a neutral nation, yet if the nation against whom such claim exists sees proper to waive the objection, and agrees to recognise the claim as valid and binding against it, the tribunal to which it is referred for settlement cannot assume for it a defence which it has expressly waived." [75]

Unless, however, there is such a waiver, the principle is of such a fundamental character that where an award disregarded it, a State, even if the award were in its favour, would hesitate to insist upon its enforcement. In the *Pelletier Case* (1885), compensation was allowed to an American claimant whose ship was seized by Haiti for an attempt at slave trading. In recommending that it should not be enforced, the United States Secretary of State, Mr. Bayard, took occasion to say:—

" Even were we to concede that these outrages in Haitian waters were not within Haitian jurisdiction, I do now affirm that the claim of Pelletier against Haiti . . . must be dropped, and dropped peremptorily and immediately by the . . . United States . . . *Ex turpi causa non oritur actio*: by innumerable rulings under Roman common law, as held by nations holding Latin traditions, and under the common law as held in England and the United States, has this principle been applied." [76]

The award was never enforced.[77]

The principle, however, only applies in so far as the claim itself is based upon an unlawful act. It does not apply to cases

[75] U.S. Domestic Commission for Claims against Mexico (1849): *Meade Claim*, 4 *Int.Arb.*, p. 3430, at p. 3432. The waiver referred to was deduced from decisions of the Mex.-U.S. Cl. Com. (1830) which dealt with a number of claims arising out of supplies furnished to the Mexican revolutionaries in their struggle for independence against Spain. In these cases, no question was raised by either the Mexican or the U. S. Commissioners as to the admissibility of the claims. The Mexican Commissioners concurred in allowing the claims without discussion, except where questions of evidence gave rise to differences of opinion. In each case, the Commissioners referred to the supplies as having been furnished for " the promotion of the great object aforesaid," *viz.*, the independence and self-government of Mexico. The *Meade Claim* arose out of similar circumstances. See *ibid.*, pp. 3426–8.

[76] U.S.F.R. (1887), pp. 606–7.

[77] See *Pelletier Case* (1885) 2 *Int.Arb.*, pp. 1749–1805.

where, though the claimant may be guilty of an unlawful act, such act is juridically extraneous to the cause of the action.[78]

E. Fraus Omnia Corrumpit

Fraud is the antithesis of good faith and indeed of law, and it would be self-contradictory to admit that the effects of fraud could be recognised by law.

In dealing with the law of necessity, it was seen that where a person has deliberately and fraudulently placed himself in a state of necessity in order to circumvent the law, he can no longer benefit from the immunity accorded to acts done under the *jus necessitatis*.[79] In a previous section, it was also pointed out that a statement would not be regarded as an admission if induced by fraud.[80]

In the present section, discussion will be confined to a few specific instances showing the vitiating effect of fraud in international law.

In the case of *The Alabama* (1872), the question arose as to whether the commissions granted by the Confederates in the American Civil War to vessels originally built in England in violation of English laws gave them the character of public ships *vis-à-vis* Great Britain, so that the latter was prevented from inquiring into their illegal origin, the President of the Geneva Tribunal, Count Sclopis, said:—

> "The offence of which this vessel was guilty . . . does not disappear as a result of an indecent ruse . . . *Dolus nemini patrocinari debet.*"[81]

The final award of the *Alabama* Arbitral Tribunal seems only to have paraphrased this opinion:—

> "The effects of a violation of neutrality, committed by means of the construction, equipment, and armament of a vessel are not done away with by any commission which the government of the belligerent power, benefited by the violation of neutrality, may afterwards have granted to that vessel; and the ultimate step, by which

[78] *Cf.* Mex.-U.S. G.C.C. (1923): *Massey Case* (1927) *Op. of Com. 1927*, p. 228, at pp. 229–30; *Id.*: *Chattin Case* (1927), *ibid.*, p. 422, at p. 423.

[79] *Supra*, p. 77.

[80] *Supra*, p. 148.

[81] *The Alabama Arbitration* (1872) U.S.A./G.B., 1 *Alabama* (*Proceedings*), p. 178 (Transl.).

the offence is completed, cannot be admissible as a ground for the absolution of the offender, nor can the consummation of his fraud become the means of establishing his innocence." [82]

What normally constitutes a right will, therefore, not be upheld if it is either begotten by fraud or is used to dissemble the effects of another fraudulent act.

Similarly, while a State is in general sovereign in deciding who shall be its subjects and in granting naturalisation to individuals, in relation to another State a naturalisation is not conclusive as to the nationality of an individual, if it can be established that such naturalisation had been obtained by fraud.[83]

A judgment, which in principle calls for the greatest respect, will not be upheld if it is the result of fraud. A State, first of all, has a right to expect from another that "no claim will be put forward that does not bear the impress of good faith and fair dealing on the part of the claimant." [84] A certain amount of exaggeration and even misrepresentation of facts on the part of the individuals whose claim their State espouses is not infrequent and does not of itself invalidate the claim.[85] But when it is alleged that an international tribunal has been "misled by fraud and collusion on the part of witnesses and suppression of evidence on the part of some of them," "no tribunal worthy of its name or of any respect may allow its decision to stand if such allegations are well-founded. Every tribunal has an inherent power to reopen and to revise a decision induced by fraud," as long as it still has jurisdiction over the case.[86] Even where the judgment has passed out of the hands of the tribunal, a State, on discovering that an award made in its favour has been induced by fraud practised upon the tribunal by the claimants, would refuse to enforce it and would restore any money received in execution of the award, as for instance,

[82] *The Alabama Arbitration* (1872) 1 *Int.Arb.*, p. 495, at p. 655.

[83] See *Salem Case* (1932) U.S.A./Egypt, 2 UNRIAA, p. 1161, at pp. 1184 *et seq.*. See also U.S.-Ven. M.C.C. (1903): *Flutie Case*, *Ven.Arb. 1903*, p. 38, and precedents therein cited.

[84] Germ.-U.S. M.C.C. (1922): *Friedman Case* (1925) *Dec. & Op.*, p. 605, at p. 613.

[85] Mex.-U.S. G.C.C. (1922): *Mallén Case* (1927) *Op. of Com. 1927*, p. 254, at pp. 255 *et seq.*, pp. 273 *et seq.*

[86] Germ.-U.S. M.C.C. (1922): *Lehigh Valley Railroad Co. Case* (1933) *Dec. & Op.*, p. 1084, at p. 1127. See *infra*, pp. 358 *et seq.*

in the *La Abra Silver Mining Co. Case* (C. 1868) and the *Benjamin Weil Case* (C. 1868).[87]

And where fraud is proven either with regard to the formation of an international tribunal or with regard to the conduct of it members, the entire proceedings will be regarded as null and void.[88] Even innocent third parties cannot claim a right derived from its decisions.[89]

[87] See *infra*, p. 320, note 82, and p. 359.

[88] Fraud was alleged against the American Commissioner on the U.S.-Ven. Cl.Com. (1866) at Caracas both in the choice of the Umpire and in the proceedings. Venezuela protested. The U.S. Administration at first was adamant. But Congress intervened at the instance of the claimants concerned. In its Report of 1883, the Committee for Foreign Affairs of the House of Representatives declared: "The alleged commission was a conspiracy; its proceedings were tainted with fraud. That fraud affects its entire proceedings. It was diseased throughout, and there is no method known to the Committee by which to separate the fraudulent part from the honest part and establish any portion in soundness and integrity. . . . Justice to Venezuela demands these proceedings should be set aside speedily" (2 *Int.Arb.*, p. 1663). Accordingly, a new convention was signed in 1885 creating the Claims Commission of Washington to re-examine all the claims.

Cf. also *infra*, p. 261, where the P.C.A. in saying that the nullity of an award in case of essential error may be partial expressly emphasised that the case was not one where allegations of bad faith had been made against the tribunal.

[89] As to how the claims of alleged bona fide possessors of certificates of award issued by the Caracas Commission were dropped, see U.S.-Ven. Convention of March 15, 1888 (5 *Int.Arb.*, p. 4815), and the interpretation given to it by the Order of the Washington Commission on August 25, 1890 (2 *Int.Arb.*, p. 1675, note 2). *Cf.* also Mr. Rice's Report, 1885, *ibid.*, p. 1672.

PART THREE

GENERAL PRINCIPLES OF LAW IN THE CONCEPT OF RESPONSIBILITY

CHAPTER 6

GENERAL NOTIONS

A. Responsibility as a Juridical Concept

THE term "responsibility" has been used by international tribunals in a great number of senses. Before discussing the legal concept of responsibility, it is necessary to ascertain what the expression properly denotes.

First, it may be possible to distinguish between the proper use of the term "responsibility" and its improper use, or at least its derivative meaning. In the latter sense, "responsibility" is often used as being synonymous with "obligation" or "liability," with which we are not at present concerned.

RESPONSIBILITY IN THE ORDINARY SENSE

In the proper sense of the term, responsibility may be "ordinary," "moral" or "legal." In its ordinary sense, responsibility means that a person is the author of an act and should, therefore, bear its consequences.[1] The term often has a depreciatory connotation, implying either that the act is reprehensible or that its consequences are prejudicial.[2] In so far as injury results to others, it means that the author of the act should himself bear the injurious consequences, *i.e.*, take them over by making reparation.[3]

[1] *Cf.* PCIJ: *Polish Agrarian Reform Case* (Interim Protection) (1933), D.O. by Anzilotti, A/B. 58, p. 182: "It is only fair that a government should bear the consequences of the wording of a document for which it is *responsible*" (Italics added). Brit.-U.S. Cl.Arb. (1910): *The Wanderer* (1921), Nielsen's *Report*, p. 459, at pp. 465–66 (*infra*, p. 202, note 20). Webster's *New International Dictionary*, Unabridged, 1948, *sub voce*, "Responsible," Def. 6: "Answerable as the primary cause, motive or agent, whether of evil or good; creditable or chargeable with the result."

[2] *Cf.* Fran.-Germ. M.A.T.: *Franz Case* (1922), 1 T.A.M., p. 781, at p. 785: "By the terms of Article 231 of the Treaty of Versailles, Germany has admitted her responsibility for the war and for its consequences" (Transl.). See Art. 231 quoted *infra*, p. 164.

[3] *Cf.* Art. 232 of the Treaty of Versailles in which this necessity of reparation ensuing from responsibility is assumed.

MORAL RESPONSIBILITY

A specific kind of responsibility is "moral responsibility" by which is meant that a person may be considered, by moral standards, as the author of an act and its consequences, and, for that reason, as incurring a moral obligation to repair those prejudicial consequences that have affected others.[4] "Moral responsibility" differs from "responsibility" in ordinary usage and "responsibility" in its legal sense, in that in the former only common standards, whilst in the latter legal standards are applied. The same distinction between common, moral and legal standards similarly exists with regard to the notion of "negligence," but again is often not clearly drawn.[5] Confusion frequently arises out of an indifferent use of terms, or failure to distinguish their various meanings.

Article 231 of the Treaty of Versailles provided that:—

"The Allied and Associated Governments affirm and Germany accepts the responsibility of Germany and her allies for causing all the loss and damage to which the Allied and Associated Governments and their nationals have been subjected as a consequence of the war imposed upon them by the aggression of Germany and her allies."

In a unanimous decision, the German-United States Mixed Claims Commission (1922) held that:—

"Article 231 of the Versailles Treaty at most amounts to no more than an acceptance by Germany of the affirmance by the Allied and Associated Governments of Germany's responsibility for all loss and damage suffered as a consequence of the war—a *moral responsibility*. Germany's *financial responsibility* for losses occurring during belligerency is limited and clearly defined in the succeeding Article and Annex pertaining thereto and other provisions of the Treaty."[6]

[4] See Art. 2 of the Mexican-U.S. Convention of September 10, 1923, establishing the Special Cl.Com. to deal with claims of American citizens to whom Mexico "*ex gratia* feels morally bound to make full indemnification" (A.J.I.L., Off. Doc., 1924, p. 143 *et seq.*). See also similar conventions signed by Mexico with France (1924), Germany, Spain (1925), Great Britain (1926), and Italy (1927) (Feller, *The Mexican Claims Commission, 1923–34*, 1935, pp. 412 *et seq.*, 442 *et seq.*, 521 *et seq.*, 467 *et seq.*, 502 *et seq.*).

Cf. also PCA: *Russian Indemnity Case* (1912), 1 H.C.R., p. 532, at p. 547; and *supra*, p. 64.

[5] See *infra*, pp. 225 *et seq.*

[6] *Administrative Decision No. II* (1923), *Dec. & Op.*, p. 5, at p. 15. Italics of the Commission.

The term "responsibility" in the Treaty was, therefore, held to mean only "moral responsibility,"[7] in the sense described above.

"ASSUMED RESPONSIBILITY"

It is submitted that when the German-United States Mixed Claims Commission (1922) spoke of "Germany's financial responsibility," it used the word "responsibility" in its derivative, and hence improper, sense. It will be found that, elsewhere in the same decision, the Commission spoke generally of the "financial obligations" of Germany.[8] The so-called "financial *responsibility* for losses occurring during belligerency" means no more than the "financial *obligation* to compensate for losses occurring during belligerency."[9] Support for this view may be found in *Administrative Decision No. V* (1924) of the same Commission, in which it declared that:—

"The Treaty[[10]] embodies in its terms a contract by which Germany accorded to the United States, as one of the conditions of peace, rights in behalf of American nationals which had no prior existence but which were created by the Treaty. While these treaty terms doubtless include obligations of Germany arising from the violation of rules of international law or otherwise and existing prior to and independent of the Treaty, they also include obligations of Germany which were created and fixed by the terms of the Treaty. (Footnote No. 19: A large proportion of the financial obligations fixed by paragraph 9 of Annex I to Section 1 of Part VIII of the Treaty of Versailles as carried by reference into the Treaty of Berlin did not arise under the rules of international law but are terms imposed by the victor as one of the conditions of peace.) All of these obligations, whatever their nature, are merged in and fixed by the Treaty."[11]

[7] *Cf. Russian Indemnity Case* (1912), *loc. cit.*, p. 547.

[8] *E.g.*, p. 11, quoting *Administrative Decision No. I*: "The financial obligations of Germany to the United States arising under the Treaty of Berlin . . . embrace: (a) all losses, damages, or injuries . . . ." *Vide passim.*

[9] *Cf. Administrative Decision No. II* (1923), *loc. cit.*, p. 15: "It is manifest that Article 231 is qualified and limited by the provisions of Article 232 and the Annex I pertaining thereto, which in express terms . . . limit the *obligation* of Germany *to make compensation* to the civilian population of the Allied and Associated Powers for such damages as fall within the terms of Article 232 and Annex I" (Italics added). The passage quoted in the text follows almost immediately this quotation and constitutes a restatement thereof.

[10] *i.e.*, the Treaty of Berlin of August 21, 1921, which inter alia, made the reparation provisions of the Treaty of Versailles applicable between the United States and Germany.

[11] *Dec. & Op.*, p. 145, at pp. 184–85.

It is clear from the above that the so-called "financial responsibility" of Germany refers to a contractual, or conventional, obligation of a pecuniary nature.

The reason why the word "responsibility" is used for the term "obligation" may, however, be readily perceived. In the above-cited passage, it will be found that the German-United States Mixed Claims Commission (1922) mentioned three kinds of obligations: obligations arising from a contract, obligations arising from the violation of rules of law, and obligations arising otherwise.[12] In so far as the Commission was concerned, all these obligations assumed a contractual nature.[13]

Attention may be drawn to the special mention by the Commission of "obligations arising out of violation of rules of law"; for it will be seen that the commission of an act in violation of law gives rise to immediate responsibility, involving a legal obligation to make reparation for all the prejudicial consequences caused to others by the act.[14] This is the proper meaning of "responsibility" in law. As the content of this contractual obligation assumed by Germany was to make reparation for the prejudicial consequences of certain acts, derivatively and by way of analogy, the situation is spoken of as one of responsibility. For this reason, immediately following the passage above quoted from *Administrative Decision No. V* (1924), the German-United States Mixed Claims Commission (1922) continued:—

> "The Commission's inquiry is confined solely to determining whether or not Germany by the terms of the Treaty accepted responsibility for the act causing the damage claimed and it is not concerned with the quality of that act or whether it was legal or illegal as measured by rules of international law."[15]

For the sake of brevity, this responsibility may be called "contractual responsibility"[16] or "assumed responsibility."

[12] *Cf.*: "While these treaty terms doubtless include obligations of Germany arising from the violation of rules of international law or otherwise . . . they also include obligations of Germany which were created and fixed by the terms of the Treaty."

[13] *Cf.* "All of these obligations whatever their nature, are merged in and fixed by the Treaty." "The Treaty embodies in its terms a contract."

[14] *Infra*, pp. 169 *et seq.*

[15] *Loc. cit.*, p. 185.

[16] This term admittedly may cause some confusion, as contractual responsibility is often used to denote responsibility *ex contractu*, *i.e.*, legal responsibility

However, from a juridical point of view, it must always be remembered that the term responsibility is here used only in a derivative meaning, and that there exists a fundamental difference, as regards their juridical nature, between this "assumed responsibility" and responsibility properly so-called, *viz.*, responsibility arising out of an unlawful act. Responsibility properly so-called, as will be seen, is an independent juridical concept subject to well defined principles as to its origin, scope and consequences, while "assumed responsibility" is in reality only a contractual obligation based on consent, the extent of the obligation being determined by the parties themselves.

While there may be a great similarity in the rules and principles applicable to the enforcement of the obligation out of this assumed responsibility and the obligation to make reparation arising out of responsibility for an unlawful act, *e.g.*, in ascertaining what are the "consequences" caused by a given act (the principle of proximate causality), it cannot be overstressed that to call the latter obligation "responsibility" is juridically only a figure of speech. Great care should, therefore, be exercised in order not to use instances of the so-called "assumed responsibility" to explain or judge cases of responsibility for unlawful acts.

> "An inaccurate use of terminology may sometimes be of but little importance, and discussion of it may be merely a quibble. But accuracy of expression becomes important when it appears that inaccuracy is due to a confusion of thought in the understanding or application of proper rules or principles of law." [17]

By way of illustration, one or two examples showing the importance of separating these two types of "responsibility" may be mentioned. First, the distinction between an obligation arising out of responsibility for an unlawful act and an obligation assumed by treaty may be of practical importance in a case of so-called State Succession. It is clearly established that the former type of obligation is not binding on a successor

arising out of the breach of a contractual obligation. *Cf.* P.C.A.: *Russian Indemnity Case* (1912) 1 H.C.R., p. 533, at pp. 542–43.

[17] Mex.-U.S. G.C.C. (1923): *International Fisheries Co. Case* (1931) D.O. by F. K. Nielsen, *Op. of Com. 1931*, p. 207, at pp. 265–66.

State, while this is not necessarily the case as regards treaty obligations.[18] Secondly, while the obligation to make reparation in case of an unlawful act arises the moment the illegal act is committed,[19] the obligation to make reparation in a case of the so-called "assumed responsibility" does not arise until the treaty, whereby the obligation is assumed, comes into force.[20] The determination of the precise moment at which the obligation arises may present considerable practical importance when considering the point of time from which the person benefiting from the obligation may assign his right, or, in a situation peculiar to international law, when the beneficiary changes his nationality.[21] Thirdly, while the obligation arising from responsibility for an unlawful act consists invariably, *ipso jure* and independently of the will of the parties, in the integral reparation of all the proximate consequences of the unlawful act committed, the object and extent of the obligation arising from the so-called "assumed responsibility," following the freedom of contract, varies from case to case according to the will of the parties. For instance, the assumed obligation may cover the reparation of consequences not of an act of man, but of an act of God; it may have as its object the enforcement of a moral responsibility[22]; the obligation may not be to make integral reparation, but merely to pay compensation for part of the loss caused by certain acts; the payment of compensation may again be limited to losses suffered by certain categories of individuals and not others, *e.g.*, civilians and not persons possessing a military status.[23]

In short, the so-called "assumed responsibility" is a purely contractual obligation, the nature of which is the same as all other contractual obligations.

18 *Cf.* Brit.-U.S. Cl.Arb. (1910): *Hawaiian Claims* (1925) Nielsen's *Report*, p. 85, see *Award*, pp. 106–61; and also *Id.*: *Robert E. Brown Case* (1923) *ibid.*, p. 162, at pp. 199 *et seq.*

19 *Infra*, p. 169 and pp. 177 *et seq.*

20 *Cf.* Germ.-U.S. M.C.C. (1922): *Administrative Decision No. V* (1924) *Dec. & Op.*, p. 145, at pp. 183–84.

21 *Cf. Administrative Decision No. V* (1924) *ibid.* The whole discussion in this decision was concerned with this subject. See particularly, pp. 186 *et seq.*, *e.g.*, "By this agreement [Treaty of Berlin] Germany is bound. The rights thus fixed constitute property the title whereof passes by succession, assignment, or other form of transfer."

For an obligation arising from an unlawful act, *cf.* Fran.-U.S. Cl.Com. (1880): *Camy Case*, 3 *Int.Arb.*, p. 2398, at p. 2400.

22 *Cf. supra*, p. 164, note 4.

23 *Cf. supra*, p. 165, note 9.

RESPONSIBILITY STRICTO SENSU

Coming now to what is submitted to be the strict meaning of the term responsibility in international law, *i.e.*, responsibility for internationally unlawful acts, the words of the Mexican-United States General Claims Commission (1923) may be cited:—

"Under International Law, apart from any convention, in order that a State may incur responsibility it is necessary that an unlawful international act be imputed to it, that is, that there exist a violation of a duty imposed by an international juridical standard." [24]

Speaking of an unlawful act, the Permanent Court of International Justice said:—

"This act being attributable to the State and described as contrary to the treaty right of another State, international responsibility would be established immediately as between the two States." [25]

Again, the Permanent Court observed that:—

"It is a principle of international law, and even a general conception of law, that any breach of an engagement involves an obligation to make reparation." [26]

"The essential principle contained in the actual notion of an illegal act . . . is that reparation must, as far as possible, wipe out all the consequences of the illegal act and re-establish the situation which would, in all probability, have existed if that act had not been committed. Restitution in kind, or, if this is not possible, payment of a sum corresponding to the value which a restitution in kind would bear; the award, if need be, of damages for loss sustained which would not be covered by restitution in kind or payment in place of it—such are the principles which should serve to determine the amount of compensation due for an act contrary to international law." [27]

The actual notion of responsibility is thus a relatively simple one. It denotes the state of being the author of an unlawful act and being answerable in law to the injured party for its

[24] *Dickson Car Wheel Co. Case* (1931). *Op. of Com. 1931*, p. 175, at p. 187.
[25] *Phosphates in Morocco Case* (Prel.Obj.) (1938), A/B. 74, p. 28.
[26] *Chorzów Factory Case* (Merits) (1928), A. 17, p. 29; *Cf. Chorzów Factory Case* (Jd.) (1927), A. 9, p. 21; Spanish Zone of Morocco Claims (1923): *Rapport III* (1924), 2 UNRIAA, p. 615, at p. 641.
[27] *Chorzów Factory Case* (Merits) (1928), A. 17, p. 47.

prejudicial consequences. International responsibility is immediately incurred by a State which, by an act imputable to it, has violated a rule of international law. This responsibility involves a legal obligation to re-establish the situation which would, in all probability, have existed but for the unlawful act. In particular, it means the obligation to make reparation for all the prejudicial consequences of the unlawful act affecting others. It is not surprising, therefore, that the Permanent Court has regarded this as a general conception of law; for, by the negation of any negation of law—to borrow Hegel's phraseology,—by the automatic sanction attached to any infraction of the legal order, that legal order provides for its own protection and its theoretical inviolability. Any infringement of the legal order involves automatically for the wrong-doer an obligation to make whole, to re-establish the *status quo erat*. Responsibility thus conceived is an indispensable element of any legal system.

Before proceeding further to examine the general principles of law governing this legal concept of responsibility, it is necessary first to elucidate the meaning of the two constitutive elements of responsibility in international law alluded to above, *viz.*:—

1. Existence of an international unlawful act;
2. Imputability of this unlawful act to the State.

B. Unlawful Act in International Law

LAW APPLICABLE

The United States Commissioner in his dissenting opinion in the *International Fisheries Co. Case* (1931) affirmed:—

"The supreme law of all members of the family of nations is not its domestic law but is international law." [28]

"Conformity by authorities of a Government with its domestic law is not conclusive evidence of the observance of legal duties imposed by international law, although it may be important evidence on that point." [29]

[28] Mex.-U.S. G.C.C. (1923): D.O. of F. K. Nielsen, *Op. of Com. 1931*, p. 207, at p. 234.
[29] *Ibid.*, p. 236. *Cf. The Alabama Arbitration* (1872), 1 *Int.Arb.*, p. 495, at p. 656.

This may be accepted as a correct statement of the law.

The Permanent Court of International Justice in one of its Advisory Opinions declared:—

> "It should . . . be observed that, while on the one hand, according to generally accepted principles, a State cannot rely, as against another State, on the provisions of the latter's Constitution, but only on international law and international obligations duly accepted, on the other hand and conversely, a State cannot adduce as against another State its own Constitution with a view to evading obligations incumbent upon it under international law or treaties in force." [30]

In this Advisory Opinion, the Court also observed that although "the application of the Danzig Constitution may . . . result in the violation of an international obligation incumbent on Danzig towards Poland, whether under treaty stipulations or under general international law, as, for instance, in the case of a denial of justice in the generally accepted sense of that term in international law," "in cases of such a nature, it is not the Constitution and other laws, as such, but the international obligation that gives rise to the responsibility of the Free City." [31] It is the violation of the international obligation, whether arising from treaty or from general international law, that constitutes the international unlawful act that gives rise to international responsibility, and not any possible violation of municipal law.[32]

It may happen, therefore, that, on the one hand, an act may be lawful in international law while not strictly in accordance with municipal law [33] and, on the other hand, an act may be held unlawful in international law despite the fact that it is lawful in municipal law.[34] In particular, an act contrary

30 *Polish Nationals in Danzig* (1932), A/B. 44, p. 24.

31 *Ibid.*, pp. 24–5.

32 N.B. The Court makes no distinction between the violations of obligations arising from treaty or from general international law.

33 *Cf.*, *e.g.*, PCIJ: *The Lotus Case* (1927), A. 10, p. 24.
Cf. also Mex.-U.S. G.C.C. (1923): *F. M. Smith Case* (1929), *Op. of Com. 1929*, p. 208, at pp. 209–10.

34 See, *e.g.*, PCIJ: *The Wimbledon* (1923), A. 1, pp. 29, 30: "In any case a neutrality order, issued by an individual State, could not prevail over the provisions of the Treaty of Peace. . . . She could not advance her neutrality orders against the obligations which she had accepted under this Article." PCIJ: *Free Zones Case* (Second Phase: Order) (1930), A. 24, p. 12: "It is certain

to international law does not become lawful by reason of the fact that it is authorised by municipal legislation which applies to nationals and aliens alike.[35] Conversely, an act which has been declared unlawful according to international law may yet be valid in municipal law and its juridical effects continue to be recognised in that legal order.[36] Indeed, it may be well to recall here the words of the Permanent Court of International Justice that: —

> "From the standpoint of International Law and of the Court which is its organ, municipal laws are merely facts which express the will and constitute the activities of States, in the same manner as do legal decisions or administrative measures." [37]

International law and municipal law belong to different spheres. The rules of the one are not applicable in the other except by incorporation or by reference. For the determination of the existence of an unlawful act in international law, it may be said, therefore, that municipal law, as such, is wholly irrelevant.

Having shown that the unlawful character of an act in international law is solely to be determined by the latter, the question now arises whether there are two types of internationally unlawful acts depending on whether the rule violated is one of international treaty or customary law with a corresponding distinction in the nature of the responsibility of the State. This distinction has so far not been admitted by international tribunals, nor is it believed to be inherent in the notion of an unlawful act or of responsibility as a legal concept.

The Rumano-German Arbitral Tribunal, for instance, in examining the meaning of the expression "acts committed" in section 4 of the Annex to Articles 297 and 298 of the Treaty of Versailles, decided that the term meant "acts contrary to the

that France cannot rely on her own legislation to limit the scope of her international obligations."

Cf. also PCIJ: *Greco-Bulgarian "Communities"* (1930) Adv.Op. No. 17, B. 17, p. 32. *Metzger & Co. Case* (1900) U.S.F.R. (1901), p. 262. Responsibility arose where an act was in accordance with local law but was in violation of treaty obligation (see pp. 275–6).

35 See PCIJ: *German Interests Case* (Merits) (1926) A. 7, p. 33; PCIJ: *Peter Pázmány University Case* (1933) A/B. 61, p. 243.

36 *Cf.* PCIJ: *Statute of the Memel Territory* (Merits) (1932) A/B. 49, p. 336.

37 PCIJ: *German Interests Case* (Merits) (1926) A. 7, p. 19.

law of nations," [38] following previous decisions of various Mixed Arbitral Tribunals and the example of the Permanent Court of International Justice.[39] The sole Arbitrator went on to point out that, in this sense, international law cannot be limited to " written law " and he indicated Article 38 of the Statute of the Permanent Court of International Justice as enumerating the sources of international law.[40] It would seem therefore that an act is internationally unlawful whether it violates a treaty, a rule of customary international law, or a general principle of law recognised by civilised nations.

In the *Russian Indemnity Case* (1912), the Permanent Court of Arbitration declined to recognise any distinction in the " juridical essence of the notion of responsibility," based on the source of the obligation that has been violated, whether contractual or legal. It regarded the notion of responsibility as a unitary concept, originating in fault, and ending in reparation.[41]

As for the Permanent Court of International Justice, in its well-known enunciation of the principle of reparation for an unlawful act [42] which, from a practical point of view, forms the most important aspect of an unlawful act, there is not the slightest suggestion of any difference between the breach of a treaty obligation and the breach of an obligation of general international law.[43] Nor has any such distinction ever been suggested in the entire jurisprudence of the Court.[44]

As is clearly indicated in the decision of the Permanent Court of Arbitration in the *Russian Indemnity Case* (1912), the municipal law distinctions of responsibility, based on the sources of the obligations violated, are the result of special laws mitigating the consequences of the breach of certain contractual obligations, and are not distinctions inherent in the legal concept

[38] *David Goldenberg & Sons Case* (1928) 2 UNRIAA, p. 901, at p. 908.

[39] *Interpretation of the Treaty of Neuilly* (1924) A. 3, p. 8. Decision by Chamber of Summary Procedure.

[40] *Loc. cit.*, pp. 908–9.

[41] 1 H.C.R. p. 532, at p. 543.

[42] *Supra*, p. 169.

[43] *Cf. supra*, p. 171, note 32.

[44] *Cf.* I.C.J.: *Corfu Channel Case* (Merits) (1949) *ICJ Reports 1949*, p. 4, at p. 45, Ind.Op. by Alvarez, on a totally different distinction between international delinquencies (acts contrary to the sentiments of humanity), prejudicial acts (acts which are harmful but not contrary to the sentiments of humanity) and unlawful acts. Such a distinction is not to be found in traditional international law and must be considered as peculiar to the " New International Law " which Judge Alvarez has undertaken to expound.

of responsibility. Any such modification established by law has to be specifically proved.[45] In principle, it may, therefore, be said that an unlawful act in international law engendering responsibility is any act on the part of the State which transgresses a rule of international law, whatever its source, the quality of the act in municipal law being wholly irrelevant.

INTERNATIONAL ACT

The question as to what constitutes an act in international law has received but little attention from international tribunals, it being generally assumed that it denotes some human activity imputable to a State, or, more correctly, to an international person.[46]

It is certain, however, that the term "act" includes both positive and negative act, that is to say, act and omission. Whenever there is a legal obligation to act, a voluntary inaction —by which is meant not necessarily an *intended* inaction but simply an inaction which is not due to impossibility of acting otherwise—would constitute a breach of that obligation, in other words, an unlawful act.[47]

An interesting question is whether municipal legislation may, as such, constitute an internationally unlawful act. This question was discussed in the *Mariposa Development Co. et al. Case* (1933). The Commission, speaking of confiscatory legislation, said that, while it did not deny that laws might be passed of such a character that their mere enactment would give rise forthwith to an international claim, "practical common sense" indicates that, ordinarily, "there should be a *locus poenitentiae* for diplomatic representation and executive forbearance, and claims should arise only when actual confiscation follows."[48] It is submitted that there can be no doubt that a municipal enactment constitutes an act of the State[49] and, as such, is capable of violating international law. Whether it does so or not depends

[45] *Loc. cit.*, at p. 543.
[46] Regarding the question of imputability; see *infra*, pp. 180 *et seq*.
[47] See Spanish Zone of Morocco Claims (1923): *Rapport III* (1924) 2 UNRIAA, p. 615, at p. 643.
[48] Panamanian-U.S. G.C.C. (1926): (1933) Hunt's *Report*, p. 533, at p. 577.
Cf. Mex.-U.S. G.C.C. (1923): *International Fisheries Co. Case* (1931) D.O. by F. K. Nielsen, *Op. of Com. 1931*, p. 207, at p. 255.
[49] *Cf.* PCIJ: *German Interests Case* (Merits) (1926) A. 7, p. 19; *supra*, p. 172.

upon what is in fact prohibited by the particular rule of international law and upon whether the municipal law actually contravenes it or merely enables some other organ of the State to do so. In the latter case, the municipal enactment amounts at most to a preparatory act, to a violation *in posse*, which would justify only diplomatic representation. In the former case, however, the unlawful act consists in, and arises from, the very adoption of the municipal enactment.[50]

The ascertainment of the particular rule of international law applicable and of the precise act impugned is not, however, always obvious in practice. Thus the Mexican-United States General Claims Commission (1923) in the *Janes Case* (1926) took occasion to explain at length that in a case of denial of justice on account of the non-prosecution of a crime committed by a private individual against a foreigner, the unlawful act in international law consists in the failure on the part of the State to live up to its international obligation to use due diligence in the protection of aliens and not in the criminal act of the individual. It said:—

"The international delinquency in this case is one of its own specific type, separate from the private delinquency of the culprit. The culprit is liable for having killed or murdered an American national; the government is liable for not having measured up to its duty of diligently prosecuting and properly punishing the offender. The culprit has transgressed the penal code of his country; the State, so far from having transgressed its own penal code (which perhaps not even is applicable to it) has transgressed a provision of international law as to State duties. The culprit cannot be sentenced in criminal or civil procedure unless his guilt or intention in causing the victim's death is proven; the Government can be sentenced once the non-performance of its judicial duty is proven to amount to an international delinquency, the theories on guilt or intention in criminal and civil law not being applicable here. The damage caused by the culprit is the damage caused to Janes' relatives by Janes' death; the damage caused by the government's

[50] *Cf.* PCIJ: *Phosphates in Morocco* (1938), Italy/France, A/B. 74, p. 26; "The alleged inconsistency of the monopoly régime with the international obligations of Morocco and of France is a reproach which applies first and foremost to the dahirs of 1920 establishing the monopoly. If, by establishing the monopoly, Morocco and France violated the treaty régime of the General Act of Algeciras of April 7, 1906, and of the Franco-German Convention of November 4, 1911, that violation is the outcome of the dahirs of 1920. In those dahirs are to be sought the essential facts constituting the alleged monopolisation."

negligence is the damage resulting from the non-punishment of the murderer." [51]

This statement, more than any other,[52] makes plain what precise act it is that is called into question in international law and is interesting both from the theoretical and the practical point of view.

Theoretically, this separation of the internationally unlawful act from the private delinquency shows, as the Commission has itself pointed out, that even in a case like the *Janes Case* there is no exception to the general principle that a State is responsible only for what it has done or failed to do, and not for the acts of private persons—the principle of individual responsibility.[53]

From a practical point of view, if the above distinction were not made, a State might be held responsible for an act which it has not committed, or for an act which was not internationally unlawful, or alternatively, for injuries which were not caused by its own unlawful act—situations which would obviously be inadmissible.

Apart from the above consideration, the determination of the precise rule violated and the precise act violating it is also the prerequisite for fixing the exact moment when an international delinquency arises. The incidence of the time of an unlawful act may be of capital importance to the question of the admissibility of an international claim *ratione temporis*.

Thus in the *Cayuga Indians Case* (1926), if the United States had been held directly responsible for the failure of New York to perform certain contracts signed with the Cayuga Nation in 1789, 1790 and 1795, the first breach of obligation on the part of the United States would have occurred in 1812, from which year onwards the Cayugas who had migrated to Canada were not paid their annuity stipulated in the contracts. In such a case, the

[51] *Op. of Com. 1927*, p. 108, at p. 115.
Cf. ICJ: *Reparation for Injuries suffered in the Service of the United Nations* (1949), Ad.Op., *ICJ Reports 1949*, p. 174, at p. 181. The Court recognises that diplomatic protection of citizens abroad rests upon the basis that " the *defendant State* has broken [" *manqué à* "] an obligation towards the *national State* in respect of its nationals." Italics added.

[52] *Janes Case, loc. cit.*, p. 116: " The Commission is not aware of an international award in which the distinction has been set forth with clearness."
Cf. ICJ: *Corfu Channel Case* (Merits) (1949) *ICJ Reports 1949*, p. 4, at p. 52, D.O. by Winiarski and citation of the L.o.N., Committee of Jurists Report.

[53] See *infra*, pp. 208 *et seq.*

claim would have been barred by Article V of the Treaty of 1853 between Great Britain and the United States.[54] However, the Tribunal found that the responsibility of the United States did not arise until, New York having definitely refused to recognise the claims of the Canadian Cayugas, the matter was brought to the notice of the Federal authorities of the United States, and the latter did nothing to carry out its obligations towards Great Britain in respect of these Canadian Cayugas. This, in the opinion of the Tribunal did not occur until 1860, and for this reason, the claim was not barred by the Treaty of 1853.[55]

Even where there is no doubt as to which obligation has been violated, there may yet be a dispute with regard to the time of a particular act. As, however, the Permanent Court of International Justice pointed out in the *Phosphates in Morocco Case* (1938):—

> "The question whether a given situation or fact is prior or subsequent to a particular date is one to be decided in regard to each specific case, just as the question of the situations or facts with regard to which the dispute arose must be decided in regard to each specific case."[56]

The incidence of time of a given act is thus a question of fact to be decided according to the circumstances of each case.

LOCAL REMEDIES

Once the unlawful act has been established, responsibility attaches immediately. Thus in the above-mentioned case, the Permanent Court also said:—

> "In its Application, the Italian Government has represented the decision of the Department of Mines as an unlawful international act, because that decision was inspired by the will to get rid of the foreign holding and because it therefore constituted a violation of the vested rights placed under the protection of the international

[54] Convention of February 8, 1853 (5 *Int.Arb.*, pp. 4743 *et seq.*).

[55] Brit.-U.S. Cl.Arb. (1910): Nielsen's *Report*, p. 203, at pp. 328–9. *Cf.* pp. 267 *et seq.*

[56] A/B. 74, p. 24. *Cf.* this case (p. 26) and the *Cayuga Indians Case* (1926), *loc. cit.*

Cf. PCIJ: *Mavrommatis Palestine Concessions Case* (1924), A. 2, p. 35; and *Phosphates in Morocco Case* (1938), S.O. of Cheng Tien-Hsi, *loc. cit.*, pp. 36–7.

conventions. That being so, it is in this decision that we should look for the violation of international law—a definite act which would, by itself, directly involve international responsibility. This act being attributable to the State and described as contrary to the treaty right of another State, international responsibility would be established immediately as between the two States. In these circumstances the alleged denial of justice, resulting either from a *lacuna* [57] in the judicial organisation or from the refusal of administrative or extraordinary methods of redress designed to supplement its deficiencies, merely results in allowing the unlawful act to subsist. It exercises no influence either on the accomplishment of the act or on the responsibility ensuing from it." [58]

It follows from the above that, in the words of the Arbitrator in the *Finnish Vessels Case* (1934):—

"There may be cases where it can be said that a breach of international law has been committed by the very acts complained of and before any recourse has been had to the municipal tribunal." [59]

In such a case, the local remedies rule,[60] which was recognised by the Arbitrator, is of a purely procedural character,[61] its

[57] "*Une carence.*"

[58] A/B. 74, p. 28.

[59] 3 UNRIAA, p. 1479, at p. 1501.

[60] It is not intended here to deal with the local remedies rule save in so far as it may confirm the proper understanding of the notion of an unlawful act in international law.

[61] *Ibid.*, at pp. 1502–3. As the arbitrator pointed out, if it were otherwise, it would be difficult to perceive how international responsibility can be established where recourse to local remedies has either been excused or dispensed with. The contrary view of Judge Hudson expressed in his D.O. in the *Panevezys-Saldutiskis Ry. Case* (1939) (PCIJ: A/B. 76, p. 47) that: "This is not a rule of procedure. . . . Until the available means of local redress have been exhausted, no responsibility can arise," seems, therefore, to be unacceptable and, besides, it was not shared by the rest of the Court either in the majority or in the minority. The majority decision referred to the "rule which in principle subordinates the presentation of an international claim to such an exhaustion" (p. 18), and clearly assumed, therefore, the existence of a claim (substance), the presentation of which (procedure) was subordinated to certain conditions. The former is concerned with the merits, the latter is a preliminary objection. As is clearly shown by the joint separate opinion of Judges De Visscher and Rostworowski, the alleged unlawful international act complained of by Estonia and considered by it as engendering the international responsibility of Lithuania was the seizure of the railway by Lithuania in 1919 (pp. 26 *et seq.*). On p. 29, these two judges by contradistinguishing this objection from the first objection which they said was of a peremptory character, clearly implied that the objections based on non-exhaustion of local remedies were of a dilatory character, thus not touching the merits of the question concerning the responsibility of Lithuania. The procedural character of this rule must also be considered as the basic assumption of Judge Van Eysinga when he maintained in his dissenting opinion that the unconditional acceptance of the compulsory jurisdiction of the court con-

function being to permit the respondent State to discharge its responsibility by doing justice in its own way, to investigate and adjudicate by its own tribunals upon the questions of law and fact of the case, and then to determine on the basis of this adjudication its international responsibility and to meet or reject the claim accordingly.[62] In this case, the mere fact that the municipal authorities empowered to award remedies were not able to atone the international responsibility of the State does not by itself give rise to a separate unlawful act on the part of the State.[63]

Cases of failure of local remedies in this sense should, therefore, be carefully separated from cases of denial of justice proper, where the international unlawful act consists in the remedial organs of the State failing to comply with the requirements of international law to provide redress for private wrongs suffered within its jurisdiction. In the latter case, the international unlawful act does not arise unless there is an established failure of local remedies.[64] The distinction is of great importance in those cases where, for instance, before a claims commission, the rule of local remedies is dispensed with.[65] Such a provision can only dispense with the rule with regard to the former category of cases, but not with regard to the latter. For in the second category of cases, where local remedies have not yet failed either by insufficient action or by

stituted a prorogation of jurisdiction dispensing with the local remedies rule (*q.v.*, pp. 30 *et seq.*).

See also Mex.-U.S. G.C.C. (1923): *Chattin Case* (1927) paragraph 8 *et passim*, *Op. of Com. 1927*, p. 422.

Cf. contra E. M. Borchard, "Theoretical Aspects of the international Responsibility of States," I (1) Z.f.a.ö.R.u.V. (1929) p. 223. Contrary to what Borchard maintained, the determination of the exact moment when international responsibility arises is of practical importance. See *supra*, p. 176, *infra*, pp. 178–180.

62 *Finnish Vessels Case* (1934), *loc. cit.*, p. 1501.

63 *Ibid.*, at p. 1501. See also Mex.-U.S. G.C.C. (1923): *Garcia and Garza Case* (1926), paragraph 8, *Op. of Com. 1927*, p. 163, at p. 169.

64 As regards the dual function of the local remedies rule, *cf.* the *Salvador Commercial Co. Case* (1902), U.S.F.R. (1902), p. 838, at pp. 870–1.

65 *E.g.*, Mexican–U.S. Convention of September 8, 1923, establishing a General Claims Commission, Art. V (A.J.I.L. (1924), Off.Doc., pp. 147 *et seq.*); Mexican–U.S. Convention of September 10, 1923, establishing a Special Claims Commission, Art. VI (A.J.I.L. 1924, Off.Doc., pp. 143 *et seq.*); Panamanian–U.S. Convention of July 28, 1926, Art. V (Hunt's *Report*, pp. 835 *et seq.*).

Cf. Mex.-U.S. G.C.C. (1923): *International Fisheries Co. Case* (1931), D.O. of F. K. Nielsen, *Op. of Com. 1931*, p. 207, at p. 239: "There has in recent years been a tendency, seemingly a very proper one, to eliminate that rule in connection with the adjudication of international controversies."

their absence, there is no internationally unlawful act and hence no claim to be presented.

While the failure of local remedies to redress an existing wrong committed by the State does not create an additional responsibility, it may happen, however, that the responsibility of the State for an existing unlawful act is aggravated by further injustices committed by its remedial organs. This would be the case when, an unlawful act having already been committed by the State, its remedial organs have not only failed to expiate the wrong by affording proper redress—which in itself would not constitute another unlawful act—but have acted in such a way as to amount " to an outrage, to bad faith, to wilful neglect of duty, or to an insufficiency of governmental action so far short of international standards that every reasonable and impartial man would readily recognise its insufficiency."[66] When this happens, there is an additional unlawful act and an additional item of responsibility.[67]

In conclusion, it is submitted that an unlawful act in international law is any act or omission which is imputable to a State,[68] and which violates an international obligation incumbent upon it, whether under treaty stipulations or under general international law, the quality of the act in municipal law being juridically irrelevant. The unlawful act exists and responsibility arises immediately the international obligation is violated,[69] the existence or non-existence of possible municipal remedies having no juridical effect either on the existence of the unlawful act or on the responsibility arising out of it.

C. Imputability in International Law

Imputability in international law is the juridical attribution of a particular act by a physical person, or a group of physical persons, to a State, or other international person, whereby it

[66] Mex.-U.S. G.C.C. (1923): *Garcia and Garza Case* (1926), *Op. of Com. 1927*, p. 163, at p. 169.

[67] Mex.-U.S. G.C.C. (1923): *Mallén Case* (1927), §§ 11 and 13, *Op. of Com. 1927*, p. 254, at pp. 261–2; *Stephens Case* (1927), §§ 8 and 10, *ibid.*, p. 297, at pp. 400–1.

[68] Perhaps, more correctly, to a subject of international law.

[69] Moreover, once an unlawful act is committed, it acquires an existence independent of the obligation which it has violated (see ICJ: *Ambatielos Case* (1952), D.O. by Sir A. D. McNair, *ICJ Reports 1952*, p. 28, at p. 63).

is regarded as the latter's own act. Imputability is a basic notion in the concept of State responsibility and is fundamentally linked with the juridical concept of the State in international law.

I. THE STATE

In this connection, the following opinion of the Venezuelan Commissioner in the cases of *Amelia de Brissot, Ralph Rawdon, Joseph Stackpole* and *Narcisa de Hammer* (1885) is instructive:—

"The responsibility of governments, in general, for damages caused to foreigners, is founded on the ground that the State being a moral person endowed to a certain degree with the same capacity and liberty as are enjoyed by the citizens who compose it, is bound as such to account for its own acts when they cause some injury to another State, or to the citizens of another State. For the same reason it is held bound to indemnify the damages caused by the persons under its dependence, and for whom it is accountable.

"But in the State a double juridical person is to be recognised—the civil person, inasmuch as it is the possessor of its patrimony and has the capacity to administer it, and the political person, so far as it is a political, independent, and sovereign entity charged with the preservation of the public order and the protection of the citizens. Considered in the first aspect, its responsibility towards the foreigners damnified or injured by the acts of its officers is purely moral, and only in the case of complicity, or of manifest denial of justice, could it become international. . . .

"With regard to the political personality, the international responsibility of the State for acts of its officers in the exercise of public authority is subject to clear and well-known rules. Such responsibility is admitted, but only in the case that upon an examination of the circumstances, the fact which has produced the damage to foreign interests may morally be imputable to the State." [70]

This opinion, on the whole, fairly expresses the legal aspect of the State in international law. As a political entity, sovereign and independent, the State is an international legal person, possessing not only the capacity to bear rights and obligations under international law, but also the capacity to exercise these rights and violating these obligations. There can

[70] U.S.-Ven. Cl.Com. (1885): 3 *Int.Arb.*, p. 2949, at pp. 2952–3.

thus be no doubt regarding the so-called international *Deliktsfähigkeit* of the State, that is to say, its capacity to commit international unlawful acts. Without this capacity, it would naturally be vain even to speak of international unlawful acts being imputed to the State. Concurrently with this international personality of the State, which is alone relevant from the point of view of international responsibility, and indeed of international law, the State also has a, and possibly several personalities under municipal law. In so far as international law is concerned, the State and its subdivisions, acting in this latter capacity, are to be treated as persons subject to municipal law.[71] In speaking of the imputability of acts to the

[71] This distinction is clearly made in Mex.-U.S. G.C.C. (1923): *Home Insurance Co. Case* (1926), *Op. of Com. 1927*, p. 51. Claims against Mexico as administrators of Mexican railways for seizure by revolutionaries of goods entrusted for transportation. Held:

"16. It is for each nation to decide for itself whether or not it will engage in owning and/or operating railroads or other transportation facilities. In this case it appears that at the time of the losses here complained of the Government of Mexico had taken possession of and was operating the railroads located in the territory under its jurisdiction. As such it was performing a governmental function, but it by no means follows that its liability as a carrier of freight and passengers for hire was in any respect greater than or different from that of a private corporation operating the same railroads. *In its capacity as carrier Mexico*, as between it and the owner of the goods carried, *was subject to the laws of the Republic applicable to other public carriers. . . .* Under the laws of Mexico a public carrier for hire is not liable for the loss or damage to shipments in its possession resulting from '*casos fortuitos*,' which includes acts of revolutionary forces, without negligence on its part. In these circumstances the Commission decides that the Government of Mexico is not liable in its capacity as carrier for the loss of the shipments of coffee here involved.

"17. *But the Government of Mexico in its sovereign capacity owed the duty to protect the persons and property within its jurisdiction* by such means as were reasonably necessary to accomplish that end" (pp. 56–7. Italics added).

Note that the Commission in recognising the dual capacity of the State does not deny that the administration of railways in such a case is a governmental function. It is not necessary therefore that the enterprise or transaction be segregated from the other machinery or administration of the State. It also shows that the Government, as organ of the State, may also function in this dual capacity.

See similarly, Fran.-Germ. M.A.T.: *Fonbank Case* (1928), 8 T.A.M., p. 489.

The distinction between the State in its political and its private aspect becomes more pronounced as one goes down the governmental hierachy of the State.

"The dual character of municipal corporations; the one governmental, legislative, or public; the other proprietary or private" was strongly stressed by the Umpire in U.S. Ven. M.C.C. (1903): *La Guaira Electric Light and Power Co. Case, Ven.Arb. 1903*, p. 178, at p. 181. In the latter capacity, the acts of the municipality are solely those of a private legal person submitted to municipal law. See p. 182.

The State in municipal law may in fact possess several legal personalities. It definitely possesses a personality in municipal public law. It is the State in this capacity, for instance, that contracts public loans with private individuals and grants concessions. As such the relations are between subjects of

State, therefore, only the imputability of acts to the State in its capacity as a sovereign and independent international person is referred to. The actual conditions of imputability mentioned by the Commissioner [72] do not, however, seem entirely satisfactory and it is proposed to examine the question afresh on the basis of international judicial practice.

II. STATE REPRESENTATION

From the fact that States are juridical persons it follows that they must act through physical persons. In the words of the Permanent Court of International Justice:—

municipal law, governed by rules of that law. See, *e.g.*, PCIJ: *Serbian Loans Case* (1929), A.20/21, p. 18. But it may also possess a purely private legal personality, *e.g.*, in purchasing certain goods under an ordinary contract of sale. See Pol.-Germ. M.A.T.: *Gwirzmann Case* (1927), 7 T.A.M., p. 732, at p. 737.

In the realm of municipal law, in contrast to that of international law, the political subdivisions of the State may also possess a legal personality distinct from that of the State. The distinction is of importance in understanding those cases which deal with transactions of foreign private individuals with political subdivisions in their separate municipal personality in matters governed by municipal laws. *Cf.*, *e.g.*, Rum.-Germ. M.A.T.: *Rosenstein Case* (1927), 7 T.A.M., p. 121, at p. 123: "The State of Hamburg, the only party to the contract of works, has a juridical personality distinct from that of the State of Germany" (Transl.). The distinction naturally is only one of municipal law. *Cf.* also Brit.-Germ. M.A.T.: *Niger Co., Ltd.* (1923), 3 T.A.M., p. 232, at pp. 235–6 (the private law personality of German Cameroon Protectorate) and Brit.-Turk. M.A.T.: *Ransomes, Sim et Jefferries, Ltd.* (1928) 8 T.A.M., p. 203.

In the field of international law, however, all these distinctions in municipal law disappear and all these juridical relations between persons of municipal law, both natural and juridical, public and private, become pure facts. *Cf.* the statement many times repeated by Commissioner Nielsen in several of his dissenting opinions that "International law, which is a law for the conduct of nations, does not concern itself with contracts," *i.e.*, contracts of municipal law. See, *e.g.*, Mex.-U.S. G.C.C. (1923): *International Fisheries Co. Case* (1931), D.O. of Commissioner Nielsen, *Op. of Com. 1931*, p. 207, at p. 230. International law only deals with the acts of the State as an international person. International responsibility only arises when the international person commits an internationally unlawful act by violating a rule of international law or an international obligation. *Cf.* Brit.-U.S. Cl.Arb. (1910): *Cayuga Indians Case* (1926), Nielsen's *Report*, p. 203, at p. 329.

72 "Fiore and Calvo concur in subordinating it to four conditions, to wit:—

"'1. That the Government may have known in due time to prevent it, the illegal act which its officer intended to commit, and did not prevent it.

"'2. That it, having been enabled to revoke in time the act of its officer, did not revoke it.

"'3. That the ignorance of the act intended by the officer may, by its circumstances, be judged as malicious or criminal.

"'4. That having been advised of the facts, it had not pressed itself to blame the acts of its agent, nor to take the proper measures to prevent in future the repetition of the same faults'" (*loc. cit.*, p. 2953).

For reasons why these conditions are considered unsatisfactory, see *infra*, p. 196, note 16.

"States can act only by and through their agents and representatives." [73]

The acts of the agents of a State are, therefore, to be considered as the acts of the State itself. Moreover, since

"an officer or person in authority represents *pro tanto* his government, which in an international sense is the aggregate of all officers and men in authority," [74]

it means that a State is represented by its government, whose acts are imputable to it as its own. But States not only act through their government but through their government exclusively.

There seems, on this point, little dissent from the view advanced by Venezuela in the *British Guiana-Venezuela Boundary Arbitration* (1899):—

"States do not act through individuals, but through governments. The acts of individual subjects of a State are not the acts of the State." [75]

Acts of private individuals, however numerous, cannot, therefore, be imputed to the State, notwithstanding the link of membership, *viz.*, nationality, between the individual and the State. As the Chilean-United States Claims Commission (1892) once said with regard to injurious acts:—

"All the authorities on international law are a unit as regards the principle that an injury done by one of the subjects of a nation is not to be considered as done by the nation itself." [76]

[73] *German Settlers in Poland* (1923), Adv.Op., B. 6, p. 22. See ICJ: *Reparation for Injuries suffered in the Service of the United Nations* (1949), Adv.Op., *ICJ Reports 1949*, p. 174, at p. 177, for a definition of "agent."

[74] Mex.-U.S. Cl.Com. (1868): *Moses Case* (1871), 3 *Int.Arb.*, p. 3127, at p. 3129. Seizure of goods by a minor official to satisfy a fine.

[75] *The Printed Argument on behalf of the United States of Venezuela before the Tribunal of Arbitration* (C. 9501; 112 *Parl.Papers* (1899), p. 35). It is true that in the present instance, the question raised was not the imputability of an unlawful act to the State, but whose act the State may claim to be its own as showing possession of land to create title for adverse holding. Yet the theory of imputability of any act to the State, whether delictual, contractual or otherwise, is fundamentally the same.

Cf. Senate of Hamburg: *Yuilles, Shortridge & Co. Case* (1861), 2 *Arb.Int.*, p. 96. See p. 105. To create desuetude of a treaty right, the non-usage must emanate from the government of the beneficiary State and not from private individuals, irrespective of their number.

With regard to acts acquisitive of title to territory, see, confirming the Venezuelan contention, *Brazil–British Guiana Boundary Case* (1904), 99 B.F.S.P., p. 930, at p. 930; PCIJ: *Eastern Greenland Case* (1933), A/B. 53, pp. 42–3.

[76] *Lovett Case*, 3 *Int.Arb.*, p. 2990, at p. 2991.

To do otherwise is, indeed,

" 'to raise a private injury to the height of a public offence, and to impute to the whole nation an offence committed by one of its members.' "[77]

The distinction to be drawn, however, between persons acting as private individuals and those acting as agents or officers of the State is purely qualitative and not quantitative, depending, as will be seen, upon the capacity in which they act, and not upon their number. The "one subject" spoken of in the first quotation is not limitative but generic and, in the very decision in which it was enunciated, the principle was applied to the acts of a body of 70 convicts who were in revolt on board a vessel while being escorted to a penal colony. The principle laid down is thus applicable generally to acts of such bodies of men as mobs, rioters, bandits, etc.[78] whose acts cannot, therefore, be regarded as acts of the State. A special word is necessary, however, with regard to acts of revolutionaries.

III. RIVAL GOVERNMENTS

Before proceeding to examine the imputability to the State of acts of the government, in other words of the aggregate of officials and men in authority, it is necessary first to consider the position of rival or revolutionary governments within a State.

Revolutionaries differ from other groups of private individuals in that they have a system of government. As defined by the American Commissioner in the *Santa Isabel Cases* (1926):—

"A revolutionist is one who, having a plan of government, is engaged in an attempt to overthrow an existing government."[79]

Are the acts of such a rival government imputable to the State? Far from being imputable to the State as its own, the

[77] *Oberlander* and *Messenger Case* (1897), U.S.A. *v.* Mexico, U.S.F.R. (1897), p. 370, at p. 387, quoting Calvo, 3 *Int.Law.*, p. 134.

[78] *Cf.* Brit.-U.S. Cl.Arb. (1910): *Home Missionary Society Case* (1920), Nielsen's *Report*, p. 421. The case cited anonymously by its reference only in support of the statement that "no government can be held responsible for the act of rebellious bodies of men" (p. 425) is the *Lovett Case* above quoted.

[79] Mex.-U.S. Special Cl.Com. (1923): D.O. of U.S. Commissioner, *Op. of Com. 1926–1931*, p. 1, at p. 19. *Cf.* Fran.-Mex. M.C.C. (1924): *Pinson Case* (1928), *Jurisprudence*, p. 1, at p. 107.

acts of revolutionaries are in fact regarded as acts of the *enemy* of the State. Both the Mexican and the American Commissioners in the Mexican-United States Claims Commission of 1868 qualified revolutionaries as enemies of the State, the Mexican Commissioner explaining that:—

"The propriety with which we employ this word when we speak of civil wars can be easily perceived. Enemies are all those against whom the nation has been compelled to employ the public force and to put itself, for its own conservation, on a footing of war. It matters little that the other nations may or may not recognise the position of the rebels as belligerents. Such a recognition can entail certain liabilities and duties to the government that deems proper to make it; but neither a new obligation can be imposed on account of it upon the contending parties, nor much less any alteration introduced in the diplomatic intercourse with the foreign powers who have not made the recognition." [80]

The acts of a revolutionary government, far from being undertaken on behalf of the State, are directly opposed to and directed against its constituted authority. They cannot be imputed to the State.[81]

Speaking of revolutions, the Umpire in the *Great Venezuelan Railroad Case* (C. 1903) said:—

"Revolutions are unlawful—are positively illegal; their object is to break down the *de jure* and *de facto* government and to destroy the existing system of law; their leaders and followers are by the laws of all civilised nations guilty of the highest crime known to the law, treason, and until success, therefore, anyone who aids or abets a revolution is a violator of the law and any citizen who omits or fails to assist the government violates his duty as a citizen." [82]

[80] *Salvador Prats Case*, 3 *Int.Arb.*, p. 2886, at p. 2896. *Cf.* Opinion of the American Commissioners, at p. 2890.

[81] Until it is supplanted by another government, the regular government is the sole organ representing the State. For this reason, it was not altogether incorrect when the Umpire of the Ital.-Ven. M.C.C. (1903), in the *Sambiaggio Case* (*Ven.Arb. 1903*, p. 666), denied the existence of *State* responsibility because the acts were those of the enemy of the *Government* (*e.g.*, p. 680). To be sure, such metonymy should not be encouraged lest it lead to confusion of thought. But international tribunals, as a whole, draw a clear distinction between the international person and its organ. "There is a well-recognised distinction between a State and a government or the governing body. The State is a person in law. . . . As a person invested with a will which is exerted through the government as the organ or instrument of society. . . ." U.S.-Ven. Cl.Com. (1885): *Garrison Case*, 4 *Int.Arb.*, p. 3548, at p. 3552.

[82] Germ.-Ven. M.C.C. (1903): *Ven.-Arb. 1903*, p. 632, at pp. 635–6.

Stronger words cannot be used to show that revolutionaries are extraneous to the legal order which constitutes the State. But this passage contains an important proviso in the words "until success," wherein lies the most important exception to the general principle: *ex injuria non oritur jus.* Therein is to be found perhaps the ultimate source of law (*lex*)—the greatest social force predominating in any given society in a more or less stable manner. The word "success" perhaps contains also the missing basic norm of those who uphold the pure theory of law. He who defies the law and defies it successfully shall himself say what is to be the law.[83]

[83] We are here speaking of course, only of the application of, and exception to the principle *ex injuria non oritur jus* in the sphere of municipal law. In the international sphere, revolutions by force do not *per se* constitute internationally unlawful acts. Internationally, therefore, in recognising a government established by force as the lawful government of a State, there is in reality no infringement of the principle *ex injuria jus non oritur.* It is only the doctrine of legitimacy once supported by the Holy Alliance and Tobar which tries to relate international law to municipal law on this point. This doctrine is now no longer valid in international law. See *infra*, pp. 188 *et seq.*

Incidentally, the Stimson doctrine which may be regarded as an application of the principle *ex injuria jus non oritur* in the sole orbit of international law is not concerned with governments formed through revolution. The distinction sometimes does not appear to be very clearly drawn by some writers, *e.g.*, Borchard and Morrison ("The Doctrine of Non-Recognition" in *Legal Problems in the Far Eastern Conflict*, 1941, pp. 157–8). This confusion is perhaps due to the use of the word "recognition" or rather "non-recognition" which has hitherto been usually applied to the non-recognition of governments.

The Stimson doctrine of non-recognition is in effect an express declaration in the international sphere not to acquiesce in, or accept, any result or situation arrived at by another State in violation of the provisions of a treaty to which one is a party. Its distinctive feature probably lies in its departure from customary practice where States often acquiesce in violations of multipartite conventions to which they are parties as long as no material interests of their own are affected. While in this sense it may be regarded as a step forward, it is in truth only "the minimum which considerations of international decency require" (A. D. McNair, "The Stimson Doctrine of Non-Recognition," 14 B.Y.I.L. (1933), p. 65, at p. 74). It does no more than abide by the logical consequences of the acceptance of the rule of law, and hardly deserves to be called a "weighty factor" in "upholding the authority of the law" (Lauterpacht, "The Principle of Non-Recognition" in *Legal Problems in the Far Eastern Conflict*, pp. 148–54).

Moreover, the same exception to the principle *ex injuria non oritur jus* as mentioned above also applies here. "It is an illusion that non-recognition can be a substitute for other more vigorous measures in the upholding of law" (T. C. Chen, *The International Law of Recognition*, 1951, p. 441). For unless there is some prospect of the wrongdoer being compelled to abandon his unlawful success, or, in other words, unless the other States are able and willing to use means more effective than this "somewhat symbolic instrument for upholding the challenged authority of international law" (Lauterpacht, *Recognition in International Law*, 1948, p. 433), non-recognition becomes no more than a pious fiction (see Schwarzenberger, *Power Politics*, 1951, p. 503), and, where it is admitted that *de facto* recognition may be given and a "substantial measure of actual intercourse" may be continued (Lauterpacht, "The Principle of Non-Recognition," *loc. cit.*, p. 148, at p. 154), it is a fiction which is not even pious (*cf.* McNair, *loc. cit.*).

As the Arbitrator said in the *Aguilar-Amory and Royal Bank of Canada (Tinoco) Cases* (1923):—

"The change by revolution upsets the rule of the authorities in power under the then existing fundamental law, and sets aside the fundamental law in so far as the change of rule makes it necessary." [84]

It follows, therefore, that a change of government may be brought about without compliance with the existing municipal law of the country.

"To speak of a revolution creating a *de facto* government, which conforms to the limitations of the old constitution is to use a contradiction in terms." [85]

It is rather the existing municipal law which must perforce be modified to conform to the successful revolution.[86] This, incidentally, demonstrates the fundamental irrelevancy of municipal law to imputability in international law, since, in determining the representative organ of the State, it is not necessary to attach importance even to the State's fundamental law.

"According to a principle of international law, denied at first theoretically in the dynastic interest by the diplomacy of European monarchies, applied, in fact, however, in a series of cases, and today universally admitted, the capacity of a government to represent the State in its international relations does not depend in any degree upon the legitimacy of its origin, so that . . . the usurper who in fact holds power with the consent express or tacit of the nation, acts and concludes validly in the name of the State treaties that the restored legitimate government is obliged to respect." [87]

"A government *de facto*, when once invested with the powers which are necessary to give it that character, can bind the State to the same extent and with the same legal effect as what is styled a government *de jure*. Indeed, as Austin has pointed out, every government, properly so called, is a government *de facto*. A government *de jure* but not *de facto*, says he, is that which *was* a government, and which, according to the view of the speaker, *ought* still to be a government, but, in point of fact, is not." [88]

[84] 1 UNRIAA, p. 369, at p. 381.
[85] *Ibid.*
[86] See Fran.-Chil. Arb.Trib. (1894): *Dreyfus Case* (1901), *Traités du XXe Siècle* (1901), p. 188, at p. 396.
[87] *Dreyfus Case* (1901), *ibid.*, at p. 394 (Transl.).
[88] *Garrison Case* (C. 1885), *loc. cit.*, at p. 3553. See also U.S.-Ven. Cl.Com. (1868): *Jansen Case*, 3 *Int.Arb.*, p. 2902, at p. 2930.

"As to what constitutes a government *de facto* is a question that must necessarily depend somewhat upon the facts and circumstances in the particular case to which it is proposed to apply the principle. Austin speaks of it as a government which presumably commands the habitual respect and obedience of the bulk of the people." [89]

"This habitual obedience of the members of a political society (of the 'bulk' of them) must, in fact, exist to constitute a government." [90]

Recognition *vel non* by foreign States, although of evidential value, is not, however, a conclusive criterion, even upon the State granting or withholding it.[91]

In so far as imputability is concerned, the problem of rival or revolutionary governments is, therefore, a relatively simple one. For, if the relevant government for the purpose of imputability is the one which commands the habitual obedience of the *bulk* of the people, "there can be but one government in the same State at the same time," [92] whose acts may be imputable to the State.

From the standpoint of international law,

"The State is a person in law. . . . As a person invested with a will which is exerted through the government as the organ or instrument of society, it follows as a necessary consequence that mere

[89] *Garrison Case, loc. cit.*, at p. 3553.

[90] Mex.-U.S. Cl.Com. (1868): *Cuculla Case*, 3 *Int.Arb.*, p. 2873, at p. 2877; see also *passim; McKenny Case, ibid.*, p. 2881, at p. 2882. Neth.-Ven. M.C.C. (1903): *Henriquez Case, Ven.Arb. 1903*, p. 896, at p. 899.

[91] *Aguilar-Amory and Royal Bank of Canada (Tinoco) Case* (1923), *loc. cit.*, pp. 380 *et seq.* Mex.-U.S. G.C.C. (1923): *Hopkins Case* (1926), *Op. of Com. 1927*, p. 42, at p. 50. Fran.-Mex. M.C.C. (1924): *Pinson Case* (1928), *Jurisprudence*, p. 1, at pp. 105–6.

On closer examination, the *Jansen Case* (C. 1868) (*loc. cit*), does not constitute an exception. The decision was based on a finding of fact that the Maximilian experiment did not succeed in forming a national government *de facto*. The non-recognition by the U.S. seemed to the Commissioner to have indicated that the U.S. would not have desired to espouse such a claim.

Cf., moreover, the same Commissioner (Wadsworth) in the *McKenny Case* (C. 1868) (*loc. cit.*, at p. 2883) and in the *Cuculla Case* (C. 1868) (*loc cit.*, at pp. 2876–7) where he definitely attributed to foreign recognition only evidential value in determining a question of *fact* whether a new government had been formed or not. "Recognition is based upon the pre-existing fact; does not create the fact" (pp. 2876–7). See also opinion of the Mexican Commissioner in the *Cuculla Case* (*loc. cit.*, p. 2880).

The *Garrison Case* (C. 1885) too is not an exception despite what was said in *loc. cit.*, p. 3553. *Cf. loc. cit.*, pp. 3560–1, where the Umpire definitely treated recognition as evidence of a fact and not as a binding conclusion on the existence of a fact.

[92] Mex.-U.S. Cl.Com. (1868): *Jansen Case*, 3 *Int.Arb.*, p. 2902, at p. 2928. See also p. 2930.

internal changes which result in the displacement of any particular organ for the expression of this will, and the substitution of another, cannot alter the relations of the society to the other members of the family of States as long as the State itself retains its personality. The State remains, although the government may change." [93]

" Nations do not die when there is a change of their rulers or in their forms of government. These are but expressions of a change of national will. ' The King is dead; long live the King!' has typified this thought for ages." [94]

Forma regiminis mutata, non mutatur ipsa civitas.[95]

It has been held, however, that

" The change must be supported by the mass of the people and rest upon their consent. Should foreign intervention aid this change we can never regard the fact as accomplished or as resting upon the favour of the people unless the new government is strong enough to maintain itself after the foreign aid shall be withdrawn." [96]

A régime that is established thanks to foreign intervention cannot be considered as the organ representing the national will, as long as it is maintained with foreign aid. Rather must it be considered as the instrument of the will of the foreign Power. The acts of such a régime are not the acts of the nation; they cannot, consequently, be imputed to the State.[97]

To the general rule that at any given time there is only one organ whose acts are imputable to the State, there is, however, an exception. During a period of revolution, it may happen that the acts of two different governments are imputable to the State; for the acts of revolutionaries who are ultimately successful are imputable to the State. This imputability covers acts done in respect of territory subject to their control, even

[93] *Garrison Case*, *loc. cit.*, p. 3552. See also *Neapolitan Indemnity*, Note of U.S. Minister to Neapolitan Secretary for Foreign Affairs, of Aug. 24, 1816 (5 *Int.Arb.*, p. 4577; full text in 5 B.F.S.P., p. 204, at p. 206); *Dreyfus Case* (1901), *loc. cit.*, at pp. 394 *et seq.*; *Aguilar-Amory and Royal Bank of Canada (Tinoco) Case* (1923), *loc. cit.*, p. 377.

[94] Brit.-Ven. Cl.Com. (1903): *Bolivar Ry. Case*, *Ven.Arb. 1903*, p. 388, at p. 394.

[95] Mex.-U.S. Cl.Com. (1868): *Baxter Case*, 3 *Int.Arb.*, p. 2934: " The State is the same, although the form of government is changed."

[96] *Jansen Case*, *loc. cit.*, p. 2927.

[97] See *Jansen Case*, *loc. cit.* The case referred to the French sponsored Maximilian attempt to establish a monarchy in Mexico. Mexico was held not accountable for the acts of that régime.

before they succeeded in establishing a general *de facto* government over the entire national territory.[98]

"The nation is responsible for the obligations of a successful revolution from its beginning, because, in theory, it represented *ab initio* a changing national will, crystallizing in the finally successful result. . . . Success demonstrates that from the beginning it was registering the national will." [99]

It may, therefore, happen that for a period of time the national will is expressed simultaneously by two rival organs, the *de jure* government on the one hand and the ultimately successful revolutionaries on the other hand. The acts of two different governments may, therefore, be imputed to the State. It must, however, be remembered that this rather anomalous situation does not arise unless the revolution is one which is ultimately successful.

So far, we have discussed revolutions which attempt to supplant the entire governmental machinery. The Mexican-United States General Claims Commission (1923) in the *Hopkins Case* (1926) pointed out, however, that:—

"The greater part of governmental machinery in every modern country is not affected by changes in the higher administrative officers." [1]

And the significance of this decision, to which there has sometimes been attributed a wider meaning than the case actually warrants, consists in showing that there may be revolutions confined to the "higher administration" only.[2] In such a case,

[98] Mex.-U.S. G.C.C. (1923): *Hopkins Case* (1926), *Op. of Com. 1927*, p. 42–51, at p. 48. The distinction between revolutions beginning in the capital and those originating from the provinces presents in reality no juridical justification or value except to the extent of pointing out that the mere possession and control of the capital is no valid criterion of a *de facto* national government representing the State as long as the revolutionary movement is not the real master of the nation. For the immateriality of the mere control of the capital, see also *Cuculla Case*, 3 *Int.Arb.*, p. 2873, at p. 2877.

[99] *Bolivar Ry. Case*, *Ven.Arb. 1903*, p. 388, at p. 394.

[1] *Op. of Com. 1927*, p. 42, at p. 44.

[2] As appears clearly from § 11 of the decision, this was the case in question concerning the Huerta usurpation in Mexico, 1913. See inter alia, *ibid.*, p. 47: "It also appears that when Huerta seized the reins of government which in his capacity as provisional president he undertook to administer he did not change the Government machinery as it had been set up under President Madero, which continued to operate in all its parts in the service of the people, and the great machinery of the personnel of all of the bureaus and agencies of the Government remained unchanged and continued to discharge their duties to and in the name of Mexico."

the unaffected part of the government remains the proper State organ; its acts are those of the State. Only the acts of those officials acting *qua* revolutionaries are subject to the rules of imputability governing acts of revolutionaries. The distinction is not, however, based on any arbitrary line drawn across the governmental hierarchy, but depends upon the nature and circumstances of each act according to whether it is accomplished in the discharge of normal governmental functions or is an act of an extraordinary nature peculiar to a state of revolution. This would seem to be the principle of the *Hopkins Case* (1926), especially if that case is examined in the light of the entire jurisprudence of the Commission. The *Hopkins Case* was not really concerned with a situation in which the whole machinery of government is involved in a revolution.[3]

Having thus determined the question of contending governments, it is now possible to resume the general discussion concerning imputability of governmental acts to the State.

IV. ACTS OF OFFICIALS

The imputability of governmental acts to the State is, in the last analysis, a problem of the imputability of acts of government officials. It has already been mentioned that a government, "in an international sense is the aggregate of all officers and men in authority."[4]

We have just seen that the question whether the acts of a government are imputable to the State under international law is in reality one of fact, namely, whether or not it wields the power and authority of the State, irrespective of its position in municipal law. As regards the imputability of the acts of each particular officer, it will be seen that, in the last analysis, this

[3] The decision contains long recitals of reasons too long to quote here (*q.v.*).
The following decisions of the same Commission have been decided in conformity with the *Hopkins Case* (1926) and serve to illustrate the application of the principle stated above: *Peerless Motor Case* (1927), *Op. of Com. 1927*, p. 303; *G. W. Cook Case* (Docket No. 663) (1927), *ibid.*, p. 318; *Parsons Trading Co. Case* (Docket No. 2651) (1927), *ibid.*, p. 324; *McPherson Case* (1927), *ibid.*, p. 325; *Craw Case* (1928), *Op. of Com. 1929*, p. 1; *National Paper and Type Co. Case* (1928), *ibid.*, p. 3; *Acosta Case* (1928) *ibid.*, p. 121; *Singer Sewing Machine Co. Case* (1928), *ibid.*, p. 123; *Parsons Trading Co. Case* (Docket Nos. 3125 and 3126) (1929), *ibid.*, p. 135; *G. W. Cook Case* (Docket No. 1366) (1929), *ibid.*, p. 266; *Moffit Case* (1929), *ibid.*, p. 288; *G. W. Cook Case* (Docket Nos. 1353 and 1795) (1930), *Op. of Com. 1931*, pp. 162 and 167.

[4] *Supra*, p. 184.

also is a question of fact, namely, whether the officer occupies a position in which he exercises the authority, or a fraction of the authority, possessed by the government as a whole. His acts, in the exercise of that fraction of State authority, constitute a manifestation of the State's will and are imputable to the State, whatever may be his nationality, his function, his rank, or whether he has acted in error, in disobedience to instructions, or in contravention of municipal law.

The irrelevancy of the nationality of the official was clearly acknowledged by the Franco-German Mixed Arbitral Tribunal in the *Damas-Hamah Case* (1924). In deciding that the taking of the claimant's railway in pursuance of orders issued by Turkish officials who were of German nationality was "a measure emanating from the Ottoman authorities" and not an act of Germany, the Tribunal said:—

> "One could not object that von Kress, as well as Dickmann, are both of German nationality, it being clear that, in this case, they acted in their capacity as officials of the Turkish government, on behalf of this government." [5]

Furthermore, the official of one State may also act at the same time as the agent of another. The imputability of his act in each case must depend on the capacity in which he acts, which is a question of fact. Thus in the *Chevreau Case* (1931), the Permanent Court of Arbitration held that:—

> "The British Government could not be held responsible for a negligence of which its consul, acting in his capacity of representative of the Consulate of another power, might have been guilty." [6]

In other words, the negligence of the consul could not be imputed to the State which in this particular case he did not in fact represent.

[5] 4 T.A.M., p. 801, at p. 804. (Transl.)

[6] 2 UNRIAA, p. 1113, at p. 1141. (Transl.) He was in fact acting for the French Consulate in that case.

Cf., however, Brit.-U.S. Cl.Arb. (1910): *The Wanderer Case* (1921), Nielsen's *Report*, p. 459. In this case, which seemingly adopted a contrary view, it may legitimately be asked if the situation was not different; for the United States officers who effected the seizure were not acting for the British Government as its agents, but in fact for the United States Government in pursuance of the authority delegated by the United States. It may be said that it was the United States which was empowered in certain circumstances to seize British vessels. In the absence of these circumstances, its officers made such a seizure. Their error is imputable to the United States but not Great Britain. For facts of the case see *infra*, p. 202, note 30.

Next, it may be convenient to enquire whether there is a distinction to be made between the various categories of agents of the State. If there ever was a faint suggestion that acts of the judicial officers of a State were so aloof and independent that they were not acts personal to the State,[7] today,

" ' There can be no doubt . . . that a State is responsible for the acts of its rulers, whether they belong to the legislative, executive or judicial department of the government, so far as the acts are done in their official capacity.' "[8]

Another problem is the question of acts done by officials of the constituent states of a federal entity, in regard to which there may be relative degrees of independence under the Constitution. An example of this question arose before the British-Venezuelan Mixed Claims Commission (1903), concerning the unlawful act of an official of the state of Bolivar, one of the states of Venezuela, and,

" In the opinion of the umpire there can be but one answer to this proposition, which is that there is responsibility on the part of Venezuela for the acts of its civil officers whether they in fact received their respective commissions directly from the National Government or indirectly and mediately through means and methods previously devised by the National Government for the care and

[7] *Cf.* Senate of Hamburg: *Yuille, Shortridge & Co. Case* (1861), 2 *Arb.Int.*, p. 78, at p. 103: " It would be altogether unjust to make the Royal Government of Portugal account for the faults committed by its tribunals. By the Constitution of the Kingdom of Portugal, the courts are perfectly independent of the Government which consequently cannot exercise any influence over their decisions; one cannot therefore make it responsible for them " (Transl.). But the decision in this case was based precisely on the acts of the judiciary. " The Supreme Court having sent the suit to the Court of Appeal, it was the judgment delivered by this jurisdiction which furnished the Royal British Government a legitimate means of complaint " (p. 107). What the Senate meant was not, therefore, that the acts of the judiciary were not the acts of the State, but rather the judicial acts of a State were to be given a stronger presumption of regularity and were not to be considered internationally unlawful save in exceptional circumstances of " denial of justice or pretence of forms to mask violence " (p. 103), or violations of treaty obligations (p. 105).
Cf. also *Id.*: *Croft Case* (1856), 2 *Arb.Int.*, p. 1, at p. 24.

[8] *Salvador Commercial Co. Case* (1902), U.S.F.R. (1902), p. 838, at p. 870, quoting Halleck.
Mex. U.S. G.C.C. (1923): *Way Case* (1928), *Op. of Com. 1929*, p. 94, at p. 106: " Under international law a nation has responsibility for the conduct of judicial officers."
Cf. also *Id.*: *Chattin Case* (1927), *Op. of Com. 1927*, p. 422, for a discussion of the various international standards of conduct governing the activities of the different branches of the government, including the judiciary (§§ 8–11). The more lenient standard applied to the judiciary (p. 427) as compared with other branches of the government is the probable explanation of the erroneous impression that acts of the judiciary are not imputable to the State.

control of the state, county, or municipality to whom power had been delegated by the National Government to make these appointments and issue commissions. The creator of these methods and means of internal administration, *viz.*, the nation, must always be responsible to the other government for the creatures of its creation." [9]

As to the rank of the official concerned,

"An examination of the opinions of international tribunals dealing with the question of a nation's responsibility for minor officials reveals conflicting views and considerable uncertainty . . . To attempt by some broad classification to make a distinction between some 'minor' or 'petty' officials and other kinds of officials must obviously at times involve practical difficulties." [10]

"I believe that it is undoubtedly a sound general principle that, whenever misconduct on the part of any such persons, whatever may be their particular status or rank under domestic law, results in the failure of a nation to perform its obligations under international law, the nation must bear the responsibility for the wrongful acts of its servants." [11]

The cases often cited to show that a distinction is apparently made between the imputability of the acts of minor and superior officials [12] were in reality instances where the claims failed because available local remedies had not been exhausted.[13] The dual character and the procedural aspect of the rule of exhaustion of local remedies have already been mentioned and need no further elaboration here.[14] Since local remedies are, in point

[9] *Davy Case*, *Ven.Arb. 1903*, p. 410, at p. 411.

[10] Mex.-U.S. G.C.C. (1923): *Massey Case* (1927), *Op. of Com. 1927*, p. 228, at pp. 230–1. Mexico contended that a State could not be held responsible for the act of a minor official (a gaol keeper) done in violation of law and of duty, if the State immediately disapproved of the act by arresting and punishing the officer.

[11] *Massey Case* (1927), *loc. cit.*, p. 234. Jurisprudence confirmed by same Commission in *Way Case* (1928), *Op. of Com. 1929*, p. 94, at p. 106; *Roper Case* (1927), *Op. of Com. 1927*, p. 205, at p. 208.

See also identical wording in U.S.-Turk. Cl. Settlement (under 1935 Act): *Malamatinis Claim* (1937), Nielsen's *Op. & Rep.*, p. 603, at pp. 608–9.

Cf. also Neth.-Ven. M.C.C. (1903): *Maal Case*, *Ven.Arb. 1903*, p. 914, at p. 916.

[12] Mexico in the *Massey Case* (1927) cited the following: U.S. Domestic Commission (1849): *Bensley Case*, 3 *Int.Arb.*, p. 3016; Mex.-U.S. Cl.Com. (1868): *Blumhardt Case*, *ibid.*, p. 3146; *Id.*: *Slocum Case* (1876), *ibid.*, p. 3140; *Id.*: *Leichardt Case*, *ibid.*, p. 3133.

[13] See *Massey Case* (1927), *loc. cit.*, §§ 9, 10, 12, 13. In § 11, the decision also pointed out that the Mex.-U.S. Cl.Com. (1868) dismissed a number of claims purely because local remedies had not been exhausted.

[14] *Supra*, pp. 179 *et seq.*

of fact, more often provided for the wrongful acts of officials in the lower strata of the governmental hierarchy, and since claims arising from their acts sometimes become barred on account of the rule that local remedies must first be exhausted, the erroneous impression has sometimes been formed that acts of minor officials are not imputable to the State. It is when this rule has been dispensed with that the irrelevancy of the rank of the officials from the point of view of imputability becomes apparent. It was in such circumstances that the Umpire in the *Moses Case* (1871) said:—

"An officer or person in authority represents *pro tanto* his government, which in an international sense is the aggregate of all officers and men in authority." [15]

Whatever his rank, his act *qua* an official is an act of the government and hence of the State.[16]

Equally unimportant from the point of view of imputability is the municipal status of the official concerned. In the *Stephens Case* (1927), an American was shot by an individual called Valenzuela, who belonged to "some Mexican guards or auxiliary forces" and was on guard duty. With regard to the status of the force to which the individual belonged, the Mexican-United States General Claims Commission (1923) said:—

"It is difficult to determine with precision the status of these guards as an irregular auxiliary of the army, the more so as they lacked both uniforms and insignia." [17]

The Commission nevertheless held that:—

"But at any rate they were 'acting for' Mexico or for its political subdivisions." [18]

"Taking account of the conditions existing in Chihuahua then and there, Valenzuela must be considered as, or assimilated to, a soldier." [19]

It is plain, therefore, that international law, in order to

15 Mex.-U.S. Cl.Com. (1868), 3 *Int.Arb.*, p. 3127, at p. 3129.

16 For this reason the conditions mentioned by the Venezuelan Commissioner in the *de Brissot Cases* (*supra*, p. 183, note 72) are unsatisfactory and are disapproved inter alia by the *Massey Case* (1927), where some of the conditions were not fulfilled. The result of those conditions would mean that to an unlawful act of the official must be added the action or omission of another official in order to make the wrong imputable to the State.

17 *Op. of Com. 1927*, p. 397, at p. 399.

18 *Ibid.*, p. 399.

19 *Ibid.*, p. 400.

determine whether or not a person is acting as a State official, whose acts may be imputed to the State, decides autonomously according to the facts of the case and not according to the municipal status of the individual concerned.[20]

Having now dealt with various considerations derived from municipal law, nationality, function, rank, status, and the like, which are deemed irrelevant from the point of view of imputability, we may proceed to examine the conditions governing the imputability of the act of an official to the State. The question is so intimately linked with the circumstances of each case that it is difficult to discern the precise standard

[20] In this connection, it may be of interest to cite the decision of the Germ.-U.S. M.C.C. (1922) in the *Damson Case* (1925), *Dec. & Op.*, p. 243. By paragraph 9 of Annex I to section I of Part VIII of the Treaty of Versailles, Germany was bound to pay indemnity for certain losses suffered by the "civilian population" of the Allied and Associated Powers. The Commission held: "The line of demarcation between the 'civilian population' and the military within the meaning of the Treaty is not an arbitrary line drawn by the statutory enactments of the nation, each nation drawing it in a different place, but a natural line determined by the occupation, at the time of the injury or damage complained of, of the individual national of each and all of the Allied and Associated Powers. . . ." The Commission recalled one of its previous decisions in which the following illustration was used:—

> "'The taxicabs privately owned and operated for profit in Paris during September, 1914, were in no sense military materials; but when these same taxicabs were requisitioned by the Military Governor of Paris and used to transport French reserves to meet and repel the oncoming German army, they became military materials, and so remained until redelivered to their owners.'" The Commission then continued:—

"The same rule, having its source in the same reason, applies to the drivers of those taxicabs. On the streets of Paris, operating their vehicles for profit, they were a part of the 'civilian population' of France. But when pressed into service and used to transport the army to the battle front where the taxicab drivers were exposed to the risks to which the 'civilian population' was not generally exposed, they became a part of the French fighting machine; they were directly engaged in a military operation launched against the enemy and were no longer embraced in the 'civilian population' of France within the meaning of the Treaty, although they may not have been enrolled in the army, or authorised to wear uniforms or bear arms, or possessed of a 'military status'" (pp. 262–3).

See also *Id.*: *Hungerford Case* (1926), *Dec. & Op.*, p. 766.

In transferring an individual from the category of civilians to that of "military," the Commission has endowed him with the quality of an agent of the State; for as the Commission said in its *Opinion Construing the Phrase "Naval and Military Works and Materials" as applied to Hull Losses and also dealing with Requisitioned Dutch Ships* (1924), *Dec. & Op.*, p. 75, at p. 99: "So long as a ship is privately operated for private profit she cannot be impressed with a military character, for only the Government can lawfully engage in direct warlike activities." In other words, he who is a military person is an agent of the Government, or else, from the point of view of international law, he cannot be reckoned among the military personnel.

While the Commission has dealt with only a very small section of government agents, yet it seems that the principle involved is susceptible of general application.

See also *Cession of Vessels and Tugs for Navigation on The Danube* (1921), 1 UNRIAA, p. 97, at pp. 106 *et seq.*

applied by international courts and tribunals. No clear statement has been found in international decisions, the closest being perhaps the following dictum of the Mexican-United States General Claims Commission (1923):—

> "In reaching conclusions in any given case with respect to responsibility for acts of public servants, the most important considerations of which account must be taken are the character of the acts alleged to have resulted in injury to persons or to property, or the nature of functions performed whenever a question is raised as to their proper discharge." [21]

There are, therefore, two pertinent considerations governing the imputability of acts of officials to the State:

1. Character of the act in question;
2. Nature of the function which the official is entrusted to discharge.

It may be of interest to compare these considerations with the criterion adopted by the Permanent Court of International Justice in the *Eastern Greenland Case* (1933) with regard to the "Ihlen declaration." On July 22, 1919, the Norwegian Foreign Minister, M. Ihlen, following a request from the Government of Denmark seeking from his Government an acknowledgment of the latter's sovereignty in Greenland, declared to the Danish Minister verbally that "The Norwegian Government will not make any difficulties in the settlement of this question." The question raised was whether the declaration was binding on Norway. In other words, the question was whether such a declaration on the part of the Foreign Minister could be considered as an act of the State itself. The Court held:—

> "The Court considers it beyond all dispute that a *reply of this nature* given by the Minister for Foreign Affairs on behalf of his government in response to a request by the diplomatic representative of a foreign Power, *in regard to a question falling within his province*, is binding upon the country to which the Minister belongs." [22]

The Court did not inquire into any municipal limitations of the power of the Foreign Minister to make such a statement, and it is well to supplement this point by a passage from the

[21] *Massey Case* (1927), *Op. of Com. 1927*, p. 228, at p. 231; *Way Case* (1928), *Op. of Com. 1929*, p. 94, at p. 105.

[22] A/B. 53, p. 71. Italics added.

Dissenting Opinion of Judge Anzilotti who agreed with the majority in the binding effect of the declaration on Norway:—

"The question of the competence of the Minister for Foreign Affairs is closely connected with the contents of the agreement in question; and these have already been determined. No arbitral or judicial decision relating to the international competence of a Minister for Foreign Affairs has been brought to the knowledge of the Court; . . . In my opinion, it must be recognised that the constant and general practice of States has been to invest the Minister for Foreign Affairs—the direct agent of the chief of the State—with authority to make statements on current affairs to foreign diplomatic representatives, and in particular to inform them as to the attitude which the government, in whose name he speaks, will adopt in a given question. Declarations of this kind are binding upon the State.

"As regards the question whether Norwegian constitutional law authorised the Minister for Foreign Affairs to make the declaration, that is a point which, in my opinion, does not concern the Danish Government: it was M. Ihlen's duty to refrain from giving his reply until he had obtained any assent that might be requisite under the Norwegian laws." [23]

The *Eastern Greenland Case* [24] confirms the view that the nature of the act and the nature of the function of the official are the two most important factors governing the imputability of acts of the official to the State, and the case also shows how these tests are to be applied. It is necessary first to determine the nature of the function of the official concerned, his "province" or his "international competence." Next the nature of the act should be ascertained. Both points are to be determined in the light of prevailing international practice. If the act, by its nature, falls within the functions of the official, it is imputable to the State, irrespective of any municipal limitation on his competence. If the act, by its nature, falls outside his functions, it is no longer imputable to the State.[25]

[23] *Ibid.*, pp. 91–2.

[24] Mervyn Jones in his *Full Powers and Ratifications*, 1946, appeared to minimise unduly the significance of the decision (pp. 147–48). See also his "Constitutional Limitations on the Treaty Making Power," (1941) 35 A.J.I.L., p. 462, at p. 473. For a different, and what appears a more correct appraisal, see Schwarzenberger, 1 *International Law*, 1949, pp. 66–9.

[25] *Cf.* "*Blockade*" *of Portendic Case* (1843). For facts see *supra*, p. 30 and pp. 137 *et seq.* The British contention used the same criteria when it argued that: "It may, indeed, be pretended, that the promise of one Minister, and

The fact that the character of the act coincides with the nature of the function with which the official is charged indicates that the act in question was performed by the official in his public capacity. Understood in this sense, it may be said that all acts of officials in their public capacity or, as it has sometimes been said, in the performance of their official duties, are imputable to the State.

To illustrate the distinction between acts of officials in their public capacity and acts of officials in their private capacity,[26] there is hardly a better example than the *Mallén Case* (1927). In this case, a deputy constable of the state of Texas, in the United States of America, attacked the same foreign consul on two different occasions. On the first occasion, his act was considered as that of a private individual not imputable to the State; on the second it was imputed to the State. The facts were as follows:—

Deputy Constable Franco of Texas harboured a personal grudge against the Mexican consul Mallén. Meeting Mallén one day at El Paso, Texas, Franco either slapped Mallén on the face or knocked his hat off, "possibly after having said some words in Spanish." Another policeman or a private citizen took him away and he was fined $5, which apparently he paid. With regard to this incident, the Mexican-United States General Claims Commission (1923) said:—

"The evidence as to the first assault . . . , though unsatisfactory as to its details, clearly indicates a malevolent and unlawful act of a private individual who happened to be an official; not the act of an

this not the Minister of Foreign Affairs, cannot bind the Government to which he belongs. But it surely must be admitted that that promise ought to bind his own particular department. If a Minister of Public Instruction, for instance, was to state what he thought likely, or certain to be done in the Department of the Ministry of War, it might indeed be said 'the Minister of Instruction cannot bind the Minister of War, and the fault is with the Ambassador who took the word of a functionary who could not be certain of what he stated, and was not responsible for it.' But here is the case of a Minister of Marine, the very person to whom Lord Granville ought to have applied for prompt and correct information as to a naval matter. . . ." (Document of August 12, 1841, 30 B.F.S.P., p. 603, at p. 611.) In giving legal effect to the assurance, even though not as an irrevocable promise (see 42 B.F.S.P., p. 1378; *supra*, pp. 138 *et seq.*), the Arbitrator recognised that a statement to a foreign Ambassador during an official interview by a naval Minister on a naval matter was one emanating from the State.

26 These locutions are used for the sake of convenience only. "Acts of officials in their private capacity" are juridically only acts of private individuals who happen at the same time to hold some official position. See next footnote.

official . . . Direct responsibility of the United States for this first assault has not been alleged." [27]

In other words, this was not an act imputable to the United States; for, in the terminology of the Commission, direct responsibility means responsibility for the acts of the Government itself.[28]

Some two months later, while in a street car in El Paso, Franco came up to Mallén, struck him savagely on the head, threatened him with a pistol after he had fallen to the floor, and, while his face was smeared with blood, took him to jail on a charge—which was not well-founded—of carrying a pistol without permission. The Commission held, in this instance, that:—

"It is essential to state that the whole act was of a most savage, brutal and humiliating character. It is also essential to note that both governments consider Franco's acts as the acts of an official on duty . . . and that the evidence establishes his showing his badge to assert his official capacity. Franco could not have taken Mallén to jail if he had not been acting as a police officer. Though his act would seem to have been a private act of revenge which was disguised, once the first thirst of revenge had been satisfied, as an official act of arrest, the act as a whole can only be considered as the act of an official. . . . The American Agency, in the conclusion of its reply brief, states: 'The Agent of the U.S. does not contend that this Government is without responsibility in this matter. An "official or other" acting in a broad sense for the United States was by an American jury, in the language of the treaty, found to have perpetrated an "injustice" upon Mr. Mallén. This circumstance is properly resented by Mexico.'" [29]

In whatever way the act may have been performed, it was "an act of arrest," which, by its nature, fell within the official's competence. It was, therefore, an "official act"

[27] *Op. of Com. 1927*, p. 254, at p. 256. See also *Id.*: *Putnam Case* (1927), *ibid.*, p. 222. Murder by an individual who was a policeman. No direct responsibility alleged. *Cf.* also *Id.*: *Gordon Case* (1930) *Op. of Com. 1931*, p. 50. Two Mexican military officers, one medical, made the private purchase of a pistol and, trying it out on a target, injured Gordon, an American. Held: "Everything then leads to the belief that *the act in question* was *outside the line of service* and the performance of the duty of a military officer, and was a private act and under those conditions the Mexican Government is not directly responsible for the injury suffered by Gordon" (p. 52). Italics added.

[28] *Chattin Case* (1927) *Op. of Com. 1927*, p. 422, at p. 426, § 8 of Decision.

[29] *Loc. cit.*, pp. 259–60.

carried out in his official capacity, *i.e.*, one imputable to the State.

Here again it must be pointed out that the specific competence of the official according to municipal law to carry out the act and to carry it out in that particular manner is irrelevant. In this case the official acted without authority, since his act was condemned by the municipal courts as an "injustice." Yet the respondent State admitted the act to be an act imputable to the State.

Indeed, when an official acts in his official capacity, his acts are imputable to the State, irrespective of whether he has acted in error,[30] without authorisation,[31] in disobedience to instructions[32] or otherwise in contravention of municipal law.[33]

It has sometimes been maintained, however, that acts of officials in disobedience of instructions and in violation of municipal law are in fact outside their competence (under municipal law) and are, therefore, not legally imputable to the State. This point of municipal competence came up for discussion in the *Youmans Case* (1926) in which 10 Mexican soldiers under an officer sent to protect some Americans at Angangueo against the violence of a mob, instead of properly

30 Brit.-U.S. Cl.Arb. (1910): *The Coquitlam* (1920) Nielsen's *Report*, p. 447. United States cutter *Corwin* seized British *S.S. Coquitlam* on June 22, 1892, bona fide believing that the latter was infringing the United States "Hovering Statutes." Held: "The good faith and fair conduct of the officers of the *Corwin* are unquestionable, but though this may be taken into account as an explanation given by the same officers to their government, it cannot operate to prevent their action being an error in judgment for which the Government of the United States is liable to a foreign government" (pp. 449–50).

Id.: *The Wanderer* (1921) *ibid.*, p. 459. Officers of *U.S.S. Concord* seized British sealing ship the *Wanderer* on June 10, 1894, bona fide believing that they had authority to do so in virtue of the Behring Sea Award and a special régime obtaining between Great Britain and the United States. Such belief proved to be erroneous. Held: "The bona fides of the United States naval officers is not questioned. It is evident that the provisions of Section 10 of the Act of Congress constituted a likely cause of error. But the United States Government is responsible for that section, and liable for the errors of judgment committed by its agents" (p. 465–66).

Cf. also *Id.*: *The Kate* (1921) *ibid.*, p. 472.

31 Brit.-U.S. Cl.Arb. (1910): *The Jessie*, *The Thomas F. Bayard*, and *The Pescawha* (1921) Nielsen's *Report*, p. 479.

32 *Cf.* Mex.-U.S. G.C.C. (1923): *Youmans Case* (1926) *Op. of Com. 1927*, p. 150, at pp. 158–59. See *infra*, pp. 203 *et seq.*

33 Indeed all cases of unlawful arrest or detention arise precisely because the action of the officials has violated rights of individuals guaranteed in the first instance by the municipal law. *Cf.*, *e.g.*, Mex.-U.S. G.C.C. (1923): *Harry Roberts Case* (1926) *Op. of Com. 1927*, p. 100, at pp. 103–4; *Way Case* (1928) *Op of Com. 1929*, p. 94, at p. 106; *Dyches Case* (1929) *ibid.*, p. 193, at p. 197; *Chazen Case* (1930) *Op. of Com. 1931*, p. 20, at p. 26.

discharging their duty, participated in the acts of violence by using their arms against the victims. The Mexican-United States General Claims Commission (1923) before which the case came had the following to say:—

"There are citations in the Mexican Government's brief of extracts from a discussion of a sub-committee of the League of Nations Committee of Experts for the Progressive Codification of International Law. The passage quoted, which deals with the responsibility of a State for illegal acts of officials resulting in damages to foreigners, begins with a statement relative to the acts of an official accomplished 'outside the scope of his competency, that is to say, if he has exceeded his powers.' An illegal act of this kind, it is stated in the quotation, is one that cannot be imputed to the State. . . . It seems clear that the passage to which particular attention is called in the Mexican Government's brief is concerned solely with the question of the authority of an officer as defined by domestic law to act for his government with reference to some particular subject. Clearly it is not intended by the rule asserted to say that no wrongful act of an official acting in the discharge of duties entrusted to him can impose responsibility on a government under international law because any such wrongful act must be considered to be 'outside the scope of his competency.' If this were the meaning intended by the rule it would follow that no wrongful acts committed by an official could be considered as acts for which his government could be held liable. We do not consider that any of these passages from the discussion of the sub-committee quoted in the Mexican brief are at variance with the view which we take that the action of the troops in participating in the murder at Angangueo imposed a direct responsibility on the Government of Mexico.

". . . Citation is also made in the Mexican brief to an opinion rendered by Umpire Lieber in which effect is evidently given to the well recognised rule of international law that a government is not responsible for malicious acts of soldiers committed in their private capacity . . . But we do not consider that the participation of the soldiers in the murder at Angangueo can be regarded as acts of soldiers committed in their private capacity when it is clear that at the time of the commission of these acts the men were on duty and under the immediate supervision and in the presence of a commanding officer. Soldiers inflicting personal injuries or committing wanton destruction or looting always act in disobedience of some rules laid down by superior authority. There could be no liability whatever for such misdeeds if the view were taken that any acts committed by soldiers in contravention of instructions must always be considered as personal acts.'' [34]

The above shows that the violation of instructions and municipal rules of law does not *ipso facto* render the act of an official an act done in his private capacity. In the case in question, the function of the agents was to preserve law and order and the act was intended as an act for the protection of aliens. The act was within the functions of the officer and men, although as the Commission said: "It cannot properly be said that adequate protection is afforded to foreigners in a case in which the proper agencies of the law to afford protection participate in murder.'' [35] In saying that there was direct responsibility in this case, the Commission regarded the acts of these soldiers, despite their violation of law and instructions, as the acts of the government and hence imputable to the State; for, as has been mentioned, in the terminology of the Commission, direct responsibility of the State means responsibility for governmental acts.[36] Moreover, it also results from the interpretation which the Commission placed on the report of the sub-committee of the League, that imputability is determined by the general function of the agent and not by his municipal authority to perform a specific act in a specific manner, thus confirming the view developed above.

The Presiding Commissioner of the Franco-Mexican Mixed Claims Commission (1924) in the *Caire Case* (1929), however, was of a different opinion. Among acts traditionally imputed to the State, those in excess of the municipal competency of the officials concerned were, according to what he considered to be a better and more modern view, not legally imputable to the State, although the latter might be held liable for their consequences. The presiding Commissioner said:—

"'There is unanimous agreement,' M. Bourquin rightly said,[37]

[34] *Op. of Com. 1927*, p. 150, at pp. 157–59.
[35] *Ibid.*, at p. 157.
[36] *Supra*, p. 201.
[37] Note of the Decision: "2. See his observations on the Report of M. L. Strisower to the Institute of International Law, inserted in the *Annuaire* of the Institute for 1927, Vol. I, pp. 501 *et seq.*, notably pp. 507–8. See also Anzilotti, *Teoria generale della responsibilità dello Stato nel diritto internazionale*, [1902], p. 167: 'Two things are certain: First, that an act of this kind is not in any

in saying that the acts committed by the officials and agents of the State engage the international responsibility of the latter, even if their author had not the competence to perform them. This responsibility finds not its justification in general principles, I mean those which govern the juridical organisation of the State. Indeed, the act of an official cannot juridically be set up as an act of State unless it was within the sphere of competency of that official. The act of an incompetent official is not an act of the State. It should not, therefore, in principle, affect the responsibility of the State. If one admits, in international law, that it is otherwise, this is for reasons peculiar to the mechanism of international life; it is because one considers that international dealings would become too difficult, too complicated and too uncertain, if one oblige foreign States to take into account the legal provisions, often complex, which fix the competencies within the State. Hence, it is evident that in the hypothesis in question the international responsibility of the State has a purely *objective* character and that it rests upon a conception of *guarantee*, where the subjective notion of fault plays no part.'

"But to be able to admit this so-called objective responsibility of the State for the acts committed by its officers or organs outside the limit of their competency, it is necessary that they should have acted at least apparently as competent officials or organs, or that, in acting, they had used the powers or means belonging to their official capacity." [38]

The *Caire Case* (1929) does not deny that States might be held liable for acts of officials which are *ultra vires* in the eyes of municipal law. But it casts grave doubt on the theoretical justification for imputing such acts to the State, in international law. There is, however, a flaw in the reasoning adopted by the presiding Commissioner in the *Caire Case* (1929), which consists in the assumption that, even in the international sphere, imputability is to be determined according to rules of municipal law "which govern the juridical organisation of the

way an act of the State, but a purely private act; Secondly, that positive international law affirms in no uncertain manner the responsibility of the State for the unlawful acts of its officials, even when they have been carried out in contravention to law and beyond the power of the respective officials'" (Transl.).

But it has been seen that international law does not necessarily regard an act of this kind as a purely private act. When it does so, it no longer holds the State responsible for it.

[38] *Jurisprudence*, p. 207, at p. 221. (Transl.)

State."[39] It may be true that acts of officials violating their instructions and exceeding their competence are not, in municipal law, imputable to the State. Within the municipal sphere, a State may, by its own laws, dissociate and exculpate itself from all unlawful acts of its agents, by enacting that such acts shall be *ultra vires* and, therefore, not imputable to the State. The situation is created wherein "The *State* can do no wrong," and any liability of the State for such acts would be purely *ex gratia*. It is difficult to appreciate, however, why international imputability should be made dependent upon municipal legislation and, therefore, upon the unfettered will of the State concerned. In such a case, the rules of imputability would vary from State to State. Moreover, if a State were to enact that none of its officials should be competent to perform an act that would result in the breach of an international obligation by that State, then no internationally unlawful act

[39] Prof. Bourquin's view is shared by other eminent writers; see, *e.g.*, Oppenheim, 1 *International Law*, § 163 (the text of § 163 has been little altered by the successive editors); C. de Visscher, "La responsabilité des Etats," 2 *Bibliotheca Visseriana*, 1924, p. 88, at pp. 91–2; Freeman, *International Responsibility of States for Denial of Justice*, 1938, pp. 23–6.

In his earlier writings (see *Teoria generale della responsabilità dello Stato*, 1902, p. 167; "La responsabilité internationale des États," 13 R.G.D.I.P. (1906), at pp. 289 *et seq.*), Anzilotti also shared this view. In his *Cours de Droit international*, 1929, however, he was of the opinion that with regard to imputability in the international sphere, rules of international law operated autonomously (pp. 254 *et seq.*, 469 *et seq.*), and that acts of officials in excess of their municipal competence, even though they might not be imputed to the State in municipal law, might be so imputed in international law (pp. 470–1). But he remained faithful to the idea of guarantee (p. 471). In doing so, Anzilotti failed to pursue to its logical conclusion his new standpoint that rules on imputability in international law operated autonomously; for the idea of guarantee might imply one of two things. Either such acts were after all not acts of the State, and the State, on being held liable for them, was held liable not for its own acts but only as a guarantor. In that case, he would be repudiating his view that international law imputed such acts to the State. Or, the guarantee is the *ratio legis* of the imputation, that is to say, because it is considered that the State should guarantee others against the risks of certain acts, they are imputed to the State so that it may be held responsible for them as if they were its own acts. Although imputability and responsibility are closely related subjects, they are nevertheless distinct. As the *de Brissot Cases* show (*supra*, p. 181), responsibility depends upon the injurious act being imputable to the State. Guarantee as a reason for imputation would indeed put the cart before the horse by making imputability dependent upon responsibility.

But the idea of guarantee is wholly unnecessary, if Anzilotti's new standpoint, which is in conformity with the majority of international decisions, is pursued to its logical conclusion. For, if on the one hand international law operating autonomously imputes such acts to the State as its own acts, and if, on the other hand, international law holds the State responsible for those acts, then the logical conclusion is that the State, here as in other instances, is held responsible only for its own acts. The question of guarantee or objective responsibility no longer arises.

would in any circumstances be imputable to it—a state of affairs which would not correspond with reality. It has been seen that other international tribunals have applied international law without regard to any restrictions imposed by the municipal law concerned, both as regards the question of imputation of acts of officials to the State, and in ascertaining the representative organ of the State.

The Permanent Court of International Justice has held that:—

> "From the standpoint of International Law and of the Court which is its organ, municipal laws are merely facts which express the will and constitute the activities of States, in the same manner as do legal decisions or administrative measures." [40]

Municipal law as such, therefore, has no operative effect in international law and, in consequence, imputability in international law should not be governed, and need not be justified, by provisions of municipal law "which govern the juridical organisation of the State." The doubt raised by the *Caire Case* (1929) concerning the imputability of acts of officials acting in fact as organs of the State but in excess of their municipal competence, being based upon considerations of municipal law, does not, therefore, appear to be justified, and the resort to the notion of guarantee or objective responsibility, which is the subject of much controversy in international law, is wholly unnecessary. International law operating autonomously is, in this, as in other cases, only holding the State responsible for its own acts, that is to say, acts which are imputable to it. Only when it is sought to give effect at one and the same time to both international law and municipal law and to reconcile any discrepancy existing between them does it become necessary to have recourse to the notion of guarantee or objective responsibility.[41]

Much space has been devoted to explaining the meaning of "unlawful act" and "imputability" in international law. This can only be justified by the consideration that without this clarification, it would be impossible to proceed, as we are about to do, to the exposition of two of the general principles of law governing responsibility, *viz.*, the principle of individual responsibility and the principle of fault.

[40] *German Interests Case* (Merits) (1926), A. 7, p. 19.
[41] *Cf. supra*, p. 206 note 39.

CHAPTER 7

THE PRINCIPLE OF INDIVIDUAL RESPONSIBILITY

It follows from the very conception of responsibility as developed above that responsibility only attaches to the person who is the author of the unlawful act. It has been said that "under international law, apart from any convention, in order that a State may incur responsibility it is necessary that an unlawful international act be imputed to it, that is, that there exist a violation of a duty imposed by an international juridical standard."[1] As a duty can of necessity only be personal, so responsibility is also personal. Indeed, the Umpire in the *Salvatore Sambiaggio Case* (C. 1903) formulated what he considered to be an "apparently axiomatic principle" as follows:—

> "The ordinary rule is that a government, like an individual is only to be held responsible for the acts of its agents or for acts the responsibility for which is expressly assumed by it. To apply another doctrine, save under certain exceptional circumstances incident to the peculiar position occupied by a government toward those subject to its power, would be unnatural and illogical."[2]

This principle that everyone should only be responsible for his own acts or those of his agents may be called the *principle of individual responsibility*.

In the section on imputability,[3] it was seen what international law regards as the acts of a State. It was shown that acts of private individuals are not acts of the State, whether the individuals are acting singly or in groups, such as mobs, rioters, or bandits. In international law, States are not held responsible for acts committed by them.

[1] *Supra*, p. 169.

[2] Ital.-Ven. M.C.C. (1903): *Ven.Arb. 1903*, p. 666, at p. 680. Venezuela held not responsible for acts of unsuccessful revolutionaries. On the question of the relative position of the State and the Government, and the metonymy of speaking of government responsibility, see *supra*, p. 186, note 81).

Cf. Jay Treaty (Art. VII) Arbitration (1794): *The Jamaica* (1798), 4 *Int. Adj.*, M.S., p. 489, at p. 497.

[3] *Supra*, at pp. 180 *et seq.*

"One nation is not responsible to another for the acts of its individual citizens, except when it approves or ratifies them. It then becomes a public concern, and the injured party may consider the nation itself the real author of the injury."[4]

"It is a well-established principle of international law that no government can be held responsible for the act of rebellious bodies of men committed in violation of its authority, where it is itself guilty of no breach of good faith, or of no negligence in suppressing insurrection. (Moore's *Int.Law Dig.*, Vol. VI, p. 956; VII, p. 957; Moore's *Arbitrations*, pp. 2991–2992; British Answer, p. 1)."[5]

As regards State responsibility in time of revolution, the Umpire in the *Aroa Mines Case* (C. 1903) and the *Henriquez Case* (C. 1903) took the view that the following provision in the treaty of 1892 between Germany and Colombia expressed the correct view of international law:—

"It is also stipulated between the contracting parties that the German Government will not attempt to hold the Colombian Government responsible, unless there be want of due diligence on the part of the Colombian authorities or their agents, for the injuries, vexations, or exactions occasioned in time of insurrection or civil war to German subjects in the territory of Colombia, through rebels, or caused by savage tribes beyond the control of the Government. (Article 20, section 3.)"[6]

From the above opinions of various international tribunals, it clearly emerges that a State is not responsible for acts of private individuals or persons who are not its agents, whether they be isolated citizens, mobs, rioters, savage tribes, rebels, or unsuccessful revolutionaries, unless it has committed some unlawful act or omission through persons whose acts are

[4] *Cotesworth & Powell Case* (1875), 2 *Int.Arb.*, p. 2050, at p. 2082. Alleged denial of justice by the courts of Colombia.

[5] Brit.-U.S. Cl.Arb. (1910): *Home Missionary Society Case* (1920), Nielsen's *Report*, p. 421, at p. 425. Native riots in Sierra Leone after imposition of a hut tax. Spanish Zone of Morocco Claims (1923): *Rapport III* (1924), and Claim 53: *Fiat, Ben Kiran* (Melilla) (1924), 2 UNRIAA, p. 615, at pp. 645 *et seq.* and 730 *et seq.*

U.S. Domestic Commission, Mex. Claims (1849): *Laguеruene Case* (1851): "Mobs and rioters are enemies of the public peace. . . . It is the duty of a government to pass laws to punish individuals who commit acts of violence, but the government is not responsibile for those acts" (3 *Int.Arb.*, p. 3027, at p. 3028).

[6] Brit.-Ven. M.C.C. (1903): *Aroa Mines Ltd. Case*, *Ven.Arb. 1903*, p. 344, at p. 373; Neth.-Ven. M.C.C. (1903): *Henriquez Case*, *ibid.*, p. 896, at p. 900.

imputable to it. In the latter event, as was clearly and forcefully pointed out by the *Janes Case* (1926), mention of which has already been made,[7] a distinction has to be drawn between the act of the individuals concerned and those of the State. The State is responsible only for its own act, and not the acts of private individuals.

Moreover, it has already been shown [8] that whilst acts of State officials in their official capacity are imputable to the State, those in their private capacity are not. The cases which have been cited in connection with the imputability of acts of State officials also establish that a State is responsible only for the former, and not the latter,[9] category of acts of its officials. The case of State responsibility for acts of officials in excess of their competence under municipal law has also been discussed and it has been shown that where a State is held responsible for such acts, they are in reality internationally imputable to it.[10] It may indeed be said that in international law imputability and State responsibility strictly coincide. In other words, there is a constant practice on the part of international tribunals holding the State responsible only for its own acts, and thus upholding the principle of individual responsibility. The only exception is perhaps an incidental remark in the *Sarropoulos Case* (1927) to the effect that a State is responsible for the consequences of a riot directed against foreigners as such.[11] The existence of such a rule of international law would constitute an exception to the principle of individual responsibility. Such responsibility would mean responsibility without an unlawful act on the part

[7] See *supra*, pp. 175 *et seq.* The principle of individual responsibility is not affected even if the principle applied in the *Janes Case* (1926) is not accepted and the theory of implied State complicity adhered to. See, *e.g.*, Brierly, "The Theory of Implied Complicity in International Claims," 9 B.Y.I.L. (1928), p. 42. Brierly considered it axiomatic that the State was responsible only for its own acts.

[8] *Supra*, pp. 200 *et seq.*

[9] See also Mex.-U.S. G.C.C. (1923): *Gordon Case* (1930), *Op. of Com. 1931*, p. 50, at p. 53: "The principle is that the personal acts of officials not within the scope of their authority do not entail responsibility upon a State."

[10] *Supra*, pp. 202 *et seq.*

[11] Greco.-Bulg. M.A.T.: 7 T.A.M., p. 47, at pp. 50–1. *Cf. Rosa Gelbtrunk Case* (1902). U.S.F.R. (1902), p. 876, at p. 879.

The absolute responsibility of the State for anti-foreign riots, although admitted in the *Règlement* of the Institut de Droit International of 1900 (18 *Annuaire* (1900), p. 254), does not seem to be admitted in the *Bases of Discussion* of the L.o.N. Conference for the Codification of International Law, which, however, place upon the State the burden of proving the absence of negligence (L.o.N.P.: C.75.M.69.1929,V., pp. 104 *et seq.*, 120).

of the State held responsible. It rests upon an idea of guarantee. This has been termed "objective" responsibility, a term which we have already encountered in the last Chapter. Such responsibility may be admitted in those cases where there is a clear rule of law establishing it. This objective responsibility is, in its juridical nature, akin to what we have called "assumed responsibility" [12]; for, in neither case, is there any responsibility as the term has been defined. What has been said of assumed responsibility applies *mutatis mutandis* to objective responsibility. In both instances, there is only a legal obligation, derived in the one case from a contractual or treaty stipulation, and in the other from a legal provision. For this reason, objective responsibility is sometimes called legal responsibility in municipal law, although it must be said that all responsibility is, in a sense, legal. It is in truth a legal obligation conditional upon the happening of some event independent of the will of the obligated party, an obligation to make reparation for the consequences of that event, to make pecuniary compensation therefor. Indeed, on this point, the scope of the obligation is not necessarily co-extensive with the consequences of the event, but varies according to the precise terms of the legal provision establishing such obligation.[13] Like assumed responsibility, it is an obligation modelled upon responsibility properly so-called; like assumed responsibility, it is called responsibility only as a figure of speech. It may be conceived as supplementary to the principle that responsibility should be individual, but should not be confused with, or taken as replacing it.

Both the principle of individual responsibility and the possibility of supplementary obligations based on express legal provisions were reaffirmed by the German Commissioner in the

[12] *Supra*, pp. 165 *et seq.*

[13] See, *e.g.*, the legal obligation upon States to make compensation for damage suffered by aliens as a consequence of mob violence, riots, insurrections, etc., if, and to the extent to which they compensate their own nationals. Fran.-Mex. M.C.C. (1924): *Pinson Case* (1928), *Jurisprudence*, p. 1, at pp. 23, 105, 131. "The State which grants its nationals compensation for loss or damage caused by insurrectionary movements, ought to grant at least the same compensation to foreigners in the same or analogous conditions" (p. 105. Transl.). The legal obligation is thus only the granting of national treatment and its scope varies according to the municipal enactments of each State. Such a situation is not possible in the case of responsibility properly so-called, where its extent cannot be affected by the municipal law of the State concerned and is in principle co-extensive with the proximate consequences of the unlawful act.

Mendel Case (1926) before the German-United States Mixed Claims Commission (1922):—

> "Certainly it is a general rule that an individual as well as a government is responsible only for its own act or the acts of its agents and not for the independent acts of a third party. Any deviation from this common-sense principle requires a special provision in municipal law as well as in international law." [14]

But the principle of individual responsibility is so fundamental and cases of "assumed responsibility" or "legal responsibility" so exceptional that the existence of any obligation to make reparation for losses caused otherwise than by a person's own act must result from a clear and categorical provision. This is fully demonstrated by the *Mendel Case,* where the Commission upheld the principle of individual responsibility, even though a literal interpretation of the relevant treaty would have justified a departure from it.

In the *Mendel Case,* certain American nationals invoked Article 297 (*e*) of the Treaty of Versailles which provided that:—

> "The nationals of Allied and Associated Powers shall be entitled to compensation in respect of damage or injury inflicted upon their property, rights or interests, including any company or association in which they are interested, in German territory as it existed on August 1, 1914, by the application either of the exceptional war measures or measures of transfer mentioned in paragraphs 1 and 3 of the Annex hereto." [15]

"Planting themselves"—as the Umpire said—"on the letter" of the provision, they claimed compensation for losses which they alleged to have suffered as minority stockholders in two German corporations. By application of "exceptional war measures or measures of transfer," as those terms were defined in the Treaty of Versailles, the property of the two corporations in German New Guinea were taken over and administered by the Commonwealth of Australia, and were finally liquidated by the Australian Government. This part of New Guinea was

[14] *Dec. & Op.*, p. 772, at pp. 780–1.
[15] The Treaty of Versailles was made applicable to the proceedings of this Commission through the Treaty of Berlin between the United States and Germany of August 25, 1921.

indisputably "German territory as it existed on August 1, 1914," but it was occupied by Australian forces as early as September, 1914. At the time of the measures complained of, *i.e.*, 1920, this territory had already been ceded by Germany to the "Principal Allied and Associated Powers," and was in the possession and control of Australia. The Commissioners disagreed on the validity of the claim, the German Commissioner favouring its dismissal on the ground of individual responsibility in terms which have just been quoted. This view was sustained by the Umpire, who formulated the same principle in the following terms:—

> "It is fundamental that in the absence of an express stipulation to the contrary a State or person can be held liable only for its own acts or those for whom it is responsible." [16]

Reasoning from this premise, the Umpire arrived at the conclusion that, failing a provision *expressis verbis*, it could not have been the intention of the makers of the Treaty to impose on Germany an obligation to make compensation for losses caused not through her own measures but by one of her former enemies.[17]

There is, therefore, a general legal principle applicable between States as well as between individuals to the effect that a person is only responsible for his own acts. The application of this principle—the principle of individual responsibility—in international law is fully demonstrated by the fact that States are only responsible for those acts which are, according to international law, imputable to them. Any exception to this

[16] *Loc. cit.*, p. 793.

[17] The following decisions of the Mixed Arbitral Tribunals interpreting the same article or similar provisions in other peace treaties signed after the First World War were cited by the Umpire in support of his interpretations: Italo-Germ. M.A.T.: *Fadin Case* (1924), Rome. Fran.-Germ. M.A.T.: *Rothbletz Case* (1924), 4 T.A.M., p. 747, at p. 749; Italo-Austrian M.A.T.: *A. Torres Case* (1924), 5 *ibid.*, p. 518, at p. 522.

To these the following cases may be added: Fran.-Germ. M.A.T.: *Sachs & Co.* (1921), 1 T.A.M., p. 215, at pp. 217, 219, 221 (Art. 297 (e) of the Treaty of Versailles). Fran.-Bulg. M.A.T.: *Société de Sucreries et Raffineries en Bulgarie* (1923), 3 *ibid.*, p. 439, at p. 444 (Art. 177 (e) of the Treaty of Neuilly). Rum.-Germ. M.A.T.: *Marcu Colleanu* (1929), 9 *ibid.*, p. 216, at pp. 220–221 (Art. 297 (e) of the Treaty of Versailles).

Cf. contra: Belg.-Austrian M.A.T.: *Mines et Charbonnages en Carniole* (1923), 3 *ibid.*, p. 811, at p. 814 (Art. 249 (e) of the Treaty of St. Germain). In this case the tribunal considered that there was a definite assumption of liability by the Treaty. The case does not, therefore, affect the validity of the principle under discussion.

principle in the form of the so-called "assumed responsibility" or "legal responsibility" cannot be presumed but must result from an express and unequivocal treaty stipulation or a clear legal provision. Moreover, as explained above, juridically such exceptions are mere obligations derived either from treaty stipulations or from positive law. They are modelled upon responsibility properly so-called, and are supplementary thereto. They in no way affect the nature or the validity of the principle of individual responsibility.

DERIVATIVE RESPONSIBILITY

It seems necessary at this juncture to mention the effect of international representation on the question of State responsibility. In cases of international representation, that is to say the representation in international relations of one international person (the "representee") by another (the "representant"), there is a responsibility falling on the representant for the acts of the representee.

This is, for instance, the case of the Mandatory with regard to Mandated Territory under the régime set up by the League of Nations. Thus in the case of the *Mavrommatis Palestine Concessions* (1924), the Permanent Court of International Justice, speaking of the Mandate for Palestine, held that:—

> "The obligations resulting from these engagements are therefore obligations which the Administration of Palestine must respect; the Mandatory is internationally responsible for any breach of them since, under Article 12 of the Mandate, the external relations of Palestine are handled by it." [18]

A similar state of affairs may be said to have existed between Poland and the Free City of Danzig during the inter-war period, "the conduct of the foreign relations of the Free City being entrusted to the Polish Government." [19]

The principle is fundamentally the same in cases of international protectorates, even though international protectorates differ from case to case. In the *Phosphates in Morocco Case* (1938), Judge van Eysinga said in his dissenting opinion:—

[18] A. 2, p. 23.

[19] PCIJ: *Danzig and the International Labour Organisation* (1930), Adv.Op., B. 16, p. 11. See Treaty of Nov. 9, 1920, between the Free City and Poland, 6 L.N.T.S., pp. 191 *et seq.*

" Disregarding the Spanish and Tangier zones, the case we have to consider is that of a State, whose international status is in a large measure determined by collective conventions and which is under the protection of one of the States parties to these conventions. The Protectorate Convention of 1912 between France and Morocco provides that, for all questions concerning relations between the Shereefian Empire and foreign Powers, France shall be competent. It is, apparently, owing to this situation that the Italian Application, although it makes a distinction between the interests and international obligations of Morocco, on the one hand, and those of France, on the other hand (see also the Italian Memorial, p. 59, No. 44, last para.), is directed solely against France, who, as is indeed said in the Application, has incurred a twofold responsibility: an indirect responsibility as the State protecting Morocco, and a personal and direct responsibility arising from the acts performed by the French authorities or in co-operation with them, for the benefit of purely French interests." [20]

With regard to the Spanish Zone of Morocco, the *Rapporteur* in the Spanish Zone of Morocco Claims (1923), declared:—

" As the protégé no longer acts without an intermediary, in the international field, and as all measures that a third State might take to secure respect of its rights from the Shereefian Government would also inevitably affect the interests of the protector, the latter ought to take upon itself the responsibility of the protégé, at least as a derivative responsibility." [21]

" It is to Spain, in its capacity of protecting Power of the Spanish zone, that the other States can and ought to address their claims based on acts taking place in this zone. If the protectorate suppresses direct diplomatic relations between the protégé and the other States, so that the latter can no longer directly approach the protégé, it is necessary that, for this limitation imposed on third States, the protector should be under a corresponding duty to answer in place of the protégé." [22]

It need hardly be mentioned here that:—

" In spite of common features possessed by Protectorates under international law, they have individual legal characteristics resulting

[20] PCIJ: A/B. 74, p. 32. See also ICJ: *United States Nationals in Morocco Case* (1952), Preliminary Objection filed by the U.S. Government (*I.C.J. Pleadings*: 1 *Morocco Case*, pp. 235–247) and Observations of the French Government thereon (*ibid.*, pp. 248–256).

[21] *Rapport III* (1924), 2 UNRIAA, p. 615, at p. 648. (Transl.)

[22] *Ibid.*, pp. 647–8. (Transl.)

from the special conditions under which they were created, and the stage of their development." [23]

" The extent of the powers of a protecting State in the territory of a protected State depends, first, upon the Treaties between the protecting State and the protected State establishing the Protectorate, and, secondly, upon the conditions under which the Protectorate has been recognised by third Powers as against whom there is an intention to rely on the provisions of these Treaties." [24]

Although this is not the place to enter into the problem of international representation, it may be said that the same considerations apply. In so far as responsibility is concerned in cases where there is representation of one international person by another in its external relations, the following conclusions seem to emerge from the above international decisions. Inasmuch as there is direct participation in the affairs of the representee by the representant, there is direct responsibility of the representant for its own acts. Inasmuch as the representee preserves its international personality and enjoys thereby an international *Deliktsfähigkeit*, with internationally unlawful acts imputable to itself and not to the representant, the representee is subject to a corresponding responsibility in the proper meaning of the term. In the latter case, inasmuch as the representee has not the capacity to exercise its rights and obligations in the international field, or in other words, in so far as its external relations are handled by the representant, there is a corresponding assumption of derivative responsibility by the representant for the internationally unlawful acts of the representee.[25] Conversely, in so far as the representee has the capacity to exercise its international rights and obligations, there is a corresponding absence of responsibility on the part of the representant.[26] Finally it may be said that where there is

23 PCIJ: *Nationality, Decrees Issued in Tunis and Morocco Case* (1923), Adv. Op., B. 4, p. 27. *Cf.* also Greco-Bulg. M.A.T.: *Arakas (The Georgios) Case* (1927), 7 T.A.M., p. 39, at p. 42.

24 PCIJ: B. 4, p. 27.

25 *Cf.* Spanish Zone of Morocco Claims (1923): *Rapport III* (1924), 2 UNRIAA, p. 615, at p. 648: " If the responsibility has not been assumed by the protector as its own, it remains the responsibility of the protégé; in no case could it have disappeared " by the establishment of the protectorate (Transl.).

26 *Cf.* Brit.-U.S. Cl.Arb. (1910): *Robert E. Brown Case* (1923), Nielsen's *Report*, p. 162. Internationally unlawful act on the part of the South African Republic; denial of justice, 1895–1898. " We may grant that a special relation between Great Britain and the South African State, varying considerably in its scope

only one international personality, as, for example, where the protectorate enjoys no international status, there is in truth no State representation, but only a direct responsibility of the national Government in all cases. The internally autonomous entity would be regarded merely as a political subdivision of the State.[27] In each case, therefore, it is necessary, as the Permanent Court of International Justice has said with regard to protectorates, to look at the relationship existing between the representing and the represented State and at how far this régime is *opposable* to third Powers.

As to the legal nature of this responsibility, a distinction can be drawn. Derivative responsibility may possess the character of a contractual or assumed responsibility (*i.e.*, obligation) where representation is based on an international treaty, as with League mandates or the Free City of Danzig. Or, it may be of the nature of a quasi-contractual responsibility (*i.e.*, obligation), where the régime of international representation results more particularly from a state of fact. Responsibility properly so-called still remains with the international person which has violated its international obligations.[28]

and significance from time to time, existed from the beginning [Sand River Convention of 1852]. No doubt Great Britain's position in South Africa imposed upon her a peculiar status and responsibility. She repeatedly declared and asserted her authority as the so-called paramount power in the region; but the authority which she exerted over the South African Republic certainly at the time of the occurrences here under consideration, in our judgment fell far short of what would be required to make her responsible for the wrong inflicted upon Brown. . . . If there had been no South African war, we hold that the United States Government would have been obliged to take up Brown's claim with the Government of the Republic and that there would have been no ground for bringing it to the attention of Great Britain. The relation of suzerain did not operate to render Great Britain liable for the acts complained of " (pp. 201–2).

27 *Cf. supra*, pp. 194–195.

28 *Cf.*, however, Spanish Zone of Morocco Claims (1923): *Rapport III* (1924), 2 UNRIAA, p. 615, at p. 649. Where the representee retains an international personality, it cannot be said, however, that the representant is the only person in existence internationally. At p. 648, the *Rapporteur* clearly recognised that the two responsibilities were juridically distinct. When the *Rapporteur* said that " As externally the situation of the protector is the same as that of a sovereign State, its responsibility ought to be the same " (p. 649), he must be understood to mean that the protecting State in its dual capacity of sovereign State and of representant of the protected State, was externally tantamount to the only sovereign State in the territory involved and the sum of its responsibilities should never be less than if there were only one sovereign State involved.

CHAPTER 8

THE PRINCIPLE OF FAULT

THE principle of fault was recognised in *The Jamaica Case* (1798) by the Mixed Claims Commission set up by Article VII of the Jay Treaty of 1794, between Great Britain and the United States. The case concerned a British ship, which was burnt on the high seas by a French privateer originally armed and equipped in the United States, a neutral in the war then raging between Great Britain and the newborn French Republic. Having decided that the case did not fall within the purview of any treaty provision, the two United States Commissioners, who formed the majority, examined the case from the point of view of customary international law. Both decided that responsibility must depend upon the existence of fault on the part of the neutral.

In disallowing the claim, Commissioner Gore said:—

"According to the principles of justice, on which is founded the law of nations, no government can be liable to compensate for an injury which they did not commit, or for not preventing a loss when out of their power to prevent it, or for not using means in their power to restore property wrongfully taken, when such property never came within the reach of those means . . .

"Indeed, nothing could be more incongruous with the principles of justice, as well as with the law of nations, than to render an individual or government under an obligation to restore that which was never in his power to restore, or under such circumstances to compensate for not restoring it, when the loss arose without the smallest fault imputable to such government or individual . . .

". . . Where there is no fault, no omission of duty, there can be nothing whereon to support a charge of responsibility or justify a complaint." [1]

It seems clear, therefore, that the Commissioner was of opinion that according to general legal principles applicable

[1] 4 *Int.Arb.* M.S., p. 489, at p. 497–99.

to States and individuals alike, responsibility must be based on a fault imputable to the person charged. It would seem, moreover, that the term "fault" derived from "*fallere*," to deceive or to fail, was used by the Commissioner synonymously with the expression "omission of duty," which stood in apposition to it.[2] This failure to observe one's duty constitutes the fault which is the sole basis of responsibility, and this fault is, therefore, equivalent to the notion of an unlawful act which, as has been explained above, is that failure to observe one's obligations which constitutes the only source of responsibility.[3] Thus, the conclusion is inescapable that responsibility, in the sense explained above, cannot exist without fault, as, indeed the Commissioner held.[4]

The principle of fault in responsibility is not, however, entirely redundant or devoid of significance; for it brings to light one element in the notion of an unlawful act which has not been fully developed—the element of freedom of action. In the above passage, it may be noted that the Commissioner put repeated emphasis on the fact that whatever might have happened, it was not committed by the respondent nor was it ever within the power of the respondent to prevent the damage or to remedy it. Indeed, as the Mexican Commissioner in the *Salvador Prats Case* (C. 1868) pointed out, albeit when speaking of the duty of protection of aliens rather than that of a neutral:—

"The duty of protection on the part of the government, either by the general principles of international law or by especial agreements of the treaties, only goes as far as permitted by possibility."[5]

[2] *Cf.* Henri Capitant, *Vocabulaire Juridique*, 1936: "*Faute*: I (Droit civil). Acte ou omission constituant un manquement intentionnel ou non intentionnel soit à une obligation contractuelle, soit à une prescription légale, soit au devoir qui incombe à l'homme de se comporter avec diligence et loyauté dans ses rapports avec ses semblables. La faute suppose le discernement, c'est-à-dire l'aptitude de l'individu à comprendre la portée de son acte. Elle oblige son auteur à réparer le dommage qu'elle peut causer à autrui."

Planiol et Ripert, 2 *Traité élémentaire de Droit civil*, 1929, p. 290: "Définition—La faute est *un manquement à une obligation préexistante*, dont la loi ordonne la réparation quand il a causé un dommage à autrui."

[3] *Supra*, pp. 169 *et seq.*, 170 *et seq.*, especially pp. 171, 180.

[4] *Cf.* the dissenting opinions of various judges of the I.C.J. in *Corfu Channel Case* (Merits) (1949) *ICJ Reports 1949*, p. 4, pp. 65, 71–72, 82–96, 127–28. These opinions are mentioned together at *infra*, p. 231, note 44. See *Buzau-Nehoiasi Railway Case* (1939) 3 UNRIAA, p. 1827, at p. 1839.

[5] Mex.-U.S. Cl.Com. (1868) 3 *Int.Arb.* p. 2886, at p. 2893. Claims on behalf of Mexican citizens against United States for destruction caused by southern Confederates.

The duty of protection in both cases was also assimilated by the *Rapporteur* in the Spanish Zone of Morocco Claims (1923) who was likewise of the opinion that the State's obligation was limited by the range of possibility. Speaking of the diligence required of a State in the protection of aliens against banditry, he said:—

"Here, the question of the degree of vigilance exercised becomes particularly important. Is the territorial State exonerated if it has done what may reasonably be asked of it, taking into account its effective situation? Or is it obliged to guarantee a certain degree of security, being responsible for any incapacity to provide it? Such a view has been upheld and applied to certain States. The correctness of this point of view, however, seems to be highly disputable, and it is far from being accepted by decisions of international tribunals. Writers are clearly against it. In the branch of international law in which the problem of the negligence of the State in preventing acts which eventually prove unlawful under international law has played a particularly important part, namely, the field of neutrality in time of maritime warfare, it has finally been recognised that the State is obliged to exercise only that degree of vigilance which corresponds to the means at its disposal. To require that these means should always measure up to the circumstances would be to impose upon the State duties which it would often not be able to fulfil. Thus, the view that the vigilance required should correspond to the importance of the interests at stake has not been able to prevail. The vigilance which, from the point of view of international law a State is obliged to exercise, may be characterised as a *diligentia quam in suis* applying by analogy a term of Roman law. This rule, conforming to the primordial principle of the independence of States in their internal affairs, actually provides States with the degree of security for their nationals, which they may reasonably expect. As soon as the vigilance exercised falls clearly below this standard in regard to the nationals of a particular State, the latter is entitled to consider itself injured in interests which should enjoy the protection of international law.

"What has just been said of the diligence required with regard to the general insecurity resulting from the activities of bandits, applies *a fortiori* to two other situations mentioned above, *viz.*, common crime and rebellion. In the first case, a diligence going further than the *diligentia quam in suis* would impose upon the State the obligation to organise a special police force for foreigners, which would certainly extend beyond the compass of recognised international obligations (apart from cases where it is a question of persons legally entitled to enjoy a special protection). In the second case, that of rebellion, etc., the responsibility is limited because the public authority is faced with exceptional resistance." [6]

When the *Rapporteur* referred to "the view that the viligance required should correspond to the interests at stake," it would seem that he had in mind *The Alabama Case* (1872) and was ready to disagree with that decision, should it be interpreted as requiring a degree of diligence which is not limited by the State's capacity. When, however, the deliberations leading up to the *Alabama* Award are examined, it will be seen that the *Alabama* Tribunal intended no such requirement.

The *Alabama* Award stated that:—

"The 'due diligence' referred to in the first and third of the said rules ought to be exercised by neutral governments in exact proportion to the risks to which either of the belligerents may be exposed, from a failure to fulfil the obligations of neutrality on their part." [7]

A review of the opinions of the various arbitrators shows that this passage in the Award was directly inspired by the opinion of the presiding Arbitrator, Count Sclopis, who, in his "Opinion on the Question of 'Due Diligence,'" said the following:—

"It is no doubt right to take into consideration a belligerent's requirement's *vis-à-vis* a neutral, but they must not be pushed to the point of hindering the neutral in the normal exercise of his rights, in the organisation of his governmental functions.

"On the other hand, I freely admit that the duties of a neutral cannot be determined by the laws that this Power might have established in its own interest. That would be an easy means to escape from positive responsibilities, which equity recognises and which the law of nations lays down . . .

"It does not seem admissible to me, however, that a belligerent can require a neutral to increase its military strength and its ordinary system of defence in order to discharge its duties of neutrality.

[6] *Rapport III* (1924) 2 UNRIAA, p. 615, at p. 644. Transl. *Cf. contra*, *The Montijo* (1875) 2 *Int.Arb.*, p. 1421, at p. 1444. See, however, the comment on *The Montijo Case* by the Umpire of Ital.-Ven. M.C.C. (1903): *Sambiaggio Case*, *Ven.Arb. 1903*, p. 666, at p. 684.

[7] 1 *Int.Arb.*, p. 495, at p. 654.

This would be a violation of the independence of each State, which, finding itself involuntarily in a special position with regard to the belligerent, is not bound to abdicate a portion of its material sovereignty. A neutral can be asked to bring the wheels of its governmental machinery into full play in order to maintain its neutrality; it cannot be reasonably expected to modify its governmental organisation in order to serve the interests of another Power.

" One must beware of making the condition of neutrals too difficult and almost impossible.

" I believe that it would be appropriate to lay down the following rule with regard to the degree of effort required of a neutral in the performance of its duties of neutrality: *It should be in direct ratio to the actual dangers which the belligerent may run through the neutral's laxity, and in inverse ratio to the direct means which the belligerent may possess for avoiding these dangers.*

" This rule leads us to a solution of the question, so often discussed in the documents presented, as to the initiative to be taken by the neutral in order to preserve its neutrality to the belligerent.

" Where the ordinary conditions in a country or the special circumstances obtaining in the neutral's territory constitute a special danger to the belligerent from, which the latter cannot have direct means of avoiding, the neutral is bound to employ its initiative so that the state of neutrality is maintained in relation to both belligerents . . ." [8]

From this it would seem to follow that the *Alabama* rule is only an elaboration or definition of the adjective " due " in the phrase " due diligence " and that the requirement of " due diligence " as a whole does not, in the opinion of the *Alabama* Tribunal, go beyond the neutral's capacity.[9] Far from being contradictory, therefore, the *Alabama* Award (1872) and the *Rapports* on the Spanish Zone of Morocco Claims (1923), on this point, both support the decision in the *Prats Case* (C. 1868), in which it was held that:—

" The duty of protection on the part of the government, either by the general principles of international law or by especial agreements of the treaties, only goes as far as permitted by possibility." [10]

[8] 1 *Alabama* (*Proceedings*), p. 168, at p. 170. (Transl.) Original italics.

[9] See also Count Sclopis: " I agree that the performance of acts that are naturally impossible cannot be required, that is the case of *vis major*; *ad impossibile nemo tenetur* . . ." (*ibid.*, p. 173. Transl.).

[10] *Supra*, p. 219.

Indeed, possibility is not only the limit of the duty of protection, but the limit of all obligations. In the *Prats Case*, the Commissioner also held that:—

"Possibility is, indeed, the last limit of all the human obligations: the most stringent and inviolable ones cannot be extended to more. The purpose of trespassing this limit should be equivalent to pretend an impossibility; and so the jurists and law writers, in establishing the maxim *ad impossibile nemo tenetur*, have merely been the interpreters of common sense." [11]

That the maxim: *Ad impossibile nemo tenetur* is related to the principle of fault, that fault depends upon the voluntary character of the act, and that responsibility does not exist without fault were explained by the same Commissioner in the following passage:—

"There is no responsibility without *fault* (*culpa*), and it is too well known that there is no *fault* (*culpa*) in having failed to do what was impossible. The *fault* is essentially dependent upon the will, but as the will completely disappears before the force, whose action cannot be resisted, it is a self-evident result that all the acts done by such force, without the possibility of being resisted by another equal or more powerful force, can neither involve a fault nor an injury nor a responsibility.

"It must not appear strange to speak of violence (*vis major*) when the question is of nations, and even of very powerful ones." [12]

In laying down categorically that there is no responsibility without fault, the *Prats Case* confirms the view that "fault" is to be identified with "unlawful act." In saying that fault is dependent upon the will, it shows that an act is essentially the expression of a will, a point which was often alluded to in the section on imputability.[13] In other words, an unlawful act must be one emanating from the free will of the wrongdoer. There is no unlawful act if the event takes place independently of his will and in a manner uncontrollable by him, in short if it results from *vis major*; for the obligation, the violation of which constitutes an unlawful act, ceases when its observance becomes impossible.

[11] *Loc. cit.*, p. 2894.
[12] *Ibid.*, p. 2895.
[13] *Supra*, pp. 189–191, 207.

Both the principle of fault and its corollary, the concept of *vis major,* were confirmed by the Permanent Court of Arbitration in the *Russian Indemnity Case* (1912). Speaking of the various kinds of responsibility alluded to in the Ottoman Memorials, the Court said:—

"It is necessary to find out whether these various terms and categories created by commentators correspond to some intrinsic differences in the very nature of law, to some distinction in the juridical essence of the notion of responsibility.—The Tribunal is of the opinion that all damages are merely reparation, the payment of compensation, for fault. From this point of view, all damages are compensatory; it matters little what name they are given. The liquidated interest allowed to the creditor of a sum of money from the date of formal demand to the debtor [*mise en demeure*] is the liquidated compensation for the fault of the debtor in arrears, exactly as the damages allowed in case of a delict, quasi-delict, or the nonfulfilment of a positive obligation, are the compensation of the loss suffered by the *creditor,*[14] the equivalent, in terms of money, of the responsibility of the faulty *debitor.*[15]—It is all the more unjustified to exaggerate the importance of civil law distinctions of responsibility, now that several systems of law have recently shown a tendency to lessen or to abolish the mitigations introduced by Roman law and its derivatives in the responsibility for money debt.—It is, indeed, certain that all fault, whatever may be its origin, may ultimately be measured in money and transformed into an obligation to pay; in the last analysis, it always results, or can result, in a money debt.—It is, therefore, not possible for the Tribunal to perceive any essential differences between the various types of responsibility. Identical in their origin—fault—they are the same in their consequences—monetary reparation." [16]

The decision of the Permanent Court of Arbitration disposes any possible doubt that "fault" is synonymous with "unlawful act." The Court referred to the fault of the debtor in arrears, and fault consisting in a delict, a quasi-delict, or in the nonfulfilment of a positive obligation. These are but the familiar civil law distinctions applied to unlawful acts. We have shown that unlawful act in international law is a unitary

[14] "*Créancier,*" *i.e.*, the party in whose favour the obligation exists.
[15] "*Débiteur,*" *i.e.*, the obligated party.
[16] 1 H.C.R., p. 532, at p. 543. (Transl.)

concept.[17] According to the Court, fault is similarly a unitary concept. "Unlawful act" as a unitary concept is the sole source of responsibility[18]; the sole origin of responsibility, according to the Court, resides in the unitary concept of fault. Fault consists in the violation of an obligation, giving rise to responsibility. Such violation we have termed "unlawful act." The two concepts may properly be identified. With fault thus conceived, it is clear that the principle requiring fault in responsibility agrees perfectly with the notion of responsibility as we have expounded it, and, furthermore, forms part and parcel of that notion.

It seems clear from what has been said that the only constitutive elements of fault are the will, the act, and the unlawfulness thereof. It should perhaps be expressly mentioned that, contrary to what is assumed by the majority of writers,[19] fault in modern jurisprudence is no longer identified exclusively with negligence or malice. As has been seen, it means any act or inaction which violates an obligation.[20] In reaching the conclusion that, in accordance with a general principle of law, responsibility in international law requires the existence of fault, we should, therefore, not be understood to imply that an internationally unlawful act must needs be committed "wilfully and maliciously or with culpable negligence," as is, for instance, maintained in Oppenheim's *International Law*,[21] quoted with approval by Judge Krylov and Dr. Ečer in their dissenting opinions in the *Corfu Channel Case* (Merits) (1949).[21a] Certain acts are not internationally unlawful unless committed with malice,[22] or culpable negligence. But what is

17 *Supra*, pp. 172 *et seq*.

18 *Supra*, pp. 169 *et seq*.

19 *e.g.*, Anzilotti, "La responsabilité internationale des états," 13 R.G.D.I.P. (1906), pp. 5 and 285, at pp. 286 *et seq.*; Schoen, *Die völkerrechtliche Haftung*, 1917, pp. 51–63; Eagleton, *The Responsibility of States*, 1928, pp. 208 *et seq.*; Ago, "Le délit international," 69 *Recueil La Haye* (1939), p. 419, at p. 486; Kelsen, *General Theory of Law and the State*, 1946. p. 66; H. Lauterpacht, *Private Law Sources*, 1927, pp. 134 *et seq.*; La Pradelle et Politis, 2 *Arb.Int.*; pp. 972 *et seq.*, *Note doctrinale*.

20 See Fauchille, I (1) *Traité de droit international public*, 1922, p. 515; Salvioli, "Les règles générales de la Paix," 46 *Recueil La Haye* (1933), p. 5, at pp. 96 *et seq*.

See also *supra*, p. 219, note 2.

21 § 154 (1st to 7th ed. inclusive).

21a *ICJ Reports 1949*, p. 4, at p. 72, and pp. 127–128 respectively. See *infra*, p. 231, note 44.

22 *e.g.*, generally speaking, acts of a municipal judicature. See Mex.-U.S. G.C.C. (1923): *Chattin Case* (1927) *Op. of Com. 1927*, p. 422, at p. 429. See also *supra*, pp. 121–122.

negligence? As defined by the British-Venezuelan Mixed Claims Commission (1903):—

"Negligence is . . . 'Such an omission by a reasonable person to use that degree of care, diligence, and skill which it was *his legal duty to use* for the protection of another person from injury as, in a natural and continuous sequence, causes unintended injury to the latter.' (Bouvier, Vol. 2, p. 478.)" [23]

Negligence, or culpable negligence, is, therefore, the failure to perform a legal duty, *i.e.*, a pre-existing obligation prescribing the observance of a given degree of diligence. Being a default in carrying out an obligation, culpable negligence constitutes fault in the sense described above. In such cases, fault does consist in culpable negligence. But culpable negligence constitutes only one category of fault, namely, default in those obligations which prescribe the observance of a given degree of diligence for the protection of another person from injury. Fault as such, however, covers a much wider field. It embraces any breach of an obligation. There are certain obligations which merely stipulate that a party should do or abstain from doing certain acts. This is so as regards most treaty obligations as well as most contractual obligations in the municipal sphere. The mere failure to comply with such obligations, unless it is the result of *vis major*, constitutes a failure to perform an obligation, and a fault entailing responsibility. In such instances, there is no need to consider whether the failure is accompanied by malice or is due to negligence.[24] A State may often be held responsible for the errors of judgment of its organs, even if such errors be bona fide.[25] In cases of this kind, the unlawful act, the fault, is free from the element of malice or culpable negligence. Thus, whether or not malice or culpable negligence is necessary to constitute an unlawful act depends not upon a general principle covering all unlawful acts but upon the particular pre-existing obligation. Malice and negligence can neither be identified with, nor are they inherent in, the notion of fault. Fault is dependent upon the

[23] *Davis Case*, *Ven.Arb. 1903*, p. 402, at p. 406. *Cf. supra*, p. 164.

[24] *Cf. e.g.*, Peruv.-U.S. Cl.Com. (1863): *Sartori Case*, 3 *Int.Arb.*, p. 3120, at p. 2123. Nor could it be said, for instance, that in *The Wimbledon Case* (1923) (PCIJ: A. 1), proof of malice or culpable negligence was required in order to establish Germany's responsibility.

[25] See *e.g.*, *supra*, p. 202, notes 30 and 31. See also Mex.-U.S. G.C.C. (1923): *Kling Case* (1930) *Op. of Com. 1931*, p. 36, at pp. 41–4, and cases cited therein.

existence of the will,[26] but not upon that of malice or negligence. Good faith and due diligence are not the limits of all obligations. Impossibility is. It is only where *vis major* has deprived a person of his free will that there is no obligation, no fault.[27]

The corollary of the principle of fault, the principle *ad impossibile nemo tenetur*, is also confirmed by the *Russian Indemnity Case* (1912):—

> " The exception of *vis major*, invoked as the first line of defence, may be pleaded in public international law as well as in private law." [28]

As was said by the Rumano-Turkish Mixed Arbitral Tribunal in the case of *Michel Macri* (1928):—

> " It is axiomatic that *force majeure*, in order to release a person from his obligation, must be of such a nature as to make it impossible for him to fulfil the obligation to which he is subject. It does not suffice that the alleged *casus fortuitus*, without preventing the fulfilment of the obligation, merely makes it more onerous." [29]

It cannot be doubted that natural impossibility extinguishes any obligation.[30] With regard to the duty of a State to protect aliens within its territorial jurisdiction, it has frequently been recognised that both in the prevention and in the repression of crimes, a State may be faced with natural limitations, and that the duty of the State does not extend beyond these limits.[31]

26 See *supra*, pp. 223 *et seq*.

27 See *infra*, p. 231, note 44, for a discussion of the majority judgment and dissenting opinions of the I.C.J. in the *Corfu Channel Case* (Merits) (1949), with regard to the notion of fault.

28 1 H.C.R. p. 532, at p. 546. (Transl.) Both the PCIJ and the PCA use the term " *vis major* " in a wide sense covering all impossibility preventing the fulfilment of an obligation. See, *e.g.*, PCIJ: *Serbian and Brazilian Loans Cases* (1929) A. 20/21, pp. 39–40, 120.

29 7 T.A.M., p. 981, at pp. 982–3. Transl. Contract claim.

30 *Cf. The Alabama Arbitration* (1872), Opinion of President of Tribunal: " I agree that the performance of acts that are naturally impossible cannot be required, that is the case of *vis major*; *ad impossibile nemo tenetur* " (1 *Alabama* (*Proceedings*), p. 168, at p. 173. Transl.).

31 *Cf.* Spanish Zone of Morocco Claims (1923): *Rapport III* (1924). The *Rapporteur* was of the opinion that, because, in the absence of special authority, it was not possible for an international tribunal to investigate into the origin of riots, revolts, civil or international wars, these occurrences must be regarded as cases of *vis major* (see *infra*, p. 228, note 35). As to crimes committed against foreigners by individuals, bandits or insurgents, the duty of prevention is limited to the observance of *diligentia quam in suis*, in any case not exceeding the means at the State's disposal (2 UNRIAA, p. 615, at pp. 641 *et seq*.). *Cf.*, *supra*, pp. 220–222. With regard to the duty of repression, the *Rapporteur* said: " It is admitted that, generally speaking, the repression of crime is not only a legal obligation of the competent authorities, but also an international duty of the State, inas-

The question of *vis major* has already been mentioned in connection with the Principle of Self-Preservation[32] where it has been shown that *jus necessitatis* is recognised in international law to the extent that "if there is absolutely no conceivable manner in which a State can fulfil an international obligation without endangering its very existence, that State is justified in disregarding its obligation, in order to preserve its existence."[33]

The application of the principle of *vis major* is, however, subject to two important qualifications. First, there must be a link of causality between the *vis major* and the failure to fulfil the obligation. Secondly, the alleged *vis major* must not be self-induced.

Evidence of the first qualification may be found in the cases of the *Serbian Loans* and the *Brazilian Loans* (1929). The Permanent Court of International Justice, considering that the gold clauses in the loan contracts merely referred to gold francs as a standard of value, refused to regard the obligation as dissolved merely because gold francs *in specie* were no longer obtainable.[34]

In the Spanish Zone of Morocco Claims (1923), the *Rapporteur*, having declared that "mob violence, revolts, and wars civil or international" constitute cases of *vis major*[35]

much as foreigners are the victims thereof. The repressive action of the State depends essentially upon its own will. But there are important elements in the repression of crime, which have to be taken into account and which are independent of the will of State authorities. The enforcement of criminal justice is, indeed, subject to natural limitations. Being above all directed at individual crimes, it is more or less powerless in case of revolt or civil war. Furthermore, it presupposes a more or less normal state of affairs in social life and organisation. As in the case of prevention, there are thus *de facto* limits to the prevention of crimes. The enforcement of civil and criminal justice can, therefore, only depend upon the means which are at the State's disposal, and upon the degree of authority which it is able to exercise. The uniform administration of a system of justice conforming to certain minima criteria of international law cannot be required in all circumstances. It must be realised that there are circumstances in which, as in the case of prevention, the activity of the State may be materially limited or even paralysed . . ." (*ibid.*, at p. 646. Transl.).

Cf. also Brit.-Mex. Cl.Com. (1926): *Buckingham Case* (1931), §§ 2, 3, *Further Dec. & Op. of Com.*, p. 323, at pp. 325–6.

See also ICJ: *Corfu Channel Case* (Merits) (1949), *infra*, p. 231, note 44.

32 See *supra*, pp. 69 *et seq.*

33 *Supra*, pp. 73–74.

34 A. 20/21, pp. 40, 120.

35 This is not inevitably so, since these events may have been caused by the State itself and on account of the second qualification of the principle of *vis major* they would not then be regarded as such. The *Rapporteur* no doubt shared this view, except that he said: "In the absence of specific agreements or treaty provisions, the necessary investigation to this end is not permissible. These events must be considered as cases of *vis major*. The principle of the independence of States excludes the possibility of their domestic or foreign

went on to inquire whether "in virtue of the theory of non-responsibility of the State for such happenings, the mere fact that the damage suffered has certain link with happenings in the nature of a rebellion or war, allows the immediate dispensing with all investigation into the responsibility which the State may have in this regard." His answer was that:—

"Even accepting the view that the responsibility of the State immediately ceases when there is a connection between the damage suffered and a revolt, etc., it would nevertheless be impossible to exclude *a limine* a claim in respect of such damage; for the question of fact, *i.e.*, the effective connection between the two, must always be examined and decided first. But there is more: the principle of non-responsibility in no way excludes the duty to exercise a certain degree of vigilance. If the State is not responsible for the revolutionary events themselves, it may nevertheless be responsible for what its authorities do or do not do to ward off the consequences, within the limits of possibility." [36]

Within the limit of possibility, therefore, the obligation subsists.[37] Consequently, there must be an effective connection between the *vis major* and the consequences of the failure to fulfil the obligation. This is a point of fact, which must be proved in case of dispute.

Evidence of the second qualification that *vis major* must not be imputable to the obligated party himself may be found in the *Norwegian Claims Case* (1922), where the Permanent Court of Arbitration held that while the exercise of the power of eminent domain by the United States might be used as a defence in

policy being made, in case of doubt, the subject of international judicial enquiry" (*Rapport III* (1924), 2 UNRIAA, p. 615, at p. 642. Transl.). The *Rapporteur's* opinion is not, therefore, incompatible with the *Michel Macri Case* (1928), *infra*, p. 230.

36 *Ibid.*, at p 642. (Transl.) *Cf.* also Belgo-Germ. M.A.T.: *Wolff Case* (1929) 7 T.A.M., p. 794, at p. 795.

37 The decision of the ICJ: *Corfu Channel Case* (Merits) (1949) *ICJ Reports 1949*, p. 4, is entirely in agreement on all points with the views expressed above. While recognising the obligation of a State in time of peace to notify the presence of minefields in its territorial waters and to warn approaching shipping, the Court held that this obligation depended on the State's having knowledge of the presence of the minefield. Responsibility depended, moreover, upon the possibility, as regards time, of notifying all shipping and warning approaching vessels after having learned of the presence of the minefield. While recognising that it would have been difficult or even impossible to give a general notification to all States the very day the coastal State learned of the presence of the minefield, the Court held: "But this would certainly not have prevented the Albanian authorities from taking, as they should have done, all necessary steps immediately to warn ships near the danger zone, more especially those that were approaching that zone" (p. 23).

disputes between private citizens as a " restraint of princes," the United States could not itself invoke it as against the Kingdom of Norway in defence of a claim by Norway.[38]

In the *Alabama Arbitration* (1872), the British Arbitrator sustained the British contention that Great Britain found herself in what counsel termed the " political impossibility " of affording greater protection and said, for instance, in his opinion expressed during the discussion of the *Florida* (Ex-*Oreto*) *Case*:—

" The equipping of the *Oreto* not amounting to a violation of neutrality, but simply to a breach of the Foreign Enlistment Act, the [British] Government did not have the right to seize it by the mere exercise of the prerogative of the Crown, or by virtue of any executive power. . . . There was not evidence on which to seize the *Oreto* and to ask her condemnation under the Foreign Enlistment Act.

"It was impossible to obtain such evidence, except by the exercise of inquisitorial powers which the Government did not possess.

" Neither was the Government of Great Britain bound to ask for, nor the Parliament to grant to it, powers inconsistent with the established principles of British law and government and with the general institutions of the country." [39]

The Tribunal did not uphold this view and, in its award, decided that:—

" The government of Her Britannic Majesty cannot justify itself for a failure in due diligence on the plea of insufficiency of the legal means of action which it possessed." [40]

In the *Michel Macri Case* (1928), the Rumano-Turkish Arbitral Tribunal spoke of a " circumstance which, by itself, excludes the application of the principle of *force majeure*."

" Indeed, this principle implies that the nonfulfilment of an obligation of the obligated party must, in order that he may be exonerated, proceed from an extraneous cause which cannot, therefore, be imputed to him." [41]

[38] 2 H.C.R., p. 39, at pp. 56, 73.

[39] 2 *Alabama* (*Proceedings*), p. 7, at p. 128. Transl.

[40] 1 *Int.Arb.*, p. 495, at p. 656.

[41] 7 T.A.M., p. 981, at pp. 983–4. (Transl.) *Cf. supra*, p. 228, note 35.

See also Fran.-Germ. M.A.T.: *Franz Case* (1922) 1 T.A.M., p. 781, at p. 785: " It is in fact an undisputed and indisputable principle that no one can invoke, in his own defence, the existence of a fact for which he is himself alone responsible " (Transl.); *Hourcade Case* (1922), *ibid.*, p. 786, at p. 788; *Lorrain Case* (1923) 3 *ibid.*, p. 623, at p. 625.

See also Brit.-Turk. M.A.T.: *Direction générale de la Navigation turque*

Turkey having entered the war before any openly hostile acts on the part of other belligerent Powers took place, the Tribunal held that she could not invoke the war as a *vis major* exonerating her from contractual obligations towards the claimant.

It follows from the above survey of international decisions that the principle of fault and its corollary, the concept of *vis major*, are general principles of law governing the notion of responsibility in the "very nature of law." Their application in the international legal order is abundantly confirmed by international judicial practice.

As has already been shown in the section on imputability,[42] the theory of responsibility without fault or of objective responsibility, in favour of which the Presiding Commissioner declared himself in the *Caire Case* (1929), was not necessary to the decision in that case and was, moreover, founded on a misconception of the problem of imputability in international law. It is not denied that there may be genuine cases of "objective responsibility," where there exists an obligation to make reparation which is conditional on the happening of certain events independent of any fault or unlawful act imputable to the obligated party. But, as explained in the Chapter on the Principle of Individual Responsibility,[43] this so-called responsibility, like "assumed responsibility," is simply a legal obligation modelled on the notion of responsibility. Such a legal obligation based on an express provision does not form part of the concept of responsibility and should be kept entirely separate from it in any discussion of the subject. Responsibility based on fault, founded on the existence of an unlawful act imputable to the actor, forms an independent juridical concept and is one of the most important institutions in any legal order.[44]

Séiri-Sèfaïn (1928) 8 T.A.M., p. 988, at p. 993. In deciding that the requisition by the British Government constituted a case of *force majeure* for the defendant company, the Tribunal added: "the supervening impossibility not being imputable to said Company . . . ."

[42] *Supra*, pp. 204 *et seq.*

[43] *Supra*, pp. 210–211.

[44] The question whether or not responsibility requires fault received a certain amount of attention in the *Corfu Channel Case* (Merits) (1949) (*I.C.J. Reports 1949*, p. 4), from the dissenting judges who, though predominantly in favour of the principle of fault in international responsibility, were not agreed as to its meaning and application. Before proceeding to examine the dissenting opinions of the various judges, it may be pointed out that the judgment of the Court is in perfect agreement with the views expressed above. The I.C.J.,

first of all, stated what was the obligation incumbent upon the defendant State (p. 22). Although the Court did not expressly mention the principle of fault, it was clearly of opinion that the duty of fulfilling this obligation would be subordinated to the condition of possibility (pp. 22–3). Finding that the defendant State had made no attempt to fulfil this obligation, the Court held that "these grave omissions involve the international responsibility" of the defendant State (p. 23). The Court's decision, therefore, agrees with the interpretation of the principle of fault developed above. Moreover, in a passage in which it held that the mere fact that an unlawful act had been committed in territory and waters under its control did not involve the prima facie responsibility of the State nor raise a presumption of responsibility shifting the burden of proof, the Court may be considered as having rejected the theory of objective responsibility. So much for the majority decision.

As for the dissenting judges, Judge Krylov and the judge *ad hoc* of the defendant State, both considered that responsibility required the existence of fault, *culpa*, but they seemed to attribute to the term "fault" the meaning of *dolus* or culpable negligence (pp. 72, 127–8). However true this may be as regards the notion of *culpa* in Roman law (even in Roman law, however, *culpa* was at first distinguished from *dolus*), the reason why this is no longer the meaning of the term "fault" in modern systems of law, especially in international law, has already been explained (*supra*, pp. 225 *et seq.*).

In a sense, therefore, Judge Azevedo was right, when he said in his dissenting opinion, of which he devoted a large portion (pp. 82–96) to an examination of the principle of fault, that: "The notion of *culpa* (*faute*) is always changing and undergoing a slow process of evolution; moving away from the classical elements of imprudence and negligence, it tends to draw nearer to the system of objective responsibility" (p. 85). The learned judge did not, however, clearly indicate the exact meaning which he attributed to the term "fault." He upheld the principle of fault, but seemed also willing to admit the system of responsibility based on risk (pp. 86, 92). He started by criticising the view—which was advanced by the parties and applied by the majority judgment—that responsibility is based on the breach of an obligation (pp. 82–3), but he also sought, first of all, to establish that "secret minelaying in time of peace" was unlawful (p. 85). He considered that there existed in international law a system of what may be called "presumed responsibility." Wherever a link of causation could be established between a State and a damage, responsibility was presumed and the State incurred the burden of exculpating itself (p. 86). Judge Azevedo's efforts appeared to be directed towards establishing a system of objective responsibility based on risk, without, however, abandoning the theory of subjective responsibility based on intention and negligence (*cf.* p. 86). Both the system of objective responsibility and that of "presumed responsibility" were rejected in the majority decision (p. 18).

Judge Badawi Pasha was also of a contrary view and, in his dissenting opinion, rejected the theory of objective responsibility based on risk (p. 65). He based international responsibility expressly on the principle of fault (p. 65). Thus he said: "Il faut donc établir une obligation internationale à la charge de l'Albanie dont le manquement lui serait imputable et serait la cause de l'explosion" (p. 65). ("The failure of Albania to carry out an international obligation must therefore be proved, and it must also be proved that this was the cause of the explosion." Translation of the Court.) The existence of an obligation must, therefore, be first established. Fault consists in the failure to carry out an obligation, in other words, an unlawful act. If the fault, which has caused damage, is imputable to the State, State responsibility will arise. "Fault," "imputability" (see *supra*, pp. 180 *et seq.*) and "causality" (see *infra*, pp. 241 *et seq.*) are, therefore, the requisite elements of responsibility. Judge Badawi Pasha's dissenting opinion, in point of law, is in agreement with the majority decision and also with the principle of fault outlined above.

CHAPTER 9

THE PRINCIPLE OF INTEGRAL REPARATION

"IT is a principle of international law, and even a general conception of law, that any breach of an engagement involves an obligation to make reparation." [1]

"The essential principle contained in the actual notion of an illegal act—a principle which seems to be established by international practice and in particular by the decisions of arbitral tribunals —is that reparation must, as far as possible, wipe out all the consequences of the illegal act and re-establish the situation which would, in all probability, have existed if that act had not been committed. Restitution in kind, or, if this is not possible, payment of a sum corresponding to the value which a restitution in kind would bear; the award, if need be, of damages for loss sustained which would not be covered by restitution in kind or payment in place of it—such are the principles which should serve to determine the amount of compensation due for an act contrary to international law." [2]

The Permanent Court of International Justice thus formulated the principle of integral reparation, inherent in the very notion of responsibility for unlawful acts, and recognised by decisions of international tribunals. That the same principle may be derived from municipal law is shown by the following quotations from the *Lusitania Cases* (1923), decided by the German-United States Mixed Claims Commission (1922):—

"It is a general rule of both the civil and the common law that every invasion of private right imports an injury and that for every

[1] PCIJ: *Chorzów Factory Case* (Merits) (1928), A. 17, p. 29. Although the Court was speaking of treaty, or contractual engagements, it cannot be doubted that the principle is applicable equally, if not *a fortiori*, to obligations *ex lege*. This interpretation is confirmed by the I.C.J. in its Adv.Op. on *Reparation for injuries suffered in the Service of the United Nations* (1949), *ICJ Reports 1949*, p. 174, at p. 184, where the principle was reiterated and applied to the breach of any engagement capable of giving rise to international responsibility. See *ibid.*, p. 208, D.O. by Badawi Pasha and also the Germ.-U.S. M.C.C. (1922) upholding "the fundamental principle that there exists a remedy for the direct invasion of every right" (*infra*, p. 234). This principle has been epitomised in the maxim *Ubi jus, ibi remedium.*

[2] PCIJ: A. 17, p. 47.

such injury the law gives a remedy. Speaking generally, that remedy must be commensurate with the injury received. It is variously expressed as ' compensation,' ' reparation,' ' indemnity,' ' recompense,' and is measured by pecuniary standards, because, says Grotius, ' money is the common measure of valuable things.' "[3]

" The legal concept of damages is judicially ascertained compensation for wrong. The compensation must be adequate and balance as near as may be the injury suffered. In many tort cases, including those for personal injury and for death, it is manifestly impossible to compute mathematically or with any degree of accuracy or by the use of any precise formula the damages sustained. . . . This, however, furnishes no reason why he who has suffered should not receive reparation therefor measured by rules as nearly approximating accuracy as human ingenuity can devise. To deny such reparation would be to deny the fundamental principle that there exists a remedy for the direct invasion of every right."[4]

" The fundamental concept of ' damages ' is satisfaction, reparation for a *loss* suffered; a judicially ascertained *compensation* for wrong. The remedy should be commensurate with the loss, so that the injured party may be made whole. The superimposing of a penalty in addition to full compensation and naming it damages, with the qualifying word exemplary, vindictive, or punitive, is a hopeless confusion of terms, inevitably leading to confusion of thought."[5]

According to both these decisions, therefore, an unlawful act implies an obligation to make integral reparation to the injured party so that he may be " made whole " again. Moreover, the second decision clearly indicates that reparation does not go beyond this limit. In particular, it refutes the idea of punitive damages:—

" That one injured is, under the rules of international law, entitled to be compensated for an injury inflicted resulting in mental suffering, injury to his feelings, humiliation, shame, degradation, loss of social position or injury to his credit or to his reputation, there can be no doubt, and such compensation should be commensurate to the injury. Such damages are very real, and the mere fact that they are difficult to measure or estimate by money standards makes them none the less real and affords no reason why

[3] *Dec. & Op.*, p. 17, at p. 19. Grotius, *De Jure Belli ac Pacis*, II, 17, xxii.
[4] *Ibid.*, at p. 21.
[5] *Ibid.*, at p. 25.

the injured person should not be compensated therefor as compensatory damages, but not as a penalty . . .

"The industry of counsel has failed to point us to any money award by an international arbitral tribunal where exemplary, punitive, or vindictive damages have been assessed against one sovereign nation in favour of another presenting a claim in behalf of its nationals." [6]

While it is true that international tribunals have mostly disallowed claims for punitive damages not on the ground that such damages can never be allowed but on the ground that they have no jurisdiction to award them,[7] this lack of jurisdiction proceeds directly from the premise that the question of punitive damages is not a justiciable issue. *A fortiori*, it does not fall within the legal notion of responsibility. As the German-United States Mixed Claims Commission (1922) said in the same Opinion:—

"Putting the inquiry only serves to illustrate how repugnant to the fundamental principles of international law is the idea that this Commission should treat as justiciable the question as to what penalty should be assessed against Germany as a punishment for its alleged wrongdoing. It is our opinion that as between sovereign nations the question of the right and power to impose penalties, unlimited in amount, is political rather than legal in its nature, and therefore not a subject within the jurisdiction of this Commission." [8]

[6] *Ibid.*, at p. 27. Ralston, Borchard, and two arbitral awards cited. See, *ibid.*, footnote 20. The decision went on (pp. 27–8) to discuss the *Moses Moke Case* (Mex.-U.S. Cl.Com. (1868): 4 *Int.Arb.*, p. 3411). While admitting that the *language* of the decision was the nearest approach to a recognition of the doctrine of exemplary damages to be found in any reported decision of a mixed arbitral tribunal, the Commission did not regard the *decision* as a recognition of this doctrine. It considered that the damages awarded in that Case, far from being punitive or exemplary, were hardly adequate even as compensation for the injury suffered (pp. 27–8).

[7] This is the decisive ground on which the Germ.-U.S. M.C.C. (1922) relied: "But it is not necessary for this Commission to go to the length of holding that exemplary damages cannot be awarded in *any* case by *any* international arbitral tribunal. A sufficient reason why such damages can not be awarded by *this* Commission is that it is without the power to make such awards under the terms of its charter—the Treaty of Berlin" (*Ibid.*, at p. 28).

Mex.-U.S. Cl.Com.: (1868): *Brooks Case*, 4 *Int.Arb.*, p. 4309, at p. 4311: "Our Commission has no punitive mission." Portugo-Germ. Arbitration (1919): *Award II* (1930), 2 UNRIAA, pp. 1076–7: "(E) *Special Indemnity claimed as a Sanction*. . . . The sanction claimed by Portugal is therefore beyond both the sphere of competency of the Arbitrators and the framework of the Treaty" (Transl.).

Cf. also PCA: *The Carthage* (1913), 1 H.C.R., p. 556, at p. 560; *The Manouba* (1913), *ibid.*, p. 565, at p. 570.

[8] *Loc. cit.*, pp. 30–1.

It may, therefore, be concluded that the notion of responsibility for an unlawful act implies the principle of integral reparation, but that, as here envisaged, it does not cover the infliction of any sanction in the form of a pecuniary penalty under the "misnomer" of punitive or exemplary damages.[9]

The exclusion of any pecuniary penalty in the actual notion of responsibility is in fundamental agreement with the proposition that the duty to make reparation should not go beyond "wiping out all the consequences of the illegal act." It has thus been held that reparation for an unlawful act should not be allowed to become a source of enrichment for the injured person[10] and the Permanent Court of International Justice in the *Chorzów Factory Case* (Merits) (1928) repeatedly said that it was necessary to guard against compensating the same damage twice over.[11] The exclusive character of the principle of integral reparation is also borne out by the rule that where no damage is proved, material or moral, no indemnity can be awarded, although this does not exclude the possibility of a declaratory judgment to determine the legality of the act in question, or to clarify judicially the respective rights of the parties.[12]

9 "In our opinion the word exemplary, vindictive, or punitive as applied to *damages* are misnomers" (*ibid.*, at p. 25).

Cf. PCA: *Russian Indemnity Case* (1912), 1 H.C.R., p. 532, at p. 543: "All damages are compensatory."

10 *Delagoa Bay Railway Arbitration* (1900), Martens, II (30) N.R.G., p. 329, at p. 413: "But, if it is just, on the one hand, to restore to the concessionary Company, as an indemnity, all the profits of which it has really been deprived by the rescission (of the concession), it would, on the other hand, be contrary to the most elementary consideration of equity to make this measure a source of enrichment for the company and to attribute to it under this name sums of money which without the rescission, would have profited not this company, but some third party money lenders" (Transl.).

Cf. also PCIJ: *Chorzów Factory Case* (Merits) (1928), A. 17, p. 31: "Excluding from the damage to be estimated, injury resulting for third parties from the unlawful act."

Mex.-U.S. G.C.C. (1923): *Francis J. Acosta Case* (1928), *Op. of Com. 1929*, p. 121, at p. 122. Reparation for wrongful refusal by Mexico to honour Mexican money orders. The Commission, in converting the amount of the money orders into U.S. currency, used the rate of exchange of the time of their purchase so as to avoid any unjust enrichment to the claimants. The Presiding Commissioner of the same Commission also pointed out in the *Cook Case* (Docket No. 663) (1927), *Op. of Com. 1927*, p. 318, that reparation should not result in an unjust enrichment to the claimant and that the amount awarded in that case did not result in such enrichment (p. 323).

11 A. 17, p. 48 *in fine*, p. 49 *in medio*, p. 59 *in principio*. See also ICJ: *Reparation for Injuries suffered in the Service of the United Nations* (1949), Adv.Op., *ICJ Reports 1949*, pp. 174, 186: "The defendant State cannot be compelled to pay the reparation due in respect of the damage twice over."

12 PCIJ: *Mavrommatis Jerusalem Concessions Case* (1925), A. 5, p. 51. "For these reasons, the Court, having heard both Parties, gives judgment as follows: I. That the concessions granted to M. Mavrommatis under the Agreements

During recent years, however, possibly due to the trend towards the establishment of an international criminal law, there has been a tendency among writers to favour the superimposition of a pecuniary penalty over and above integral reparation in case of an internationally unlawful act. Thus, the present editor of Oppenheim's *Treatise on International Law*, Professor Lauterpacht, abandoning the author's view, upheld by previous editors, that the only legal consequence of responsibility in international law was integral reparation and that the idea of a penalty must be excluded, now maintains that "this view hardly accords with principle or practice."[13]

Professor Lauterpacht does not, however, indicate with what principle the view appearing in the previous editions of the Treatise conflicts, and the cases cited by him do not, on closer analysis, sustain his view.[14] In another of his works, Professor

signed on January 27, 1914, between him and the City of Jerusalem, regarding certain works to be carried out at Jerusalem, are valid; That the existence, for a certain space of time, of a right on the part of M. Rutenberg to require the annulment of the aforesaid concessions of M. Mavrommatis was not in conformity with the international obligations accepted by the Mandatory for Palestine; That no loss to M. Mavrommatis, resulting from this circumstance has been proved; That therefore the Greek Government's claim for an indemnity must be dismissed."

ICJ: *Corfu Channel Case* (Merits), *ICJ Reports 1949*, p. 4, at pp. 26, 35 and 36. See also the discussion on declaratory judgments by Azevedo in his dissenting opinion, *ibid.*, p. 97. Also see *ibid.*, pp. 113–114.

Martini Case (1930), 2 UNRIAA, p. 975, at pp. 1001–2; see below, note 14.

Trail Smelter Arbitration (1935): *Final Award* (1941) 3 UNRIAA, p. 1905, at p. 1962.

Brit.-U.S. Cl.Arb. (1910): *Fijian Land Claims*: *Brower Case* (1923), Nielsen's *Report*, p. 612. One shilling nominal damages awarded for the loss of some worthless barren rock islands. In such a case it may be said that there existed a physical loss, although it had no practical value.

Cf. United States and Paraguay Navigation Co. Case (1860), 2 *Int.Arb.*, p. 1485. The American Commissioner, in rejecting the claim, said: "A formal award, made by a mixed commission, under treaty, giving to the claimants 'one cent damages,' would be simply ridiculous. Such a technicality would be unbecoming the dignity of nations and repugnant to the spirit of the public law" (pp. 1506–7). In this case there was in fact no injury, although the U.S. Government argued that there was an admission of responsibility on the part of Paraguay.

13 Oppenheim, 1 *International Law*, 6th and 7th ed., edited by Lauterpacht, § 156a. 5th ed., edited by Lauterpacht, p. 286, note 1. *Cf. contra*, § 156 of 1st, 2nd, 3rd and 4th eds.

See also Eagleton, "The Measure of Damages in International Law," 39 *Yale L.J.* (1929–1930), p. 52; Briggs, "The Punitive Nature of Damages in International Law and State Responsibility for Failure to Apprehend, Prosecute or Punish," in *Essays in Political Science in Honour of W. W. Willoughby*, ed. by Mathews and Hart, 1937, pp. 339–53.

14 Prof. Lauterpacht cited *The Carthage Case* (1913), the *Janes Case* (1926), the *Greco-Bulgarian Frontier Incident* (1926), *The I'm Alone Case* (1933, 1935), and the *Martini Case* (1930).

The quotation from *The Carthage Case* (1913), *viz.*, "The establishment

Lauterpacht seems to have deduced the possibility of imposing a pecuniary penalty upon States from the fact of their submission to law,[15] but this is a *petitio principi*, since everything depends upon what the law says. According to the Permanent Court of International Justice and other international tribunals, international law imposes only the duty of integral reparation, and this apparently was also the conclusion of Professor Lauterpacht in his *Private Law Sources and Analogies of International Law*, in which, assuming an analogy between international responsibility and civil responsibility in private law, he said: "In international law, as in private law, *restitutio in integrum* is regarded as the object of redress." [16]

of the fact that a State had failed its obligations 'constitutes in itself a serious penalty,' " is based on the erroneous translation of the French word "sanction" into "penalty" in English. "Sanction," in French as in English, may be moral, civil or penal. No one would, for instance, maintain that Art. 36 (2) (*c*) of the Statute of the I.C.J. confers upon the Court a right to inflict "penalties." The award as a whole clearly shows that the P.C.A. in that case disclaimed any punitive function (see 1 H.C.R., p. 556).

The decision in the *Martini Case* (1930) (2 UNRIAA, p. 975), far from inflicting a "punishment" upon the defendant State, following the jurisprudence of the P.C.I.J., awarded no damages because no loss was incurred, even though it found that the Venezuelan judiciary committed a "manifest injustice." It expressly adopted the principle of integral reparation formulated by the P.C.I.J. and, in annulling the obligations arising from the unlawful judgment, it was only "wiping out all the consequences of the illegal act." It ordered a restitution in kind, but did not inflict a "punishment."

In the *Janes Case* (1926), *Greco-Bulgarian Frontier Incident* (1926) and *The I'm Alone Case* (1933, 1935), reparation for moral damage was awarded. If reparation for moral damage is erroneously called vindictive damages, the difference would be purely terminological. But Prof. Lauterpacht considers that "*la réparation morale contient un élément distinct de châtiment*" ("Règles générales du droit de la Paix," 62 *Recueil La Haye* (1937) p. 99, at p. 355). This is the "confusion of thought" which, as the Germ.-U.S. M.C.C. (1922) said, would inevitably result from a "confusion of terms" (*supra*, p. 234). The reason why reparation for moral damage (*le préjudice moral*) is strictly compensatory and not punitive has already been set out at length by the Germ.-U.S. M.C.C. (1922) (*Dec. & Op.*, pp. 24–8; for quotations, see *supra*, pp. 234–235) and need not be repeated here.

Moreover, with particular reference to the *Janes Case* (1926), the Mex.-U.S. G.C.C. (1923) expressly warned us that "it would seem a fallacy to sustain that, if in case of non-punishment by the government it is not liable for the crime itself then it can only be responsible, in a punitive way, to a sister government, not to a claimant" (*Op. of Com. 1927*, p. 108, at p. 117), and it said that in all cases of denial of justice, including that resulting from the non-prosecution of a common crime against an alien, a nation is never held liable for anything else than the *damage caused* by what the executive, legislative, or judiciary committed or omitted itself (*ibid.*). The award was, therefore, in compensation of an actual damage caused by the organs of the State.

See Schwarzenberger, "The Problem of an International Criminal Law" (1950) 3 C.L.P., p. 263, at pp. 276 *et seq.*

15 Lauterpacht, "Règles générales du droit de la Paix," *loc. cit.*, at pp. 356–7.

16 1927, p. 149.

However, while the juridical principle of integral reparation is well established and quite simple in conception, its practical application to life may present problems of infinite complexity [17] and international judicial decisions bear witness to a certain amount of flexibility in its application. Conjecture, in cases where the evidence as to the exact amount of the injury is defective,[18] and compromise, where the judges disagree, cannot be entirely excluded.[19] Here as elsewhere, human endeavours can only aspire to approximate accuracy and truth, but not to the absolute.

It would be beyond the compass of the present work concerned with "the general principles of law" to set out in detail the judicial application of the principle of integral reparation. It

[17] *Cf. e.g.*, *Delagoa Bay Railway Case* (1900) 2 *Int.Arb.*, p. 1874; Martens, II (30) N.R.G., p. 329. The elaborate system for assessing the exact amount of damage is set out in the Award and illustrates how damages may be more or less carefully assessed.

[18] *Cf.* Mex.-U.S. Cl.Com. (1868): *Emilio Roberts Case*: "It is often much more difficult for us to fix the amount of the claim, in a reasonable manner, than to give judgment about the justice of the same claim. Claimants almost always exaggerate enormously, and try to present the facts in the light most favourable to themselves, without paying great respect to the truth. The authorities having in charge the collection of the defensive evidence, very seldom pay attention to the estimate of damages, and use all their efforts in contradicting the principle of the claim. For this reason, we, the Commissioners, are compelled to proceed solely by simple conjectures and inferences, drawn from the few facts we have before us, and to make a very ample use of the discretionary power which pertains to our office." Memorial and Opinion, docket 594, MS., U.S. Department of State. Quoted from Whiteman, 2 *Damages*, p. 833. The conjecture can, however, only relate to the extent of the injury. Its existence must not be conjectural but must be proved to the satisfaction of the court.

[19] The amount of $15,500,000 awarded in *The Alabama Arbitration* (1872) seems to have been arrived at in the following manner. The amount claimed by the United States for damage caused by the *Alabama*, the *Florida* and the *Shenandoah*, the "inculpated cruisers," at the final stage of the proceedings was $14,437,000; the amount which the British Agent regarded as just was $7,074,000. Splitting the difference, the Swiss Arbitrator Staempfli proposed the round figure of $10,905,000. To this were added first, an uncontested sum of $988,000 as compensation for crews and equipment of whaling vessels, and secondly, interest at 7 per cent. from January 1, 1864, to the final date fixed for the payment of the award. In this way he arrived at a round figure of $20,000,000. Sir Alexander Cockburn seemed completely in agreement with this method of splitting the difference, but he maintained that, first, interest should not be allowed and, secondly, taking the American claim as a basis for computing damages, there should be deducted certain items which the tribunal had already decided as not allowable. In this way he arrived at the figure of $10,121,044. The tribunal did not indicate how it reached the figure of $15,500,000, but the American Agent Bancroft Davis in his report to the American Secretary of State thought that it was arrived at by splitting the difference of the figures proposed by the two arbitrators. See 2 *Arb.Int.*, p. 713, at pp. 886–8.

Mex.-U.S. Cl.Com. (1868): *Brooks Case*, 4 *Int.Arb.*, p. 4309, at p. 4311.

Brit.-U.S. Cl.Arb. (1910): *Cayuga Indians Case* (1926), Nielsen's *Report*, p. 203, at p. 331.

must, however, be mentioned that the statement that integral reparation must "wipe out all the consequences of the illegal act," only refers to the proximate consequences thereof. Here we touch upon "a well known principle of the law of damages that *causa proxima non remota inspicitur,*" [20] which forms the subject of the next Chapter.

[20] Brit. U.S. Cl.Arb. (1910): *The Newchwang* (1921), Nielsen's *Report*, p. 411, at p. 419.

CHAPTER 10

THE PRINCIPLE OF PROXIMATE CAUSALITY [1]

IN May, 1921, an American sent four locomotives into Mexico. Rochín, a Mexican official, wrongfully sent a telegram ordering that they should not be allowed to return to the United States. During their forced stay in Mexico, they became involved in various vicissitudes culminating in their ruin or destruction. Can their fate be regarded as the consequence of the unlawful act of the Mexican official? This was one of the questions that arose in the *H. G. Venable Case* (1927), which came before the Mexican-United States General Claims Commission (1923).

" What was the damage caused by Rochín's telegram? Linked up with subsequent occurrences, his telegram may have been the cause of all the mishap of the claimant relative to the three engines which on September 3, 1921 [date of the telegram], were in good condition, and of part of the mishap with the fourth engine which had been wrecked in August . . . It is clear, however, that only those damages can be considered as losses or damages caused by Rochín which are immediate and direct results of his telegram." [2]

This case clearly shows that, in law, the term " consequences " has a technical meaning. The use of the adjectives " immediate and direct " is not, however, altogether happy. As the Portugo-German Arbitral Tribunal said in the *Angola Case* (1928, 1930):—

" The problem of responsibility for indirect damage has often been considered by international tribunals and writers on international law. In the well-known *Alabama Case*, the arbitrators

[1] Or " effective causality." *Cf. infra*, p. 253, note 25.

[2] *Op. of Com. 1927*, p. 331, at p. 338. The bulk of the damages was awarded on the ground of gross insufficiency of governmental action subsequent to the Rochín telegram, and not on the ground of this initial unlawful act. The Commission quoted the *Lacaze Case* (1864), 2 *Arb.Int.*, p. 290, at p. 298: " All compensation for losses should reasonably and equitably include only those which are the immediate and direct consequence of the act which has caused them, without being possible ever to extend to those which are only the mediate or indirect consequence thereof, and still less to expectancies of eventual profits " (Transl.).

declared that they would not take into consideration this kind of loss. This decision has been criticised, and in subsequent cases, arbitrators have quite often allowed compensation for damages that are not direct. And, indeed, it would not be equitable to let the injured party bear those losses which the author of the initial illegal act has foreseen and perhaps even intended, for the sole reason that, in the chain of causation, there are some intermediate links. But, on the other hand, every one agrees that, even if the strict principle that direct losses alone give rise to a right to reparation is abandoned, it is none the less necessary to exclude losses unconnected with the initial act, save by an unexpected concatenation of exceptional circumstances which could only have occurred with the help of causes which are independent of the author of the act and which he could in no way have foreseen. Otherwise, there would be an inadmissible extension of responsibility. Thus, notwithstanding the provisions of the treaty of August 25, 1921, between the United States of America and Germany, which requires Germany to compensate losses caused to American citizens 'directly or indirectly,' the arbitrators, charged with the application of this treaty, have not hesitated to refuse all indemnity in respect of injuries which, though standing in causal relation to the acts committed by Germany, also resulted from other and more proximate causes." [3]

The proper criterion, according to the Portugo-German Arbitral Tribunal is, therefore, not the directness of the consequences, but their foreseeability or proximate causality in relation to the wrongful act. The decisions of the German-United States Mixed Claims Commission (1922) to which this Tribunal referred are *Administrative Decision No. II* (1923) and the Opinion in *War Risk Insurance Premium Claims* (1923), in which the same view is brought out with much greater force. In the latter decision, the Umpire held that the arguments of counsel for the claimants were partly based on "a confusion of the legal concept of the proximate cause of a loss with that of the consequential and indirect damages flowing therefrom." [4]

In *Administrative Decision No. II* (1923), the Umpire declared:—

"The proximate *cause* of the loss must have been in legal contemplation the act of Germany. The proximate *result* or

[3] *Award I* (1928), 2 UNRIAA, p. 1011, at p. 1031. (Transl.)
[4] *Dec. & Op.*, p. 33, at p. 46.

consequence of *that act* must have been the loss, damage, or injury suffered . . . This is but an application of the familiar rule of proximate cause—a rule of general application both in private and public law—which clearly the parties to the Treaty had no intention of abrogating. It matters not whether the loss be directly or indirectly sustained so long as there is a clear, unbroken connection between Germany's act and the loss complained of. It matters not how many links there may be in the chain of causation connecting Germany's act with the loss sustained, provided there is no break in the chain and the loss can be clearly, unmistakably, and definitely traced, link by link, to Germany's act. But the law cannot consider . . . the 'causes of causes and their impulsions one on another.' Where the loss is far removed in causal sequence from the act complained of, it is not competent for this tribunal to seek to unravel a tangled network of causes and of effects, or follow, through a baffling labyrinth of confused thought, numerous disconnected and collateral chains, in order to link Germany with a particular loss. All indirect losses are covered, provided only that in legal contemplation Germany's act was the efficient and proximate cause and source from which they flowed." [5]

" The use of the term [indirect damages] to describe a particular class of claims is inapt, inaccurate and ambiguous. The distinction sought to be made between *damages* which are direct and those which are indirect is frequently illusory and fanciful and should have no place in international law. The legal concept of the term 'indirect' when applied to an act proximately causing a loss is quite distinct from that of the term 'remote.' The distinction is important." [6]

It is only true to say that in the majority of cases, in which the epithets "direct" and "indirect" are applied to describe the consequences of an unlawful act, they are in fact being used synonymously with "proximate" and "remote." [7] The

[5] *Dec. & Op.*, p. 5, at pp. 12–13. Italics of the Commission.

[6] Germ.-U.S. M.C.C. (1922): *War Risk Insurance Premium Claims* (1923), *ibid.*, p. 33, at p. 58.

[7] *Cf. e.g.*. Spanish Zone of Morocco Claims (1923): Claim 25: *Rzini-Beni Madan, Cattle* (1924), 2 UNRIAA, p. 615, at pp. 696–697. The *Rapporteur* considered that a *lucrum cessans* which was "alien" to the act complained of, in other words, had no causal relation therewith, was certainly included in the notion of "indirect or consequential damages" disclaimed by the British representative. In this very case, the *Rapporteur* clearly indicated, however, that he was guided by the principle of integral reparation, of putting the claimant back "in the same position he would have found himself" had the act complained of not been committed (*ibid.*). See also Claim I: *Rzini-Tetuan, Orchards* (1924), *ibid.*, at pp. 651–659. Having held that it was the claimant

decisions of the Portugo-German Arbitral Tribunal (1919) and the German-United States Mixed Claims Commission (1922) categorically show, however, that "indirect damage"—in the strict sense of the term—cannot as a group be excluded from reparation.[8] Moreover, they show that it is "a rule of general application both in private and public law," equally applicable in the international legal order, that the relation of cause and effect operative in the field of reparation is that of proximate causality in legal contemplation. In order that a loss may be regarded as the consequence of an act for purposes of reparation, either the loss has to be the proximate consequence of the act complained of, or the act has to be the proximate cause of the loss.

who had voluntarily renounced the pursuit of his cultivation, the *Rapporteur* said that the immediate cause of the loss of a harvest was this decision freely taken, which could only have been the mediate consequence of the alleged insecurity in the district. This distinction between mediate and immediate causality is, in substance, the same as the distinction between proximate and remote causality made by the Germ.-U.S. M.C.C. (1922) and the Portugo-German Arbitral Tribunal. With regard to *lucrum cessans*, the *Rapporteur* also indicated in the same case that it would not be excluded as indirect or consequential damages if it were shown to have "serious chances" of being achieved. The Mex.-U.S. Cl.Com. (1868) in the *Rice Case* (4 *Int.Arb.*, p. 3248) seemed to regard "consequential damages" as meaning *lucrum cessans*. Although differing in terminology from the *Rapporteur*, the *Rice Case* was in substantial agreement with him. It allowed damages for loss arising from "the direct and habitual lawful pursuit of gain, or the fairly certain profit of the injured person, or the profit of an enterprise judiciously planned according to custom and business," and disallowed expectancies from "a mere device of speculation, however probable its success would have been or may appear to the projector" (p. 3248). But the sole Arbitrator in the *Whaling and Sealing Claims*: *The Cape Horn Pigeon Case* (1902), while in substantial agreement with the above cases, refused to call a fairly certain *lucrum cessans* an indirect or consequential damage. He said: "In this case, it is not a matter of *indirect* damage, but of direct damage, the amount of which ought to be assessed" (U.S.F.R. (1902), Appendix I, p. 467, at p. 471. (Transl.) Italics of the Tribunal). See *infra*, pp. 247–248.

A reading of the *Lacaze Case* (1864) (*loc.cit.*, *supra*, p. 241, note 2) and the *Mallén Case* (1927) (Mex.-U.S. G.C.C. (1923) *Op. of Com. 1927*, p. 254, §§ 13, 14), cited by the Commission in the *Venable Case* (1927) will show that what the Mex.-U.S. G.C.C. (1923) had in mind was also the effectiveness of the causation rather than its immediacy or mediacy.

Cf. also Fran.-Ven. M.C.C. (1902): *Pieri Dominique et Cie* (1905), Ralston's *Report*, p. 185, at p. 206: "There can be no allowance for any losses accruing to the claimant in the sale of his houses, such losses not being the direct and approximate result of any cause of which the respondent Government has responsibility, and it is only for such results that indemnity can be awarded." *Direct*, *approximate*, *efficient*, *proximate* are, indeed, often used in this connection synonymously.

However, proximate damages cannot be identified either with *damnum emergens* or "necessary" or "inevitable" damages, even *grosso modo*, as seems to have been assumed by Ecer in I.C.J.: *Corfu Channel Case* (Compensation) (1949), *I.C.J. Reports 1949*, p. 244, at p. 254.

[8] For a discussion of *The Alabama Case* (1872) which adopted a contrary solution see Germ.-U.S. M.C.C. (1922): *War Risk Insurance Premium Claims* (1923), *Dec. & Op.*, p. 33, at pp. 48 *et seq.*, under "*The Alabama Claims decisions considered and applied.*"

Hence the maxim: *In jure causa proxima non remota inspicitur.* Even in cases of "assumed responsibility," with which the German-United States Mixed Claims Commission (1922) was concerned, derogation from this principle is not to be presumed.[9]

In an age when the very principle of causation has been challenged by philosophers, it would seem that the Umpire of the German-United States Mixed Claims Commission (1922) purposely used the phrase "in legal contemplation" when invoking the principle of proximate causality. This principle is a legal nexus of cause and effect and it is necessary to elucidate what is the proper criterion for determining proximate causality in legal contemplation.

It is possible to discern in international judicial decisions the use of two criteria to determine proximate causality, the one objective the other subjective.

The objective criterion, *i.e.*, that the consequences should be normal, seems to be the criterion favoured by the German-United States Mixed Claims Commission (1922). In its decision in the *Life Insurance Claims* (1924), the Commission had to deal with claims of life insurance companies for losses suffered by them through the accelerated maturity of their policies resulting from premature deaths caused by acts of Germany. Speaking of the rules which should govern reparation for injuries causing death, the Commission first recalled the rule of proximate causality which it had laid down in *Administrative Decision No. II* (1923) and then said:—

"Applying this test, it is obvious that the members of the families of those who lost their lives on the *Lusitania*, and who were accustomed to receive and could reasonably expect to continue to receive pecuniary contributions from the decedents, suffered losses which, because of the natural relations between the decedents and the members of their families, flowed from Germany's act as a *normal consequence* thereof, and *hence attributable to Germany's act as a proximate cause*. The usages, customs, and laws of civilised

[9] See Germ.-U.S. M.C.C. (1922): *War Risk Insurance Premium Claims* (1923), *Dec. & Op.*, p. 33.

Also Rum.-Hung. M.A.T.: *Beligradeanu Case* (1928), 8 T.A.M., p. 967, at p. 971.

Greco-Germ. M.A.T.: *Antippa (The Spyros) Case* (1926), 7 T.A.M., p. 23, at p. 28. U.S.A.: Brit. Cl.Arb. (1927): *The Lisman* (1937), 3 UNRIAA, p. 1767, at p. 1792.

countries have long recognised losses of this character as proximate results of injuries causing death. . . .

"But the claims for losses here asserted on behalf of life insurance companies rest on an entirely different basis. Although the act of Germany was the immediate cause of maturing the contracts of insurance by which the insurers were bound, *this effect* [italics of the Commission] so produced was a circumstance incidental to, but not flowing from, such act as the normal consequence thereof, and was, therefore, *in legal contemplation remote—not in time—but in natural and normal sequence* . . . In striking down the natural man, Germany is not in legal contemplation held to have struck every artificial contract obligation, of which she had no notice, directly or remotely connected with that man. The accelerated maturity of the insurance contracts was *not a natural and normal consequence of* Germany's act in taking the lives, and *hence not attributable to that act as a proximate cause.*" [10]

The contrast in which the German-United States Mixed Claims Commission (1922) placed these two types of consequence brings out with great clarity what the Commission meant by proximate cause in legal contemplation. If a loss is a normal consequence of an act, it is attributable to the act as a proximate cause. If a loss is not the normal and natural consequence of an act, it is not attributable to the act as a proximate cause.[11] As to what constitutes a normal and natural consequence of an act,

[10] *Dec. & Op.*, p. 103, at pp. 133–4. Italics added.

[11] See also, *e.g. id.*: *Beha Case* (1928), *Dec. & Op.*, p. 901. Claims on behalf of American holders of insurance policies who failed to obtain the full amount of their insurance claims because of the insolvency of the Norske Lloyd Insurance Co., Ltd., due to the destruction by Germany of property insured by it belonging to other than American nationals. Held: "Assuming the truth of the facts upon which this argument rests, the vice in it is that the inability of these American policyholders to collect from the Norwegian insurer indemnity in full *was not the natural and normal* consequences of the acts of Germany in destroying property not American owned which happened to be insured by the same Norwegian insurer. . . . The destruction by Germany of non-American-owned property insured by this Norwegian insurer which resulted in its insolvency *cannot, in legal contemplation, be attributed as the proximate cause* of damages sustained by American nationals resulting from their inability, because of the insurer's insolvency, to collect full indemnity for the loss of their property not touched by Germany" (pp. 902–3).

For other illustrations of the distinction between the proximate and the remote consequences of an act, see *id.*: *Eisenbach Brothers & Co.* (1925), *Dec. & Op.*, p. 267. The sinking of a ship is the proximate consequence of the planting of a mine. *Id.*: *Neilson (The Mohegan) Case* (1926), *Dec. & Op.*, p. 670. Chased by a submarine, a merchantman strained its engines. The damage is the proximate consequence of the act of the submarine. See also *id.*: *Crder of May 7, 1925, Announcing Rules applicable to Debts, Bank Deposits, Bonds, etc.*, *Dec. & Op.*, p. 854.

an arbitrator or judge may seek guidance and authority from "usages, customs and laws of civilised countries."

Arbitrators or judges may, however, also have recourse to science for determining the normal and natural consequences of a given act. In the *Maninat Case* (1905), which came before the Franco-Venezuelan Mixed Claims Commission (1902), and arose out of the unlawful infliction of a machete wound, the Umpire said:—

> "When it comes to the actual trial of actions for personal injuries, there are two difficult questions, to the solution of which the testimony of the medical expert may be directed. One of these is how far the defendant's negligence is responsible for some subsequently developed infirmity or disease or, in other words, how far a given injury may be said to be the natural and proximate cause of a subsequently developed condition and therefore render the defendant liable for that condition." [12]

Quoting medico-legal authority, the Umpire said:—

> "'The general rule is easily stated, to wit: if the subsequent disease or infirmity is one which would occur as the natural result of the injury, and it is not shown that any other independent cause existed of which it might have been the result, then the author of the original injury is liable for the subsequent disease or infirmity.'" [13]

The Umpire, having found on medical evidence that the subsequent death was due to traumatic tetanus, and that the latter was due to the trauma inflicted by the machete, concluded:—

> "Since his death resulted through a line of natural sequences from a wound inflicted under the circumstances named, the responsibility of the respondent government is the same as though death had been the immediate result of the machete stroke." [14]

The objective criterion of normality or naturalness of the consequence may be applied not only to *damnum emergens* but also to *lucrum cessans*. In the case of *The Cape Horn Pigeon* (1902), the sole Arbitrator held that:—

[12] Ralston's *Report*, p. 44, p. 77.

[13] *Ibid.*, at p. 77, quoting Allan McLane Hamilton and others, 2 *A System of Legal Medicine*, p. 379.

[14] *Ibid.*, at p. 78. *Cf.* Mex.-U.S. G.C.C. (1923): *Mallén Case* (1927), *Op. of Com., 1927*, p. 254, § 13.

"The general principle of civil law, according to which damages ought not only to include compensation for injuries suffered, but also for loss of profit, is equally applicable in international disputes. . . . In order that it may be applied, it is not necessary for the amount of the *lucrum cessans* to be calculable with certainty. It is sufficient to show that the act complained of has prevented the making of a profit which would have been possible *in the ordinary course of events* (*dans l'ordre naturel des choses*)." [15]

The principle of proximate causality has indeed sometimes been stated simply as that of normal consequence. Thus in the *Antippa (The Spyros) Case* (1926), the Greco-German Mixed Arbitral Tribunal said:—

[15] U.S.F.R. (1902), Appendix I, p. 467, at p. 470–1. (Transl.) Italics added.

Cf. PCIJ: *Chorzów Factory Case* (Merits) (1928), A. 17, p. 47: "Re-establish the situation which would, *in all probability*, have existed if that act had not been committed." See also pp. 53 *et seq.* The Court was definitely of the opinion that *lucrum cessans* may be taken into account in assessing compensation, based on the "normal development" of the undertaking.

Cf. Brit.-U.S. Cl.Arb. (1910): *The Wanderer* (1921), Nielsen's *Report*, p. 459; *The Favorite* (1921), *ibid.*, p. 515; *The Kate* (1921), *ibid.*, p. 472; *The Horace B. Parker* (1925), *ibid.*, p. 570, at p. 571: "It is enough to say that a long line of decisions of international tribunals has established as the measure of damages for such cases loss of use of the vessel, to be measured by the loss of *probable* catch. For this purpose the catch of other vessels or the average catch under the conditions at hand has often been taken as the measure. Indeed this tribunal has so held in three prior cases. *The Wanderer* . . .; *The Favorite* . . .; *The Kate*. . . ." Cases of interference with fishing vessels. The basic criterion is the same as with other cases of *lucrum cessans*.

What is normal in one case is normal in another only when conditions are the same. In accordance with the principle that damages should not be a source of profit to the injured person, prospective gains are not allowed when they are highly problematical or when special circumstances show that the injured person would probably *not* obtain what others might.

Cf., e.g., The Canada (1870), 2 *Int.Arb.*, p. 1733. Seizure of a whaling ship. "But the undersigned can in no case admit a right to prospective profits; for the ship and the whole capital might have been lost in the voyage, or the expedition might have been entirely unsuccessful and without profit. In this particular case the objection is still stronger, because the *Canada* was commanded by a captain who, very little after sunset, when darkness could have hardly set in, ran his vessel upon a reef, with the existence and position of which he ought to have been well acquainted" (p. 1746).

The distinction is clearly drawn in the *Rice Case* (C. 1868), 4 *Int.Arb.*, p. 3248, at p. 3248: "As to the portion of the damages claimed which may be imagined to arise out of consequential damages, the umpire desires to lay down as one of the requisites for consequential damages, that there must be a manifest wrong, the effect of which prevents the direct and habitual lawful pursuit of gain, or the fairly certain profit of the injured person, or the profit of an enterprise judiciously planned according to custom and business. A mere device of speculation, however probable its success would have been or may appear to the projector, cannot enter into the calculation of consequential damages." See also *Shufeldt Case* (1930), 2 UNRIAA, p. 1079, at p. 1099: "The *damnum emergens* is always recoverable, but the *lucrum cessans* must be the direct fruit of the contract and not too remote or speculative."

"According to principles recognised both by municipal and by international law, the indemnity due from one who has caused injury to another comprises all loss which may be considered as the *normal consequence* of the act causing the damage." [16]

In addition to this objective criterion based on the normality of the consequences, it is possible to discern the use of a subjective criterion in international judicial decisions—namely, that of foreseeability and intention.

The criterion of foreseeability was applied by Sir Cecil Hurst (then Mr. C. J. B. Hurst) and Mr. R. Newton Crane, British and American Commissioners respectively, in their "Joint Report No. II of August 12, 1904," in connection with the *Samoan Claims Award* (1902). In this Report, they submitted what they considered to be the proper method for computing the damages payable to German nationals as a result of the military activities of Great Britain and the United States at Samoa in 1899, following the Arbitral Award [17] rendered by King Oscar II in 1902 in favour of Germany. As regards remote damages, the Commissioners said:—

"4. (vi). On this question of the damages in cases such as the foregoing being too remote, it may be useful if we state the principles which, in our opinion should be followed.

"There is, it is true, a striking absence of international precedent or authority that we can appeal to, but in the continual litigation in the courts of our respective countries rules have gradually been established as to the damages that can or cannot be recovered in cases of wrongdoing. We have no ground for thinking that the rules obtaining in foreign countries are different, nor does there seem to be any reason why as between nations liability for wrongdoing should not be assessed in accordance with the rules observed in municipal courts, and which are found to work substantial justice as between all parties.

"We may go further and affirm that so far as the records of International Commissions dealing with claims of a similar character to those under consideration are accessible, they indicate that these principles have been followed in such tribunals.

"The effect of these rules, stated briefly, is that the damages for which a wrongdoer is liable are the damages which are both, in fact,

[16] 7 T.A.M., p. 23, at p. 28. (Transl.) Italics of the tribunal.
[17] U.S.F.R. (1902), p. 444. See *supra*, pp. 140–141.

caused by his action, and cannot be attributed to any other cause, and which a reasonable man in the position of the wrongdoer at the time would have foreseen as likely to ensue from his action." [18]

While it may be true that the criterion of foreseeability by a reasonable man may be just as objective a test as that of normality, it can hardly be denied that in allowing the judge to determine the relation of cause and effect from the point of view of the wrongdoer at the time of the act and not of a judge investigating the facts after the event, there is a great concession to the subjective elements involved. Moreover we may venture to submit that this criterion comes closer to the *ratio legis* of the principle of proximate causality. Coupled with the principle of fault, it would render a person responsible for all foreseeable and, *a fortiori*, all intended consequences of any of his voluntary acts which are unlawful. That this subjective element of foreseeability and intention is the *ratio* of the principle seemed to be the view of the Portugo-German Arbitral Tribunal in the *Angola Case* (1928, 1930). It may be recalled that this Tribunal made the following statement in its first award:—

> "And, indeed, it would not be equitable to let the injured party bear those *losses which the author of the initial illegal act has foreseen and perhaps even intended*, for the sole reason that, in the chain of causation, there are some intermediate links. But, on the other hand, every one agrees that, even if the strict principle that direct losses alone give rise to a right to reparation is abandoned, it is none the less necessary to exclude losses unconnected with the initial act, save by an unexpected concatenation of exceptional circumstances which could only have occurred with the help of causes which are independent of the author of the act and *which he could in no way have foreseen*." [19]

While the foreseeability of its consequence by the doer of an act may be regarded as one of the *rationalia* of responsibility, the standard which the law in fact applies is perforce much more objective. The proximate consequences of an act are not necessarily those which its author actually foresaw, but need

[18] MS., U.S. Department of State, National Archives, 210 Despatches, Great Britain, Ambassador Choate to Secretary Hay, August 18, 1904, No. 1429, enclosure. Quoted at some length in Whiteman, 3 *Damages*, p. 1778, at pp. 1779–80.

[19] 2 UNRIAA, p. 1011, at p. 1031. (Transl.) Italics added.

only be those which the judges consider he could and should have foreseen. In practice, therefore, it is still the standard of the reasonable man. In the *Angola Case*, speaking of the causal connection between the unjustified German incursions into Angola and the subsequent native uprising, the Tribunal, after mentioning the responsibility of Portugal for its extension, said:—

> "It is certain, however, that the German aggression was, in itself, capable of causing trouble among the native population, that it was in the natural order of things that the blacks, subdued only so few years previously, would avail themselves of the opportunity to revolt. No doubt, the Germans could not have foreseen the spreading of this revolt by reason of the special circumstances which have just been mentioned, but they should have reckoned with the serious effects which their military action, in a country only recently pacified, would have had on the authority of Portugal." [20]

In its *Award II* (1930), the Tribunal said:—

> "This uprising, considered as a harmful act, thus constitutes . . . an injury which the author of the initial act, namely, the German command, should have foreseen as a necessary consequence of its military operations." [21]

For these consequences which should have been foreseen, Germany was held responsible.[22]

By thus introducing what may be called a minimum standard of foreseeability, in the nature of an irrebuttable presumption, the two criteria, objective and subjective, are in practice merged.

While, however, the objective criterion of normality and the subjective criterion of reasonable foreseeability generally coincide in the determination of proximate causality, the subjective criterion alone applies in the case of exceptional consequences intended by the author of the act. If intended by the author, such consequences are regarded as consequences of the act for which reparation has to be made, irrespective of whether such consequences are normal, or reasonably foreseeable.

In the *Frances Irene Roberts Case* (C. 1903), which concerned an unjustifiable and inexcusable attack upon an American

[20] *Ibid.*, at p. 1032. (Transl.)
[21] *Ibid.*, at p. 1075. (Transl.)
[22] *Award I* (1928), *ibid.*, at p. 1032.

citizen and his family, the United States-Venezuelan Mixed Claims Commission (1903) decided that:—

"The act was committed by duly constituted military authorities of the Government. It was never, so far as the evidence shows, disavowed or the guilty parties punished. Under these circumstances well established rules of international law fix a liability beyond that of compensation for the direct losses sustained. *Other consequences are presumed to have been in the contemplation of the parties committing the wrongful acts* and in that of the Government whose agents they were. The derangement of Mr. Quirk's plans, the interference with his favourable prospects, his loss of credit and business, are all proper elements to be considered in the compensation to be allowed for the injury he sustained. To the amount hereintofore designated is added, in view of the considerations above mentioned, the sum of $5,000." [23]

The same Commission in the *Dix Case*, in laying down the principle of proximate causality, made an express reservation with regard to consequences intended by the wrongdoer:—

"Governments, like individuals, are responsible only for the proximate and natural consequences of their acts. International as well as municipal law denies compensation for remote consequences, in the absence of evidence of deliberate intention to injure." [24]

[23] *Ven.Arb. 1903*, p. 142, at p. 145. Italics added. Soldiers under the command of officers pillaged claimant's plantation, and threatened "to return and kill the claimant and destroy the place." Superior authorities unable to afford the protection sought, claimant left his plantation thus sacrificing property and very promising prospects. *Cf.* Spanish Zone of Morocco Claims (1923): Claim I: *Rzini-Tetuan Orchards* (1924), 2 UNRIAA, p. 615, at pp. 651–659 (see *supra*, p. 243, note 7).

[24] *Ven.Arb. 1903*, p. 7, at p. 9. In the course of a civil war, claimant, to escape possible further requisitions, sold his cattle at a loss. The claim was for compensation to cover this loss. Held: "The military authorities, under the exigencies of war, took part of his cattle, and he is justly entitled to compensation for their actual value. But there is in the record no evidence of any duress or constraint on the part of the military authorities to compel him to sell his remaining cattle to their parties at an inadequate price. Neither is there any special animus shown against Mr. Dix, nor any deliberate intention to injure him because of his nationality" (*ibid.*, at p. 9). This part of the claim was disallowed.

Cf. Belgo-Germ. M.A.T.: *De Maret Case* (1924), 4 T.A.M., p. 103, at p. 105. Germany was held not responsible for loss sustained through stocks of raw material being sold by their Belgian owner to avoid German requisition.

It is interesting to compare these cases with the *F. I. Roberts Case* quoted above.

See also Germ.-U.S. M.C.C. (1922): *Life-Insurance Claims* (1924), *Dec. & Op.*, p. 103, at p. 137: "The great diligence and research of American counsel have pointed this Commission to no case decided by any municipal or international tribunal awarding damages to one party to a contract claiming a loss as a result of the killing of the second party to such contract

In conclusion, it may be said that the principle of integral reparation in responsibility has to be understood in conjunction with that of proximate or effective [25] causality which is valid both in municipal and international law. By virtue of the latter principle, the duty to make reparation extends only to those damages which are legally regarded as the consequences of an unlawful act. These are damages which would normally flow from such an act, or which a reasonable man in the position of the wrongdoer at the time would have foreseen as likely to result, as well as all intended damages.

by a third party without any *intent* of disturbing or destroying such contractual relations." See *supra*, pp. 245–246. See also *Id.*: *Hickson Case* (1924), *Dec. & Op.*, p. 439.

[25] It is possible to consider the nexus between an act and all its consequences "in legal contemplation" as one of "effective causality," reserving the term "proximate causality" to the normal and reasonably foreseeable sequence of events. As long as the meaning of the terms is properly understood, the choice of the name is of little importance.

PART FOUR

GENERAL PRINCIPLES OF LAW IN JUDICIAL PROCEEDINGS

PART FOUR

GENERAL PRINCIPLES OF LAW IN JUDICIAL PROCEEDINGS

THE general principles of adjective law were well expressed by the Greco-Bulgarian Mixed Arbitral Tribunal in the *Arakas (The Georgios) Case* (1927). Speaking of the decision of a Bulgarian Military Commission sitting as a prize court, the Tribunal said:—

" It is true that each State is free to organise its prize courts and to regulate their procedure; but these courts possess a special character; for, although dependent upon municipal law and municipal administration, they have certain international aspects, on account of the nature of their functions and of the correct application which they have to make of international law. It is necessary that a *judicial procedure* should be followed, *in the course of which both parties are heard*, and the decisions, which are in truth judgments, must be based, not only on municipal law and national interest, but also on international law. . . .

" The Commission was able to sit legally as a Prize Court, but it does not appear from its decision of December 11, 1912, that a judicial procedure was followed. The text of the decision does not indicate whether the Commission took the neutral character of the ship into account, nor whether it examined the question, raised in Article 3 of the XIth Hague Convention of 1907, according to which ' small boats employed in local trade (and this seems to apply to the *Georgios*, by reason of its small tonnage) are exempt from capture.'

" The vessel being neutral, it was necessary to resolve certain essential preliminary questions before declaring it contraband of war. . . .

" The Bulgarian Commission, in the decision submitted to our Tribunal in the present case, affirmed that the goods were destined for the Turkish army of Marmara and Gallipoli, without *indicating the evidence* or information upon which it relied. . . .

" Nothing in the Bulgarian decision indicates its source of information or the reasons which might explain it or which served as its legal basis. These serious omissions might justify the view that the decision is a violation of the principle that *no one should be judge in his own cause*. . . .

" The Tribunal, despite these obvious defects in the decision of the Bulgarian Military Commission, is eager, as always, to show the *greatest respect for the principle of res judicata* and prefers to seek the solution of the problem submitted to it, in the application of another international legal criterion, without having to confirm or to invalidate the decision of the Commission." [1]

The Tribunal thus admitted the existence of certain independent criteria as to what constitutes "judicial procedure." "Judicial procedure" has the character of a legal concept independent of particular rules of law applicable to it. In the course of judicial proceedings both parties must be heard—*audiatur et altera pars*. The body sitting as a judicial organ must be legally competent. There exists a principle that no one should be judge in his own cause—*nemo judex in sua propria causa*. The judge must not neglect the examination of any relevant point of fact or of law. The decision must be based on the law applicable, and should be a proper judgment. It is preferable, to say the least, that the factual and juridical bases of the decision should be indicated. Finally, there should always be the greatest respect for the principle of *res judicata*.

The *Arakas Case* serves as a useful starting point for examining the validity of these criteria as general principles of law.

[1] 7 T.A.M., p. 39, at pp. 43–5. (Transl.) Italics added. This case is wrongly placed under the heading *Vlassios D. Katrantsios* c. *Etat bulgare* in the T.A.M.

CHAPTER 11

JURISDICTION

A. Extra Compromisum Arbiter Nihil Facere Potest

" THERE are certain elementary conceptions common to all systems of jurisprudence, and one of these is the principle that a court of justice is never justified in hearing and adjudging the merits of a cause of which it has no jurisdiction. . . .

" The requirement of jurisdiction, which is universally recognised in the national sphere, is not less fundamental and peremptory in the international. . . .

" Ever mindful of the fact that their judgments, if rendered in excess of power, may be treated as null, international tribunals have universally regarded the question of jurisdiction as fundamental." [1]

Judge John Bassett Moore thus formulated the necessity of jurisdiction as one of the principles " common to all systems of jurisprudence " in one of his dissenting opinions.

The Mexican-United States General Claims Commission (1923) gave the following definition of the term jurisdiction:—

" Jurisdiction is the power of a tribunal to determine a case in accordance with the law creating the tribunal or a law prescribing its jurisdiction." [2]

The same principle as that mentioned by Judge Moore has been formulated as follows by the Franco-Venezuelan Mixed Claims Commission (1902):—

" The limits of this honorable commission are found and only found in the instrument which created it. . . . An arbitral tribunal is one of large and exclusive powers within its prescribed limits, but it is as impotent as a morning mist when it is outside these limits." [3]

[1] PCIJ: *Mavrommatis Palestine Concession Case* (Jd.) (1924), D.O. by Moore, A. 2, pp. 57–60.

[2] *Elton Case* (1929), *Op. of Com. 1929*, p. 301, at p. 306. See *Salem Case* (1932), D.O. by Nielsen, 2 UNRIAA, p. 1161, at p. 1205; ICJ: *Corfu Channel Case* (Prel.Obj.) (1948), D.O. by Daxner, *ICJ Reports 1947–1948*, p. 12, at p. 39.

[3] *French Company of Venezuelan Railroads Case* (1905), Ralston's *Report*, p. 367, at p. 444. Jay Treaty (Art. VII) Arbitration (1794): *The Betsey*

An illustration of this principle may be found in what became known as the "*Umpire Cases*" before the Granadine-United States Claims Commission (1857). These cases were submitted to the Umpire of the Commission by the national commissioners for his decision on certain preliminary questions. The Umpire, instead of confining himself to the preliminary questions, rendered his awards on the merits of the claims, thereby overstepping the limits of his power as prescribed by the Convention setting up the Commission. The Granadine Commissioner entered a protest and the decisions were set aside by a subsequent Commission and the cases examined *de novo*.[4]

Mention may also be made of the *Northeastern Boundary Arbitration* (1831) between Great Britain and the United States. The royal Arbitrator King William I of the Netherlands, from whom a "decision" was sought as to the boundary of the disputed territory as described in treaties between the parties, found that the relevant treaties were obscure and proposed a new frontier line. The American Minister at The Hague therefore deemed it his duty "to enter a Protest against the proceeding, as constituting a departure from the powers delegated by the High Interested Parties." The British Government, although disposed to acquiesce in the award, did not insist upon regarding it as final and after the resolution of the United States Senate in June, 1832, declaring it not binding, the matter was ultimately settled by a compromise in the Treaty of Washington of August 9, 1842.[5]

A well-known case where a final award was successfully attacked on the ground of excess of jurisdiction is that of the *Orinoco Steamship Co.* (1910) decided by the Permanent Court of Arbitration. An agreement was signed on February 13, 1909, between the United States and Venezuela submitting to the Court for review the decision of February 22, 1904, by Umpire Barge of the United States-Venezuelan Mixed Claims Commission (1903) on the claims of the above-mentioned company against Venezuela. The Court held inter alia that:—

(1797), 4 *Int.Adj.*, M.S., p. 179, at pp. 193–4, 200, quoted *infra*, p. 277. Pol.-Germ. M.A.T.: *Tiedemann Case* (1926), 7 T.A.M., p. 702, at p. 706, quoted *infra*, p. 356.

[4] 2 *Int.Arb.*, pp. 1396–1420. See also *infra*, pp. 291 *et seq.*

[5] 1 *Int.Arb.*, pp. 85–161.

"Whereas by the agreement of February 13, 1909, both Parties admit at least implicitly, as vices involving the nullity of an arbitral award, excessive exercise of jurisdiction and essential error in the judgment. . . .

"Whereas, following principles of equity in accordance with law, when an arbitral award embraces several independent claims, and consequently several decisions, the nullity of one is without influence on any of the others, more especially when, as in the present case, the integrity and the good faith of the arbitrator are not questioned; this being ground for pronouncing separately on each of the points at issue. . . .

"Whereas the agreement of February 17, 1903, did not invest the arbitrators with discretionary powers, but obliged them to give their decisions upon a basis of absolute equity without regard to objections of a technical nature, or of the provisions of local legislation. . . .

"*Whereas excessive exercise of jurisdiction may consist, not only in deciding a question not submitted to the arbitrators, but also in disregarding the imperative provisions of the agreement as to the path along which they are to reach their decisions, notably with regard to the law or the legal principles to be applied.*" [6]

The Court, therefore, declared void several items in the award of 1904 which, although admissible according to absolute equity, were rejected for technical reasons or objections based on local law.[7]

The above cases show that not only unauthorised decisions (lack of jurisdiction), but also decisions arrived at in disregard of the constitution of the Tribunal, either as to the object of the submission or the legal principles to be applied (excess of competence), are null. In other words the principle of competence requires that a tribunal should decide strictly in accordance with its constitutional law, on pain of nullity.

Violation of the principle may consist not only in positive acts, but also failure either to apply the prescribed principles of law or to decide a case that falls within the Tribunal's jurisdiction. Thus in *The Betsey Case* (1797) Commissioner Gore said:—

"To refrain from acting, when our duty calls us to act, is as wrong as to act where we have no authority. We owe it to the

[6] 1 H.C.R., p. 504, at pp. 505–6. (Transl.) Italics added.
[7] *Ibid.*, at p. 508.

respective governments to refuse a decision in cases not submitted to us—we are under equal obligation to decide on those cases that are within the submission." [8]

Refusal to exercise jurisdiction in such a case would indeed amount to a denial of justice.[9]

As Judge Kellog observed in the *Free Zones Case* (Second Phase: Order) (1930):—

"The question of jurisdiction can always be raised at any stage of the proceeding. It is not even necessary that it be raised by one of the litigant Parties. It may and should be raised by the Court on its own initiative, as was done in the *Eastern Carelia Case.*" [10]

While the Permanent Court of International Justice could, and often did, raise "*proprio motu* the question whether the Court has jurisdiction" [11] there are, as the Court had occasion to point out, important distinctions to be drawn between the Court and municipal tribunals with regard to the points raised by Judge Kellog. Thus in the case of the *Minority Schools in Upper Silesia* (1928), the Court declared:—

"The Court's position, in regard to jurisdiction, cannot be compared to the position of municipal courts, amongst which jurisdiction is apportioned by the State, either *ratione materiae* or in accordance with a hierarchial system. This division of jurisdiction is, generally speaking, binding upon the Parties [*Cette repartition est, en general, d'ordre public*] and implies an obligation on the part of the Courts *ex officio* to ensure its observance. Since in such cases the raising of an objection by one Party merely draws the attention of the Court to an objection to the jurisdiction which it must *ex officio* consider, a Party may take this step at any stage of the proceedings." [12]

Unlike the position under municipal law, however, as was pointed out in the same judgment,

"The Court's jurisdiction depends on the will of the Parties." [13]

8 Jay Treaty (Art. VII) Arbitration (1794): 4 *Int.Adj.*, M.S., p. 179, at p. 193.
9 *Cf.* PCIJ: *Chorzów Factory Case* (Jd.) (1927), A. 9, p. 30.
10 P.C.I.J.: A. 24, p. 43. *Id.*: *Minority Schools in Upper Silesia Case* (1928), D.O., by Huber, A. 15, pp. 53–4.
11 *e.g.*, P.C.I.J.: *Administration of the Prince of Pless Case* (Prel.Obj.: Order) (1933), A/B. 52, pp. 15, 16. See also *Ottoman Debt Arbitration* (1925), 1 UNRIAA, p. 529, at p. 565. ICJ: *Anglo-Iranian Oil Co. Case* (Jd) (1952), Ind.Op. of McNair, *ICJ Reports 1952*, p. 93, at pp. 116–7.
12 PCIJ: A. 15, p. 23.
13 *Ibid.*, at p. 22. See also ICJ: *Anglo-Iranian Oil Co. Case* (Jd.) (1952), *ICJ Reports 1952*, p. 93, at p. 103.

On the one hand, the Court will thus refuse to decide a dispute even indirectly when the interested States have not given their consent, as in the case concerning the status of *Eastern Carelia* (1923) where it said in its reply to a request for an Advisory Opinion:—

"It is well established in international law that no State can, without its consent, be compelled to submit its disputes with other States either to mediation or to arbitration, or to any other kind of pacific settlement." [14]

On the other hand, the Court always considers itself competent once the Parties

"have accepted its jurisdiction, since there is no dispute which States entitled to appear before the Court cannot refer to it. Article 36 of the Statute, in its first paragraph, establishes this principle in the following terms:

"'The jurisdiction of the Court comprises all cases which the Parties refer to it and all matters specifically provided for in treaties and conventions in force.'

"This principle only becomes inoperative in those exceptional cases in which the dispute which States might desire to refer to the Court would fall within the exclusive jurisdiction reserved to some other authority. . . .

"The acceptance by a State of the Court's jurisdiction in a particular case is not, under the Statute, subordinated to the observance of certain forms, such as, for instance, the previous conclusion of a special agreement.

"Thus, in Judgment No. 5 the Court has accepted as sufficient for the purpose of establishing its jurisdiction a mere declaration made by the Respondent in the course of the proceedings agreeing that the Court should decide a point which, in the Court's opinion, would not otherwise have come within its jurisdiction.[15] And there seems to be no doubt that the consent of a State to the submission of a dispute to the Court may not only result from an express declaration, but may also be inferred from acts conclusively establishing it. It seems hard to deny that the submission of arguments on the merits, without making reservations in regard to the question of jurisdiction, must be regarded as an unequivocal indication of the desire of the State to obtain a decision on the merits of the suit. . . .

[14] PCIJ: B. 5, p. 27.
[15] *The Mavrommatis Jerusalem Concessions* (1925), A. 5, pp. 26–8.

"The Court . . . holds that there is nothing . . . in the principles governing the Court's jurisdiction to prevent questions not falling within the category of those in respect of which compulsory jurisdiction is established, from being submitted to the Court by agreement between the Parties, notwithstanding the fact that the suit has been brought on the basis of the clause conferring compulsory jurisdiction. The Court, in this connection, refers to what it observed in Judgment No. 5, already referred to. . . .

"If, in a special case, the Respondent has, by an express declaration, indicated his desire to obtain a decision on the merits and his intention to abstain from raising the question of jurisdiction, it seems clear that he cannot, later on in the proceedings, go back upon that declaration. This would not hold good only if the conditions under which the declaration had been made were such as to invalidate the expression of intention, or if the Applicant had, in the subsequent proceedings, essentially modified the aspect of the case, so that the consent, given on the basis of the original claim, could not reasonably be held to apply to the claim in the form which it now assumes. And, in the Court's opinion, there is no reason for dealing otherwise with cases in which the intention of submitting a matter to the Court for decision has been implicitly shown by the fact of arguing the merits without reserving the question of jurisdiction." [16]

This principle established by the Permanent Court of International Justice was confirmed by the International Court of Justice in its first decision. The new World Court, recalling the jurisprudence of the Permanent Court, dismissed an Albanian preliminary objection to its competence by holding that:—

[16] PCIJ: *Minority Schools in Upper Silesia Case* (1928), A. 15, pp. 22–25, *Cf.* D.O.s of Huber, Nyholm, Negulesco, *ibid.*, at pp. 51–52, 54, 56, 69, 73. Jurisprudence of the court confirmed by PCIJ: *Société commerciale de Belgique Case* (1939), A/B. 78, p. 174. *Cf.* also ICJ: *Corfu Channel Case* (Merits) (1949), *ICJ Reports 1949*, p. 4. The reservation by the defendant of the right to discuss the assessment of compensation was considered, account taken of its previous attitude, as "an implied acceptance of the Court's jurisdiction to decide this question" (p. 25). See also ICJ: *Haya de la Torre Case* (1951), cited *infra*, p. 265, note 20. The ICJ, in the *Anglo-Iranian Oil Co. Case* (Jd.) (1952), held, however, that no element of consent to the jurisdiction of the Court could be deduced from the fact that the party "submits also objections which have no direct bearing on the question of jurisdiction," but "are clearly designed as measures of defence" in case its objection to jurisdiction were rejected, as that party had consistently denied the jurisdiction of the Court (*ICJ Reports 1952*, p. 93, at p. 114). The Court held: "The principle of *forum prorogatum*, if it could be applied to the present case, would have to be based on some conduct or statement regarding the jurisdiction of the court" (*ibid.*).

"The letter of July 2, 1947, addressed by the Albanian Government to the Court, constitutes a voluntary acceptance of its jurisdiction." [17]

Accordingly other sources of jurisdiction did not require to be considered. This letter, addressed to the Court by the Albanian Government, acknowledged the receipt of a copy of the British unilateral application instituting proceedings concerning the Corfu Channel Incident. While maintaining that the unilateral application was irregular, it went on to say:—

"It [*i.e.*, the Albanian Government] is prepared, notwithstanding this irregularity in the action taken by the Government of the United Kingdom, to appear before the Court . . . The Albanian Government wishes to emphasise that its acceptance of the Court's jurisdiction for this case cannot constitute a precedent for the future." [18]

The International Court of Justice, in declaring this letter to constitute "a voluntary and indisputable acceptance of the Court's jurisdiction," said:—

"While the consent of the parties confers jurisdiction on the Court, neither the Statute nor the Rules requires that this consent should be expressed in any particular form . . . Furthermore, there is nothing to prevent the acceptance of jurisdiction, as in the present case, from being effected by two separate and successive acts, instead of jointly and beforehand by a special agreement." [19]

For this reason the Court dismissed Albania's preliminary objection in regard to jurisdiction.[20]

What has been said in the preceding pages shows that in the application of the general principles of law, the *ratio* of the principle has to be considered. A general principle of law may

[17] ICJ: *Corfu Channel Case* (Prel.Obj.) (1948), *ICJ Reports 1947–1948*, p. 12, at p. 26.

[18] *Ibid.*, at p. 19.

[19] *Ibid.*, at pp. 27–28.

[20] *Cf.* ICJ: *Corfu Channel Case* (Order of March 26, 1948), *ICJ Reports 1947–1948*, p. 53. On the day on which judgment was delivered, a special agreement was concluded between the parties and became the basis of further proceedings before the Court. See also ICJ: *Haya de la Torre Case* (1951), *ICJ Reports 1951*, p. 71, at p. 78: "All the questions submitted to it have been argued by them on the merits, and no objection has been made to a decision on the merits. This conduct of the Parties is sufficient to confer jurisdiction on the Court". *Cf.* ICJ: *Anglo-Iranian Oil Co. Case* (Jd.) (1952), *ICJ Reports 1952*, p. 93, at pp. 113–14 (*supra*, p. 264, note 16).

apply in one legal system and not another, not because the latter rejects it, but because the circumstances justifying its application in the one system are absent from the other. Therefore, in applying the same principle to a third system, it is necessary to ascertain whether, and to what extent, the circumstances justifying its application exist. Here the general principle is that a tribunal is incompetent to act beyond its jurisdiction. Where the limits of jurisdiction are binding upon the parties, the question of competence may be raised, either by the parties or *proprio motu* by the tribunal, whether municipal or international, at any stage of the proceedings.[21] But where the parties have the power to confer jurisdiction upon the tribunal or to extend it, once they have concurred in doing so in a given matter, either simultaneously or successively, either by express words or by acts conclusively establishing it, neither party may subsequently question the tribunal's competence. In such cases, it may be said that, since the procedural acts of the parties will, in proper cases, be interpreted as acceptance of the tribunal's jurisdiction, the possibility of raising such an objection will gradually disappear as the proceedings develop.

B. Jurisdiction over Incidental Questions

Where a tribunal has jurisdiction in a particular matter, it is also competent with regard to all relevant incidental questions, subject to express provision to the contrary. For instance, in virtue of Article 250 of the Treaty of Trianon, the Hungaro-Serb-Croat-Slovene Mixed Arbitral Tribunal was competent to adjudicate upon claims of Hungarian nationals for the restitution of their property. In the case of the *Compagnie pour la Construction du Chemin de Fer d'Ogulin à la Frontière, S. A.* (1926), the ownership of the property claimed was in dispute and the defendant contested the Tribunal's jurisdiction to decide the question of disputed ownership. The Tribunal held that the question of ownership was an incidental question and:—

"Incidental questions arising in the decision of a case ought to be examined by the judge competent to decide on the principal issue, unless the law provides otherwise; nothing in the Treaty of

[21] *Cf.* Pol.-Germ. M.A.T.: *Tiedemann Case* (1926), 7 T.A.M., p. 702, at p. 708. See *infra*, pp. 355 *et seq.*

Trianon excludes examination of the preliminary question concerning ownership from the jurisdiction conferred upon the Mixed Arbitral Tribunals by Article 250 of the said Treaty; in these circumstances, the Tribunal is competent to consider the application." [22]

In the *German Interests Case* (Jd.) (1925), the Permanent Court of International Justice held that:—

"It is true that the application of the Geneva Convention is hardly possible without giving an interpretation of Article 256 of the Treaty of Versailles and the other international stipulations cited by Poland. But these matters then constitute merely questions preliminary or incidental to the application of the Geneva Convention. Now the interpretation of other international agreements is indisputably within the competence of the Court if such interpretation must be regarded as incidental to a decision on a point in regard to which it has jurisdiction . . .

"The jurisdiction possessed by the Court under Article 23 in regard to differences of opinion between the German and Polish Governments respecting the construction and application of the provisions of Articles 6 to 22 concerning the rights, property and interests of German nationals is not affected by the fact that the validity of these rights is disputed on the basis of texts other than the Geneva Convention." [23]

It should, however, be mentioned that the effect of a decision on incidental questions is not exactly the same as that of a decision on the principal question, as will be seen in the Chapter dealing with the principle of *res judicata*.[24]

C. Competence to Indicate Interim Measures of Protection

What may perhaps be regarded as another form of extension of jurisdiction is the power of a tribunal to indicate provisional

[22] 6 T.A.M., p. 505, at p. 507. Transl. Pol.-Germ. M.A.T.: *Kunkel Case* (1925), *ibid.*, p. 974, at p. 977. *Zeltweg-Wolfsberg and Unterdrauburg-Woellan Railways Case* (Prel.Obj.) (1934), 3 UNRIAA, p. 1795, at p. 1803. *Cf.*, however, Greco-Bulg. M.A.T.: *Société Dospat-Dag Case* (1924), 4 T.A.M., p. 477; *Hatiboglou Case* (1925), 5 *ibid.*, p. 905.

[23] A. 6, p. 18. See also PCIJ: *Mavrommatis Palestine Concessions Case* (Jd.) (1924), A. 2, p. 28; *German Interests Case* (Merits) (1926), A. 7, pp. 25, 42; *Free Zones Case* (Jgt.) (1932), A/B. 46, pp. 114, 154–56; *Zeltweg-Wolfsberg and Unterdrauburg-Woellan Railways Case* (Prel.Obj.) (1924), 3 UNRIAA, p. 1795, at p. 1803.

Cf. also PCIJ: *Chorzów Factory Case* (Jd.) (1927), A. 9, p. 23; ICJ: *Corfu Channel Case* (Merits) (1949), *ICJ Reports 1949*, p. 4, at p. 23 *et seq.*

[24] *Infra*, pp. 350 *et seq.*

measures of protection. In the *Anglo-Iranian Oil Co. Case*, while the question of the Court's jurisdiction was still pending, the International Court of Justice indicated on July 5, 1951, certain interim measures of protection to be observed by the Parties on a basis of reciprocity.[24a] These measures lapsed when the Court subsequently decided on July 22, 1952, that it had no jurisdiction to deal with the merits of the case.[24b] As to the competence of the Court to indicate these measures, the Court said:—

"The Court derived its power to indicate these provisional measures from the special provisions contained in Article 41 of the Statute."[24c]

Article 41 I of the Statute of the International Court of Justice, following that of the Permanent Court of International Justice, provides that:—

"The Court shall have the power to indicate, if it considers that circumstances so require, any provisional measures which ought to be taken to preserve the respective rights of either party."[25]

The Permanent Court considered that this provision was but an application of the "principle universally accepted by international tribunals" that:—

"Parties to a case must abstain from any measure capable of exercising a prejudicial effect in regard to the execution of the decision to be given and, in general, not allow any step of any kind to be taken which might aggravate or extend the dispute."[26]

The Rules of Procedure of almost all the Mixed Arbitral Tribunals established by the Peace Treaties after the First World War contained provisions which permitted the granting of interim orders of protection,[27] and, in the case of the British-

24a (Interim Protection), *ICJ Reports 1951*, p. 89.
24b (Jd.), *ICJ Reports 1952*, p. 93, at p. 114.
24c *Ibid.*, at p. 102. See also Same Case (Interim Protection), *ICJ Reports 1951*, p. 89, at p. 93.
25 The corresponding article of the Statute of the P.C.I.J. used the word "reserve" instead of "preserve," but this is believed to be due to a printer's error at the early stage of drafting. See Hudson, *The P.C.I.J.*, 1943, p. 199.
26 *Electricity Co. of Sofia and Bulgaria* (Interim Protection) (1939), A/B. 79, p. 199. See *supra*, p. 140.
27 Amongst the 34 Rules of Procedure published in T.A.M., only those of the Brit.-Germ. (1 T.A.M., p. 109), Jap.-Germ. (*ibid.*, p. 124) and the Jap.-Austrian (*ibid.*, p. 821) M.A.Ts. did not contain such provisions.

German Mixed Arbitral Tribunal, the Rules of Procedure of which contained no such provision, the tribunal nevertheless ordered interim measures of protection in the *Gramophone Co., Ltd., Case* (1922).[28] In that particular case, the Tribunal was satisfied that it had jurisdiction as to the merits.[29] Where a tribunal has jurisdiction as to the merits, its competence to indicate interim measures of protection does not appear to be disputed.

The question to be examined here, however, is how far a tribunal has the power to indicate provisional measures of protection before it is fully satisfied that it has jurisdiction in a case. This question arose in connection with the proceedings before the Mixed Arbitral Tribunal and the same applies even as regards the World Court. There can be no doubt that, when a tribunal is requested to indicate interim measures of protection, it must always consider whether it is "competent to adjudicate upon it." [30] But almost without exception, the Rules of Procedure of the various Mixed Arbitral Tribunals provided that the Tribunal could exercise this power "at any stage of the proceedings, even before the filing of the suit instituting proceedings." [31] As the Czechoslovak-Hungarian Mixed Arbitral Tribunal said in the case of *Count Hadik Barcoczy* (1928), speaking of Article 33 of its Rules of Procedure [32]:—

> "This provision gives the Tribunal, or, if necessary, its President, the power to order interim measures of protection even before the filing of the suit, that is to say even before the Tribunal is in possession of the necessary information to enable it to examine if it has jurisdiction over the claim." [33]

But the Rules of Procedure of the Mixed Arbitral Tribunals were laid down by the Tribunals themselves and could neither diminish nor increase their power derived from the Peace

[28] 1 T.A.M., p. 857.
[29] *Ibid.*, at p. 859.
[30] PCIJ: *Administration of the Prince of Pless Case* (Interim Protection) (1933), A/B. 54, p. 153.
[31] See Art. 32 of the Rules of the Fran.-Germ. M.A.T. (1 T.A.M., p. 44) which was literally reproduced in those of 10 other M.A.Ts. The Rules of 13 other M.A.Ts. were similar on this point. Those of the Brit.-Austrian, Brit.-Bulg., and Brit.-Hung. M.A.Ts. (1 T.A.M., pp. 662, 639, 655 respectively) simply said: "at any stage of the proceedings" (Art. 65).
[32] 3 T.A.M., p. 193.
[33] 35 R.G.D.I.P. (1928), p. 61, at p. 63. (Transl.)

Treaties. They were, however, modelled more closely upon municipal law than upon international law.[34] And as Judges Badawi Pasha and Winiarski said, in their joint Dissenting Opinion in the *Anglo-Iranian Oil Co. Case* (Interim Protection) (1951) before the International Court of Justice:—

> "The question of the jurisdiction of the national tribunal does not arise . . . In municipal law, there is always some tribunal which has jurisdiction. In international law it is the consent of the parties which confers jurisdiction on the Court." [35]

In practice, however, it appears that the Mixed Arbitral Tribunals were in agreement that:—

> "The question of jurisdiction [as to the merits] is closely linked with that of interim measures of protection." [36]

In the Statute of the International Court of Justice, Article 41 is placed at the beginning of Chapter III on Procedure. It comes immediately after the Article dealing with the institution of proceedings, but before the various articles concerned with the actual procedure before the Court, commencing with Article 42 which deals with the representation of the parties by agents. An interpretation of the Statute by the systematic method would seem to indicate that once a case is brought before the Court,[37] but before any other procedural steps have been taken,[38] the Court may exercise its power to indicate interim measures of protection.

In the *Anglo-Iranian Oil Co. Case* (Interim Protection) (1951), the International Court of Justice held that it was

[34] *Cf.* Rabel, "Rechtsvergleichung und Internationale Rechtsprechung," 1 Z.f.P. (1927), p. 13. Guggenheim, "Les mesures conservatoires dans la procédure arbitrale et judiciaire," 40 *Recueil La Haye* (1932), p. 645, p. 726 *et seq.* In contrast, the more cautious wording of Art. 41 of the Statute of the I.C.J. was originally inspired by similar provisions in the so-called "Bryan treaties" concluded by the U.S. with a number of countries in 1914. See Report of the Advisory Committee of Jurists which drafted the Statute of the P.C.I.J., *Procès-verbaux*, p. 735.

[35] *ICJ Reports 1951*, p. 89, at pp. 96–97.

[36] Pol.-Germ. M.A.T.: *Tiedemann Case* (Interim Protection) (1923), 3 T.A.M., p. 596, at p. 600. (Transl.) See *Anglo-Iranian Oil Co. Case* (Interim Protection) (1951), D.O. by Badawi Pasha and Winiarski, *loc. cit.*, p. 96.

[37] In the *Polish Agrarian Reform Case* (Interim Protection) (1933), the P.C.I.J. held that "the essential condition which must necessarily be fulfilled . . . is that such measures should have the effect of protecting the rights forming the subject of the dispute submitted to the Court" (A/B. 58, p. 177). The dispute must, therefore, have first been submitted to the Court.

[38] See *infra*, pp. 271–2.

competent to indicate interim measures when it found that the dispute was not one which could *a priori* be accepted as falling "completely outside the scope of international jurisdiction."[39]

With great respect, it is submitted that the pertinent consideration was not "international jurisdiction," but the jurisdiction of the Court itself, in the light of all relevant instruments. Judges Badawi Pasha and Winiarski in their joint Dissenting Opinion were of the view that:—

> "The power given to the Court by Article 41 [of its Statute] is not unconditional; it is given for the purposes of the proceedings and is limited to those proceedings. If there is no jurisdiction as to the merits, there can be no jurisdiction to indicate interim measures of protection."[40]

But, at the same time, they recognised that:—

> "Clearly, it could not be claimed that, in the event of a challenge of its jurisdiction, the Court should finally pronounce on this question before indicating interim measures of protection; in such a case as this the request might well become pointless."[41]

The very basis of the request that *interim* protection is necessary being the urgency of the matter,[42] as the Czechoslovak-Hungarian Mixed Arbitral Tribunal said:—

> "To refuse interim measures of protection for the sole reason that the jurisdiction of the Tribunal is challenged would open a very simple way for any party wishing to avoid any interim measures of protection being taken against him. The power of the Tribunal under Article 33 of its Rules of Procedure would thus be rendered absolutely futile."[43]

Had the International Court of Justice, in the *Anglo-Iranian Oil Co. Case* (Interim Protection) (1951), held, as it could have done, that it was competent to indicate such measures because, upon a "*summaria cognitio*, which is characteristic of a procedure of this kind,"[44] it is considered that the dispute could not be

[39] *ICJ Reports 1951*, p. 89, at p. 93.
[40] *Ibid.*, at p. 97.
[41] *Ibid.*, at p. 96.
[42] *Cf.* I.C.J.: Rules, Art. 61, para. 2.
[43] *Barcoczy Case* (1928), *loc. cit.*, p. 66.
[44] *Polish Agrarian Reform Case* (Interim Protection) (1933), D.O. by Anzilotti, A/B. 58, p. 181.

excluded *a priori* from *its* jurisdiction,[45] the Court would, it seems, have been more in line with precedents. It is true that little guidance can be derived from the practice of the Permanent Court of International Justice. Yet, some help may be found in the case of the *Denunciation of the Treaty of 1865 between China and Belgium* (Interim Protection) (1927). At that time, the President of the Permanent Court was empowered by the Rules of Court then in force, to indicate interim measures of protection. In making the Order he relied on the following considerations:—

"Belgium and China have signed and ratified the Protocol of signature of December 16th, 1920, relating to the adoption of the Statute of the Court;

". . . These two Powers have recognised as compulsory the Court's jurisdiction, in accordance with Article 36, paragraph 2, of the Court's Statute; and . . . sub-paragraph (d) of this paragraph covers legal disputes concerning the nature or extent of the reparation to be made for the breach of an international obligation. . . ."[46]

Since the President also stated that by its final decision "the Court will either declare itself to have no jurisdiction or give judgment on the merits,"[47] he was evidently of the opinion that he was competent to indicate such measures, even before the question of jurisdiction had been decided, but when prima facie the dispute came within, or at least did not fall outside, the Court's jurisdiction.[48] As the Czechoslovak-Hungarian Mixed Arbitral Tribunal tersely and more explicitly put it:—

"All that is required is that the Court does not patently and evidently lack jurisdiction."[49]

The precedents of the Mixed Arbitral Tribunals were, however, discounted by Judges Winiarski and Badawi Pasha, who, in their joint dissenting opinion, put forward the view that:—

45 *Cf.* B. Cheng, "The Anglo-Iranian Dispute," 5 *World Affairs* (New Series) (1951), p. 387, at pp. 396–9.

46 A. 8, p. 7.

47 *Ibid.*

48 See also P.C.I.J.: *Administration of the Prince of Pless Case* (1933), A/B. 54, p. 153; *Polish Agrarian Reform Case* (1933), A/B. 58, p. 179.

49 *Barcoczy Case* (1928), *loc. cit.*, p. 65. (Transl.) See also Pol.-Germ. M.A.T.: *Frauenverein Szamothly Case* (1925), 6 T.A.M., p. 326, at p. 327; *Ulmenstein Case* (1925), *ibid.*, p. 328, at p. 329; *Follmer et al. Cases* (1925), *ibid.*, pp. 332–3.

"The Court ought not to indicate interim measures of protection unless its competence, in the event of this being challenged, appears to the Court to be nevertheless *reasonably probable.* Its opinion on this point should be reached after a summary consideration; it can only be provisional and cannot prejudge its final decision." [50]

Differences of opinion may, therefore, exist, as to whether there must be a probability that the Court has jurisdiction or whether a mere possibility is sufficient. What is certain, however, is that an international tribunal need not be convinced, nor reasonably certain, that it would have jurisdiction before it can indicate interim measures of protection. The reason why an international tribunal may exercise this power even when its jurisdiction as to the merits is yet uncertain must be sought in the fact that the duty of the parties to the dispute to maintain the *status quo* already exists independently of any judicial intervention [51] and that the Court's indication is rather in the nature of a "judicial suggestion." [52]

Moreover, when indicating such interim measures of protection, international tribunals will observe

"a principle which, although it may not have been included in the rules of procedure, is not any the less worthy of consideration, namely, the principle that the possible injury that may be caused by the proposed interim measures of protection must not be out of proportion with the advantage which the claimant hopes to derive from them." [53]

Finally, it need hardly be mentioned that, should the Court eventually come to the conclusion that it has no jurisdiction

[50] *Loc. cit.*, p. 97. Italics added.

[51] See *supra*, p. 140.

[52] *Cf.* the wording of Art. 41, para. 2 of the Statute of the I.C.J., and see the *travaux préparatoires* relating to the corresponding article in the Statute of the P.C.I.J., *e.g.*, Report of the Advisory Committee of Jurists, *Procès-verbaux*, pp. 735–6; speech of Elihu Root in the Committee of Jurists (March, 1929), created by the Council of the L.o.N. to examine the Statute of the P.C.I.J., L.o.N.P.: C.166.M.66.1929.V., pp. 63–4. See Hammarskjöld, *Juridiction internationale*, 1938, pp. 299 *et seq.*; *contra* Hudson, *The P.C.I.J.*, 1943, pp. 425–7. See, however, pp. 415 *et seq.* of Hudson's work published in 1934. *Cf.* Pol.-Germ. M.A.T.: *Comité central de la Mission intérieure de l'Eglise Evangélique allemande Case* (1926), 6 T.A.M., p. 331.

[53] Belg.-Bulg. M.A.T.: *Cie d'Électricité de Sofia et de Bulgarie* (1923), 2 T.A.M., p. 924, at pp. 926–7. (Transl.) See also *Barcoczy Case* (1928), *loc. cit.*, pp. 66–7.

over the dispute, any interim measures that may have been indicated, if not immediately revoked by the tribunal,[54] would automatically lose their effect.[55]

[54] See I.C.J.: *Anglo-Iranian Oil Co. Case* (Jd.) (1952), p. 93, at p. 114. Also, Pol.-Germ. M.A.T.: *Frauenverein Czarnkow Cases* (1925), 6 T.A.M., p. 348.

[55] *Cf. Barcoczy Case* (1928), *loc. cit.*, p. 66.

Chapter 12

POWER TO DETERMINE THE EXTENT OF JURISDICTION

(COMPÉTENCE DE LA COMPÉTENCE)

If jurisdiction is of such vital importance in judicial procedure, who is competent to determine the extent of the jurisdiction of a judicial body? As might be expected, this question arose at the very dawn of modern international arbitration, in *The Betsey Case* (1797).[1] This was the first case to be submitted to the Mixed Commission set up under Article VII of the Jay Treaty (1794) between Great Britain and the United States. A leading feature of the case was that the Lords Commissioners of Appeal in Prize Causes—the then final English Court of Appeal in Prize—had affirmed the original condemnation. The presentation of this claim caused, in the words of the Agent for the United States, "a momentous crisis!" The British Commissioners withdrew from the Board in order to prevent any decision.

The specific point at issue was whether the decision of the Lords Commissioners of Appeal affirming the decision of the lower prize courts, should be regarded as in all respects final and conclusive, thus precluding any further examination of the case by the Commission, but the wider question arose whether the Commission had the power itself to determine the extent of its own jurisdiction.

The United States Commissioner Gore said:—

"A power to decide whether a claim preferred to this board is within its jurisdiction, appears to me inherent in its very constitution, and indispensably necessary to the discharge of any of its duties. That a board should be constituted with powers to conclude the contracting parties, both as to the justice of the claim and the amount of money to be paid in compensation thereof, and should have no power to decide whether the subject-matter of complaint

[1] 4 *Int.Adj.*, M.S., p. 179.

be submitted to it, is with me so palpable a contradiction, that the disrespect which, in my judgment, such a position reflects on the high contracting parties, and the attempt to support the reverse by argument, or other authority than the instrument itself, can be apologised for only by the very sincere esteem I entertain for those who make the objection." [2]

The British Commissioner having withdrawn, the matter was taken up on the diplomatical level. Lord Grenville suggested that the opinion of Lord Chancellor Loughborough should be sought. The latter when consulted, described as "absurd," "the doubt respecting the authority of the Commissioners to settle their own jurisdiction," and declared:—

"They must necessarily decide upon cases being within, or without, their competency." [3]

Thus an opinion based on ordinary common sense prevented the Mixed Commission at London set up under Article VII of the Jay Treaty from coming to a premature end over this issue, like the Commission at Philadelphia set up under Article VI of the same Treaty.[4]

For a more recent authority, Advisory Opinion No. 16 of the Permanent Court of International. Justice may be referred to. The Court expressed the view that:—

"As a general rule, any body possessing jurisdictional powers has the right in the first place itself to determine the extent of its jurisdiction." [5]

By reason of the judicial nature of its functions,[6] the power to determine its own competence and, in proper cases, to raise the question of jurisdiction is "inherent . . . in every legal

[2] *Ibid.*, at p. 183.
[3] *Ibid.*, at p. 85. See pp. 82–7.
[4] 3 *Int.Adj.*, M.S.
[5] *Interpretation of the Greco-Turkish Agreement* (1928), B. 16, p. 20. See *Zeltweg-Wolfsberg and Unterdrauburg-Woellan Railways Case* (Prel.Obj.) (1934), 3 UNRIAA, p. 1795, at p. 1803.
[6] Germ.-U.S. M.C.C. (1922): *Lehigh Valley Railroad Co. Case* (1933), *Dec. & Op.*, p. 1084, at p. 1122: "The Agreement [creating the Commission] is to be read in the light of its language and its purpose; and where it is silent, the powers and duties of the Commission are to be determined according to the nature of the function entrusted to it. I have no doubt that the Commission is competent to determine its own jurisdiction by the interpretation of the agreement creating it. Any other view would lead to the most absurd results—results which obviously the two Governments did not intend."

Tribunal. This power can only be taken away by a provision framed for that express purpose." [7]

But how is this power to be reconciled with the maxim: *Extra compromisum arbiter nihil facere potest* dealt with in the previous Chapter? The question was raised and, indeed, answered in *The Betsey Case* (1797), in which Commissioner Gore said:—

"The answer is obvious, it is that of the law of nations, of the common law of England and of common sense—a party is not bound by the decision of arbitrators in a case not within the submission—such decision would be a dead letter—it would be as no decision." [8]

When determining its own competence, is a tribunal to interpret its powers extensively or restrictively? In the *Free Zones Case* (Judgment) (1932), the Permanent Court of International Justice said:—

"The Court does not dispute the rule invoked by the French Government, that every Special Agreement, like every clause conferring jurisdiction upon the Court, must be interpreted strictly." [9]

Nevertheless:—

"That rule could not be applied in such a way as to give the Special Agreement, under the guise of strict interpretation, a construction according to which it would not only fail entirely to enunciate the question really in dispute, but would, by its very terms, have prejudged the answer to that question." [10]

[7] Brit.-U.S. Cl.Arb. (1910): *Rio Grande Case* (1923), Nielsen's *Report*, p. 332, at p. 342.

The Hague Convention, 1907 (Art. 73) and the Statutes of both the P.C.I.J. (Art. 36 IV) and the I.C.J. (Art. 36, 6) provide that the respective Courts shall decide their own jurisdiction in case of disputes. See also Chil.-U.S. Cl.Com. (1892): *Didier Case*, 4 *Int.Arb.*, p. 4329, at p. 4331. U.S.-Ven. M.C.C. (1903): *Flutie Case*, *Ven.Arb. 1903*, p. 38, at p. 41. *Société Radio-Orient Case* (1940), 3 UNRIAA, p. 1871, at p. 1878. I.C.J.: *Ambatielos Case* (1952), Ind.Op. of Spiropoulos (*ICJ Reports 1952*, p. 28, at p. 55), D.O. of Klaestad (*ibid.*, p. 83).

[8] 4 *Int.Adj.*, M.S., p. 179, at p. 194; see also Opinion of Commissioner Pinkney, *ibid.*, p. 200.

[9] A/B. 46, pp. 138–9.

Cases adopting restrictive interpretation; Colombian-U.S. Cl.Com. (1864): *Riggs Case*, *Oliver Cases*, *Doglas Case* ("Bond Cases"), 4 *Int.Arb.*, pp. 3612–6. *Cf.* a discussion of these cases by Commissioner Little in U.S.-Ven. Cl. Com. (1885): *Howland Case*, 4 *Int.Arb.*, p. 3616. See *infra*, p. 278, note 12.

Cf. also I.C.J.: *Corfu Channel Case* (Merits) (1949), D.O. by Badawi Pasha, by Krylóv, by Ečer, *ICJ Reports 1949*, p. 4, at pp. 67, 73, 128, respectively.

[10] A/B. 46, p. 139.

In the *Chorzów Factory Case* (Jd.) (1927), the Court held that:—

" When considering whether it has jurisdiction or not, the Court's aim is always to ascertain whether an intention on the part of the Parties exists to confer jurisdiction upon it. The question as to the existence of a doubt nullifying its jurisdiction need not be considered when, as in the present case, this intention can be demonstrated in a manner convincing to the Court." [11]

The task of the tribunal is therefore the same as in any case of treaty interpretation, namely to discover the intention of the parties. Thus the Arbitrator in the Greco-Bulgarian Arbitration under Article 181 of the Treaty of Neuilly (1919) held that:—

" [An arbitral] clause should be interpreted in the same way as other contractual stipulations. If analysis of the text and examination of its purpose show that the reasons in favour of the competence of the arbitrator are more plausible than those which may be shown to the contrary, the former should be adopted." [12]

[11] A. 9, p. 32.

[12] *Rhodope Forests Case* (Prel. Question) (1931), 3 UNRIAA, p. 1389, at p. 1403. (Transl.) See also U.S.-Ven. Cl.Com. (1885): *Howland Case*, 4 *Int.Arb.*, p. 3616, at pp. 3629, 3634 *et passim*. The middle course of the " ordinary standard of interpretation " adopted. See also I.C.J.: *Anglo-Iranian Oil Co. Case* (Jd.) (1952), D.O. by Hackworth, *ICJ Reports 1952*, p. 93, at p. 140.

CHAPTER 13

NEMO DEBET ESSE JUDEX IN PROPRIA SUA CAUSA

IN *The Virginius Incident* (1873) the *S.S. Virginius* flying the American flag was captured on the high seas by a Spanish man-of-war, and 53 of her passengers and crew, including Americans, British and Cubans, were summarily tried and executed.[1] The Spanish Government inquired of the British Government whether the latter would be willing to arbitrate between the United States and Spain for the settlement of the incident. In a despatch to the British Minister in Spain, dated November 17, 1873, declining the invitation, the British Foreign Secretary, Earl Granville, said:—

> "They [Her Majesty's Government] consider, moreover, that they are disqualified from acting as arbitrators, inasmuch as they are themselves parties to the claim which would have to be arbitrated upon." [2]

Indeed, as was stated in the Report on the Project concerning the establishment of an international Court of Arbitral Justice during the Second International Peace Conference, 1907:—

> "It is a universally accepted doctrine that no one can be judge in his own cause and all systems of law adopt it." [3]

The existence of this general principle of law is hardly questioned or, indeed, open to question and its application extends beyond purely judicial procedures.[4] In its Advisory

[1] See Moore, 2 *Dig.*, pp. 895–903.

[2] 65 B.F.S.P. (1873–1874), p. 102, at p. 103.

[3] IIe Conférence internationale de la Paix: 1 *Actes et Documents*, 1907, p. 367 (Transl.). *Rapporteur*, James Brown Scott.

[4] *Cf.* U.S.-Ven. M.C.C. (1903): *Rudloff Case*, *Ven.Arb. 1903*, p. 182. Opinion of Commissioner Bainbridge: "The jurisprudence of civilised States and the principles of natural law do not allow one party to a contract to pass judgment upon the other, but guarantee to both the hearing and decision of a disinterested and impartial tribunal" (p. 197). Commissioner Grisanti, for the Commission: "The municipal council of the Federal District had no right to annul of its own free will the referred-to contract in the resolution of

Opinion No. 12 (1925), the Permanent Court of International Justice was asked the question whether representatives of the interested States on the Council of the League of Nations might vote in a decision concerning differences between themselves. Answering the question in the negative, the Court stated:—

"The well-known rule that no one can be judge in his own suit holds good."[5]

On this point, the position of national arbitrators taking part in international judicial proceedings comes to mind. The Court was perhaps not unmindful of this point when it said:—

"It may perhaps be well to observe that since the Council consists of representatives of States or Members, the legal position of the representatives of the Parties upon the Council is not comparable to that of national arbitrators upon courts of arbitration."[6]

In other words, the legal position of national arbitrators is not that of representatives of their respective countries, parties to the dispute.

Except perhaps for the isolated instance of Sir Alexander

November 13, 1895; because, as the municipality was one of the contracting parties, it could not at the same time judge as to the validity of the nullity of the same. To obtain said nullity the municipality should apply for a lawsuit to the competent tribunals" (p. 200).

Salvador Commercial Co. Case (1902), U.S.F.R. (1902), p. 838, at pp. 871–2: "It is abhorrent to the sense of justice to say that one party to a contract, whether such party be a private individual, a monarch, or a government of any kind, may arbitrarily, without hearing and without impartial procedure of any sort, arrogate the right to condemn the other party to the contract, to pass judgment upon him and his acts, and to impose upon him the extreme penalty of forfeiture of all his rights under it, including his property and his investment of capital made on the faith of that contract. Before the arbitrament of natural justice all parties to a contract, as to their reciprocal rights and their reciprocal remedies, are of equal dignity and are equally entitled to invoke for their redress and for their defence the hearing and the judgment of an impartial and disinterested tribunal." This case also shows that in the application of this principle, one must look to the substance and not to the form. It is not the formal non-identity that is vital, but the real existence of impartial and disinterested judges.

U.S.-Ven. M.C.C. (1903): *Turnbull/Manoa Co., Ltd./Orinoco Co., Ltd. Cases*, *Ven.Arb. 1903*, p. 200, at p. 244. Umpire Barge considered the rule that "nobody can be judge in his own cause" as a rule of equity, and from this rule there sprang a "rule of the law of almost all civilised nations" that "in cases of bilateral contracts, the nonfulfilment of the pledged obligations by one party does not annul the contract *ipso facto*, but forms a reason for annulment, which annulment must be asked of the tribunals, and the proper tribunal alone has the power to annul such a contract."

5 "*Mosul Case*" (1925), B. 12, p. 32.

6 *Ibid.*, at p. 32.

Cockburn's [7] dissenting opinion in *The Alabama Case* (1872) in which he considered himself to have sat on the Tribunal at Geneva "in some sense as the representative of Great Britain," [8] the view of the Permanent Court that national arbitrators are not legally representatives of their State is supported by consistent international judicial practice.

In the words of Gore, the United States Commissioner, in *The Betsey Case* (1797):—

"Although I am a citizen of but one, I am constituted a judge for both. Each nation has the same, and no greater, right to demand of me fidelity and diligence in the examination, exactness and justice of the decision." [9]

Special mention may be made in this connection of the decision of the United States Commissioner Hassaurek in the claims of Captain Clark, known also as *The Medea* and *The Good Return Cases*.[10] 50 per cent., 21½ per cent., and 28½ per cent. of the claim were presented by the United States against New Granada, Ecuador and Venezuela, respectively as successor States of Colombia. Notwithstanding an earlier opinion of Umpire Upham of the Granadine-United States Claims Commission (1857) in favour of the United States,[11] the United States Commissioner Hassaurek decided against the United States, when the claim was presented to the Ecuadorian-United States Claims Commission (1862).

In his opinion Hassaurek said:—

"The Commissioners should consider themselves not the attorneys for either the one or the other country, but the judges appointed for the purpose of deciding the questions submitted to them, impartially, according to law and justice, and without

[7] *Cf.* as a matter of interest J. B. Moore's opinion of Cockburn's "disturbing effects" upon the "even and accustomed flow" of the "majestic stream of the common law, united with international law," as represented by the latter's opinion in the case of *The Queen* v. *Keyn* (*The Franconia*) (1877) 2 Exch.Div., p. 63 (PCIJ: *The Lotus* (1927), D.O. by J. B. Moore, A. 10, p. 75).

[8] 2 *Alabama* (*Proceedings*), p. 7, at pp. 51 and 72 (Transl.). *Cf.*, however, *ibid.*, p. 52, where he said: "As *judge* and as an English lawyer, I maintain . . ." (Transl. Italics added). *Cf.* also Cockburn during the discussions: "We *are* here as *judges*" (1 *Int.Arb.*, p. 648. See 1 *Alabama* (*Proceedings*), p. 16).

[9] 4 *Int.Adj.*, M.S., p. 179, at p. 191.

[10] For a narrative of these cases, see *supra*, pp. 155 *et seq.*

[11] 3 *Int.Arb.*, pp. 2730–2731. Opinion was, however, set aside ultimately because of irregularity in the submission. See 2 *Int.Arb.*, pp. 1396–1405. See *supra*, p. 260, *infra*, pp. 291 *et seq.* At the time of Hassaurek's decision, this was not yet effected.

reference to which side their decision will affect favourably or unfavourably." [12]

It is, therefore, perhaps not without reason that Justice is always represented as being blindfolded.[13]

Furthermore, another American national Commissioner in the *McKenny Case* before the Mexican-United States Claims Commission (1868) clearly emphasised his legal independence from his own country in his capacity as arbitrator. This claim arose out of the destruction of property during the Zuloaga and Miramon régime. The Commissioners, especially the United States Commissioner, Wadsworth, refused to consider the Zuloaga and Miramon régime as a *de facto* government of Mexico although at one time it enjoyed temporary recognition by the United States. Commissioner Wadsworth said:—

"Certainly I do not consider that the recognition of Zuloaga by the Government of the United States (conceding this to be the fullest extent claimed) settles the question for Mexico or this commission; but it is argued by counsel that the act of the United States Government in recognising Zuloaga is conclusive upon Mr. Commissioner Wadsworth, because he is the 'judicial representative of the United States in this commission,' and that for this reason he is precluded from even inquiring into the propriety of the recognition by the United States of the Government of Zuloaga. It is scarcely necessary to remark that this view is founded upon a total misconception of the nature and character of the office of a commissioner under the convention between the United States and Mexico. Mr. Commissioner Wadsworth is not a 'judicial representative of the United States in this commission,' nor 'a judicial officer' of that government. The authority which he possesses he derives from both the United States and Mexico, and is obliged to exercise it impartially for the benefit of both. He would possess neither office nor authority without the consent and concurrence of both nations, and is no more bound by the official acts or municipal regulations of the United States than by those of Mexico. He derives his appointment to a place on the board—a place created by the action of both governments—from the Government of the United States, indeed, but is no more bound by this appointment to represent

12 3 *Int.Arb.*, p. 2731, at pp. 2733–4.

13 See allusion to this symbolism by the Venezuelan Commissioner in Fran.-Ven. M.C.C. (1902): *Cie générale de l'Orénoque Case* (1905), Ralston's *Report*, p. 244, at p. 287.

the interests of the United States than those of Mexico, and no more bound by the acts of that government than his colleague on the board, or their umpire. He is an impartial arbiter selected by the United States, but deriving all his powers from the United States and Mexico, nor more the officer of the former than of the latter." [14]

From the fact that national arbitrators in international tribunals are not agents of their respective States but independent and impartial judges for both parties appearing before them, as is evidenced by consistent practice, it is clear that their presence on the tribunal is compatible with the principle *nemo debet esse judex in propria sua causa*. In the section on imputability, the relation between the State and its representatives was considered.[15] It may be said that in so far as a national acts as a representative of his State, *qua* party to a dispute, he is an organ of one of the parties, and is identifiable with it. But in so far as the same national is divested of his capacity as an organ of his State *qua* party to the dispute, especially when he has been appointed to act impartially even in matters involving his own State, he may be regarded as unconnected with the dispute. This may apply not only to individuals but even to what is normally a State organ. Thus in the *Arakas Case* (1927), cited at the beginning of Part IV, when the Mixed Arbitral Tribunal held that the silence of the judgment of the Bulgarian Military Commission sitting as a prize court as to the grounds for its decision might "justify the view that the decision is a violation of the principle that no one should be judge in his own cause," [16] it evidently did not mean that this principle would be violated merely because the body which decided the case was an organ of the Bulgarian State. It can only be reasonably understood to mean that the absence of a statement of the grounds of the decision might give rise to the belief that the Commission had not acted in an impartial and independent capacity, but merely as an organ of the State *qua* party to the suit. If this interpretation is correct,[17] it may

[14] 3 *Int.Arb.*, p. 2881, at pp. 2883–4.
[15] *Supra*, Chap. 6, C. pp. 180 *et seq.*
[16] *Supra*, p. 258.
[17] *Cf. supra*, p. 279, note 4. According to those decisions, if the States concerned *qua* parties to a contract had applied to one of their own courts, the principle under discussion would not have been violated. And yet it cannot

be said that there was no violation of the principle *nemo debet esse judex in propria sua causa* even when the French Court of Cassation was chosen by Nicaragua and France as arbitrator in a dispute between the two countries.[18]

The *raison d'être* of the principle may be taken to be what Commissioner Gore said in *The Betsey Case* (1797), namely that:—

"Justice is impartial." [19]

The principle *nemo judex in propria sua causa* undoubtedly constitutes the most elementary and essential guarantee of impartiality in the administration of justice by disqualifying both parties from acting as judges of the dispute between them, since parties are by definition partial and not impartial.

The above survey should suffice to show that this general legal principle is not only recognised in international law but is not infringed by the institution of national judges, because the legal position of the latter is not that of representatives of the country to which they belong, but that of independent and impartial judges for both parties. In the Permanent Court of International Justice, judges were allowed to retain their seats on the Bench when their State appeared before the Court as a party and this is still the rule in the International Court of Justice.[20]

The Report of the Advisory Committee of Jurists for the Establishment of the Permanent Court explained that:—

"As they have given a solemn undertaking to administer justice impartially and conscientiously, there is no danger that they will fail in their duty by showing any partiality towards the State whose subjects they are. Chosen as they are from amongst men of the highest moral character, one may rest assured that their scruples

be denied that such courts would be part of the State machinery. Their capacity as independent and impartial judges would, however, distinguish them from the parties to the dispute.

18 *The Phare Case* (1880), 5 *Int.Arb.*, p. 4870. It need hardly be mentioned that the circumstances in which the British Government declined to act as arbitrator in *The Virginius Incident* were different, since in that case, it was the British Government as such or, at all events, its representative, that was asked to be the arbitrator.

19 4 *Int.Adj.*, M.S., p. 179, at p. 187. *Cf. supra*, p. 279, note 4.

20 Statute: Art. 31. *Cf.* however, Rules of Court of both the P.C.I.J. and the I.C.J. Art. 13 of both prevents a judge whose country appears before the Court from exercising the functions of president in respect of that case.

Cf. also Project for the Establishment of a Court of Arbitral Justice, Deuxième Conférence internationale de la Paix, 1907, 1 *Actes et Documents*, pp. 347–97; 2 *Actes et Documents*, pp. 603–6.

in the administration of justice will be increased in the event of their having before them as a party the State whose subjects they are." [21]

The fact remains, however, that, in the work of the Advisory Committee of Jurists, as the Report admitted, "one of the most difficult questions was that of the inclusion on the Court of judges of the nationality of the contesting parties." [22]

There are three cases in which national judges participate in the work of the Court.

The first concerns regular judges whose State appears before the Court as a party. Article 31, paragraph 1, of the Statute provides:—

"1. Judges of the nationality of each of the parties shall retain their right to sit in the case before the Court."

In justification of this provision, the Report of the Advisory Committee of Jurists said that the withdrawal of the judges in such cases might reduce their number by too many, especially if several States had a joint interest in the same proceedings. The character of the Court as a World Court might thus be impaired.[23] This is undoubtedly true. It is indeed possible to go even further. At the time of the establishment of the Permanent Court there existed many international treaties to which the majority of nations were parties and this is even more true today. When a case involves the interpretation of one of these treaties, every party to such treaty may intervene in virtue of Article 63 of the Court's Statute.[24] If judges who are nationals of the parties were disqualified from sitting, the Court would hardly be able to function.[25] While it does not apply to *ad hoc* tribunals between two or a small number of States, the above consideration seems to provide a valid reason why national judges should be allowed to retain their seat in a World Court.

21 *Procès-verbaux*, pp. 720–1.
22 *Ibid.*, p. 720. For an account of the discussion in the Committee, see *ibid.*, pp. 121, 168–9, 172, 197–8, 222, 528–39.
23 *Ibid.*, p. 721.
24 Both of the P.C.I.J. and of the I.C.J.
25 This was also pointed out by Wang Chung-Hui, a former judge of the P.C.I.J., at a meeting of the Committee of Jurists set up to examine the project for the new Court, UNCIO: 14 *Documents*, pp. 126, 130.

Paragraph 2 of Article 31 envisages the second type of case and provides:—

"2. If the Court includes upon the Bench a judge of the nationality of one of the parties, any other party may choose a person to sit as judge . . ."

The Report of the Advisory Committee of Jurists said:—

" Although with men of the high moral character of our judges there would be no occasion to fear any lapse from impartiality, public opinion in the State without a judge on the Bench might consider that this inequality would affect it adversely, not as a State, but in its position as a contesting party."[26]

Although the validity of the premise that there would be an inequality if the Court included among its members a national of only one of the parties is open to question from a legal point of view, this provision may perhaps be regarded as justified by the consideration that there should not only be equality in substance but also equality in form so that justice will not only be done but will also appear to be done.[27]

The third case is provided for by paragraph 3 of Article 31:—

" 3. If the Court includes upon the Bench no judge of the nationality of the parties, each of these parties may proceed to choose a judge as provided in paragraph 2 of this Article."

In justification of this provision, the Report said:—

" States attach much importance to having one of their subjects on the Bench when they appear before a Court of Justice." [28]

But the correctness of this statement is open to doubt and this desire of States, if it exists, is not fully acceded to even by the Committee. Should several States appear together on the same side, they are reckoned, for the purpose of the present provision, as one party only (Article 31, paragraph 5), so that some of the States would not have a judge of their nationality on the Bench.[29] Besides, in several cases before the Permanent Court,

[26] *Procès-verbaux*, pp. 721–22.
[27] See *infra*, p. 289, note 38.
[28] *Procès-verbaux*, p. 722.
[29] See PCIJ: *Austro-German Customs Union* (Order) (1931), A/B. 41, p. 88, at p. 89: " All governments which, in the proceedings before the Court, come

e.g., Advisory Opinion of March 3, 1928,[30] Advisory Opinion of December 11, 1931,[31] and Advisory Opinion of February 4, 1932,[32] and in the *Corfu Channel Case* (1948, 1949) before the International Court of Justice,[33] the party which had no judge of its own nationality on the Court appointed as judge *ad hoc* a person who was not one of its own subjects. Indeed, since the revision of the Statute of the Permanent Court in accordance with the Protocol of September 14, 1929, there is no restriction, based on nationality, in the Statute of the Permanent Court, and, following it, in that of the International Court, on the choice of the judge *ad hoc*. Prior to this revision, if a party had a deputy-judge of its nationality on the Court, it could appoint only him as *ad hoc* judge. From the point of view of the Statute and of States, therefore, it seems that it is not essential that the judge *ad hoc* should be a national of the State appointing him. But the reason given for the importance which States attach to having one of their subjects on the Bench appears to be that:—

> " It is highly desirable that the judges should be able to the last minute during the deliberations, to put forward and explain the statements and arguments of the States [" *de l'Etat* "], and to ensure that the sentence, however painful it may be in substance, should be drawn up so as to avoid ruffling national susceptibilities in any way." [34]

The Report added:—

> " If the opposing views are both represented on the Bench, they counter-balance one another." [35]

Were this so, it must be said that the Report is inconsistent, if, indeed, it has not fallen into an outright misconception of the legal position of the judge who is a national of one of the parties. Although this passage may be slightly ambiguous, it seems only reasonable to consider that the word " States,"

to the same conclusion, must be held to be in the same interest for the purpose of the present case." The Court held that there was no ground for the appointment of judges *ad hoc* either by Austria or Czechoslovakia in that case.

30 *Jurisdiction of the Danzig Courts* (1928), B. 15.

31 *Polish War Vessels in Danzig* (1931), A/B. 43.

32 *Polish Nationals in Danzig* (1932), A/B. 44.

33 *ICJ Reports 1947–48*, p. 15; *ICJ Reports 1949*, p. 4 and p. 244.

34 Report of the Adv.Com.of Jurists, *Procès-verbaux*, p. 721.

35 *Ibid.*, p. 721.

especially since it is used in the singular in the French text, refers to the respective States of the national judges. The Report assumed, therefore, that the national judge would take it upon himself to put forward the statements and arguments of his own State, and that the views of the two national judges would naturally be "opposing." This cannot be called consistent with the assurance of impartiality which the Report wished to give a few lines earlier. It comes nearer to the view of one of the co-authors of the article that national judges are "national representatives" of the parties who would "protect their interests," [36] which, in the light of the international judicial decisions we have reviewed, would appear to be an erroneous conception of the office of the national judge. If this be the purpose of allowing both parties having no judge of their nationality on the Bench each to appoint a judge *ad hoc,* the purpose is not a legitimate one. Unless the prevention of offensive wording in the judgment constitutes a sufficient justification, this right of the parties needs serious reconsideration.

It would thus appear that the presence of national judges does not conflict with the principle *nemo judex debet esse in propria sua causa.* In the present framework of the international society, where the family of nations is but small in number, it may even be difficult to avoid it in a world court. This does not mean, however, that the institution of national judges is an ideal implementation of the principle that no one should be judge in his own cause. As the examples have shown, the misconception that national judges represent their own State, however unfounded, may easily arise. Moreover, the link of nationality between the judge and one of the parties affords too convenient a ground for insinuations of partiality, however rare and improper.[37] As the Report of the Advisory Committee for the establishment of the Permanent Court aptly said:—

[36] *Ibid.*, p. 528. *Cf. contra*, pp. 123, 367, 369.

[37] *Cf.* Fran.-Ven. M.C.C. (1902): *Cie Générale de l'Orénoque Case* (1905), Ralston's *Report*, p. 244, see pp. 284–5, 286–7, 314. The French Commissioner in his written opinion openly accused the Venezuelan Commissioner: "Because his patriotism may have led him to become a lawyer representing his country instead of the man who was called upon to pass judgment" (p. 284). The Venezuelan Commissioner rightly pointed out that such observations "are entirely foreign to the impersonal character which discussions between arbitrators must have when a difference of opinion divides them while investigating and deciding upon a case" (p. 286).

"Justice, however, must not only be just, but appear so. A judge must not only be impartial, but there must be no possibility of suspecting his impartiality." [38]

And it cannot be doubted that even where the principle *nemo judex debet esse in propria sua causa* obtains, and where the judge is in fact impartial, the fewer special links there are between the judge and one of the parties to the dispute, the less chance is there of suspicion, and the stronger is the appearance that justice is being done.[39]

[38] *Procès-verbaux*, p. 721.

Germ.-U.S. M.C.C. (1922): *Lehigh Valley Railroad Co. Case* (1936), *Dec. & Op.*, p. 1175, at pp. 1176–77: "In international arbitration it is of equal importance that justice *be done* and that *appearances* show clearly to everybody's conviction that justice *was done*." Original italics. Because he considered that the second requirement was not satisfied, the German Commissioner was willing to accede to the conclusion of his colleagues in the Commission to set aside a previous decision decided in favour of Germany.

[39] *Cf.* Statutes of the P.C.I.J. and the I.C.J. articles 17, 24, concerning incompatibility, disqualification and abstentions of judges.

Cf. also, Articles 24, 25, 26, 27 of the Rules of the Central American Court of Justice, 8 A.J.I.L. (1914), Supplement, pp. 184, 185.

CHAPTER 14

AUDIATUR ET ALTERA PARS

In the foregoing Chapter, it was said that:—

"Justice is impartial." [1]

Referring to the Commission of which he was a member, Commissioner Gore said:—

"That board could never be denominated impartial or just, that did not see with equal eye the party that claimed and the party that resisted." [2]

Indeed, it may be said that there are two cardinal characteristics of a judicial process, the impartiality of the tribunal and its corollary, the juridical equality between the parties in their capacity as litigants.[3]

This equality of the parties is, to say the least, gravely impaired when one of the parties has not been able to appear before the tribunal. Thus, reviewing the work of the arbitral tribunals (*Schiedsgerichte*) set up by the German occupation army in Belgium during the First World War, before which the City of Antwerp as defendant was not able to be represented by counsel, the Belgo-German Mixed Arbitral Tribunal said:—

"The absence of the defendant party destroyed the equilibrium between the parties which would have existed before the ordinary tribunals and would, therefore, have resulted in excessive sentences on the City of Antwerp." [4]

After mentioning the extremely summary character of the procedure of the *Schiedsgericht* and the slender requirement of proof, it added:—

[1] *Supra*, p. 284.
[2] Jay Treaty (Art. VII) Arbitration (1794): *The Betsey* (1797), 4 *Int.Adj.* M.S., p. 179, at p. 185.
[3] *Cf.* the solicitude of the Advisory Committee of Jurists in the elaboration of the Statute of the P.C.I.J. to maintain the equality of parties, *supra*, p. 286, note 26.
[4] *Ville d'Anvers Case* (Indemnity) (1926), 6 T.A.M., p. 749, at p. 752. (Transl.) See *Ville d'Anvers Case* (Merits) (1925), 5 *ibid.*, p. 712.

"It is obvious that in making as liberal a use of its freedom of appraisement, the Schiesdsgericht greatly reduced the guarantees which the application of the ordinary procedure would have ensured to the absent defendant." [5]

Thus, while the Mixed Arbitral Tribunal did not deny the possibility of a judgment in default, provided that the absent defendant was afforded some guarantees of a just decision based on sufficient evidence, it regarded it only as an exception to the principle that there should be equality of the parties as translated into practice by the representation of both parties before the Tribunal. Indeed, in the same opinion, it qualified the absence of the defendant as a "fundamental defect" in the procedure.

As the decision in the *Salvador Commercial Co. Case* (1902) indicated, the "due process of judicial proceedings," involves "notice, full opportunity to be heard, consideration and solemn judgment." [6] Attention may also be drawn to the *Arakas Case* (1927) already cited at the beginning of Part IV, which, when mentioning that "it is necessary that a judicial procedure should be followed," added, as a matter of logical sequence, "in the course of which both parties are heard." [7] This feature of judicial proceedings has long been expressed in the well-known maxim *audiatur et altera pars* or *audi alteram partem*, which may be regarded as a general principle of law translating into practice the fundamental requirement of equality between the parties in judicial proceedings.

Actual refusal to hear one of the parties in an international judicial proceeding may be said never to have happened. Mention may, however, be made of the "*Umpire Cases*" before the Granadine-United States Claims Commission (1857). Certain preliminary questions were submitted to the Umpire and "some remarks were made as to a hearing on the merits." In the words of a subsequent statement issued by the Umpire, "as no further measures were taken for a hearing, at the last moment, as the Commission was expiring, I filed the awards." [8]

[5] *Ibid.*, at p. 752. (Transl.)
[6] U.S.F.R. (1902), p. 838, at p. 871. See *supra*, p. 279, note 4.
[7] *Supra*, p. 257.
[8] *The Medea, The Good Return, The La Constancia, Danels, Gibbes Cases*, 2 *Int. Arb.*, p. 1397, at p. 1405.

The Granadine Commissioner filed a protest in which he stated:—" Said decisions or awards are, in the opinion of Mr. Hurtado, null and void according to the stipulations of the treaty and to the universal principle of justice that no party can be condemned before having been heard in defence." [9] The Umpire in his subsequent statement said: " On the subsequent protest, as the Commission had expired, it did not seem to me the cases could be opened again, except on an extension of the Commission, when, perhaps for cause shown, it might be done." [10] The Commission having been extended by the Convention of 1864, the new Umpire in a decision of 1866 held that:—

> " Serious doubts arise as to the sufficiency and regularity of the proceedings which resulted in the decision of the Umpire, Mr. Upham, and as '*in rebus dubiis tutior pars est eligenda,*' it appears to me that the reconsideration of these cases is the most reasonable course to adopt." [11]

While the previous Umpire may have exceeded his competency and thus caused his decisions to be considered null,[12] the insufficiency of proceeding consisting in the failure to hear the arguments on the merits before passing judgment upon them seems also to be considered as a cause of nullity.[13]

[9] *Ibid.*, at pp. 1401–1402.
[10] *Ibid.*, at p. 1405.
[11] *Ibid.*, at p. 1408.
[12] See *supra*, at p. 260.
[13] *Cf.* also Greek representative before the Council of the League of Nations in the Greco-Bulgarian Frontier Incident (1925) after a Commission of Inquiry had decided that Greece should pay 20,000,000 leva to Bulgaria for movable property carried off by Greek troops (7 L.N.O.J. (1926), p. 196, at pp. 204–205, see also p. 210): " The Greek Government complains, however, that the Commission did not invite it to submit its own comments on the Bulgarian demands. In international law there are no rules. There are nevertheless general rules of law which are followed by all civilised countries; no one can be condemned without a hearing. *Audiatur et altera pars.*" The Greek Government was accordingly granted an opportunity to be heard, although the decision was not revised (*ibid.*, at pp. 172–3, see " Annex," *ibid.*, at pp. 175–6). It must be remembered that in so far as the principle was originally not observed the whole settlement, as the President of the Council put it, followed " a procedure of conciliation which had almost a family character " (*ibid.*, at p. 177) and with regard to the decision on the amount of compensation by the Commission of Enquiry, it was purposely sought to avoid even a " quasi-judicial procedure " (*ibid.*, at p. 172). Indeed it may be said that the hearing of the parties is such a strong characteristic of judicial proceedings that where, in other methods of settling disputes, this principle is followed the procedure takes on a judicial hue and becomes " quasi-judicial." The actual experience of this case shows that even in other methods of pacific settlement of disputes, it would be preferable from the outset to follow the principle *audiatur et*

A simple way of implementing this principle is to allow each of the two parties to present its case to the Tribunal and let the latter decide on the basis of the record so formed. However, unless each of these parties is allowed a further opportunity of commenting on the pleadings of its opponent, as the sole Arbitrator in *The Canada Case* (1870) pointed out, the Tribunal might have " to come to a decision upon the evidence produced, notwithstanding any errors, omissions, or misstatements which may possibly have been made by one party or the other." [14]

Therefore rules of procedure often provide for a second statement from each of the parties in refutation of the previous statement by its opponent,[15] or even for a third one.[16] In the Hague Convention of 1907 for the Pacific Settlement of International Disputes,[17] in the Statute of the Permanent Court,[18] and in the Statute of the International Court,[19] the procedure is divided into two phases. In the first, there will be communicated to the Court and to the opposing party a written memorial and a written counter-memorial, with the possibility of further written replies. In the second phase, the arguments of the parties will be further developed orally before the Court.

All these rules are merely different methods designed to ensure that the judge should hear and consider what each party may have to say on the dispute as fully as possible—not only on the question at issue, but also on the statements of its opponent. They constitute a more or less elaborate implementation of the fundamental principle: *audiatur et altera pars*.

While the possibility of commenting on the pleadings of an opponent has the advantage of enabling possible errors, omissions,

altera pars. *Cf.* International Commission of Inquiry under the Hague Convention for the Pacific Settlement of International Disputes, 1899 (Art. 10 IV), 1907 (Art. 19 I): " On the inquiry both sides must be heard."

[14] 2 *Int.Arb.*, p. 1733, at p. 1742. For the *Compromis*, see 5 *ibid.*, pp. 4687–8.

[15] *E.g.*, *Brazil-French Guiana Boundary Arbitration* (1900), Treaty of April 10, 1897, Arts. III, IV, V. (Martens, II (25) N.R.G. (1896–1899), pp. 335–6.) *The Bulama Arbitration* (1870), G.B./Portugal, Protocol of January 13, 1869, Arts. III, IV (5 *Int.Arb.*, pp. 4793–5).

[16] *E.g.*, Treaty of Washington, May 8, 1871, for the submission of *The Alabama* Claims, Arts. III–V (1 *Int.Arb.*, pp. 547–53). The Exchange of Notes between the U.S.A. and Guatemala providing for Arbitration of the P. W. Shufeldt Claim, Nov. 2, 1929, Arts. 4–7 (2 UNRIAA, p. 1079, at pp. 1081–1082).

[17] Art. 63.

[18] Art. 43.

[19] Art. 43.

or misstatements to be checked, this advantage would naturally be lost if the parties were to withhold material evidence or reserve their main arguments until the last moment, when the final pleadings are being filed or exchanged.[20] This may be considered as the reason why many rules of procedure divide the pleadings into two parts, the first (*l'instruction*) devoted to the filing of pleadings and accompanying documents, the second (*les débats*) to the discussion of the material thus far submitted, either orally or in writing, without it being possible at this stage to file any new evidence or to advance any new argument without leave of the Tribunal or the agreement of the other party.[21] In deciding whether further pleadings or amendments to pleadings are to be admitted, the Tribunal has to balance the desire to be in possession of all material facts and

[20] See *Brazil-French Guiana Boundary Arbitration* (1900), *Pasicrisie int.*, p. 564. For reference to *compromis*, see *supra*, p. 293, note 15. France was of the opinion that: " To bring to light for the first time in the second memorial some devices held back in reserve until such time when one could no longer be in a position to challenge them would seem to us to be contrary to the spirit of the special agreement " (p. 570. Transl.).

Cf. also complaint of the American agent on the tardiness with which some British affidavits were filed in Brit.-U.S. Cl.Arb. (1910): *Fishing Claims*—Group I (1925), Nielsen's *Report*, p. 554, at p. 563. See also *ibid.*, p. 555. Panamanian-U.S. G.C.C. (1926), Hunt's *Report*, pp. 22–3.

Cf., however, P.C.A.: *Palmas Case* (1928), 2 H.C.R., p. 83, at pp. 94–5.

[21] *E.g.*, Hague Convention of 1907 for the Pacific Settlement of International Disputes, Arts. 63, 67. See also Arts. 65, 68. *Cf.* also the corresponding Arts. 39, 42, 43 of the Hague Convention of 1899.

Similarly Art. 48 of the Rules of Procedure of the Fran.-Germ. M.A.T. (1 T.A.M., pp. 44–61) which were followed by a number of other M.A.T.

Also Exchange of Notes between the U.S.A. and Guatemala providing for Arbitration of the P. W. Shufeldt Claim, November 2, 1929, Arts. 4–7 (2 UNRIAA, p. 1079, at pp. 1081–2).

The Statute of the I.C.J., like that of the P.C.I.J., is less strict in this respect (Art. 43). As the Adv.Com. of Jurists has said, the emphasis is more on the division of the procedure into a written and an oral phase rather than on the distinction between " *l'instruction* " and " *les débats* " (*Procès-verbaux*, pp. 736–7). Thus " it may happen that the pleadings [*l'instruction*] continue in the oral phase " (*ibid.*, p. 737). A greater latitude is left to the Court to regulate the conduct of the case (Art. 48. *Cf.* Art. 52).

In 1926, when the Rules of Court were being revised, the Registrar proposed the addition of a provision to the effect that upon the termination of the written proceedings, " no more documents may be filed by the parties except at the request of the Court " (PCIJ: Ser. D, 1st addendum to No. 2, p. 100). This proposal was not adopted (*ibid.*, pp. 100–2). In 1936, however, Art. 48 of the Rules of Court was adopted. This allows the Court to receive or refuse, unless the other party consents to accept, further documents after the termination of the written proceedings. This provision, as the President said when the revision was being discussed, was to enable the Court ' to short circuit the possible bad faith of a party who might, for instance, try without justification to delay as much as possible the moment at which it produced an important document " (PCIJ: Ser. D, 3rd addendum to No. 2, p. 191).

Art. 48 of the Rules of Court of the I.C.J. is similar to Art. 48 of the Rules of Court (1936) of the P.C.I.J.

to hear all the arguments of the parties against the public need that there should be an early settlement of all disputes (*interest reipublicae ut sit finis litium*), not to mention the consideration that time-limits once set should in principle be observed. Practical difficulties may thus arise, the solution of which must depend upon the circumstances of each case.[22] But the principle *audi alteram partem* asserts itself so that whenever there is such new evidence, alteration of the legal basis of the claim, or amendment of the original submission, the other party is always assured of an opportunity to reply thereto, or comment thereon.[23]

[22] *Cf.*, *e.g.*, Brit.-U.S. Cl.Arb (1910): *Rio Grande Case* (1923), Nielsen's *Report*, p. 332, at p. 334. In view of Arts. 63 and 65 of the Hague Convention, 1907, which were applicable to its proceedings, the Tribunal experienced a certain amount of embarrassment in dealing with the British Reply, an optional one, which was filed after the period of *l'instruction* had been closed, *i.e.*, after the session of the tribunal had commenced. The parties finally came to an agreement on this question of procedure.

It was to avoid such difficulties that the P.C.I.J. did not wish to adopt too rigid a rule in 1926, lest " they . . . run the risk of a case between two States being decided on a purely formal administration of justice." (PCIJ: Ser. D, 1st addendum to No. 2, p. 101). See *supra*, p. 294, note 21 *in fine*. *Cf. Rhodope Forests Case* (Merits) (1933), 3 UNRIAA, p. 1405, at p. 1406.

[23] *Cf.* PCIJ: *Eastern Greenland Case* (1933). One of the parties wished to introduce fresh documents in its oral rejoinder. If the Court admitted them without permitting at the same time a supplementary oral statement from the other party, the latter would not have an opportunity to comment on them. The Court by the decision of February 3, 1933, while reserving its right to refuse the fresh documents also " reserves the right to furnish the Danish agent with an opportunity to make observations on the fresh documents produced by Norway in her oral rejoinder " (PCIJ: Ser. C. 66, p. 2615; A/B. 53, pp. 25–6).

In 1936, Art. 48 of the Rules of Court (P.C.I.J.) was added. While introducing the restriction that in principle no new documents may be submitted after the termination of the written proceedings, it provided also that when, exceptionally, the Court sanctions the production of new documents, " an opportunity shall be given to the other party of commenting upon it." See similarly I.C.J.: Rules of Court, Art. 48.

Other examples: Treaty of Washington of May 8, 1871, between the U.S.A. and G.B. for the submission to arbitration of *The Alabama Claims*, Art. V (1 *Int.Arb.*, pp. 547–53); Brit.-Mex. Cl.Com. (1926): Rules of Procedure Art. 15 (d) (*Dec. & Op. of Com. 1931*, pp. 9–18).

Fran.-Germ. M.A.T.: *Banque de l'Indochine Case* (1930), 10 T.A.M., p. 38. While permitting France to change the legal basis of her claim, in the course of the oral proceedings, from Art. 296 of the Treaty of Versailles to Arts. 299 and 304 of the same treaty, the M.A.T. held: " The argument and the submissions which have just been summarised have not been advanced by the applicant's agent until the hearings have begun. The respondent has not been able, therefore, to make his reply after a thorough examination of the new line of argument, with which he is now faced. For these reasons, the Court, in the interest of the proper administration of justice and without prejudice to the questions of fact and law already discussed in the course of the written proceedings, deems it necessary to invite the agent of the French Government to set out in a memorial the new points of view which

The principle *audi alteram partem* must, however, be understood only as meaning that each party must have an *opportunity* to be heard. A procedure is not necessarily vitiated, or rendered unjudicial, if a party is not heard, either through refusal to appear before a competent tribunal after due notification, or through wilful failure to present his case, where there is no valid reason for such failure, such as *vis major*.

In the *Electricity Company of Sofia and Bulgaria Case* (Order) (1940), where Bulgaria, the defendant, abstained, "without valid reasons," from presenting a rejoinder after the original time limit for doing so had already been once extended, the Permanent Court of International Justice decided that Bulgaria "cannot thus by its own volition prevent the continuation of the proceedings instituted and the due exercise of the powers of the Court in accordance with the Statute and the Rules,"[24] and the Court proceeded without having received the Bulgarian Rejoinder. Had the Bulgarian Government persisted in its attitude, and had the work of the Court not been disrupted by the tide of war, it cannot be doubted that the Court would have been able eventually to deliver a judgment by default without hearing any more from that Government. A similar position would have arisen in the *Denunciation of the Treaty of November 2nd, 1865, between China and Belgium Case* (1927, 1928, 1929), had the case not been withdrawn by the applicant and had the respondent Government persisted in its refusal to appear, provided of course that the Court found itself competent.[25] Article 53 of the Statute of the Permanent Court provided as follows for the case of judgment by default:—

he has orally advanced. This memorial will be communicated to the respondent who will be allowed time to frame his reply" (p. 40. Transl.).

PCIJ: *Chorzów Factory Case* (Merits) (1928), A. 17, p. 7: "These [German] submissions have, in the course of the written or oral proceedings, undergone modifications which will be indicated below. As the Court has not in the present suit availed itself of the right conferred upon it under Art. 28 of the Statute to make orders as to 'the form and time in which each party must conclude its arguments,' it, in this case, allows the parties, in accordance with established precedent, to amend their original submissions, not only in the case and counter-case (Art. 40 of the Rules), but also both in the subsequent documents of the written proceedings and in declarations made by them in the course of the hearings (Art. 55 of the Rules), *subject only to the condition that the other party must always have an opportunity of commenting on the amended submissions.*" Italics added.

24 A/B. 80, p. 9. The case was unable to proceed following the occupation of the seat of the Court by the German army in May, 1940. See PCIJ: Ser. E. 16, pp. 149 *et seq.* It was withdrawn by the Belgian Government in 1945 (p. 153).

25 PCIJ: A. Nos. 8, 14, 16, 18.

"Whenever one of the parties shall not appear before the Court, or shall fail to defend his case, the other party may call upon the Court to decide in favour of his claim.

"The Court must, before doing so, satisfy itself, not only that it has jurisdiction in accordance with Articles 36 and 37, but also that the claim is well founded in fact and law."

The corresponding article in the Statute of the International Court of Justice (Art. 53) contains only slight phraseological amendments to the earlier version.[26]

The International Court of Justice had occasion to apply this provision in the *Corfu Channel Case* (1949). In that part of the proceedings relating to the assessment of the amount of compensation due from Albania to the United Kingdom, Albania "failed to defend its case" and the International Court proceeded without the participation of Albania.[27] When, at the last moment, on the expiry of the last time-limit for filing its observations, Albania asked for a modification of the procedure and a prolongation of the appointed time limit, the Court pointed out that it had given enough opportunity to the Albanian Government to defend its case, and that instead of availing itself of this opportunity it had omitted to file its submissions and had declined to appear at the public hearing. In those circumstances, it decided that it could not grant the Albanian request. Having then found that the amount of damages claimed by the United Kingdom was justified, the Court allowed the claim.[28]

As, however, the Permanent Court explained in its Reply to a request for an Advisory Opinion on the status of *Eastern Carelia* (1923), in examining a question of fact, where one of the interested parties refused to take part,

"The Court would, of course, be at a very great disadvantage in such an enquiry."[29]

The Court also indicated that for lack of sufficient material it

[26] It need hardly be mentioned that as jurisdiction in international law is founded on consent (PCIJ: *Eastern Carelia* (1923), Reply of Court to Request for Advisory Opinion, B. 5, p. 27), procedure by default occurs only very exceptionally.

[27] (Order of Nov. 19, 1949), *ICJ Reports 1949*, pp. 237 *et seq*.

[28] *Corfu Channel Case* (Compensation) (1949) *ICJ Reports 1949*, p. 244, at p. 248.

[29] B. 5, p. 28.

would not be able to "arrive at any judicial conclusion upon the question of fact." [30]

"The Court, being a Court of Justice, cannot, even in giving advisory opinions, depart from the essential rules guiding their activity as a Court." [31]

The Court regarded the above consideration as a cogent reason for declining to deliver an advisory opinion amounting in substance to deciding a dispute between the parties. This was particularly so when such a decision turned on a question of fact, where one of the parties, having no obligation to do so, did not consent to the jurisdiction of the Court or appear before it.[32]

It may indeed be submitted that besides the fundamental idea of equality between the parties, another *ratio* of the principle *audiatur et altera pars* is that it ensures the presentation of sufficient *data* concerning the case for the judge to "arrive at a judicial conclusion"; for, as will be seen presently, while a judicial authority is supposed to know the law, the facts of the case have as a rule to be proved by the parties. As the Court said:—

"It should not be left to the Court itself to ascertain what they are." [33]

The decision of the Court not to give its opinion demonstrates the fundamental nature of the principle *audiatur et altera pars.* Exceptions should not be allowed save where a party, which is under an obligation to present itself and has been afforded the opportunity to do so, fails to comply with such obligation without valid reason and neglects to exercise the right and privilege of being heard.

[30] *Ibid.*

[31] *Ibid.*, at p. 29.

[32] See ICJ: *Interpretation of Peace Treaties* (1st Phase) (1950), Adv.Op., *ICJ Reports 1950*, p. 65, in which the *Eastern Carelia Case* (1923) was distinguished (p. 72). *Cf.* D.O. of Winiarski, *ibid.*, pp. 90 *et seq.*

[33] B. 5, p. 28. Herein lies perhaps the essential procedural difference between a judicial body properly so-called and a commission of inquiry as for example those provided for in the Hague Conventions of 1899 and 1907 for the Pacific Settlement of International Disputes, the task of which is essentially that of establishing the facts (Part III), as distinct from International Arbitration (Part IV). It may, however, be mentioned that even in Commissions of Inquiry the principle *audiatur et altera pars* should also be respected. See the Hague Convention, 1899, Art. 10 IV; the Hague Convention, 1907, Art. 19 I: "On the inquiry both sides must be heard."

Chapter 15

JURA NOVIT CURIA

In the *Brazilian Loans Case* (1929), the Permanent Court of International Justice said:—

> "The Court . . . is a tribunal of international law, and . . . in this capacity, is deemed to know what this law is." [1]

This is but a recognition of a well-known principle of judicial procedure in municipal law: *jura novit curia*, on which we need not dwell at length.

Questions of law, as distinct from questions of fact, need not be raised by the parties themselves, but the Court can and should examine them *proprio motu*.[2] It is the task of the Court itself to ascertain the law, of which it is the organ, and to apply it to the dispute, without being confined to the contentions advanced by the parties.[3] While it is undoubtedly bound by the law, "it is not bound by the arguments of the parties." [4]

"From a general point of view, it cannot lightly be admitted that the Court, whose function it is to declare the law, can be called upon to choose between two or more constructions determined beforehand by the Parties, none of which may correspond to the opinion at which it may arrive. Unless otherwise expressly provided,

[1] A. 20/21, p. 124.

[2] PCIJ: *International Commission of the River Oder Case* (1929), A. 23, pp. 18–19. The Polish Government did not contend that the Barcelona Convention had not been ratified by Poland until the oral proceedings. The Six Governments asked the Court to reject the Polish contention *in limine*, for having been submitted at such an advanced stage of the proceedings. Dismissing the objection as untenable, the Court held: "The fact that Poland has not ratified the Barcelona Convention not being contested, it is evident that the matter is purely one of law such as the Court should examine *ex officio*."

Cf. supra, pp. 257–8.

[3] PCIJ: *The Lotus* (1927) A. 10. In its task of ascertaining whether there was a rule of international law precluding Turkey from instituting the prosecution against the first officer of the French ship *Lotus*, the Court expressly said that: 'In the fulfilment of its task of itself ascertaining what the international law is, it has not confined itself to a consideration of the arguments put forward" (p. 31).

[4] Rum.-Germ. M.A.T.: *Colleanu Case* (1929), 9 T.A.M., p. 216, at p. 221 (Transl.).

See also ICJ: *Corfu Channel Case* (Merits) (1949), D.O. by Winiarski, *ICJ Reports* 1949, p. 1, at pp. 51–56.

it must be presumed that the Court enjoys the freedom which normally appertains to it, and that it is able, if such is its opinion, not only to accept one or other of the two propositions, but also to reject them both." [5]

Express agreements of course constitute the law between the parties and, in so far as they are relevant to the case, form part of the law which the judge deciding a dispute between the parties will have to apply.[6] Needless to say a Court must always act in accordance with the terms of the instrument conferring jurisdiction upon it.[7] But this does not constitute an exception to the principle *jura novit curia*; for the Tribunal has still to decide the meaning and effect of the agreement of the parties which forms part of the law to be applied.

The principle, however, applies only to the law of which

[5] PCIJ: *Free Zones Case* (Jgt.) (1932), A/B. 46, p. 138.
Cf. also PCIJ: *Chorzów Factory Case* (Interpretation) (1927), A. 13, pp. 15–16.
ICJ: *Corfu Channel Case* (Merits) (1949), D.O. by Azevedo, *ICJ Reports 1949*, p. 1, at p. 84: "Il ne faut pas oublier que si à l'égard des faits l'accord des parties est valable, encore qu'une cour internationale, plus libre que les juges internes en matière de preuve, pourrait faire des réserves, *il serait tout à fait irrecevable en ce qui est du droit à appliquer*" (Italics added). "It is true . . . that an agreement between the parties on the facts is valid, even though an international court, having more freedom in regard to evidence than a municipal judge, might make reservations; such an agreement would be quite inadmissible in regard to the law to be applied" (Transl. of the Court). ICJ: *Asylum Case* (1950), *ICJ Reports 1950*, p. 266, at p. 278: "The Court, whose duty it is to apply international law in deciding the present case, cannot attach decisive importance to any of these documents." The latter contained views contrary to those now maintained by the respective parties before the Court.

[6] See, *e.g.*, British Guiana-Venezuela Boundary Arbitration Treaty (1897), Art. IV: "In deciding the matters submitted, the Arbitrators shall . . . be governed by the following rules, which are agreed upon by the High Contracting Parties as Rules to be taken as applicable to the case, and by such principles of international law not inconsistent therewith as the Arbitrators shall determine to be applicable to the case." Amongst the Rules were "(a) Adverse holding or prescription during a period of fifty years shall make a good title" (C.9533—1899, pp. 3–4).
The Alabama Arbitration Treaty (1871), Art. VI, establishing what have become known as the Three Rules of Washington concerning the duties of neutrals (1 *Int.Arb.*, pp. 547–53). It may be noted that in this case the British Government made an express reservation that these rules were not part of the law at the time the acts complained of occurred, but that it agreed that in adjudging the claims arising from these occurrences "the Arbitrators should assume that Her Majesty's Government had undertaken to act upon the principles set forth in these rules." Moreover, both parties agreed to observe these rules in future and to invite other maritime powers to accede to them (*ibid.*).

[7] *Cf. e.g.*, Germ.-U.S., M.C.C. (1922): *Administrative Decision No. II* (1923), *Dec. & Op.*, p. 5, at p. 5. I.M.T. (Nuremberg) (1945): "*German Major War Criminals Case*" (1946), 1 *I.M.T. (Nuremberg)*, pp. 174, 216, 218 *et seq.* "The law of the Charter is decisive and binding upon the Tribunal" (p. 218). See *supra*, pp. 259 *et seq.*, especially p. 261.

the Tribunal is the organ. Although an international tribunal may be bound to apply municipal law when circumstances so require, it

"is not obliged also to know the municipal law of the various countries. All that can be said in this respect is that the Court may possibly be obliged to obtain knowledge regarding the municipal law which has to be applied. And this it must do, either by means of evidence furnished it by the Parties or by means of any researches which the Court may think fit to undertake or to cause to be undertaken." [8]

Indeed,

"From the standpoint of International Law and of the Court which is its organ, municipal laws are merely facts which express the will and constitute the activities of States." [9]

They are treated as facts which have to be proved like any other fact.[10]

[8] PCIJ: *Brazilian Loans Case* (1929), A. 20/21, p. 124.
[9] PCIJ: *German Interests Case* (Merits) (1926), A. 7, p. 19.
[10] *Cf.* Fran.-Germ. M.A.T.: *Heim et Chamant Case* (1922) 3 T.A.M., p. 50, at p. 55.

CHAPTER 16

PROOF AND BURDEN OF PROOF

IN a previous Chapter mention was made of the opinion of the Permanent Court of International Justice that the Court, as a judicial body, should not be left to ascertain the facts of the case.[1] It falls primarily upon the parties, therefore, to place the facts of the case before the Court, although a Court may also require points not dealt with by the parties to be further elucidated.[2] When this has been done,

> " [The Court] must consider the totality of the allegations and evidence laid before [it] by the Parties, either *motu proprio* or at [its] request and decide what allegations are to be considered as sufficiently substantiated." [3]

It may be said that the aim of an international tribunal is to arrive at a moral conviction [4] of the truth and reality of all the relevant facts of the case upon which its decision is to be based.[5]

"It is for the Arbitrator to decide both whether allegations do or—as being within the knowledge of the tribunal—do not need

[1] *Supra*, p. 298.
[2] *Cf.* P.C.A.: *Palmas Case* (1928), 2 H.C.R., p. 83, at p. 85.
[3] *Ibid.*, at p. 95.
[4] *Cf.*, *e.g.*, Germ.-Ven. M.C.C. (1903): *Faber Case, Ven.Arb. 1903*, p. 600, at p. 622: ". . . Judge J. C. Bancroft Davis said, in *Caldera Cases* (15 C.Cls.R. 546) (a Dissenting Opinion, p. 666): 'In the means by which justice is to be attained the Court is freed from the technical rules of evidence imposed by the common law, and is permitted to ascertain truth by any method which produces *moral conviction*. This proposition is self-evident. . . .' "
Germ.-U.S. M.C.C. (1922): *Drier Case* (1935), *Dec. & Op.*, pp. 1037, 1079; Brit.-Mex. Cl.Com. (1926): *Mexico City Bombardment Claims* (1930), D.O. by British Commissioner, *Dec. & Op. of Com.*, p. 100, at p. 109.
[5] *Cf.*, *e.g.*, Mex.-U.S. G.C.C. (1923): *Parker Case* (1926), *Op. of Com.* 1927, p. 35, at p. 39: " The greatest liberality will obtain in the admission of evidence before this Commission with the view of discovering the whole truth with respect to each claim submitted."
Brit.-Mex Cl.Com. (1926): *Cameron Case* (1929), *Dec. & Op. of Com.*, p. 33, at p. 34: " Ascertain the truth in a manner which is not subject to any restriction."
PCIJ: *Oscar Chinn Case* (1934), S.O. by van Eysinga, A/B. 63, pp. 146-147: " The Court is not tied to any system of taking evidence, . . . Its task is to co-operate in the objective ascertainment of the truth."
ICJ: *Corfu Channel Case* (Merits) (1949), *ICJ Reports 1949*, p. 1, at p. 20. The I.C.J. spoke of " its search for the truth."

evidence in support and whether the evidence produced is sufficient or not." [6]

While international tribunals are thus "entirely free to estimate the value of statements made by the Parties," [7] their activity in this regard is nevertheless governed by a large number of general principles of law recognised by States *in foro domestico.* In the succeeding pages some of the general principles of law concerning proof and burden of proof applied by international tribunals will be examined.

JUDICIAL NOTICE

First of all, as the above quotation indicates, certain allegations of the parties that are within the knowledge of the tribunal need no evidence in support.[8] "*Judicial notice*" is taken of the facts averred.[9] Proof may thus be dispensed with as regards facts which are of common knowledge or public notoriety [10] or which, in the circumstances of the case, are self-evident.[11]

[6] *Palmas Case* (1928), 2 H.C.R., p. 83, at p. 95.

[7] PCIJ: *German Interests* (Merits) (1926), A. 17, p. 73. Fran.-Mex. M.C.C. (1924): *Pinson Case* (1928), *Jurisprudence*, p. 1, at p. 14: "In the matter of evidence, I consider . . . as fundamental the complete freedom of the Franco-Mexican Commission in admitting any evidence which it deems fit and in determining its value" (Transl.). See further *infra*, pp. 307–8.

[8] *Supra*, p. 302. In that case, the Treaty of Utrecht invoked by one of the parties was not in the record produced but was nevertheless taken into consideration by the Tribunal because its text "is of public notoriety and accessible to the Parties" (*Palmas Case* (1928), 2 H.C.R., p. 83, at p. 96.

[9] See Sandifer, *Evidence Before International Tribunals*, 1939, pp. 269–278.

[10] Germ.-U.S. M.C.C. (1922): *Mendel Case* (1926). Concerning what took place with regard to the former German colony of New Guinea before, during and since the First World War, the Commission said: "From the record therein and *from historical sources and official reports of which the Commission takes judicial notice* it appears . . . ." (*Dec. & Op.*, p. 772, at p. 784. Italics added).

Cf. Charter of the I.M.T. (Nuremberg), Art. 21. Charter of the I.M.T. for the Far East, Art. 13 (d). Judicial notice is to be taken of facts of common knowledge and also official government documents of the United Nations.

[11] *e.g.*, Portugo-German Arbitration (1919): *The Cysne* (1930), 2 UNRIAA, p. 1011, at p. 1056: "As has been maintained by the claimant, the captor of a neutral prize *must*, in principle, take it to port [1] ([1] Art. 48, Declaration of London). If he makes use of the *exceptional* right to destroy his capture, he *must* prove [2] ([2] Art. 51, Declaration of London) that he had acted in the face of such necessity as is envisaged in Art. 49. *But this proof*, contrary to the Portuguese contention, *is unnecessary*, *if it is obvious* that the captor, because of its type, was not in a position to escort the seized vessel or to detach a prize crew. This was certainly the case with a German submarine, Mark 1915, operating in the western parts of the Channel [3] ([3] . . . . .). Its extreme vulnerability and the weakness of its armament would practically exclude the possibility of its escorting the prize. Moreover, the small number of German submarines [4] ([4] . . . . .), did not make it possible for a unit to leave its sector in order to escort a prize of little importance, without involving danger,

In this connection it may be mentioned that the information obtained by a tribunal through an inspection of the places concerned in proceedings ("*descente sur les lieux*"), a procedure which has sometimes been applied in international arbitral and judicial proceedings,[12] presents considerable affinity with judicial notice.

PRESUMPTIONS

Proof may also be dispensed with as regards facts, the truth of which, though not within judicial knowledge, is presumed by the tribunal. Without going so far as to holding them to be true, it is legitimate for a tribunal to presume the truth of certain facts or of a certain state of affairs, leaving it to the party alleging the contrary to establish its contention. These presumptions serve as initial premises of legal reasoning.

in the sense of Art. 49 of the Declaration of London, to the success of the operations in which she was engaged. The crews of submarines, reduced to the strict minimum, were too small for detaching prize crews, especially when operating at a great distance from the German coast. It must therefore be conceded to Germany that the German submarine 41 was, in fact, in the exceptional situation envisaged in Art. 49 of the Declaration of London" (Transl. Italics added). *N.B.*—proof was considered unnecessary, even when Art. 51 of the Declaration of London prescribes that the captor has to "establish" that he was acting in a case of necessity. An argument may thus be based on logical deduction from the circumstances of the case.

12 *Cf.* PCIJ: *Meuse Case* (1937) A/B. 70, p. 9; Order of May 13, 1937, Ser. C. 81, pp. 553–4. This Order was made under Arts. 48 and 50 of the Statute. On the suggestion of the Belgian Government which met with no opposition on the part of the Government of the Netherlands, the Court decided to visit the places concerned in the proceedings and there witnessed practical demonstrations of the operation of locks and of installations connected therewith. Manley O. Hudson, one of the judges who took part in the inspection, writing afterwards in 31 A.J.I.L. (1937), p. 696, "Visits by International Tribunals to Places concerned in Proceedings," said: "The Court viewed the Belgian suggestion, not as an offer to present evidence, but as an invitation to the Court to procure its own information" (p. 697). The procedure may thus be regarded as a means for edifying the judicial knowledge.

Cf. also *Tillett Case* (1890). Concerning the question of treatment in prison of Antwerp, the Arbitrator went to inspect the place itself "in order, by means of a full knowledge of the case, to solve certain questions which seemed doubtful to me." (92 B.F.S.P. (1899–1900), p. 105, at p. 105. Transl.)

Other international precedents of "*descente sur les lieux*" include the *Meerauge Boundary Arbitration* (1902), Martens, III (3) N.R.G., p. 71, at p. 72. P.C.A.: *Grisbadarna Case* (1909), Norway/Sweden, *Recueil des Comptes rendus de la visite des lieux et des Protocols des séances du Tribunal arbitral, constitué en vertu de la Convention du 14 mars 1908, pour juger la question de la délimitation d'une certaine partie de la frontière maritime entre la Norvège et là Suède*, 1909.

Cf. also the use of experts to inspect the places, ICJ: *Corfu Channel Case* (Order of December 17, 1948) *ICJ Reports 1947–1948*, p. 124; (Merits) (1949) *ICJ Reports 1949*, p. 4, at p. 9. The opinion of the Court's experts, although no doubt of great weight, differs, however, in nature from the information acquired by the Court itself (*cf., e.g., ICJ Reports 1949*, p. 4, at p. 21).

International tribunals have applied a number of *presumptions founded on general principles of law.* In the first place, international tribunals constantly have recourse to the rebuttable presumption of the regularity and validity of acts and recognise that this is a general principle of law. Thus, the Umpire in the German-Venezuelan Mixed Claims Commission (1903) held that:—

> "*Omnia rite acta praesumuntur.* This universally accepted rule of law should apply with even greater force to the acts of a government than those of private persons."[13]

Similarly, according to another general principle of law, good faith is to be presumed,[14] whilst an abuse of right is not. "It rests with the party who states that there has been such misuse to prove his statement."[15] In the sphere of international law, it follows from these important presumptions that, as the *Rapporteur* in the Spanish Zone of Morocco Claims (1923) said:—

> "The international responsibility of the State is not to be presumed."[16]

[13] *Valentiner Case, Ven.Arb. 1903*, p. 562, at p. 564. U.S. Domestic Commission: Mexican Claims (Act of 1849): *Felix Case*, 3 *Int.Arb.*, p. 2800, at p. 2811: Regularity and Validity of a municipal judgment presumed. Mex.-U.S. G.C.C. (1923): *Robinson Smith Putnam Case* (1927) *Op. of Com. 1927*, p. 222, at p. 225: Municipal judgment to be respected save for "a clear and notorious injustice, visible, to put it thus, at a mere glance." Mex.-U.S. Cl.Com. (1868): *Black & Stratton Case*, 3 *Int.Arb.*, p. 3138: Confiscation by Mexican Officials. Fran.-Ven. M.C.C. (1902): *Frierdich & Co. Case*, Ralston's *Report*, p. 31, at p. 42: "The general presumption is that public officers perform their official duties, and that their official acts are regular. . . . Where some preceding act or pre-existing fact is necessary to the validity of an official act, the presumption in favour of the validity of the official act is presumptive proof of such preceding act or pre-existing fact." Ital.-Ven. M.C.C. (1903): *Guerrieri Case, Ven.Arb. 1903*, p. 753, at p. 754. The Neth.-Ven. M.C.C. (1903): *Bembelista Case, Ven.Arb. 1903*, p. 900, at p. 901. Fran.-Mex. Cl.Com. (1924): *Nájera Case* (1928) *Jurisprudence*, p. 156, at p. 177: Regularity and validity of an option of nationality accepted by the Government concerned. *Salem Case* (1932) 2 UNRIAA, p. 1161, at p. 1186: Regularity and validity of naturalisation presumed. Mex.-U.S. G.C.C. (1923): *Chazen Case* (1930), *Op. of Com. 1931*, p. 20, at p. 32: An auction sale. ICJ: *Corfu Channel Case* (Merits) (1949) D.O. by Ečer, *ICJ Reports 1949*, p. 4, at pp. 119–20, 127, 129.

[14] Fran.-Ven. M.C.C. (1902): *Frierdich & Co. Case*, Ralston's *Report*, p. 31, at p. 42. PCIJ: *Lighthouses Case* (1934) S.O. by Séfériadès, A/B. 62, p. 47. PCIJ: *Mavrommatis Jerusalem Concessions Case* (1925) A. 5, p. 43. P.C.A.: *Norwegian Claims Case* (1922) 2 H.C.R., p. 39, at p. 57.

[15] PCIJ: *German Interests Case* (Merits) (1926) A. 7, p. 30: see French text which is more explicit. PCIJ: *Free Zones Case* (Second Phase: Order) (1930) A. 24, p. 12.

[16] Claim 28: *Haj Mohamed Harrej* (*Tanger, Horses*) *Case* (1924), 2 UNRIAA, p. 615, at p. 699. (Transl.) *Cf.* ICJ: *Corfu Channel Case* (Merits) (1949) D.O. by Ečer, *ICJ Reports 1949*, p. 4, at p. 119: "I consider therefore that

The party alleging a violation of international law giving rise to international responsibility has the burden of proving its assertion.[17]

If good faith and the observance of law may be regarded as the general rule and not the exception, as indeed they should be, the above presumptions may be said to belong to a still wider principle that what exists as a general rule will be presumed while he who alleges an exception to this general rule incurs the burden of substantiating his allegation. As Commissioner Gore said in the case of *The Neptune* (1797):—

> "Whoever will derive to himself advantage by the exception to a general rule, or by an interference with the generally acknowledged rights of another, is bound to prove that his case is completely within the exception." [18]

Since sovereignty and independence of States constitute the cardinal rule of international law,

> "Restrictions upon the independence of States cannot . . . be presumed." [19]

The party alleging such restrictions or wishing to derive a right therefrom must prove the exception to the general rule.[20] In general, it may be said that what is normal, customary or the more probable is presumed, and that anything to the contrary has to be proved by the party alleging it.[21]

in international law there is a presumption in favour of every State, corresponding very nearly to the presumption in favour of the innocence of every individual in municipal law. There is a *presumptio juris* that a State behaves in conformity with international law."

17 *Cf.* Portugo-German Arbitration (1919): *Claims for Losses suffered in Belgium* (1930) 2 UNRIAA, p. 1011, at p. 1040, § 4.

18 Jay Treaty (Art. VII) Arbitration (1794): 4 *Int.Adj.*, M.S., p. 372, at p. 407. The right of the neutral to carry on commerce with either of the parties at war being recognised by the Tribunal, the party who alleges contraband must prove his allegation. See also Brit.-U.S. Cl.Arb. (1910): *The Wanderer* (1921) Nielsen's *Report*, p. 459, at p. 462.

19 PCIJ: *The Lotus* (1927), A. 10, p. 18. *Id.*: *Free Zones Case* (Second Phase: Order) (1930), A. 24, p. 12.

20 *Cf.* P.C.A.: *North Atlantic Coast Fisheries Case* (1910), 1 H.C.R., p. 141, at p. 157. The general principle being that territory is conterminous with sovereignty, if the United States asserts that the right to regulate the fishery industry in British waters does not reside independently in Great Britain, she incurs the burden of proving such an exception to the general rule.

21 PCIJ: *Eastern Greenland Case* (1933), A/B. 53, p. 49: "The geographical meaning of the word 'Greenland,' *i.e.*, the name which is habitually used in the maps to denominate the whole island, must be regarded as the ordinary meaning of the word. If it is alleged by one of the parties that some unusual or exceptional meaning is to be attributed to it, it lies on that party to establish its contention." See also, *ibid.*, p. 52.

THE ADMISSION AND THE APPRAISAL OF EVIDENCE

Allegations of the parties of the truth of which the tribunal does not take judicial notice or which are not presumed by it, have to be proved, unless they are admitted by the other party.[22] Those which are not proved need not be taken into consideration by the tribunal: *Idem est non probari non esse.*[23] The conviction of the Tribunal as to the truth of the assertions of the parties is secured by means of evidence. In the *Faber Case* (C.1903), the following definition of evidence is to be found:—

"'In its wider and universal sense it [evidence] embraces all means by which any alleged fact, the truth of which is submitted to examination, may be established or disproved. (1 Green, Ev., sec. 1).'"[24]

Apart from special provisions, international tribunals claim, and indeed exercise, complete freedom in the admission and evaluation of evidence in order to arrive at the moral conviction of the truth of the whole case.[25] With regard to the appraisal of evidence, however, as the American Commissioner in the Mexican-United States General Claims Commission (1923) said in one of his concurring opinions:—

22 Exceptionally, however, the admission by the other party of a fact alleged does not relieve the party alleging it from bringing adequate proof, in cases where the truth of the fact alleged is a condition *sine qua non* for the right of action of a party or for the jurisdiction of the tribunal. See Mex.-U.S. G.C.C. (1923): *Hatton Case* (1928), *Op. of Com. 1929*, p. 6, at p. 8. *Cf.* ICJ: *Corfu Channel Case* (Merits) (1949), D.O. by Azevedo, *ICJ Reports 1949*, p. 1, at p. 84.

23 *Cf.*, *e.g.*, ICJ: *Corfu Channel Case* (Merits) (1949), *ICJ Reports 1949*, p. 1, at pp. 15–7: "Although the United Kingdom Government never abandoned its contention that Albania herself laid the mines, very little attempt was made by the British Government to demonstrate this point. . . . . Although the suggestion that the minefield was laid by Albania was repeated in the United Kingdom statement in Court on January 18, 1949, and in the final submissions read in Court on the same day, this suggestion was in fact hardly put forward at that time except *pro memoria*, and no evidence in support was furnished. In these circumstances, the Court need pay no further attention to this matter. . . .

"The Court need not dwell on the assertion of one of the counsel for the Albanian Government that the minefield might have been laid by the Greek Government. It is enough to say that this was a mere conjecture which, as counsel himself admitted, was based on no proof."

24 Germ.-Ven. M.C.C. (1903): *Ven.Arb. 1903*, p. 600, at p. 622.

25 Fran.-Mex. Cl.Com. (1924): *Pinson Case* (1928), *Jurisprudence*, p. 1, at p. 94. See also *ibid.*, p. 48. *Shufeldt Case* (1930), 2 UNRIAA, p. 1079, at p. 1083. Neth.-Ven. M.C.C. (1903): *Evertsz Case*, *Ven.Arb. 1903*, p. 904, at p. 905. P.C.A.: *Palmas Case* (1928), 2 H.C.R., p. 83, at pp. 95–6. U.S.: War Claims Arbiter (Act of 1928): *Administrative Decision No. II* (1928) 23 A.J.I.L. (1929), p. 659, at pp. 667–8.

See also case cited *supra*, p. 302, notes 4 and 5, p. 303, note 7.

"This Commission cannot apply strict rules of evidence such as are prescribed by domestic law, but it can and must give application to well-recognised principles underlying rules of evidence and of course it must employ common-sense reasoning in considering the evidential value of the things which have been submitted to it as evidence." [26]

Speaking for the Commission in a subsequent case, the same Commissioner said:—

"With respect to matters of evidence they [international tribunals] must give effect to common-sense principles underlying rules of evidence in domestic law." [27]

General principles of law prevailing *in foro domestico* relating to evidence must, therefore, be applied. In this connection, it may be mentioned that the above cases disprove the theory which tends to regard the general principles of law recognised by civilised nations as a kind of mathematical highest common factor among the various systems of municipal law, including all their particularities introduced on account of special circumstances. It shows, on the contrary, that a much broader approach has to be adopted in order to arrive at the common underlying principles, without regard to the particularities of individual systems.[28]

As, however, the appraisal of evidence is an intellectual process depending upon the circumstances of each case, any attempt to itemize broad principles governing such subjective mental activity must perforce be somewhat hazardous.[29] In

[26] *Mallén Case* (1927), C.O. by American Commissioner, *Op. of Com. 1927*, p. 254, at p. 268.

[27] *Kling Case* (1930), *Op. of Com. 1931*, p. 36, at p. 45. *Id.*: *Dillon Case* (1928), C.O. by American Commissioner, *Op. of Com. 1929*, p. 61, at p. 65. P.C.A.: *Norwegian Claims Case* (1921), *Counter Case of the U.S.*, Washington, 1922, p. 4.

[28] *Cf.* also Brit.-Mex. Cl.Com. (1926): *Mexico City Bombardment Claims* (1930), D.O. by British Commissioner, *Dec. & Op. of Com.*, p. 100, at p. 109: "Under the rules governing the procedure of the Commission we are not bound by the laws of evidence prevailing in Mexico or in England or in any other country. But it is our duty to apply general principles of justice and equity and to give to any oral evidence or document produced before us such evidential value as we consider in all the circumstances of the case it ought to carry."

[29] *Cf.* British India: Appellate High Court: *The Queen* v. *Madhub Chunder Giri* (1873), Sutherland 21, *The Weekly Reporter* (1874), Criminal Rulings, p. 13, at p. 19, c. 2, *per* Birch J.: "For weighing evidence and drawing inferences from it, there can be no canon. Each case presents its own peculiarities and common sense and shrewdness must be brought to bear upon the facts elicited in every case."

particular, it should be pointed out that the following principles inferred from the practice of international tribunals are not to be considered as in any sense absolute. They can either support one another to increase the value of the evidence, or they may cancel each other out so that the value of the evidence is diminished. The determining factor can thus only be ascertained after judiciously weighing all the relevant considerations.

STATEMENTS AND AFFIDAVITS OF THE CLAIMANT

Generally speaking, unless the fact or state of affairs be within judicial notice or presumed, the mere *ex parte* statements of the facts by the interested party in a dispute are not considered as evidence and do not constitute sufficient proof of the facts alleged. In the *Odell Case* (1931), before the British-Mexican Claims Commission (1926), the claimant alleged that he had been forced to conduct a military train and was subsequently injured in the derailment of the train caused by Mexican revolutionary forces. No other evidence was adduced relative to the whole incident. Held:—

"The Commissioners do not deny that the description of the derailment, as given by the claimant, and taken as a whole, bears a certain appearance of truth, but a judicial decision cannot be based on this personal impression alone. . . . A decision which imposes upon a State a financial liability towards another State, cannot rest solely upon the unsupported allegations of the claimant. . . . If an international tribunal were to accept all these allegations without evidence, it would expose itself to the not unjustifiable criticism of placing jurisdiction as between nations below the level prevailing in all civilised States for jurisdiction as between citizens." [30]

Even where absolute sincerity and good faith are not in doubt, the statement of the facts in the pleadings by one of the interested parties, being a partial statement drawn up specially to present the case in the best possible light, cannot be considered

[30] *Further Dec. & Op. of Com.*, p. 61, at pp. 62–3. *Cf.* also I.C.J.: *Corfu Channel Case* (Merits) (1949), *ICJ Reports 1949*, p. 4, cited *supra*, p. 307, note 23.

Cf., however, Mex.-U.S. G.C.C. (1923): *Hatton Case* (1928), *Op. of Com. 1929*, p. 6, at p. 10: "The proof of the value of the animals taken is meagre, but since it has not been contested, the claimant should have an award for the amount asked." *N.B.*, the amount was not contested. *Cf. infra*, p. 319. note 80.

as evidence and regarded as conclusive.[31] A tribunal must base its decisions upon allegations of the truth of which it is convinced, and not upon those which merely have a semblance of truth.[32] It appears from the above decision that a departure from this principle would be a violation of the international minimum standard for the administration of justice.

Moreover, allegations of the interested parties may often contain exaggerations and even misrepresentations on account of the personal interest at stake, a factor which must be taken into account,[33] although, as the Mexican-United States General Claims Commission (1923) has indicated, "exaggerations and even misrepresentations of facts on the part of claimants are not so uncommon as to destroy the value of their contentions." [34]

As we shall see, an oath is regarded as a considerable safeguard of veracity.[35] In the *National Paper and Type Co. Case* (1928), counsel for the claimant argued before the Mexican-United States General Claims Commission (1923) that since the memorial containing the allegations of fact had been sworn to by the claimant, there was in fact an affidavit in support of the allegations before the Commission. The Commission ruled, however, that the verification of the memorial prescribed by the rules of the Commission would not justify the view that "a pleading might be regarded at once as a pleading and as evidence." [36]

Sworn statements emanating from the claimants, may, however, be legitimately considered by a tribunal.[37] But with regard to affidavits in general and uncorroborated affidavits of the claimants in particular, the British-Mexican Claims Commission (1926) said:—

"In its decision on the demurrer, filed by the Mexican Agent in the name of Mrs. V. C. [*sic*] Cameron, the Commission has made

[31] Brit.-U.S. Cl.Arb. (1910): *Studer Case* (1925), Nielsen's *Report*, p. 547, at p. 552.

[32] *Cf. infra*, pp. 325, 326.

[33] *White Case* (1864), 2 *Arb.Int.*, p. 305, at p. 322. Mex.-U.S. G.C.C. (1923): *Chattin Case* (1927), *Op. of Com. 1927*, p. 422, at p. 438.

[34] *Mallén Case* (1927) *Op. of Com. 1927*, p. 254, at p. 256. *Id.*: *Walter H. Faulkner Case* (1926), *ibid.*, p. 86, at pp. 90–91.

[35] *Infra*, pp. 312 *et seq.*

[36] *Op. of Com. 1929*, p. 3, at p. 4.

[37] Mex.-U.S. G.C.C. (1923): *Dillon Case* (1928), C.O. by American Commissioner *Op.of Com. 1929*, p. 61, at p. 65. See also *ibid.*, pp. 62–63.

known its attitude as to affidavits in general. The unanimous view of the Commissioners was expressed as follows:—

> " ' It is true, no doubt that affidavits contain evidence which can be described as secondary evidence and is often of a very defective character. In many cases, it may be, affidavit evidence may possess little value, but the weight to be attached to that evidence is a matter for the Commissioners to decide according to the circumstances of a particular case. Affidavits must and will be weighed with the greatest caution and circumspection, but it would be utterly unreasonable to reject them altogether.'
>
> "...
>
> " It may be useful for the further guidance of the Agents, that the Commission announces that its majority has come to the conclusion, in general, that unsupported affidavits of claimants possess the very defective character of which the quotation speaks, and that only in cases of the rarest exception, they can be accepted as sufficient evidence. Such documents are sworn without the guarantee of cross examination by the other party; in nearly all cases a false statement will remain without penalty, and, as they are signed by the party most interested in the judgment, they cannot have the value of unbiased and impartial outside evidence." [38]

Personal interest of the deponent and the uncontrolled character of his affirmation are, therefore, important considerations which generally deprive a claimant's affidavit of much of its probative force. Thus the British-Mexican Claims Commission (1926) dismissed a large number of claims based solely on uncorroborated affidavits of the claimant,[39] and, as it said in the *Engleheart Case* (1931):—

> " An unsupported affidavit of the claimant cannot be considered as outside evidence, it is part of the claim itself." [40]

[38] *Mexico City Bombardment Claims* (1930), *Dec. & Op. of Com.*, p. 100, at pp. 102–103. The decision referred to is that on the claim of Mrs. V. L. Cameron, *ibid.*, p. 33, at p. 35.

[39] *Tracy Case* (1930), *Dec. & Op. of Com.*, p. 118, at p. 121; *Leigh Case* (1931), *Further Dec. & Op. of Com.*, p. 80, at p. 83; *Lynch Case* (Claim No. 32) (1931), *ibid.*, p. 101, at p. 103; *Payne Case* (1931), *ibid.*, p. 110, at p. 111; *Read Case* (1931), *ibid.*, p. 154, at p. 156; *Delamain Case* (1931), § 6, *ibid.*, p. 222, at p. 224; *Mackenzie and Harvey Case* (1931), *ibid.*, p. 277, at p. 280; *David Bruce Russell Case* (1931), *ibid.*, p. 278, at p. 280; *Debenture Holders of the New Parral Mines Syndicate and Blunt Case* (1931), *ibid.*, p. 281, at p. 286; *Bryant Case* (1931), *ibid.*, p. 361, at p. 362.

Pan.-U.S. G.C.C. (1926): *Agnes Ewing Brown Case* (1933), Hunt's *Report*, p. 85, at p. 94.

[40] *Further Dec. & Op. of Com.*, p. 65, at p. 66.

In the *Office belge de Vérification Case* (1926), however, the Belgo-German Mixed Arbitral Tribunal was of the opinion that, in the absence of other means of proof, the affidavit of the claimant could possess a special probative value on account of his recognised respectability (*honorabilité*) or on account of reasons adduced by him to explain why the production of better evidence was not possible.[41]

TESTIMONIAL EVIDENCE [42]

Testimony by third persons not interested in the claim is free from the defect of personal interest mentioned above which weakens the probative value of the statements by an interested party and, even if unsworn, is entitled, as the United States-Venezuelan Mixed Claims Commission (1903) said, to "such consideration as they may seem to deserve." [43] The same Commission also recognised, however, that:—

"Legal testimony presented under the sanction of an oath administered by competent authority will undoubtedly be accorded greater weight than unsworn statements." [44]

[41] 6 T.A.M., p. 704, at p. 706. Affidavits of the National Bank of Belgium, of an insurance company, etc. *Cf.* however, *infra*, p. 320, note 82, 2nd paragraph.

See also Mex.-U.S. G.C.C. (1923): *Dillon Case* (1928), *Op. of Com. 1929*, p. 61, at p. 62: "According to the affidavit of the claimant, and no evidence to the contrary having been produced, it is to be assumed that during all the time of his detention the claimant was kept incommunicado . . . and that no information was given him concerning the purpose of his arrest and detention." The affidavits were, however, considered insufficient evidence of other alleged ill-treatment in jail. The inherent difficulty in proving a negative fact seems to have been taken into account by the Commission. *Cf.*, however, the apparently more stringent requirement of proof in P.C.A.: *Chevreau Case* (1931), 2 UNRIAA, p. 1113, at p. 1133.

[42] *i.e.*, evidence by means of witnesses, as distinguished from documentary evidence.

[43] *Lasry Case*, *Ven.Arb. 1903*, p. 37, at p. 38.

Mex.-U.S. G.C.C. (1923): *Parker Case* (1926), *Op. of Com. 1927*, p. 35, at p. 37.

Cf. Brit.-Mex. Cl.Com (1926): *Bartlett Case* (1931), *Further Dec. & Op. of Com.*, p. 51, at p. 52.

[44] *Lasry Case*, *Ven.Arb.* 1903, p. 37, at p. 38.

Cf. an opinion on the legal effect of a solemn affirmation to speak the truth as a guarantee of veracity, D.O. by Mexican Commissioner, Brit.-Mex.Cl.Com. (1926): *Stacpoole Case* (1930) *Dec. & Op. of Com.*, p. 124, at pp. 128–29. The dissenting commissioner was clearly wrong, however, in considering an affidavit by the claimant as a "confession" in civil law countries and in believing that the subscription to a solemn affirmation always implied the possibility of cross-examination. He seemed also to have neglected entirely the moral effect of an oath or solemn affirmation.

Cf. Mex.-U.S. Special Cl.Com. (1923): *Naomi Russell Case* (1931), Opinion of American Commissioner who spoke of the "moral sanction" and "legal sanction," *Op. of Com., 1926–1931*, p. 144 at p. 54.

An oath always enhances the probative value of a statement whether emanating from a disinterested person, or from an interested party.[45] Thus in the *Fouilloux Case* (1922), the Franco-German Mixed Arbitral Tribunal, in the absence of any satisfactory evidence as to the value of the articles which were the subject of the claim, accepted the statement of the claimant after administering to him an oath in Court as to the sincerity and veracity of his claim.[46] An oath may be a sufficient consideration to give to the statement of a disinterested person satisfactory probative value and the character of being true. Thus the British-Mexican Claims Commission (1926), in accepting the affidavit of a third person as sufficient corroborative evidence, said:—

> " He is himself not interested in the decision on the claim, and it is difficult to see why he should have committed perjury." [47]

The allegation of the claimant supported by the affidavit of even one creditable witness is thus often considered as sufficiently established in the absence of countervailing evidence,[48] although it has sometimes been contended that the testimony of one single witness cannot constitute full proof.[49] While trustworthy

[45] *Cf.* Brit.-Mex.Cl.Com. (1926): *Kidd Case* (Demurrer), *Dec. & Op. of Com.*, p. 50, at p. 51: " From one point of view, an affidavit sworn by a father concerning the birth of his child has more value than the statement [*sic*] he may make to the Registrar of Births, since the latter statements are not made upon oath." *Cf. infra*, p. 317, note 65.

[46] 3 T.A.M. p. 108, at p. 110. *Cf.* also Ital.-Ven.M.C.C. (1903): *Cervetti Case*, *Ven.Arb. 1903*, p. 658. In the absence of satisfactory evidence, the facts of the case were elucidated by means of examining the claimant under oath by the Commission.

[47] *Stacpoole Case* (1930), *Dec. & Op. of Com.*, p. 124, at p. 126.

[48] *Stacpoole Case* (1930) *ibid. Id*: *Ward Case* (1931), *Further Dec. & Op. of Com.*, p. 107. The same Commission in the *Payne Case* (1931) (*ibid.*, 110, at p. 111) recalled that in the *Mexico City Bombardment Claims* (1930), § 5 (*Dec. & Op. of Com.*, p. 100, at pp. 102–103), they accepted the depositions of those claimants only when they were corroborated by the affidavit of an independent witness, while rejecting that of another claimant whose deposition was not so corroborated. *Cf.* also the Mex.-U.S. G.C.C. (1923) in the *Chattin Case* (1927) (*Op. of Com. 1927*, p. 422, at pp. 438–39) explaining why the uncorroborated statement of claimants concerning ill-treatment in prison could not in general be accepted without reserve and why in the *Harry Roberts Case* (1926) (*ibid.*, p. 100) it was accepted only because it was corroborated by a contemporaneous statement of the American Consul.

[49] Brit.-Mex.Cl.Com. (1926): *Cameron Case* (Demurrer) (1929), Separate Opinion of Mexican Commissioner, *Dec. & Op. of Com.*, p. 33, at p. 49: " As a general rule the testimony of a single witness, however honourable he may be, cannot constitute full proof." The old adage *Testis unus testis nullus*, generally abandoned in modern legal systems, is not valid in international law where the judge enjoys complete freedom in assessing the evidence.

affidavits have been accepted as satisfactory evidence by international tribunals in the absence of rebutting evidence,[50] their defective character, as has already been mentioned, is not unrecognised by international tribunals.[51] As the sole Arbitrator in the *Walfisch Bay Case* (1911) observed:—

> "All the evidence alluded to has been produced out of court, in the sense that the arbitrator has not been able to conduct any cross-examination and without being disputed, inasmuch as the party prejudiced by it has not cross-examined the witness either, circumstances which, though they do not deserve blame and appear easily explicable in the present case, certainly diminish the value of the evidence." [52]

It follows *a contrario* that where the testimony of a witness has successfully undergone the interrogation of the Court and the cross-examination by the opposing party, its value as evidence will be considerably enhanced.[53]

In general, in so far as they can be established, the antecedents and character of a person would influence the probative value to be attributed to his testimony,[54] and if conscious

[50] *Cf.* also Neth.-Ven. M.C.C. (1903): *Evertsz Case, Ven.Arb. 1903*, p. 904, at p. 905.

[51] See *supra*, pp. 310 *et seq. Cf.* also Chil.-U.S. Cl.Com. (1892): *E. C. Murphy Case*, 3 *Int.Arb.*, p. 2262, at p. 2265: see, however, D.O. by American Commissioner, *ibid.*, at p. 2272.

[52] *Award*, Recital XLVII (Cd. 5857, p. 29). *Cf.* Chil.-U.S. Cl.Com. (1892): *Thorndike Case*, 3 *Int.Arb.*, p. 2274, at pp. 2275–76.

[53] *Cf.* Brit.-Mex. Cl.Com. (1926): *Cameron Case* (1929), *Dec. & Op. of Com.*, p. 33. S.O. by British Commissioner: "Cross-examination in the true sense of the word means that a witness has to face the ordeal of an open court in which he is verbally cross-questioned by counsel, both with regard to the facts of the case, and his own antecedents and credibility. The value of this method of ascertaining the truth lies in the personal contact between the witness, who has no idea of what questions may be asked him, and the personality of the advocate who puts the questions to him. The effect of the evidence of a witness subjected to this ordeal may be completely destroyed. In this sense the evidence of a witness who has been cross-examined is of greater weight than an *ex parte* statement" (p. 43). The British Commissioner in a preceding passage appeared to construe the meaning of interrogation by the court too narrowly. While cross-examination may not be the exact term, interrogation may consist in questions freely put by the judge to the witness and in such a case what the British Commissioner has said with regard to cross-examination "in the true sense of the word" should apply all the more to the interrogation by the court. Interrogation by the court and cross-examination by the opposing party are admitted in the procedure of the P.C.I.J. (Statute, Art. 43 V, Rules (1936), Art. 53), I.C.J. (Statute, Art. 43 (5), Rules, Art. 53), the I.M.T. at Nuremburg (Charter, Arts. 16 (*e*), 17), and for the Far East (Charter, Arts. 9 (*d*), 11).

[54] *Cf.* Hague Commission of Inquiry: *The Tubantia* (1922), 2 H.C.R., p. 135 at p. 140. The Commission took into consideration that the witness was a person who had served a prison sentence. *White Case* (1864) 2 *Arb.Int.*, p. 305, at p. 322: "It appears indisputably from the documents that White,

untruth is found in a testimony, no weight will be attached to such statements.[55]

The purpose of evidence being to prove the truth of an alleged fact, testimony is useful only inasmuch as it purports to testify knowledge of its truth and reality. Thus the Mexican-United States General Claims Commission (1922) has held that:—

"Affidavits constitute full proof either when stating acts of the affiant or acts that said affiant knew directly, but when they contain hearsay evidence or only refer to rumours, their value diminishes considerably, at times to such an extent as to become void."[56]

For this reason, testimony even by persons directly or indirectly interested in a case may be accorded due weight if they are the persons best informed of the facts,[57] while testimony even by "respectable" persons would be given little, if any, weight,

being at the time of his arrest a foreigner without occupation, without income and without fixed address, was not at all in a situation to warrant particular credence for his words" (Transl.).

On the other hand, the "known respectability" of a person may enhance the probative value of his testimony, see *supra*, p. 312.

[55] *Cf. White Case* (1864), *ibid.*, at p. 323. Having given examples of the deponent's "voluntary alterations of the truth," the award said: "One should not then attach any weight to the assertions of a man who shows so little respect for the truth" (Transl.).

Cf. also Germ.-U.S. M.C.C. (1922): *Lehigh Valley Railroad Co. Case* (1939), *Op. & Dec.*, p. 1.

[56] *McCurdy Case* (1929) *Op. of Com. 1929*, p. 137, at p. 141. Brit.-Mex. Cl.Com. (1926): *Shone Case* (1930), *Dec. & Op. of Com.*, p. 136, at p. 140. See also ICJ: *Corfu Channel Case* (Merits) (1949), *ICJ Reports 1949*, p. 4, at pp. 16–17, regarding the statements of the witness Kovacic. See also Krylov's D.O., *loc. cit.*, p. 68.

Cf. Walfisch Bay Case (1911), Cd. 5857, Recital XLIX. See also Recital LI (i).

Compare Brit.-Mex. Cl.Com. (1926): *Tracy Case* (1930) (*Dec. & Op. of Com.*, p. 118, at p. 121) with Mex.-U.S. G.C.C. (1923): *Pomeroy's El Paso Transfer Co. Case* (1930) (*Op. of Com. 1931*, p. 1, at p. 4). In the former case the affidavit of the president of a company on matters relating to the affairs of the company was accepted by the Commission, while in the latter case it was considered as of little value; for, in the latter case, the witness did not assume office till after the events in question had taken place. Consequently his knowledge of them was considered "second hand." A comparison of these two cases shows the importance of personal knowledge.

See also Chil.-U.S. Cl.Com. (1892): *Murphy Case*, 3 *Int.Arb.*, p. 2262, at p. 2271. Mex.-U.S. G.C.C. (1923): *Mallén Case* (1927), C.O. by American Commissioner, *Op. of Com. 1927*, p. 254, at p. 269.

[57] Mex.-U.S. G.C.C. (1923): *Dillon Case* (1928), C.O. by American Commissioner, *Op. of Com. 1929*, p. 61, at p. 65. *The Montijo Case* (1875), 2 *Int. Arb.*, p. 1421, at p. 1434. Brit.-Mex. Cl.Com. (1926): *Mexico City Bombardment Claims* (1930), D.O. by British Commissioner, *Dec. Op. of Com.*, p. 100, at p. 109; *Scrope Case* (Merits) (1931), *Further Dec. & Op. of Com.*, p. 269, at pp. 270–1. Mex.-U.S. G.C.C. (1923): *Dyches Case* (1929), *Op. of Com. 1929*, p. 193, at p. 195.

if based on hearsay.[58] For the same reason, testimony should, as far as possible, be individual[59] and spontaneous.[60] The competency of the witness to grasp the exact truth of the things to which he testifies is naturally also an important consideration in estimating the value of his testimony.[61] The testimony of experts will, therefore, usually possess greater probative force.[62] Moreover, witnesses are only expected to testify to facts within their knowledge. The legal conclusion to be drawn from these facts is a matter for the tribunal.[63]

With regard to the testimony generally, it may be said in the words of the British-United States Arbitral Tribunal (1910) that " Allowance must be made for infirmities of memory," [64]

58 Mex.-U.S. Cl.Com. (1868) *Cramer Case* (1876) 4 *Int.Arb.*, p. 3250, at p. 3250: " Anyone who carefully reads the evidence of the three witnesses, one of whom was the United States consul, will acquire the conviction that it was obtained principally from hearsay." Claims dismissed for insufficiency of proof.

59 *Cf.* Mex.-U.S. G.C.C. (1923): *Pomeroy's El Paso Transfer Co. Case* (1930), *Op. of Com. 1931*, p. 1, at p. 5: " It is not denied that the statement of a person who confirms what another states in detail may have some value, but it is unquestionably true that in order to form a definite opinion each witness must set forth in his own manner the things he saw or knew since the comparison of different statements throws a light upon the facts equivalent to a confrontation of witnesses."

60 *Cf.* Mex.-U.S. Cl.Com. (1868): *Ignacio Torres Case*, 4 *Int.Arb.*, p. 3798, at pp. 3799–800: " The civil law discountenances suggestive questions as much as the common law disapproves of leading questions. At least this is the case in those countries in which the civil law is the basis of the legal fabric, and with which I am acquainted; and I must suppose that it is so likewise in Mexico. The whole disapproval of leading or suggestive questions in the different law systems is dictated by morality and a simple sense of justice, which can no longer be disregarded, whatever used to be done in times happily past."

61 *Cf.* Portugo-German Arbitration (1919): *Naulilaa Incident* (1928), 2 UNRIAA, p. 1011, at p. 1020: Reservation made by tribunal on the probative force of the depositions of a person regarding conversations held in a language which he hardly understood although he was supposed to be an interpreter. *Cf.* also *ibid.*, p. 1024.

62 Mex.-U.S. G.C.C. (1923): *I. R. Clark Case* (1928), *Op. of Com. 1929*, p. 131, at pp. 131–2: " Whatever may be the facts with respect to this particular matter, careful consideration must be given in connection therewith to what may be called expert testimony accompanying the memorial. This is an affidavit of a physician. . . ."

ICJ: *Corfu Channel Case* (Merits) (1949), *ICJ Report 1949*, p. 4, at p. 21. Pan.-U.S. G.C.C. (1926): *De Sabla Case* (1933), Hunt's *Report*, p. 379, at p. 448. Spanish Zone of Morocco Claims (1923), *Rapport VI* (1925), 2 UNRIAA, p. 615, at p. 735.

Cf. ICJ: *Corfu Channel Case* (Compensation) (1949) D.O. by Ečer *ICJ Reports 1949*, p. 244, at p. 253.

63 Mex.-U.S. G.C.C. (1923): *Hatton Case* (1928) *Op. of Com. 1929*, p. 6, at p. 7: *Re* nationality.

Mex.-U.S. Special Cl.Com. (1923): *Naomi Russell Case* (1931) Opinion of American Commissioner, *Op. of Com. 1926–1931*, p. 44, at p. 54.

64 Brit.-U.S. Cl.Arb. (1910): *Studer Case* (1925) Nielsen's *Report*, p. 547, at p. 552. Brit.-Mex. Cl.Com. (1926): *Cameron Case* (1929) *Dec. & Op. of Com.* p. 33, at p. 35. *Abu Dhabi Oil Arbitration* (1951) 1 I.C.L.Q. (1952), p. 247, at pp. 259–60.

and, between two testimonies, that which is nearer in time to the event attested will ordinarily be given greater credence.[65] While a circumstantial account of things and events would give the impression of veracity,[66] too detailed testimony may, in certain circumstances, also arouse suspicion.[67] While a certain amplification by a witness in his account through the addition of details does not destroy the value of his testimony,[68] inconsistencies, obscurities and patent errors contained in a deposition will obviously diminish its probative force.[69] Moreover, those who testify to things which are most unlikely,[70] obviously erroneous or naturally impossible will of course not be believed.[71]

As regards the credibility of witnesses in general, while it has been seen that persons who are not interested in the claim are generally considered impartial, where special relations exist between the witnesses and the party in whose favour they testify, such relations may be taken into account in weighing their testimony. In a claim presented on behalf of an individual, even though in international law this is regarded as the claim of his State,[71a] the personal, business or other relations between the individual claimant and the third persons whose testimony is offered may be legitimately considered by the tribunal.[72] In the *Walfisch Bay Case* (1911), which involved national claims, the Arbitrator, finding that:—

> " The witnesses brought forward by one or the other depend in some way or other, by reason of nationality, residence, or office, on the State in whose favour they are giving evidence,"

[65] Brit.-Mex. Cl.Com. (1926): *Tracy Case* (1930) *Dec. & Op. of Com.*, p. 118, at p. 122; *Clapham Case* (1931), *Further Dec. & Op. of Com.*, p. 159, at p. 161. Chil.-U.S. Cl.Com. (1892): *Murphy Case*, 3 *Int.Arb.*, p. 2262.

[66] Brit.-Mex. Cl.Com. (1926): *Delamain Case* (Merits) (1931), *Further Dec. & Op. of Com.*, p. 222, at p. 224.

[67] Mex.-U.S. Cl.Com. (1868): *Ignacio Torres Case*, 4 *Int.Arb.*, p. 3798, at p. 3799.

[68] Hague Commission of Inquiry: *The Tubantia* (1922), 2 H.C.R., p. 135, at p. 137.

[69] Brit.-Mex. Cl.Com. (1926): *Shone Case* (1930), *Dec. & Op of Com.*, p. 136, at p. 140.

[70] Belgo-German M.A.T.: *Cattoor Case* (1924), 4 T.A.M., p. 702, at p. 704.

[71] ICJ: *Corfu Channel Case* (Merits) (1949), D.O. by Krylov, *ICJ Reports 1949*, p. 4, at p. 68.

[71a] See PCIJ: *Mavrommatis Palestine Concessions* (1924) A. 2, p. 12.

[72] Mex.-U.S. G.C.C. (1923): *Parker Case* (1926), *Op. of Com. 1927*, p. 35, at p. 37. *Cf.* Czechoslovak-German M.A.T.: Rules of Procedure, Art. 39 (1 T.A.M., pp. 948–57). Persons in the direct line of descent of the parties, brothers and sisters, uncles and nephews, and spouses, even when divorced, are disqualified as witnesses although they may be heard, not under oath, for the sake of information.

Cf. however, *supra*, p. 315.

stated that this fact,

"though it does not properly constitute a legal objection, is a ground for a reasonable presumption that they may accentuate their assertions, whether they wish it or not, in a definite sense."[73]

As regards testimonial evidence in general, therefore, the same Arbitrator adopted a method of appraisal which, he said,

"is in accordance with the rules of sane criticism, in conformity with the leading system in modern law and the only one acceptable in the proceedings of an international arbitration, in which no principle or positive rule imposes any other limit on the powers of the arbitrator,"

whereby, testimonial evidence introduced by either one of the parties,

"the value of which, being in favour of the high party which invokes it, should be weighed more carefully than is necessary when it is unfavourable to that party."[74]

In conclusion, it may be said that a tribunal in deciding whether to give credence to an allegation "should take into consideration all the circumstances of the affair, the inherent probability or otherwise of the alleged facts and the likelihood of, and opportunity for, fraud or exaggeration"[75] or error; and in examining testimonial evidence in general should consider "a person's sources of information and his capacity to ascertain and his willingness to tell the truth."[76]

DOCUMENTARY EVIDENCE

"Testimonial evidence," it has been said, "due to the frailty of human contingencies is most liable to arouse distrust."[77] On the other hand, documentary evidence stating, recording, or sometimes even incorporating the facts at issue, written or executed

[73] *Award*, Recital XLVIII, Cd. 5857, p. 29. *Cf.*, on the other hand, Hague Commission of Inquiry: *The Tubantia* (1922) 2 H.C.R., pp. 135, 140: "The manner in which this witness has attempted to offer his testimony in favour of a foreign government is not likely to inspire the necessary confidence."

[74] *Award*, Recital XLVI, Cd. 5857, p. 29.

[75] Brit.-Mex. Cl.Com. (1926): *Mexico City Bombardment Claims* (1930), D.O. by British Commissioner, *Dec. & Op. of Com.*, p. 100, at p. 109.

[76] Mex.-U.S. G.C.C. (1923): *Kling Case* (1930), *Op. of Com. 1931*, p. 36, at p. 47.

[77] See Mex.-U.S. Special Cl.Com. (1923): *Naomi Russell Case* (1931), *Op. of Com. 1926–31*, p. 44, at p. 184.

either contemporaneously or shortly after the events in question by persons having direct knowledge thereof, and for purposes other than the presentation of a claim or the support of a contention in a suit, is ordinarily free from this distrust and considered of higher probative value. As we have seen, however, an international tribunal "can assuredly also apply common-sense reasoning with respect to the value of what might be called purely documentary evidence." [78] On account of the great variety in the nature and form of documentary evidence it would be still more difficult here to give to such common-sense reasoning any precise formulation without falling into dangerous over-generalisation. It may, however, be said that similar considerations to those which influence the probative force of testimonial evidence apply *mutatis mutandis* to documentary evidence, particularly with respect to hearsay.[79]

With regard to the appraisal of evidence as a whole, it may be said that the amount of evidence required to sustain an allegation may vary with the nature of the allegation, its relative importance in the case, the strength of the legal and logical presumptions for or against such an allegation and the relative ease or difficulty for the parties to produce evidence in support or in rebuttal. Thus the Portugo-German Arbitral Tribunal (1919) has held that:—

"In their appraisal of the evidence, the arbitrators will be obliged to be strict with regard to the prejudicial act, its author, and its date; for these are the very conditions of their competency. They may be less severe with regard to the amount of damage and be satisfied with simple presumptions; taking into account particular difficulties the injured owners may have in establishing what took place in Belgium in their absence during the German occupation." [80]

[78] *Naomi Russell Case* (1931), *ibid.*, at p. 88.

[79] *Cf.* Brit.-Mex. Cl.Com. (1926): *Cameron Case* (Demurrer) (1929), S.O. by British Commissioner, *Dec. & Op. of Com.*, p. 33, at p. 44. The presumption in favour of government documents does not cover hearsay statements of fact. P.C.A.: *Palmas Case* (1928), 2 H.C.R., p. 83, at pp. 108–9, 111, with regard to maps based not on authentic information carefully collected but on existing maps.

[80] *Claims for Losses suffered in Belgium* (1930) 2 UNRIAA, p. 1011, at p. 1040. (Transl.)

Cf. Mex.-U.S. G.C.C. (1923): *McCurdy Case* (1929) *Op. of Com. 1929*, p. 137, at pp. 140–1: "In this case it is endeavoured to prove misconduct, in a grave degree, of Mexican officials and therefore the Agency advancing the

"BEST EVIDENCE" RULE

As a general rule, to quote the Final Report of the sole Commissioner of the United States Domestic Commission established pursuant to the Convention with Spain of February 17, 1834:—

"Each claimant was required to produce the highest evidence, which the nature of his claim admitted, to establish the allegations of his memorial." [81]

Where evidence of better quality should be available and its non-production is not satisfactorily explained, this will weigh against the party whose allegations may either be proved or disproved by such evidence.[82] Where documentary evidence should be available, this must be produced.[83] The party whose negligence has resulted in failure to produce documentary evidence must bear the consequences of such non-production.[84]

charge should submit evidence of the highest and most conclusive character." ICJ: *Corfu Channel Case* (Merits) (1929) *ICJ Reports 1949*, p. 4, at p. 17. A charge of less gravity, it seems, may be substantiated with less evidence.

Cf. also the slender requirement of proof in a question of minor importance in the issue of the case, Mex.-U.S. G.C.C. (1923): *Acosta Case* (1928) *Op. of Com. 1929*, p. 121, at p. 121. See also *supra*, p. 309, note 30.

81 U.S. Domestic Commission, Spanish Claims (Act of 1836): *Final Report* (1838) 5 *Int.Arb.*, p. 4542, at p. 4544.

82 Mex.-U.S. G.C.C. (1923): *McCurdy Case* (1929) *Op. of Com. 1929*, p. 137, at p. 141; *Pomeroy's El Paso Transfer Co. Case* (1930) *Op. of Com. 1931*, p. 1, at p. 6.

Cf. Mex.-U.S. Cl.Com. (1868): *La Abra Silver Mining Co. Case* (1875) 2 *Int.Arb.*, p. 1324. Umpire relied on "respectable" testimony, although he recognised that evidence, presumably available, in the form of books or reports from the company had, without explanation, not been produced (p. 1328). The claim was subsequently discovered to be a fraud and the money awarded was returned to Mexico. See *infra*, p. 359.

83 Brit.-Mex. Cl.Com. (1926): *Mexico City Bombardment Claims* (1930) D.O. by British Commissioner, *Dec. & Op. of Com.*, p. 100, at p. 109: "Thus, in the case of a contract, there is a principle which is almost universally admitted and with which I am in entire agreement, that, in general, both the existence and the terms of the contract must be established by a written document signed by the parties, for in making a contract it should always be possible to reduce it to writing, and this, moreover, is the common practice of civilised mankind." See footnote 84.

U.S. Domestic Commission, Spanish Claims (Act of 1836): *Final Report* (1838) 5 *Int.Arb.*, p. 4542, at p. 4544.

See also the first two cases cited in the preceding footnote.

84 *Pomeroy's El Paso Transfer Co. Case* (1930) *loc. cit.*, at p. 6. Claim for payment from Mexican Government for alleged services rendered at latter's order. No evidence submitted except two affidavits from members of the claimant company. Held that at least a written order should have been required from the Mexican authorities. The decision in this case concerned only the problem of proof. Even for an international agreement between two States the written form is not necessary (see PCIJ: *Legal Status of Eastern Greenland Case* (1933) D.O. by Anzilotti, A/B. 53, p. 91). *Aguilar-Amory and Royal Bank of Canada (Tinoco) Case* (1923) 1 UNRIAA, p. 369, at p. 393. *Cf. Lamu Case* (1889) 5 *Int.Arb.* p. 4940, at p. 4942.

"But in the case of a tort or a criminal matter it is obviously almost always impossible to have any document attesting the facts." [85]

Much, however, depends upon the circumstances of the case as to the amount of evidence that may be available.[86] While a Government cannot rely on its own lack of power to procure evidence as an excuse for the non-production of available evidence when such power could easily be obtained,[87] the collecting of evidence for an international dispute is not a valid reason for violating the rights of another State.[88]

In general, therefore, as the British-Mexican Claims Commission (1926) said with regard to the amount of evidence to be adduced by the claimant:—

"He is to create the conviction that he has earnestly tried to place all existing evidence at our disposal," [89]

although, as was said by the same Commission in the *Odell Case* (1931):—

"The Commission also realise that the weighing of outside evidence, if any such be produced, may be influenced by the degree to which it was possible to produce proof of a better quality. In cases where it is obvious that everything has been done to collect stronger evidence and where all efforts to do so have failed, a court

[85] Brit.-Mex. Cl.Com. (1926): *Mexico City Bombardment Claims* (1930), D.O. by British Commissioner, *Dec. & Op. of Com.*, p. 100, at p. 109.

[86] Thus in a case where the claimant complained of being injured by the derailment of a train, the Brit.-Mex. Cl.Com. (1926) said: "The wrecking of a military train by revolutionaries in the neighbourhood of one of the principal towns of the country, is a fact that could hardly have passed unnoticed. It must have left some trace in the archives of the Railway Company and in the contemporary press. Mr. Odell relates that on the fatal spot itself he was attended to by a surgeon, that the Superintendent of the Railway Company at Puebla also spoke to him at the scene of the derailment, that he was as soon as possible taken to the Hospital at Puebla, that he resumed work nine months later, and that finally, in June, 1912, he was given a certificate of dismissal on account of his disability to serve. It is difficult to believe that none of those sources could furnish confirmation of one or more of the facts alleged by the claimant". (*Odell Case* (1931) *Further Dec. & Op. of Com.*, p. 61, at pp. 63–4). *Cf.* U.S.-Ven. M.C.C. (1903): *Gage Case*, *Ven.Arb. 1903*, p. 164, at p. 167: "From the nature of the facts as to the treatment of prisoners by their gaoler, it will always be difficult to find other witnesses besides the prisoners themselves."

[87] Germ.-U.S. M.C.C. (1922): *Lehigh Valley Railroad Co. Case* (1933) *Dec. & Op.*, p. 1084, at pp. 1126–7.

[88] *Cf.* ICJ: *Corfu Channel Case* (Merits) (1949), *ICJ Reports, 1949*, p. 1, at pp. 34–35.

[89] *Gill Case* (1931), *Further Dec. & Op. of Com.*, p. 85, at p. 90.

can be more easily satisfied than in cases where no such endeavour seems to have been made." [90]

The general principle requiring the best available evidence is thus tempered by considerations of possibility.[91]

CIRCUMSTANTIAL EVIDENCE

In cases where direct evidence of a fact is not available, it is a general principle of law that proof may be administered by means of circumstantial evidence. In the *Corfu Channel Case* (Merits) (1949), before the International Court of Justice, Judge Azevedo said in his dissenting opinion:—

"A condemnation, even to the death penalty, may be well-founded on indirect evidence and may nevertheless have the same value as a judgment by a court which has founded its conviction on the evidence of witnesses.

"It would be going too far for an international court to insist on direct and visual evidence and to refuse to admit, after reflection, a reasonable amount of human presumptions with a view to reaching that state of moral, human certainty with which, despite the risks of occasional errors, a court of justice must be content." [92]

This part of his opinion is in agreement with the majority decision, which, in admitting proof by inferences of fact (*présomptions de fait*) or circumstantial evidence, held that:—

"This indirect evidence is admitted in all systems of law, and its use is recognised by international decisions. It must be regarded as of special weight when it is based on a series of facts linked together and leading logically to a single conclusion . . . The proof may be drawn from inferences of fact [*présomptions de fait*], provided that they leave *no room* for reasonable doubt." [93]

[90] *Ibid.*, p. 61, at p. 63.
[91] *Cf.* also ICJ: *Corfu Channel Case* (Merits) (1949); *ICJ Reports, 1949*, p. 4, at p. 18. In case one State is the victim of an unlawful act committed within the exclusive territorial jurisdiction of another State, "the fact of this exclusive territorial control exercised by one State within its frontiers has a bearing upon the methods of proof available to establish the knowledge of that State as to such events. By reason of this exclusive control, the other State, the victim of a breach of international law, is often unable to furnish direct proof of facts giving rise to responsibility. Such a State should be allowed a more liberal recourse to inferences of facts and circumstantial evidence."
[92] *ICJ Reports, 1949*, p. 4, at pp. 90–91.
[93] *Ibid.*, at p. 18. Italics of the Court. From the established fact that Albania kept a strict watch over the Corfu Channel during the whole period when the mines could have been laid there, and the established fact that any laying of mines in the Channel during that period would have been detected from the observation posts set up in Albania, the "Court draws the conclusion that the

PRIMA FACIE EVIDENCE

Sometimes, in view of its particular nature, conclusive proof of a certain fact is impossible. With regard to the nationality of claimants, for instance, the British-Mexican Claims Commission (1926) held:—

"It would be impossible for any international commission to obtain evidence of nationality amounting to certitude unless a man's life outside the State to which he belongs is to be traced from day to day. Such conclusive proof is impossible and would be nothing less than *probatio diabolica*. All that an international commission can reasonably require in the way of proof of nationality is prima facie evidence sufficient to satisfy the Commissioners and to raise the presumption of nationality, leaving it open to the respondent State to rebut the presumption by producing evidence to show that the claimant has lost his nationality through his own act or some other cause."[94]

In cases where proof of a fact presents extreme difficulty, a tribunal may thus be satisfied with less conclusive proof, *i.e.*, prima facie evidence.

laying of the minefield which caused the explosions on October 22nd, 1946, could not have been accomplished without the knowledge of the Albanian Government" (p. 22). In other words, knowledge by the Albanian Government was considered proved. Judge Badawi Pasha and also the *ad hoc* judge in their dissenting opinions, concurred in the use of circumstantial evidence, although both emphasised that the conclusion adopted must be the only rational one to be drawn from the established circumstances (pp. 60, 120). Judge Krylov alone doubted if State responsibility could be proved by indirect evidence (p. 69).

In cases before the Brit.-Mex.Cl.Com. (1926), knowledge of the Mexican authorities of certain acts was inferred from their public notoriety in the locality. See *McNeill Case* (1931), *Further Dec. & Op. of Com.*, p. 96, at p. 100; *The Sonora (Mexico) Land and Timber Co. Case* (1931), *ibid.*, p. 292, at p. 296; *Taylor Case* (1931), *ibid.*, p. 297, at p. 298.

See other examples of the use of circumstantial evidence: Hague Commission of Inquiry: *The Tubantia* (1922) 2 H.C.R., p. 135. Germ.-U.S. M.C.C. (1922); *Taft Case* (1926), *Dec. & Op.*, p. 801. In the latter case, the desired inference from the facts was rebutted by conclusive counter-evidence. Portugo-German Arbitration (1919): *The Cysne Case* (1930), 2 UNRIAA, p. 1011, at p. 1056; *supra*, p. 303, note 11.

Spanish Zone of Morocco Claims (1923): Claim I: *Rzini (Tetuan Orchards) Case* (1924), 2 UNRIAA, p. 615, at p. 654.

94 *Lynch Case* (1929), *Dec. & Op. of Com.*, p. 20, at p. 21. The Commissioners were of the opinion that where a fact can be more easily and conclusively established, *e.g.*, birth, death, etc., a stricter degree of proof would be required (*ibid.*).

See, also, Hungaro-Serb-Croat-Slovene M.A.T.: *Cie pour la Construction du Chemin de Fer d'Ogulin à la Frontière, S.A., Case* (1926), 6 T.A.M., p. 505. Restitution of articles under Art. 250, Treaty of Trianon. Claimants having produced sufficient proof to establish at least a presumption in favour of their ownership, the Tribunal could not admit "that the Serb-Croat-Slovene State is legally entitled to exact the absolute proof of ownership, this *probatio diabolica* being generally impossible" (p. 509. Transl.).

"Prima facie evidence has been defined as evidence 'which unexplained or uncontradicted, is sufficient to maintain the proposition affirmed.'" [95]

It does not create a moral certainty as to the truth of the allegation, but provides sufficient ground for a reasonable belief in its truth, rebuttable by evidence to the contrary.[96] The absence of evidence in rebuttal is an essential consideration in the admission of prima facie evidence. Where the opposite party can easily produce countervailing evidence, its non-production may be taken into account in weighing the evidence before the Commission.[97] As the American Commissioner said in the *Naomi Russell Case* (1931), when referring to those "common-sense principles underlying" the rules of evidence in domestic law:—

"It [the Commission] can analyse evidence in the light of what one party has the power to produce and the other party has the power to explain or contravert. And in appropriate cases it can draw reasonable inferences from the non-production of evidence." [98]

Again, in the *Kling Case* (1930), the Mexican-United States General Claims Commission (1923) said:—

"A claimant's case should not necessarily suffer by the non-production of evidence by the respondent. It was observed by the Commission in the *Hatton Case, Op. of Com., Wash., 1929*, pp. 6, 10, that, while it was not the function of a respondent government to make a case for the claimant government, certain inferences could

[95] Mex.-U.S. G.C.C. (1923): *Kling Case* (1930) *Op. of Com. 1931*, p. 36, at p. 49, quoting 23 *Corpus Juris*, p. 9.

[96] *E.g.*, Brit.-Mex. Cl.Com. (1926): *Lynch Case* (1929), *Dec. & Op. of Com.*, p. 20, at p. 22. In the absence of evidence impugning the accuracy of a consular certificate, this, although it "cannot be considered as absolute proof of nationality," was "accepted as prima facie evidence." Compare this case with the *Cameron Case* (Demurrer) (1929), decided by the same Commission, *ibid.*, p. 33, at p. 36: "The certificate of consular registration put in by the British Agent does raise a presumption of British nationality, though that presumption is rebutted by another document put in by the Mexican Government." Though the latter was not conclusive, the former was considered weakened to such an extent that British nationality was considered not to have been established.

[97] *Cf.* Fran.-Ven. M.C.C. (1902): *Brun Case*, Ralston's *Report*, p. 5 at p. 25: "The Umpire might hesitate to adopt these findings if it were not true, and had not been always true, that the respondent Government could ascertain and produce before this mixed commission the exact facts regarding the positions and movements of its own soldiers, and the position and movements of the insurgent forces at the time in question."

[98] Mex.-U.S. Special Cl.Com. (1923): *Naomi Russell Case* (1931), *Op. of Com. 1926–1931*, p. 44, at p. 88.

be drawn from the non-production of available evidence in the possession of the former. See also the *Melczer Mining Co. Case*, *ibid.*, pp. 228, 233. The Commission has discussed the conditions under which, when a claimant government has made a prima facie case, account may be taken of the non-production of evidence by the respondent government, or of unsatisfactory explanation of the non-production of evidence. Case of *L. J. Kalklosch*, *ibid.*, p. 126. [In this case, the Commission said: ' In the absence of official records the non-production of which has not been satisfactorily explained, records contradicting evidence accompanying the Memorial respecting wrongful treatment of the claimant, the Commission can not properly reject that evidence ' (p. 130)]." [99]

Whilst it is true, as the German Commissioner observed in the *Lehigh Valley Railroad Co. Case* (1936) that:—

" Mere suspicions never can be a basic element of juridical findings," [1]

where counter-proof can easily be produced but its non-production is not satisfactorily explained,

" it may therefore be assumed that such evidence as could have been produced on this point would not have refuted the charge in relation thereto." [2]

The inference in every case must, however, be one which can reasonably be drawn.[3] The situation, as established by prima facie evidence, coupled with the adverse presumption arising from the non-production of available counter-evidence, is thus sufficient to create a moral conviction of the truth of an allegation. This was regarded as a general principle of law by the American Commissioner who said in his concurring opinion in the *Daniel Dillon Case* (1928):—

" Evidence produced by one party in a litigation may be supported by legal presumptions which arise from the non-production

[99] *Op. of Com. 1931*, p. 36, at pp. 44–5. See other cases therein cited. See also *Aguilar-Amory and Royal Bank of Canada (Tinoco) Case* (1923) 1 UNRIAA, p. 369, at p. 393.

[1] Germ.-U.S. M.C.C. (1922), *Dec. & Op.*, p. 1175, at p. 1176. See also *supra*, pp. 309–10.

[2] Mex.-U.S. G.C.C. (1923): *Melczer Mining Co. Case* (1929), *Op. of Com. 1929*, p. 228, at p. 233.
Neth.-Ven.M.C.C. (1903): *Evertsz Case*, *Ven.Arb. 1903*, p. 904, at p. 905.

[3] *Cf.* ICJ: *Corfu Channel Case* (Merits) (1949), *ICJ Reports, 1949*, p. 4, at pp. 32, 129.

of information exclusively in the possession of another party, and this well-known principle of domestic law is one which it seems to me an international tribunal is justified in giving application in a proper case."[4]

An attempt has been made above to elicit some of the "common-sense principles underlying rules of evidence" as they have been applied by international tribunals. It is quite natural, if not inevitable, that these principles should be the same in different legal systems, since, in the final analysis, they merely represent the concrete embodiment of the long experience of judges in seeking to ascertain the truth. To sum up, the words of the British Commissioner in the *Mexico City Bombardment Claims* (1930) may be quoted:—

"If, after giving due weight to all these considerations, it [the Commission] feels a reasonable doubt as to the truth of any alleged fact, that fact cannot be said to be proved. But if the Commissioners, acting as reasonable men of the world and bearing in mind the facts of human nature, do feel convinced that a particular event occurred or state of affairs existed, they should accept such things as established."[5]

In dubio pro reo.[6]

BURDEN OF PROOF

We may now turn to the question of burden of proof and inquire whether international tribunals admit the existence of any general principles of law governing its incidence.

In this connection, the *Parker Case* (1926), decided by the Mexican-United States General Claims Commission (1923), needs to be carefully examined; for the language used by the Commission in that case has sometimes given rise to the impression[7] that, contrary to the view generally accepted by

4 Mex.-U.S. G.C.C. (1923): *Op. of Com., 1929*, p. 61, at p. 65.

5 Brit.-Mex. Cl.Com. (1926): D.O. by British Commissioner, *Dec. & Op. of Com.* p. 100, at p. 109.

6 Span.-U.S. Cl.Com. (1871): *Zaldivar Case* (1882), 3 *Int.Arb.*, p. 2982. U.S.-Ven. M.C.C. (1903): *Gage Case, Ven.Arb. 1903*, p. 164, at p. 167. ICJ: *Corfu Channel Case* (Merits) (1949), D.O. by Ečer, *ICJ Reports 1949*, p. 4, at pp. 120, 124, 129.

7 See Fran.-Mex. Cl.Com. (1924): *Pinson Case* (1928), *Jurisprudence*, p. 1, at pp. 94–5.

international tribunals, it gave a negative answer to the question.[8]

In the first place, the Commission held as follows:—

"The Commission expressly decides that municipal restrictive rules of adjective law or of evidence cannot be here introduced and given effect by clothing them in such phrases as 'universal principles of law,' or 'the general theory of law,' and the like. On the contrary, the greatest liberality will obtain in the admission of evidence before this Commission with a view of discovering the whole truth with respect to each claim submitted. . . . As an international tribunal, the Commission denies the existence in international procedure of rules governing the burden of proof borrowed from municipal procedure."[9]

It may, however, be pointed out that, with regard to principles of adjective law in general, the reference in the decision to "'universal principles of law,' or 'the general theory of law,' and the like," relates only to the misuse of these terms to cover "municipal restrictive rules of adjective law or of evidence" and in no way excludes *a priori* the existence of true general principles of adjective law applicable to all legal systems; for the same Commission clearly recognised that "with respect to matters of evidence they [international tribunals] must give effect to common-sense principles underlying rules of evidence in domestic law."[10]

With regard to the incidence of the burden of proof in particular, international judicial decisions are not wanting which expressly hold that there exists a general principle of law placing the burden of proof upon the claimant and that this principle is applicable to international judicial proceedings. In *The Queen Case* (1872), for instance, it was held that:—

"One must follow, as a general rule of solution, the principle of jurisprudence, accepted by the law of all countries, that it is for the claimant to make the proof of his claim."[11]

[8] *Op. of Com.*, *1927*, p. 35, at pp. 39–40.
[9] *Ibid.*, at p. 39.
[10] See *supra*, p. 308.
[11] 2 *Arb.Int.*, p. 706, at p. 708. (Transl.)
See Lord Phillimore in the Advisory Committee of Jurists for the Establishment of the PCIJ, *Procès-verbaux*, p. 316. Speaking of the "principes du droit commun qui sont applicables aux rapports internationaux," he said: "Another principle of the same kind is that by which the plaintiff must prove his contention under penalty of having his case refused."
Fran.-Germ. M.A.T.: *Firme Ruinart Père et Fils Case* (1927), 7 T.A.M.,

It may, therefore, be asked whether the Mexican-United States General Claims Commission (1923) really maintained that the maxim *onus probandi actori incumbit* did not express a general principle of law or that in any event it was not applicable to international judicial proceedings, thus contradicting *The Queen Case* (1872). The answer would appear to be in the negative. It would seem that the Commission did not use the term " burden of proof " in its usual sense. Thus after saying that " as an international tribunal, the Commission denies the existence in international procedure of rules governing the burden of proof borrowed from municipal procedure," the Commission continued:—

> " On the contrary, it holds that it is the duty of the respective Agencies to co-operate in searching out and presenting to this tribunal all facts throwing any light on the merits of the claim presented." [12]

From the context of this passage, it is clear that the Commission used the term " burden of proof " in the sense of a duty to produce evidence, and to disclose the facts of the case. But the term is used in a different sense when it is asked on whom the burden of proof falls, or when it is said that the burden of proof rests upon this or the other party.

To illustrate the distinction between these two meanings of the term, the *Taft Case* (1926), decided by the German-United States Mixed Claims Commission (1922) may be mentioned. In this case, the claimants alleged that their ship the *Avon* had been sunk by a German submarine. On behalf of the claimants, " all available evidence tending however remotely to establish the loss of the *Avon* through an act of war has been diligently assembled and presented by able counsel," while on behalf of

p. 599, at p. 601: The Tribunal, " in the absence of any contrary provision of the Treaty, can only rely on the usual principle that lays the burden of proof on the plaintiff " (Transl.).

Greco-Turk. M.A.T.: *Banque d'Orient Case* (1928), 7 T.A.M., p. 967, at p. 973.

See also cases cited *infra passim.*

12 *Op. of Com. 1927*, p. 35, at p. 39. The following passages from the same decision are to the same effect: " The Parties before this Commission are sovereign Nations who are in honour bound to make full disclosures of the facts in each case so far as such facts are within their knowledge, or can reasonably be ascertained by them " (p. 40). " Article 75 of the said Hague Convention of 1907 affirms the tenet adopted here by providing that the parties undertake to supply the tribunal, as fully as they consider possible, with all the information required for deciding the case " (p. 40).

the defendant, "a full disclosure has been made to the Commission by the German Agent" of the activities of German submarines operating at the material time in the vicinity of the *Avon's* projected course. In his conclusion the Umpire held, however, that:—

> "Weighing the evidence as a whole . . . , the claimants have failed to discharge the burden resting upon them to prove that the *Avon* was lost through an act of war." [13]

Thus although both parties had scrupulously observed the duty of disclosing all material facts relative to the merits of the claim, it was held that the claimants had failed to discharge their burden of proof. Burden of proof, however closely related to the duty to produce evidence, therefore implies something more.[14] It means that a party having the burden of proof must not only bring evidence in support of his allegations, but must also convince the Tribunal of their truth, lest they be disregarded for want, or insufficiency, of proof.

The real intention of the Mexican-United States General Claims Commission (1923) may be gathered from what it went on to say, after the above quoted passage:—

> "The Commission denies the 'right' of the respondent merely to wait in silence in cases where it is reasonable that it should speak. . . . On the other hand, the Commission rejects the contention that evidence put forward by the claimant and not rebutted by the respondent must necessarily be considered as conclusive. But, when the claimant has established a prima facie case and the respondent has afforded no evidence in rebuttal the latter may not insist that the former pile up evidence to establish its allegations beyond a reasonable doubt without pointing out some reason for doubting. While ordinarily it is encumbent [*sic*] upon the party who alleges a fact to introduce evidence to establish it, yet before this Commission this rule does not relieve the respondent from its obligation to lay before the Commission all evidence within its possession to establish the truth, whatever it may be. . . . In any case where evidence which would probably influence its decision is peculiarly within the knowledge of the claimant or of the respondent government, the

[13] *Dec. & Op.*, p. 801, at p. 805.

[14] The Mex.-U.S. G.C.C. (1923) itself seems also to have accepted this view, since, despite the fact that it identified the principle it enunciated with Art. 75 of the Hague Convention of 1907, it said that that Convention contained no provision as to burden of proof (*loc. cit.*, p. 40).

failure to produce it, unexplained, may be taken into account by the Commission in reaching a decision." [15]

This, then, is not so much a denial of the validity of the maxim *onus probandi actori incumbit* as a general principle of law, but rather a statement that in proper cases the Commission might be satisfied with prima facie evidence whenever the allegations, if unfounded, could be easily disproved by the opposing party. Strictly speaking, however, this is a question of the quantum of evidence required to sustain an allegation or a claim, and not of the burden of proof.

That the Commission in the *Parker Case* (1926) was not speaking of burden of proof, and that in practice it admitted the validity of the general principle *onus probandi actori incumbit* may also be gathered from its decision in the *Pomeroy's El Paso Transfer Co. Case* (1930). In this case, although the deciding Commissioner was of the opinion that:—

"The Mexican Agency has not fully complied, in regard to evidence, with the duties imposed upon it by this arbitration as defined by the Commission in paragraphs 5, 6, 7 of its decision in the case of *William A. Parker*," [16]

he disallowed the claim because:—

"In this case it appears that the evidence submitted by the claimant government is not sufficient to establish a prima facie case." [17]

Indeed, the Commission on several occasions held that:—

"The mere fact that evidence produced by the respondent government is meagre, cannot in itself justify an award in the absence of concrete and convincing evidence produced by the claimant government." [18]

This is all that is meant by the general principle of law that the burden of proof is upon the claimant.

15 *Loc. cit.*, pp. 39–40.
16 *Op. of Com. 1931*, p. 1, at p. 4.
17 *Ibid.*, at p. 7.
18 *Melczer Mining Co. Case* (1929), *Op. of Com. 1929*, p. 228, at p. 233. See also *Archuleta Case* (1928), *ibid.*, p. 73, at p. 77; *Costello Case* (1929), *ibid.*, p. 252, at p. 264.

Thus, in spite of appearance to the contrary, the *Parker Case* (1926), when properly understood, does not deny the validity and applicability of the general principle *onus probandi actori incumbit* in international judicial proceedings. In the first place, when the Tribunal denied the existence of any general legal principles governing the incidence of the burden of proof, it was not using the term in its commonly accepted meaning. Moreover, the Tribunal in practice applied the principle *onus probandi actori incumbit*.

Another point raised by the *Parker Case* (1926) may also be mentioned. The Commission said:—

"The absence of international rules relative to a division of the burden of proof between the parties is especially obvious in international arbitrations between governments in their own right, as in those cases the distinction between a plaintiff and a respondent often is unknown, and both parties often have to file their pleadings at the same time." [19]

To this the *Chevreau Case* (1931) provides a ready answer. The case which was between France and Great Britain concerned alleged unlawful arrest and improper treatment of a French national.

"The Arbitrator, before examining these various grievances, deems it his duty to make some observation concerning the burden of proof. While the British Government asserts that the burden is upon the French Government as the plaintiff, the latter maintains that in the present case there is neither plaintiff nor defendant. In this connection, it calls attention to an Order issued on August 15, 1929, by the Permanent Court of International Justice, where it was said that, the case in issue having been submitted by a *compromis*, there was neither plaintiff nor defendant. But on that point, in the opinion of the Arbitrator, there is a misunderstanding. The Order only refers to a question of procedure and decides nothing in regard to questions relating to the burden of proof. The matter is complicated, and if Article 3 of the *compromis* imposes upon both Parties the duty of 'determining to the satisfaction of the Arbitrator the authenticity of all points of fact offered to establish or disapprove responsibility,' that provision, in the Arbitrator's opinion, is not intended to exclude the application of the ordinary rules of evidence.

[19] *Loc. cit.*, p. 40.

It only shows that there can also be a duty to prove the existence of facts alleged in order to deny responsibility." [20]

Thus, despite the fact that there was no procedural distinction between the plaintiff and defendant, the burden of proof was laid upon France, who was the claimant in fact.[21]

That, in any given case, it is possible to determine the effective positions of the parties without reference to questions of procedure is shown by the *Corfu Channel Case* (Jurisdiction) (1948), where, without considering the form in which the case was submitted, the International Court of Justice held that:—

"There is in fact a claimant, the United Kingdom, and a defendant, Albania." [22]

The *Corfu Channel Case* was first brought before the Court by a unilateral application of the United Kingdom (May 22, 1947). When the Albanian Preliminary Objection to the Court's jurisdiction was rejected by the Court on March 25, 1948, the two parties notified the Court on the same day of the conclusion of a Special Agreement. That Special Agreement formed the basis of subsequent proceedings before the Court in that case.[23] But the respective positions of the parties as regards burden of proof was not thereby altered. As far as the British claim was concerned, the burden of proof was undoubtedly laid upon the United Kingdom.[24] The Court expressly held that the mere fact that an act contrary to international law had occurred in Albanian territory did not shift the burden of proof to Albania.[25]

Indeed, it may be said that the term *actor* in the principle *onus probandi actori incumbit* is not to be taken to mean the plaintiff from the procedural standpoint, but the real claimant in view of the issues involved. The ultimate distinction between the claimant and the defendant lies in the fact that the claimant's submission requires to be substantiated, whilst that of the defendant does not.

It may in fact happen that the claimant is procedurally the defendant, as in the *United States Nationals in Morocco Case*

20 P.C.A.: 2 UNRIAA, p. 1113, at pp. 1124–25.
21 *Cf.* PCIJ: *Oscar Chinn Case* (1924), A/B 63. See particularly, p. 81.
22 *ICJ Reports 1947–1948*, p. 15, at p. 28.
23 (Order of March 26, 1948), *ibid.*, p. 53, at p. 55.
24 (Merits), *ICJ Reports 1949*, p. 4, at pp. 13 *et seq.*
25 *Ibid.*, p. 18.

(1952), between France and the United States.[26] In that case, the United States was in fact in the position of a claimant, in that it claimed special rights and privileges in the French Zone of Morocco and alleged that certain acts of the Moroccan authorities were contrary to such rights and privileges. France, in denying the existence of these rights and privileges and maintaining the legality of the acts of the Moroccan authorities, was in fact in the position of a defendant; for she could rely on the principle that neither restrictions on sovereignty nor international responsibility are to be presumed.[27]

For political reasons, however, the French Government, in order to bring the dispute before the Court, took the initiative and applied to the International Court of Justice under the Optional Clause, thus abandoning, as it said in its Memorial,[28] its logical position as defendant and placing itself, from the procedural standpoint, in the position of a plaintiff. Thereupon, the United States claimed that the burden of proof lay upon France because the latter had assumed the position of plaintiff, and because of "the nature of the legal issues involved." [29]

This, however, was not the view taken by the Court. What the Court in fact did in its judgment was to examine each of the United States claims, and rejected them to the extent to which they were not supported by treaties which the United States was entitled to invoke against Morocco.[30] The United States also adduced "custom and usage" as a basis for some of its alleged special rights and privileges. The Court here specifically laid the burden of proof upon the United States and rejected the allegation for want of sufficient evidence of such a custom binding upon Morocco.[31] In the operative part of the judgment, the Court referred to only one of the Submissions of the French Government. But, even in this case, its rejection of the French Submission that the Decree of December 30, 1948, issued by the French Resident General in Morocco, was lawful, was in fact only a favourable decision on the United States Submission that the Decree violated the treaty rights of the

[26] *ICJ Reports 1952*, p. 176. See the present writer's "Rights of United States Nationals in the French Zone of Morocco," 2 I.C.L.Q. (1953), p. 354.
[27] See *supra*, pp. 305–6.
[28] *ICJ Pleadings*, 1 *Morocco Case*, pp. 29–30.
[29] *Ibid.*, p. 180; *ICJ Reports 1952*, p. 176, at p. 180.
[30] *Cf. ICJ Reports 1952*, p. 176, at pp. 212–13.
[31] *Ibid.*, at pp. 200, 202.

United States derived from the Act of Algeciras of 1906 and its treaty of 1836 with Morocco. Thus, notwithstanding its procedural position of respondent, the burden of proof was laid upon the United States, the claimant in fact.

There may, however, be cases where there is genuinely no distinction between claimant and defendant. Thus in the case of a territorial dispute, both parties put forward rival claims. It will then be incumbent upon each party to substantiate its contention. In the *Palmas Case* (1928), the Arbitrator held that:—

> "Each party is called upon to establish the arguments on which it relies in support of its claim to sovereignty over the object in dispute." [32]

This is not, however, an exception to the general principle that the burden of proof falls upon the claimant, but is due to the fact that both parties are in the position of claimants before the tribunal.

Taking into consideration that the *actor*, whether termed claimant or plaintiff, is to be determined according to the issues involved rather than the incidents of procedure, what has been said above shows that there is in substance no disagreement among international tribunals on the general legal principle that the burden of proof falls upon the claimant, *i.e.*, "the plaintiff must prove his contention under penalty of having his case refused." [33] *Actore non probante reus absolvitur.*

The burden of proof so far discussed relates to the proof of the factual basis of the claim as a whole, although in a single action, there may be several claims, as well as counter-claims. This may be called the ultimate burden of proof.[34] The term burden of proof may, however, also be used in a more restricted sense as referring to the proof of individual allegations advanced by the parties in the course of proceedings. This burden of proof may be called procedural. As has been seen at the beginning of the present Chapter, in this sense of the term, the burden of proof rests upon the party alleging the fact, unless the truth of the fact is within judicial knowledge or is presumed by the

[32] P.C.A.: 2 H.C.R., p. 83, at p. 90.

[33] *Supra*, p. 327, note 11.

[34] *Cf.* A. T. Denning, "Presumptions and Burdens," 61 L.Q.R. (1945), pp. 379–83.

Tribunal. In the absence of convincing evidence, the Tribunal will disregard the allegation.[35]

In conclusion, it may be said that the aim of a judicial inquiry is to establish the truth of a case, to which the law may then be applied. While the greatest latitude is enjoyed by international tribunals in the carrying out of their task, their activity is nevertheless governed by certain general principles of law based on common sense and developed through human experience. These principles create certain initial presumptions, guide the weighing of evidence and determine the incidence of the burden of proof.

[35] *Supra*, pp. 307 *et seq.*

Chapter 17

THE PRINCIPLE OF RES JUDICATA

Speaking of the principle of *res judicata,* Judge Anzilotti stated in his dissenting opinion in the *Chorzów Factory Case* (Interpretation) (1927):—

"It appears to me that if there be a case in which it is legitimate to have recourse, in the absence of conventions and custom, to 'the general principles of law recognised by civilised nations,' mentioned in No. 3 of Article 38 of the Statute, that case is assuredly the present one. Not without reason was the binding effect of *res judicata* expressly mentioned by the Committee of Jurists entrusted with the preparation of a plan for the establishment of a Permanent Court of International Justice, amongst the principles included in the above-mentioned article (Minutes, p. 335)." [1]

There seems little, if indeed any question as to *res judicata* being a general principle of law or as to its applicability in international judicial proceedings. Thus the Trial Smelter Arbitral Tribunal (1935) stated in its *Final Award* (1941):—

"That the sanctity of *res judicata* attaches to a final decision of an international tribunal is an essential and settled rule of international law.

"If it is true that international relations based on law and justice require arbitral or judicial adjudication of international disputes, it is equally true that such adjudication must, in principle, remain unchallenged, if it is to be effective to that end." [2]

A. Meaning

As to the meaning of *res judicata,* the Permanent Court of International Justice held in the *Société commerciale de Belgique Case* (1939), that:—

[1] PCIJ: A. 13, p. 27. See *Procès-verbaux*, pp. 315, 316.

[2] 3 UNRIAA, p. 1905, at pp. 1950–51. See also P.C.A.: *Pious Fund Case* (1902) 1 H.C.R., p. 1; Fran.-Ven. M.C.C. (1902): *Fabiani Case*, Ralston's *Report*, p. 81; P.C.A.: *Orinoco Steamship Co. Case* (1910) 1 H.C.R., p. 226. PCIJ: *Jaworzina Frontier* (1923) Adv.Op., B. 8, p. 38; *Monastery of St. Naoum* (1924) Adv.Op., B. 9, pp. 21, 22; *Polish Postal Service in Danzig* (1925) Adv.Op., B. 11, p. 24; *Société Commerciale de Belgique Case* (1939) A/B. 78, p. 174. ICJ: *Haya de la Torre Case* (1951) *ICJ Reports 1951*, p. 71, at pp. 77. 80, 82.

"Recognition of an award as *res judicata* means nothing else than recognition of the fact that the terms of that award are definitive and obligatory." [3]

Res judicata, therefore, has two effects.

First, that which is *res judicata* is definitive. Once a case has been decided by a valid and final judgment, the same issue may not be disputed again between the same parties, so long as that judgment stands.

" ' The general principle announced in numerous cases is that a right, question, or fact distinctly put in issue and directly determined by a court of competent jurisdiction, as a ground of recovery, cannot be disputed, etc.,' " [4] " the essence of the final judgment being, as it has been expressed ' to close the mouth on the one side and the ear on the other.' " [5]

This negative effect of *res judicata* has long been expressed in the maxim: *Non bis in idem* or *Bis de eadem re non sit actio.*[6, 7] It only attaches, however, to a final judgment of a competent tribunal. Where a tribunal has merely declared itself to have no jurisdiction to entertain a suit, this does not prevent the

[3] A/B. 78, p. 175.

[4] Fran.-Ven. M.C.C. (1902): *Cie générale de l'Orénoque Case* (1905) Ralston's *Report*, p. 244, at p. 355.

[5] Germ.-U.S. M.C.C. (1922): *Lehigh Valley Railroad Co. Case* (1935) Opinion of the German Commissioner, *Dec. & Op.*, p. 1159, at p. 1166. The view of the German Commissioner on this point was sustained by the Umpire. See *ibid.*, at p. 1175.

[6] *Cf.* also Fran.-Germ. M.A.T.: *Banque Meyer Case* (1923) 3 T.A.M., p. 639. Claimant who had the alternative, under Art. 304 *litt.* b, para. 2, of the Treaty of Versailles, of choosing between his own national courts and the M.A.T., having chosen of his own accord his national court and having obtained a judgment acquiring the force of *res judicata*, may not, for the same claim, return before the M.A.T. Generally, however, a decision of municipal law does not constitute *res judicata* in international law, because of the dualism of international law and municipal law; see *Bužau-Nehoiaşi Railway Case* (1939), 3 UNRIAA, p. 1827, at p. 1836, and *supra*, pp. 275 *et seq.*

See Span.-U.S. Cl.Com. (1871): *Machado Case*, 3 *Int.Arb.*, p. 2193, at p. 2194.

Cf. also the maxim *non bis in idem* applied to prevent the submission of a claim finally settled by diplomatic agents of the interested governments. Brit.-U.S. Cl.Com. (1853): *McLeod Case* (1855), Hornby's *Report*, p. 428, at p. 455; Pan.-U.S. G.C.C. (1926): *Chase Case* (1933), Hunt's *Report*, p. 341, at pp. 374, 375. *Cf.* also in this regard Fran.-Ven. M.C.C. (1902): *Fabiani Case*, Ralston's *Report*, p. 81; see *infra*, p. 344, note 28.

[7] Reservation by a party to the dispute to his acceptance of the award is of no significance. Germ.-U.S. M.C.C. (1922): *Drier Case* (1935) *Dec. & Op.*, p. 1037, at p. 1080. *Cf.* also *ibid.*, p. 1057, opinion of German Commissioner.

same issue from being presented before another tribunal which may be competent.[8]

Secondly, *res judicata*, that is to say, what has been finally decided by a tribunal, is binding upon the parties. As Article 37 II of the Hague Convention for the Pacific Settlement of International Disputes, 1907, provides:—

"Recourse to arbitration implies an engagement to submit in good faith to the award."

The binding effect of the award is thus inherent in the very institution of arbitration or judicial settlement.[9] Furthermore, as the Permanent Court of International Justice held in the *Société Commerciale de Belgique Case* (1929), between Belgium and Greece:—

[8] Brit.-U.S. Cl.Arb. (1910): *The Newchwang* (1921) Nielsen's *Report*, p. 411, at p. 415. See also *Alsop Case* (1911) 5 A.J.I.L. (1911), p. 1079, at p. 1085.
The Trail Smelter Arbitral Tribunal, in its *Final Award* (1941), referred to the *Fabiani Case* decided by the Fran.-Ven. M.C.C. (1902). It mentioned, amongst other contentions of the claimants in the *Fabiani Case*, that: "It was argued, on behalf of claimants, that 'the doctrine and jurisprudence are for a long time unanimous upon this incontestable principle that a declaration of incompetency can never produce the effect of *res judicata* upon the foundation of the law'" ("Foundation of the law": "*Le fonds du droit*," *i.e.*, "The merits of the case"). The Trail Smelter Arbitral Tribunal went on to say: "Umpire Plumley rejected these contentions" (3 UNRIAA, p. 1905, at p. 1951). Neither from the above quoted passage, nor from Umpire Plumley's decision in the *Fabiani Case*, should the inference be drawn that he rejected, as such, the principle invoked by the claimants. He only held that it was not applicable to the claimants' case. The Fabiani claim had previously been submitted to the President of the Swiss Confederation and an award was made in 1896. Certain items of the claim which were dismissed in 1896 were submitted to the Fran.-Ven. M.C.C. (1902), of which Plumley was Umpire. What Plumley rejected was the contention that the previous arbitrator dismissed some of the claims through lack of jurisdiction. "It is the opinion of the Umpire that the hon. arbitrator had complete and absolute dominion over the whole Fabiani controversy" (Ralston's *Report*, p. 81, at p. 125). On the point here under discussion, Umpire Plumley's decision is adequately summed up by the head note which he himself prepared for the Report: "The Umpire holds . . . that no jurisdictional questions were before the Swiss arbitrator; none were urged by either party, and none in fact were determined" (*ibid.*, p. 81. See actual decision, *ibid.*, at pp. 125–7). Umpire Plumley's opinion, therefore, was that the previous arbitrator had dismissed the claims on the merits of the case and not for lack of jurisdiction. There was, therefore, *res judicata*. The validity of the principle invoked by the claimants was not questioned. See *infra*, p. 344, note 28 and p. 355, note 66.

[9] See Rum.-Hung. M.A.T.: *Ungarische Erdgas A. G. Case* (1925), 5 T.A.M., p. 951, at p. 955: "The very fact that a State takes part in the establishment of an international tribunal and consents to submit to its jurisdiction implies already the willingness on the part of the State to take its place among those amenable to the Court's jurisdiction. It is precisely by an exercise of its sovereignty that it voluntarily and willingly assumes this position, which by its nature, carries not only rights but also duties, such as . . . compliance with judgments that will be given" (Transl.).

"If the awards are definitive and obligatory, it is certain that the Greek Government is bound to execute them and to do so as they stand." [10]

The obligation to carry out a judgment possessing the force of *res judicata* follows logically from the definitive and obligatory character of the judgment, and the party bound by it cannot seek to subordinate its execution to conditions not admitted in the judgment.[11] Indeed, in the very first case which came before the Permanent Court, it was decided that the Court neither could nor should contemplate the possibility of its judgments not being complied with.[12] In the case of a judgment declaring an act to be unlawful, this decision entails an obligation on the State which has committed the act to put an end to the illegal situation created thereby.[13] This positive effect of *res judicata* imposing an obligation on the parties to carry out the judgment is not, however, impaired, if the obligation is prevented from being performed through *force majeure*,[14] nor does it preclude the possibility of arrangements between the parties concerned modifying by common consent the obligation imposed by the judgment, as, for instance, by taking into account the debtor's capacity to pay.[15]

B. Limits

As regards the limits of the general principle of *res judicata*, the British-United States Claims Arbitral Tribunal (1910) held that:—

"It is a well established rule of law that the doctrine of *res*

[10] A/B. 78, p. 176.

[11] *Ibid.* See also *supra*, p. 337, note 7.

[12] PCIJ: *The Wimbledon* (1923), A.1, p. 32.

[13] ICJ: *Haya de la Torre Case* (1951), *ICJ Reports 1951*, p. 71, at p. 82. See *infra*, p. 347. See further, *supra*, pp. 233 *et seq.*

[14] *Cf. Société commerciale de Belgique Case* (1939), A/B. 78, pp. 177–8. Germ.-U.S. M.C.C. (1922): *Lehigh Valley Railroad Co. Case* (1933), *Dec. & Op.* p. 1084, at p. 1124. *Cf.* also ICJ: *Haya de la Torre Case* (1951), *ICJ Reports 1951*, p. 71, at pp. 79, 81, 82, 83.

[15] *e.g.*, *Société commerciale de Belgique Case* (1939), A/B. 78, p. 176. In this case, the Court, in view of the declarations of both parties agreeing to such a course, even commented: "Such a settlement is highly desirable" (p. 178). In PCIJ: *Serbian Loans Case* (1929), A. 20/21, there was a provision (Art. II) in the Special Agreement itself which provided for the eventual modification of the obligation imposed by the judgment, either by mutual agreement or arbitration to be based on pure considerations of equity (pp. 15–6).

judicata applies only where there is identity of the parties and of the question at issue." [16]

The second element of identification, *i.e.*, question at issue, has sometimes been subdivided into the object (*petitum*) and the grounds (*causa petendi*) of the case.[17] Thus in its *Final Award* (1941) the Trail Smelter Arbitral Tribunal (1935) held that:—

"There is no doubt that in the present case, there is *res judicata.* The three traditional elements for identification: parties, object and cause (PCIJ: Judgment 11, Series A, No. 13, D.O. by Anzilotti, p. 23) are the same (*Cf.* PCIJ: Series B, No. 11, p. 30)." [18]

These "material limits" of *res judicata* may be briefly examined.

That the authority of *res judicata* is conclusive and binding only upon the parties concerned has long been expressed in the maxim: *Res inter alios judicata aliis neque nocet neque prodest,*[19] and does not seem to be disputed.[20] Article 59 of the

[16] Brit.-U.S. Cl.Arb. (1910): The *Newchwang* (1921), Nielsen's *Report*, p. 411, at p. 415.

As the P.C.I.J., speaking of the decision of the P.C.A. in the *Pious Fund Case* (1902), said: "It must be remembered that the Court of Arbitration applied the doctrine of *res judicata* because not only the Parties but also the matter in dispute was the same (*il y a non seulement identité des Parties en litige, mais également identité de la matière*" (*Polish Postal Service in Danzig* (1925), Adv.Op., B. 11, p. 30). See P.C.A.: *Pious Fund Case* (1902), 1 H.C.R., p. 1, at p. 5.

Cf. Fran.-Ven. M.C.C. (1902): *Cie générale de l'Orénoque Case* (1905), Ralston's *Report*, p. 244, at p. 357

Cf. Digest, 44. 2, De Exceptione rei judicatae 3: *Julianus libro tertio digestorum respondit exceptionem rei judicatae obstare, quotiens eadem quaestio inter easdem personas revocatur.*"

[17] PCIJ: *Chorzów Factory Case* (Interpretation) (1927), D.O. by Anzilotti, A. 13, p. 23: "Art. 59 [Statute of the PCIJ] . . . determines the material limits of *res judicata* when stating that 'the decision of the Court has no binding force except between the Parties and in respect of that particular case': we have here the three traditional elements for identification, *persona*, *petitum*, *causa petendi*, for it is clear that 'that particular case' (*le cas qui a été decidé*) covers both the object and the grounds of the claim [*la chose demandée et la cause de la demande*]."

[18] 3 UNRIAA, p. 1905, at p. 1952.

[19] See *Digest* 42, 1, 63; 44,2,1; *Justinian Code* 7, 56, 2; 7, 60.

[20] See *Brazil-British Guiana Boundary Arbitration* (1904), 99 B.F.S.P., p. 930, at p. 931.

Mex.-U.S. Cl.Com. (1868): *Norton Case*, 3 *Int.Arb.*, p. 2160. Claim against Mexico assigned by one American national to another. "Towards third persons and to all courts, the assignor, once possessor of the right, has lost it as completely as if he had never held it, to such an extent that if he were sued in such a case and the judgment were against him, no exception *rei judicatae* could be alleged against the assignee, who might justly term such a sentence *res inter alios acta*" (p. 2163). The assignee may, therefore, present the same claim even though there be identity of *petitum* and *causa petendi*.

See also ICJ: *Corfu Channel Case* (Merits) (1949), D.O. by Azevedo, *ICJ Reports, 1949*, p. 4, at p. 90.

Statute of the International Court, as likewise did the same article in the Statute of the Permanent Court, expressly provides that:—

> " The decision of the Court has no binding force except between the parties. . . ." [21]

However, although what is not *res judicata* between the parties has no authoritative and binding effect, there is nothing to prevent a decision in another case from being accorded " such consideration as the logic of its reasoning might give " [22] and

[21] *Cf.* also Art. 84 of the Hague Convention of 1907 for the Pacific Settlement of International Disputes (Convention of 1899, Art. 56): " The award is not binding except on the parties in dispute."

Interpretation of a multipartite convention—Paragraph II of the same Art. 84 is very similar to Art. 63 of the Statutes of the P.C.I.J. and the I.C.J., which provides for notification of the parties to a multipartite convention whenever its construction is in question in a case in which they are not involved. " Every State so notified has the right to intervene in the proceedings; but if it uses this right, the construction given by the judgment will be equally binding upon it." As the Report adopted by the Council of the League of Nations on October 27, 1920, remarked, *a contrario* if such a State for any reason abstains from intervening, the construction given by the judgment will not be binding upon it (PCIJ: 2 *Documents*, p. 50). Note, however, that intervention is admissible only " if it actually relates to the subject-matter of the pending proceedings " (ICJ: *Haya de la Torre Case* (1951), *ICJ Reports 1951*, p. 71, at p. 76).

[22] *Cf.* Germ.-Ven. M.C.C. (1903): *Faber Case*, *Ven.Arb. 1903*, p. 600, at p. 622.

Judicial Precedents—While the P.C.I.J. expressly recognised that the object of Art. 59 of its Statute was " to prevent legal principles accepted by the Court in a particular case from being binding upon other States or in other disputes (A. 7, p. 19; A. 13, p. 21), it felt free to recall its previous decisions between other parties on particular points of law whenever the same questions arose (see, *e.g.*, A. 10, p. 16; A. 17, p. 63; A. 20, p. 17; B. 10, p. 21; B. 14, p. 28; B. 16, p. 35; A/B. 47, p. 249; A/B. 65, p. 49; A/B. 77, p. 82). Indeed, reliance on judicial precedents, established either by themselves or by other tribunals, is a frequent practice of both national and international tribunals. In Anglo-Saxon systems of law, certain precedents are recognised as binding. The institution of binding judicial precedents is, however, juridically distinct from the principle of *res judicata*. While precedents are concerned with questions of law *in abstracto*, *res judicata* is essentially the solution of a concrete dispute over the respective rights and obligations of the parties. The requirement of the identity of parties for the application of the *exceptio rei judicatae* has the effect of preventing the rights of third parties from being conclusively settled without being involved in litigation. They are not precluded by what is *res inter alios judicata* from submitting their own disputes, even involving the same points of law, or same subject matter, to fresh judicial consideration. Whether it is wise to do so, or whether the tribunal will or may decline to follow precedents, constitute separate questions.

Independently of the Hague Convention (Art. 84), and the Statutes of the P.C.I.J. and the I.C.J. (Art. 59), a system of binding judicial precedents does not exist in international law. See *e.g.*, opinion of Commissioner Hassaurek of the Ecuad. U.S. M.C.C. (1862) in which he registered his dissent from the decision of Umpire Upham of the Grenadine-U.S. M.C.C. (1857) in an identical case (3 *Int.Arb.*, p. 2731, at p. 2733; see *supra*, p. 156). International arbitrators have also considered themselves free to depart from precedents previously established by their own commission. It is significant that in the *McManus Case* (1874)

the weight of judicial precedents in international judicial practice can hardly be overestimated.[23] The rationale of the principle *res inter alios judicata aliis neque nocet neque prodest,*

(4 *Int.Arb.*, p. 3411) before the Mex.-U.S. Cl.Com. (1868) an English Umpire, Sir Edward Thornton, adopted a different principle with regard to forced loans, from that applied by a previous Umpire of the Commission, Lieber, and he explained in the *Francis Rose Case*: " If these matters are to be settled entirely by such precedents the umpire does not understand why, where there has been a decision upon the matter by a previous umpire, the question should be referred to the present umpire at all. It can only be with the intention that he should express his unbiased opinion upon the matter " (4 *Int.Arb.*, p. 3421, at p. 3421). *Cf.* also the work of the Span. U.S. Cl.Com. (1871) where there was also a departure from precedents by a new Umpire in the *Thompson Case* (1882) (4 *Int.Arb.*, p. 3754, at pp. 3779–80). Reversal of jurisprudence happens not only where there is a change in the person of the arbitrators, but also where the composition of the tribunal has remained identical (Brit.-Germ. M.A.T.: *Gunn Case* (1922) 2 T.A.M., p. 202, at pp. 203–4). This point has been mentioned for its factual interest; juridically the continuity of the tribunal is of course not affected by a change of its members (Span.-U.S. Cl.Com. (1871): *Young, Smith & Co. Case*, Opinion of American Commissioner, 3 *Int.Arb.*, p. 2184, at p. 2187). But of course, a change of jurisprudence " will not be done without serious reasons " (*Gunn Case* (1922), *loc. cit.*, p. 204). As the Fran.-Mex. Cl.Com. (1924) said in the *Pinson Case* (1928), a Tribunal would not disown its previous viewpoints of the law save in exceptional cases which deserve a different solution (*Jurisprudence*, p. 1, at p. 6).

An instance of what *appears* to be an application of the rule *stare decisis* may be found in the *Hawaiian Claims* (1925), in which the Brit.-U.S. Cl. Arb.Trib. (1910) went so far as to say, on the question of State succession to responsibility arising out of international unlawful acts: " We think the cases are governed by the decisions of this tribunal in the case of *Robert E. Brown* " (Nielsen's *Report*, p. 85, at p. 160). In this case, however, Great Britain, claimant, did not argue that the previous decision was wrong. She accepted the law applied as correct since she benefited from the rule in question in the *Robert E. Brown Case*. She only asked the tribunal to distinguish the present case from the previous one. The tribunal found no ground for such distinction.

" *Administrative Decisions* "—What has been said above concerning judicial precedents is not opposed to the possibility of " administrative decisions " of a general character being rendered by a tribunal set up to adjudge a number of specific claims between the same parties. The question from the juridical and practical points of view was discussed by the Fran.-Mex. Cl.Com. (1924) in the *Pinson Case* (1928) (*Jurisprudence*, p. 1, at pp. 5–6). The Commission cited the practice of the Germ.-U.S. M.C.C. (1922). It is necessary to point out, however, that the latter considered its " administrative decisions " to be more of an administrative than of a judicial character, destined principally for the guidance of the agents and counsel of the respective parties in the preparation and presentation of the various claims. (*Cf. Dec. & Op.*, pp. 3, 5, 61, etc.). In the practice of the Germ.-U.S. M.C.C. (1922), " each claim has been treated as initiating a separate case and has eventuated in a separate decision (a decision of it as a separate case: even though as a convenience the Commission in one document frequently dismissed a number of claims and less frequently rendered awards in a number of cases, each received the same treatment as if the decision thereof had been expressed in a record devoted to it alone.) " (*Lehigh Valley Railroad Co. Case* (1933), *Dec. & Op.*, p. 1084, at p. 1123.) This being so, the dictum of Sir Edward Thornton in the *Rose Case*, quoted above, applies. If the Fran.-Mex. Cl.Com. (1924) in the above-mentioned case seemed to attribute greater force to decisions of a general character (*loc. cit.*, p. 6), it must be remembered that it conceived them as being juridically admissible only through some sort

[23] See note 23 on p. 343.

while it is to be found essentially in the maxim *res inter alios acta*,[24] is also based, at least partly, on the general principle *audi alteram partem* in judicial proceedings,[25] which has been examined in a previous Chapter.

With regard to the second limit of *res judicata*, identity of the "question at issue," or, as it has been variously termed, identity of the "matter in dispute," or "the particular case," we have already mentioned that it has sometimes been sub-divided into two separate elements, *petitum* and *causa petendi*.[26] An examination of international decisions, however, throws some doubt upon the accuracy of this sub-division, especially in border-line cases.

There is no doubt that where two claims differ radically in their object, a decision on the first would not constitute *res judicata* for the subsequent case. But *petitum*, as an element for identification of *res judicata*, does not seem to apply to certain cases, especially in regard to the negative effects of *res judicata*. This appears clearly from the following dictum of the Spanish-United States Claims Commission (1871):—

"The Umpire is of opinion that the question whether this claim No. 125, is a new one or the same as No. 12 depends upon whether new rights are asserted in this claim.

"In case No. 12 the claimant appealed to the Commission for indemnification and compensation on account of the seizure and detention of a certain estate and the destruction or loss while in the hands of Spanish authorities of the personal property upon the same estate. This case was decided on its merits by the Umpire, M.

of joinder of the various claims (*cf. loc. cit.*, p. 5). In the above mentioned decision, the Germ.-U.S. M.C.C. (1922) denied that it was "the arbiter of a single suit or action consisting of thousands of counts, each count representing the claim of an American national or of the Government of the U.S." (*loc. cit.*, p. 1122).

23 See preceding footnote. *Cf.* also ICJ (PCIJ): Statutes, Art. 38 I (*d*). Germ.-U.S. M.C.C. (1922): *Administrative Decision No. II* (1923), *Dec. & Op.*, p. 5, at p. 7.

24 *Cf. supra*, p. 340, note 20.

25 *Cf. e.g.*, *Fur Seal Arbitration* (1893), 1 *Int.Arb.*, p. 755. An incidental question in this case was whether Russia held and exercised any exclusive right in the Behring Sea after the Anglo-Russian Treaty of 1825. The President of the Tribunal, in concurring in the majority opinion that Russia held and exercised no such rights, observed that he intended only to state the position in so far as it had been presented for consideration by the two governments before the Tribunal, and that he by no means intended to prejudge Russia's own view of the facts, as that power had not been heard by the Tribunal, nor placed in such a situation as to make her views known to it (p. 917).

Cf. supra, p. 341, note 21, regarding intervention in case of interpretation of multipartite treaty. *Cf.* also the right of intervention under Art. 62 of the Statute of the I.C.J. (also P.C.I.J.).

26 *Supra*, p. 340.

Bartholdi, April 22, 1876, and this decision must be regarded as a negative of all right of the claimant at the time to demand indemnity before this Commission on account of the seizure referred to. It is now contended that, although the injury complained of in the present case, No. 125, is the same seizure of the same property, the claimant's right to recover indemnity on account of this seizure ought to be examined again by the Commission inasmuch as the claimant in the former case only asked for the rents, issues, profits, and income of the land, and that in this he demands the value of the land; but this conclusion cannot be accepted. Even if the claimant did not at the time of the former case ask indemnity of the Commission for the value of the lands, the claimant had the same power to do so as other claimants in other cases where it has been done, and he cannot have relief by a new claim before a new Umpire." [27]

The whole question is regarded as settled and it may not be the subject of a second action. *Eadem res*, in the maxim *bis de eadem re non sit actio*, should, therefore, be construed as the entire claim without regard to the fact whether the various and separate items therein contained have all been presented or not.[28] Even with regard to the positive effect of *res judicata*, the *petitum*, notwithstanding the general principle *non ultra*

[27] *Delgado Case* (1881) 3 *Int.Arb.*, p. 2196, at p. 2199.
Span.-U.S. Cl.Com. (1871): *Machado Case* (1880) 3 *Int.Arb.*, p. 2193, at p. 2194: "The question whether this claim No. 129 is a new one, or the same as No. 3, does not depend upon whether the items included be the same in both cases, but that the test is whether both claims are founded on the same injury."

[28] In addition to the cases cited above, *cf.* Franc.-Ven.M.C.C. (1902): *Antoine Fabiani Case*, Ralston's *Report*, p. 81, (*supra*, p. 338, note 8). By the Protocol of 1891, France and Venezuela agreed "to submit to an arbitrator the claims of M. Antoine Fabiani against the Venezuelan Government." The Arbitrator, the President of the Swiss Confederation gave his decision in 1896, awarding reparation amounting to about one tenth of what was claimed (5 *Int.Arb.*, p. 4878). That part of the claim which had been dismissed was presented again before the Franc.-Ven.M.C.C. (1902), the claimant contending that the Swiss Arbitrator had dismissed it for lack of jurisdiction. The Umpire held that no jurisdictional questions were involved in the first arbitration, the Arbitrator having merely decided upon the claim in accordance with the protocol. While recognising that the protocol had placed certain restriction upon the scope of the claim, he held that: "the process by which this agreement is reached being concessions by each, each concession cancels the other, so that, outside the protocol, of the original contention *there is left nothing. All of the original controversy* is found finally resting in the protocol *or in oblivion*" (p. 135. Original italics.) The whole controversy or what was left of it, had therefore been finally and conclusively settled by the award of the Swiss Arbitrator. It is true that the negative exclusive effect of the settlement lay more in the protocol than in the award, but it seems certain that the same *ratio* prevents the splitting up of a claim into numerous items to be successively presented. See p. 133.

petita,[29] does not always set a true limit to the *res judicata*,[30] since the principle *non ultra petita* may, under certain circumstances, be subject to an exception and the judgment would, therefore, go beyond the actual *petitum*.[31]

As to the *causa petendi* as an element of identification, it seems, as indicated by the *Delgado Case* (1881) quoted above, that where new rights are asserted, there is a new case which ought not to be barred by a previous decision even if the parties and the object be identical. In this connection, it need hardly be mentioned that a claim based on a distinct injury is an assertion of a new right—a right that has been violated—and would be considered as a new case.

In the *Delgado Case* (1881), the Umpire went on to say after the above quoted passage:—

" However, it is further contended that the Spanish Government has, by a decree of November, 1873, ordered the restoration of the claimant's property, and that the rights acquired under this decree were not asserted before the Umpire in case No. 12.

" The Umpire hereby decides that the part of the claim which is founded on the decree of November, 1873, may be presented again with further argument on the question whether the Commission has jurisdiction to hear and determine a case of violation of the rights

29 That the principle of *non ultra petita* is a general principle of judicial procedure has been recognised in numerous cases. ICJ: *Corfu Channel Case* (Compensation) (1949), *ICJ Reports, 1949*, p. 244, at p. 249. Judge Ečer pointed out in his D.O. that the Court was applying the general principle *non ultra petita*, a principle within the meaning of Art. 38 I (*c*) of the Statute. In ICJ: *Asylum Case* (Interpretation) (1950), the Court said: " One must bear in mind the principle that it is the duty of the Court . . . to abstain from deciding points not included in [the final] submissions [of the parties] " (*ICJ Reports, 1950*, p. 395, at p. 402). Other instances, see Spanish Zone of Morocco Claims (1923): *Rapport IV* (1924) 2 UNRIAA, p. 615, at p. 650; Rum.-Germ. M.A.T.: *Gologan Case* (1926) 5 T.A.M., p 945, at p. 950; Franc.-Mex.M.C.C. (1924): *Pinson Case* (1928) *Jurisprudence*, p. 1, at p. 137.

30 *Contra* D.O. by Anzilotti in PCIJ: *Chorzów Factory Case* (Interpretation) (1927) A. 13, p. 25.

31 *Cf*. Spanish Zone of Morocco Claims (1923): Claim No. 21: *Holliday* (*Ouad Hélu*) (1924) 2 UNRIAA, p. 615, at pp. 692–93. Expropriation of a piece of land. Claimant claimed for 3,600 sq. metres. A later survey made by him showed the area to be 3,780 sq. metres. A survey made at the request of the *Rapporteur* and with the agreement of the Spanish authorities and the representative of the claimant showed an area of 3,980 sq. metres. " The *Rapporteur* adopts the measurement of the survey established at his request and recognised as exact by the two parties. In a case of expropriation, where it would be incumbent upon the authorities to prepare the surveys, an error committed by the owner in the establishment of a private survey cannot cause him a prejudice. This rule ought, in the opinion of the *Rapporteur*, to prevail over the principle mentioned by the *Rapporteur* in certain other cases according to which he should not go beyond the claims " (p. 692. Transl.).

asserted, but that the part which is alleged to be founded on other injuries be dismissed." [32]

While the *causa petendi* thus seems to be a decisive criterion of identification, it should, however, be observed that this does not mean that a case may be presented a second time in a new light. Thus in the *Danford Knowlton & Co. and Peter V. King & Co. Case* (1881), the Spanish-United States Claims Commission (1871) held that:—

"In case of seizure a claim can be presented on account of that injury, but that confiscation of the same property cannot, as a distinct injury, be made the foundation of a new claim under a new number." [33]

Seizure and confiscation cannot, therefore, be considered as separate *causae petendi.*

The use of the criteria *petitum* and *causa petendi* as elements of identification of the "same question at issue," especially as applied to the negative effect of *res judicata*, is, therefore, subject to considerable reservation. Despite its lack of precision, it may be asked whether the more generic criterion of the "same question at issue" is not more correct.[34] In order to illustrate what have been considered by international tribunals as separate questions at issue, the following cases may be cited, in addition to those mentioned above.

In the case of the *Newchwang* (1921), which concerned a collision between two vessels, it was held that the liability of the respective owners did not constitute identical questions, whatever the *de facto* connection between the two actions. Decision on the liability of one owner did not, therefore, preclude subsequent proceedings to determine the liability of the other.[35]

32 Span.-U.S. Cl.Com. (1871): 3 *Int.Arb.*, p. 2196, at p. 2200.
Cf. also *Id.*: *John F. Machado Case* (1880), 3 *ibid.*, p. 2193 (*supra*, p. 344, note 27).

33 3 *ibid.*, p. 2194, at p. 2195.

34 It is of interest to mention that the same difficulty existed in Roman law. As Buckland says in his *Manual of Roman Private Law*, 1939, p. 403: "The notion of *eadem res* raises many difficult questions." Edouard Cuq in his *Manuel des Institutions juridiques des Romains*, 1917, p. 886, does not believe that the criteria of object and cause should be cumulatively applied to determine the identity of question, while Girard in his standard work, *Manuel élémentaire de Droit romain*, 1929, p. 1107, definitely considers identity of question to be the correct criterion, the criteria of object and cause being inexact.

35 Brit.-U.S. Cl.Arb. (1910): Nielsen's *Report*, p. 411, at p. 415.

In the case of the *Compagnie générale de l'Orénoque* (1905), it was decided that counter-claims, as well as claims that might be presented by way of set off, constituted independent actions. Even though they could have been pleaded in a previous action, if in fact they were not presented and considered, subsequent action upon them was not precluded by the previous decision.[36]

Finally, it should be mentioned that the criterion of "question" was also applied by the International Court of Justice in the *Haya de la Torre Case* (1951). In its judgment in the *Asylum Case* (1950), the Court had held that the granting of diplomatic asylum to Haya de la Torre by the Colombian Government in its Embassy in Lima was not in conformity with the 1928 Havana Convention on asylum, in force between Colombia and Peru.[37] In the words of the Court:—

> "This decision entails a legal consequence, namely that of putting an end to an illegal situation: the Government of Colombia which had granted the asylum irregularly is bound to terminate it."[38]

The irregularity of the asylum and the obligation to terminate it must thus be regarded as *res judicata*. In the subsequent *Haya de la Torre Case* (1951), however, which concerned the duty of Colombia to surrender Haya de la Torre to the Peruvian authorities, the Court held that:—

> "The question of the surrender of the refugee was not decided by the judgment of November 20 [in the *Asylum Case*]. *This question is new. . . . There is consequently no res judicata upon the question of surrender.*"[39]

The duty to terminate the asylum and the duty to surrender the fugitive constituted, therefore, separate questions. Hence, judgment on the one did not bar proceedings in respect of the other.[40] In this connection, it might perhaps be pointed out that the Court considered that "surrender is not the only way of terminating asylum."[41]

36 Fran.-Ven. M.C.C. (1902): Ralston's *Report*, p. 244, at pp. 357–9.
37 *ICJ Reports 1950*, p. 266, at p. 288.
38 *Haya de la Torre Case* (1951), *ICJ Reports 1951*, p. 71, at p. 82.
39 *Ibid.*, at p. 80. Italics added.
40 *Cf.*, however, incidental allusion to the *petitum* (*ibid.*, at pp. 76–7).
41 *Ibid.*, at p. 82.

C. Scope

The Permanent Court of International Justice in its Advisory Opinion concerning the *Polish Postal Service in Danzig* (1925) stated:—

> "Once a decision has been duly given, it is only its contents that are authoritative, whatever may have been the views of its authors,"[42]

and, indeed, whatever their subsequent views may be.[43] But not everything contained in the decision acquires the force of *res judicata*. As the Court said in the same Advisory Opinion:—

> "Now it is certain that the reasons contained in a decision, at least in so far as they go beyond the scope of the operative part, have no binding force as between the Parties concerned.
>
> "It is perfectly true that all the parts of a judgment concerning the points in dispute explain and complete each other and are to be taken into account in order to determine the precise meaning and scope of the operative portion. This is clearly stated in the award of the Permanent Court of Arbitration of October 14, 1902, concerning the Pious Funds of the Californias[[44]], which has been repeatedly invoked by Danzig. The Court agrees with this statement. But it by no means follows that every reason given in a decision constitutes a decision. . . . Now, although it is not quite clear why the High Commissioner, in paragraph 6 of his decision, expressed his opinion on the scope of the utilisation of the Polish postal service, there can be no doubt that the said opinion is irrelevant to the point actually decided by him and therefore has no binding force. This conclusion . . . is drawn from the very nature of judicial decisions."[45]

Views expressed by the Tribunal in its judgment which are not relevant to the actual decision on the question at issue, therefore, have no binding force and are not *res judicata*.

As the Franco-Venezuelan Mixed Claims Commission (1902) held in the case of the *Compagnie Générale de l'Orénoque* (1905):—

[42] B. 11, p. 28.
[43] *Ibid.*, at p. 31.
[44] *Q. v.*, 1 H.C.R., p. 1, at p. 5.
[45] *Loc. cit.*, pp. 29–30.

"It is only the particular matter in controversy which is decided."[46]

In the same case, the Commission, basing the principle of *res judicata* upon the Anglo-Saxon notion of estoppel, also said:—

"Every matter and point distinctly in issue in said cause, and which was directly passed upon and determined in said decree, and which was its ground and basis, is concluded by said judgment, and the claimants themselves and the claimant government in their behalf are forever *estopped* from asserting any right or claim based in any part upon any fact actually and directly involved in said decree.

"'The general principle, announced in numerous cases is that a right, question, or fact *distinctly put in issue and directly determined*, by a court of competent jurisdiction, as a ground of recovery, can not be disputed, etc.'"[47]

What the Commission said affords an explanation why what the Permanent Court of Arbitration said in the *Pious Fund Case* (1902), as quoted above,[48] is compatible with Judge Anzilotti's statement in his dissenting opinion in the *Chorzów Factory Case* (Interpretation) (1927). In that dissenting opinion, Judge Anzilotti maintained that:—

"It is certain that the binding effect attaches only to the operative part [*le dispositif*] of the judgment and not to the statement of reasons [*les considerants*]."[49]

But, he added:—

"When I say that only the terms [*le dispositif*] of a judgment are binding, I do not mean that only what is actually written in the

[46] Ralston's *Report*, p. 244, at p. 357.
Cf. PCIJ: *Polish Postal Service in Danzig* (1925), Adv.Op., B. 11, p. 30: "In the decision of December 23, 1922, as well as in every other decision of the High Commissioner, the operative portion is clearly distinguished from the statement of reasons; the Court is unable to see any ground for extending the binding force attaching to the declaratory judgment on the point decided to reasons which were only intended to explain the declaration contained in the operative portion of this judgment *and all the more so if these reasons relate to points of law on which the High Commissioner was not asked to give a decision.*" Italics added. In other words, it was not a point at issue.

[47] *Loc. cit.*, p. 355. Original italics. U.S. cases and authorities cited.

[48] *Supra*, p. 348.

[49] PCIJ: A. 13, p. 24. *Cf. Junghans Case* (2nd Phase) (1940), 3 UNRIAA, p. 1883, at p. 1889.

operative part [*le dispositif*] constitutes the Court's decision. On the contrary, it is certain that it is almost always necessary to refer to the statement of reasons [*les motifs*] to understand clearly the operative part [*le dispositif*] and above all to ascertain the *causa petendi*. But, at all events, it is the operative part [*le dispositif*] which contains the Court's binding decision." [50]

The difference is, therefore, only one of approach, the meeting point of the various views, including that of the Permanent Court of International Justice, is perhaps to be found in the following statement of the Franco-Venezuelan Mixed Claims Commission (1902):—

"Every matter and point distinctly in issue in said cause, and which was directly passed upon and determined in said decree, and which was its ground and basis, is concluded by said judgment." [51]

This formula has the advantage of including amongst the questions concluded by the judgment those which are its "ground and basis." This leads us to the question whether preliminary and incidental questions decided in a judgment form part of the *res judicata*, particularly when they are the basis of the decision on the principal question.

DECISIONS ON PRELIMINARY AND INCIDENTAL QUESTIONS

In his dissenting opinion in the *Chorzów Factory Case* (Merits) (1928), M. Ehrlich, the Polish national judge, said:—

"It is generally admitted that the principles of litispendency and *res judicata* do not apply to questions decided as incidental and preliminary points." [52]

For this reason Judge Ehrlich upheld the Polish contention that the decision of the Permanent Court in the *German Interests Case* (Merits) (1926) on the preliminary and incidental question of the right of ownership of the Oberschlesische Stickstoffwerke A.-G. over the Chorzów factory was not *res judicata*, although

[50] *Ibid.*, at p. 24. It may perhaps be mentioned that in a number of countries, notably on the Continent of Europe, judgments are drawn up in three distinct parts: (1) recital of facts (*les faits*), (2) statement of reasons (*les motifs*), and (3) the operative part (*le dispositif*). The P.C.I.J. on the whole followed this method, as does the I.C.J.

[51] *Supra*, p. 349.

[52] PCIJ: A. 17, p. 76.

in that decision the Court had held that the action of Poland towards the Oberschlesische (whose factory she took over) was not in conformity with her obligations towards Germany. He maintained that in the subsequent suit for indemnity, the Court should have taken account of a judgment which the (Polish) Civil Court of Katowice, the competent municipal tribunal, had rendered in the meantime, denying the right of ownership of the Oberschlesische to the factory. For a full discussion of the various points involved, reference may be made to the various decisions of the Permanent Court concerning the Chorzów factory [53] but the question was actually disposed of in the *Chorzów Factory Case* (Interpretation) (1927), in which it was said:—

"The Court, by that judgment [*German Interests Case* (Merits) (1926), Judgment No. 7], decided that the attitude of the Polish Government in regard to the Oberschlesische was not in conformity with the provisions of the Geneva Convention. This conclusion, which has now indisputably acquired the force of *res judicata*, was based, amongst other things, firstly, on the finding by the Court that, from the standpoint of international law, the German Government was perfectly entitled to alienate the Chorzów factory, and, secondly, on the finding that, from the standpoint of municipal law, the Oberschlesische had validly acquired the right of ownership to the factory—and these findings constitute a condition essential to the Court's decision. The finding that, in municipal law, the factory did belong to the Oberschlesische is consequently included amongst the points decided by the Court in Judgment No. 7, and possessing binding force in accordance with the terms of Article 59 of the Statute. The very context in which the passage in question occurs is calculated to establish the right of ownership of the Oberschlesische from the standpoint of municipal law." [54]

The finding of the Court on a preliminary and incidental point not primarily within the competency of the Court, but constituting "a condition essential to the Court's decision," thus possesses binding force in accordance with the terms of Article 59 of the Statute. Does this mean that the principle

[53] PCIJ: *German Interests* (Merits) (1926), A. 7, particularly pp. 42–3; *Chorzów Factory Case* (Jd.) (1927), A. 9; *Chorzów Factory Case* (Interpretation) (1927), A. 13; *Chorzów Factory Case* (Merits) (1928), A. 17, particularly pp. 31–4.

[54] A. 13, p. 20.

affirmed by Judge Ehrlich is thus refuted, at least in so far as the decision on the incidental and preliminary point is a "condition essential" to the principal decision?

In order to arrive at a proper understanding of the judgment in this case, it is necessary to examine the pleadings of both parties, even though the Court had said that "it cannot be bound by formulae chosen by the parties concerned, but must be able to take an unhampered decision."[55]

Poland, while not disputing that the decision of the Court in the *German Interests Case* (Merits) (1926) on the question of her attitude towards the Oberschlesische Stickstoffwerke A.-G. had acquired the force of *res judicata,* maintained that the judgment did not and could not prejudice the right of the competent municipal tribunal to determine the right of ownership of the Oberschlesische over the Chorzów factory.[56] Germany, on the other hand, maintained that the decision of the Court on this preliminary and incidental question, although not binding once and for all on the question of the right of ownership, was nevertheless binding for the purpose of that judgment.[57]

Germany argued as follows:—

"It is true that the Court has not the competence to 'establish' a right of civil law, as the Polish Government says in p. 6[[58]] of their Observations. But it can not be doubted that, inasmuch as it is necessary, for the solution of an international conflict, to decide, as an incidental question, a point of civil law, the Court is competent to decide it for the purposes and within the limits of the international suit which is laid before it and upon which it is called upon to give a final decision.

"Since all international decisions are, as a general rule, dependent upon incidental decisions on preliminary points, there would be no possibility of really solving any international conflict if the defeated Party were free to dispute afresh points which are pertinent to the decision and have been decided in an incidental manner by characterising them as mere opinions with no binding effect, and to

[55] *Ibid.*, at pp. 15–6.

[56] *Observations of the Polish Government*, PCIJ: Ser. C. 13–V, p. 50. *Cf.* also speech by Sobolewski for Poland, *ibid.*, pp. 29, 30.

[57] *Cf. Exposé of the German Government*, para. 8, PCIJ: Ser. C. 13–V, pp. 58–9.

[58] *i.e.*, PCIJ: Ser. C. 13–V, p. 49.

subordinate its acceptance of the judgment to a further investigation by itself of the decision on incidental questions.'' [59]

The logical conclusion to be drawn from the German contention is that, if the Court had decided in the *German Interests Case* (Merits) (1926) that the attitude of the Polish Government in regard to the Oberschlesische Stickstoffwerke A.-G. was not in conformity with Article 6 and the following articles of the Geneva Convention, there was an unlawful act on the part of Poland *vis-à-vis* Germany. The existence of this unlawful act, which necessarily implied that the Oberschlesische was the owner of the Chorzów factory, was *res judicata* and could no longer be disputed. For the purpose of that decision the former decision on the incidental question was final and conclusive, although it did not preclude a contrary decision by a competent tribunal on that incidental question. Such a decision would not influence the effect of *res judicata* of the previous decision concerning the existence of the unlawful act. In other words, the former decision could not be rendered nugatory by the subsequent decision.

To sum up, when preliminary and incidental questions, which do not normally come within the competence of a tribunal, fall within its competence because they are necessary for the determination of the principal question,[60] decisions on these questions are not conclusive and binding unless they are an essential condition to the judgment on the principal suit. Such binding force is, however, limited to that judgment. The same question may be the subject of dispute between the same parties again either as an incidental question in another suit, or as a principal question before the competent tribunal. But whatever the outcome of these subsequent proceedings, the force of *res judicata* of the previous decision can in no way be affected. It is submitted that the decision of the Court in the *Chorzów Factory Case* (Interpretation) (1927), regarding the binding effect of its decision in the *German Interests Case* (Merits) (1926) on an incidental question should be understood in this sense. It is in this sense that the words of Judge Anzilotti in this connection should also be understood:—

[59] *Ibid.*, at pp. 59–60. (Transl.)
[60] *Cf. supra*, pp. 266–7.

"Under a generally accepted rule which is derived from the very conception of *res judicata,* decisions on incidental or preliminary questions which have been rendered with the sole object of adjudicating upon the Parties' claims (*incidenter tantum*) are not binding in another case." [61]

Thus understood, the principle invoked by Judge Ehrlich and Judge Anzilotti is not inconsistent with the decision of the Court in the *Chorzów Factory Case* (Interpretation) (1927).[62]

Two points may, however, be mentioned with regard to what has been said above concerning the binding character of decisions on incidental and preliminary questions.

First, as the German Exposé in the *Chorzów Factory Case* (Interpretation) (1927) explained:—

"The Polish interpretation would only be right if the operative part of Judgment No. 7 contained a reservation." [63]

Secondly, when a declaratory judgment establishing the existence of an unlawful act includes a decision on a preliminary and incidental question, does the general rule explained above, that such a decision is not binding upon the parties in another suit, apply to proceedings for damages in respect of the unlawful act? [64] The question was answered in the negative by the Permanent Court of International Justice. That is to say, a

[61] PCIJ: *Chorzów Factory Case* (Interpretation) (1927), D.O. by Anzilotti, A. 13, p. 26.

[62] Additional support for this interpretation of the *Chorzów Factory Case* (Interpretation) (1927) may be found in the subsequent decision of the Court on the question of damages (*Chorzów Factory Case* (Merits) (1928)). In the latter decision, as Judge Ehrlich pointed out in his dissenting opinion (A. 17, p. 75), the Court did not rely on the incidental question of ownership being *res judicata*, but on the consideration that the judgment on damages was only a sequel to the judgment on responsibility, which was *res judicata*. *Cf. infra*, pp. 354–5, especially p. 355, note 65. In this connection it may be legitimate to note that in the *Chorzów Factory Case* (Merits) (1928), Judge Anzilotti not only did not register any dissent, but, as President of the Tribunal, was, in accordance with the Court's practice, an *ex officio* member of the Committee of Three entrusted with the drafting of the judgment.

[63] PCIJ: Ser. C. 13–V, p. 59. Transl.

A case of such reservation occurred in Spanish Zone of Morocco Claims (1923): *Claims* 18–20 (1924), 2 UNRIAA, p. 615, at p. 686. Having made it clear that he had decided the incidental question of ownership of Rzini, on whose behalf the claims were put forward by Great Britain against Spain, only provisionally, the *Rapporteur* said: "If, in future, a final decision of a competent tribunal should evict Rzini or his *ayants-droit* entirely or partially from his ownership of one or all of the lands in question, there can be no doubt that the British Government would refund the Spanish Government, or make Rzini refund the money wrongly received" (Transl.).

[64] See PCIJ: *Chorzów Factory Case* (Interpretation) (1927), D.O. by Anzilotti A. 13, p. 27.

decision on an incidental point in a judgment establishing the existence of an unlawful act may not be disputed in a subsequent action for indemnity based on such unlawful act.[65] This is entirely consistent with what has been submitted above.

Decisions on incidental and preliminary points which do not normally fall within the competence of the tribunal are to be distinguished, however, from judgments of a tribunal on preliminary questions which are primarily within its competency. Such a preliminary judgment acquires the full force of *res judicata* on the question actually decided. It cannot, for instance, be doubted that the decision of the Permanent Court in the *Panevezys-Saldutiskis Railway Case* (1939) upholding the Lithuanian preliminary objection on the ground of failure to exhaust local remedies possesses all the attributes of *res judicata* on that particular question. It need hardly be mentioned that, since the Court thus declined to entertain the claim, the force of *res judicata* in this instance did not affect the merits of the case.[66]

Where a case proceeds after a preliminary judgment, is the tribunal irrevocably bound by that judgment? The question was raised in the *Tiedemann Case* (1926) before the Polish-German Mixed Arbitral Tribunal. While recognising the silence of its Rules of Procedure on this point, the Mixed Arbitral Tribunal expressed the belief that these Rules did not intend to depart from a rule generally accepted by Continental legal systems that the judge was bound by the decisions which he had taken before the final judgment.

"The Tribunal considers that, in the interests of legal stability, it is important that what has been decided ought, in principle, to be treated as final." [67]

[65] PCIJ: *Chorzów Factory Case* (Merits) (1928), A. 17, p. 32: "The Court, having been of opinion that the Oberschlesische's right to the Chorzów Factory justified the conclusion that the Polish Government's attitude in respect of that company was not in conformity with Art. 6 and the following articles of the Geneva Convention, must necessarily maintain that opinion when the same situation at law has to be considered for the purpose of giving judgment in regard to the reparation claimed as a result of the act which has been declared by the Court not to be in conformity with the Convention." Anzilotti did not dissent. See *ibid.*, pp. 31–4, and *passim* with regard to the Court's conception of reparation as part of the question of responsibility and a necessary conse quence of the existence of an unlawful act. *Cf.* also Judgment No. 8 (A. 9).

[66] A/B. 76, *e.g.*, p. 22. See *supra*, pp. 337–8.

[67] 7 T.A.M., p. 702, at p. 706. (Transl.)

The Tribunal did, however, make a reservation. In Chapter 11 it was pointed out that a tribunal is incompetent to act outside its jurisdiction, and that jurisdiction is so fundamental a requirement that, where it cannot be extended by the will of the parties, the question may be raised by the tribunal *proprio motu* or by the parties at any stage of the proceedings.[68] The reservation made by the Tribunal reflects this principle. It said:—

"But the question appears in a very special light when the preliminary judgment is a judgment affirming the competency of the Tribunal and when the latter recognises subsequently, but before the judgment on the merits, that it is in fact incompetent. In such a case, if it is obliged to consider itself bound by its first decision, it would be led to pass judgment on a matter which it acknowledges to be beyond its jurisdiction. . . . In other words, to remain faithful to the principle of respect for *res judicata*, it would have to commit a manifest abuse of its power." [69]

The Tribunal was, therefore, of the opinion that in such a case the preliminary judgment might be set aside. It continued:—

"In fact, in order that there be *res judicata*, there must be a valid judgment. Now, writers generally admit . . that this condition is not fulfilled when the decision has been reached outside its competency by a tribunal of a special or exceptional character. Particularly in the field of international arbitration, decisions which an arbitrator has reached by going beyond the limits fixed by the arbitral agreement, are considered as null because they are in excess of his power. . . . If this view is adopted, that is to say, if the decision rendered by an incompetent arbitrator is considered as devoid of binding force between the parties, it would be contrary to all reason to deny the arbitral tribunal, which has wrongly declared itself competent, the right to go back on this preliminary decision, when, before the judgment on the merits, it is shown that the decision is erroneous." [70]

The Tribunal thus took the view that such a decision should, in any event, be considered as null and void, and could not, therefore, be binding.

[68] *Supra*, pp. 259 *et seq.*, at p. 266.
[69] *Loc. cit.*, at p. 706. (Transl.)
[70] *Ibid.*, at p. 706. (Transl.)

D. Nullity and Voidability

Having thus considered one exception to the principle of *res judicata,* it seems proper, before concluding this Chapter, to enumerate the various causes of nullity and voidability of final judgments, since they are directly related to the principle of *res judicata,* of which they constitute exceptions. It is not, however, proposed to examine the actual procedure whereby, in international adjudications, a final judgment may be anulled, revised or otherwise set aside.

I. Incompetence.—As shown by the *Tiedmann Case* (1926) quoted above, lack, or excess, of competence are causes of nullity of a final judgment. This question has already been examined at length in Chapter 11.[71]

II. Violation of the Principle nemo debet esse judex in propria sua causa.[72]—No international decision has to our knowledge been challenged on this ground, but it follows from the recognition of this principle in international law that it may be a reason for impugning a judicial decision. As, however, jurisdiction in international law is dependent upon the will of the parties, it is difficult to conceive that a State would submit itself to a tribunal of this character. Were it to do so it may be asked whether such voluntary submission would not constitute a waiver preventing the parties from invoking the principle after the final decision. The principle nevertheless has its application, in so far as the theory of *res judicata* is concerned, in measuring the regularity and validity of those judicial decisions where such special circumstances do not exist.[73]

III. Violation of the Principle audiatur et altera pars.—The failure to afford an opportunity to the parties to be heard as a cause of nullity of the judgment has also been discussed in a previous Chapter and requires no repetition.[74]

[71] *Supra*, pp. 259 *et seq.*, 277 and 356.
[72] *Supra*, pp. 279 *et seq.*
[73] See *e.g.*, Greco-Bulg. M.A.T.: *Arakas* (*The Georgios*) *Case* (1927), cited *supra*, pp. 257–8.
[74] Chap. 14, *supra*, pp. 290 *et seq.*

IV. Fraud and Corruption.—Fraud and corruption on the part of a tribunal would nullify its entire proceedings. One rare instance of such an occurrence in modern international arbitration is the United States-Venezuelan Claims Commission (1866) which met at Caracas. When the fraud was discovered, its proceedings were considered entirely null and void and, by an agreement between the United States and Venezuela, concluded in 1885, a new Commission was set up at Washington to re-examine all the claims anew.[75]

V. Fraud of the Parties and Collusion of Witnesses.—The best-known example of fraud and collusion of witnesses is provided by the so-called "*Sabotage Cases*" which came before the German-United States Mixed Claims Commission (1922). It seems that the defendant, in order to conceal its responsibility, deliberately filed false pleadings, and suborned witnesses on a large scale in order to procure false testimony, thus discrediting reliable and genuine evidence produced by the claimants.[76] In consequence thereof, the Commission in 1930 dismissed the claims for lack of sufficient evidence.[77] Alleging the fraud practised on the Commission, the claimants petitioned for a reopening of the case. By a decision of 1933, the Commission affirmed that it still had jurisdiction over the case, as it was not yet *functus officio*. As such, it considered that it had "inherent power to reopen and to revise a decision induced by fraud."[78] In its decision of 1935, it held that there should be a preliminary proceeding to determine whether or not the case should be reopened:—

"It is, of course, conceivable that the Commission should hear argument on both the propriety of reopening the case and the merits at one and the same time. Much may be said pro and con such a procedure. Nevertheless, I suppose that if the parties were in agreement that this course should be followed, the Commission would acquiesce. There is no such agreement. Germany insists that the preliminary question be determined separately. I am of opinion

[75] See *supra*, p. 160, notes 88, 89.

[76] For the extent of the fraud, see Germ.-U.S. M.C.C. (1922); *Lehigh Valley Railroad Co. Case* (1939), Opinion of the American Commissioner, *Op. & Dec.*, p. 1, at pp. 21–310.

[77] *Lehigh Valley Railroad Co. Case* (1930), *Dec. & Op.*, pp. 967–94.

[78] *Lehigh Valley Railroad Co. Case* (1933), *ibid.*, p. 1084, at p. 1127.

this is her right. She now has a judgment. Before that judgment may be set aside, and a new hearing held upon the merits, it is incumbent upon the claimants to sustain the affirmative of the issues made by their petition. The next hearing, therefore, will be upon the question of reopening *vel non*, and not upon the merits." [79]

This decision also shows that juridically the setting aside of a decision is distinct from the subsequent rehearing or revision of a case although the two are often not separated in practice. It is with the first problem that we are directly interested inasmuch as it constitutes an exception to the principle of *res judicata*. Finally, in his decision of June 15, 1939, the Umpire found that:—

"As set forth in the American Commissioner's opinion, he and the Umpire agreed in the conclusion that the motion should be granted because the United States had proved its allegation that fraud in the evidence presented by Germany misled the Commission and affected its decision in favour of Germany." [80]

And, as the German Commissioner insisted that the Commission should also examine the evidence tendered by the United States to determine whether the claims had been made good, this was also done in the same decision and the cases of the claimants were found to be good.[81] Awards were subsequently entered in favour of the claimants.[82]

Mention may also be made of the *La Abra Silver Mining Co. Case* and the *Benjamin Weil Case*, in which awards were made in favour of the claimants by the Mexican-United States Mixed Claims Commission (1868). Subsequent investigation by the United States having shown that the claims were obtained by fraud on the part of the claimants, the sum received by the United States Government in respect of these claims was refunded to the Mexican Government.[83]

[79] *Lehigh Valley Railroad Co. Case* (1935), *Dec. & Op.*, p. 1159, at p. 1175.
[80] *Lehigh Valley Railroad Co. Case* (1939), *Op. & Dec.*, p. 1, at p. 311.
[81] *Ibid.*, at p. 311–2.
[82] *Cf.* Germ.-U.S. M.C.C. (1922): *Final Report of H. H. Martin, Acting Agent of the U.S.*, 1941, pp. 81 *et seq.*
[83] For an account of these cases, see 2 *Int.Arb.*, pp. 1324–1348. See also U.S.F.R. 1902, correspondence between U.S. Secretary of State Hay and Mexican Ambassador Azpíroz returning to Government of Mexico unpaid balance of amount awarded to the La Abra Co. (pp. 781–2) and to Weil (pp. 783–4). See particularly, letter of Hay to Azpiroz of March 28, 1900 (p. 781), which summed up the history of the investigation of fraud. The remainder of the amount

But, while fraud on the part of the tribunal nullifies the whole proceedings, it would seem that fraud on the part of the parties and witnesses constitutes a cause of nullity only to the extent to which it has affected the decision.[84] In other words, the Tribunal must have been led into error by the fraud of the party or parties. In this sense, it may be correct to say that the setting aside of a judgment for reason of fraud of the parties is merely a form of revision on the ground of error.[85] Unlike the first four causes of nullity enumerated above, error through fraud of the parties does not, strictly speaking,

received for these claims was returned on March 6, 1902 (see *Counter Case of the United States, Appendix, United States and Venezuelan Arbitration at The Hague* (*Orinoco Steamship Co. Case*), p. 92). See also, *supra*, p, 320, note 82.

See also U.S. Domestic Commission, Mexican Claims (Act of 1849): *Gardiner Case.* This case was concerned also with alleged dispossession of mines in Mexico. With counterfeit official documents, account books, correspondence, and perjury committed by himself and his accomplices, claimant obtained an award for $400,000. Fraud having been established by Congressional investigation committees, action was brought before the Court of New York for recovery of the sums awarded, which court reversed and annulled the award (2 *Int.Arb.*, pp. 1255–1266).

84 *Cf. supra*, pp. 358–9. The Germ.-U.S. M.C.C. (1922) granted the American motion for a rehearing, "because the U.S. had proved its allegation that fraud in the evidence presented by Germany *misled the Commission* and *affected its decision* in favour of Germany." Italics added. Referring to another occasion on which the Umpire had used the expression "misled," the German Commissioner said in his opinion of September 13, 1934: "The next restriction flows from the Umpire's Decision when he states, he admits such fraud, *as misled the Commission.* Thus the Umpire asks for causality between fraud and decision." (*Dec. & Op.*, p. 1138.) The American Commissioner, in his Opinion of June 15, 1939 (*Op. & Dec.*, p. 21), said: "It is perfectly patent that the decision at Hamburg cannot be set aside on account of fraud in the pleadings alone. . . ." Indeed, exaggeration of claims is not infrequent even in international proceedings, especially those preferred on behalf of individuals. As long as the tribunal is not misled, there is no cause of nullity. In the above mentioned opinion, the American Commissioner minutely examined the fraud in the pleadings and the fraud in the evidence and analysed their effect on the previous decision rendered at Hamburg. The Umpire concurred in this opinion.

85 *Cf. Lehigh Valley Railroad Co. Case* (1933), *Dec. & Op.*, p. 1084, at pp. 1127–28: "If it [the Tribunal] may correct its own errors and mistakes, *a fortiori* it may, while it still has jurisdiction of a cause, *correct errors into which it has been led by fraud and collusion.*" Italics added.

Since, as the Trail Smelter Arbitral Tribunal (1935) said, "the formula of 'essential error' originated in a text voted by the International Law Institute in 1876" (*infra*, p. 362), it may be mentioned that Article 27 of the Project of Rules for the Procedure of International Arbitration (1 *Annuaire* (1877), pp. 126 *et seq.*), in which "essential error" was regarded as a cause of nullity of arbitral awards, originated from Article 24 of the Geneva Project of the Institute (7 R.D.I.L.C. (1875), pp. 418–25). The latter Article spoke only of "essential error caused by the production of false documents." It was, as the *Rapporteur* of the second Commission in The Hague session said, because the Commission considered that essential error should also include error induced by false testimony (1 *Annuaire* (1877), pp. 86–7) that the term "essential error" was adopted without further qualification. It seems, therefore, that, at least in the opinion of the Institute, the term "essential error" covered primarily, if indeed not solely, error produced through false documents and testimony.

constitute a cause of nullity but only a cause of voidability. While the first four cases prevent a valid decision from being given, error through fraud of the parties only enables an otherwise valid decision to be set aside. The same applies to "manifest and essential error" and error through lack of essential evidence, which will be considered in the next two sections.

VI. Manifest and Essential Error.—The Trail Smelter Arbitral Tribunal (1935) in its Final Award (1941) held that:—

> "A mere error in law is no sufficient ground for a petition tending to revision." [86]

In the *Drier Case* (1935), dealing with a petition for rehearing on grounds of alleged injustice and judicial error, the German-United States Mixed Claims Commission (1922) held that:—

> "No power resides in the Commission to redress an alleged injustice inherent in its awards. . . . The only reason which may now be considered is the third, which asserts manifest juridical error in the award." [87]

As, however, the Umpire of the same Commission said in the *Lehigh Valley Railroad Co. Case* (1933):—

> "I think it clear that where the Commission has misinterpreted the evidence, or made a mistake in calculation, or where its decision does not follow its fact findings, or where in any other respect the decision does not comport with the record as made, or where the decision involves a material error of law, the Commission not only has power, but is under the duty, upon a proper showing, to reopen and correct a decision to accord with the facts and the applicable legal rules. My understanding is that the Commission has repeatedly done so where there was palpable error in its decision." [88]

The Trail Smelter Arbitral Tribunal (1935) quoting the above passage without its last sentence, considered it to be in the nature of a dictum and "in so far as it does not refer to the correction of possible errors arising from a slip or accidental omission, it does not express the opinion generally prevailing as to the position in international law," the implication being that

[86] 3 UNRIAA, p. 1905, at p. 1957.
[87] *Dec. & Op.*, p. 1037, at p. 1078.
[88] *Dec. & Op.*, p. 1084, at p. 1124–5.

the power claimed and exercised was too wide.[89] When, however, the omitted sentence is taken into account, and leaving aside the question of the correcting of clerical errors in a judgment, there seems to be no substantial disagreement between the two tribunals, especially when the above quoted passage from the decision in the *Drier Case* (1935) by the same Umpire is considered.[90] Moreover the Trail Smelter Arbitral Tribunal (1935) itself decided that a judgment might be impugned for "manifest errors" in law, "such as would be committed by a tribunal that would overlook a relevant treaty or base its decision on an agreement admittedly terminated."[91] As a concrete example, the Tribunal cited the *Schreck Case* (1874),[92] in which Umpire Thornton reconsidered and revised his decision because he found that he had clearly committed an error in law.[93] It may therefore be said that these international tribunals agree that "manifest" or "palpable" errors in law may constitute a ground for revising a judgment.

As for the qualification "essential" which has been used with regard to errors,[94] the Trail Smelter Arbitral Tribunal (1935) had the following to say:—

"The formula 'essential error' originated in a text voted by the International Law Institute in 1876. From its inception, its very authors were divided as to its meaning. . . . The Tribunal is of opinion that the proper criterion lies in a distinction not between 'essential' errors in law and other such errors, but between 'manifest' errors . . . and other errors in law."[95]

[89] *Final Award* (1941), 3 UNRIAA, p. 1905, at p. 1957.

[90] *Supra*, p. 361. Also *loc. cit.*, p. 1080.

[91] *Final Award* (1941), *loc. cit.*, p. 1957.

[92] The claimant's name has been variously reported in *Int.Arb.* under both "Schreck" and "Shreck."

[93] Mex.-U.S. Cl.Com. (1868): 2 *Int.-Arb.*, pp. 1357–8; also 3 *ibid.*, pp. 2450–3. Because a claimant was born in Mexico, the Umpire took it for granted that he was of Mexican nationality. The Agent of the United States produced the appropriate law of Mexico, by which it appeared that the assumption was clearly erroneous.

[94] *Cf.* use of the "essential error" formula, P.C.A.: *The Orinoco Steamship Co. Case* (1910), 1 H.C.R., p. 226, at p. 230: "Whereas by the agreement of February 13, 1909, both parties have at least implicitly admitted, as vices involving the nullity of an arbitral decision, excessive exercise of jurisdiction and essential error in the judgment."

PCIJ: *Monastery of Saint-Naoum* (1924), Adv.Op., B. 9, p. 21. The Court used this expression but was non-committal as to its effect.

[95] *Final Award* (1941), *loc. cit.*, p. 1957. *Cf. supra*, p. 360, note 85. The Tribunal appears to have overstated any divergence of opinion amongst the authors of the resolution.

Yet it cannot be doubted that even where an error in law may be manifest, it needs also to be material to the actual question decided in order to constitute a ground for setting the judgment aside.

More limited than a manifest error in law as an admissible ground of revision is perhaps an alleged error in fact. As mentioned above, the seeming liberality of the German-United States Mixed Claims Commission (1922) in the matter of revision has already been the subject of criticism. Yet in the *Drier Case* (1935), the same Commission held with regard to an alleged error in the allowance of damages that:—

> "The error committed by the Commissioners, if error there was, was not an error as to a matter of law but of fact. . . . The Commission has no function to sit as a tribunal to grant new trials for errors of fact, particularly where those errors involve opinion as to value." [96]

It cannot be doubted that a final decision may not be set aside merely because the appraisal of fact by the tribunal may be the subject of well-founded criticism, just as it cannot be for a "*mere* error in law." [97] It does not, however, appear from the above quotation that the German-United States Mixed Claims Commission (1922) categorically rejected error in fact as a ground for setting aside a final judgment. Indeed, it seems from the following passage in the same decision that, where an error in fact is manifest or results from judicial abuse, it may still be a cause for setting aside a final judgment.

> "From what has been said, it is evident that the award is regular upon its face, and that there does not appear upon the record any matter from which it can fairly be concluded that the Commissioners either abused their discretion in appraising the evidence

[96] *Dec. & Op.*, p. 1037, at p. 1079. The Trail Smelter Arbitral Tribunal (1935) in its *Final Award* (1941) (3 UNRIAA, p. 1905, at pp. 1938 *et seq.*), was dealing with an alleged error of interpretation of the Convention and seemed to avoid dealing with the question of error of fact.

[97] P.C.A.: *Orinoco Steamship Co. Case* (1910), 1 H.C.R., p. 226, at p. 231. Span.-U.S. Cl.Com. (1871): *Young, Smith & Co. Case*, 3 *Int.Arb.*, p. 2184, at p. 2187. Fran.-Germ. M.A.T.: *de Neuflize Case* (1927), 7 T.A.M., p. 629, at pp. 632–3, cited *infra*, p. 372, note 31. *Cf.* the rather free translation which the Trail Smelter Arbitral Tribunal (1935) in its *Final Award* (1941) (*loc. cit.*, p. 1957) gave to the passage quoted from *de Neuflize Case* (1927) as " . . . in order to justify revision it is not enough that there has taken place an error on a point of law or in the appreciation of a fact, or in both." See also *infra*, p. 372.

or were guilty of manifest error in reaching the amount of their award." [98]

VII. Fresh Evidence.—Error produced through lack of knowledge, at the time of the judgment, of facts which would have exercised a decisive influence upon the decision may be regarded as a particular form of error in fact. The Hague Conventions of 1899 and 1907 for the Pacific Settlement of International Disputes (Articles 55, 83 respectively), the Statutes of the Permanent Court of International Justice (Article 61) and of the International Court of Justice (Article 61), and the Rules of Procedure of practically every Mixed Arbitral Tribunal set up in pursuance of the Treaties of Peace after the First World War [99] consider after-discovered or newly discovered evidence as a ground for revising a judgment. The aim is to provide a remedy against possible injustice arising from errors of fact which have become demonstrable for the first time after the judgment.[1]

[98] *Drier Case* (1935), *Dec. & Op.*, p. 1037, at p. 1080.

Cf. PCIJ: *Monastery of Saint-Naoum* (1924), Adv.Op., B. 9, p. 21. The Court used the term "essential error" as a cause of revision to cover the case of a possible error in fact. *Cf.* also P.C.A.: *Orinoco Steamship Co. Case* (1910), 1 H.C.R., p. 226, at p. 230, where the P.C.A. also used the term "essential error" to cover possible cases of "errors in law and fact."

[99] *e.g.*, Fran.-Germ. M.A.T.: Rules of Procedure (2.IV.1920), Arts. 79–82 (1 T.A.M., pp. 44–61); Belgo-Germ. M.A.T.: Rules of Procedure (19.X.1920), Art. 76 (*ibid.*, pp. 33–44); Brit.-Austrian M.A.T.: Rules of Procedure (16.VIII.1921), Art. 91 (*ibid.*, pp. 622–39); Czech.-Germ. M.A.T.: Rules of Procedure (9.XI.1921), Art. 63 (*ibid.*, pp. 948–57); S.C.S.-Germ. M.A.T.: Rules of Procedure (27.III.1921), Art. 64 (*ibid.*, pp. 266–75): Italo-Germ. M.A.T.: Rules of Procedure (20.XII.1921), Art. 68 (*ibid.*, pp. 796–812); Rum.-Germ. M.A.T.: Rules of Procedure (9.III.1922), Arts. 69–70 (*ibid.*, pp. 939–48); Fran.-Turk M.A.T.: Rules of Procedure (1.XII.1929), Art. 67 (5 *ibid.*, pp. 984–93); Greco-Turk. M.A.T.: Rules of Procedure (24.XII.1925), Arts. 125–6 (*ibid.*, pp. 994–1012). Each of the above represents a different version of the same principle. As regards this particular provision, the Rules of Procedure of the Greco-Germ. M.A.T. (16/3.VIII.1920) and of the Siamese-Germ. M.A.T. (22.XII.1920) are the same as that of the Fran.-Germ. M.A.T. The Rules of Procedure of the Brit.-Germ. M.A.T. (4.IX.1920) did not originally contain a provision for revision for after-discovered evidence, but it was adopted in an amendment of February 20, 1925 (5 *ibid.*, pp. 616–7). Among the Rules of Procedure of the M.A.T. reproduced in the T.A.M., those to which Japan was a party alone did not contain such a provision, although Art. 41 of the Rules of Procedure (12.XI.1920) of the Japano-Germ. M.A.T. (1 *ibid.*, pp. 124–7) provided that: "The Tribunal may, on application or of its own motion, rectify any apparent error in the decision." In so far as the present provision is concerned, the version in the Rules of Procedure of the M.A.T. to which Germany was a party is in general identical with that in the Rules of Procedure of those M.A.T. which the same Allied or Associated Power later set up with Germany's former allies, *e.g.*, provisions concerning revision in the Rules of Procedure of the Fran.-Germ. M.A.T. and the Fran.-Austrian, Fran.-Bulg., Fran.-Hung. M.A.T. are identical.

[1] *Cf.* S.C.S.-Germ. M.A.T.: *Ventense Case* (1923), 7 T.A.M., p. 79, at p. 82.

In the *Moore Case* (1871), the Mexican-United States Claims Commission (1868) held, in the absence of express provision in the *compromis*, that:—

"Whenever the evidence produced on a motion for rehearing before the Commission is of a certain and conclusive character, such as ought undoubtedly to produce a change in the minds of the Commissioners and convince them of petitioner's right to an award, we are disposed to grant the motion and award according to public law, equity and justice." [2]

The Trail Smelter Arbitral Tribunal (1935), referring to the Rules of Procedure of the Franco-German Mixed Arbitral Tribunal concerning this question, said in its *Final Award* (1941):—

"These rules themselves are expressive of the opinion generally prevailing as to the position in international law." [3]

Article 79 of the Rules of Procedure of the Franco-German Mixed Arbitral Tribunal provided that:—

"The application for revision shall be made to the Tribunal. It may be made only when it is based upon the discovery of some new fact of such a nature as to be a decisive factor, which fact was, at the time of closing of the record (*clôture des débats*), unknown to the Tribunal itself and also to the party claiming revision."

Certain elements are common to all these provisions for the revision of a final judgment on the ground of after-discovered evidence.

First, there must be the discovery of some fact.

"The use of the word 'discovery'"—as the Franco-Bulgarian Mixed Arbitral Tribunal held—"implies unquestionably the existence of the fact, which was unknown to the Tribunal, at the time when it gave the decision which is now impugned." [4]

Evidence of a *new* fact which has come into existence only after the decision is, therefore, inadmissible as a ground for revision.[5]

[2] 2 *Int.Arb.*, p. 1357. On the jurisdictional question, see *infra*, p. 370, note 24.
[3] 3 UNRIAA, p. 1905, at p. 1957, note 1.
[4] *Battus Case* (1929), 9 T.A.M., p. 284, at p. 286. (Transl.)
[5] *Battus Case* (1929), *ibid.* See also Fran. Germ. M.A.T.: *Creange Case* (1924), 5 T.A.M., p. 114, at p. 116; *Guillaume Case* (Revision) (1928), 8 *ibid.*, p. 764, at p. 765; *Otzenberger Case* (1929), 9 *ibid.*, p. 272, at p. 274.

As to what constitutes a fact, the Franco-German Mixed Arbitral Tribunal held that:—

"The notion of *fact* ought not to be put in absolute opposition to that of *law* which are not always easily distinguishable the one from the other, but it should be understood in a more liberal sense, covering also means of proof which have bearing on the law and exceptionally the law itself, where the principle *jura novit curia* does not apply and the burden of proving the law is upon the party wishing to rely upon it."[6]

Secondly, this fact must be of such a nature as would have exercised a decisive influence upon the judgment rendered. In other words, the judgment would have been materially different if this fact had then been known.[7]

Thirdly, the fact must have been unknown to the tribunal and to the party claiming such revision at the time of closing the record (*clôture des débats*) or of the decision.[8] The previous ignorance of the new fact adduced has to be proved.[9]

In most of the above Conventions, Statutes and Rules, a preliminary procedure is provided for deciding the existence of the new fact and whether it possesses the above attributes.[10] If it were found wanting in any one of the three conditions, the application for revision would be denied and the previous judgment left undisturbed.[11]

Moreover, the Statute of the World Court expressly provides that the previous ignorance of the party of the newly discovered fact must not have been due to its own negligence.[12] In the *Moore Case* (1871), cited above, where the Mexican-United

6 Fran.-Germ. M.A.T.: *Heim and Chamant Case* (1922), 3 T.A.M., p. 50, at p. 55. (Transl.)

7 *Cf. Heim and Chamant Case* (1922), *ibid.*, at p. 55. Belgo-Germ. M.A.T.: *La Suèdoise Case* (1924), 4 T.A.M., p. 315, at p. 316.

8 *Cf.* Belgo-Germ. M.A.T.: *Betz Case* (1929), 9 T.A.M., p. 654, at p. 655.

9 Fran.-Germ. M.A.T.: *de Tayrac Case* (1929), 9 T.A.M., p. 492, at p. 494.

10 ICJ (PCIJ): Statute, Art. 61 II; The Hague Convention, 1907 (1899), Art. 83 III (Art. 55 III). Among the Rules of Procedure of the M.A.Ts., similar provisions existed except those of the Rum.-Germ. (1 T.A.M., p. 939–48); Rum.-Hung. (*ibid.*, pp. 826–35); Fran.-Turk (5 *ibid.*, pp. 984–93) and the Belgo.-Turk. (7 *ibid.*, pp. 288–97) M.A.T.s which left the procedure of revision entirely to be regulated by the tribunal.

11 *e.g.*, Fran.-Germ. M.A.T.: *de Neuflize Case* (1927), 7 T.A.M., p. 629.

12 Art. 61. See also the Rules of Procedure of the Greco-Turk., Rum.-Turk. M.A.T.s (5 T.A.M., pp. 994–1012), and the Rules of Procedure of those M.A.T.s to which Great Britain was a party, *e.g.*, Brit.-Austrian M.A.T. (1 T.A.M., pp. 622–39).

States Claims Commission (1868) allowed revision for newly discovered evidence, the Commission went on to say:—

"If there be an exception to this practice, it must be where there has been some gross laches of the claimant, or where, to allow the motion, at the time and under the circumstances, injustice would probably be done to the government defending." [13]

In this connection, it may be recalled that:—

"The lack of an instrument which would have been ready to hand it required cannot excuse the failure to obtain the testimony thereby obtainable." [14]

The requirement that there should be no negligence on the part of the claimant is in agreement with the rationale of the power of a Tribunal to grant revision for after-discovered evidence. In the *Lehigh Valley Railroad Co. Case* (1933), the Umpire of the German-United States Mixed Claims Commission (1922) said:—

"I come now to the question of jurisdiction to reopen for the presentation of what is usually known in judicial procedure as after-discovered evidence. I am of opinion that the Commission has no such power.

"In cases where a retrial is granted or a reopening and rehearing indulged for the submission of so-called after-discovered evidence, this is usually by a court. It is to the interest of the public that litigation be terminated, and municipal tribunals have the power to set a case for trial and to compel the parties to proceed. While they will not compel a litigant to proceed without hearing his reasons for delay, neither party has a right to hold the case open until he feels that he has exhausted all possible means of obtaining evidence. If such right existed, courts would be unable to function. By analogy, if this Commission had the power to make an order to close the proofs in any case and compel the parties to proceed, either party who was not then ready, because it had not exhausted its sources of information and evidence might well have an equity to ask a reopening that it might be permitted to offer evidence theretofore unavailable.

[13] 2 *Int.Arb.*, p. 1357.

[14] Germ.-U.S. M.C.C. (1922): *Lehigh Valley Railroad Co. Case* (1933), *Dec. & Op.*, p. 1084, at p. 1127. It is, therefore, no excuse for a State to plead insufficiency of power under municipal law to compel witness to testify within its jurisdiction when it could easily have passed the necessary legislation. *Cf. supra*, pp. 230 and 321.

" But the situation here is quite otherwise. . . . No time limit whatsoever was set in the original agreement for the closing of proofs. . . . The Commission has from its inception been sensible of its lack of power to compel the closing of the record and the final submission of any case. . . .

" The agreement does not contemplate that when the two Agents signify their readiness to submit a case and do submit it upon the record as then made to their satisfaction, obtain a hearing and decision thereon, the Commission shall have power to permit either Agent to add evidence to the record and to reconsider the case upon a new record thus made." [15]

Thus, it may be said that where a party has all the time it desires to prepare a case before submission, the non-discovery of some essential fact gives rise to at least a presumption of negligence. Where a tribunal has no power to close the record for submission by definite dates, it would, therefore, normally also have no power to grant revision for after-discovered evidence.

There remain, however, two questions which are not resolved by the above decision. First, is the presumption of negligence rebuttable? In other words, if it is established that in fact there has been no negligence, would the tribunal have the power to reopen the judgment? Secondly, separating the question of procedure, which concerns the power of the tribunal, from the question of substance, which relates to the voidability of the judgment, it may be asked whether a judgment may still be impugned, even when there is no tribunal competent to revise it. This applies to two types of cases. Either there may never have been a tribunal competent to revise the judgment. Or, if there had been, its power has expired. Thus, in the above mentioned Conventions, Statutes and Rules of Procedure, which permit revision by the tribunal, there is in every case a time limit set, beyond which a request may not be received.[16]

[15] *Dec. & Op.*, p. 1084, at pp. 1125–7. See also *Id.*: *Philadelphia-Girard National Bank Case*, *ibid.*, p. 939.

[16] I.C.J. (P.C.I.J.): Statute, Art. 61 (4), (5): 10 years from the date of the decision and six months from the discovery of the new fact.

The Hague Conventions leave the period to be fixed by the parties in the special agreement. The Special Agreement between the U.S.A. and Mexico of 1902 in the *Pious Fund Case* limited the period to eight days from the announcement of the award (Art. 13). In the *North Atlantic Coast Fisheries*

After this time limit has been exceeded, it is certain that the tribunal will no longer be competent to entertain a motion for revision.[17] But in all these cases, where there is no competent tribunal to reopen a judgment, is a judgment to stand if it is shown to have been erroneous by reason of some after-discovered evidence, which with all due diligence could not have been discovered earlier by the interested party?

In this connection, the *Lazare Case* (1885),[18] although not furnishing a complete answer, is instructive, in that it shows clearly the distinction that has to be made between the question of jurisdiction and the question of substance. In this case between Haiti and the United States, the former, soon after the award, petitioned the Arbitrator, Judge Strong, for a rehearing, on the ground of newly discovered evidence. The Arbitrator declined. In a subsequent letter to the Haitian Minister at Washington,[19] he stated that the petition was refused solely on the ground that his power over the award was at an end, notwithstanding that the newly discovered evidence was of such a character that it would "materially have affected" his decision had it been presented to him during the hearing of the case, and before his powers under the protocol had terminated.[20]

Counsel for Haiti appealed to the United States Department of State. Following a Senate resolution, the United States Government re-examined the case and Secretary of State Bayard reported that the award should be set aside on account of (i) certain papers in the Department of State which were not shown to have been laid before the Arbitrator; (ii) irregularities in the Arbitrator's proceedings; (iii) errors in the award;

Case, the Special Agreement between Great Britain and the U.S.A. (1908) limited the period to only 5 days from the promulgation of the award (Art. 10).

As for the M.A.T., out of a total of 34 Rules of Procedure published in the T.A.M., a majority of 18 (M.A.T.s to which France, Greece, Czechoslovakia, S.C.S. Kingdom, Rumania and Siam were parties) fixed the time at one year from the notification of the decision; 9 (M.A.T.s to which Belgium, Italy, Poland and, in one instance, France were parties) at two years; 4 (M.A.T.s to which Great Britain was a party) at six months; the Rules of Procedure of the Greco-Turk and the Rumano-Turk M.A.T.s fixing the delay at 60 days from the notification of the judgment or from the discovery of the new fact or means of proof and the Rules of Procedure of the Belgo-Hungarian M.A.T. being alone in fixing the delay at three years from the date of the notification of the award.

17 Fran.-Bulg. M.A.T.: *Battus Case* (1929) 9 T.A.M., p. 284, at p. 286. See also p. 287, where the question was more explicitly put as one of jurisdiction.

18 2 *Int.Arb.*, pp. 1749–1805.

19 February 18, 1886 (*ibid.*, at p. 1793). United States: S.Ex.Doc. 64, 49 Cong. 2 sess. 43.

20 *Ibid.*, at p. 1801.

(iv) the alleged newly discovered evidence; and (v) the above mentioned letter of Judge Strong to the Haitian Minister.[21] In the conclusion of his report, Secretary of State Bayard said inter alia that the announcement by the President in his annual message that the arbitration had been closed and a final award given could not preclude a re-examination of the case, and that whenever it was discovered that a claim against a foreign government could not be honourably and honestly pressed, such claim should be dropped no matter what stage had been reached in the proceedings.[22]

Although no formal action appears subsequently to have been taken, the Haitian Government, which, it seems, was informally apprised of the report, accepted it as finally disposing of the matter and the award was never enforced.

In the above pages, having first examined the various aspects of the principle of *res judicata*, we have also enumerated the various grounds of nullity or for the setting aside of a judgment or part thereof.[23] What is otherwise a final judgment possessing the force of *res judicata* may be declared null or set aside by the tribunal for any of the above reasons if it still has jurisdiction over the case.[24] It may similarly be

[21] *Ibid.*, at pp. 1800–1801.

[22] *Ibid.*, at p. 1804.

[23] It need hardly be recalled that nullity and *a fortiori* error may affect only part of a judgment, unless the nullity is due to fraud or corruption of the Tribunal. See *supra*, pp. 261, 358, 360.

[24] The jurisdictional point must be decided first before a Tribunal embarks upon the reopening and rehearing of a case. In the so-called "*Sabotage Cases*", the Germ.-U.S. M.C.C. (1922), before having dealt with the question of the jurisdiction of the Commission to entertain the petition, gave a decision on December 3, 1932 (*Dec. & Op.*, p. 999), denying, on its merits, a petition for rehearing. A new Umpire in the subsequent proceedings of the same case commented that: "As the matter is now viewed in retrospect, it would have been fairer to both the parties definitely to pass in the first instance upon the question of the Commission's power to entertain the supplementary petition for re-hearing" (*Dec. & Op.*, p. 1084, at p. 1118). In this decision (*Lehigh Valley Railroad Co. Case* (1933)), the new Umpire examined the jurisdiction of the Commission to grant a rehearing, the occasion being the filing of yet another petition to reopen the case. The Trail Smelter Arbitral Tribunal (1935) when faced with a petition for revision, referring to the latter decision, said: "The Tribunal is of opinion that this procedure should be followed" (*Final Award* (1941) 3 UNRIAA, p. 1905, at p. 1954).

Jurisdiction to reopen.—This question is by no means clear in international judicial practice. The Trail Smelter Arb. Trb. (1935) considered that before it rendered the final judgment and completed its task, it had jurisdiction to reopen a previous decision (*Final Award* (1941) *ibid.*, at p. 1954).

Apart express provision to the contrary, it seems, however, that where a tribunal has finished its task and finally adjourned, it becomes *functus officio* and would no longer be competent to grant a rehearing (*e.g.*, *Lazare Case*

renounced by the party in whose favour the judgment has been given.[25] It may also be reconsidered by another tribunal if both parties agree to submit the question to arbitration.[26]

In virtue of the principle, *res inter alios judicata neque nocet neque prodest,* it seems reasonable that only a party to the suit may request either the annulment or the revision of a judgment. In a case concerning revision for after-discovered evidence, the Franco-German Mixed Arbitral Tribunal held that:—

"The request for revision presented to the Tribunal has been submitted by a person not directly involved in the suit leading to the impugned decision; this fact alone suffices to reject as inadmissible this request for revision filed by a party which is, in truth, a third party." [27]

(1885) 2 *Int.Arb.*, p. 1749, at p. 1793; *supra*, pp. 369 *et seq.*). In the case of a claims commission, it seems that it becomes *functus officio* with the expiration of the term or with the completion of its task. See *e.g.*, Umpire Upham in the so-called "*Umpire Cases*" (1857): "As the Commission had expired, it did not seem to me the cases could be opened again, except on an extension of the Commission" (2 *Int.Arb.*, p. 1396, at p. 1405; *supra*, p. 292, note 10). He seemed to be of opinion, therefore, that if the term had not expired or had it been extended, the case might be reopened.

The Germ.-U.S. M.C.C. (1922) in the *Lehigh Valley Railroad Co. Case* (1933), although it declined to hold the view that it was a continuing tribunal trying one single case divided into numerous counts (*Dec. & Op.*, p. 1084, at pp. 1123–4; *supra*, p. 341, note 22, paragraph 5), was of opinion that as long as it sat, it would not be *functus officio* and would be competent to reopen a previous decision of fraud or manifest error (p. 1127; *supra*, p. 358, note 78), but that it had no power to reopen for after-discovered evidence (pp. 1125–7; *supra*, p. 368, note 15.

Umpire Thornton of the Mex.-U.S. Cl.Com. (1868), in the *Weil* and *La Abra Silver Mining Co. Cases* (Rehearing) (1876), held that he was debarred by the Convention from rehearing cases which he had already decided (2 *Int.Arb.*, p. 1324, at p. 1329), although the Commission was still sitting. He did, however, revise the *Schreck Case* (1874) for error in law (*supra*, p. 362, note 93). Although he distinguished the two cases on the ground that in the latter no new evidence was involved, the two National Commissioners of the same Commission seemed to agree, however, that the Commission had jurisdiction to grant rehearings even where no new evidence was involved; for they allowed revision for after-discovered evidence in the *Moore Case* (1871) (*supra*, p. 365, note 2).

In the *Young, Smith & Co. Case* the American Commissioner of the Span.-U.S. Cl.Com. (1871) held that: "Every Court has control of its judgments until the end of the term during which they are rendered" (3 *Int.Arb.*, p. 2184, at p. 2186) and the Umpire entertained a motion for rehearing presented to him through the National Commissioners (p. 2185). He was of opinion, however, that he, as Umpire, was incompetent to grant such a motion, unless it had been submitted to him through the National Commissioners (*Price Case* (1878) 3 *Int.Arb.*, p. 2189). A new Umpire expressed a similar opinion in the *de Acosta y Foster Case* (1881) (3 *Int.Arb.*, p. 2187).

[25] *e.g.*, *Lazare Case* (1885), see *supra*, pp. 369 *et seq.*; *La Abra Silver Mining Co. Case* and *Weil Case*, see *supra*, p. 359.

[26] *e.g.*, P.C.A.: *Orinoco Steamship Co. Case* (1910) 1 H.C.R., p. 226.

[27] *Société française de Banque et de Dépôt Case* (1928) 8 T.A.M., p. 766, at p. 767. (Transl.).

The principle of *res judicata* that all final judgments should be considered as conclusive and binding, that no dispute once settled should be revived, is, however, of such fundamental importance to legal stability that the above exceptions to the principle do not operate *ipso jure*. Each party may rely upon a final judgment until and unless it has been declared null or set aside.[28] Even where a tribunal still retains control over a decision, it must, unless the parties otherwise agree, first set aside the former decision in accordance with law before embarking upon any reconsideration of the case.[29] It seems certain, at all events, that, in virtue of the principle *nemo debet esse judex in propria sua causa,* neither of the parties may, against the wishes of the other, unilaterally regard a final judgment as null or vitiated by error and, therefore, refuse to comply with it. In case of dispute, the question should be submitted to an independent judicial authority.[30]

Before concluding this Chapter, it may be pointed out that nullity or revision of a final judgment is distinct from reconsideration of a judgment subject to appeal. In the latter case, the object is to decide whether a judgment which is not yet final has been well or ill decided and to reform it, if necessary, by a hierarchically superior court.[31] In the case of appeal, the principle of *res judicata* is not juridically affected; for a decision is not final until it is no longer subject to appeal. On the other hand, the causes of nullity and revision mentioned above constitute direct exceptions to the principle of *res judicata,* affecting the validity of a final judgment, and, for this reason, form an integral part of the general theory of *res judicata.*

28 *Cf. supra*, pp. 337 *et seq.*

29 *Cf. supra*, pp. 358–9.

30 *Cf. supra*, p. 279, note 4. The same *ratio* should apply all the more to a judicial decision.

31 *Cf.* Fran.-Germ. M.A.T.: *de Neuflize Case* (1927) 7 T.A.M., p. 629, at pp. 632–3: "Revision—the only remedy available against a judgment of the Mixed Arbitral Tribunals—should not be confused with, or assimilated to, appeal or cassation. In the case of a judgment which is not subject to appeal, revision does not depend on whether the case has been well or ill decided. Therefore, it cannot be based either on criticisms directed against a certain construction of the law or on differences of opinion concerning the appraisal of facts, or even on a combination of both these considerations. . . . Indeed, in revision, there could be no question of examining whether or not the Tribunal has correctly interpreted a given set of facts. This constitutes precisely the task of an appellate judge. . . ." (Transl.). *Id.*: *Heim et Chamant Case* (1922) 3 T.A.M., p. 50, at p. 54. S.C.S.-Germ. M.A.T.: *Ventense Case* (1923) 7 T.A.M., p. 79, at pp. 82–3. *Cf.* also P.C.A.: *Orinoco Steamship Co. Case* (1910) 1 H.C.R., p. 226, at p. 231. *Cf. supra*, p. 363.

Chapter 18

EXTINCTIVE PRESCRIPTION

The principle of extinctive prescription has been defined as follows:—

"When a right of action becomes extinguished because the person entitled thereto neglects to exercise it after a period of time, this extinction of the right is called prescription of action." [1]

In the *Sarropoulos Case* (1929), perhaps not unmindful of a decision reached the previous year by a majority vote of the League of Nations Committee of Experts for the Progressive Codification of International Law,[2] the Greco-Bulgarian Mixed Arbitral Tribunal, while conceding that "positive international law has not so far established any precise and generally accepted rule either as to the principle or to the duration of prescription," nevertheless held that "prescription, an integral and necessary part of every system of law, is deserving of recognition in international law." [3]

Other international tribunals have been more categorical, and the United States-Venezuelan Mixed Claims Commission (1885) described prescription as "an universally recognised principle," "equally obligatory upon every tribunal seeking to administer justice." [4]

The *Pious Fund Case* (1902), between the United States

[1] Ital.-Ven. M.C.C. (1903): *Gentini Case*, quoting Savigny, *Ven.Arb. 1903*, p. 720, at p. 726. (Transl.) See also U.S. Ven. M.C.C. (1903): *Spader Case*, quoting Vattel: "Prescription is the exclusion of all pretensions to right—an exclusion founded on the length of time during which that right has been neglected" (*Ven.Arb. 1903*, p. 161, at p. 162).

[2] To the effect that extinctive prescription did not form part of international law and, therefore, did not need to be considered as a subject for codification Minutes of the 4th Session, 1928, pp. 18–22. See also, pp. 47, 48. *Cf.* also U.N. International Law Commission, 2nd Session, Report on Arbitration Procedure, A/CN.4/18, March 21, 1950, para. 75. See further the present writer's "General Principles of Law as a subject for International Codification," 4 *Current Legal Problems* (1951), p. 35, at pp. 46 *et seq.*

The cases cited herein show that, in fact, the principle has often been invoked and applied in international adjudications as part of positive international law.

[3] 7 T.A.M., p. 47, at p. 51. Transl.

[4] *Cadiz Case*, 4 *Int.Arb.*, p. 4199, at p. 4203. By reason of the above "universally recognised principle," the Commission dismissed the claim on which, in the words of the Umpire, the claimants had been "sleeping . . . for nearly half a century" without any endeavour to collect it.

and Mexico decided by the Permanent Court of Arbitration,[5] has sometimes been relied upon as showing that the principle of prescription is not recognised in international law. This was done, for instance, by Italy in the *Gentini Case* before the Italo-Venezuelan Mixed Claims Commission (1903).[6] Jackson H. Ralston, Umpire of the Commission—formerly Agent of the United States in the *Pious Fund Case*—took occasion to point out that what the United States contended and what the Permanent Court of Arbitration upheld in that case was that the claim of the United States before an international tribunal could not be defeated by Mexican statutes of limitation, such municipal statutes having no authority whatsoever over international courts.[7] The Umpire went on to say that "the Permanent Court of Arbitration has never denied the principle of prescription, a principle well recognised in international law, and it is fair to believe that it will never do so."[8]

Even here it should be added that, although, as also held in the *Spader Case*, "it is doubtless true that municipal statutes of limitation can not operate to bar an international claim,"[9] based exclusively on international law, this should not be taken to exclude their application to an international claim where certain aspects of the case are properly governed by municipal law.[10]

The controversy surrounding the application of the principle of prescription in international law has involved international tribunals in extended discussion explaining the rationale of prescription as a principle of law recognised by all nations and why, as such, it should be received into, or rather must "by very necessity" form part of, the international legal order.

[5] 1 H.C.R., p. 429.

[6] *Gentini Case*, *loc. cit.*, at p. 725. Case concerned with claim for alleged forced loans, etc., presented for the first time after thirty years since their alleged occurrence. Case dismissed because "claimant has so long neglected his supposed rights as to justify a belief in their non-existence" (p. 730).

[7] *Loc. cit.*, at p. 725.

[8] *Ibid.*

[9] *Ven.Arb. 1903*, p. 161, at p. 162.

[10] See Mex.-U.S. G.C.C. (1923): *Cook Case* (1927), *Op. of Com. 1927*, p. 318, at p. 319. Belgo-Germ. M.A.T.: *Joestens Case* (1927) 7 T.A.M., p. 564.

Incidentally, the criticism of the *Cook Case* (1927) in Lauterpacht, *The Function of Law*, 1933 (pp. 93–4) does not seem justified. The Commission, far from denying the principle of prescription was precisely referring to it when it spoke of a "well-recognised *principle* of international practice." It only said that "there is, of course, no *rule* of international law" of the character of a municipal statute of limitation, a statement which is perfectly correct. *Cf. infra* the *Williams Case* and the *Gentini Case*.

Thanks to this discussion, prescription stands out as one of the most instructive examples showing how general principles of law operate as a source of international law. Now that we are approaching the end of our inquiry, which is concerned with the application of general principles of law by international tribunals, it is fitting that we should deal in greater detail with this typical example in order to illustrate the process of this operation.

The following quotation from the opinion of Commissioner Little in the *Williams Case*, for instance, is not only instructive as to the principle of prescription, but also as to the use of general principles of law in international law. Speaking for the United States-Venezuelan Claims Commission (1885), the learned Commissioner said:—

"The opposition (perhaps as strenuous now as at any former period) to international prescription among modern writers . . . seems to us to arise in good measure from confusion of terms, and to be therefore largely apparent, rather than real. In other words, the difference between the two schools, as we conceive, partly at least, 'lies in the terms'. Prescription is confounded with limitation. . . . They are always distinct. The former relates to substance, is the same in all jurisdictions, and aims at justice in every case, while the latter pertains to process, varies as a rule in all jurisdictions, and from time to time often arbitrarily in the same one, and admits occasional individual injustice. . . . Prescription was recognised when limitation was yet unknown. Bracton knew of it at common law before the English statutes on the subject. Courts of equity, where limitation acts do not apply, have invariably given lapse of time due weight in adjudications. They have always refused to enforce stale demands without undertaking to fix precise times for imparting the infirmity. Each case is left, under general principles, to be adjudged, as to time, according to its own character and circumstances. And the doctrine has been applied to the State acting for its citizens. . . . It is this prescription which underlies, varies from, antedates and, as Phillimore says, forms the model for municipal limitation regulations that the writers asserting the existence of the doctrine in the international law refer to and treat of." [11]

[11] 4 *Int.Arb.*, p. 4181, at pp. 4190–4. Account for mirrors supplied was presented twenty-six years after the sale without cause for delay. Defendant maintained that account was settled at the time of purchase. The Commission, presuming account to have been settled, dismissed the claim.

Prescription is, therefore, the principle underlying municipal rules of limitation. It is always necessary to distinguish, as did the Umpire in the *Gentini Case*, between principles and rules, even though the distinction is only a relative one. The Umpire adopted the following distinction:—

> " A ' rule ' . . . ' is essentially practical and, moreover, binding . . . ; there are rules of art as there are rules of government ' while principle ' expresses a general truth, which guides our action, serves as a theoretical basis for the various acts of our life, and the application of which to reality produces a given consequence. ' " [12]

Since principles express general truth, general principles of law express general juridical truth. They form the theoretical bases of positive rules of law. The latter are the practical formulation of the principles and, for reasons of expediency, may vary and depart, to a greater or lesser extent, from the principle from which they spring.[13] The application of the principle to the infinitely varying circumstances of practical life aims at bringing about substantive justice in every case; the application of rules, however, results only in justice according to law, with the inescapable risk that in individual cases there may be a departure from subjective justice.[14]

Since the general principles of law form the basis of positive rules of law, in seeking these principles, there is no inherent reason why they cannot be found by a process of induction from the positive law of any single system, and indeed this always appears to be the inevitable starting point.[15] But the comparative method of studying the legal systems of different nations is no doubt a valuable and even conclusive test whether a given principle represents a general juridical truth and not what has been derisively called the "*plaisante justice qu'une rivière borne!*" [16]

12 *Loc. cit.*, p. 725. (Transl.). Umpire was quoting Bourguignon & Bergerol's *Dictionnaire des Synonymes*.

13 *Cf. Williams Case, loc. cit.*, pp. 4191–2.

14 See *supra*, p. 375.

15 See, as an illustration of this process, the Hurst-Crane Report (1904), *supra*, p. 249; also *supra*, p. 316, note 60. See also *Abu Dhabi Oil Arbitration* (1951) 1 I.C.L.Q. (1952) p. 247, at p. 251: " But, albeit English Municipal Law is inapplicable *as such*, some of its rules are in my view so firmly grounded in reason, as to form part of this broad body of jurisprudence—this modern law of nature ' " (original italics).

16 Blaise Pascal, *Pensées*, Ed. Brunschwicg, fragment 294: "*Plaisante justice qu'une rivière borne! Vérité en deçà des Pyrénées, erreur au delà.*"

Nevertheless, whether they are sought in one legal system, or in different legal systems, they cannot be found by stopping short at mere positive rules. It is necessary to go further and fathom their underlying theoretical basis. In other words, the *ratio legis* must be sought. An explicit example of this process may be found in the following quotation from the *Gentini Case*, concerning the principle of prescription:—

"On examining the general subject we find that by all nations and from the earliest period it has been considered that as between individuals an end to disputes should be brought about by the efflux of time. Early in the history of the Roman law this feeling received fixity by legislative sanction. In every country have periods been limited beyond which actions could not be brought. In the opinion of the writer these laws of universal application were not the arbitrary acts of power, but instituted because of the necessities of mankind, and were the outgrowth of a general feeling that equity demanded their enactment; for very early it was perceived that with the lapse of time the defendant, through death of witnesses and destruction of vouchers, became less able to meet demands against him, and the danger of consequent injustice increased, while no hardships were imposed upon the claimant in requiring him within a reasonable time to institute his suit. In addition, another view found its expression with relation to the matter in the maxim '*Interest republica ut sit finis litium.*' . . .

"As appears to the writer, all the arguments in favour of it as between individuals exist equally as well when the case of a national is taken up by his government against another, subject to considerations and exceptions noted at the end of this opinion. For may not a government equally with an individual lose its vouchers, particularly when, if any exist, they are in the hands of far distant subordinate agents? . . . May the claimant against the government, with more justice than if he claimed against his neighbour, virtually conceal his supposed cause of action till its investigation becomes impossible. Does equity permit it?" [17]

The process applied in the *Gentini Case* of tracing a general principle from rules of positive law universally applied *in foro domestico* through the general feeling of mankind for the requirements of equity and to equity itself, is a striking

[17] *Loc. cit.*, pp. 726–7.

reminder of Descamps' proposal for the application in international law of "objective justice" or "equity" as evidenced by the "*conscience juridique des peuples civilisés*" and confirms the belief drawn from the *travaux préparatoires* of the Statute of the Permanent Court of International Justice that this proposal is not very different from the ultimately adopted formula of "the general principles of law recognised by civilised nations" in Article 38 I (c) of the Court's Statute.[18]

In the opinion of the Umpire in the *Gentini Case*, prescription is a principle founded on equity and aimed at the attainment of justice. It has grown out of the necessities of mankind and has been sanctioned by the general juridical feeling of all nations since the earliest times. It may be said that these are the considerations which properly impart to the principle its character of universal validity. The *ensemble* of circumstances justifying the principle constitutes its *raison d'être* and, whenever these circumstances are present, the principle applies. *Ubi eadem ratio, ibi idem jus.*[19] And, as the same Umpire said in a subsequent case:—

> "When the reason for the rule of prescription ceases, the rule ceases,"[20]

thus applying the well-known maxim: *cessante ratione legis cessat lex.*

Before amplifying what the Umpire in the *Gentini Case* held to be the *ratio* of prescription, it may be pointed out that the application of the principle in international law may be excluded by express treaty provision as in *The Macedonian Case* (1863).[21] But in the absence of such positive rules the principle is applicable wherever those circumstances calling for its application, exist.

A review of the various international decisions dealing with the subject will show that the *raison d'être* of prescription may be found in the concurrence of two circumstances:—

18 See *supra*, p. 14. See also *supra*, p. 2, note 4.

19 *Cf.* ICJ: *Interpretation of Peace Treaties* (2nd Phase) (1950), D.O. by Azevedo, *ICJ Reports 1950*, p. 221, at p. 253.

20 Ital.-Ven. M.C.C. (1903): *Tagliaferro Case*, *Ven.Arb. 1903*, p. 764, at p. 765.

21 2 *Int.Arb.*, p. 1449. The Convention of November 10, 1858, excluded the plea of prescription from the consideration of the Arbitrator (5 *Int.Arb.*, p. 4691). *Cf.*, however, how the Arbitrator in computing damages nevertheless took into consideration the initial delay with which the claimant Government first brought the claim against the defendant Government (pp. 1464–5).

1. Delay in the presentation of a claim;
2. Imputability of the delay to the negligence of the claimant.

These two requirements for prescription can already be seen in the definition which was given at the beginning of the present Chapter.[22] The reason why a concurrence of these two circumstances gives rise to prescription will now be examined.

I. DELAY.—Prolonged delay in the presentation of a claim may perhaps itself be regarded as a sufficient reason for prescription. It has been seen that in the *Gentini Case* the Umpire, after giving the reason why the principle of prescription had grown up in municipal law, added that:—

> "In addition, another view found its expression with relation to the matter in the maxim '*Interest republica ut sit finis litium.*' "[23]

The Umpire went on to quote Savigny's view which would seem to indicate that the second consideration is the "most general and decisive" reason for the enactment of prescriptive legislation in municipal law.[24] But the Umpire, consonant with previous international decisions, relied on the first reason indicated for the application of the principle in international law. Indeed, it is doubted if international society is sufficiently integrated to admit a doctrine of international public policy. Although there may be a recent tendency to do so as is shown by the *Sarropoulos Case* (1927),[25] previous international decisions have not primarily relied merely on prolonged delay in order to justify prescription, but rather on the presumptions which in the experience of human affairs naturally arise from

[22] *Supra*, p. 373, note 1.

[23] *Supra*, p. 377. See also *Cadiz Case*, 4 *Int.Arb.*, p. 4199. The Umpire included prescription among principles "having their origin in public policy" (p. 4203).

[24] *Loc. cit.*, p. 726.

[25] Greco.-Bulg. M.A.T.: 5 T.A.M., p. 47. The facts of the case show that the M.A.T. was not justifying prescription in this case by presumptive evidence; for, as the Tribunal held, the facts did not appear to be disputed (5 T.A.M., p. 47, at p. 49). The Tribunal said: "The security and the stability of human affairs require the fixing of a time beyond which rights and obligations may no longer be disputed" (p. 51. Transl.).

However, though considering that prescription should be recognised in international law, the Tribunal relied actually on other grounds for the disposition of the case, namely, lack of jurisdiction.

such delay, a distinction that is not without its practical con sequences.[26]

As the United States-Venezuelan Claims Commission (1885) said in the *Williams Case*:—

"It is 'ordinary prescription' subject to be rebutted, with which we are especially concerned."[27]

In other words, it is prescription based upon certain rebuttable presumptions arising from long delay in the presentation of the claim that is applied in international law. The same Commission said:—

"Prescription is a 'rule' of inference . . . that *something* at least has transpired which, in the *natural order*, as the Civilians say, forms a basis and demand for its operation. It is no more the creature of legislative will than is any other deduction."[28]

The "natural basis" of prescription arising from the delayed presentation of a claim is twofold.[29] In the first place, the delay gives rise to a presumption against the existence of the alleged right forming the basis of the claim.[30] Secondly, it raises a presumption in favour of the defence. It is considered that long lapse of time inevitably destroys or obscures the evidence of the facts and, consequently, delay in presenting the claim places the other party in a disadvantageous position. For, if it had not previously been warned of the existence of the claim, it would probably not have accumulated and preserved the evidence necessary for its defence.[31]

But when do these two presumptions arise? In other words, how long must the delay be in order to justify prescription?

"A definite answer it would be difficult to frame. But in general we should say, where, all the evidence considered, it appears from long lapse of time and as a result thereof ordinarily to have been apprehended, that material facts including means of ascertainment

[26] *Cf. infra*, pp. 382–3.
[27] *Loc. cit.*, p. 4196.
[28] *Loc. cit.*, p. 4192. Italics of the Commission.
[29] See Brit.-Ven. M.C.C. (1903): *Stevenson Case, Ven.Arb., 1903*, p. 327, at p. 328.
[30] See also U.S.-Ven. M.C.C. (1903): *Spader Case, Ven.Arb. 1903*, p. 161, at p. 162, quoting Domat. Quoted also in *Williams Case, loc. cit.*, p. 4188.
See also *Gentini Case, loc. cit.*, p. 726. This case was actually dismissed on the ground that "the claimant has so long neglected his supposed rights as to justify a belief in their non-existence" (p. 730).
[31] *Gentini Case, loc. cit.*, p. 726, quoted *supra*, p. 377. *Cadiz Case, loc. cit.*, p. 4203.

pertaining to support or defence are lost, or so obscured as to leave the mind, intent on ascertaining the truth, reasonably in doubt about them, or in 'danger of mistaking the truth,' a basis for the presumption exists." [32]

The presumptions arising from the delayed presentation of a claim are, however, only presumptions of fact and are rebuttable.[33] They do not constitute a sufficient reason for barring an action, unless the second element justifying prescription is also present—imputability of the delay to the negligence or laches of the claimant.

II. Negligence or Laches of the Claimant.—Continuing from the above quoted passage, the United States-Venezuelan Claims Commission (1885) said:—

"If such situation be fairly imputable to a claimant's *laches* in withholding his demand, or, in Vattel's phrase, 'when by his own fault he has suffered matters to proceed to such a state that there would be danger of mistaking the truth,' prescription operates and resolves such facts against him; but if not so imputable, what the finding must be becomes a question of the preponderance of testimony merely, leaving each party to the misfortune time may have wrought for him in the support or in the defence of the claim." [34]

Laches or negligence are, therefore, indispensable to justify prescription. As the same Commission held:—

"Abandoned or neglected property or rights only are prescriptable." [35]

Vigilantibus, non dormientibus, jura subveniunt.[36]

When the presumptions against the existence of the right and in favour of the defence have arisen from the delayed

[32] *Williams Case, loc. cit.*, p. 4196. *Cf. ibid.*: "While prescription names and can name no particular periods, since Sir Matthew Hale's enunciation to that effect twenty years have been looked upon as about the time, in the ordinary run of affairs, required to give rise to the presumption. And the general acceptance of that time is evidence of its reasonable foundation. Still it must be said the constantly increasing multiplicity of business transactions and intercourse tends to suggest a shorter period." The *Sarropoulos Case* (1927) also suggested twenty years (*loc. cit.*, p. 51), however, for different reasons (see *supra*, p. 379, note 25).

[33] See *supra*, p. 380.

[34] *Williams Case, loc. cit.*, p. 4196.

[35] *Loc. cit.*, p. 4195.

[36] *Cf. Williams Case, loc. cit.*, p. 4195; *Gentini Case, loc. cit.*, p. 727.

presentation of the claim, the imputability of this delay to the claimant renders the presumption conclusive and the examination of the merits of the case unnecessary. The action is then said to be prescribed.[37]

Having thus explained the circumstances justifying the application of the principle of prescription, it may be desirable, before concluding this Chapter, to give a few instances where the principle of prescription does not apply because these justifying circumstances are not present.

We have seen that one of the bases of the principle of prescription is the presumption arising from the delay in the presentation of the claim. The delay must be such as would cause the evidence to become so obscured as to create a likelihood of mistaking the truth.

When such a situation has not yet been reached, a delayed demand escapes prescription, although delays will always excite criticism, since "honest claims and honest defences suffer by them; only dishonest ones profit." This, in the view of the United States-Venezuelan Claims Commission (1885), was what happened in the *Carlos Butterfield & Co. Case* (1890), where it appeared that there was a gap of less than six years between the events complained of (1854–5) and the notification of the claim.[38]

In certain cases, where the evidence has been well established and there can be no doubt as to truth, there will be no prescription, although the claim is not presented for a long time.

"In the *Gentini Case* . . . the Umpire referred to the fact that under certain circumstances prescription would not be recognised as a defence, mentioning specifically that of bonds 'as to which a public register has been kept.'"[39]

37 *Cf. Williams Case, loc. cit.*, p. 4199: "Upon these principles, too lengthily discussed, without awaiting further proof called for in defence from Venezuela, we disallow claim No. 36. It was withheld too long. The claimants' verification of the old urgent account of 1841 twenty-six years after its date, without cause for the delay, supposing it to be competent testimony, is not sufficient under the circumstances of the case to overcome the presumption of settlement."

38 See *Williams Case*, 4 *Int.Arb.*, p. 4181, at p. 4197. *Carlos Butterfield & Co. Case* (1890) 2 *Int.Arb.*, p. 1185. The original delay was about six years. Another aspect of the case was that the claim had been for over thirty years intermittently taken up and let fall again. On this point, *cf. infra*, pp. 385 *et seq.*

39 Ital.-Ven. M.C.C. (1903): *Giacopini Case, Ven.Arb. 1903*, p. 765, at p. 766.

In the *Tagliaferro Case*, although the claim was over 30 years old and had not previously been presented to the respondent Government, the same Umpire held that prescription did not apply. The acts complained of were connected with the unjust imprisonment by the military authorities of the defendant State and the failure of its judicial authorities to grant redress. In the opinion of the Umpire, if the complaint were groundless, "judicial, military, and prison records must exist to demonstrate the fact." [40]

Where the facts are not disputed, prescription also does not operate.

"It is said there are old claims about which there is and can be no dispute as to the facts. It is enough to say as to such, that the present holding does not stand in their way. The statement of Mr. Crallé, Acting Secretary of State, to which our attention has been directed, namely, 'Governments are presumed always ready to do justice; and whether a claim be a day or a century old, so that it is well founded, every principle of natural equity and of sound morals requires that it should be paid,' may not in itself perhaps be opposed to prescription. Conceded that a claim 'is well founded,' there would seem to be no occasion for prescriptive or other evidence in regard to it. The objection to the remark, in the connection in which it was employed, is, that it assumed the truth of the matter in controversy, to wit, the validity of the claim, for the ascertainment of which the principle was invoked. As to any admitted or indisputable fact, the public law, not resting 'upon the niceties of a narrow jurisprudence, but upon the enlarged and solid principles of State morality,' we are inclined to think, would not oppose the lapse of time, except for the protection of intervening rights, should there be such, even where municipal prescription might." [41]

Similarly, prescription will not operate where the second requirement—negligence or laches of the claimant [42]—is lacking; for

[40] Ital.-Ven. M.C.C. (1903): *Tagliaferro Case*, *Ven.Arb. 1903*, p. 764, at pp. 764–5.
It may, however, be possible to regard this case as one where the claim was brought to the notice of the defendant at the very beginning by the fact that the individuals immediately applied to the judicial authorities for redress. The headnote of the case, prepared by Ralston, the Umpire who decided the case, seems to support this view (p. 764). See *infra*, p. 384, note 48.
See also Brit.-U.S. Cl.Com. (1853): *The John Case* (1854), Hornby's *Report*, p. 216. For summary, see 4 *Int.Arb.*, pp. 3793–8; for its bearing on the present point, see 2 *Int.Arb.*, pp. 1736–7.

[41] *Williams Case*, 4 *Int.Arb.*, p. 4181, at pp. 4197–8.

[42] *Supra*, p. 381.

"Where there is valid reason for the withholding the case is different."[43]

"Incapacity, disability, want of legal agencies, prevention by war, well-grounded fear, and the like" constitute valid reasons.[44] *Contra non valentem agere nulla currit praescriptio.* Needless to say, where the delay has been occasioned by the defendant, there can be no question of prescription.[45]

Moreover,

"The presentation of a claim to the competent authority within proper time will interrupt the running of prescription."[46]

"It has been urged with plausibility that this occurs on the claimant invoking the aid of his government, because then he ceases to have control of his claim. But notice to the plaintiff State is of itself no protection to the defendant State. The latter's means of defence may be dissipated while the claim lies in the archives of the former, and thus its right to defend impaired in the sense above indicated. If it be said the plaintiff State is an interested party and time should not begin to run against it till its discovery of the injury, it may be answered that where one of two States is liable to be placed at a disadvantage by the conduct of a citizen it should be that one whose citizen he is. We think the due notification to the debtor government marks the proper date. This puts that government on notice, and enables it to collect and preserve its evidence and prepare its defence."[47]

The essential thing is that the defendant should be put on notice, within a reasonable time from the occurrences complained of, either by the individuals concerned or by their home State. Thus in the *Giacopini Case*, the Umpire, without departing from the principle of prescription which he recognised in the *Gentini Case* said:—

"In the present case, full notice having been given to the defendant, no danger of injustice exists, and the rule of prescription fails."[48]

43 *Williams Case*, 4 *Int.Arb.*, p. 4181, at p. 4195.

44 *Williams Case*, *ibid.*

45 Brit.-Ven. M.C.C. (1903): *Stevenson Case*, *Ven.Arb. 1903*, p. 327, at p. 329. See also *supra*, p. 150.

46 Ital.-Ven. M.C.C. (1903): *Gentini Case*, *Ven.Arb. 1903*, p. 720, at p. 730.

47 *Williams Case*, *loc. cit.*, at p. 4197. See also Mex.-U.S. G.C.C. (1923): *Faulkner Case* (1926), S.O. by American Commissioner, *Op. of Com. 1927*, p. 86, at p. 96. *Cf.* Brit.-U.S. Cl.Arb. (1910): *Cayuga Indians Case* (1926), referred to in the next footnote.

48 Ital.-Ven. M.C.C. (1903): *Giacopini Case*, Ralston: *Ven.Arb. 1903*, p. 765, at p. 767. Claimant's property was taken by Venezuelan troops thirty-two years

If a claim has been notified to the defendant, but has not been pressed for a long time, will prescription again start to run?

" There are so many things that may induce one government not to press pending demands against another, disconnected with the demands themselves, consideration for the condition and welfare of the debtor State itself being prominent among them, that we are disposed to think the true and, so far as we are advised, the usual way is to regard time in such cases, in the absence of circumstances evincing abandonment, as no respecter of persons." [49]

Unless, therefore, a claim can be considered as waived or abandoned,[50] if it has been duly notified to the plaintiff, prescription will not run even though it is not continually

prior to the presentation of the claim. But in the same month as the event occurred, he sought the help of the local tribunal to establish judicially the facts of the case. The tribunal directed notice to be given to the " Fiscal " of Venezuela before taking evidence. The latter attended the court proceedings and vigorously cross-examined the witnesses; he asked for and was given by the judge a copy of the evidence. In the same year the claimant informed the Italian Legation of the claim. But both he and Legation did not seem to have made any claim for all this time. *Cf.* headnote, prepared by the Umpire, " Held, the Government knowing in this manner of the existence of the claim had ample opportunity to prepare its defence " (p. 767).

Cf. Cayuga Indians Case (1926), Nielsen's *Report*, p. 203, at pp. 329–30. The case on this point is in substantial agreement with the *Giacopini Case*, although the ambiguous language of the Arbitral Tribunal may give the erroneous impression that as long as the individual claimants have persistently pressed their government to take up their case even if the government is guilty of laches, the action cannot be prescribed. This impression is reinforced by the Tribunal's introducing the principle *contra non valentem nulla currit praescriptio*. Such a view would be contrary to that held by the U.S.-Ven. Cl.Com. (1885) in the *Williams Case*, quoted *supra*, p. 384. See also American Agent's criticism, Nielsen's *Report*, pp. 271–2.

A review of the facts of the case will show, however, that the decision is in line with other international decisions on this matter. The private claim of the Canadian Cayugas against New York for payment of certain perpetual annuities dated back to 1811. New York held that American Cayugas were alone entitled to them and had paid each instalment to the American Cayugas. This claim was presented to the legislature of New York in 1849. The Brit. U.S. Cl.Arb. Tribunal recognised that there was an equity in favour of New York before 1849 and refused to allow the claim for annuities 1811–49 (pp. 330–1). But as the Tribunal said, New York could no longer be prejudiced by the delay of Great Britain after 1849, as at that time the facts of the case were brought to its notice and a public commission charged with its examination had recommended that the claim should be paid (p. 330). The claim for the annuities after 1849 was allowed by the Tribunal.

Thus looking at the substance of the case, its disposition agrees with the general principle of prescription in international law. The Tribunal did apply it when a defendant was not put on notice. It refused to apply it when it had been notified, even by the private claimant, or when the facts had been clearly established.

49 *Williams Case*, 4 *Int.Arb.*, p. 4181, at p. 4199.

50 *Cf.* Mex.-U.S. Cl.Com. (1839): *Charles Turner Case*, 3 *Int.Arb.*, p. 3126.

pressed for some reason which is at least plausible. This view is supported by *The Canada Case* (1870).[51]

In sum, prescription appears as the rational basis of certain rules of law admitted in all legal systems and its application in every juridical order is dictated by the sense of justice and equity common to civilised mankind and indeed by necessity. When not expressed in formulated rules, the principle is directly applicable to the facts of life whether intranational or international, wherever those circumstances justifying its *raison d'être* obtain. In every case, where such circumstances exist, conformity with the principle is regarded as bringing about substantive justice, while departure therefrom works injustice. Indeed, it is the characteristic of the general principles of law and of their essence that their binding character is derived not so much from some extrinsic authority, but rather from their inherent value; for they are the paths which civilised mankind has learned in its long experience in the municipal sphere to be those leading to justice and which it would perforce have to follow if it wished to establish Law and Justice among Nations.

[51] 2 *Int.Arb.*, p. 1733, at p. 1745.

Cf. Sir Edward Thornton dismissing a claim brought for the first time to the notice of the defendant State 15 years after the event, Mex.-U.S. Cl.Com. (1868): *Mossman Case* (1875) 4 *Int.Arb.*, p. 4180.

It may also be mentioned that in *The Canada Case* (1870), it was maintained by the U.S. that the interruption in the prosecution of the claim could not be construed as an admission of the justice of the Brazilian position, since "the acquiescence of a sovereign Government can never be assumed from lapse of time"; and in support of this contention, the case of the U.S. cited the well-known common law maxim, *nullum tempus occurrit regi.* J. B. Moore, commenting on this contention said rightly: "This maxim, which merely expresses the law as between sovereign and subject, possesses no international authority, . . . and its invocation added little or nothing to the reply of the United States to the suggestion of acquiescence" (2 *Int.Arb.*, p. 1736). In municipal law the State may be placed in a privileged position *vis-à-vis* its individual subjects. International law is based upon the equality of the States.

The same observation may be addressed to the *Alsop Case* (1911) 5 A.J.I.L. (1911), p. 1079, see pp. 1099–1100, in so far as it held that prescription, the term used in the award being actually "principle of limitation of actions," did not apply against, or between, sovereign States.

As regards the distinction between prescription and limitations, see *supra*, p. 375. But inasmuch as the case relied on the ground that the delay of the claimant in pressing for the payment of a debt acknowledged by the debtor State in a contract was reasonable because the debtor State was clearly not in a position to pay and no advantage could be derived from attempts to make it do so, and the only course open to the claimant was to wait until the financial situation of the debtor State improved, this decision confirms *The Canada Case* (1870) and the general proposition set out above.

CONCLUSIONS

THE purpose of the foregoing pages, as stated in the Introduction, has been to demonstrate the practical application by international courts and tribunals of various general principles of law recognised by civilised nations. It is to be hoped that they have adequately shown the extent to which these principles are applied in international law. As we have seen, the Anglo-American Board of Commissioners set up under Article VII of the Jay Treaty of 1794, which heralded the era of modern international arbitration, already had frequent occasion to invoke and apply them, though not always under the name of general principles of law.[1] Thereafter, and up to the time of the establishment of the Permanent Court of International Justice, references to, and the application of, "principles of jurisprudence accepted by the law of all countries"[2] and the like[3] are frequently to be found.

Moreover, the express mention of "the general principles of law recognised by civilised nations" among the sources of international law by the Statute of the World Court is an example followed by numerous arbitration treaties concluded since the establishment of the Permanent Court,[4] and the definition of the sources of international law set out in Article 38 of the Statute of the Court "has been repeatedly treated as authoritative

[1] See *e.g.*, *supra*, pp. 70–1, 218, 275–77.

[2] *The Queen Case* (1872), *supra*, p. 327.

[3] *e.g.*, *Closure of Buenos-Aires Case* (1870), 2 *Arb.Int.* p. 637, at p. 659: "Universal jurisprudence." U.S.-Ven. Cl.Com. (1885): "An universally recognised principle," *supra*, p. 373. *Delagoa Bay Railway Case* (1900), Martens, 2 (30) N.R.G., p. 329, at pp. 401–2: "General principles of the common law of modern nations." Germ.-Ven. M.C.C. (1903): "This universally accepted rule of law," *supra*, p. 305. U.S.-Ven. M.C.C. (1903): *Heny Case*, *Ven.Arb. 1903*, p. 14, at p. 23: "Principles of law generally adopted by all nations." *Walfisch Bay Case* (1911), Cd. 5857, p. 23. See also *ibid.*, "rules in conformity with the leading systems in modern law," *supra*, p. 318.

[4] They have been analysed and conveniently set out in the following publications: L.o.N., *Arbitration and Security (Systematic Survey of the Arbitration Conventions and Treaties of Mutual Security deposited with the L.o.N.)*, 2nd ed., 1927, L.o.N.P., C.653.M.216.1927.V.29, pp. 40 *et seq.*; Max Habicht, *Post-War Treaties for the Pacific Settlement of International Disputes*, 1931, pp. 1048 *et seq.*; U.N., *Systematic Survey of Treaties for the Settlement of International Disputes, 1928–1948*, 1948, pp. 116 *et seq.* The above analyses show how consistently the formula of the Statute has been followed.

by international arbitral tribunals."[5] The Permanent Court itself and, after it, the International Court, have on many occasions applied these principles as an integral part of international law,[6] and individual judges, in their separate opinions, have often had express recourse to them.[7]

From the evidence thus provided by the practice of international courts and tribunals, it has been possible to trace the practical application of a number of general principles in the sphere of international law.

In Part One the application of a principle of law which is recognised by the public law of the various nations—*Salus populi suprema lex*—was examined. In the international sphere, it gives rise to a number of rights of the State *vis-à-vis* individuals subject to its authority, by permitting the State's superior interest of self-preservation to override the interests of individuals. It also gives rise to a number of rights of the State *vis-à-vis* other States, notably by affording it the right of protecting its own existence and other legal rights against any unlawful attack, and also by permitting it in exceptional cases of extreme necessity to disregard a minor right of another State. We have also seen how in its practical application, the principle has its limitations, so that the State's

[5] U.N., *Survey of International Law*, Memorandum submitted by the Secretary-General, 1949, A/CN.4/1/Rev.1, p. 22. See, *e.g.*, Germ. U.S. M.C.C. (1922): *Administrative Decision No. II* (1923) *Dec. & Op.*, p. 5, at pp. 7–8. Rum.-Germ. Arb. (1919): *David Goldenberg & Sons Case* (1928) 2 UNRIAA, p. 901, at p. 909.

[6] PCIJ: *German Interests Case* (Jd.) (1925). The Court indicated that its law of procedure included not only rules contained in the Statute and the Rules of Court but also " the general principles of law " (A. 6, p. 19). On other occasions, it spoke of " essential rules guiding their [the Court's] activity as a Court " (B. 5, p. 28; *supra*, p. 298). *Cf.* also, *supra*, pp. 299–300. It has also applied the principle of interpretation *contra proferentem* as " a familiar rule for the construction of instruments " (A. 20/21, p. 114; *supra*, p. 108, note 14), " the well known rule that no one can be judge in his own suit " (B. 12, p. 32; *supra*, p. 280), " the principle that, as a general rule, any body possessing jurisdictional powers has the right in the first place to determine the extent of its jurisdiction " (B. 16, p. 20; *supra*, p. 276). Elsewhere, it spoke of conclusions " drawn from the very nature of judicial decisions " (B. 11, p. 30; *supra*, p. 348), and reparation as a " general conception of law " (A. 17, p. 29; *supra*, p. 233).
ICJ: *Corfu Channel Case* (Merits) (1949) *ICJ Reports 1949*, p. 4, at p. 18 (*supra*, p. 322); *Corfu Channel Case* (Compensation) (1949), *ibid.*, p 244, at p. 249 (*supra*, p. 345, note 29).

[7] *e.g.*, PCIJ: D.O. by Anzilotti (A. 13, p. 27); S.O. by Séfériadès (A/B. 62, pp. 49–50); D.O. by Anzilotti (A/B. 70, p. 50); Ind. Op. by Hudson (A/B. 70, pp. 76 *et seq.*); S.O. by Séfériadès (A/B. 71, p. 138); D.O. by Hudson (A/B. 77, p. 125). ICJ: D.O. by Krylov, *ICJ Reports 1949*, pp. 71 and 219; S.O. by McNair, *ICJ Reports 1950*, pp. 149 *et seq.*; S.O. by Read, *ibid.*, p. 167; S.O. by Alvarez, *ICJ Reports 1951*, pp. 147 *et seq.*; D.O. by Carneiro, *ICJ Reports 1952*, p. 161.

interest of self-preservation may be reconciled with the interests of individuals and the interests of other States. The application of this general principle of law in the international sphere supports the view that "international law, like law in general, has the object of assuring the co-existence of different interests which are worthy of legal protection," [8] and shows that law, instead of being a mere agglomeration of abstract rules, is a purposeful discipline.

In Part Two, dealing with the Principle of Good Faith, it was seen that international law requires obedience to a standard of honesty, loyalty, and fair dealing, in short of morality, in international conduct, particularly in the field of treaty relations, in the exercise of rights and in the fulfilment of obligations. The enforcement of the principle of good faith in the law of nations as well as in the law obtaining amongst individuals is a striking illustration of the well-known words of Lord Coleridge in *The Queen* v. *Dudley and Stephens* (1884): "Though law and morality are not the same, and many things may be immoral which are not necessarily illegal, yet the absolute divorce of law from morality would be of fatal consequence." [9]

Part Three dealt with the concept of responsibility, which in its true meaning is substantially similar to responsibility in municipal private law. Its juridical essence is that it imposes an obligation upon every subject of law who commits an unlawful act to wipe out all the consequences of that act and to re-establish the situation which would, in all probability, have existed if that act had not been committed. It is a logical consequence flowing from the very conception of law and is an integral part of every legal order.

Finally, in Part Four certain general principles pertaining to judicial proceedings, common to all systems of law, were examined. They are the essential rules which govern the activity of every tribunal as a Court of Justice. They ensure the fulfilment of the fundamental purpose of all judicial proceedings, the final settlement of a dispute by an impartial

[8] P.C.A.: *Palmas Case* (1928), 2 H.C.R., p. 83, at p. 130. See also Spanish Zone of Morocco Claims (1923): *Rapport III* (1924), 2 UNRIAA, p. 615, at p. 640.

[9] England: 19 Q.B.D., p. 273, at p. 287.

authority in a manner just and equitable to the parties on the basis of respect for law.

A consideration of the subject-matter covered by these general principles of law shows the important position they hold in the international juridical order, and indeed in any juridical order. They lie at the very foundation of the legal system and are indispensable to its operation.

These general principles of law fulfil three different functions. First, they constitute the source of various rules of law, which are merely the expression of these principles. Secondly, they form the guiding principles of the juridical order according to which the interpretation and application of the rules of law are orientated. Thirdly, they apply directly to the facts of the case wherever there is no formulated rule governing the matter. In a system like international law, where precisely formulated rules are few, the third function of general principles of law acquires special significance and has contributed greatly towards defining the legal relations between States.

It is of no avail to ask whether these principles are general principles of international law or of municipal law; for it is precisely of the nature of these principles that they belong to no particular system of law, but are common to them all.[10] The general principles of law envisaged by Article 38 I (c) of the Statute of the World Court are indeed the fundamental principles of every legal system. Their existence bears witness to the fundamental unity of law, a purposeful discipline which seeks to establish peace and justice in human relations by reconciling different interests, by maintaining a certain moral standard in human conduct, by requiring the *restitutio in prestinum* wherever the juridical order is disturbed and by providing means for the peaceful and impartial settlement of disputes on the basis of respect for law. Indeed, an unmistakable feature of international arbitral and judicial decisions is the assumption by international courts and tribunals that this

10 See further the *Abu Dhabi Oil Arbitration* (1951), 1 I.C.L.Q. (1952), p. 247. The Arbitrator, denying the name law to the system applied by the Ruler of Abu Dhabi, tried to find the "proper law" applicable in construing an agreement between the parties. He found them in such general principles of law, although he did not call them so. He considered them as "a sort of 'modern law of nature,'" possessing "ecumenical validity" (p. 251).

universal concept of law exists, independently of any particular system. International law is precisely the application of this universal concept, which has long been applied in the relations between individuals, to the relations between States. Thus the Hague Convention for the Pacific Settlement of International Disputes, 1907, describes international arbitration as having for its object the settlement of international disputes "on the basis of respect of law."[11] The establishment of the international legal order, by the consent of States to their relations, or certain of their relations,[12] being conducted and judged on the basis of respect for law, means that law together with all its principles becomes applicable to these relations.

Law having been applied between individuals ever since men began to form into societies, and having been developed and elaborated in the course of time into highly technical and rigorous systems in the municipal sphere, it is natural that, in seeking the general principles of this universal concept in order to apply them to relations between States, we should look to the municipal sphere.[13] Assuming a basic analogy between individuals and nations, between international relations and relations between individuals, international courts and tribunals apply to international relations those principles underlying municipal rules of law which have been found to work substantial justice between individuals, whenever circumstances similar to those justifying their application in the municipal sphere exist. Where, however, the circumstances differ, the principle will not be applied.[14]

[11] Art. 37 (Hague Convention 1899, Art. 15). See also Art. 73. See a discussion of this provision, Brit. U.S. Cl.Arb. (1910): *Cayuga Indians Case* (1926), Nielsen's *Report*, p. 203, at pp. 320–1. See also Brit.-U.S. Cl.Com. (1871): *The Sir William Peel*, *The Volant*, *The Science Case*, D.O. by Frazer, 4 *Int.Arb.*, p. 3935, at p. 3953.

[12] International law governs in reality only a part of the international conduct of the States. Its operation is excluded from those matters which were formerly called matters of honour or vital interests and which now fall under the heading of domestic jurisdiction. International law is truly extended to the whole field of international intercourse only when States agree to submit all their disputes to arbitration, to be decided "on the basis of respect for law." *Cf.* two interesting speeches by President W. H. Taft before the American Society for Judicial Settlement of International Disputes, *Proceedings of International Conference* (1910), pp. 351 *et seq.*, at p. 353; *Proceedings of the 2nd National Conference* (1911), p. 6, at pp. 8, 14, 20.

[13] *Cf.* ICJ: *Corfu Channel Case* (Merits) (1949), D.O. by Azevedo, *ICJ Reports 1949*, p. 4. at p. 104.

[14] See *e.g.*, *supra*, pp. 262 *et seq.*, 367 *et seq.*, 382 *et seq.* For this reason, the application of general principles of law sometimes requires careful consideration of the special circumstances peculiar to the legal system in which they

As to the branches of municipal law where it is legitimate to look for such general principles, there is no *a priori* reason why there should be any restriction in this respect. Among the general principles of law which have been examined, those relating to the concept of responsibility are essentially those to be found in private law, but the principle *salus populi suprema lex* is eminently one to be found in the public law of the various nations. Similarly, principles relating to judicial proceedings are generally regarded as relating to public and not to private law.

Moreover, " since the general principles of law form the basis of positive rules of law, in seeking these principles there is no inherent reason why they cannot be found by a process of induction from the positive law of any single system, and indeed this always appears to be the inevitable starting point. But the comparative method of studying the legal systems of different nations is no doubt a valuable and even conclusive test whether a given principle represents a general juridical truth, and not what has been derisively called the '*plaisante justice qu'une rivière borne.*' "[15] In practice, however, express recourse to a comprehensive comparative method is extremely rare.

Municipal law thus provides evidence of the existence of a particular principle of law. But this is not equivalent to the application of municipal law in the international juridical order. The two are always distinct. Thus in the *Russian Indemnity Case* (1912), while the Permanent Court of Arbitration looked for the " juridical essence of the notion of responsibility " " in the very nature of law " amongst municipal systems, it was not applying private law to an international dispute; for it was fully conscious of the fact and expressly stated that, in the present dispute, " the law applicable is public international law."[16] It applied what it considered to be a juridical concept in the very nature of law as exemplified by municipal law. That concept did not, however, belong exclusively to municipal law, and was free from any special elements which positive law in the various municipal systems might have attached to it.[17]

are to be applied. *Cf.* German contention in *Interpretation of Art. 11 of the London Protocol of August 9, 1924 (German Reparation) Case* (1926), 2 UNRIAA, p. 755, at p. 761.

15 *Supra*, p. 376.

16 1 H.C.R., p. 532, at p. 541.

17 *Ibid.*, p. 543.

The *Russian Indemnity Case* (1912) is a further illustration of what has been said in connection with the ascertainment of general principles of law underlying municipal rules of evidence, namely, "the above cases disprove the theory which tends to regard the general principles of law recognised by civilised nations as a kind of mathematical highest common factor among the various systems of municipal law, including all their peculiarities introduced on account of special circumstances." [18] Indeed, as Judge Sir Arnold McNair has said, "It would be difficult to reconcile such a process with the application of 'the general principles of law.'" [19] "It shows, on the contrary, that a much broader approach has to be adopted in order to arrive at the common underlying principles, without regard to the particularities of individual systems." [20]

Just as it is possible in the municipal sphere to modify general principles of law to meet particular circumstances, it is possible to do so in the international sphere. In this connection, there has been much discussion among writers concerning the hierarchical order between general principles of law and rules of law formulated through the will of the States, namely, treaties and customs. The problem has to be approached from two different angles. From the juridical point of view, the superior value of general principles of law over customs and treaties cannot be denied; for these principles furnish the juridical basis of treaties and customs and govern their interpretation and application. From the operative point of view, however, the hierarchical order is reversed. Rules of law though in derogation of general principles of law are binding. But the possibility of establishing rules in derogation of general principles of law must not be exaggerated. It may be compared to the theoretical omnipotence of the British Parliament to legislate except in order to make a woman a man, and a man a woman.[21] The establishment of rules of law is always governed by internal and external limitations.[22] States in their desire to regulate their relations on the basis of respect for law will naturally and of

[18] *Supra*, p. 308.

[19] S.O. by McNair in ICJ: *International Status of South-West Africa* (1950), Adv.Op., *ICJ Reports 1950*, p. 128, at p. 148.

[20] *Supra*, p 308. See also *supra*, p. 377

[21] De Lolme quoted in Dicey, *Law of the Constitution*, 1948, p. 43.

[22] *Cf. mutatis mutandis*, Dicey, *op. cit.*, pp. 76 *et seq.*

necessity take such general principles as the foundation of their international intercourse. For these general principles are "rooted in the good sense and common practice of civilized nations"[23] and are, as has been observed, "the paths which civilized mankind has learned in its long experience in the municipal sphere to be those leading to justice and which it would perforce have to follow if it wished to establish Law and Justice among Nations."[24]

[23] *Abu Dhabi Oil Arbitration* (1951), 1 I.C.L.Q. (1952), p. 247, at p. 251.
[24] *Supra*, p. 386.

APPENDICES

APPENDIX 1

DRAFT CODE OF GENERAL PRINCIPLES OF LAW *

Article 1. Good Faith shall govern relations between States.

In particular, every State shall fulfil its obligations and exercise its rights in good faith.

Article 2. A State is responsible for any failure on the part of its organs to carry out the international obligations of the State, unless such failure is due to *vis major*.

Vis major, in order to relieve the State of its obligation, must be of such a nature as to make it impossible for the State to fulfil that obligation, and this impossibility must not be imputable to the State itself.

Article 3. Responsibility involves an obligation on the part of the State concerned to make integral reparation for the damage caused, in so far as it is the proximate result of the failure to comply with the international obligation.

The State shall, wherever possible, make restitution in kind. If this is not possible, a sum corresponding to the value which restitution in kind would bear shall be paid. Whenever restitution in kind, or payment in lieu of it, does not cover the entire loss suffered, damages shall be paid in order that the injured party may be fully compensated.

The damage suffered shall be deemed to be the proximate result of an act if it is the normal and natural consequence thereof, or if it would have been foreseen by a reasonable man in the position of the author of the act, or if it is the intended result of the act.

Article 4. Any claim by one State against another shall be deemed invalid if the claimant State has, by its own negligence, failed to present the claim for so long as to give rise to a danger of mistaking the truth.

Article 5. Every tribunal has the power, in the first instance, to determine the extent of its jurisdiction, in the absence of express provisions to the contrary.

* See the present writer's "General Principles of Law as a Subject for International Codification," in 4 C.L.P. (1951), p. 35.

Article 6. The jurisdiction of a tribunal extends to all relevant matters incidental to the principal question in respect of which it is competent, in the absence of express provisions to the contrary.

Article 7. Parties to a dispute are disqualified from acting as judges or arbitrators in such dispute.

Where a judge or arbitrator is the national of, or has been selected by, one of the parties to the dispute, he shall not consider himself as an agent of that party, but must decide the case submitted to him impartially without fear or favour.

Article 8. In judicial proceedings, the tribunal shall ensure that both parties have an adequate and equal opportunity to be heard.

Article 9. The above provision shall not affect the right of the tribunal to decide by default, if one of the parties, without valid reason, fails to appear before the tribunal, or to defend his case.

In such an event the tribunal must decide according to the merits of the case, after satisfying itself that it has jurisdiction.

Article 10. The tribunal shall, within the limits of its jurisdiction, examine points of law *proprio motu*, without being limited to the arguments of the parties.

Article 11. Parties to a case must abstain from any act which might aggravate or extend the dispute and, in particular, from any measure calculated to have a prejudicial effect in regard to the carrying out of the decision to be given.

Article 12. The decision of an international tribunal is final. Any question which has been resolved by a valid and final decision may not be reopened between the same parties.

Article 13. The decision of an international tribunal is binding only upon the parties to the dispute.

Decisions on incidental or preliminary questions are only binding for the purposes of the particular dispute.

Article 14. A judgment may be annulled:—

(a) if the tribunal which gave the judgment lacked jurisdiction or exceeded its jurisdiction;

(b) if the tribunal, or any member thereof is proved to have been guilty of fraud or corruption in connection with the particular case; or

(c) if the tribunal failed to give both parties an equal and adequate opportunity to be heard.

Article 15. A judgment may be revised on the grounds of:—

(a) manifest and essential error;

(b) after-discovered evidence; or

(c) fraud of the parties or collusion of witnesses.

Article 16. A tribunal may annul or revise its own judgment, either *proprio motu*, or on the application of one of the parties, for any of the reasons mentioned in the two preceding Articles provided that it still has jurisdiction over the dispute.

Appendix 2

MUNICIPAL CODES WHICH PROVIDE FOR THE APPLICATION OF THE GENERAL PRINCIPLES OF LAW, EQUITY, OR NATURAL LAW

(In chronological order according to date of promulgation)

British India. In British India, as Sir Courtenay Ilbert pointed out, "in matters for which neither the authority of Hindu or Mohamedan text-books or advisers nor the regulations and other enactments of the Government supplied sufficient guidance, the judges of the civil courts were usually directed to act in accordance with 'justice, equity, and good conscience'" (*The Government of India*, 1915, p. 360). The earliest provision relating to gaps in the law is probably Section XXI of the Bengal Regulation III of 1793, which provided that: "In cases coming within the jurisdiction of the zillah and city courts for which no specific rule may exist, the judges are to act according to *justice, equity, and good conscience.*"

Other early provisions are, for instance, Bombay Regulation III (1799), Section XX; Fort St. George Regulation II (1802), Section XVII. *Cf.* also the Charter granted by the Governor and Company of Merchants, Trading to the East Indies, to the Mayor, Aldermen and Burgesses of Madras on December 30, 1687, for the Establishment of a Municipality and Mayor's Court at Madras.

As to the place of natural law in Anglo-Saxon legal systems in general, see, for instance, Sir Frederick Pollock's *Essays in the Law*, 1922.

French Civil Code (1804). In the French Civil Code, Article 4 provides that: "Judges who refuse to decide a case on the pretext of silence, obscurity or insufficiency of the law are liable to be prosecuted for a denial of justice." In the draft of the Code, there was an article immediately preceding the present Article 4, which may be considered as complementary to it, wherein it was provided that: "In civil matters, in the absence of a specific provision, the judge is a *minister of equity.* Equity is the return to *natural law* or to accepted usages, in the event of the silence of positive law" (*Livre préliminaire du Projet de l'An VIII*, Titre V, Art. 11; P. A. Fenet, 2 *Recueil complet des travaux préparatoires du Code civil*, 1836, p. 7).

Articles 1 and 4 of *Titre I* of the *Livre préliminaire* of the same draft also recognised that there was an "Universal and immutable law," and that the law of each country consisted partly of this universal law (Fenet, 2 *op. cit.*, pp. 3–4). See also Portalis' *Discours préliminaire* and *Exposé des Motifs* (1 *ibid.*, pp. 469–476; 6 *ibid.*, pp. 360–361).

AUSTRIAN CIVIL CODE (1811): " Art. 7: If a case cannot be solved either by the text or the natural sense of a written provision, recourse shall be had to similar cases expressly provided for in other provisions of the law and to principles of analogous provisions. If the case still remains in doubt, it shall be decided according to the principles of *natural law*, taking into careful consideration all the circumstances of the case."

PERUVIAN CIVIL CODE (1852): " Preliminary Charter, Art. IX: Judges may not suspend or refuse the administration of justice by reason of *lacunae*, obscurities or inadequacies in the legal provisions; in such cases, they shall decide having regard: 1. to the spirit of the law; 2. to other provisions relating to analogous cases; and 3. to the *general principles of law*. . . ."

See F. N. Irvine, " El centenario de la promulgación del Código Civil de 1852," 39 *Revista del Foro* (1952), p. 215, at pp. 224 *et seq.* The author recalls that the Albert Code of Sardinia, promulgated in 1837 had previously used the expression " the general principles of law." Art. 15 of the Sardinian Code (1837) provided that: " If a case cannot be solved either by the letter or the spirit of the written law, recourse shall be had to similar cases expressly provided for in other legal provisions and to principles which form the basis of analogous provisions. If the case still remains in doubt, recourse shall be had to the *general principles of law*, taking into consideration all the circumstances of the case."

Superseded by Peruvian Civil Code (1936). See *infra*, p. 407.

CHILEAN CIVIL CODE (1855): " Art. 24: In cases in which the foregoing rules of interpretation cannot be applied, obscure or contradictory passages shall be interpreted so as to best conform to the general spirit of the legislation and *natural equity*."

ECUADORIAN CIVIL CODE (1860): " Art. 18: (6) In cases in which the foregoing rules of interpretation cannot be applied, obscure or contradictory passages shall be interpreted so as to best conform to the general spirit of the legislation and *natural equity*.

" (7) In the absence of a rule, those governing analogous cases shall apply; when there is none, recourse shall be had to the *general principles of universal law*."

This provision has remained unaltered in subsequent editions of the Code (1871, 1889, 1930 and 1950).

El Salvadorian Civil Code (1860): " Art. 24: . . . In cases in which the foregoing rules of interpretation cannot be applied, obscure or contradictory passages shall be interpreted so as to best conform to the general spirit of the legislation and *natural equity.*"

This provision has remained unaltered in subsequent editions of the Code (1880, 1893, 1904, 1912, 1926 and 1947).

Italian Civil Code (1865): " Provisions on the Publication, Interpretation, and Application of the Law in General, Art. 3: Whenever a case cannot be decided on the basis of a precise provision of the written law, recourse shall be had to provisions governing similar and analogous cases or matters; if the case still remains doubtful, it shall be decided according to the *general principles of law.*"

See Giorgio del Vecchio, *Sui principi generali del diritto*, Roma, 1929.

Superseded by Italian Civil Code (1942). See *infra*, p. 407.

Portuguese Civil Code (1867): " Art. 16: If questions concerning rights or obligations cannot be solved either by the text or the spirit of the written law, or by means of principles applied in analogous cases and provided for in other provisions of the law, recourse shall be had to the *principles of natural law*, taking into account the factual circumstances."

Argentine Civil Code (1869): " Art. 16: If a civil question cannot be solved either by the letter or by the spirit of the written law, recourse shall be had to principles contained in analogous provisions; and if the case still remains doubtful, it shall be decided according to the *general principles of law*, account being taken of the circumstances of the case."

See R. M. Salvat, *Tratado de Derecho Civil Argentino*, Parte general, Buenos Aires, 1950.

Colombian Civil Code (1873), Amendment of 1887: " Law 153 of 1887, Art. 4: *Principles of natural law* and the rules of jurisprudence shall serve to illustrate the constitution in doubtful cases. Constitutional doctrine is, in its turn, a rule for the interpretation of laws.

" Art. 8: When there is no written provision exactly applicable to the dispute, laws governing analogous cases or matters shall be applied, and, in their absence, constitutional doctrine and the *general rules of law.*"

See also Arts. 5, 10 and 13.

Mixed Civil Code of Egypt (1875): " Art. 11: In cases where the law is silent, insufficient or obscure, the judges shall observe *principles of natural law* and *rules of equity.*" (Also *Règlement d'Organisation judiciaire*, Art. 34.)

See S. Messina, *Traité de Droit civil égyptien mixte*, 3 vols., Alexandrie, 1927–1930, Vol. I. Also S. Messina, "Lacunes de la loi en droit égyptien mixte," 12 *L'Egypte contemporaine* (1921), pp. 353–388.

Abrogated by Law 115 of 1948. See *infra*, p. 407.

GUATEMALAN CIVIL CODE (1877): "Art. 18: Judges may not suspend or refuse the administration of justice by reason of *lacunae*, obscurities or inadequacies in the legal provisions; in such cases, they shall decide having regard: 1. to the spirit of the law; 2. to other provisions relating to analogous cases; and 3. to the *general principles of law*. . . ."

Superseded by Guatemalan Civil Code (1937). See *infra*, p. 407.

EGYPTIAN CODE ON THE ORGANISATION OF NATIVE COURTS (1883): "Art. 29: In the absence of an express provision of the written law, the judge shall follow *principles of equity*, and, in commercial matters, he shall furthermore follow commercial usages."

Abrogated by Law 147 of 1949. See *infra*, p. 407.

MEXICAN CIVIL CODE OF THE FEDERAL DISTRICT AND TERRITORIES (1884), repealing that of 1870: "Art. 20: When a judicial controversy cannot be decided, either by the text or by the natural sense or spirit of the law, it shall be decided in accordance with the *general principles of law*, all the circumstances of the case being taken into consideration."

Superseded by Mexican Civil Code (1926). See *infra*, p. 406.

SPANISH CIVIL CODE (1888): "Art. 6: Any court which shall refuse to render a decision on the pretext of silence, obscurity, or insufficiency of the law shall be held liable therefor.

"When there is no provision exactly applicable to the point at issue, the custom of the place shall be applied, and, in the absence thereof, the *general principles of law*."

See D. J. M. Manresa, 1 *Commentarios al Código civil español*, Madrid, sixth ed., 1943, pp. 134 *et seq.*

CUBAN CIVIL CODE (1889): "Art. 6: Any court which shall refuse to render a decision on the pretext of silence, obscurity, or insufficiency of the law shall be held liable therefor.

"When there is no provision exactly applicable to the point at issue, the custom of the place shall be applied, and, in the absence thereof, the *general principles of law*."

Paraguayan Civil Code (1889): "Art. 16: If a civil question cannot be solved either by the letter or by the spirit of the written law, recourse shall be had to principles contained in analogous provisions; and if the case still remains doubtful, it shall be decided according to the *general principles of law*, account being taken of the circumstances of the case."

Uruguayan Civil Code (1893): "Art. 16: When a civil question arises, which cannot be solved by either the letter or the spirit of the law governing the matter, recourse shall be had to principles underlying analogous provisions, and if the case still remains doubtful, it shall be decided according to the *general principles of law* and the most widely accepted doctrine, account being taken of the circumstances of the case."

German Civil Code (1896). In the first draft, there was a provision whereby, in the absence of a specific rule, the judge should have recourse to analogy, and, where this was not possible, to principles drawn from the legal order as a whole. This provision was, however, omitted as being, inter alia, a matter of course. See Plank, 1 *Kommentar zum B.G.B.*, 4th ed., 1913, p. lix.

Puerto Rican Civil Code (1902): "Section 7: Any court which shall refuse to render a decision on the pretext of silence, obscurity or unintelligibility of the laws, or for any other reason, shall be held liable therefor.

"When there is no statute applicable to the case at issue, the court shall decide in accordance with *equity*—which means that *natural justice*, as embodied in the *general principles of jurisprudence* and in accepted and established usages and customs, shall be taken into consideration."

Panamanian Civil Code (1903): "Art. 32: In cases in which the foregoing rules of interpretation cannot be applied, obscure or contradictory passages shall be interpreted so as to best conform to the general spirit of the legislation and *natural equity*."

Superseded by Panamanian Civil Code (1917). See *infra*, p. 406.

Swiss Civil Code (1907): "Art. 1: The written law is applicable to all matters which come within the letter or the spirit of any of its provisions.

"When no legal provision is applicable, the judge shall decide according to customary law and, in default of a custom, according to *rules which he would lay down if he had himself to act as legislator*.

"He shall be guided by solutions established by writers and judicial decisions." See also Art. 4.

See *Exposé des Motifs de l'Avant projet du Département fédéral de Justice et de Police*, by Eugène Huber, Berne, t. I, 1901, especially at pp. 24, 31. E. Lehr, *Code civil du Canton de Zurich de 1887*, Paris, 1890, Introduction, pp. xxviii–xxxiv. Before the unification of the Civil Law in Switzerland, in the Cantons of Tessin and Basle-City, in the absence of positive law, the judge was to apply "general principles of the common law," in Lucerne and Valais, "general principles of law," in Berne, Fribourg, and Basle-Country, "equity."

See also Ivy Williams, *The Sources of Law in the Swiss Civil Code*, Oxford, 1923. Gény, 2 *Méthode d'Interprétation, etc.*, 2e éd., 1919, pp. 308–339 (*Les Pouvoirs du Juge d'après le Code Civil Suisse du 10 décembre 1907*). At pp. 326–327, Gény said: "La formule de l'Article Ier du Code Civil Suisse de 1907 pourrait être proposée comme contenant le résumé le plus adéquat de mes développements," speaking of his "libre recherche scientifique."

The formula contained in the last part of paragraph 2 of Art. I of the Swiss Civil Code, dating back to Aristotle (*Nicomachean Ethics*, Bk. V, Chap. XIV), was adopted by the Draft Scheme of the Five Neutral Powers for the Establishment of the PCIJ (Art. 2 *in fine*). The Swiss Civil Code by its immense prestige (*cf. infra*, Turkish Civil Code), exercised a profound influence upon Continental legal thinking. One may also see in Art. 1 paragraph III of the Swiss Civil Code a forerunner of Art. 38 I (d) of the Statute of the International Court of Justice.

BRAZILIAN CIVIL CODE (1916): "Art. 7: Cases not herein regulated shall be governed by provisions concerning analogous cases, and, where there is no such provision, by the *general principles of law*."

See Bevilaqua, *Theoria geral do direito civil*, Rio de Janeiro, 1908. A leading civilist in his own country, Bevilaqua, a member of the Advisory Committee of Jurists for the establishment of the PCIJ, incorporated the idea contained in this article in his draft scheme for the PCIJ; see Explanatory Notes *ad* Art. 24 of his draft scheme (PCIJ: 1 *Documents*, p. 371) and Art. 24 itself (*ibid.*, p. 353).

Amended in 1942. See below.

BRAZILIAN CIVIL CODE (1916), Amendment of 1942: "Law of Introduction to the Code, Art. 4: When the written law does not provide for a particular case, it shall be decided by the judge in accordance with analogy, custom and the *general principles of law*.

VENEZUELAN CIVIL CODE (1916): "Art. 4: . . . If a dispute cannot be decided by reference to an express provision of the law, provisions governing similar cases or analogous matters shall be taken into consideration; and if the case still remains in doubt, it shall be decided in accordance with the *general principles of law.*"

This provision remained unaltered in the 1922 Code, which has, however, been superseded by Venezuelan Civil Code (1942). See *infra*, p. 407.

PANAMANIAN CIVIL CODE (1917): "Art. 24: When t' ere is no statute exactly applicable to the point in issue, the laws which regulate analogous cases or subject-matter shall be applied, and, in the absence thereof, the constitutional doctrine, the *general principles of law*, and customs which are general and in accordance with Christian morals."

THAI (SIAMESE) CIVIL CODE (1925): "Art. 4: The law shall be applied to all cases which come within the letter or spirit of any of its provisions.

"Where no provision is applicable, the case shall be decided according to the local custom.

"If there is no such custom, the case shall be decided by analogy to the provision most nearly applicable, and, in default of such provision, by the *general principles of law.*"

MEXICAN CIVIL CODE (1926), repealing that of 1884: "Art. 19: Judicial disputes of a civil nature shall be decided according to the letter of the law or its judicial interpretation. In the absence of a law, they shall be decided according to the *general principles of law.*"

TURKISH CIVIL CODE (1926): "Art. 1." Same as the Swiss Civil Code. The Swiss Civil Code was considered so good that it was adopted, save for slight modifications, *in toto* by Turkey. The Turkish Minister of Justice in his *Exposé des Motifs*, paid the handsome compliment to the Swiss Civil Code as being "the most recent, the most perfect, and the most democratic" (Exposé des Motifs par le Ministre de la Justice, Mehmed Essad, in *Code Civil Turk*, Éd. Rizzo, Constantinople, 1926, p. xiv).

DRAFT HUNGARIAN CIVIL CODE (1928): "§ 6: In questions of law not regulated by the provisions of the law, the court shall decide according to the spirit of the law of this country, the *general principles of law*, and the *findings of the science of law.*"

See G. Auer, "Über die Freiheit des richterlichen Ermessens im Vorentwurfe zu dem ungarischen bürgerlichen Gesetzbuche," 29 *Zeitschrift für vergleichende Rechtswissenschaft* (1912), pp. 299–314.

CHINESE CIVIL CODE (1929): "Art. 1: In civil matters if there is no provision of law applicable to a case, the case shall be decided according to custom. If there is no such custom, the case shall be decided in accordance with the *general principles of law.*"

PERUVIAN CIVIL CODE (1936), repealing that of 1871: "Art. XXIII: Judges may not refuse to administer justice by reason of inadequacies in the legal provisions. In such cases, they shall apply the *principles of law.*"

See also Peruvian Commercial Code (1902), Art. 50.

GUATAMALAN CIVIL CODE (1937), consolidating the Code of 1933 with the unrepealed part of the 1877 Code: "Art. 2430: In cases in which the foregoing rules of interpretation cannot be applied, obscure or contradictory passages shall be interpreted so as to best conform to the general spirit of the legislation and *natural equity.*"

GREEK CIVIL CODE (1940). See N. G. Michaélidès, "L'œuvre créatrice de la jurisprudence grecque en cas de silence de la loi," 4 *R.D.I.* (*hellénique*) (1951), p. 163, at p. 178: "In cases not provided for by statute, the practical solutions adopted by the courts are based either upon an extensive interpretation of legal provisions or contractual clauses, or upon their application by analogy, or upon the *general principles of law* " (Transl. See, particularly, pp. 172–177). See also A. Bournias, "La méthode depuis le Code Civil de 1804 au point de vue des sources du droit positif hellénique," *ibid.*, p. 323, at p. 327.

ITALIAN CIVIL CODE (1942), repealing that of 1865: "Provisions in General, Art. 12 II: Whenever a case cannot be decided on the basis of a precise provision of the written law, recourse shall be had to provisions governing similar and analogous cases or matters.

"If the case still remains doubtful, it shall be decided according to the *general principles of the juridical order of the State.*"

For comments on the change, or rather impending change, see Giorgio del Vecchio, *Reforma del Codice civile e principî generali di diritto*, Roma, 1938.

VENEZUELAN CIVIL CODE (1942), repealing that of 1922: "Art. 4: When there is no specific legislative provision applicable, provisions governing similar cases or analogous matters shall be taken into consideration; and, if doubt still remains, the *general principles of law* shall be applied."

EGYPTIAN CIVIL CODE (1948): "Art. 1: In the absence of an express provision, the judge shall follow the rules of custom; if they do not exist, the principles of Islamic law, and, if they in turn do not exist, he shall follow principles of *natural law and equity.*"

PHILIPPINE CIVIL CODE (1949), repealing that of 1889 (*i.e.*, the *Spanish Civil Code*, 1888, *q.v.*): "Art. 9: No judge or court shall decline to render judgment by reason of the silence, obscurity or insufficiency of the laws.

" Art. 10: In case of doubt in the interpretation or application of laws, it is presumed that the law-making body intended *right and justice* to prevail."

Furthermore, the new Philippine Code of 1949 contains an extremely interesting new Chapter (Chapter 2) of eighteen articles (Arts. 19–36) on " Human Relations," of which the first article is as follows: " Art. 19. Every person must, in the exercise of his rights and in the performance of his duties, act with justice, give everyone his due, and observe honesty and good faith."

IRAQI CIVIL LAW, No. 40 (1951): " Art. 1: The written law is applicable to all matters which come within the letter or the spirit of any of its provisions.

" When no provision is applicable, justice shall be administered by the courts or tribunals according to custom, and, in default of such custom, according to those principles of Islamic law, irrespective of any particular sect, that are most in harmony with the principles of the Civil Code, and, in default of such principles, according to the *general principles of justice.*

" The courts shall be guided in all matters of principle by solutions adopted by judicial decisions and writers in Iraq and in other countries, the laws of which are similar to Iraqi law."

APPENDIX 3

BIBLIOGRAPHY

A. General Works on International Decisions

Annual Digest (and Reports) of Public International Law Cases. 1919–. London, 1929–.

A.S.I.L.: *Contribution of the P.C.I.J. to the Development of International Law.* 24 *Proceedings* (1930), pp. 34–78.

BECKETT, W. E.: *Decisions of the P.C.I.J. on Points of Law and Procedure of General Application.* 11 B.Y.I.L. (1930), pp. 1–54.

—— *Les questions d'intérêt général au point de vue juridique dans la jurisprudence de la C.P.J.I.* 39 *Recueil La Haye* (1932), pp. 135–269.

—— *Les questions d'intérêt général au point de vue juridique dans la jurisprudence de la C.P.J.I. (juillet 1932—juillet 1934).* 50 *Recueil La Haye* (1934), pp. 193–305.

BLÜHDORN, Rudolf: *Le fonctionnement et la jurisprudence des tribunaux arbitraux mixtes créés par les traités de Paris.* 41 *Recueil La Haye* (1932), pp. 141–243.

BEUS, J. G. de: *The Jurisprudence of the General Claims Commission, U.S. and Mexico.* The Hague, 1938.

BISHOP, W. W.: *Cases and Materials on International Law.* Michigan, 1949.

BORCHARD, E. M.: *The Opinions of the Mixed Claims Commission, U.S. and Germany.* 19 A.J.I.L. (1925), pp. 133–143; 20 A.J.I.L. (1926), pp. 69–80.

—— *Decisions of the Claims Commission, U.S. and Mexico.* 20 A.J.I.L. (1926), pp. 536–542; 21 A.J.I.L. (1927), pp. 516–522; 25 A.J.I.L. (1931), pp. 735–740.

BRIGGS, H. W.: *The Law of Nations. Cases, Documents, and Notes.* London, 1953.

COBBETT, P.: *Cases on International Law.* 2 vols. London, 1937, 1947.

DARBY, W. E.: *Modern Pacific Settlements involving the Principle of International Arbitration.* London, 1904.

DEREVITZKY, P.: *Les principes du droit international tels qu'ils se dégagent de la jurisprudence de la C.P.J.I.* Paris, 1932.

DICKINSON, E. de Witt: *A Selection of Cases and Readings on the Law of Nations, Chiefly as It is Interpreted and Applied by British and American Courts.* New York, 1929.

—— *Cases and Materials on International Law.* Brooklyn, 1950.

FACHIRI, A. P.: *Decisions, Opinions and Awards of International Tribunals.* 7 B.Y.I.L. (1926), pp. 197–205; 8 B.Y.I.L. (1927), pp. 145–156; 10 B.Y.I.L. (1929), pp. 231–243; 13 B.Y.I.L. (1932), pp. 144–156.

FELLER, A. H.: *The German-Mexican Claims Commission.* 27 A.J.I.L. (1933), pp. 62–79.

—— *The Mexican Claims Commissions 1923–1934.* New York, 1935.

FENWICK, C. G.: *Cases on International Law.* Chicago, 1951.

FITZMAURICE, G. G.: *The Law and Procedure of the I.C.J.* I. *General Principles and Substantive Law.* 27 B.Y.I.L. (1950), pp. 1–41. II. *Treaty Interpretation and Certain Other Treaty Points.* 28 *ibid.* (1951), pp. 1–28.

FONTES IURIS GENTIUM:
- Ser. A, Sec. 1, Tom. 1: *Digest of the Decisions of the P.C.I.J.* (1922–1930). Berlin, 1931.
- Ser. A, Sec. 1, Tom. 2: *Digest of the Decisions of the P.C.A.* (1902–1928). Berlin, 1931.
- Ser. A, Sec. 1, Tom. 3: *Digest of the Decisions of the P.C.I.J.* (1931–1934). Berlin, 1935.

FRANCQUEVILLE, Bernard de: *L'œuvre de la C.P.J.I.* Tome 2: *Avis et arrêts.* Paris, 1928.

GARNER, J. W.: *Decisions of the German-American M.C.C.* 5 B.Y.I.L. (1924), pp. 222–225; 6 B.Y.I.L. (1925), pp. 204–210; 9 B.Y.I.L. (1928), p. 164; 12 B.Y.I.L. (1931), pp. 171–173; 14 B.Y.I.L. (1933), pp. 181–182.

—— *Decisions of the American-Mexican M.C.C.* 8 B.Y.I.L. (1927), pp. 179–186; 9 B.Y.I.L. (1928), pp. 156–164; 11 B.Y.I.L. (1930), pp. 220–226; 12 B.Y.I.L. (1931); pp. 166–173.

GENET, R.: *Précis de Jurisprudence de la C.P.J.I.* Paris, 1933.

GREEN, L. C.: *International Law Through the Cases.* London, 1951.

HACKWORTH, G. H.: *Digest of International Law.* 8 Vols. USGPO, 1940–1944.

HAMBRO, EDVARD.: *The Case Law of the International Court.* Leyden, 1952.

HUDSON, M. O.: *The First (Second, etc.) Year of the P.C.I.J. (World Court).* A.J.I.L. from Vol. 17 (1923) onwards.

HUDSON, M. O.: *Cases and Other Matters on International Law.* St. Paul, Minn., 3rd ed., 1951.

—— *The World Court 1921–1938. A Handbook of the P.C.I.J.* 5th ed., Boston, 1938. Chaps. 5 and 6.

KAECKENBEECK, G.: *The Character and Work of the Arbitral Tribunal of Upper Silesia.* 21 *Grotius Transactions* (1935), pp. 27–44.

KIESSELBACH, W.: *Problems of the German-American Claims Commission.* Wash., 1930.

LALIVE, J.-F.: *La jurisprudence de la Cour internationale de Justice.* 6 *Annuaire Suisse* (1949), pp. 163–202.

LA PRADELLE, A. de: *Les grands cas de la jurisprudence internationale.* Paris, 1939.

LA PRADELLE, A. de, et POLITIS, N.: *Recueil des Arbitrages internationaux.* 2 tomes. Paris, 1924, 1932.

LAUTERPACHT, H.: *The Development of International Law by the P.C.I.J.* London, 1934.

MACKENZIE, N., and LAING, L. H.: *Canada and the Law of Nations. A Selection of Cases in International Law, affecting Canada and Canadians.* Toronto, 1938.

MCKERNAN, L. W.: *Special Mexican Claims.* 32 A.J.I.L. (1938), pp. 457–466.

MOORE, J. B.: *A Digest of International Law.* 8 vols. Washington, 1906.

—— *International Adjudications.* Ancient Series, 1 vol. New York, 1936. Modern Series, 6 vols. New York, 1929–1933.

—— *History and Digest of the International Arbitrations to which the U.S. has been a party.* 6 vols. Washington, 1898.

NEGULESCO, D.: *La jurisprudence de la C.P.J.I. Six conférences à l'Institut des Hautes Etudes internationales de la Faculté de droit de Paris, avril 1939.*

NIELSEN, F. K.: *International Law as applied to Reclamations, Mainly in Cases between the U.S. and Mexico.* Wash., 1933.

P.C.I.J., The. Issued by the Registry of the Court. The Hague, 1939. Chap. 10.

PFANKUCHEN, Ll.: *A Documentary Textbook in International Law.* New York, 1940.

RALSTON, J. H.: *The Law and Procedure of International Tribunals.* Rev. ed., California, 1926.

—— *Supplement to 1926 Revised Edition.* California, 1936.

Recueil La Haye. Tables Générales du Recueil des Cours publiés de 1923 à 1937 inclus, Paris, 1939. Table de Jurisprudence, pp. 601–618.

RUZÉ, R.: *La jurisprudence des T.A.M. institués par les traités de paix.* 3 (3) R.D.I.L.C. (1922), pp. 22–66.

SCOTT, J. B.: *Cases on International Law.* St. Paul, Minn., 1922.

SCOTT, J. B., and JAEGER, W. H. E.: *Cases on International Law.* St. Paul, Minn., 1937.

SNOW, F.: *Cases and Opinions on International Law.* 1893.

SCHMID, K.: *Die Rechtsprechung des Ständigen Internationalen Gerichtshofs in Rechtssätzen dargestellt.* Stuttgart, 1932.

SCHÜCKING, W.: *Das Werk vom Haag.* München, 1914.

SCHWARZENBERGER, G.: *The development of International Economic and Financial Law by the P.C.I.J.* 54 *Juridical Review* (1942), pp. 21–40, 80–100.

—— *International Law.* Vol. 1: *International Law as applied by International Courts and Tribunals.* 2nd ed., London, 1949.

—— *Trends in the Practice of the World Court.* 4 C.L.P. (1951), pp. 1–34.

—— *A Manual of International Law.* 3rd ed., London, 1952.

SOHN, L. B.: *Cases and other Materials on World Law.* Brooklyn, 1950.

STEINER, H. A.: *Fundamental Conceptions of International Law in the Jurisprudence of the P.C.I.J.* 30 A.J.I.L. (1936), pp. 414–438.

STOWELL, E. C., and MUNRO, H. F.: *International Law Cases.* 2 vols. Boston, 1916.

STRUYCKEN, A. J. N. M.: *Analyses des sentences rendues par les Tribunaux d'arbitrage, constitués conformément aux stipulations des Conventions de La Haye de 1899 et 1907. 1899–1934.* The Hague, 1934.

STUYT, A. M.: *Survey of International Arbitrations, 1794–1938.* The Hague, 1939.

TEYSSAIRE, J., and SOLÈRE, P.: *Les tribunaux arbitraux mixtes.* Paris, 1931.

WHARTON, F.: *A Digest of the International Law of the U.S.* 3 vols. USGPO, 1886.

B. Works on General Principles of Law

BALLADORE-PALLIERI, Giorgio: *I "principî generali del diritto riconosciuti dalle nazioni civili" nell'art. 38 dello Statuto della Corte permanente di Giustizia internazionale.* Torino, 1931.

BISSCHOP, W. R.: *Sources of International Law.* 26 *Grotius Transactions* (1940), pp. 235–260. See also 27 *op. cit.* (1942), pp. 214–312.

BORCHARD, E. M.: *La théorie et les sources du droit international.* 3 *Recueil Gény*. Paris, 1936, pp. 328–361.

ALCALÁ CARRERA, Eulalia: *Los Principios generales de Derecho como Fuente de Derecho Internacionale.* México, 1948.

CEGLA, WOLF W.: *Die Bedeutung der allgemeinen Rechtsgrundsätze für die Quellenlehre des Völkerrechts.* Berlin, 1936.

CHENG, Bin: *General Principles of Law as a Subject for International Codification.* 4 C.L.P. (1951), pp. 35–53.

CORBETT, P. E.: *The Consent of States and the Sources of the Law of Nations.* 6 B.Y.I.L. (1925), pp. 20–30.

FINCH, G. A.: *The Sources of Modern International Law.* Washington, 1937.

GOUET, YVON: *La coutume en droit constitutionnel interne et en droit constitutionnel international. Envisagée principalement dans ses rapports avec les autres modes de constatation du droit.* Paris, 1932.

GRAPIN, Pierre: *Valeur internationale des principes généraux du droit. Contribution à l'étude de l'art. 38, alinéa 3, du Statut de la C.P.J.I.* Thèse, Paris, 1934.

GUTTERIDGE, H. C.: *Comparative Law.* Cambridge, 1946, Chap. 5.

HÄRLE, Elfried: *Die allgemeinen Rechtsgrundsätze im Völkerrecht.* 11 (2) Z.ö.R. (1931), pp. 206–246.

—— *Die Entscheidungsgrundlagen des Weltgerichtshofes. Eine Auslegung des Art. 38 des Statuts des Ständigen Internationalen Gerichtshofes unter besonderer Berücksichtigung der allgemeinen Rechtsgrundsätze.* Dissertation, Basel, 1931.

—— *Die allgemeinen Rechtsgrundsätze im Völkerrecht.* 33 *Die Friendens-Warte* (1933), pp. 129–131.

—— *Die allgemeinen Entscheidungsgrundlagen des Ständigen Internationalen Gerichtshofes. Eine kritisch-würdigende Untersuchung über Artikel 38 des Gerichtshof-Statuts.* Berlin, 1933.

—— *Les principes généraux de droit et le droit des gens.* 3 (16) R.D.I.L.C. (1935), pp. 663–687.

HEILBORN, P.: *Les sources du droit international.* 2 *Recueil La Haye* (1926), pp. 1–63.

HEYDTE, F. A. von der: *Glossen zu einer Theorie der allgemeinen Rechtsgrundsätze.* 33 *Die Friedens-Warte* (1933), pp. 289–300.

HUDSON, M. O.: *Law Applicable by the P.C.I.J.* Harvard Legal Essays written in Honor of and presented to Joseph Henry Beale and Samuel Williston, 1934, pp. 133–137.

I.[DELSON], V.R.: *Arbitrations (Law applicable by reference to the Statute of the P.C.I.J.).* 15 B.Y.I.L. (1934), pp. 146–147.

INSTITUT DE DROIT INTERNATIONAL: *Les principes généraux de droit comme source du droit des gens.*
Rapport de M. Verdross. 37 *Annuaire* (1932), pp. 283–298.
Observations de MM. Le Fur, Nippold, Kosters, Brierly, Borchard, Salvioli, Fedozzi, de la Barra et de la Brière. *Loc. cit.*, pp. 298–319.
Discussions orales. *Loc. cit.*, p. 320.
Rapport final de M. Verdross. *Loc. cit.*, pp. 320–328.
Délibérations en séance plénière et en section. 40 *Annuaire* (1937), pp. 183–189.

KOPELMANAS, L.: *Quelques réflexions au sujet de l'art. 38, 3°, du Statut de la C.P.J.I.* 43 R.G.D.I.P. (1936), pp. 285–308.

—— *Custom as a Means of the Creation of International Law.* 18 B.Y.I.L. (1937), pp. 127–151.

—— *Essai d'une théorie des sources formelles du droit international.* 21 (1) R.D.I. (1938), pp. 101–150.

KÜNTZEL, Walter: *Ungeschriebenes Völkerrecht.* Heidelberg, 1936.

LASALA, Llanas Manuel de: *Fuentes del derecho internacionál según el Estatudo del Tribunal permanente de Justicia.* R.D.I. (Gve) (1924), pp. 288–301.

LAUTERPACHT, H.: *Private Law Sources and Analogies of International Law (With Special References to International Arbitration).* London, 1927.

LE FUR, L.: *Le droit naturel et le droit rationnel ou scientifique. Leur rôle dans la formation du droit international.* 1 (3) R.D.I. (1927), pp. 658–698.

—— *La coutume et les principes généraux du droit comme sources du droit international public.* 3 *Recueil Gény.* Paris, 1936, pp. 362–374.

MERIGGLI, Léa: *Considérations sur le problème des sources du droit des gens.* 3 (15) R.D.I.L.C. (1934), pp. 492–529.

PASCHING, Walter: *Allgemeine Rechtsgrundsätze über die Elemente des völkerrechtlichen Vertrages.* 14 Z.ö.R. (1934), pp. 26–61.

RAESTAD, Arnold: *"Droit coutumier" et principes généraux en droit international.* Conférences faites à l'Inst. Nobel. 4 (3) A.S.J.G. (N.T.I.R.) (1933), pp. 62–84.

RIPERT, Georges: *Les règles de droit civil applicables aux rapports internationaux.* 44 *Recueil La Haye* (1933), pp. 569–663.

ROUSSEAU, Charles: *Principes généraux du droit international public.* Tome 1: Introduction, Sources. Paris, 1944.

RUIZ MORENO, Isidoro: *Las fuentes del derecho internacional público.* 2 *Revista* (*Buenos Aires*) (1947), pp. 163–189.

SCELLE, G.: *Essai sur les sources formelles du droit international.* 3 *Recueil Gény.* Paris, 1936, pp. 400–430.

SCERNI, Mario: *I principî generali di diritto riconosciuti dalle nazioni civili nella giurisprudenza della Corte Permanente di Giustizia Internazionale.* Padova, 1932.

SCHEUNER, Ulrich: *L'influence du droit interne sur la formation du droit international.* 68 *Recueil La Haye* (1939), pp. 95–206.

SØRENSEN, Max: *Les sources du droit international. Étude sur la jurisprudence de la C.P.J.I.* Thèse. Copenhague, 1946.

SPIROPOULOS, Jean: *Die allgemeinen Rechtsgrundsätze im Völkerrecht. Eine Auslegung von Art. 38³ des Statuts des Ständigen Internationalen Gerichtshofs.* Kiel, 1928.

STUYT, A. M.: *The General Principles of Law as Applied by International Tribunals to Disputes on Attribution and Exercise of State Jurisdiction.* The Hague, 1946.

VELLANI, G. E.: *La revisione dei trattati e i principî generali del diritto.* Modena, 1930.

VERDROSS, Alfred: *Die Verfassung der Völkerrechtsgemeinschaft.* Wien und Berlin, 1926.

—— *Die allgemeinen Rechtsgrundsätze als Völkerrechtsquelle.* Wien, 1931.

—— *Les principes généraux de droit comme source du droit des gens.* 37 *Annuaire* (1932), pp. 283–298.

—— *Les principes généraux du droit et le droit des gens.* 13 (2) R.D.I. (1934), pp. 484–498.

—— *Les principes généraux de droit dans la jurisprudence internationale.* 52 *Recueil La Haye* (1935), pp. 195–259.

—— *Les principes généraux du droit comme source du droit des gens.* 3 *Recueil Gény.* Paris, 1936, pp. 383–388.

—— *Les principes généraux du droit applicables aux rapports internationaux.* 45 R.G.D.I.P. (1938), pp. 44–52.

VISSCHER, Charles de: *Contribution à l'étude des sources du droit international.* 3 (14) R.D.I.L.C. (1933), pp. 395–420.

—— *Contribution à l'étude des sources de droit international.* 3 *Recueil Gény.* Paris, 1936, pp. 389–399.

WOLFF, Karl: *Les principes généraux du droit applicables dans les rapports internationaux.* 36 *Recueil La Haye* (1931), pp. 479–550.

C. Select Specialised Bibliography *

PART ONE

THE PRINCIPLE OF SELF-PRESERVATION

Chapter 1. Territorial Application of the Principle of Self-preservation

A. Exclusion and Expulsion of Aliens

A.S.I.L.: *Admission and Restrictions upon the Admission of Aliens.* 5 *Proceedings* (1911), pp. 66–116.

—— *Expulsion of Aliens.* 5 *Proceedings* (1911), pp. 119–150.

Boeck, Ch. de: *L'expulsion et les difficultés internationales qu'en soulève la pratique.* 18 *Recueil La Haye* (1927), pp. 447–647.

Borchard, E. M.: *The Diplomatic Protection of Citizens Abroad.* New York, 1927. §§ 26–32.

Bouvé, C. L.: *A Treatise on the Laws governing the Exclusion and Expulsion of Aliens in the United States.* Washington, 1912.

Catzeflis, E.: *De quelques aspects de l'expulsion.* 2 *R.D.I.* (*Égyptienne*) (1946), pp. 55–72.

Fraser, C. F.: *Control of Aliens in the British Commonwealth of Nations.* London, 1940.

Institut de Droit International: *De quelle manière et dans quelles limites les gouvernements peuvent-ils exercer le droit d'expulsion vis-à-vis des étrangers.* 10 *Annuaire* (1888–1889), pp. 227–246.

—— *Droit d'admission et d'expulsion des étrangers.* 11 *Annuaire* (1889–1892), pp. 273–321; 12 *Annuaire* (1892–1894), pp. 184–226.

Konvitz, M. R.: *The Alien and the Asiatic in American Law.* Ithaca, N.Y., 1946.

Politis, N.: *Le problème des limitations de la souveraineté et la théorie de l'abus des droits dans les rapports internationaux.* 6 *Recueil la Haye* (1925), pp. 1–121, at pp. 101 *et seq.*

Puente, J. Irizarry y: *Exclusion and Expulsion of Aliens in Latin America.* 36 A.J.I.L. (1942), pp. 252–270.

* General treatises and textbooks on international law are not here included, for a list of which see G. Schwarzenberger's *A Manual of International Law*, Part III, 7: *The Doctrine of International Law.* The *Study Outlines* of the *Manual*, as well as the bibliography compiled by L. C. Green in G. Schwarzenberger's *International Law*, Vol. 1, may also be consulted for further reference.

RÉPERTOIRE DE DROIT INTERNATIONAL: "*Expulsion*" par André Blondel.

SPIROPOULOS, J.: *Expulsion and Internment of Enemy Nationals.* Leipzig, 1922.

B. MEASURES TO PROMOTE PUBLIC WELFARE

(The Taking of Private Property for Public Use)

A.S.I.L.: *Treatment of Private Property of Aliens on Land in Time of Peace.* 27 *Proceedings* (1933), pp. 103–109.

—— *Treatment of Private Property of Aliens on Land in Time of War.* 27 *Proceedings* (1933), pp. 110–127.

BINDSCHEDLER, R. L.; *Verstaatlichungsmassnahmen und Entschädigungspflicht nach Völkerrecht.* Zurich, 1950.

BORCHARD, E. M.: *The Diplomatic Protection of Citizens Abroad.* New York, 1927. §§ 104–105.

BULLINGTON, J. P.: *The Land and Petroleum Laws of Mexico.* 22 A.J.I.L. (1928), pp. 50–69.

BULLOCK, C. Ll.: *Angary.* 3 B.Y.I.L. (1922–23), pp. 99–129.

CHENG, Bin: *The Anglo-Iranian Dispute.* 5 (New Series) *World Affairs* (1951), pp. 387–405.

CRAWFORD, H. P.: *Expropriation of Petroleum Companies in Mexico.* U.S. Dept. of Commerce, Comparative Law Series, April, 1938, pp. 105–115.

DEÁK, Fr.: *The Hungarian-Rumanian Land Dispute.* New York, 1928.

DOMAN, N. R.: *Compensation for Nationalised Property in Post-War Europe.* 3 I.L.Q. (1950), pp. 323–342.

DRUCKER, Alfred: *The Nationalisation of United Nations Property in Europe.* 36 *Grotius Transactions* (1950), pp. 75–114.

DUNN, F. S.: *The Diplomatic Protection of Americans in Mexico.* New York, 1933. Chap. 11: Oil. Chap. 12: Agrarian Reform.

—— *International Law and Private Property Rights.* 28 *Columbia L.R.* (1928), pp. 166–180.

FACHIRI, A. P.: *Expropriation and International Law.* 6 B.Y.I.L. (1925), pp. 159–171.

—— *International Law and the Property of Aliens.* 10 B.Y.I.L. (1929), pp. 32–55.

FAWCETT, J. E. S.: *Some Foreign Effects of Nationalisation of Property.* 27 B.Y.I.L. (1950), pp. 355–375.

FRIEDMAN, S.: *Expropriation in International Law.* London, 1953.

GAITHER, R. B.: *Expropriation in Mexico.* New York, 1940.

GORDON, W. C.: *The Expropriation of Foreign Owned Property in Mexico.* Washington, 1941.

HARVARD RESEARCH IN INTERNATIONAL LAW (1939): *Comment* ad Art. 21 of the *Draft Convention on Rights and Duties of Neutral States in Naval and Aërial War.* 33 A.J.I.L. (1939), Supplement, pp. 359–385.

HERZ, J. H.: *Expropriation of Foreign Property.* 35 A.J.I.L. (1941), pp. 243–262.

HUNGARIAN OPTANTS IN TRANSYLVANIA, DISPUTE *re* APPLICATION OF AGRARIAN REFORM LAW. See 8 and 9 L.N.O.J. (1927 and 1928) Indexes.

HYDE, C. C.: *Confiscatory Expropriations.* 32 A.J.I.L. (1938), pp. 759–766.

—— *Compensation for Expropriations.* 33 A.J.I.L. (1939), pp. 108–112.

JENNINGS, W. I.: *The Right of Angary.* 3 *Cambridge L.J.* (1927–1929), pp. 49–57.

KUHN, A. K.: *Nationalization of Foreign owned Property in its Impact on International Law.* 45 A.J.I.L. (1951), pp. 709–712.

KUNZ, J. L.: *The Mexican Expropriations.* New York, 1940.

LAUTERPACHT, H.: *Angary and Requisition of Neutral Property.* 27 B.Y.I.L. (1950), pp. 455–459.

LE CLÈRE, J.: *Les mesures coercitives sur les navires de commerce étrangers: Angarie, Embargo, Arrêt de Prince.* Paris, 1949.

MCNAIR, A. D.: *Problems connected with the Position of the Merchant Vessel in Private International Law, with particular reference to the Power of Requisition.* 31 *Grotius Transactions* (1945), pp. 30–58.

MEXICO, GOVERNMENT OF: *The True Facts about the Expropriation of the Oil Companies' Properties in Mexico.* Mexico City, 1940.

PETRASCO, N. N.: *La réforme agraire roumaine et les réclamations hongroises.* Paris, 1931.

RE, Edward D.: *Foreign Confiscations in Anglo-American Law.* New York, 1951.

Réforme, La, agraire en Roumanie, et les Optants hongrois de Transylvannie devant la Société des Nations. Études redigiés par MM. A. Alvarez, J. Appleton, Et. Barton, J. Basdevant, H. Barthélémy, J. Brierly, R. Cassin, J. Diena, L. Duguit, A. Higgins, Ed. His, G. Jèze, L. Le Fur, J. Limburg, Ch.

Lyon-Caen, J. de Montmorency, P. Pic, M. Picard, N. Politis, A. Prudhomme, R. Redslob, A. Rolin, W. Schucking, M. Sibert, A. Sottile, K. Strupp, Donnedieu de Vabres, Ch. de Visscher, A. Wahl, Y. de la Brière, H. Capitant, A. Cavaglieri, Descamps, P. Fedozzi, H. La Fontaine, S. Gemma, G. Jèze, A. Lenard, Barbosa de Magalhaes, Th. Niemeyer, A. Salandra, Q. Saldana, G. Salvioli, M. Sibert, M. de Taube, L. Trotabas et J. de Yanguas. 2 vols., Paris, 1927, 1928.

ROBLES, Garcia: *La question du pétrole au Mexique et le droit international.* Paris, 1939.

SCHWARZENBERGER, G.: *The Protection of Human Rights in British State Practice.* 1 C.L.P. (1948), pp. 152–169.

—— *The Protection of British Property Abroad.* 5 C.L.P. (1952), pp. 295–323.

WILLIAMS, J. Fischer: *International Law and the Property of Aliens.* 9 B.Y.I.L. (1928), pp. 1–30.

WILSON, G. G.: *Taking over and Return of Dutch Vessels 1918–1919.* 24 A.J.I.L. (1930), pp. 694–702.

WISE, J. C.: *The Rights of Visit and Search, Capture, Angary and Requisition.* 16 A.J.I.L. (1922), pp. 391–399.

WISE, M. K.: *Requisition in France and Italy. The Treatment of National Private Property and Services.* New York, 1944.

WOOLSEY, L. H.: *Expropriation of Oil Properties by Mexico.* 32 A.J.I.L. (1938), pp. 519–526.

—— *The Taking of Foreign Ships in American Ports.* 35 A.J.I.L. (1941), pp. 497–506.

WORTLEY, B. A.: *Expropriation in International Law.* 33 *Grotius Transactions* (1947), pp. 25–49.

C. MEASURES TO ENSURE PUBLIC SAFETY

ARIAS, H.: *The Non-Liability of States for Damages suffered by Foreigners in the Course of a Riot, an Insurrection, or a Civil War.* 7 A.J.I.L. (1913), pp. 724–765.

A.S.I.L.: *The Right of a Government to Impose Burdens and Limitations upon the Alien for Governmental Purposes, that is, for the Benefit of the Community.* 5 *Proceedings* (1911), pp. 214–225.

—— *The Confiscation of Alien Property.* 20 *Proceedings* (1926), pp. 14–25.

—— *Responsibility of States for Injuries suffered by Foreigners within their Territories on account of Mob Violence, Riots and Insurrection.* 21 *Proceedings* (1927), pp. 49–81.

A.S.I.L.: *The " Minimum Standard " of the Treatment of Aliens.* 33 *Proceedings* (1939), pp. 51–74.

Borchard, E. M.: *The Diplomatic Protection of Citizens Abroad.* New York, 1927. §§ 98–103, 106, 108.

Brandon, M.: *Legal Control over Resident Enemy Aliens in Time of War.* 44 A.J.I.L. (1950), pp. 382–387.

Dickinson, E. D.: *Closure of Port in Control of Insurgents.* 24 A.J.I.L. (1930), pp. 69–78.

Downey, Jr., William Gerald: *The Law of War and Military Necessity.* 47 A.J.I.L. (1953), pp. 251–262.

Eagleton, C.: *Responsibility for Damages to Persons and Property of Aliens in undeclared War.* 32 A.S.I.L. *Proceedings* (1938), pp. 127–140.

Gaithings, J. A.: *International Law and American Treatment of Alien Enemy Property.* Washington, 1940.

Goebel, J.: *The International Responsibility of States for Injuries sustained by Aliens on account of Mob Violence, Insurrection and Civil War.* 8 A.J.I.L. (1914), pp. 802–852.

Harvard Research in International Law (1939): *Comment* ad Art. 22 of the *Draft Convention on Rights and Duties of Neutral States in Naval and Aërial War,* 33 A.J.I.L. (1939), Supplement, pp. 386–391.

Institut de Droit International: *Devoirs et droits des puissances étrangères et leurs ressortissants, au cas de mouvement insurrectionnel, envers les gouvernements établis et reconnus qui sont aux prises avec l'insurrection.* 17 *Annuaire* (1898), pp. 71–95; 18 *Annuaire* (1900), pp. 41–45, 181–229.

—— *Responsabilité des États à raison des dommages soufferts par des étrangers en cas d'émeute ou de guerre civile.* 17 *Annuaire* (1898), pp. 96–137; 18 *Annuaire* (1900), pp. 47–49, 233–256.

Padelford, N. J.: *International Law and Diplomacy in the Spanish Civil Strife.* New York, 1939.

Podestà Costa, L. A.: *International Responsibility of the State for Damages suffered by Aliens during Civil War.* 31 *I.L.A. Rep.* (1923), pp. 119–124.

Rodick, B. C.: *The Doctrine of Necessity in International Law.* New York, 1923.

Roth, A. H.: *The Minimum Standard in International Law applied to Aliens.* Leiden, 1949.

Rouggier, A.: *Les guerres civiles et le droit des gens.* Paris, 1903.

SATOW, Ernest: *The Treatment of Enemy Aliens.* 2 *Grotius Transactions* (1916), pp. 1–10.

SPAIGHT, J. M. : *The Doctrine of Air Force Necessity.* 7 B.Y.I.L. (1925), pp. 1–7.

—— *Legitimate Objectives in Air Warfare.* 21 B.Y.I.L. (1944), pp. 158–164.

—— *Air Power and War Rights.* London, 1947.

WEHBERG, H. : *La guerre civile et le droit international.* 63 *Recueil La Haye* (1938), pp. 7–127.

WILSON, R. R. : *A Case of International Responsibility during Martial Rule.* 36 A.J.I.L. (1942), pp. 657–661.

—— *Treatment of Civilian Alien Enemies.* 37 A.J.I.L. (1943), pp. 30–45.

WOOLSEY, L. H. : *Closure of Ports by the Chinese Nationalist Government.* 44 A.J.I.L. (1950), pp. 350–356.

WRIGHT, Q. : *Responsibility for Losses in Shanghai.* 26 A.J.I.L. (1932), pp. 586–590.

See also Bibliography to Part Three, *infra*, pp. 429 *et seq.*

CHAPTER 2. EXTERNAL APPLICATION OF THE PRINCIPLE OF SELF-PRESERVATION

A. NECESSITY

BORSI, U. : *Ragione di guerra e stato di necessità nel diritto internazionale.* 10 *Rivista* (1916), pp. 157–194.

CAVAGLIERI, A. : *Lo stato di necessità nel diritto internazionale.* Roma, 1917.

CAVARRETTA, G. : *Lo stato di necessità nel diritto internazionale.* Palermo, 1910.

GLASER, S. : *Quelques remarques sur l'état de nécessité en droit international.* 35 *Revue de droit pénal et de criminologie* (1952), pp. 570–603.

HAZAN, E. T. : *L'état de nécessité en droit pénal interétatique et international.* Paris, 1949.

KOHLER, J. : *Not kennt kein Gebot. Die Theorie des Notrechtes und die Ereignisse unserer Zeit.* Berlin und Leipzig, 1915.

RODICK, B. C. : *The Doctrine of Necessity in International Law.* New York, 1928.

SPERDUTI, G. : *Introduzione allo studio delle funzioni della necessità nel diritto internazionale.* 35 *Rivista* (1943), pp. 19–103.

STILZ, Richard: *Notstand im Völkerrecht.* Coburg, 1930.

VISSCHER, Ch. de: *Les lois de la guerre et la théorie de la nécessité.* 24 R.G.D.I.P. (1917), pp. 74–108.

WEIDEN, P.: *Necessity in International Law.* 24 *Grotius Transactions* (1938), pp. 105–132.

B. SELF-DEFENCE

ARNOLD-FOSTER, W.: *Order and Self-defence in the World Community.* 5 *Problems of Peace* (1930), pp. 230–255.

DESCAMPS, Baron: *Le droit international nouveau. L'Influence de la condamnation de la guerre sur l'évolution juridique internationale.* 31 *Recueil La Haye* (1930), pp. 399–557, at pp. 469–486.

EAGLETON, C.: *The attempt to define aggression.* International Conciliation, No. 264 (Nov., 1930).

GIRAUD, Emile: *La théorie de la légitime défense.* 49 *Recueil La Haye* (1934), pp. 691–865.

HETZ, W. G.: *Die Theorie der Notwehr.* 35 *Die Friedens-Warte* (1935), pp. 137–142.

JELF, E. A.: *What is War? What is Aggressive War?* 19 *Grotius Transactions* (1934), pp. 103–114.

JEMTEL, Yves Le: *L'assistance hostile dans les guerres maritimes modernes.* Paris, 1938.

JENNINGS, R. Y.: *The Caroline and McLeod Cases.* 32 A.J.I.L. (1938), pp. 82–99.

KOHLER, J.: *Notwehr und Neutralität.* 8 Z.f.V. (1914), pp. 576–580.

KULSRUD, C. J.: *The Seizure of the Danish Fleet, 1807.* 32 A.J.I.L. (1938), pp. 280–311.

KUNZ, J. L.: *Individual and Collective Self-Defence in Art. 51 of the Charter of the United Nations.* 41 A.J.I.L. (1947), pp. 872–879.

MOCH, C.: *Du droit de légitime défense et des traités d'alliance défensive.* Mémoire présenté au XVIIIe Congrès universel de la Paix, Stockholm, 1910.

POTTER, P. B.: *Preventive War critically considered.* 45 A.J.I.L. (1951), pp. 142–145.

VIGNOL, René: *Définition de l'agresseur dans la guerre.* Paris, 1933.

WRIGHT, Q.: *The Meaning of the Pact of Paris.* 27 A.J.I.L. (1933), pp. 39–61.

—— *The Concept of Aggression in International Law.* 29 A.J.I.L. (1935), pp. 373–395.

See also Bibliography to C. Self-help.

C. SELF-HELP

A.S.I.L.: *Enforcement of Treaty Obligations by Self-help and Self-defence.* 26 *Proceedings* (1932), pp. 90–101.

BALLIS, W.: *The Legal Position of War: Changes in its Practice and Theory from Plato to Vattel.* The Hague, 1937.

BEAUFORT, D.: *La guerre comme instrument de secours ou de punition.* La Haye, 1933.

BORCHARD, E. M.: *The Diplomatic Protection of Citizens Abroad.* New York, 1927. §§ 194–197.

BOURQUIN, M.: *Le problème de la sécurité internationale.* 49 *Recueil La Haye* (1934), pp. 473–541.

BRIÈRE, Yves de la: *Évolution de la doctrine et de la pratique en matière de représailles.* 22 *Recueil La Haye* (1928), pp. 241–293.

BRIERLY, J. L.: *International Law and Resort to Armed Forces.* 4 *Cambridge L.J.* (1930–1932), pp. 308–319.

—— *Vital Interests and the Law.* 21 B.Y.I.L. (1944), pp. 51–57.

CLARK, G.: *The English Practice with regard to Reprisals by Private Persons.* 27 A.J.I.L. (1933), pp. 694–723.

CLARK, J. Reuben, Jr.: *The Right to Protect Citizens by Landing Forces.* Washington, 1929.

COLBERT, Evelyn Speyer: *Retaliation in International Law.* New York, 1948.

EAGLETON, C.: *Faut-il proscrire seulement les guerres d'agression ou toutes les guerres?* 39 R.G.D.I.P. (1932), pp. 498–511.

GIRAUD, E.: *A Memorandum on Pacific Blockade up to the Time of the Foundation of the League of Nations.* 8 L.N.O.J. (1927), pp. 841–845.

HAMBRO, E.: *L'exécution des sentences internationales.* Paris, 1936.

HINDMARSH, A. E.: *Self-help in Time of Peace.* 26 A.J.I.L. (1932), pp. 315–326.

HINDMARSH, A. E.: *Force in Peace. Force Short of War in International Relations.* Cambridge (Mass.), 1933.

HOGAN, A. E.: *Pacific Blockade.* Oxford, 1908.

INSTITUT DE DROIT INTERNATIONAL: *Le régime de représailles en temps de paix.* 38 *Annuaire* (1934), pp. 1–161, 623–694, 708–711.

LAMBERT, J.: *La vengeance privée et les fondements du droit international.* Paris, 1936.

LEGNANO, Giovanni da: *De Bello, De Represalis et De Duello.* Translation by J. L. Brierly. Oxford, 1917.

MACCOBY, Simon: *Reprisals as a Measure of Redress Short of War.* 2 *Cambridge L.J.* (1928), pp. 60–73.

MCNAIR, A. D.: *The Legal Meaning of War and the Relations of War to Reprisals.* 11 *Grotius Transactions* (1925), pp. 29–51.

POLITIS, N.: *Les représailles entre membres de la S.d.N.* 31 R.G.D.I.P. (1924), pp. 5–16.

POTTER, P. B.: *L'intervention en droit international moderne.* 32 *Recueil La Haye* (1930), pp. 611–689.

REGOUT, R.: *La doctrine de la guerre juste de St. Augustin à nos jours d'après les théologiens et les canonistes catholiques.* Paris, 1935.

SCHWARZENBERGER, G.: *Jus Pacis ac Belli? Prolegomena to a Sociology of International Law.* 37 A.J.I.L. (1943), pp. 460–479.

—— *International Law in Early English Practice.* 25 B.Y.I.L. (1948), pp. 52–90, at pp. 65–68.

—— *Power Politics.* London, 1951, Chap. 12.

SÉFÉRIADÈS, M. S.: *La question des représailles armées en temps de paix, en l'état actuel du droit des gens.* 3 (17) R.D.I.L.C. (1936), pp. 138–164.

STOWELL, E. C.: *Intervention in International Law.* Washington, 1921.

—— *La théorie et la pratique de l'intervention.* 40 *Recueil La Haye* (1932), pp. 91–151.

THÉRY, René: *La notion d'agression en droit international.* Paris, 1937.

TUCKER, R. W.: *The Interpretation of War under Present International Law.* 4 I.L.Q. (1951), pp. 11–38.

WINFIELD, P. H.: *The Grounds of Intervention in International Law.* 5 B.Y.I.L. (1924), pp. 149–162, at pp. 151–154.

PART TWO

THE PRINCIPLE OF GOOD FAITH

CHAPTER 3. GOOD FAITH IN TREATY RELATIONS

A.S.I.L.: *Nature and Interpretation of Treaties: Treaties made under Duress.* 26 *Proceedings* (1932), pp. 45–53.

—— *The Doctrine of Rebus sic Stantibus.* 26 *Proceedings* (1932), pp. 53–68.

AUFRICHT, Hans: *Suppression of Treaties in International Law.* 37 *Cornell L.Q.* (1952), pp. 655–700.

BALLADORE-PALLIERI, G.: *La formation des traités internationaux,* 74 *Recueil La Haye* (1949), pp. 469–545.

BASDEVANT, J.: *La conclusion et la rédaction des traités et des instruments diplomatiques autres que les traités.* 15 *Recueil La Haye* (1926), pp. 539–643.

BERGER, Peter: *Zur Klausel "rebus sic stantibus."* 4 Ö.Z.f.ö.R. (1951), pp. 27–61.

BRIERLY, J. L.: *Some Considerations on the Obsolescence of Treaties.* 11 *Grotius Transactions* (1925), pp. 11–20.

BURCKHARDT, W.: *La clausula rebus sic stantibus en droit international.* 3 (14) R.D.I.L.C. (1933), pp. 5–30.

CAMERA, J. S.: *The Ratification of International Treaties.* Toronto, 1949.

CHAILLEY, P.: *La nature juridique des traités internationaux selon le droit contemporain.* Paris, 1932.

CHANG Yi-Ting: *The Interpretation of Treaties by Judicial Tribunals.* New York, 1933.

CHENG, C. H.: *Essai critique sur l'interprétation des traités dans la doctrine et la jurisprudence de la Cour permanente de Justice internationale.* Thèse, Paris, 1941.

DEHOUSE, F.: *La ratification des traités.* Paris, 1935.

EHRLICH, L.: *L'interprétation des traités.* 24 *Recueil La Haye* (1928), pp. 5–143.

FACHIRI, A. P.: *Interpretation of Treaties.* 23 A.J.I.L. (1929), pp. 745–752.

FITZMAURICE, G. G.: *Do Treaties need Ratification?* 15 B.Y.I.L. (1934), pp. 113–137.

FRANGULIS, A. F.: *Théorie et pratique des traités internationaux.* Paris, 1936.

FRÖHLICH, Max: *Die Sittlichkeit in völkerrechtlichen Verträgen.* Dissertation, Zurich, 1924.

GENET, R.: *Le problème de la clause "rebus sic stantibus." Caducité ou révision?* 37 R.G.D.I.P. (1930), pp. 287–311.

HARVARD RESEARCH IN INTERNATIONAL LAW (1935): Part 3: *Law of Treaties.* 29 A.J.I.L. (1935), Supplement.

HILL, C.: *The Doctrine of "rebus sic stantibus" in International Law.* Columbia, Missouri, 1934.

HOIJER, O.: *Les traités internationaux.* 2 tomes. Paris, 1928.

HUANG, T. Y.: *The Doctrine of rebus sic stantibus in International Law.* Shanghai, 1935.

HYDE, C. C.: *The Interpretation of Treaties by the P.C.I.J.* 24 A.J.I.L. (1930), pp. 1–19.

—— *Judge Anzilotti on the Interpretation of Treaties.* 27 A.J.I.L. (1933), pp. 502–506.

INSTITUT DE DROIT INTERNATIONAL: *De l'interprétation des traités.* 43 (I) *Annuaire* (1950), pp. 366–460. 44 (I) *ibid.* (1952), pp. 197–223. 44 (II) *ibid.* (1952), pp. 359–406.

INTERNATIONAL LAW COMMISSION: Documents No. A/CN.4/23: *Report on the Law of Treaties* (J. L. Brierly);

—— A/CN.4/31: *Bibliography on the Law of Treaties* (Secretariat);

—— A/CN.4/37: *Memorandum on the Soviet Doctrine and Practice with respect to the Law of Treaties* (Secretariat);

—— A/CN.4/41: *Report on Reservations to Multilateral Conventions* (J. L. Brierly);

—— A/CN.4/43: *Second Report on the Law of Treaties* (J. L. Brierly);

—— A/CN.4/54: *Third Report on the Law of Treaties* (J. L. Brierly);

—— A/CN.4/58: *Fourth Report of the International Law Commission*, Chap. VI.

JELLINEK, G.: *Die rechtliche Natur der Staatenverträge.* Wien, 1880.

JONES, J. M.: *Full Powers and Ratification.* Cambridge, 1946.

KUNZ, J. L.: *The Meaning and the Range of the Norm Pacta sunt Servanda.* 39 A.J.I.L. (1945), pp. 180–197.

LAUTERPACHT, H.: *Restrictive Interpretation and the Principles of Effectiveness in the Interpretation of Treaties.* 26 B.Y.I.L. (1949), pp. 48–85.

McNAIR, A. D.: *The Law of Treaties.* Oxford, 1938.

—— *La terminaison et la dissolution des traités.* 22 *Recueil La Haye* (1928), pp. 463–537.

McNair, A. D.: *Les effets de la guerre sur les traités*. 59 *Recueil La Haye* (1937), pp. 527–585.

Myers, D. P.: *Violation of Treaties: Bad Faith, Non-execution and Disregard*. 11 A.J.I.L. (1917), pp. 794–819.

Nisot, J.: *La force obligatoire des traités signés, non encore ratifiés*. 57 *Clunet* (1930), pp. 878–883.

Otétéléchano, Jean: *De la valeur obligatoire des traités internationaux. Pacta sunt servanda*. Paris, 1916.

Politis, N.: *La morale internationale*. New York, 1944.

Ray, J.: *Des conflicts entre principes abstraits et stipulations conventionnelles*. 48 *Recueil La Haye* (1934), pp. 635–707.

Scaransella, G.: *Il principio "inadimplenti non est adimplendum" nel diritto internazionale. Jus. Gentium* (*Rivista*) (1951), pp. 23–29.

Scelle, G.: *Théorie juridique de la révision des traités*. Paris, 1936.

Stinson, J. W.: *La sanction du droit des gens et la force obligatoire des traités*. 3 (5) R.D.I.L.C. (1924), pp. 424–441.

Taube, M. de: *L'inviolabilité des traités*. 32 *Recueil La Haye* (1930), pp. 295–389.

Tobin, H. J.: *The Termination of Multipartite Treaties*. New York, 1933.

Tomšič, Ivan: *La reconstruction du droit international en matière des traités. Essai sur le problème des vices du consentement dans la conclusion des traités internationaux*. Paris, 1931.

Vellani, G. E.: *La revisione dei trattati e i principî generali del diritto*. Modena, 1930.

Visscher, Paul de: *De la conclusion des traités internationaux*. Bruxelles, 1943.

Vitta, E.: *La validité des traités internationaux*. 14 *Bibliotheca Visseriana* (1940), pp. 1–250.

Whitton, J. B.: *The Sanctity of Treaties* (*Pacta sunt servanda*). International Conciliation, No. 313 (October, 1935).

Wilcox, F. O.: *The Ratification of International Conventions*. London, 1936.

Wilson, R. R.: *Some Aspects of Treaty Interpretation*. 33 A.J.I.L. (1939), pp. 541–545.

You, P.: *Le préambule des traités internationaux*. Fribourg, 1941.

Yü Tsune-Chi: *The Interpretation of Treaties*. New York, 1927.

Chapter 4. Good Faith in the Exercise of Rights

Allen, C. K.: *Legal Morality and the Jus Abutendi.* 40 L.Q.R. (1924), pp. 164–184.

Gutteridge, H. C.: *Abuse of Right.* 5 *Cambridge L.J.* (1933), pp. 22–45.

Kiss, A. C.: *L'abus de droit en droit international.* Paris, 1953.

Lauterpacht, H.: *The Function of Law in the International Community.* Oxford, 1933; Chap. XIV.

Leibholz, G.: *Das Verbot der Willkür und des Ermessensmissbrauches im völkerrechtlichen Verkehr der Staaten.* 1 Z.f.a. ö.R.u.V. (1929), pp. 77–125.

Politis, N.: *Le problème des limitations de la souveraineté et la théorie de l'abus des droits dans les rapports internationaux.* 6 *Recueil La Haye* (1925), pp. 1–121.

Salvioli, G.: *Les règles générales de la paix.* 46 *Recueil La Haye* (1933), pp. 1–164, Chap. 2, § 9.

Scerni, M.: *L'abuso di diritto nei rapporti internazionali.* Roma, 1930.

Schlochauer, H. J.: *Die Theorie des Abus de Droit im Völkerrecht.* 17 Z.f.V. (1933), pp. 373–394.

Séléa, Trifu: *La notion de l'abus du droit dans le droit international.* Thèse, Paris, 1940.

Sperduti, G.: *Il principio della buona fede e l'ammissione di nuovi membri nelle Nazioni Unite.* 7 *La Communità internazionale* (1952), pp. 42–63.

Spiropoulos, J.: *L'abus du droit de vote par un membre du Conseil de Sécurité.* 1 (1) *R.D.I.* (*hellénique*) (1948), pp. 3–14.

Chapter 5. Other Applications of the Principle of Good Faith

A.S.I.L.: *The Effect of the Unfriendly Act or Inequitable Conduct of the Citizens upon the Right to Protection.* 4 *Proceedings* (1910), pp. 99–122.

Borchard, E. M.: *The Diplomatic Protection of Citizens Abroad.* New York, 1927. Part 4, Chap. 3.

Bourgeois, L.: *La morale internationale.* 19 R.G.D.I.P. (1922), pp. 5–22.

Broom, H.: *A Selection of Legal Maxims.* London, 1939.

Cababe, M.: *Principles of Estoppel.* London, 1888.

Casperez, A.: *Estoppel and the Substantive Law, or the Principles of Keeping Faith and Finality.* 4th ed., Calcutta, 1915.

DUMBAULD, Ed.: *Interim Measures of Protection in International Controversies.* The Hague, 1932.

—— *Relief pendente lite in the P.C.I.J.* 31 A.J.I.L. (1945), pp. 391–405.

FRIEDE, W.: *Das Estoppel-Prinzip im Völkerrecht.* 5 (3) Z.f.a.ö. R.u.V. (1935), pp. 517–545.

GUGGENHEIM, P.: *Les mesures conservatoires dans la procédure arbitrale et judiciaire.* 40 *Recueil La Haye* (1932), pp. 649–764.

HAMMARSKJÖLD, Å.: *Quelques aspects de la question des mesures conservatoires en droit international positif.* 5 Z.f.a.ö.R.u.V. (1935), pp. 5–33.

KEETON, G. W., and SCHWARZENBERGER, G.: *Making International Law Work.* London, 1946. Chap. 4.

KRAUS, H.: *La morale internationale.* 16 *Recueil La Haye* (1927), pp. 389–539.

MCNAIR, A. D.: *The Legality of the Occupation of the Ruhr.* 5 B.Y.I.L. (1924), pp. 17–37, at pp. 31 *et seq.*

POLITIS, N.: *La morale internationale.* New York, 1944.

ROLIN, Henri A.: *Force obligatoire des ordonnances de la C.P.J.I. en matière de mesures conservatoires.* 2 *Mélanges Mahaim,* 1935, pp. 280–298.

SCHWARZENBERGER, G.: *Power Politics.* London, 1951. Chap. 14: *The Functions of International Morality.* See also bibliography thereto.

VERDROSS-DROSSBERG, A.: *La bonne foi comme fondement du droit international public.* 5 *R.D.I.* (*hellénique*) (1952), pp. 17–21.

WITENBERG, J.-C.: *L'estoppel, un aspect juridique du problème des créances américaines.* 60 *Clunet* (1933), pp. 529–538.

PART THREE

GENERAL PRINCIPLES OF LAW IN THE CONCEPT OF RESPONSIBILITY

AGO, R.: *La colpa nell'illecito internazionale.* Scritti giuridici in onore di S. Romano. 1939.

—— *Le délit international.* 68 *Recueil La Haye* (1939), pp. 419–554.

ANZILOTTI, D.: *Teoria generale della responsabilità dello Stato nel diritto internazionale.* Firenze, 1902.

Anzilotti, D.: *La responsabilité internationale des États à raison des dommages soufferts par des étrangers.* 13 R.G.D.I.P. (1906), pp. 5–29, 285–309.

Arias, H.: *The non-liability of States for Damages suffered by Foreigners in the Course of a Riot, an Insurrection, or a Civil War.* 7 A.J.I.L. (1913), pp. 724–765.

A.S.I.L.: *Responsibility of States for Damage done in Their Territories to the Person or Property of Foreigners.* 21 *Proceedings* (1927), pp. 23–49.

—— *Responsibility of States for Injuries suffered by Foreigners within their Territories on account of Mob Violence, Riots and Insurrection.* 21 *Proceedings* (1927), pp. 49–63.

—— *Responsibility of States for Damages done in their Territory to the Person or Property of Foreigners.* 22 *Proceedings* (1928), pp. 67–92.

—— *Responsibility for Damages to Persons and Property of Aliens in undeclared War.* 32 *Proceedings* (1938), pp. 127–140.

—— *The "Minimum Standard" of the Treatment of Aliens.* 33 *Proceedings* (1939), pp. 51–63.

Biscottini, G.: *Volontà ed attività dello Stato nell' ordinamento internazionale.* 34 *Rivista* (1942), pp. 3–43.

Borchard, E. M.: *The Diplomatic Protection of Citizens Abroad or the Law of International Claims.* New York, 1927.

—— *Government Responsibility in Tort.* 34 *Yale L.J.* (1924), pp. 1–45, 129–143, 229–258; 36 *Yale L.J.* (1927), pp. 1–41, 757–807, 1039–1100.

—— *Theories of Governmental Responsibility in Tort.* 28 *Columbia L.R.* (1929), pp. 734–775.

—— *Theoretical Aspects of the International Responsibility of States.* 1 Z.f.a.ö.R.u.V. (1929), pp. 223–250.

—— *The Local Remedy Rule.* 28 A.J.I.L. (1934), pp. 729–733.

Brierly, J. L.: *The Theory of Implied State Complicity in International Claims.* 9 B.Y.I.L. (1928), pp. 42–49.

Burckhardt, W.: *Die völkerrechtliche Verantwortlichkeit der Staaten.* Bern, 1924.

Calvo, Ch.: *De la non-responsabilité des États à raison des pertes et dommages éprouvés par des étrangers en temps de troubles intérieures ou de guerres civiles.* 1 R.D.I.L.C. (1869), pp. 417–427.

Camuzet, L.: *L'indemnité de guerre en droit international.* Paris, 1928.

Cheng, Bin.: *The Anglo-Iranian Dispute.* 5 (New Series) *World Affairs* (1951), pp. 387–405.

DECENCIÈRE-FERRANDIÈRE, A.: *La responsabilité internationale des États à raison des dommages subis par des étrangers.* Paris, 1925.

DUMAS, J.: *La responsabilité des États à raison des crimes et délits commis sur leur territoire au préjudice d'étrangers.* 36 *Recueil La Haye* (1931), pp. 187–261.

DUNN, F. S.: *The Protection of Nationals.* Baltimore, 1938.

EAGLETON, C.: *The Responsibility of States in International Law.* New York, 1928.

—— *Measure of Damages in International Law.* 39 *Yale L.J.* (1929), pp. 52–75.

—— *Une théorie au sujet du commencement de la responsabilité de l'État.* 3 (11) R.D.I.L.C. (1930), pp. 643–659.

EUSTHATHIADÈS, C. Th.: *La responsabilité internationale des États pour les actes des organes judiciaires et le problème du déni de justice en droit international.* 2 tomes. Paris, 1936.

FACHIRI, A. P.: *The Local Remedies Rule in the Light of the Finnish Ships Arbitration.* 17 B.Y.I.L. (1936), pp. 19–36.

FAIRMAN, C.: *Competence to bind the State to a Unilateral Engagement.* 30 A.J.I.L. (1936), pp. 439–462.

FITZMAURICE, G. G.: *The Meaning of the Term "Denial of Justice."* 13 B.Y.I.L. (1932), pp. 93–114.

FRIEDMANN, W.: *The Growth of State Control over the Individual and its Effect upon the Rules of International State Responsibility.* 19 B.Y.I.L. (1938), pp. 118–150.

GAMMANS, N.: *The Responsibility of the Federal Government for Violations of the Rights of Aliens.* 8 A.J.I.L. (1914), pp. 73–80.

GARDE, Castillo J.: *El acto ilicito internacional.* 3 R.D.I. (*española*) (1950), pp. 121–144.

GARNER, J. W.: *International Responsibility of States for Judgment of Courts and Verdicts of Juries amounting to Denial of Justice.* 10 B.Y.I.L. (1929), pp. 181–189.

GREEN, L.: *Rationale of Proximate Cause.* Kansas City, 1927.

HACKWORTH, G. H.: *Responsibility of States for Damages caused in their Territory to the Person or Property of Foreigners.* 24 A.J.I.L. (1930), pp. 500–516.

HARVARD RESEARCH IN INTERNATIONAL LAW: Drafts of Conventions prepared in anticipation of the First Convention on the Codification of International Law: 2. *The Law of Responsibility of States for Damage done in their Territory to the Person or Property of Foreigners.* 23 A.J.I.L. (1929), Special Supplement, pp. 133–239.

HAURIOU, A.: *Les dommages indirects dans les arbitrages internationaux.* 31 R.G.D.I.P. (1925), pp. 203–231.

HOIJER, Olof: *La responsabilité internationale des États.* Paris, 1930.

INSTITUT DE DROIT INTERNATIONAL: *Responsabilité des États à raison des dommages soufferts par des étrangers en cas d'émeute ou de guerre civile.* 17 *Annuaire* (1898), pp. 96–137; 18 *Annuaire* (1900), pp. 47–49, 233–256.

—— *La responsabilité internationale des États à raison des dommages causés sur leur territoire à la personne ou aux biens des étrangers.* 33 (1) *Annuaire* (1927), pp. 455–562; 33 (3) *Annuaire* (1927), pp. 81–168, 330–335.

—— *Protection diplomatique des nationaux à l'étranger.* 36 (1) *Annuaire* (1931), pp. 256–491; 37 *Annuaire* (1932), pp. 235–282; 479–529.

JESSUP, P. C.: *Responsibility of States for Injuries to Individuals.* 46 *Columbia L.R.* (1946), pp. 904–928.

JONES, J. Mervyn: *Constitutional Limitations on the Treaty Making Power.* 35 A.J.I.L. (1941), pp. 462–481.

KELSEN, H.: *Unrecht und Unrechtsfolge im Völkerrecht.* 12 Z.ö.R. (1932), pp. 481–608.

—— *Collective and Individual Responsibility for Acts of State in International Law.* 1 *Jewish Y.B.I.L.* (1948), pp. 226–239.

KIESSELBACH, Wilhelm: *Problems of the German-American Claims Commission.* Washington, 1930. Chap. VIII.

LEAGUE OF NATIONS (Conference for the Codification of International Law): *Responsibility of States for Damage done in Their Territories to the Person or Property of Foreigners,* Report of the Sub-Committee on. Committee of Experts for the Progressive Codification of International Law. L.o.N.P.: C.196.M.70.1927.V., pp. 92–105.

—— First Codification Conference. *Schedules of Points* drawn up by the Preparatory Committee. L.o.N.P.: V.Legal.1928.V.1.

—— *Bases of Discussion* drawn up for the Conference by the Preparatory Committee. Vol. 3: *Responsibility of States for Damage caused in their Territory to the Person or Property of Foreigners.* L.o.N.P.: V.Legal.1929.V.3.

—— *Bases of Discussion.* Supplement to Vol. 3. *Replies of Canada and the U.S.A.* L.o.N.P.: V.Legal.1929.V.10.

—— *Acts of the Conference for the Codification of International Law,* held at The Hague from March 13 to April 12, 1930. Vol. 4: Minutes of the Third Committee: *Responsibility of States for Damage caused in their Territory to the Person or Property of Foreigners.* L.o.N.P.: V.Legal.1930.V.17.

LISSITZYN, O. J.: *The Meaning of the Term "Denial of Justice" in International Law.* 30 A.J.I.L. (1936), pp. 632–646.

MONACO, R.: *La responsabilità internazionale dello Stato per fatti di individui.* 31 *Rivista* (1939), pp. 3–30, 193–261.

PERSONAZ, J.: *La réparation du préjudice en droit international.* Paris, 1939.

PODESTÀ COSTA, L. A.: *La responsabilitad del Estado por daños irrogados à la persona o à les bienes de extranjeros en lunchas civiles.* Buenos Aires, 1922.

REITZER, L.: *La réparation comme conséquence de l'acte illicite en droit international.* Paris, 1938.

ROBINSON, Nehemia: *Reparation and Restitution in International Law as affecting Jews.* 1 *Jewish Y.B.I.L.* (1948), pp. 186–205.

ROTH, A.: *Schadensersatz für Verletzungen Privater bei völkerrechtlichem Delikt.* Berlin, 1934.

RUEGGER, P., und BURCKHARDT, W.: *Die völkerrechtliche Verantwortlichkeit des Staates für die auf seinem Gebiete begangenen Verbrechen.* Zürich, 1924.

SALVIOLI, G.: *La responsabilité des États et la fixation des dommages-intérêts par les tribunaux internationaux.* 28 *Recueil La Haye* (1929), pp. 235–289.

SCHOEN, P.: *Die völkerrechtliche Haftung der Staaten aus unerlaubten Handlungen.* Ergänzungsheft 2 zur 10 Z.f.V. (1917), pp. 1–143.

SCHWARZENBERGER, G.: *The Protection of British Property Abroad.* 5 C.L.P. (1952), pp. 295–323.

SIBERT, M.: *Contribution à l'étude des réparations pour les dommages causés aux étrangers en conséquence d'une législation contraire au droit des gens.* 48 (1) R.G.D.I.P. (1941–1945), pp. 5–34.

SILVANIE, H.: *Responsibility of States for Acts of Insurgent Governments.* 33 A.J.I.L. (1939), pp. 78–103.

SOLDATI, A.: *La responsabilité des États dans le droit international.* Paris, 1934.

SPIROPOULOS, J.: *Die Haftung der Staaten für "indirekten Schaden" aus völkerrechtlichen Delikten.* 35 Z.I.R. (1925–1926), pp. 59–134.

STARKE, J. G.: *Imputability in International Delinquencies.* 19 B.Y.I.L. (1938), pp. 104–117.

STRUPP, K.: *Das völkerrechtliche Delikt.* Stuttgart, 1920.

TÉNÉKIDÈS, C. G.: *L'épuisement des voies de recours internes comme condition préalable de l'instance internationale.* 3 (14) R.D.I.L.C. (1933), pp. 514–535.

VISSCHER, Ch. de: *La responsabilité des États.* 2 *Bibliotheca Visseriana* (1924), pp. 87–119.

—— *Le déni de justice en droit international.* 52 *Recueil La Haye* (1935), pp. 369–441.

WHITEMAN, Marjorie M.: *Damages in International Law.* 3 vols. USGPO, 1937–1943.

WITENBERG, J.-C.: *La recevabilité des réclamations devant les juridictions internationales.* 41 *Recueil La Haye* (1932), pp. 5–135.

YNTEMA, H. E.: *The Treaties with Germany and Compensation for War Damages.* IV: The Measure of Damage in International Law. 24 *Columbia L.R.* (1923–1924), pp. 134–153.

ZANNAS, P. A.: *La responsabilité internationale des États pour les actes de négligence.* Thèse, Genève. Montreux, 1952.

ZELLWEGER, Ed.: *Die völkerrechtliche Verantwortlichkeit des Staates für die Presse unter besonderer Berücksichtigung der Schweizerischen Praxis.* Zürich, 1949.

Addendum:

BISSONNETTE, P. A.: *La satisfaction comme mode de réparation en droit international.* Thèse, Genève, 1952.

FREEMAN, A. V.: *The International Responsibility of States for Denial of Justice.* London, 1938.

PART FOUR

GENERAL PRINCIPLES OF LAW IN JUDICIAL PROCEEDINGS

CHAPTERS 11—17

BALASKO, A.: *Causes de nullité de la sentence arbitrale en droit international public.* Paris, 1938.

BASDEVANT, Jèze, et POLITIS, N.: *Les principes juridiques sur la compétence des juridictions internationales.* 44 R.D.P.S.P. (1927), pp. 45 *et seq.*

BOREL, E.: *Les voies de recours contre les sentences arbitrales.* 52 *Recueil La Haye* (1935), pp. 5–104.

B.[RIERLY], J. L.: *The Hague Conventions and the Nullity of Arbitral Awards.* 9 B.Y.I.L. (1928), pp. 114–117.

BRUNS, Viktor: *Der Internationale Richter.* Publication de l'Institut suédois de droit international, Nr. 1. Uppsala, 1934.

CALDWELL, R. H.: *A Study of the Code of Arbitral Procedure adopted by the Hague Peace Conferences of 1899 and 1907.* Carnegie thesis, 1921.

CARLSTON, K. S.: *The Process of International Arbitration.* New York, 1946.

CASTBERG, F.: *L'excès de pouvoir dans la justice internationale.* 35 *Recueil La Haye* (1931), pp. 357–472.

DARBY, W. E.: *International Tribunals: A Collection of the Various Schemes which have been propounded and of Instances in the 19th Century.* London, 1904.

DENNIS, W. C.: *Compromise—the Great Defect of Arbitration.* 11 *Columbia L.R.* (1911), pp. 493–513.

FUSCO, G. S.: *Note sulla cosa giudicata internazionale.* 31 *Rivista* (1939), pp. 361–377.

GARNER, J. W.: *Appeal in Cases of Alleged Invalid Arbitral Awards.* 26 A.J.I.L. (1932), pp. 126–132.

GARNIER-COIGNET, J.: *Procédure judiciaire et procédure arbitrale.* 6 R.D.I. (1930), pp. 123–147.

GUYNAT, A.: *Procédure orale devant la C.P.J.I.* 37 R.G.D.I.P. (1930), pp. 312–323.

HAGUE PEACE CONFERENCE: 2nd Conference 1907. *Project relative to a Court of Arbitral Justice, Draft Convention and Report Adopted, . . .* 1907, *with an Introductory Note by J. B. Scott.* Washington; Carnegie, 1920.

HAMMARSKJÖLD, Å.: *Juridiction internationale.* Leiden, 1938.

HERTZ, W. G.: *Essai sur le problème de la nullité.* 3 (20) R.D.I.L.C. (1939), pp. 450–500.

HILL, N. L.: *National Judges in the P.C.I.J.* 25 *A.J.I.L.* (1931), pp. 670–683.

—— *The Influence of Disputants over Procedure in International Courts.* 21 *Virginia L.R.* (1934), pp. 205–218.

HUDSON, M. O.: *The P.C.I.J.* New York, 1943.

—— *International Tribunals, Past and Future.* Washington, 1944.

HYDE, C. C.: *Maps as Evidence in International Boundary Disputes.* 27 A.J.I.L. (1933), pp. 311–316.

INSTITUT DE DROIT INTERNATIONAL: *Procédure arbitrale internationale.* 1 (6) R.D.I.L.C. (1874), pp. 84–153, 330–335, 421–453, 587–592; 1 (7) R.D.I.L.C. (1875), pp. 277–282, 418–426; 1 *Annuaire* (1877), pp. 126–133.

INSTITUT DE DROIT INTERNATIONAL: *Procédure arbitrale.* 33 (2) *Annuaire* (1927), pp. 565–668; 33 (3) *Annuaire* (1927), pp. 319–322, 345–347.

INSTITUT FÜR AUSLÄNDISCHES ÖFFENTLICHES RECHT UND VÖLKERRECHT: *Statut et Règlement de la C.P.J.I.* Berlin, 1934.

INTERNATIONAL LAW COMMISSION: Documents No. A/CN.4/18: *Report on Arbitration Procedure* (G. Scelle);

—— A/CN.4/29: *Bibliography on Arbitral Procedure* (Secretariat);

—— A/CN.4/35: *Memorandum on Arbitral Procedure* (Secretariat);

—— A/CN.4/36: *Memorandum on the Soviet Doctrine and Practice with respect to Arbitral Procedure* (Secretariat);

—— A/CN.4/46: *Second Report on Arbitration Procedure* (G. Scelle).

—— A/CN.4/57: *Supplementary Note to the Second Report on Arbitration Procedure* (G. Scelle).

—— A/CN.4/58: *Fourth Report of the International Law Commission*, Chap. II.

KAUFMANN, E.: *Probleme der internationalen Gerichtsbarkeit.* Leipzig, 1932.

LA FONTAINE, H.: *International Judicature.* Baltimore, 1915.

LALIVE, J. F.: *Quelques remarques sur la preuve devant la Cour permanente et la Cour internationale de Justice.* 7 *Annuaire Suisse* (1950), pp. 77–103.

LAMMASCH, H.: *Die Rechtskraft internationaler Schiedssprüche.* Norske Nobelinstitut. Publ., Tome 2, Fasc. 2. Kristiania, 1913.

LA PRADELLE, A. de: *L'excès de pouvoir de l'arbitre.* 2 R.D.I. (1928), pp. 5–64.

LAUTERPACHT, H.: *The Legal Remedy in Case of Excess of Jurisdiction.* 9 B.Y.I.L. (1928), pp. 117–120.

—— *Dissenting Opinion of National Judges and the Revision of the Statute of the Court.* 11 B.Y.I.L. (1930), pp. 182–186.

LIMBURG, J.: *L'autorité de la chose jugée des décisions des juridictions internationales.* 30 *Recueil La Haye* (1929), pp. 523–618.

MAKOWSKI, J.: *L'organisation actuelle de l'arbitrage international.* 36 *Recueil La Haye* (1932), pp. 267–384.

MÉRIGNHAC, A.: *Traité théorique et pratique de l'arbitrage international.* Paris, 1895.

—— *De l'autorité de la chose jugée en matière de sentence arbitrale.* 5 R.G.D.I.P. (1898), pp. 606–625.

MORELLI, G.: *La théorie générale du procès international.* 61 *Recueil La Haye* (1937), pp. 257–373.

NIPPOLD, O.: *Die Fortbildung des Verfahrens in völkerrechtlichen Streitigkeiten.* Leipzig, 1907.

NOVACOVITCH, M.: *Les compromis et les arbitrages internationaux du 12e au 15e siècle.* Paris, 1905.

NYS, E.: *La révision de la sentence arbitrale.* 2 (12) R.D.I.L.C. (1910), pp. 595–641.

POLITIS, N.: *La justice internationale.* Paris, 1924.

ROSENNE, S.: *Res Judicata: Some Recent Decisions of the International Court of Justice.* 28 B.Y.I.L. (1951), pp. 365–371.

RUNDSTEIN, S.: *La C.P.J.I. comme instance de recours.* 43 *Recueil La Haye* (1933), pp. 5–113.

SALVIOLI, G.: *Les rapports entre le jugement sur la compétence et celui sur le fond dans la jurisprudence internationale.* 36 R.G.D.I.P. (1929), pp. 108–115.

SANDIFER, D. V.: *Evidence before International Tribunals.* Chicago, 1939.

SCHÄTZEL, W.: *Rechtskraft und Anfechtung von Entscheidungen internationaler Gerichte; eine kritische Studie der internationalen Praxis, besonders der Rechtsprechung der Gemischten Schiedsgerichte.* Leipzig, 1928.

SCHWARZENBERGER, G.: *La fuerza obligatoria de las sentences internacionales.* 24 *Revista (Habana)* (1945), pp. 204–219.

SÉFÉRIADÈS, M. S.: *Le problème de l'accès des particuliers à des juridictions internationales.* 51 *Recueil La Haye* (1935), pp. 5–119.

STIEGER, H.: *Die Unparteilichkeit bei Schlichtung von Staatskonflikten.* Luzern, 1929.

STRUPP, K.: *Die internationale Schiedsgerichtsbarkeit.* Berlin, 1914.

TAUBE, M. de: *Les origines de l'arbitrage international: Antiquité et Moyen Âge.* 42 *Recueil La Haye* (1932), pp. 5–115.

TÉNÉKIDÈS, C. G.: *Rapport de droit interne et de droit international en matière de chose jugée.* 3 (15) R.D.I.L.C. (1934), pp. 683–711.

TRAININ, A.: *La procédure à Nuremberg.* 24 *R.D.I.* (*Gve*) (1946), pp. 77–81.

TUANMO-CHENG: *Le rôle de la nationalité dans la composition et le fonctionnement de la C.I.J.* Thèse, Paris, 1950.

VERDROSS, A.: *L'excès de pouvoir du juge arbitral dans le droit international public.* 3 (9) R.D.I.L.C. (1928), pp. 225–242.

WITENBERG, J.-C.: *L'organisation judiciaire, la procédure et la sentence internationales: traité pratique.* Paris, 1937.

—— *Onus probandi devant les juridictions arbitrales.* 55 R.G.D.I.P. (1951), pp. 321–342.

WOOLSEY, L. H.: *The Sabotage Claims against Germany.* 33 A.J.I.L. (1939), pp. 737–740; 34 A.J.I.L. (1940), pp. 23–35; 35 A.J.I.L. (1941), pp. 282–304.

WRIGHT, Q.: *Due Process and International Law.* 40 A.J.I.L. (1946), pp. 398–406.

YOTIS, C.: *La question ultra petita à propos d'un arbitrage entre la Grèce et la Bulgarie.* 53 *Clunet* (1926), pp. 879–889.

CHAPTER 18. EXTINCTIVE PRESCRIPTION

CAVAGLIERI, A.: *Il decorso del tempo ed i suoi effetti sui rapporti giuridici internazionali.* 18 *Rivista* (1926), pp. 169–204.

INSTITUT DE DROIT INTERNATIONAL: *La prescription libératoire en droit international public.* 32 *Annuaire* (1925), pp. 1–49, 467–487, 558–560.

—— *Retard et négligence dans la présentation d'une réclamation.* 36 (1) *Annuaire* (1931), pp. 435–441.

JOHNSON, D. H. N.: *Acquisitive Prescription in International Law.* 27 B.Y.I.L. (1950), pp. 332–352.

KING, B. E.: *Prescription of Claims in International Law.* 15 B.Y.I.L. (1934), pp. 82–97.

POLITIS, N.: *La prescription libératoire en droit international.* 3 *R.D.I.* (*Gve*) (1925), pp. 3–10.

Prescription in International Law. 17 *Harvard L.R.* (1903–1904), pp. 346–347.

RALSTON, J. H.: *Prescription.* 4 A.J.I.L. (1910), pp. 133–144.

ROCH, W. *La prescription libératoire s'applique-t-elle en droit international public?* 27 *R.D.I.* (*Gve*) (1949), pp. 254–264.

ROLIN, A.: *Prescription extinctive.* Note doctrinale sur l'affaire du "Macedonian." 2 *Arb.int.*, pp. 205–209.

SØRENSEN, M.: *La prescription en droit international.* 3 A.S.J.G. (N.T.I.R.) (1932), pp. 145–170.

VERYKIOS, P. A.: *La prescription en droit international public.* Paris, 1934.

WITENBERG, J.-C.: *Recevabilité des réclamations devant les juridictions internationales.* 41 *Recueil La Haye* (1932), pp. 5–136, at pp. 9–30.

INDEX

For EU product safety concerns, contact us at Calle de José Abascal, 56–1°, 28003 Madrid, Spain or eugpsr@cambridge.org.

www.ingramcontent.com/pod-product-compliance
Lightning Source LLC
LaVergne TN
LVHW052211200926
848481LV00001B/76

* 9 7 8 0 5 2 1 0 3 0 0 0 7 *